Class Counts combines theoretical discussions of the concept of class with a wide range of comparative empirical investigations of class and its ramifications in developed capitalist societies. What unites the topics is not a preoccupation with a common object of explanation, but rather a common explanatory factor: class. Four broad themes are explored: class structure and its transformation; the permeability of class boundaries; class and gender; and class consciousness. The specific empirical studies include such diverse topics as the sexual division of labor in housework, gender differences in managerial authority, friendship networks in the class structure, the expansion of self-employment in the United States in the past two decades, and the class consciousness of state and private-sector employees. The results of these studies are then evaluated in terms of how they confirm certain expectations within the Marxist tradition of class analysis and how they pose challenging surprises.

Studies in Marxism and Social Theory

Class Counts

Studies in Marxism and Social Theory

Edited by G. A. COHEN, JON ELSTER AND JOHN ROEMER

The series is jointly published by the Cambridge University Press and the Editions de la Maison des Sciences de l'Homme, as part of the joint publishing agreement established in 1977 between the Fondation de la Maison des Sciences de l'Homme and the Syndics of the Cambridge University Press.

   The books in the series are intended to exemplify a new paradigm in the study of Marxist social theory. They will not be dogmatic or purely exegetical in approach. Rather, they will examine and develop the theory pioneered by Marx, in the light of the intervening history, and with the tools of non-Marxist social science and philosophy. It is hoped that Marxist thought will thereby be freed from the increasingly discredited methods and presuppositions which are still widely regarded as essential to it, and that what is true and important in Marxism will be more firmly established.

Also in the series

Class Counts

Comparative Studies in Class Analysis

Erik Olin Wright

CAMBRIDGE
UNIVERSITY PRESS

Maison des Sciences de l'Homme

Published by the Press Syndicate of the University of Cambridge
The Pitt Building, Trumpington Street, Cambridge CB2 1RP
40 West 20th Street, New York, NY 10011-4211, USA
10 Stamford Road, Oakleigh, Melbourne 3166, Australia
and Editions de la Maison des Sciences de l'Homme
54 Boulevard Raspail, 75270 Paris Cedex 06

First published 1997

Printed in Great Britain at the University Press, Cambridge

A catalogue record for this book is available from the British Library

Library of Congress cataloguing in publication data

Wright, Erik Olin.
Class Counts: Comparative Studies in Class Analysis / Erik Olin Wright
    p.   cm. – (Studies in Marxism and social theory)
ISBN 0 521 55387 3 (hc.) – ISBN 0 521 55646 5 (pbk.)
1. Social classes. 2. Social mobility. 3. Class consciousness.
I. Title. II. Series.
HT 609.W698   1996
305.5 – dc20   96-11871 CIP

ISBN 0 521 55387 3 hardback
ISBN 0 521 55646 5 paperback
ISBN 2 7351 2-7351 0705 1 hardback (France only)
ISBN 2 7351 2-7351 0706 X paperback (France only)

CE

For Marcia

Summary of contents

ix

Contents

Part V Conclusion

Figures

Tables

Elsie: "WHAT'S THAT, DADDY?"
Father: "A COW."
Elsie: "WHY?"

Punch (1906)

Preface

Like Elsie wondering why a cow is a "cow," I have spent an inordinate amount of time worrying about what makes a class a "class." Here is the basic problem. The Marxist concept of class is rooted in a polarized notion of antagonistic class relations: slave-masters exploit slaves, lords exploit serfs, capitalists exploit workers. In the analysis of developed capitalist societies, however, many people do not seem to fit neatly this polarized image. In everyday language, many people are "middle class," and even though Marxists generally do not like that term, nevertheless, most Marxist analysts are uncomfortable with calling managers, doctors, and professors, "proletarians." Thus, the problem is this: how can the social categories which are commonly called "middle" class be situated within a conceptual framework built around a polarized concept of class? What does it mean to be in the "middle" of a "relation"? The diverse strands of research brought together in this book are all, directly or indirectly, ramifications of struggling with this core conceptual problem.

My empirical research on these issues began with my dissertation on class and income, completed in 1976. In that project I used data gathered by the Michigan Panel Study of Income Dynamics, the Quality of Employment Survey and several other sources. None of these had been gathered with Marxist concepts in mind. When the data analysis failed to generate anticipated results, I could therefore always say, "of course, the data were gathered in 'bourgeois categories' and this may explain why the hypotheses were not confirmed." It was therefore a natural next step to generate new data, data that would be directly tailored to quantitatively "testing" hypotheses on class and its consequences within the Marxist tradition, data that would leave me no excuses. This was the central idea behind my first grant proposal for this project to the National Science Foundation in 1977.

The original NSF proposal was framed as an attempt to generate a set of data in which the Marxist and Weberian traditions of class analysis could directly engage each other. I argued in the proposal that there was a tremendous gap between *theoretical debates* in class analysis – which largely revolved around a dialogue between Marx and Weber – and *quantitative research* – which largely ignored Marxism altogether. To close this gap required two things: first, generating systematic data derived from a Marxist conceptual framework, and second, gathering the data comparatively. Since Marxist class analysis is, above all, rooted in the concept of class structure (rather than simply individual class attributes), we needed a sample of countries which varied structurally in certain ways in order to seriously explore Marxist themes.

As often occurs in research proposals, because of the need to frame issues in ways which the reviewers of the proposals will find compelling, this way of posing the agenda of the research did not really reflect my core reasons for wanting to do the project. Adjudication between general frameworks of social theory can rarely be accomplished in the form of head-to-head quantitative combat, since different theoretical frameworks generally are asking different questions. Furthermore, the gaps between concepts, questions and measures are nearly always too great for a direct adjudication between rival frameworks to yield robust and convincing results. The Marx/Weber debate, therefore, was always a somewhat artificial way of justifying the project, and it certainly has not (in my judgment) proven to be the most interesting line of empirical analysis. My theoretical motivations had much more to do with pushing Marxist class analysis forward on its own terrain – exploring problems such as cross-national variation in the permeability of class boundaries, the effects of class location and class biography on class consciousness, the variations across countries in patterns of ideological class formation, and so on.

Nevertheless, from the start a disproportionate amount of energy in the project in the United States as well as in many of the other countries has been devoted to the problem of *adjudicating conceptual issues* rather than *empirically investigating theoretical problems*. I have worried endlessly about the optimal way of conceptualizing the "middle class" which would both be coherent (i.e. be consistent with more abstract principles of Marxist theory) and empirically powerful. This preoccupation has sometimes displaced substantive theoretical concerns and it has been easy to lose sight of the real puzzles that need solving. Rather than delve deeply into the problem of trying to explain why workers in different countries display different degrees of radicalism, I have often worried more about how properly to define the category "working class" to be used in such an investigation. It was as if I felt that if only I could get the *concepts* right, then the theoretical issues would fall into place (or at least become more tractable). It now seems to me that often it is better to forge ahead and muddle through with somewhat less certain concepts than to devote such an inordinate amount of time attempting to reconstruct the concepts themselves. To paraphrase a comment once made about Talcott Parsons, it is a bad idea to keep repacking one's bags for a trip that one never takes. It is better to get out the door even if you may have left something important behind.

The initial plan when I began the comparative class analysis project was to do a survey of class structure and class consciousness in the US and Italy jointly with a close friend from graduate school, Luca Perrone. In fact, one of the initial motivations for the project was our mutual desire to embark on a research project that would make it easy for us to see each other regularly. By the time the final NSF grant was awarded, Sweden had been added to the project as the result of a series of lectures I gave in Uppsala in 1978. Soon, scholars in other countries learned of the project, and through a meandering process, asked if they could replicate the survey. By 1982 surveys were completed or underway in the United Kingdom, Canada, and Norway, and shortly thereafter additional surveys were carried out in Australia, Denmark, Japan, New Zealand and West Germany. Tragically, Luca Perrone died in a skin diving accident in 1981 and so an Italian project was never completed. In the early 1990s an additional round of projects was organized in Russia, South Korea, Spain, Taiwan and, most recently, Portugal. A second US survey was fielded in 1991 and a new Swedish survey in 1995.

Without really intending this to happen, the US project became the coordinating node of a rapidly expanding network of class analysis projects around the world. Originally, this was meant to be a focussed, short-term project. In 1977 I had absolutely no intention of embarking on a megaproject that would eventually involve more than fifteen countries and millions of dollars. I thought that the project would take a few years, four or five at the most, and then I would return to other issues. It is now seventeen years later and the end is just now in sight.

Has it really been worth it to spend this amount of time and resources on a single research enterprise? If twenty years ago, when I was finishing my dissertation and contemplating whether or not to launch the class analysis project, I was told that I would still be working on it in 1995, I would have immediately dropped the project in horror. Certainly there have been times during the years of this project when I was fed up with it, tired of worrying endlessly about the minutiae of measurement and only asking questions that could be answered with coefficients. Nevertheless, in the end, I do think that it has been worthwhile sticking with this project for so long. This is not mainly because of the hard "facts" generated by the research. If you simply made a list of all of the robust empirical discoveries of the research, it would be easy to conclude that the results were not worth the effort. While I hope to show in this book that many of these findings are interesting, I am not sure that by themselves they justify nearly two decades of work.

The real payoff from this project has come, I think, from the effects of thinking about the same ideas, concepts and puzzles for so long. I have returned countless times to the problem of the difference between Marxist and Weberian ideas about class, the meaning of exploitation and domination as analytical and normative issues in class analysis, the conceptual status of the "middle" class in a relational class framework, and so on. It is not that the simple "facts" generated by the regression equations directly inform these issues, but repeatedly grappling with the data has forced me to repeatedly grapple with these ideas. The long and meandering class analysis project has kept me focussed on a single cluster of ideas for much longer than I would have otherwise done, and this has led – I hope – to a level of insight which I otherwise would not have achieved.

There are several limitations in the analyses in this book which should be mentioned. First, even though this is a book about class written from a Marxist perspective, there are no empirical analyses of two important segments of the class structure: substantial owners of capital, and the more marginalized, impoverished segments of population, often loosely labeled the "underclass." When I refer to the "capitalist class" in the empirical analyses I am, by and large, referring to relatively small employers, not to wealthy owners of investment portfolios. There is certainly no analysis of anything approaching the "ruling class." Similarly, the analysis of the working class largely excludes the unemployed and people who are outside of the labor force (discouraged workers, people on welfare, etc.). The irony, of course, is that within the Marxist tradition the critique of capitalism is directed above all against the wealthiest segments of the capitalist class, and the moral condemnation of capitalism is grounded to a significant extent on the ways it perpetuates poverty. The limitations of sample surveys simply make it impossible to seriously explore either of these extremes within the class structure with the methods we will use in this study.

Second, aside from relatively brief sections in Chapter 2 and Chapter 14, there is almost no discussion of the problem of race and class in the book. Given how salient the problem of race is for class analysis in the United States, this is a significant and unfortunate absence. However, the relatively small sample size meant that there were too few African-Americans in the sample to do sophisticated analyses of the interactions of race and class. What is more, even if we had had a significantly larger sample, the restriction of the American sample to the labor force and housewives would have precluded investigation of the crucial race/class issue of the "underclass." Given these limitations, I felt I would not be able to push the empirical analysis of race and class forward using the data from the Comparative Class Analysis Project.

Third, there is a methodological problem that affects the book as a whole. Most of the data analyses reported in this book were originally prepared for journal articles. The earliest of these appeared in 1987, the last in 1995. As often happens when a series of quite different analyses are generated from the same data over an extended period of time, small shifts in variable construction and operational choices are made. In preparing the book manuscript, therefore, I had to make a decision: should I redo most of the previously completed analyses in order to render all of the chapters strictly consistent, or should I simply report the findings in their original form and make note of the shifts in operationalizations? There is no question that, in the absence of constraints, the first of these options would be the best. But I figured that it would probably delay the completion of the book by a minimum of six months and probably more, and given that there would be no substantive improvement in the ideas and insights of the research, this just did not seem worthwhile. So, in Ralph Waldo Emerson's spirit that "foolish consistency is the hobgoblin of small minds," I have retained nearly all of the original analyses (except in a few cases where I discovered actual errors of one sort or another).

Finally, in revising, extending and integrating the various empirical studies I had to decide whether or not to attempt to bring the discussion of relevant literatures up to date. The analyses wander all over the map – from friendships, to housework, to class consciousness, to the transformations of class structures. Since on some of these topics I was hardly a real expert even at the time I wrote the original papers, the thought of once again reviewing the literature on all of these disparate topics was extremely daunting. In any case, I was not prepared to redo the analyses in light of any new literature I might have discovered, and thus I decided to forgo the task entirely. In a number of cases, therefore, the discussions of the broader sociological literature is likely to be somewhat dated.

This project would not have been possible without the financial support from the National Science Foundation, which funded the initial gathering and public archiving of the data and much of the data analysis. The Wisconsin Alumni Research Foundation also provided generous research support for data analysis throughout the research. In the late 1980s, grants from the Spencer Foundation and the MacArthur foundation made it possible to conduct the second US survey in conjunction with the Russian class analysis project.

There are countless people to whom I am deeply indebted for the research embodied in this book. Without the love and comradeship of Luca Perrone, the project would never have been launched in the first place. His quirky spirit is present throughout the book.

Michael Burawoy has been my most steadfast and supportive critic over the years, encouraging me both to be a hard-nosed quantomaniac and to keep the big ideas and political purposes always in mind. In reading the draft of parts of this book he urged me to keep the overblown concept-mongering to a minimum; too much grandiose theorizing, he warned, would distract readers from the empirical message of the research. I am afraid that I have only partially followed his advice: I have not excised metatheoretical and conceptual discussions from the book, but they are generally cordoned off in specific chapters.

My collaborators in the various national projects in the Comparative Class Analysis Project contributed enormously to the development of this research. Göran Ahrne, the principal director of the Swedish project in the 1980s, was especially involved in formulating questions and designing the intellectual agenda of the project from the start and always provided sensible skepticism to my Marxist theoretical impulses. Howard Newby, Gordon Marshall, David Rose, John Myles, Wallace Clement, Markku Kivenen, Raimo Blom, Thomas Colbjornson, Håkon Leilesfrud, Jens Hoff, John Western, Julio Carabaña, Gunn Elisabeth Birklund, and Chris Wilkes were all involved in the various international meetings where the project was framed and analyses were discussed.

A series of extremely talented graduate student research assistants were directly involved in many of these specific data analyses. In particular, I would like to thank Cynthia Costello, Joey Sprague, David Haken, Bill Martin, George Steinmetz, Donmoon Cho, Kwang-Young Shin, Karen Shire, Cressida Lui and Sungkyun Lee. Two post-doctoral fellows from the Australian project who spent two years in Madison – Mark Western and Janeen Baxter – infused the data analysis with great energy and imagination just at a time when my own enthusiasm was beginning to wane.

A number of colleagues have provided invaluable feedback on specific pieces of the analysis. Robert Hauser, Rob Mare, Michael Hout and Charles Halaby were always generously helpful at rescuing me when I ventured out of my depth in statistical techniques. Joel Rogers has been extremely helpful in skeptically asking "so, what's the main point?" and providing an insightful sounding board for testing out the various punchlines in the book.

Finally, I would like to thank my wife, Marcia, for refusing to let the work on this book and other projects completely take over my life. She has managed with great skill the delicate balancing act of being supportive of my academic work and yet not letting it get out of hand to encroach on everything else.

Acknowledgments

Some of the chapters in this book partially draw on previously published papers from the Comparative Class Analysis Project. In most cases, these earlier papers were substantially revised for this book: Chapter 3: "Proletarianization in Contemporary Capitalism" (with Joachim Singelmann), *American Journal of Sociology*, supplement to vol. 83, 1982, and "The Transformation of the American Class Structure, 1960–1980" (with Bill Martin), *American Journal of Sociology*, July 1987. Chapter 4: "The Fall and Rise of the Petty Bourgeoisie" (with George Steinmetz), *The American Journal of Sociology*, March 1989. Chapter 6: "The Permeability of Class Boundaries to Intergenerational Mobility: a Comparative Study of the United States, Canada, Norway and Sweden" (with Mark Western), *American Sociological Review*, June 1994. Chapter 7: "The Relative Permeability of Class Boundaries to Cross-Class Friendships: a comparative Analysis of the United States, Canada, Sweden and Norway" (with Donmoon Cho) *American Sociological Review*, February, 1992. Chapter 10: "Women in the Class Structure," *Politics & Society*, March, 1989. Chapter 11: "The Noneffects of Class on the Sexual Division of Labor in the Home: a Comparative Analysis of Sweden and the United States" (with Karen Shire, Shu-Ling Huang, Maureen Dolan and Janeen Baxter), *Gender & Society*, June 1992. Chapter 12: "The Gender Gap in Authority: a Comparative Analysis of the United States, Canada, The United Kingdom, Sweden, Norway and Japan" (with Janeen Baxter) *The American Sociological Review*, June, 1995. Chapter 14: "Class Structure and Class Formation" (with Carolyn Howe and Donmoon Cho), in Melvin Kohn (ed.), *Comparative Sociology*, (Beverly Hills: Sage ASA Presidential Volume), 1989. Chapter 15: "Ideology and State Employment: a Comparative Analysis of the United States and Sweden" (with Donmoon Cho)

Politics & Society, June 1992. Chapter 16: "Temporality and Class Analysis: a Comparative Analysis of Class Structure, Class Trajectory and Class Consciousness in Sweden and the United States" (with Kwang-Yeong Shin), *Sociological Theory*, Spring, 1988.

1 Class analysis

The empirical research in this book covers a wide range of substantive topics: from friendship patterns and class mobility to housework and class consciousness. What unites the topics is not a preoccupation with a common object of explanation, but rather a common explanatory factor: class. This is what class analysis attempts to do – explore the relationship between class and all sorts of social phenomena. This does not mean, of course, that class will be of explanatory importance for everything. Indeed, as we will discover, in some of the analyses of this book class turns out not to be a particularly powerful factor. Class analysis does not imply a commitment to the thesis that all social phenomena can be explained primarily in terms of class, or even that class is always an important determinant. Rather, class analysis is based on the conviction that class is a pervasive social cause and thus it is worth exploring its ramifications for many social phenomena. This implies deepening our understanding of the limits of what class can explain as well as of the processes through which class helps to determine what it does explain.

Understood in this way, class analysis is what might be called an "independent variable" specialty. It is a discipline like endocrinology in medicine. If you are an endocrinologist you are allowed to study a vast array of problems – sexuality, personality, growth, disease processes, etc. – in addition to the internal functioning of the endocrine system, so long as you explore the relationship between the endocrine system and those explananda. Endocrinology is monogamous in its explanatory variable – the hormone system – but promiscuous in its dependent variables. Furthermore, in endocrinology it is not an embarrassment to discover that for some problems under investigation hormones turn out not to be very important. It is an advance in our

1

knowledge of endocrinology to know what hormones do not explain as well as to know what they do. Oncology, in contrast, is a dependent variable discipline. As an oncologist you can study any conceivable cause of cancer – toxins, genetics, viruses, even psychological states. Oncology is monogamous in its dependent variable but promiscuous in its independent variables. And, in oncology, it is not an embarrassment to discover that certain potential causes of cancer turn out to be not very important.

The most elaborated and systematic theoretical framework for class analysis is found in the Marxist tradition. Whatever one might think of its scientific adequacy, classical Marxism is an ambitious and elegant theoretical project in which class analysis was thought to provide the most fundamental explanations of what can be termed the epochal trajectory of human history. The aphorism "class struggle is the motor of history" captures this idea. In effect, the Marxist theory of history – or what is commonly called "historical materialism" – is like a medical theory which combined endocrinology and oncology by arguing that hormonal mechanisms provide the central explanations ("the motor") for the dynamic development ("history") of cancers. The argument of classical historical materialism was never that everything that happens in history is explainable by class analysis, although many critics of Marxism have accused Marxists of proposing such a monocausal theory. The claim is more restricted, yet still ambitious: that the overall trajectory of historical development can be explained by a properly constructed class analysis.[1]

Many, perhaps most, contemporary Marxist scholars have pulled back from these grandiose claims of orthodox historical materialism. While the idea that history has a comprehensible structure and that the dynamics of capitalism are fraught with contradictions that point toward a socialist future may form part of the intellectual backdrop to

[1] As in all aspects of Marxism there is, needless to say, much dispute about the degree of determinism implied by class analysis within historical materialism. Some people argue that Marx was never an economic determinist at all; others argue that he defended a specific form of economic and class determinism, one which was grounded in assumptions of human agency. In any event, whether the analysis is deterministic or not, class analysis is at the core of the explanations of epochal historical trajectories in Marx. For the most sophisticated and profound account of historical materialism as a serious, explanatory theory, see G.A. Cohen (1978). For some important clarifications and amendments to the arguments in this book, see Cohen (1988). For a general assessment of the claims of historical materialism and the prospects for its reconstruction, see Wright, Levine and Sober (1992).

Marxist scholarship, most actual research brackets these ideas and, instead, focusses on the ways in which class affects various aspects of social life. Class analysis thus becomes the core of a wide-ranging agenda of research on the causes and consequences of class relations.

Marxist-inspired class analysis, of course, is not the only way of studying class. There is also Weberian-inspired class analysis, stratification-inspired class analysis, eclectic common sense class analysis. Before embarking on the specific empirical agenda of this book, therefore, we need to clarify the basic contours of the class concept which will be used in the analyses. In particular, we need to clarify the concept of *class structure*, since this plays such a pivotal role in class analysis. This is the basic objective of this chapter.

The concept of "class structure" is only one element in class analysis. Other conceptual elements include *class formation* (the formation of classes into collectively organized actors), *class struggle* (the practices of actors for the realization of class interests) and *class consciousness* (the understanding of actors of their class interests). The task of class analysis is not simply to understand class structure and its effects, but to understand the interconnections among all these elements and their consequences for other aspects of social life.

In chapter 13 we will explore a general model of the interconnections among these elements. The discussion in this chapter will be restricted to the problem of class structure. This is not because I believe that class structure is always the most important explanatory principle within class analysis. It could certainly be the case, for example, that the variation in class formations across time and place in capitalist societies may be a more important determinant of variations in state policies than variations in the class structures associated with those class formations. Rather, I initially focus on class structure because it remains *conceptually* pivotal to clarifying the overall logic of class analysis. To speak of *class* formation or *class* struggle as opposed to simply *group* formation or struggle implies that we have a definition of "class" and know what it means to describe a collective actor as an instance of class formation, or a conflict as a class conflict instead of some other sort of conflict. The assumption here is that the concept of class structure imparts the essential content of the adjective "class" when it is appended to "formation," "consciousness," and "struggle." Class formation is the formation of collective actors organized around class interests within class structures; class struggle is the struggle between such collectively

organized actors over class interests; class consciousness is the understanding by people within a class of their class interests. In each case
one must already have a definition of class structure before the other
concepts can be fully specified. Elaborating a coherent concept of class
structure, therefore, is an important conceptual precondition for
developing a satisfactory theory of the relationship between class
structure, class formation and class struggle.

1.1 The parable of the shmoo

A story from the *Li'l Abner* comic strips from the late 1940s will help to
set the stage for the discussion of the concept of class structure.[2] Here
is the situation of the episode: Li'l Abner, a resident of the hill-billy
community of Dogpatch, discovers a strange and wonderful creature,
the "shmoo," and brings a herd of them back to Dogpatch. The
shmoo's sole desire in life is to please humans by transforming itself
into the material things human beings need. They do not provide
humans with luxuries, but only with the basic necessities of life. If you
are hungry, they can become ham and eggs, but not caviar. What's
more, they multiply rapidly so you never run out of them. They are
thus of little value to the wealthy, but of great value to the poor. In
effect, the shmoo restores humanity to the Garden of Eden. When God
banished Adam and Eve from Paradise for their sins, one of their
harshest punishments was that from then on they and their descen-
dants were forced to "earn their bread by the sweat of their brows."
The shmoo relieves people of this necessity and thus taps a deep
fantasy in Western culture.

In the episode from *Li'l Abner* reproduced below, a manager
working for a rich capitalist, P.U., does a study to identify the poorest
place in America in order to hire the cheapest labor for a new factory.
The place turns out to be Dogpatch. P.U. and the manager come to
Dogpatch to recruit employees for the new factory. The story unfolds
in a sequence of comic strips from 1948 (Al Capp 1992: 134–136):

---

[2]   The use of these episodes from *Li'l Abner* as an illustration for the moral critique of
      capitalism was introduced to me by the British philosopher G. A. Cohen in a lecture
      he gave on British television in August 1986.

The presence of shmoos is thus a serious threat to both class relations and gender relations. Workers are more difficult to recruit for toilsome labor and no longer have to accept "guff" and indignities from their bosses. Women are no longer economically dependent on men and thus do not have to put up with sexist treatment.[3]

In the episodes that follow, P.U. and his henchman organize a campaign to destroy the shmoo. They are largely successful, and its sinister influence is stopped. American capitalism can continue, unthreatened by the specter of the Garden of Eden.

The saga of the shmoo helps to clarify the sense in which the interests of workers and capitalists are deeply antagonistic, one of the core ideas of Marxist class analysis. How do shmoos affect the material interests of people in these two classes?[4] This depends upon the level

[3] Given the prevailing ideologies of the time, it is quite remarkable that Al Capp indicated the implications of the shmoo for gender domination. The implications for workers, after all, fell neatly within the theoretical arguments of Marxism which, in the 1940s, were quite familiar to many intellectuals. The feminist critique of male domination was much less familiar.

[4] By "material interests" here I simply mean the interests people have in their material standard of living, understood as the package of toil, consumption and leisure. Material interests are thus not interests in maximizing consumption *per se*, but rather interests in the trade-offs between toil, leisure and consumption. Material interests, as I will discuss them here, also excludes purely status goods – goods which get their value strictly from being enjoyed by only a few people. If the interests of capitalists are not simply to have high material standards of living, but to have high*er* standards of living than others in order to have higher status, then they would be opposed to shmoos even if shmoos provided people with every conceivable luxury. I am also excluding from "material interests" such things as the desire for domination for its own sake. Material interests are thus simply the interests one has in one's own standard of living. For a more extended discussion of the problem of material interests see Wright (1989a: 280–288).

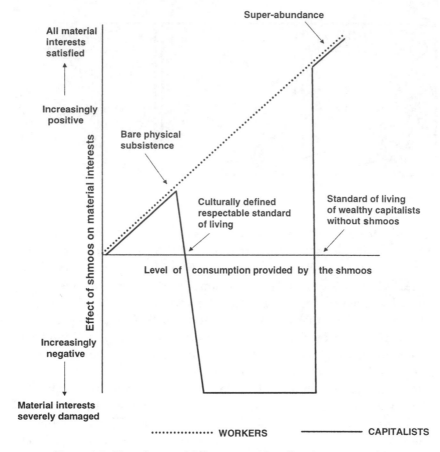

Figure 1.1 *How shmoos of different capacities affect the interests of workers and captialists*

of generosity of the shmoo as indicated in Figure 1.1. If the shmoo provides less than bare physical subsistence, it probably has a positive effect on the material interests of both workers and capitalists. For workers it makes their lives a little bit less precarious; for capitalists, such sub-subsistence shmoos could be considered a subsidy to the wage bill. All other things being equal, capitalists can pay lower wages if part of the subsistence of workers is provided outside of the market.[5] At the other extreme, if shmoos provide for superabundance, gratifying every material desire of humans from basic necessities to the

---

5   Housewives might be considered a kind of quasi-shmoo providing "free" goods at less than a subsistence level (since a worker's family cannot live exclusively on the labor of the housewife).

most expensive luxuries, then they would also positively serve the material interests of capitalists. Between these two extremes, however, the impact of the shmoo on the material interests of the two classes diverges. The welfare of workers is continuously improved as the generosity of shmoos increases, whereas for capitalists, after a point, their material interests are adversely affected. Once shmoos provide workers with a respectable standard of living, workers no longer have to work in order to live at an acceptable standard. As P.U.'s manager states in panic, "Do you realize what the shmoo means? Nobody'll have to work hard any more!!" This does not mean, of course, that no workers would be willing to work for an employer. Work fills many needs for people besides simply providing earnings, and in any case, so long as the shmoo does not provide superabundance, many people will have consumption desires beyond the shmoo level of provision. Nevertheless, workers would be in a much more powerful bargaining position with modestly generous shmoos at home, and it will be more difficult, in P.U.'s words, to get them to "do the long, dreary, back-breaking labor at our canning factories."[6]

As a result of these differences in the impact of the shmoo on the material interests of workers and capitalists, people in these two classes have very different preferences with respect to the fate of the shmoo. Consider four possible distributions of modestly generous shmoos: everyone gets a shmoo; only capitalists get shmoos; only workers get shmoos; and the shmoos are destroyed so no one gets them. Table 1.1 indicates the preference orderings for the fate of modestly generous shmoos on the assumption that both workers and capitalists are rational and only interested in their own material welfare.[7] They are thus neither altruistic nor spiteful. For capitalists,

---

[6] There is an interesting difference in the analysis of the effect of the shmoo offered by the Dogpatch resident and by P.U.'s manager. The Dogpatch resident proclaims, "But nobody whut's got shmoos has t'work any more," whereas the manager declares, "Nobody'll have to work *hard* anymore." The manager understands that the issue is the extraction of labor effort – exploitation – not simply getting people to show up for "work." The Dogpatchian only identifies an effect in the *labor market*; the manager identifies an effect in the *labor process*. To state the matter sociologically, the Dogpatchian provides a Weberian analysis, the manager a Marxist one.

[7] These preference orderings also assume homogeneous attributes among capitalists and workers. If there are big capitalists and small capitalists, or skilled workers and unskilled workers, then the preference orderings might get much more complicated. Highly skilled workers, for example, might benefit more from a supply of cheap goods produced by unskilled workers without shmoos than by an improved living standard with shmoos.

Table 1.1. *Rank ordering of preferences for the fate of the shmoo by class location*

Rank order	Capitalist class	Working class
1	Only capitalists get shmoos	Everyone gets shmoos
2	Destroy the shmoos	Only workers get shmoos
3	Everyone gets shmoos	Only capitalists get shmoos
4	Only workers get shmoos	Destroy the shmoo

their first preference is that they alone get the shmoos, since they would obviously be slightly better off with shmoos than without them. Their second preference is that no one gets them. They would rather have the shmoo be destroyed than everyone get one. For workers, in contrast, their first preference is that everyone gets the shmoos. Workers will be slightly better off if capitalists have shmoos as well as workers, since this will mean that capitalists will have slightly more funds available for investment (because they will not have to buy basic necessities for themselves). Workers' second preference is that workers alone get the shmoos, their third preference is that only capitalists get the shmoos, and their least preferred alternative is that the shmoos be destroyed.

The preference ordering of workers corresponds to what could be considered universal human interests. This is one way of understanding the classical Marxist idea that the working class is the "universal class," the class whose specific material interests are equivalent to the interests of humanity as such. This preference ordering also corresponds to what might be called Rawlsian preferences – the preferences that maximize the welfare of the worst off people in a society. With respect to the shmoo, at least, the material self-interests of workers corresponds to the dictates of Rawlsian principles of Justice.

What the story of the shmoo illustrates is that the deprivations of the propertyless in a capitalist system are not simply an unfortunate by-product of the capitalist pursuit of profit; they are a necessary condition for that pursuit. This is what it means to claim that capitalist profits depend upon "exploitation."[8] Exploiting classes have an in-

---

[8] This does not imply that the degree of exploitation is the only determinant of the degree of profits, or even that profits are solely "derived" from exploitation. All that is being claimed is that exploitation is one of the necessary conditions for profits in a capitalist economy.

terest in preventing the exploited from acquiring the means of subsistence even if, as in the case of the shmoo story, that acquisition does not take the form of a redistribution of wealth or income from capitalists to workers. To put it crudely, capitalism generates a set of incentives such that the capitalist class has an interest in destroying the Garden of Eden.

While in real capitalism capitalists do not face the problem of a threat from shmoos, there are episodes in the history of capitalism in which capitalists face obstacles not unlike the shmoo. Subsistence peasants have a kind of shmoo in their ownership of fertile land. While they have to labor for their living, they do not have to work for capitalists. In some times and places capitalists have adopted deliberate strategies to reduce the capacity of subsistence peasants to live off the land specifically in order to recruit them as a labor force. A good example is the use of monetized hut taxes in South Africa in the nineteenth century to force subsistence peasants to enter the labor market and work in the mines in order to have cash to pay their taxes. More generally, capitalist interests are opposed to social arrangements that have even a partial shmoo-like character. Capitalist class interests are thus opposed to such things as universal guaranteed basic income or durably very low rates of unemployment, even if the taxes to support such programs were paid entirely out of wages and thus did not directly come out of their own pockets.[9] This reflects the sense in which capitalist exploitation generates fundamentally antagonistic interests between workers and capitalists.

1.2 The concept of exploitation

The story of the shmoo revolves around the linkage between class divisions, class interests and exploitation. There are two main classes in the story – capitalists who own the means of production and workers who do not. By virtue of the productive assets which they own (capital and labor power) they each face a set of constraints on how they can best pursue their material interests. The presence of shmoos fundamentally transforms these constraints and is a threat to the material

---

[9] This does not mean, of course, that capitalists as *persons* could not be enthusiastic supporters of shmoos and shmoo-like social policy. Engels, after all, was a wealthy capitalist and was an enthusiastic supporter of Marx and revolutionary socialism. But in supporting shmoos, or socialism, capitalists are acting against their *class* interests.

interests of capitalists. Why? Because it undermines their capacity to exploit the labor power of workers. "Exploitation" is thus the key concept for understanding the nature of the *interests* generated by the class relations.

Exploitation is a loaded theoretical term, since it suggests a moral condemnation of particular relations and practices, not simply an analytical description. To describe a social relationship as exploitative is to condemn it as both harmful and unjust to the exploited. Yet, while this moral dimension of exploitation is important, the core of the concept revolves around a particular type of *antagonistic interdependence of material interests* of actors within economic relations, rather than the injustice of those relations as such. As I will use the term, class exploitation is defined by three principal criteria:

(a) *The material welfare of one group of people causally depends on the material deprivations of another.*

(b) *The causal relation in (a) involves the asymmetrical exclusion of the exploited from access to certain productive resources.* Typically this exclusion is backed by force in the form of property rights, but in special cases it may not be.[10]

(c) *The causal mechanism which translates exclusion (b) into differential welfare (a) involves the appropriation of the fruits of labor of the exploited by those who control the relevant productive resources.*[11]

This is a fairly complex set of conditions. Condition (a) establishes the antagonism of material interests. Condition (b) establishes that the antagonism is rooted in the way people are situated within the social organization of production. The expression "asymmetrical" in this criterion is meant to exclude "fair competition" from the domain of

---

[10] An example of an exclusion from productive resources which is not backed by force but which, nevertheless, could be the basis for exploitation, is the unequal distribution of talents. While one could stretch the notion of "coercive" exclusion to cover talents (since the untalented are coercively prohibited from owning the talented as slaves), in the actual functioning of capitalist societies, the relevant exclusion is not primarily guaranteed by force.

[11] The expression "appropriation of the fruits of labor" refers to the appropriation of that which labor produces. It does *not* imply that the value of those products is exclusively determined by labor effort, as claimed in the labor theory of value. All that is being claimed here is that a surplus is appropriated – a surplus beyond what is needed to reproduce all of the inputs of production – and that this surplus is produced through labor effort, but not that the appropriate metric for the surplus is labor time. For a discussion of this way of understanding the appropriation of the fruits of labor, see Cohen (1988: 209–238).

possible exploitations. Condition (c) establishes the specific mechanism by which the interdependent, antagonistic material interests are generated. The welfare of the exploiter depends upon the *effort* of the exploited, not merely the deprivations of the exploited.[12]

If only the first two of these conditions are met we have what can be called "nonexploitative economic oppression," but not "exploitation." In nonexploitative economic oppression there is no transfer of the fruits of labor from the oppressed to the oppressor; the welfare of the oppressor depends simply on the exclusion of the oppressed from access to certain resources, but not on their effort. In both instances, the inequalities in question are rooted in ownership and control over productive resources.

The crucial difference between exploitation and nonexploitative oppression is that in an exploitative relation, the exploiter *needs* the exploited since the exploiter depends upon the effort of the exploited. In the case of nonexploitative oppression, the oppressors would be happy if the oppressed simply disappeared. Life would have been much easier for the European settlers in North America if the continent had been uninhabited by people.[13] Genocide is thus always a potential strategy for nonexploitative oppressors. It is not an option in a situation of economic exploitation because exploiters require the labor of the exploited for their material well-being. It is no accident that culturally we have the abhorrent saying, "the only good Indian is a dead Indian," but not the saying "the only good worker is a dead worker" or "the only good slave is a dead slave." It makes sense to say "the only good worker is an obedient and conscientious worker," but not "the only good worker is a dead worker." The contrast between

---

12 There are situations in which conditions (a) and (c) are present, but not (b). For example, in what is sometimes called a "tributary mode of production," a centralized, authoritarian state apparatus appropriates surplus from peasants through taxation without directly being involved in production at all. The peasants are surely being exploited in this situation, but the state elite is not a fully-fledged "class" insofar as their social location and power is not determined by their location within the social relations of production. One could, perhaps, stretch the meaning of condition (b) somewhat by treating the direct appropriation of the peasants' product by the state elite as a form of "exclusion" of peasants from productive resources (since the surplus itself is a productive resource). But the core mechanism involved does not center on the social relations *of production*, but the direct control of violence by the state, and thus the state elite is not a "class" in the standard sense.

13 This is not to deny that in certain specific instances the settlers benefited from the knowledge of Native Americans, but simply to affirm the point that the displacement of the indigenous people from the land was a costly and troublesome process.

North America and South Africa in the treatment of indigenous peoples reflects this difference poignantly: in North America, where the indigenous people were oppressed (by virtue of being coercively displaced from the land) but not exploited, genocide was the basic policy of social control in the face of resistance; in South Africa, where the European settler population heavily depended upon African labor for its own prosperity, this was not an option.

Exploitation, therefore, does not merely define a set of *statuses* of social actors, but a pattern of on-going *interactions* structured by a set of social relations, relations which mutually bind the exploiter and the exploited together. This dependency of the exploiter on the exploited gives the exploited a certain form of power, since human beings always retain at least some minimal control over their own expenditure of effort. Social control of labor which relies exclusively on repression is costly and, except under special circumstances, often fails to generate optimal levels of diligence and effort on the part of the exploited. As a result, there is generally systematic pressure on exploiters to moderate their domination and in one way or another to try to elicit some degree of consent from the exploited, at least in the sense of gaining some level of minimal cooperation from them. Paradoxically perhaps, exploitation is thus a constraining force on the practices of the exploiter. This constraint constitutes a basis of power for the exploited.

People who are oppressed but not exploited also may have some power, but it is generally more precarious. At a minimum oppressed people have the power that comes from the human capacity for physical resistance. However, since their oppressors are not economically constrained to seek some kind of cooperation from them, this resistance is likely very quickly to escalate into quite bloody and violent confrontations. It is for this reason that the resistance of Native Americans to displacement from the land led to massacres of Native Americans by white settlers. The pressure on nonexploitative oppressors to seek accommodation is very weak; the outcomes of conflict therefore tend to become simply a matter of the balance of brute force between enemies. When the oppressed are also exploited, even if the exploiter feels no moral compunction, there will be economic constraints on the exploiter's treatment of the exploited.

Describing the material interests of actors generated by exploitation as antagonistic does not prejudge the moral question of the justice or injustice of the inequalities generated by these antagonisms. One can believe, for example, that it is morally justified to prevent poor people in third world countries from freely coming into the United States and still recognize that there is an objective antagonism of material interests between US citizens and the excluded would-be third world migrants. Similarly, to recognize the capital–labor conflict as involving antagonistic material interests rooted in the appropriation of labor effort does not necessarily imply that capitalist profits are unjust; it simply means that they are generated in a context of inherent conflict.

Nevertheless, it would be disingenuous to claim that the use of the term "exploitation" to designate this form of antagonistic interdependency of material interests is a strictly scientific, technical choice. Describing the appropriation of labor effort as "exploitation" rather than simply a "transfer" adds a sharp moral judgment to the analytical claim. Without at least a thin notion of the moral status of the appropriation, it would be impossible, for example, to distinguish such things as legitimate taxation from exploitation. Taxation involves coercive appropriation, and in many instances there is arguably a conflict of material interests between the taxing authorities and the taxpayer as a private individual. Even under deeply democratic and egalitarian conditions, many people would not voluntarily pay taxes since they would prefer to enhance their personal material interests by free-riding on other people's tax payments. Right-wing libertarians in fact do regard taxation as a form of exploitation because it is a violation of the sanctity of private property rights and thus an unjust, coercive appropriation. The motto "taxation is theft" is equivalent to "taxation is exploitation." The claim that the capitalist appropriation of labor effort from workers is "exploitation," therefore, implies something more than simply an antagonism of material interests between workers and capitalists; it implies that this appropriation is unjust.

While I feel that a good moral case can be made for the kind of radical egalitarianism that provides a grounding for treating capitalist appropriation as unjust, it would take us too far afield here to explore the philosophical justifications for this claim.[14] In any case, for purposes of sociological class analysis, the crucial issue is the recognition of the antagonism of material interests that are linked to class relations by virtue of the appropriation of labor effort, and on this basis I will refer to this as "exploitation."

---

[14] For an insightful discussion of radical egalitarian values that provides a basis for regarding capitalist appropriations as exploitative, see Cohen (1988: ch. 11).

1.3 A note on exploitation as the appropriation of surplus

So far in this discussion, no mention has been made of the idea of exploitation as the appropriation of "surplus," the traditional way that Marxists elaborate the concept of "exploitation." Sometimes this idea is specified in terms of surplus *labor*, sometimes surplus *value*, and sometimes simply the surplus *product*. Regardless of which of these formulations is adopted, the idea seems fairly simple. The total social product can be divided into two broad categories: one part is needed to reproduce all of the inputs used up in production – labor power (i.e. the ability to work), raw materials, machines, etc. The other part is· a "surplus" – the amount of the social product beyond the costs of production. If this surplus is appropriated by a group of people other than those who produced it, and this appropriation was not at the behest of the producers, then the producers are generally regarded as "exploited."

The rhetoric of the production and appropriation of surplus is an attractive one for talking about exploitation. The existence of a social surplus is closely linked to the accumulation of capital, and describing exploitation in terms of surplus thus ties exploitation to a central aspect of the dynamics of capitalism. The idea of a surplus also has an appealing physical quality to it, which makes the appropriation of surplus seem more concrete than the appropriation of labor effort.

On closer inspection, however, the concept of "surplus" is not so simple. The basic problem is providing a clear meaning to the expression "the costs of producing and reproducing labor power," for unless this idea is clear, the concept of "surplus" is ambiguous.[15] How should this latter concept be defined? One solution simply equates the cost of labor power to whatever is the empirical consumption of people (i.e. the earnings they receive in a labor market minus whatever savings they make). The "surplus" would then simply be the value of the product left over after personal consumption and replacement of means of production.[16] This solution, however, defines away the possibility that some wage-earners might appropriate surplus in the

---

[15] Recall that the "surplus" is the total social product (measured physically or in some other way, such as value or price) minus the amount of the product needed to (a) cover the costs of means of production and raw materials used up in production, and (b) cover the costs of reproducing the labor power used in production. The first of these costs of production poses fewer conceptual difficulties than the second.

[16] The consumption of capitalists, insofar as they are not merely rentier coupon clippers, should also be excluded from the surplus. Capitalists may also work – they

form of high earnings and spend it all for an extravagant life-style. Intuitively, it seems reasonable to describe a Chief Executive Officer with a $1 million/year salary as being an exploiter, as appropriating surplus within those wages, regardless of whether or not part of this income was saved from personal consumption.

An alternative is to treat the costs of producing/reproducing labor power as just the costs of "basic subsistence," set at some culturally appropriate standard, rather than the costs of all empirical consumption. This might vary somewhat across different categories of people since certain kinds of labor power might require higher consumption in order to be effectively produced and reproduced, but the concept would still be distinct from empirical earnings. This second strategy has the advantage of not eliminating by definitional fiat the possibility that high wages can be a source of exploitation, but it has the disadvantage of no longer providing a clear operational solution to distinguishing "surplus" from the "costs" of labor power. If subsistence were defined at the level of mere biological survival, then perhaps it would have an unambiguous meaning, but once subsistence is understood as "basic subsistence set at some culturally appropriate standard," then the concept seems to become open-ended and arbitrary.

One way of resolving this problem is to define "basic subsistence" counterfactually. Imagine a world in which all people who sell their labor power have exactly the same genetic and socio-economic endowments.[17] That is, they all had an equal capacity to learn and to acquire skills, they all had the same economic resources, and they all faced the same social conditions. No workers were culturally or socially deprived relative to other workers, they all had equal access to credit in order to borrow funds to get advanced training, and there were no institutional restrictions on access to training. Medical schools, for example, would accept every qualified applicant (and these qualifications, in turn, were accessible to everyone on the assumption of equal endowments). Under these conditions, people would choose how much training to get on the basis of the amount of effort they wanted

perform labor of various sorts – and thus the reproduction of their labor power should count as a "cost of production."

[17] The reason for positing equal genetic endowments is to remove all impediments to the acquisition of skills by workers, so that differences in the wages linked to skills across people would simply be a function of differences in the real costs of acquiring and maintaining skills. If certain skills require certain special genetic endowments, and those endowments are rare, then this would not be the case.

to spend, given the costs of borrowing and the earnings they could expect to get from the training. As a result, the variation in labor market earnings across occupations would simply reflect the different costs (including effort) of acquiring the skills and performing the activities of the occupation. There would be nothing morally objectionable in the differences in earnings across occupations under such circumstances. If it should happen that the wage levels of an occupation were above these costs because of an undersupply of some type of labor power, then more people would seek the relevant training and the wages would accordingly fall. In this world of perfect competition in labor markets and unfettered capacity of workers to acquire skills, we can then define "basic subsistence" as the competitive equilibrium wage rate.[18]

Of course, we do not live in such a world, and because of this the pressures which would reduce wages of all occupations to this counterfactual level are blocked in various ways. In some cases, as in the medical profession in the US, there are deliberate institutional mechanisms to restrict the supply of doctors. More broadly, unequal endowments (social, economic and genetic) and restrictions on access to credit mean that for many jobs earnings will not equilibrate to the costs of producing and reproducing labor power. In such cases, part of the social surplus is distributed to people in the form of higher earnings.[19]

Because of the complexity of understanding the idea of "surplus" in terms of a counterfactual notion of competitively determined costs of production, I will generally discuss exploitation in terms of the extraction and appropriation of effort. This way of framing the concept also highlights the linkage between production and exchange which is at the heart of the theory of exploitation. There will be places, however,

---

[18] In this way of defining "basic subsistence," a combination of improvements in productivity and class struggles could raise the level of real wages for all workers above bare biological subsistence. The counterfactually defined "surplus," therefore, is the surplus above the *historically achieved* costs of producing/reproducing labor power under the assumption of purely competitive labor markets.

[19] A similar problem can occur for the costs of producing/reproducing the means of production. Under conditions of monopoly production of some physical input into production, the empirical *price* of that input will be above the price those inputs would have had under competitive market conditions. This "monopoly rent" in the price is a way that a seller of the input in question is able to appropriate surplus. Empirical prices within exchange relations, therefore, can constitute a mechanism for the appropriation and distribution of surplus to capitalists as well as to privileged categories of wage-earners.

such as in the discussion of "skill exploitation," where the more conventional language of appropriation of the surplus will be convenient. When I talk about exploitation in these terms, therefore, the surplus should be understood in this counterfactual manner.

1.4 Class and exploitation

Within the Marxist tradition of class analysis, class divisions are defined primarily in terms of the linkage between property relations and exploitation. Slave masters and slaves constitute classes because a particular property relation (property rights in people) generates exploitation (the appropriation of the fruits of labor of the slave by the slave master). Homeowners and the homeless would not constitute "classes" even though they are distinguished by property rights in housing since this division does not constitute a basis for the exploitation of the homeless by homeowners.[20]

In capitalist society, the central form of exploitation is based on property rights in the means of production. These property rights generate three basic classes: *capitalists* (exploiters), who own the means of production and hire workers; *workers* (exploited), who do not own the means of production and sell their labor power to capitalists; and *petty bourgeois* (neither exploiter nor exploited), who own and use the means of production without hiring others.[21] The Marxist account of how the capital–labor relation generates exploitation is a familiar one: propertyless workers, in order to acquire their means of livelihood, must sell their labor power to people who own the means of production.[22] In this exchange relation, they agree to work for a specified

[20] If homeowners exchanged housing in vacant rooms for domestic service, then the property rights in housing might become the basis for a class relation. The sheer fact of homeownership and homelessness, however, does not itself constitute a form of exploitation and thus is not a class division. It is only when this property right is translated into a power relation between actors within which labor is appropriated that it becomes exploitative.

[21] As Roemer (1982) argues, it is possible that some petty bourgeois might be exploited or even be exploiters through uneven exchange in the market. A petty bourgeois working with highly capital intensive means of production, for example, may be able to appropriate the fruits of labor of others through exchange.

[22] To be somewhat more precise, in order to acquire the means of subsistence, at least some members of a propertyless family (defined as the unit of shared consumption) must sell labor power to employers. In some times and places, this has meant that the male "breadwinner" entered the labor market while the female "housewife" stayed home. In contemporary advanced capitalism, generally all adult members of households sell their labor power.

length of time in exchange for a wage which they use to buy their means of subsistence. Because of the power relation between capitalists and workers, capitalists are able to force workers to produce more than is needed to provide them with this subsistence. As a result, workers produce a surplus which is owned by the capitalist and takes the form of profits. Profits, the amount of the social product that is left over after the costs of producing and reproducing all of the inputs (both labor power inputs and physical inputs) have been deducted, constitute an appropriation of the fruits of labor of workers.

Describing this relation as exploitative is a claim about the basis for the inherent conflict between workers and capitalists in the employment relation. It points to the crucial fact that the conflict between capitalists and workers is not simply over the *level of wages*, but over the *amount of work effort* performed for those wages. Capitalists always want workers to expend more effort than workers willingly want to do. As Bowles and Gintis (1990) have argued, "the whistle while you work" level of effort of workers is always suboptimal for capitalists, and thus capitalists have to adopt various strategies of surveillance and control to increase labor effort. While the intensity of overt conflict generated by these relations will vary over time and place, and class compromises may occur in which high levels of cooperation between labor and management take place, nevertheless, this underlying antagonism of material interests remains so long as the relationship remains exploitative.

For some theoretical and empirical purposes, this simple image of the class structure may be sufficient. For example, if the main purpose of an analysis is to explore the basic differences between the class structures of feudalism and capitalism, then an analysis which revolved entirely around the relationship between capitalists and workers might be adequate. However, for many of the things we want to study with class analysis, we need a more nuanced set of categories. In particular, we need concepts which allow for two kinds of analyses: first, the analysis of the variation across time and place in the class structures of concrete capitalist societies, and second, the analysis of the ways individual lives are affected by their location within the class structure. The first of these is needed if we are to explore macro-variations in a fine-grained way; the second is needed if we are to use class effectively in micro-analysis.[23]

---

[23] For an extended discussion of the limitations of the overly abstract polarized concept of class structure, see Wright (1989a: 271–278).

Both of these tasks involve elaborating a concept of class structure in capitalist societies that moves beyond the core polarization between capitalists and workers. More specifically, this involves solving two general problems in class structural analysis: first, the problem of locating the "middle class" within the class structure, and second, locating people not in the paid labor force in the class structure.[24]

1.5 The problem of the "middle class" among employees

If we limit the analysis of class structure in capitalism to the ownership of, and exclusion from, the means of production, we end up with a class structure in which there are only three locations – the capitalist class, the working class and the petty bourgeoisie (those who own means of production but do not hire workers) – and in which around 85–90% of the population in most developed capitalist countries falls into a single class. While this may in some sense reflect a profound truth about capitalism – that the large majority of the population are separated from the means of production and must sell their labor power on the labor market in order to survive – it does not provide us with an adequate conceptual framework for explaining many of the things we want class to help explain. In particular, if we want class structure to help explain class consciousness, class formation and class conflict, then we need some way of understanding the class-relevant divisions within the employee population.

In ordinary language terms, this is the problem of the "middle class" – people who do not own their own means of production, who sell their labor power on a labor market, and yet do not seem part of the "working class." The question, then, is on what basis can we differentiate class locations among people who share a common location of nonownership within capitalist property relations? In the analyses in this book, I will divide the class of employees along two dimensions: first, their relationship to authority within production, and second, their possession of skills or expertise.[25]

---

[24] There are additional problems in the elaboration of the concept of class structure which will be discussed later in this book. The location of state employees in the class structure will be discussed in chapter 15. The issue of the temporal dimension of class locations – the fact that some jobs are organized within careers that span class boundaries – will be discussed in chapters 5 and 6.

[25] The conceptual discussion here differs in a number of ways from the way I approached these questions in my earlier book, *Classes* (Wright 1985). In that book I argued that the rationale for considering authority and skills to be dimensions of the

Authority

There are two rationales for treating authority as a dimension of class relations among employees. The first concerns the role of *domination* within capitalist property relations. In order to insure the performance of adequate effort on the part of workers, capitalist production always involves an apparatus of domination involving surveillance, positive and negative sanctions and varying forms of hierarchy. Capitalists do not simply *own* the means of production and *hire* workers; they also *dominate* workers within production.

In these terms, managers and supervisors can be viewed as exercising delegated capitalist class powers in so far as they engage in the practices of domination within production. In this sense they can be considered *simultaneously* in the capitalist class *and* the working class: they are like capitalists in that they dominate workers; they are like workers in that they are controlled by capitalists and exploited within production. They thus occupy what I have called *contradictory locations within class relations*. The term "contradictory" is used in this expression rather than simply "dual" since the class interests embedded in managerial jobs combine the inherently antagonistic interests of capital and labor. The higher one moves in the authority hierarchy, the greater will be the weight of capitalist interests within this class location. Thus upper managers, and especially Chief Executive Officers in large corporations will be very closely tied to the capitalist class, while the class character of lower level supervisor jobs will be much closer to that of the working class.

The second rationale for treating the authority dimension as a criterion for differentiating class locations among employees centers on the relationship between their earnings and the appropriation of surplus. The strategic position of managers within the organization of production enables them to make significant claims on a portion of the social surplus (defined in the counterfactual manner discussed above) in the form of relatively high earnings.[26] In effect this means that the

class structure was that the control of organizational assets (i.e. authority) and skill assets were the basis for distinctive forms of exploitation. For reasons which I elaborated in a subsequent essay (Wright 1989a: ch. 8) this no longer seems a satisfactory way of specifying the class character of the "middle class." While the formulation presented here lacks the symmetry of the earlier strategy of analysis, I believe it is conceptually sounder.

[26] In earlier work I argued that by virtue of this appropriation of surplus by managers they should be seen as exploiters. The problem with this formulation is that

wages and salaries of managerial labor power are above the costs of producing and reproducing their labor power (including whatever skills they might have).

The specific mechanism through which this appropriation takes place can be referred to as a "loyalty rent." It is important for the profitability of capitalist firms that managers wield their power in an effective and responsible way. The difficulty is that a high level of surveillance and threats is generally not an effective strategy for eliciting this kind of behavior, both because managerial performance is generally rather hard to monitor and because repressive controls tend to undermine initiative rather than stimulate creative behavior. What is needed, then, is a way of generating some level of real commitment on the part of managers to the goals of the organization. This is accomplished by relatively high earnings linked to careers and promotion ladders within authority hierarchies. These higher earnings involve a redistribution of part of the social surplus to managers in order to build their loyalty to the organization. Of course, negative sanctions are still present in the background: managers are sometimes fired, they are disciplined for poor work by failing to get promotions or raises, etc. But these coercive forms of control gain their efficacy from their link to the strong inducements of earnings that, especially for higher level managers, are significantly above the costs of producing the skills of managers.[27] Managers thus not only occupy contradictory locations within class relations by virtue of domination, they occupy what might

---

managers also contribute to the surplus through their own laboring activity, and thus their surplus income may simply reflect a capacity to appropriate part of the surplus which they contribute to production. Instead of being "exploiters," therefore, many managers may simply be less exploited than other employees. Because of this ambiguity, therefore, it is better simply to see managers as occupying a *privileged* position with respect to the process of exploitation which enables them to appropriate part of the social surplus in the form of higher incomes.

[27] This rent component of the earnings of managers has been recognized in "efficiency wage" theory which acknowledges that the market-clearing wage may be suboptimal from the point of view of the goals of the employer. Because of the difficulty in enforcing labor contracts, employers have to pay employees more than the wages predicted by theories of competitive equilibria in order to gain compliance. While this mechanism may generate some small "employment rents" for all employees, it is especially salient for those employees who occupy strategic jobs requiring responsible, diligent performance of duties. For the mainstream economics discussion of efficiency wages, see Akerloff and Yellen (1986). For arguments that extend efficiency wage theory to Marxist arguments about the "extraction" of labor effort from workers, see Bowles and Gintis (1990).

be termed a *privileged appropriation location within exploitation relations*. Both of these differentiate them from the working class.

Skills and expertise

The second axis of class differentiation among employees centers on the possession of skills or expertise. Like managers, employees who possess high levels of skills/expertise are potentially in a privileged appropriation location within exploitation relations. There are two primary mechanisms through which this can happen. First, skills and expertise are frequently scarce in labor markets, not simply because they are in short supply, but also because there are systematic obstacles in the way of increasing the supply of those skills to meet the requirements of employing organizations. One important form of these obstacles is credentials, but rare talents could also constitute the basis for sustained restrictions on the supply of a particular form of labor power.[28] The result of such restrictions on supply is that owners of the scarce skills are able to receive a wage above the costs of producing and reproducing their labor power. This "skill rent" is a way by which employees can appropriate part of the social surplus.

Second, the control over knowledge and skills frequently renders also the labor effort of skilled workers difficult to monitor and control. The effective control over knowledge by such employees means that employers must rely to some extent on loyalty enhancing mechanisms in order to achieve desired levels of cooperation and effort from employees with high levels of skills and expertise, just as they have to do in the case of managers. Employees with high levels of expertise, therefore, are able to appropriate surplus both because of their strategic location within the organization of production (as controllers of knowledge), and because of their strategic location in the organization of labor markets (as controllers of a scarce form of labor power).

Understood in this way, the possession of skills and expertise defines a distinctive location within class relations because of a specific kind of power they confer on employees. It may also be the case that

---

[28] Credentials would not constitute a restriction on the supply of a particular kind of skill if there were no obstacles for individuals acquiring the credentials. A variety of such obstacles exist: restrictions on the number of slots in the training programs; restrictions in credit markets to get loans to obtain the training; inequality in the distribution of "cultural capital" (including such things as manners, accent, appearance, etc.) and "social capital" (especially such things as access to networks and information); and, of course, inequalities in genetic endowments.

expertise, skills and knowledge are associated with various kinds of "symbolic capital" and distinctive life-styles, as Bourdieu (1984) and others have noted. While these cultural correlates of class may be of considerable explanatory importance for a variety of sociological questions, they do not constitute the essential rationale for treating skills and expertise as a dimension of class location within a materialist class analysis (except in so far as symbolic capital plays a role in acquiring skills and credentials). That rationale rests on the claim that experts, like managers, occupy a privileged appropriation location within exploitation relations that differentiates them from ordinary workers.

Throughout this book I will frequently use "skills and expertise" as a couplet. The term "skill" by itself sometimes is taken to refer simply to manual skills, rather than the more general idea of enhanced or complex labor power, contrasted to "raw" or undeveloped labor power. This enhancement can take many forms, both physical and cognitive. It may provide great flexibility to engage in a variety of work settings, or it may be highly specialized and vulnerable to obsolescence. Enhanced labor power is often legally certified in the form of official credentials, but in some circumstances skills and expertise may function effectively without such certification. The important theoretical idea is that skills and expertise designate an asset embodied in the labor power of people which enhances their power in labor markets and labor processes.

A map of middle-class class locations

Adding position within authority hierarchies and possession of scarce skills and expertise to the fundamental dimension of capitalist property relations generates the map of class locations presented in Figure 1.2. With appropriate modifications depending upon our specific empirical objectives, this is the basic schema that underlies the investigations of this book. It is important to stress that this is a map of class *locations*. The cells in the typology are not "classes" as such; they are locations within class relations. Some of these are contradictory locations within class relations, others are privileged appropriation locations within exploitation relations and still others are polarized locations within capitalist property relations. By convention the polarized locations – "capitalists" and "workers" in capitalism – are often called "classes," but the more precise terminology would be to describe these as the fundamental locations within the capitalist class structure. The

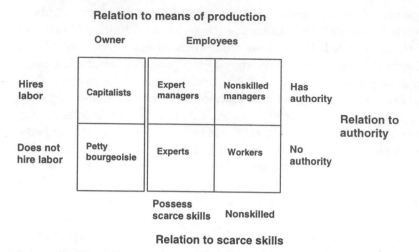

Figure 1.2 *Basic class typology*

typology is thus not a proposal for a six-class model of the class structure of capitalism, but rather a model of a class structure which differentiates six locations within class relations.

In some of the empirical analyses we will discuss, we will combine some of the locations in this typology, typically to generate a four category typology consisting of capitalists, petty bourgeois, "middle-class" locations (contradictory locations and privileged appropriation locations among employees) and workers. In other analyses we will modify the typology by adding intermediary categories along each of the dimensions. On the relation to means of production dimension this involves distinguishing between proper capitalists, small employers who only have a few employees, and the petty bourgeoisie (self-employed people with no employees). On the authority dimension this means differentiating between proper managers – people who are involved in organizational decision making – and mere supervisors, who have power over subordinates but are not involved in policy-making decisions. And, on the skill dimension this involves distinguishing between occupations which typically require advanced academic degrees, and other skilled occupations which require lower levels of specialized training. The result will be the twelve-location class-structure matrix presented in Figure 1.3.

This way of specifying the distinctiveness of the class location of managers and experts is similar in certain respects to Goldthorpe's

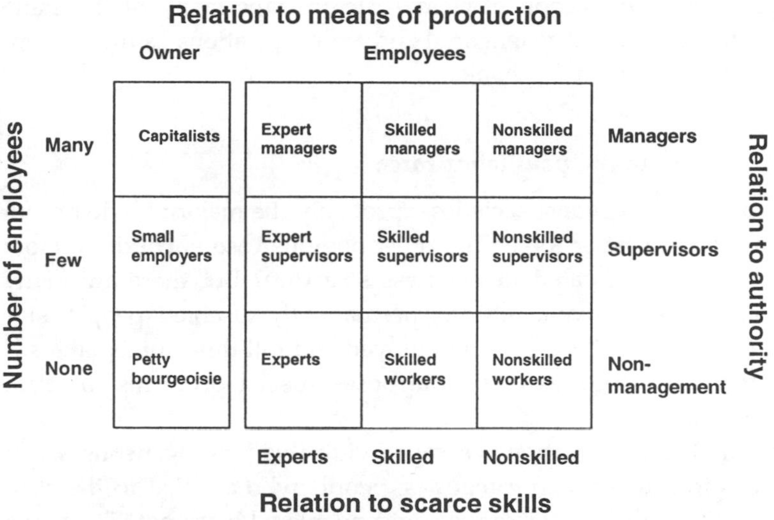

Relation to means of production

Figure 1.3 *Elaborated class typology*

(1982) treatment of the concept of the "service class." Goldthorpe draws a distinction between two kinds of employment relations: one based on a labor contract, characteristic of the working classes; and one based on what he terms a "service relationship," characteristic of managers and experts. In the latter, employees enter a career structure, not simply a job, and their rewards are in significant ways prospective, rather than simply payments for labor performed. Such a service relation, Goldthorpe argues, is "likely to be found where it is required of employees that they exercise *delegated authority or specialized knowledge and expertise* in the interests of their employing organization. In the nature of the case ... their performance will depend upon the degree of moral commitment that they feel toward the organization rather than on the efficacy of external sanctions" (Goldthorpe and Erikson 1993: 42). This characterization is closely related to the idea that, because of their strategic power within organizations, the cooperation of middle-class employees is achieved in part through the payment of loyalty rents embodied in their earnings. The main difference between Goldthorpe's conceptual analysis and the one adopted here is, first, that Goldthorpe does not link his analysis of service-class jobs to the problem of exploitation and antagonistic interests, and second, that he treats the authority dimension of managerial positions simply in terms of heightened responsibilities, not domination. Nevertheless, Goldthorpe's conceptualization of class structure taps many of the same relational properties of managerial and expert positions as the conceptualization adopted in this book.

1.6 People not in the paid labor force

Many people in capitalist societies – probably the majority – do not fill jobs in the paid labor force. The most obvious case is children. How should babies be located in the class structure? But there are many other categories as well: retirees, permanently disabled people, students, people on welfare, the unemployed and full-time homemakers.[29] Each of these categories of people poses special problems for class structure analysis.

As a first approximation we can divide this heterogeneous set of situations into two broad categories: people who are tied to the class structure through family relations, and people who are not. To be in a "location" within class structure is to have one's material interests shaped by one's relationship to the process of exploitation. One way such linkages to exploitation are generated by class structures is through *jobs*. This is the kind of class location we have been exploring so far. I will refer to these as *direct class locations*. But there are other mechanisms by which people's lives are linked to the process of exploitation. Of particular importance are the ways in which family structures and kinship relations link an individual's material interests to the process of exploitation. Being born into a wealthy capitalist family links the child to the material interests of the capitalist class via family relations. It makes sense, then, to say that this child is "in" the

---

[29] The claim that the people in these categories do not participate directly in production is simple enough for the unemployed, retirees and children, but it is problematic for housewives, since housewives obviously work and produce things in the home. This has led some theorists (e.g. Delphy, 1984) to argue that the work of housewives should be treated as domestic labor performed within a domestic mode of production in which housewives occupy a distinctive class location, the domestic worker. Others have argued that household production is a subsidiary part of the capitalist mode of production. It has even been argued (Fraad, Resnick and Wolff, 1994) that household production is a special form of feudal production in which housewives are feudally exploited by their husbands since the husbands directly "appropriate" use-values from their wives. All of these views in one way or another attempt to treat the gender and kinship relations within a family as if they were a form of class relations. This amalgamation of class and gender undercuts the explanatory specificity of both class and gender and does not, I believe, enhance our capacity to explain the processes in question. In any case, since the analysis in this book is restricted to people in the paid labor force, we will bracket these issues.

capitalist class. If that child, as a young adult, works in a factory but stands to inherit millions of dollars of capitalist wealth and can rely on family resources for various needs, then that person would simultaneously be in two class locations: the capitalist class by virtue of family ties and the working class by virtue of the job.

I will refer to these situations as *mediated class locations*. Family ties are probably the most important basis for mediated class locations, but membership in certain kinds of communities or the relationship to the state may also provide such linkages. In each case the question one asks is "how do the social relations in which a person's life is embedded link that person to the various mechanisms of class exploitation and thus shape that person's material interests?" Many people, of course, have both direct and mediated class locations. This is of particular importance in developed capitalist economies for households in which both spouses are in the labor force, for this creates the possibility that husbands and wives will have different direct class locations, and thus each of them will have different direct and mediated locations. Understanding such "cross-class families" is the core problem of chapter 10.

There are, however, people for whom family ties provide at most extremely tenuous linkages to the class structure. Most notably, this is the situation of many people in the so-called "underclass." This expression is used in a variety of ways in contemporary policy discussions. Sometimes it is meant to be a pejorative term rather like the old Marxist concept of "lumpenproletariat"; at other times it is used more descriptively to designate a segment of the poor whose conditions of life are especially desperate and whose prospects for improvement are particularly dismal. In terms of the analysis of this chapter, one way of giving this concept a more precise theoretical status is to link it to the concepts of exploitation and oppression: an "underclass" can be defined as a category of social agents who are economically oppressed but not consistently exploited within a given class system.[30]

[30] Although he does not explicitly elaborate the term "underclass" in terms of a theory of exploitation and economic oppression, the definition proposed here is consistent with the more structural aspects of way the term is used by William Julius Wilson (1982, 1987) in his analysis of the interconnection between race and class in American society. Wilson argues that as legal barriers to racial equality have disappeared and as class differentiation within the black population has increased, the central determining structure of the lives of many African-Americans is no longer race as such, but class. More specifically, he argues that there has been a

Different kinds of class structures will generate different forms of an "underclass." In many parts of the world today and throughout much of human history, the pivotal resource which defines the underclass is land. Landlords, agrarian capitalists, peasants and exploited agrarian producers all have access to land; people who are excluded from such access constitute the underclass of agrarian societies. In these terms, many Native Americans were transformed into an underclass in the nineteenth century when they were pushed off of the land onto the reservations.

In contemporary advanced capitalism, the key resource which defines the predicament of the underclass is labor power itself. This might seem like an odd statement since in capitalism, at least since the abolition of slavery, everyone supposedly owns one "unit" of labor power, him or herself. The point is that some people do not in fact own *productively saleable* labor power. The situation is similar to a capitalist owning outmoded machines. While the capitalist physically controls these pieces of machinery, they cease to be "capital" – a capitalistically productive asset – if they cannot be deployed within a capitalist production process profitably. In the case of labor power, a person can physically control his or her own laboring capacity, but that capacity can cease to have economic value in capitalism if it cannot be deployed productively. This is the essential condition of people in the "underclass." They are oppressed because they are denied access to various kinds of productive resources, above all the necessary means to acquire the skills needed to make their labor power saleable. As a result, they are not consistently exploited.[31]

Understood in this way, the underclass consists of human beings who are largely expendable *from the point of view of the logic of capitalism.*

substantial growth of an urban underclass of people without marketable skills and with very weak attachments to the labor force, living in crumbling central cities isolated from the mainstream of American life and institutions.

[31] It is perhaps controversial to amalgamate the exclusion of the contemporary urban underclass from human capital and other job resources with the exclusion of Native Americans from the land. In the latter case there was a zero-sum character to access to the resource in question and massive coercion was used to enforce the exclusion, whereas in the case of education, skills and even good jobs, it is not so obvious that the resources in question are a fixed quantity and that access is being denied through force. Thus the factual inequalities of access to these resources may not in fact be instances of coercively enforced exclusions which benefit certain groups of people at the expense of others. The plight of the underclass might still be a matter of serious moral concern, but it would not count as an instance of nonexploitative oppression analogous to the condition of Native Americans.

Like Native Americans who became a landless underclass in the nineteenth century, repression rather than incorporation is the central mode of social control directed toward them. Capitalism does not need the labor power of unemployed inner city youth. The material interests of the wealthy and privileged segments of American society would be better served if these people simply disappeared. However, unlike in the nineteenth century, the moral and political forces are such that direct genocide is no longer a viable strategy. The alternative, then, is to build prisons and to cordon off the zones of cities in which the underclass lives.

1.7 Marxist versus Weberian class analysis

As a set of empirical categories, the class structure matrix in Figures 1.2 and 1.3 could be deployed within either a Weberian or Marxist framework. The control over economic resources is central to both Marxist and Weberian class analysis, and both frameworks could be massaged to allow for the array of categories I am using. Indeed, a good argument could be made that the proposed class structure concept incorporates significant Weberian elements, since the explicit inclusion of skills as a criterion for class division and the importance accorded income privileges for both managers and credentialed experts are hallmarks of Weberian class analysis. In a real sense, therefore, the empirical categories in this book can be seen as a hybrid of the categories conventionally found in Marxist and Weberian class analysis.[32] In what sense, therefore, does this class structure analysis remain "Marxist"?

To answer this question we need to compare the theoretical foundations of the concept of class in the Marxist and Weberian traditions.[33] The contrast between Marx and Weber has been one of the grand themes in the history of Sociology as a discipline. Most graduate school programs have a sociological theory course within which Marx versus Weber figures as a central motif. However, in terms of class analysis,

---

[32] It should not be so surprising to see Marxist and Weberian elements conjoined in class analysis. After all, Weber's class analysis was deeply indebted to the Marxist legacy which was part of the general intellectual discourse of his time. In spite of the fact that Weber constantly distanced himself from Marxism, particularly because of its tendencies toward economic determinism which were especially pronounced in his day, when Weber talks of classes he is speaking in a rather Marxian voice.

[33] For discussions of the contrast between Marxist and Weberian class analysis, see for example, Parkin (1979), Burris (1987), Giddens (1973), Wright (1979: ch. 1).

posing Marx and Weber as polar opposites is a bit misleading because in many ways Weber is speaking in his most Marxian voice when he talks about class. The concept of class within these two streams of thought share a number of important features:

- Both Marxist and Weberian approaches differ from what might be called simple gradational notions of class in which classes are differentiated strictly on the basis of inequalities in the material conditions of life.[34] This conceptualization of class underwrites the common inventory of classes found in popular discourse and the mass media: upper class, upper middle class, middle class, lower middle class, lower class, underclass. Both Marxist and Weberian class analysis define classes *relationally*, i.e. a given class location is defined by virtue of the social relations which link it to other class locations.

- Both traditions identify the concept of class with the relationship between people and economically relevant assets or resources. Marxists call this relation to the means of production; Weberians refer to "market capacities." But they are both really talking about very similar empirical phenomena.

- Both traditions see the causal relevance of class as operating, at least in part, via the ways in which these relations shape the material interests of actors. Ownership of the means of production and ownership of one's own labor power are explanatory of social action because these property rights shape the strategic alternatives people face in pursuing their material well-being. What people *have* imposes constraints on what they can *do* to get what they *want*. To be sure, Marxists tend to put more weight on the objective character of these "material interests" by highlighting the fact that these constraints are imposed on individuals, whereas Weberians tend to focus on the subjective conditions, by emphasizing the relative contingency in what people want. Nevertheless, it is still the case that at their core, both class concepts involve the causal connection between (a) social relations to resources

---

[34] The contrast between "gradational" and "relational" concepts of class was first introduced into sociology by Ossowski (1963). For a more extended discussion of gradational concepts of class, see Wright (1979: ch. 1).

and (b) material interests via (c) the way resources shape strategies for acquiring income.

How then do they differ? The pivotal difference is captured by the contrast between the favorite buzz-words of each theoretical tradition: *life chances* for Weberians, and *exploitation* for Marxists. The reason why production is more central to Marxist than to Weberian class analysis is because of its salience for the problem of exploitation; the reason why Weberians give greater emphasis to the market is because it so directly shapes life chances.

The intuition behind the idea of life chances is straightforward. "In our terminology," Weber (in Gerth and Mills 1958:181–2) writes:

> "classes" are not communities; they merely represent possible, and frequent, bases for communal action. We may speak of a "class" when (1) a number of people have in common a specific causal component of their life chances, in so far as (2) this component is represented exclusively by economic interests in the possession of goods and opportunities for income, and (3) is represented under conditions of the commodity or labor markets. [These points refer to "class situation," which we may express more briefly as the typical chance for a supply of goods, external living conditions and life experiences, in so far as this chance is determined by the amount and kind of power, or lack of such, to dispose of goods or skills for the sake of income in a given economic order. The term "class" refers to any group of people that is found in the same class situation]... But always this is the generic connotation of the concept of class: that the kind of chance in the *market* is the decisive moment which presents a common condition for the individual's fate. "Class situation" is, in this sense, ultimately "market situation."

In short, the kind and quantity of resources you own affects your opportunities for income in market exchanges. "Opportunity" is a description of the feasible set individuals face, the trade-offs they encounter in deciding what to do. Owning means of production gives a person different alternatives from owning credentials, and both of these are different from simply owning unskilled labor power. Furthermore, in a market economy, access to market-derived income affects the broader array of life experiences and opportunities for oneself and one's children. The study of the life chances of children based on parents' market capacity is thus an integral part of the Weberian agenda of class analysis.

Within a Weberian perspective, therefore, the salient issue in the

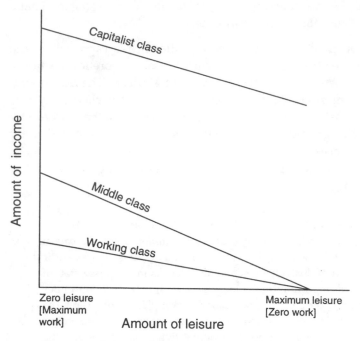

Figure 1.4 *Leisure vs. consumption trade-offs faced by people in different economic classes*

linkage of people to different kinds of economic resources is the way this confers on them different kinds of economic opportunities and disadvantages and thereby shapes their material interests. One way of representing this idea in a simple way is by examining the income–leisure trade-offs faced by people in different classes as pictured in Figure 1.4. In this figure, everyone faces some trade-off between leisure and income: less leisure yields more income.[35] However, for the propertied class it is possible to have high income with no work (thus

[35] For simplicity, the leisure–consumption trade-off is pictured here as a linear relation. For the working class and the middle class the slope of the line thus represents a linear wage rate. Of course, in the real world, because of such things as overtime on the one hand, and substandard wages for part-time work on the other, the relation would not be linear. The slope of the capitalist class curve in the figure is given as roughly the same as that of the middle class. If we consider all capitalists, not simply those with great entrepreneurial talent, there is no reason to assume *a priori* that their imputed hourly wage (i.e. the part of their earnings that is derived from labor time rather than from their property) would be greater than that of the middle class (skilled employees and managers). In any event, for our present purposes the main point about the capitalist curve is that it does not intersect the x-axis.

the expressions "the leisure class" or the "idle rich"), whereas for both the middle class and the working class in this stylized drawing, zero work corresponds to zero income. The middle class has "greater" opportunities (life chances) in the market than workers because the slope they face (i.e. the wage rate) is steeper. Some workers in fact might actually have a higher standard of living than some people in the middle class, but the trade-offs they face are nevertheless less desirable. These common trade-offs, then, are the basis for a potential commonality of interests among members of a class, and thus constitute the basis for potential common action.

Within a Marxist framework, the feature of the relationship of people to economic resources which is at the core of class analysis is "exploitation." Both "exploitation" and "life chances" identify inequalities in material well-being that are generated by inequalities in access to resources of various sorts. Thus both of these concepts point to conflicts of interest over the *distribution* of the assets themselves. What exploitation adds to this is a claim that conflicts of interest between classes are generated not simply by what people *have*, but also by what people *do* with what they have.[36] The concept of exploitation, therefore, points our attention to conflicts within production, not simply conflicts in the market.

This contrast between the Marxist and Weberian traditions of class analysis is summarized in Figure 1.5. Weberian class analysis revolves around a single causal nexus that works through market exchanges. Marxist class analysis includes the Weberian causal processes, but adds to them a causal structure within production itself as well as an account of the interactions of production and exchange. Part of our analysis of the class location of managers, for example, concerns the "loyalty rent" which managers receive by virtue of their position within the authority structure of production. This reflects the way in which location within the relations of production and not simply within market relations affects the "life chances" of managers. Our analysis of the shmoo – and more broadly, the analysis of such things as the way transfer payments of the welfare state affect the market

[36] The conceptual distinction between life chances and exploitation being argued for here runs against the arguments of John Roemer (1985), who insists that exploitation is strictly a way of talking about the injustice of the effects of what people have (assets) on what people get (income). In this sense, he collapses the problem of exploitation into the problem of life chances and thus dissolves the distinction between Marxist and Weberian class analysis. The notion of the extraction of labor effort disappears from his analysis of exploitation.

I. Simple gradational class analysis

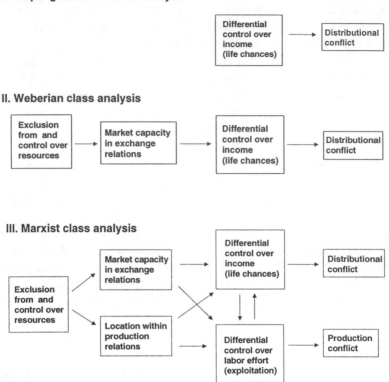

II. Weberian class analysis

III. Marxist class analysis

Figure 1.5 *Three models of class analysis*

capacity of workers – illustrates how market capacity has an impact on the extraction of labor effort within production. The Marxist concept of class directs our attention both theoretically and empirically towards these interactions.

A Weberian might reply that there is nothing in the Weberian idea of market-based life chances that would *prevent* the analysis of the extraction of labor effort within production. A good and subtle Weberian class analyst could certainly link the analysis of market capacities within exchange relations to power relations within the labor process, and thus explore the causal structures at the center of Marxist class analysis. In systematically joining production and exchange in this way, however, the Weberian concept would in effect become Marxianized. Frank Parkin (1979: 25), in a famous gibe, said, "Inside every neo-Marxist there seems to be a Weberian struggling to get out." One could just as easily say that inside every left-wing Weberian there is a Marxist struggling to stay hidden.

There are three main reasons why one might want to ground the concept of class explicitly in exploitation rather than simply market-based life chances. First, the exploitation-centered class concept affirms the fact that production and exchange are intrinsically linked, not merely contingently related. The material interests of capitalists and workers are *inherently* shaped by the interaction of these two facets of the social relations that bind them together. This provides us with the way of understanding the class location of managers as determined not simply by their position within the market for managerial labor power, but also by their position within the relations of domination in production. More broadly, the exploitation-based class concept points our attention to the fact that class relations are relations of power, not merely privilege.

Second, theorizing the interests linked to classes as grounded in inherently antagonistic and interdependent practices facilitates the analysis of social conflict. Explanations of conflict always require at least two elements: an account of the opposing *interests* at stake in the conflict and an account of the *capacity* of the actors to pursue those interests. A simple opposition of interests is not enough to explain active conflict between groups. Exploitation is a powerful concept precisely because it brings together an account of opposing interests with an account of the rudimentary capacity for resistance. Exploiters not only have a positive interest in limiting the life chances of the exploited, but also are *dependent* upon the exploited for the realization of their own interests. This dependency of the exploiter on the exploited gives the exploited an inherent capacity to resist. Exploitation, there-fore, does not simply predict an opposition of interests, but a tendency for this antagonism of interests to generate manifest conflicts between classes. This understanding of the inherent power of exploited classes is marginalized when class is defined strictly in terms of market relations.

Finally, the exploitation-centered class analysis implies that classes can exist in nonmarket societies, whereas Weberian class analysis explicitly restricts the relevance of class to markets. For Marxist class analysis, the relationship between slave master and slave or lord and serf are instances of class relations because they all involve exploitation linked to property rights in the forces of production.[37] The relationship

---

[37] The classic Marxist description of feudalism is a society in which the lords appropriate surplus products directly from the serfs through the use of what is generally called "extra-economic coercion." This coercion either takes the form of

between bureaucratic exploiters and producers in command economies can also be considered a form of class relations since the capacity of the state bureaucratic elite to appropriate surplus rests on their effective control over the society's productive resources (Wright 1994: ch. 6). For Weberian class analysis these are not class relations, but rather examples of castes or estates or some other form of inequality of power, since the differences in "life chances" of the slave and slave master, the lord and serf, the bureaucratic appropriator and producer, are not the result of their meeting within a market. The Weberian restriction of the concept of class to market societies, therefore, directs our attention away from the underlying commonality of these relations across different kinds of social systems.

There is, of course, no metatheoretical rule of sociology which says that every sociologist must choose between these two ways of grounding class analysis. It certainly might be possible to construct an eclectic hybrid between Marxist and Weberian class analysis by seeing exploitation as defining the central cleavages within a class structure and differential market capacities as defining salient *strata within classes*. Strata within the capitalist class would be defined by differential capacity to appropriate surplus; strata within the working class would be determined by differences in incomes and working conditions generated by different market capacities. In such a hybrid class analysis, what I have been calling the "middle class" might be more appropriately described as privileged strata within the working class.

Nevertheless, throughout this book I will interpret the class-structure matrix we will be using within a neo-Marxist class analysis framework. In the end, the decision to do this rather than adopt a more eclectic stance comes at least in part from political commitments, not simply dispassionate scientific principles. This does not mean that Marxist

---

forcing the peasant to work part of the week on the land of the lord, or exacting some portion of the produce of the peasant. An alternative characterization is to say that in feudalism the lord and the serf are joint owners of the labor power of the serf. This gives the lord property rights in the laboring capacity of serfs. Slavery, in these terms, is simply the limiting case in which the slave has lost all property rights in his or her own labor power. This joint ownership of the serf's labor power is reflected in the laws which tie serfs to the land and which prevent the flight of serfs to the city. Such flight is simply a form of theft: the fleeing serf, like the fleeing slave, has stolen property from the lord. The use of extra-economic coercion, then, is simply the means of enforcing these property rights, no different from the use of extra-economic coercion to prevent workers from taking over a factory. For an extended discussion of this way of understanding feudalism, see Wright (1985: 77–78).

class analysis is pure ideology or that it is rigidly dictated by radical egalitarian values. My choice of analytical framework is also based on my beliefs in the theoretical coherence of this approach – which I have argued for in this chapter – and in its capacity to illuminate empirical problems, which I hope to demonstrate in the rest of this book. But this choice remains crucially bound up with commitments to the socialist tradition and its aspirations for an emancipatory, egalitarian alternative to capitalism.

Readers who are highly skeptical of the Marxist tradition for whatever reasons might feel that there is no point in struggling through the masses of numbers, graphs and equations in the rest of this book. If the conceptual justifications for the categories are unredeemably flawed, it might be thought, the empirical results generated with those categories will be worthless. This would be, I think, a mistake. The empirical categories themselves can be interpreted in a Weberian or hybrid manner. Indeed, as a practical set of operational categories, the class structure matrix used in this book does not dramatically differ from the class typology used by Goldthorpe (1980) and Erikson and Goldthorpe (1993). As is usually the case in sociology, the empirical categories of analysis are *under*determined by the theoretical frameworks within which they are generated or interpreted. This means that readers who are resolutely unconvinced about the virtues of understanding classes in terms of exploitation can still engage the empirical analyses of this book as investigations of classes differentially situated with respect to life chances in the market.

1.8 The empirical agenda of the book

Broadly speaking, the empirical studies in this book explore three interconnected problems in class analysis: (1) Characteristics of and variations in class structure itself; (2) The relationship between class and gender as aspects of social structure; (3) The linkage between class structure and aspects of class consciousness.

Class structure

The research in parts I and II all concern various problems in the analysis of class structure itself. Chapter 2 sets the stage for the rest of the book by presenting basic descriptive data on the overall shape of the class structure in a number of advanced capitalist societies. Here we are not so much interested in testing specific hypotheses about cross-national variations than in carefully describing various aspects of these variations. As a result, in some ways this chapter is less interesting theoretically as the empirical chapters which follow.

Chapter 3 examines changes in the distribution of people in the American class structure between 1960 and 1990 and decomposes these changes into a part that can be attributed to shifts in class distributions within economic sectors and a part to shifts in the distribution of people across economic sectors. The basic results are quite striking. The working class expanded slightly in the 1960s, but has declined at an accelerating pace since then, especially because of a decline in the working class within sectors. Supervisors increased significantly in the 1960s and modestly in the 1970s, but declined in the 1980s. In contrast, managers, experts and expert managers have all increased throughout this period. The petty bourgeoisie and small employer class categories declined both within and across sectors in the 1960s, but since then have had a more complex trajectory, leading in the 1980s to a quite significant expansion of the petty bourgeoisie and a nearly steady state for small employers. While our data do not allow us to test alternative explanations for these changes, I offer a tentative explanation in terms of the combination of technological change and the ramifications of long-term economic stagnation in an increasingly competitive international capitalist economic system.

Chapter 4 examines in much greater detail one of the trends in Chapter 3, the initial decline and then steady expansion of self-employment. Two different strategies of data analysis are presented: first, a time series analysis of annual changes in the rate of self-employment in which we test whether or not changes in self-employment can be attributed to changes in the rate of unemployment; and second, an examination of the sectoral patterns of changes in self-employment in which we document that the upsurge in self-employment which began in the mid-1970s is a broad trend throughout the economy, not simply in the service sector.

Part II explores the degree of permeability of class boundaries in four countries: the United States, Canada, Norway and Sweden. Class structures vary not simply in the distribution of people into class locations, but in the extent to which the lives of people are narrowly confined to specific class locations or involve social contacts and experiences across class boundaries. Chapter 5 lays out the theoretical and methodological issues involved in studying the permeability of these boundaries. The following chapters examine three forms of permeability: the permeability of class boundaries to intergenerational mobility (Chapter 6), the permeability of boundaries to friendships (Chapter 7), and the permeability of boundaries to cross-class marriages (Chapter 8). To somewhat oversimplify the main punchlines of the research, for each of these forms of permeability in all four countries, the authority boundary is the most permeable and, generally, the property boundary is the least permeable.

Class and Gender

Since the late 1970s, one of the main challenges to class analysis has come from feminist scholars who have argued for the centrality of gender as an explanatory principle in social theory and research. Many feminists have been especially critical of claims to "class primacy," which are often attributed to Marxist scholarship (in spite of the fact that few Marxists today actually defend class primacy as a general principle).

In more recent years there has been something of a truce on the issue of class and gender as most people recognize that there is no point in arguing for all-encompassing abstract claims about the "primacy" of particular causal factors in social explanations. Primacy is a tractable issue only with respect to specific explananda, and even then it is often more fruitful to explore the forms of interaction of different causal processes than to focus on which is "more important."[38] Rather than seek any kind of metatheoretical priority to class analysis over gender analysis (or vice versa), it is more important to understand the interconnections of class and gender in specific explanatory problems.

This dialogue between Marxism and certain strands of feminism constitutes the backdrop to the analyses of class and gender in Chapters 9–12. Chapter 9 defends a conceptualization of class and gender in which they are treated as analytically distinct relations which interact in various social settings. The chapter then frames the empirical agenda by discussing a menu of five different forms in which this interaction takes place.

Chapter 10 examines the conceptual and empirical problem of the class location of married women. In Chapter 8, where we explore the permeability of class boundaries to cross-class marriages, the class character of households is defined in terms of the individual job-classes

---

[38] For a general discussion of the problem of explanatory primacy, see Wright, Levine and Sober (1992).

of both husbands and wives. Some scholars have challenged this way of understanding the class location of married women in the labor force. They have argued that families, not individuals, occupy locations in class structures, and thus all members of a family must share the same class position. Since the class interests of families are most decisively shaped by the class character of the husband's job, the argument goes, all members of the family, including married women with paid jobs, should be seen in the husband's class. This chapter explores the conceptual foundations of this argument and various other conceptualizations, and then proposes a strategy for empirically comparing the alternatives.

Chapter 11 examines an explanatory problem that is of considerable importance within gender analysis: the gender division of labor in the home. Many feminists have argued that the sexual division of labor within families is at the very core of the social practices which produce and reproduce gender hierarchy in the society at large. In this chapter we examine the relationship between the class composition of households and the amount of housework husbands perform in Sweden and the United States. The results are quite simple: class has almost no effect on husbands' performance of housework in either country.

Chapter 12 explores a specific aspect of gender distributions within class structures – the differential probabilities of men and women having workplace authority. It is hardly news that men are more likely to have authority within the workplace. What we explore in this chapter is first, the extent to which there are cross-national variations in this "gender gap" in authority; second, the extent to which this gender gap can be accounted for by a range of individual attributes of men and women (such as job experience, age, education, part-time employment, sector, occupation, and a few other variables); and third, the extent to which there is evidence of a "glass ceiling" within authority hierarchies (i.e. the gender gap in authority increases as one moves up hierarchies). The basic answer to the first question is that there are quite substantial cross-national variations, with the United States and Australia having the smallest gender gaps, followed by Canada and the UK, then the two Scandinavian countries in the analysis, Norway and Sweden, and finally Japan, which has by far the largest gender gap in authority of all of these countries. The answer to the second question is that very little of the gender gap in authority or the cross-national differences in the gap can be explained by the distribution of attributes of men and women. The gaps thus appear to be largely due to direct discrimination within employment. The answer to the third question is perhaps the most surprising: there is virtually no evidence that a genuine glass ceiling exists, at least into the middle ranges of authority hierarchies.

Class structure and class consciousness

One of the main reasons for studying class structure is because of its importance in explaining other elements of class analysis, especially class formation, class consciousness and class struggle. Chapter 13 lays out a general model of the interconnection of these elements of class analysis. More specifically, the chapter tries to clarify the relationship between the micro- and macro-levels of class analysis. This involves first discussing in general metatheoretical terms the distinction between micro- and macro-analysis, and then elaborating a micro-model of the relationship between class *location*, individual class *practices* and class *consciousness*, and a macro-model of the relationship between class *structure*, class *struggle* and class *formation*.

Chapter 14 applies the framework in Chapter 13 to a study of class consciousness and class formation in the United States, Sweden and Japan. These three countries are striking contrasts in the patterns of what we will call "ideological class formation." Sweden is quite ideologically polarized between a working-class coalition and a bourgeois coalition with a relatively large and distinct middle-class coalition in between. Ideological differentiation is sharpest along the property dimension of the class structure matrix, but is systematic and marked along the authority and skill dimensions as well. In the United States the bourgeois coalition penetrates much more broadly into the class locations among employees and the overall pattern of class formation is less ideologically polarized than in Sweden, but the basic shape of ideological differentiation across the class structure matrix is still quite similar in the two countries. In Japan the patterns are drastically different: the degree of polarization is much more muted than in either the US or Sweden, and among employees the ideological cleavages occur mainly along the skill-expertise dimension rather than the authority dimension.

Chapter 15 examines the problem of class location and class consciousness in the state. The state sector poses a number of interesting problems for class analysis, since class relations inside of the state are not directly built on the relation between capitalists and workers. I argue that the state employment in capitalist societies should be divided into two subsectors: first, an embryonic form of a post-capitalist, statist mode of production, and second, the apparatuses of the political superstructure of capitalism. This chapter then explores for Sweden and the United States the relationship between class location within the private sector of employment and these two state subsectors and class consciousness.

Finally, Chapter 16 examines the relationship between class location, class biography and class consciousness in Sweden and the United States. Two aspects of class consciousness are distinguished: class identity and what I call class-interest consciousness. The former I describe as a backward-looking aspect of consciousness since identities are rooted in a person's overall biography. Interest consciousness, on the other hand, is forward looking, since one's interests depend to a large extent on one's expectations about the future. This leads to the specific prediction that class identity should be more closely linked empirically to one's overall biographical trajectory in the class structure than to one's current class location, whereas class-interest consciousness should be more closely tied to class location.

This is a highly heterogeneous set of empirical problems. What emerges cumulatively from the research is not a simple punchline about the superiority of Marxist approaches to class over its rivals, or the universal explanatory power of class relative to other social causes. Rather, the bottom line message of the research is two-fold: first, within the family of developed capitalist societies there is considerable variation in both the structural properties of the system of class relations and the effects of class, and second, in spite of these variations, the fundamental class division based on ownership of the means of production remains a consistently important division within nearly all of the analyses of the book.

Part I

The class structure of capitalism and its transformations

2 Class structure in comparative perspective

The starting point for class analysis is the problem of class structure. The investigation of class structure provides us with a way both of situating the lives of individuals for micro-class analysis and of describing variations in societies across time and place for macro-class analysis. In Chapter 1 we explored the theoretical foundations for this concept. In this chapter we will descriptively map out the broad contours of the class structure in several developed capitalist countries.

In practical terms, this task involves pigeonholing people into specific categories on the basis of responses they give to a questionnaire about their work. It is not possible to directly observe a "class structure" as such. What one observes are individuals who occupy specific places in a social structure. By asking them appropriate questions and aggregating their responses, we generate descriptions of the class structure as a whole. To some readers this may seem like a fairly sterile scholastic exercise. Taxonomy, classification, pigeonholing – these are surely the tedious preoccupations of narrow academic specialists. What is worse, squeezing individuals into simple categories seems to obliterate the richness and complexity of their lives. Class becomes a static set of simple boxes rather than a complex, dynamic process. Wouldn't it be better to pursue qualitative field research with relatively loose and flexible concepts capable of adapting to the complexity of the situation?

There is some truth in these criticisms. The categories we will be using are highly simplified representations of the complexity of class relations. The categories do become "fixed" in that once a set of criteria are adopted they are applied to all people in the same way in different countries. As a result, there will inevitably be many cases in which individuals are being squeezed uncomfortably into slots. The appropriate question, however, is not "do the categories we develop faithfully mirror the complexity of the world?" but rather, "are these categories capable of advancing our knowledge of specific problems in class analysis?" Do these categories, however crude they might be, enable us to identify interesting puzzles? Do they help to reveal places where existing theories run into trouble, and provide at least some relevant evidence for the reconstruction of those theories? In the end, as Engels once said, "the proof of the pudding is in the eating."

This chapter will be concerned primarily with describing the overall appearance of the pudding. In the rest of the book we will eat it and see how well it tastes.

2.1 The basic contours of the class structure

Figure 2.1 presents the distribution of the employed labor force into the twelve class locations described in Chapter 1 for six countries: the United States, Canada, the United Kingdom, Sweden, Norway and Japan.[1] The details of the operationalization of these categories and a discussion of a range of methodological problems in making these estimates are presented in the methodological appendix to this chapter. We will first look at the patterns across the property dimensions of the class structure and then turn to class distributions among employees.

The property dimension

The capitalist class, defined as self-employed people who employ ten or more employees, comprises no more than about 2% of the labor

---

[1]   The other countries in the Comparative Class Analysis Project have been excluded for a variety of reasons. In the case of Russia, Korea, Taiwan and Spain, the data from their projects did not become available until after most of the analyses in the book were completed. Four of the other countries – Germany, Finland, New Zealand and Denmark – are excluded from the analyses of the book either because of various problems in the comparability of certain parts of their data or because important sections of the questionnaire were dropped. Analysis of the data of the final country, Australia, appears in one chapter of the book (Chapter 10). I am not including Australia in the present chapter because I am not confident in the reliability of the data for its overall class distribution. In particular, the proportion of managers (not simply supervisors, but decisionmaking managers) in the Australian sample is nearly twice that of any other country in the project. This very high density of managers is not consistent with other limited survey data on Australia. For this reason, I am not including the Australian data in the general discussion of class distributions in this chapter.

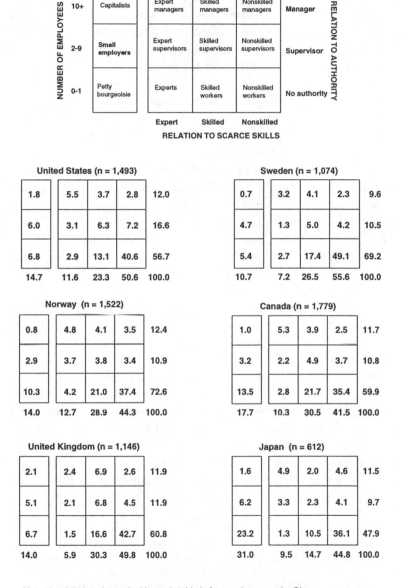

Figure 2.1 *Class distributions in six countries*

force in any of these countries, and less than 1% in two of them (Sweden and Norway). Of course, this figure does not include those capitalists who are not technically "employers." Many people who own significant amounts of capitalist wealth may be employed as top executives of corporations, others are employed in jobs completely unrelated to their capitalist wealth, and some are formally out of the labor force, living as pure rentiers off the income from their wealth. A few are even professors. Unfortunately, with the comparative data in this project it is not possible to estimate the proportion of the population who would fall into the segment of the capitalist class which is not self-employed. In any case, this would probably only add at most a few percentage points to these figures.[2]

As would be expected, there are considerably more small employers, defined here as self-employed individuals employing two to nine employees, than proper capitalists. The range is between about 3% of the labor force in Canada and Norway and about 6% in the United States and Japan. Putting these two class locations together, between roughly 4% and 8% of the labor forces of these six developed capitalist countries are in class locations which are, to a greater or lesser extent, directly connected to the capitalist class.

Considering the differences in other aspects of the political economies of these countries which might be thought relevant to the size of their capitalist classes – the size of their domestic markets, the recentness of industrialization, their position in the world economy, the role of the state – this is a relatively small range of variation. Sweden, which is arguably the least capitalistic of these six countries, still has 5.4% of its labor force in either the small employer or capitalist class location; the United States, the most purely capitalistic of these countries, has 7.8% of its labor force in these locations. This does constitute a real difference, but it is not striking.

There is much more variation across these countries in the size of the petty bourgeoisie (self-employed people with no more than one employee), which ranges from about 5% of the labor force in

2   According to Lawrence Mishel and David Frankel (1991: p. 162), in the richest 1% of US households defined by the income distribution, 47.8% of household income came from capital assets in 1988. For the next richest 4%, this figure drops to 23.2%. The average assets per household for the richest 0.5% of American households in 1989 was over $8 million, and of the next 0.5% over $2.5 million. These data suggest that the wealthy capitalist class defined strictly in terms of holdings of financial assets – i.e. individuals whose livelihood is substantially dependent upon income derived from capital holdings – constitutes probably no more than 2–3% of the population.

Sweden to over 23% in Japan. Japan is clearly the outlier.[3] Further-more, as indicated in Table 2.1, this high proportion of the labor force in the petty bourgeoisie in Japan compared to the other five countries occurs within nearly every major economic sector. In most of these sectors, the percentage of people in the petty bourgeoisie is at least twice as high as in the other countries in our analysis, and in some sectors it is more than three times as high.[4] Our first general conclusion, then, is that *Japan has a much larger petty bourgeoisie than any of the other countries, and this petty bourgeoisie is present throughout the Japanese economy.* The persistence of economic activity not directly organized by capitalist firms is thus consider-ably stronger in Japan than in the other advanced capitalist coun-tries we are studying.

Among the other five countries, there are two principal contrasts in class distributions across the property boundary: Canada has some-what larger self-employment (17.7%) and Sweden somewhat smaller (10.7%) than the other countries. The higher rate of self-employment in Canada is entirely due to the agricultural sector: Canada has proportio-nately the largest agricultural sector among these five countries, and, within that sector, there is a higher rate of self-employment in

---

[3] The figures for Japan are not simply artifacts of the sample in our survey. On the basis of official government statistics, 19% of the labor force in Japan was self-employed (i.e. employers and petty bourgeois combined) in 1986 compared to no more than about 13% in any of the other countries.

[4] The precise magnitudes of these contrasts between Japan and the other five countries may be affected by two peculiarities of the Japanese sample. First, the Japanese sample is restricted to Tokyo and its immediate environs and thus it largely excludes the agricultural sector. Since self-employment is generally much higher in agriculture than in other sectors of the economy, this suggests that the overall size of the Japanese petty bourgeoisie may be somewhat higher than our estimates. In the official statistics of the Japanese Ministry of Labor, the agricultural sector in Japan has a self-employment rate of 93.5% and constitutes 8.3% of the national employed labor force. If we accept our estimates of self-employment in the nonagricultural sector (31%) this would make the total self-employment rate 36.5% in Japan. Second, for unexplained reasons, the Japanese survey has undersampled state employees. Whereas just over 9% of the Japanese labor force was employed by the state in 1986 according to official census figures (Yearbook of Labor Statistics 1986), in the Japanese sample this figure is only 4.9%. Since self-employment is entirely located in the private sector, this sample bias will have the effect of overstating the difference in the size of the petty bourgeoisie between Japan and the other countries. These two factors – the absence of agriculture from the sample and the undersample of state employees – probably more or less cancel each other out. As Table 2.1 indicates, even in the private, nonagricultural sector, the petty bourgeoisie is two to three times greater than in the other countries in the sample.

Table 2.1. *Percentage of employers and petty bourgeoisie within different sectors*

	Total all sectors	Broad economic sectors						Nonagricultural & private sectors		
		Extractive	Transformative	Distributive	Business	Personal	Social & political	Non-agric.	Private sector	Private sector, non-agric.
Sweden										
Petty bourgeoisie	5.4	38.6	4.4	5.2	5.0	10.0	0.0	3.4	9.3	6.1
Employers	5.4	15.8	5.3	10.8	12.5	5.7	0.3	4.7	9.1	8.4
Total self-employed	10.7	54.4	9.7	16.0	17.5	15.7	0.3	8.1	18.4	14.5
(% labor force in sector)		(5.3)[a]	(31.7)	(18.1)	(3.7)	(6.5)	(34.6)	(95.1)	(58.2)	(53.3)
Norway										
Petty bourgeoisie	10.3	58.8	5.9	10.4	12.5	14.6	2.1	6.8	16.5	11.3
Employers	3.7	5.2	2.8	8.9	3.4	4.9	0.2	3.6	6.0	6.0
Total self-employed	14.0	63.9	8.7	19.3	15.9	19.5	2.2	10.3	22.5	17.3
(% labor force in sector)		(6.4)	(25.7)	(22.2)	(5.8)	(8.1)	(31.8)	(94.4)	(61.7)	(56.1)
United Kingdom										
Petty bourgeoisie	6.7	12.0	5.2	10.1	7.2	16.1	1.1	6.4	10.3	10.0
Employers	7.2	18.0	5.8	6.7	13.3	17.8	1.1	6.8	11.2	10.6
Total self-employed	14.0	30.0	11.0	16.8	20.5	33.9	2.1	13.2	21.5	20.6
(% labor force in sector)		(4.5)	(31.0)	(21.3)	(7.4)	(10.6)	(25.2)	(95.6)	(64.9)	(62.5)

Table 2.1. (*Continued*)

	Total All Sectors	Broad Economic Sectors						Nonagricultural & Private Sectors		
		Extrac-tive	Trans-forma-tive	Distri-butive	Busi-ness	Per-sonal	Social & political	Non-agric.	Private Sector	Priv Sector, non-Agric.
United States										
Petty Bourgeoisie	6.8	17.8	4.8	5.4	10.8	16.3	3.0	6.4	8.3	7.8
Employers	7.8	31.2	6.5	9.8	8.0	14.6	1.7	7.1	9.5	8.7
Total self-employed	14.7	49.1	11.3	15.2	18.8	30.9	4.6	13.5	17.8	16.1
(% labor force in sector)		(4.4)	(28.0)	(20.5)	(10.0)	(11.2)	(25.8)	(97.3)	(82.4)	(79.7)
Canada										
Petty Bourgeoisie	13.5	71.3	6.4	8.9	9.0	20.9	2.0	7.1	18.9	10.3
Employers	4.2	5.1	4.9	5.6	5.1	4.5	1.8	4.1	5.8	5.9
Total self-employed	17.7	76.4	11.3	14.5	14.1	25.4	3.7	11.1	24.7	16.2
(% labor force in sector)		(10.0)	(22.9)	(22.0)	(8.8)	(7.5)	(28.7)	(91.6)	(71.3)	(63.0)
Japan										
Petty Bourgeoisie	23.2	100.0	16.7	27.4	13.3	43.1	20.7	22.9	24.4	24.1
Employers	7.8	0.0	9.1	8.3	6.7	7.7	6.9	8.1	8.2	8.5
Total self-employed	31.0	100.0	25.8	35.7	20.0	50.8	27.6	31.0	32.6	32.6
(% labor force in sector)		(0.7)[b]	(34.7)	(27.5)	(10.5)	(11.4)	(15.2)	(99.3)	(95.1)[c]	(94.4)

a. The figures in parentheses are the percentages of the sample in the sector.

b. There are virtually no respondents in the extractive sector (which is mainly agriculture) in Japan because the Japanese sample is restricted to Tokyo and its immediate environs.

c. For unexplained reasons, the Japanese survey has undersampled state employees. In the sample, 4.9% of respondents are employed by the state, whereas in published data the figure is 9.1%.

Canada than elsewhere.[5] As Table 2.1 indicates, within the nonagricultural sectors taken together, the rate of self-employment in Canada is only 11%, which is about the average of the other countries. The large Canadian petty bourgeoisie is therefore a consequence of the persistence of a relatively large agricultural sector that continues to be organized around relatively small family farms to a greater extent than elsewhere. The smaller Swedish rate of self-employment is also largely due to the sectoral composition of the labor force, although in the Swedish case this is not because of agriculture but because of state employment. In Sweden nearly 42% of the labor force is employed directly by the state. This is in contrast to less than 20% in the United States and intermediary levels in the other countries. Since there are no self-employed people in the state sector, all things being equal, a large sector of state employment will reduce the relative size of the petty bourgeoisie in a country. When we examine the private sector separately, the petty bourgeoisie in the United States is actually slightly smaller than that of Sweden: 8.3% of the labor force in the US compared to 9.3% in Sweden. Our second general descriptive conclusion, then, is that *among the five countries other than Japan, most of the variation in class distributions across the property dimension of the class structure is due to variations in the sectoral composition of the labor force –* specifically the size of the state sector and agricultural sector – rather than sharply different class distributions within sectors.

Employees

At first glance it appears in Figure 2.1 that there is a fair amount of variation in the class distributions among employees across these six countries. The expert-manager category is more than twice as large in Japan, Canada and the United States as in the United Kingdom, and the working class is more than 30% larger in Sweden than in Norway, Japan and Canada. These cross-national differences, however, may be somewhat misleading for two reasons. First, because of the variation across countries in self-employment (especially the high self-employment rate in Japan), some cross-national differences among subcategories of employees will simply reflect these broader variations in self-

---

[5]   It is also worth noting that in Canada the self-employed in agriculture are overwhelmingly petty bourgeois. The contrast with the United States is especially striking: in American agriculture over 60% of the self-employed are employers, compared to only about 7% in Canada.

employment rather than anything specific to the class distributions among employees as such. This suggests that we should examine the class distributions separately among employees. Second, for reasons that are discussed in the methodological appendix, some of the differences across countries in these distributions are quite vulnerable to measurement problems, especially in the skill/expertise dimension of the class-structure matrix. It is notoriously difficult to precisely compare skill levels across different national economies, and this potentially could distort observed national differences in the relative size of certain locations in the class structure.

For purposes of comparing class distributions among employees, therefore, it may be somewhat more reliable to combine the polarized class locations with the intermediary categories immediately adjacent to them. In this modified class map of employees (Figure 2.2), the cross-national variability is considerably attenuated. In five of the six countries – the United States, Norway, Canada, the United Kingdom and Japan – 13–15% of all employees are in the extended expert-manager class location, and 71–74% are in the extended working-class category. Given how different are the work organizations and histor-ical experiences of these countries, it is really quite striking that their class distributions among employees are so similar.

The one country which does differ modestly from these figures is Sweden, in which 79.2% of the employee labor force is in the extended working-class location and only 9.6% is in the extended expert-manager class location. Unlike in the case of the relatively small Swedish petty bourgeoisie, this difference between Sweden and the other countries is not the result of the distribution of the Swedish labor force across economic sectors or state employment – Sweden has a higher proportion of employees in the working class and the extended working-class category than other countries within every sector.[6] The Swedish distributions are also not the result of anything special about the relationship between class and gender in Sweden – Sweden has a higher proportion of workers among men than in all the other countries and a higher proportion among women than in all the countries except for Japan. Age composition and the size distribution

[6] In a formal test of sectoral composition effects on differences in the class structures of Sweden and the United States, most of the differences were shown to be due to the differences between the two countries in class distributions *within* sectors rather than differences in the distributions of the labor force *across* sectors. See Wright (1985: 213–216).

Modified class map for employees

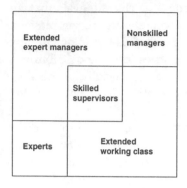

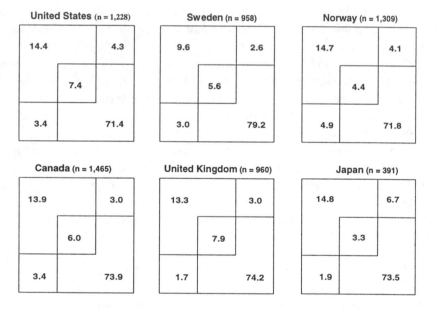

Figure 2.2 *Modified class distributions among employees in six countries*

of firms also do not appear to account for the difference between the Swedish class distributions and those of other countries. It appears, therefore, that the observed difference in class distributions between Sweden and the other countries is not the result of some compositional property of the Swedish economy, but is directly a result of differences between the Swedish class structure and that of the other countries.

At the heart of the distinctiveness of the Swedish class distributions is the fact that in Sweden a smaller proportion of its employee labor force occupies manager and supervisor positions than in any of the other countries. This contrast is particularly sharp between the United States and Sweden: in the US nearly 35% of all employees are in jobs with some kind of real workplace authority; in Sweden the figure is only 22.5%.[7] This difference between the two countries goes a long way toward explaining why the Swedish working class is larger than the American. If the United States had the same overall distribution of authority as in Sweden, but had its current distribution of skills within categories of authority, then 56.5% of American employees would be in the working-class corner of the class-structure matrix (and 79.9% would be in the extended working class). In contrast, if the United States had the same overall distribution of skills as in Sweden, but had its current authority distribution within skill categories, the American working class would only increase to 49.1% of employees (and the extended working class would increase to 74.8%).[8] In terms of accounting for the relative size of the working class, the central contrast between Sweden and the United States is thus the distribution of workplace authority in the two countries.

It is beyond the scope of the data in this project to explain why Swedish workplaces have smaller numbers of managers and supervisors than their American counterparts. One way of getting a limited handle on this problem is to examine the authority distributions within specific occupations. These data are presented in Table 2.2. For high-status occupations – professionals, technicians, teachers, managers – there is only a modestly higher proportion of people with authority in

---

[7] Gordon (1994) reports much greater differences in the percentage of "employment devoted to management and administrative tasks" in the United States and Sweden. By his estimates the ratio of managers/administrators to clerical, services and production workers is five times greater in the US than in Sweden. Gordon, however, defines his categories strictly in terms of occupational classifications rather than in terms of direct measures of the exercise of authority. This poses two problems. First, much of the variation in authority occurs outside of jobs formally designated "manager." Second, many *jobs* are quite heterogeneous with respect to occupational content. For example, how should an engineer who is also part of management be treated occupationally? In the United States, the presence of managerial functions generally takes precedence over other occupational attributes in classifying jobs into occupational categories, whereas in many other countries, professional and technical functions take precedence over managerial functions.

[8] These estimates are made using the shift-share decomposition technique described in chapter 3. For a full description of these decompositions of the differences in the class structure between Sweden and the US, see Wright (1985: 217ff.).

Table 2.2. *Distribution of supervisory authority within occupational categories*

| Occupation | Percentage of employees with supervisory authority | | Ratio US : Sweden |
	United States	Sweden	
Professionals	54.9	51.2	1.1:1
Teachers	23.2	15.6	1.5:1
Technicians	58.3	40.2	1.45:1
Managers	85.1	79.5	1.1:1
Clerks	25.9	13.1	2.0:1
Sales	15.6	21.8	0.7:1
Foremen	93.2	75.5	1.2:1
Crafts	39.2	8.7	4.5:1
Operatives	18.6	8.9	2.1:1
Laborers	15.8	16.7	0.95:1
Skilled services	51.9	17.5	3.0:1
Unskilled services	23.3	5.9	3.9:1

the United States compared to Sweden.[9] Except in the case of laborers, the differences between the two countries are much greater in those occupations which are usually thought of as part of the "working class" – clericals, crafts, operatives and service workers. And among these occupations, by far the biggest difference between the United States and Sweden is among craftworkers: in the US 39.2% occupy supervisory positions compared to only 8.7% in Sweden.

What these results seem to indicate is that the critical difference between Sweden and the United States is the extent to which the supervisory aspect of managerial functions has been delegated to positions which would otherwise be part of the working class. In particular, skilled working-class positions – craft occupations – tend to be assigned supervisory authority over other workers in the United States much more frequently than in Sweden.

While it is impossible to provide a rigorous explanation of these

[9] The term "manager" is used both to designate an occupation and to designate a structural location within the relations of power within authority hierarchies. Here we are referring to the percentage of employees in managerial occupations who also exercise managerial or supervisory powers. Even in the United States, nearly 15% of the people whose occupation is classified as "manager" do not appear to have any supervisory or decisionmaking powers.

differences without looking at historical data on both structural transformations within production and political strategies of workers and
capitalists in both countries, I can offer some speculations on the
mechanisms at work. One important factor may center around the role
and power of labor unions in the two countries. The labor movement
in Sweden has been able to eliminate legal restrictions on its ability to
organize wage-earners much more successfully than in the United
States. In particular, in the United States employees who are part of
"management" are generally legally excluded from the union bargaining unit. This means that it is in the interests of American
capitalists to integrate into the lower levels of management at least
some jobs within pivotal categories of wage-earners, categories which
otherwise would remain working class (Institute for Labor Education
and Research 1982: 315). In Sweden, since managers and supervisors
also have high rates of unionization, there is no incentive for employers
to use the authority hierarchy as a way of undercutting the labor
movement. The extension of supervisory functions to segments of the
working class may thus be one facet of the general efforts by capital to
weaken the union movement in the United States.

A second factor which might explain the leaner managerial hierarchies in Sweden compared to the United States centers on the nature of
the "class compromise" that has been in place in Sweden over the last
forty years or so. Sweden was, at least until the late 1980s, the pre-
eminent example of what is often called the "social democratic
compromise" between labor and capital. In this compromise, workers
agree to moderate their militancy, especially on the shop floor, and
cooperate with management in exchange for guarantees that wages
will rise more or less in step with productivity increases and that
unemployment will be kept at a minimum.[10] To the extent that such a
compromise is firmly in place, problems of social control within the
labor process will be reduced. The result is a lower need for extensive
"guard labor," to use the expression of Bowles, Gordon and Weisskopf
(1990: 194–196). In the United States, in contrast, there is a much more
conflictual relation between labor and management on the shop floor
and a much weaker "social contract" embedded in the workplace and
state policies. American workplaces, therefore, typically require a fairly
elaborate apparatus of social control involving intensive monitoring

[10] For an extended theoretical discussion of the logic of this compromise and the
conditions for its stability, see Przeworski (1985).

and a relatively heavy reliance on negative sanctions. One of the consequences is the employment of lots of supervisors, including supervisors of supervisors. There may thus be fewer supervisory employees in Sweden than in the United States at least in part because the differences in the labor movements, class compromises, and problems of labor discipline in the two countries make it less necessary for Swedish capitalists to devote so many positions and resources to social control activities.[11]

Whatever is the explanation for the distinctiveness of the Swedish class distribution among employees, the main conclusion from the results in Figure 2.2 is that the differences across countries are not dramatic. The working class and the locations closest to the working class constitute around three-quarters of the employee labor force in these countries, and the privileged segments of the "middle class" – the extended expert-manager category – constitute about 10–15%.

2.2 Class and gender

Any analysis of the linkage between class and gender must confront the problem of the appropriate unit of analysis for analyzing class distributions. As we will discuss in detail in Chapter 10, one view, advanced forcefully by John Goldthorpe (1983), holds that families, not individuals, occupy locations in class structures. Since families are units of shared consumption, all members of a family, Goldthorpe argues, share a common interest in the family's command of economically relevant resources, and therefore it does not make sense to say that different members of a family household are "in" different classes. Goldthorpe therefore argues in favor of what he calls the "conventional" practice of assigning the class location of the "head of household," typically the male breadwinner, to all members of the family including married women in the labor force.

An alternative approach is to treat individuals as the incumbents of class locations. In this view, class locations are constructed within the

---

[11] This interpretation is quite similar to that proposed by Gordon (1994) in his study of variations across OECD countries in what he calls the "intensity of supervision." On the basis of regression equations on national levels of supervision on job security, bargaining power and income security, Gordon (1994: 379) concludes that "economies in which workers have relatively greater income and job security and relatively more coordinated bargaining power rely much less heavily on monitoring as a mechanism for enhancing labor effort."

Table 2.3. *Class distributions of men and women in the United States and Sweden using individual job-class and family-class criteria*

	Job-class			Family-class	
	Men	Women	Total	Women	Total
United States					
1 Capitalists and small employers	10.2	5.2	7.9	5.8	8.2
2 Petty bourgeoisie	6.4	7.5	6.9	6.8	6.6
3 Expert and skilled with authority	24.9	9.5	17.8	18.0	21.8
4 Nonskilled with authority	5.3	12.7	8.7	8.7	6.8
5 Experts without authority	3.3	2.7	3.0	3.7	3.5
6 Skilled employees without authority	18.4	8.6	13.9	10.7	15.0
7 Nonskilled without authority (workers)	31.5	53.7	41.6	46.2	38.2
Sweden					
1 Capitalists and small employers	7.8	1.6	5.2	2.1	5.5
2 Petty bourgeoisie	7.0	2.9	5.3	6.0	6.6
3 Expert and skilled with authority	9.7	10.0	15.7	18.5	19.2
4 Nonskilled with authority	9.4	5.3	7.7	7.2	8.5
5 Experts without authority	2.3	2.7	2.5	4.4	3.2
6 Skilled employees without authority	17.8	14.0	16.3	19.0	18.3
7 Nonskilled without authority (workers)	35.9	63.5	47.3	42.8	38.7

social relations of production, not consumption, and since jobs are typically filled by individuals in capitalist society, individuals are the appropriate unit of analysis. The class location of married women in the labor force, therefore, is not derived from that of their husbands, and families can be internally heterogeneous in terms of class location.

These two ways of thinking about the class location of married women generate quite different pictures of the class structure, as illustrated in Table 2.3 for the United States and Sweden. (The job-class distributions in this table are not exactly the same as elsewhere in this chapter because different operational criteria had to be used for the comparison with family-class.)[12] This table reports class distributions

---

[12] The data on the class of the respondent's spouse contained much less information on

for individual job-classes and for family-classes. Following the "conventional wisdom" announced by Goldthorpe, for men family-class is identical to job-class, while for women, *family*-class is defined by their own individual *job*-class if they are single or if their spouse is not in the labor force but by their husband's *job*-class if their husband is in the labor force.

As one would expect, the class distributions for men and women are much more similar when class location is defined by family-class than when it is defined by job-class.[13] For example, in the United States 31.5% of men and 53.7% of women are in the working class when this is defined by individual job-classes, but the figure for women drops to 46.2% when we use the family-class specification of class location. The contrast is even sharper in Sweden: 35.9% of men and 63.5% of women are in the working class defined in terms of job-classes, whereas only 42.8% of women are in the working class defined in terms of family-class. The result is that the comparison of the overall class structures in these two countries is decisively different depending upon which conception of class structure is used: in terms of job-classes we would conclude that the working class is significantly larger in Sweden than in the United States – 47.3% of the employed labor force in Sweden compared to 41.6% in the United States – whereas if we used the family-class criterion, we would conclude that the working class was essentially the same size in the two countries – 38.7% in Sweden compared to 38.2% in the United States. Sweden thus has more proletarianized *jobs*, but not more proletarianized *households*, than the United States.

We will systematically engage the theoretical and empirical issues raised by these alternative views in Chapter 10. In the rest of the present chapter we will stick with the practice of treating individuals as the relevant unit of analysis. The class-by-gender distributions we

authority, and thus we were not able to operationalize the distinction between managers and supervisors for spouses. The criterion for the combined manager-supervisor category which differentiated it from people without authority was also somewhat thinner in the operationalization of family-class than in the operationalization of individual job-class. In order for the individual job-class distributions to be operationally comparable to the family-class distributions in Table 2.3 we adopted the same criteria for job-class and family-class.

13 In a family-class framework, the entire difference in the class distributions between men and women comes from the gender differences in the class distributions among unmarried people.

examine in Table 2.4, therefore, should be interpreted as the class distributions of jobs held by men and by women in the labor force.

As one would expect, when individuals rather than families are taken as the unit of analysis within class structures, the class distributions among women and men are sharply different in all six countries:

1 A much smaller proportion of women than of men in all six countries are in the expert-manager class location and the extended expert-manager category. A minimum of 80% of all expert managers are males, and in several countries this figure is well over 90%.

2 In all countries except Canada, men are at least twice as likely as women to be expert supervisors (in Canada 2.2% of both men and women are expert supervisors), and in all countries except Sweden men are at least 1.9 times more likely than women to be skilled supervisors (in Sweden a slightly higher percentage of women are skilled supervisors than men). Gender inequalities in access to authority is thus a significant property of the class structures of all of these countries. We will explore this issue in detail in Chapter 12.

3 In all countries except for Japan, men are much more likely to be capitalists or small employers than are women. In Sweden, for example, 1.5% of women are small employers or capitalists compared to 8% of men, and in the United States the figures are 5.1% and 10.1%. The result is that 70–85% of all employers and capitalists are men in these countries. Japan is the only exception to this, with 7.5% of the women in the sample being small employers or capitalists compared to 8.0% of men.[14]

4 There is much less gender inequality within the petty bourgeoisie than within the two employer categories of the self-employed. While in four of the six countries (Sweden, Norway, Canada and the UK) there is still a higher percentage of men than women who are petty bourgeois, the differences are smaller than for employers and capitalists, and in the United States and Japan the

[14] If we treat unpaid family workers as "self-employed," then the data from the Japanese Ministry of Labor confirm the fact that a higher proportion of women in Japan are self-employed than men: 31.7% compared to 20.4%. If we restrict the category self-employed to those who are legally defined as self-employed, then the rate for men in Japan is 17.7% and for women 12.3% in the official statistics.

Table 2.4. *Class-by-gender distributions*

	United States		Sweden		Norway		Canada		United Kingdom		Japan	
	Female	Male	Female	Male	Female	Male	Female	Male	Female	Male	Female	Male
I. Class distributions within genders												
1 Capitalists	0.8	2.7	0.0	1.1	0.0	1.3	0.1	1.5	0.6	3.1	1.9	1.4
2 Small employers	4.3	7.4	1.5	6.9	1.7	3.7	1.9	4.1	1.9	7.4	5.6	6.6
3 Petty bourgeoisie	7.4	6.4	2.9	7.2	7.4	12.2	7.9	17.5	5.4	7.7	28.2	19.4
Total self-employed	12.6	16.5	4.4	15.3	9.1	17.2	10.0	23.0	7.9	18.1	35.7	27.5
4 Expert managers	2.3	8.1	0.2	5.3	0.8	7.3	2.2	7.5	1.1	3.2	0.0	8.7
5 Skilled managers	2.2	5.0	1.5	5.9	2.9	5.0	3.2	6.1	3.6	9.1	0.8	2.9
6 Nonskilled managers	3.8	1.9	1.8	2.7	1.2	5.1	2.3	2.6	3.6	1.9	0.4	7.8
7 Expert supervisors	1.7	4.4	0.4	1.9	0.7	5.7	2.2	2.2	0.9	2.9	0.0	5.8
8 Skilled supervisors	3.9	8.3	5.8	4.5	2.3	4.8	3.2	6.1	4.3	8.5	0.4	7.8
9 Nonskilled supervisors	9.5	5.3	2.2	5.6	3.0	3.7	4.7	3.1	5.4	4.0	1.9	5.8
10 Experts	2.9	3.0	3.3	2.3	3.5	4.6	2.7	2.8	1.5	1.5	0.0	2.3
11 Skilled workers	7.8	17.7	15.9	18.5	23.0	19.7	19.9	23.0	13.1	19.0	9.0	11.0
12 Nonskilled workers	53.3	29.8	55.2	44.8	53.5	27.0	51.1	24.4	58.7	31.7	51.9	24.0
Extended expert managers (4, 5, 7)	5.2	17.5	2.2	13.2	4.4	18.0	6.2	15.2	5.6	15.3	0.8	17.5
Extended working class (9, 11, 12)	70.6	52.8	82.5	62.1	79.5	50.3	75.6	50.4	77.1	54.6	62.8	41.3
N	686	807	452	622	596	926	730	1,049	467	679	266	346

Table 2.4. (Continued)

II. Gender distributions within classes
(% female within each class location)

	United States	Sweden	Norway	Canada	United Kingdom	Japan
1 Capitalists	20.6	0.0	0.0	5.9	12.5	50.0
2 Small employers	33.1	14.0	22.7	24.6	15.3	39.5
3 Petty bourgeoisie	49.8	22.4	28.0	24.2	32.5	52.8
Total self-employed	39.4	17.4	25.4	23.2	23.1	50.0
4 Expert managers	19.7	2.9	6.8	16.8	18.5	0.0
5 Skilled managers	27.4	15.9	27.0	18.6	21.5	16.7
6 Nonskilled managers	62.7	32.0	13.0	38.6	56.7	3.6
7 Expert supervisors	24.2	14.3	7.0	41.0	24.1	0.0
8 Skilled supervisors	28.7	48.1	24.1	26.4	25.6	7.1
9 Nonskilled supervisors	60.5	22.2	34.6	51.5	48.1	20.0
10 Experts	45.2	51.7	32.8	40.8	41.2	0.0
11 Skilled workers	27.2	38.5	23.0	37.6	32.1	37.5
12 Nonskilled workers	60.3	55.2	53.5	59.3	56.0	62.4
Extended expert managers (4, 5, 7)	23.2	10.9	13.5	22.1	20.0	3.2
Extended working class (9, 11, 12)	53.2	49.1	50.4	51.1	49.2	53.9
Total	45.9	42.1	39.2	41.0	40.8	43.5

proportion of women who are petty bourgeois is actually higher than the proportion of men.

5 In all countries, women are much more concentrated in the working class than are men. Across the six countries, roughly 50–60% of women are in the nonskilled working-class location compared to 25–45% of men. The result is that while women are generally only about 40–45% of the employed labor force in these countries, they constitute a clear majority – 55–60% – of the working class.

Men are thus generally much more likely to be in privileged and powerful class locations than are women in all six countries.

There are two significant variations in these gender patterns across countries:

1 As we will explore in detail in Chapter 12, gender differences on the authority dimension of the class structure vary considerably across these countries. The gender gap in authority is much greater in Japan than in any of the other countries, and greater in the two Scandinavian countries than in the three English-speaking countries. Only 3.2% of the extended expert manager category in Japan are women, compared to 11–13% in the two Scandinavian countries and 20–23% in the three English-speaking countries. While males dominate the extended expert-managerial category in all countries, women have made greater inroads in some countries than in others.

2 The gender patterns in self-employment also vary significantly across the six countries. In Sweden, Norway, Canada and the United Kingdom, 17–25% of self-employed people are women, compared to 39% in the United States and 50% in Japan. This same configuration occurs when we look more restrictively at capitalists and small employers: 50% of all capitalists (defined as self-employed people employing more than nine people) in Japan are women, about 20% in the United States, 12.5% in the UK and 6% or less in the other three countries.

At first glance, these results for Japan seem quite contradictory: Japan has by far the greatest gender inequality among expert managers but the least among capitalists and small employers. This anomaly is reduced, however, when we look more closely at the nature of self-employment in Japan compared to the other countries. As explained in

Table 2.5. *Distribution of self-employed people into different household class situations*[a]

WOMEN	United States	Sweden	Norway	Canada	UK[b]	Japan
Capitalist class						
Independent	42.8	0.0	0.0	0.0	33.3	40.0
Spouse is employer	42.8	0.0	0.0	0.0	66.7	40.0
Spouse is petty bourgeois	0.0	0.0	0.0	100.0	0.0	0.0
Unpaid family worker	14.2	0.0	0.0	0.0	n.a.	20.0
N	7	0	0	1	3	5
Small employers						
Independent	65.5	57.1	50.0	35.7	44.4	0.0
Spouse is employer	10.3	28.6	30.0	50.0	44.4	33.3
Spouse is petty bourgeois	3.4	0.0	20.0	0.0	11.1	0.0
Unpaid family worker	20.7	14.3	0.0	14.3	n.a.	67.7
N	30	7	10	14	9	15
Petty bourgeoisie						
Independent	72.5	46.2	56.8	50.0	48.0	38.7
Spouse is employer	7.8	0.0	0.0	3.4	24.0	9.3
Spouse is petty bourgeois	7.8	23.1	11.4	25.9	28.0	4.0
Unpaid family worker	11.8	30.8	31.8	20.7	n.a.	48.0
N	51	13	44	58	25	75

the methodological appendix, we classified "unpaid workers in a family business or farm" as self-employed and placed them in a specific class location depending upon the number of paid employees in the family firm. Most unpaid family workers work in traditional family enterprises which are often organized in a highly patriarchal manner. Furthermore, some women who identify themselves as employers rather than "unpaid" family workers nevertheless still work in traditional family enterprises in which their husbands are also employers.

Table 2.5 divides capitalists, small employers and petty bourgeoisie into four subcategories: (1) independents (those who are not married to a self-employed person and are not themselves unpaid workers in a family business); (2) those whose spouse is an employer; (3) those whose spouse is a petty bourgeois; (4) those whose spouse is an

Table 2.5 (*Continued*)

MEN	United States	Sweden	Norway	Canada	UK[b]	Japan
Capitalist class						
Independent	95.2	85.7	83.3	93.8	100.0	80.0
Spouse is employer	4.8	0.0	8.3	6.3	0.0	20.0
Spouse is petty bourgeois	0.0	14.3	8.3	0.0	0.0	0.0
Unpaid family worker	0.0	0.0	0.0	0.0	n.a.	0.0
N	21	7	12	16	21	5
Small employers						
Independent	91.7	90.7	88.2	86.0	88.0	73.9
Spouse is employer	3.3	4.7	2.9	9.3	6.0	13.0
Spouse is petty bourgeois	3.3	4.7	8.8	4.7	6.0	0.0
Unpaid family worker	1.7	0.0	0.0	0.0	n.a.	13.0
N	60	43	34	43	50	23
Petty bourgeoisie						
Independent	88.2	86.7	85.0	91.2	90.4	82.1
Spouse is employer	0.0	2.2	0.0	0.0	1.9	10.4
Spouse is petty bourgeois	5.9	11.1	7.1	7.1	7.7	1.5
Unpaid family worker	5.9	0.0	8.0	1.6	n.a.	6.0
N	51	45	113	182	52	67

a. Entries are the percentage of people within different kinds of individually defined self-employed class locations who are in various household class situations.

b. The UK survey did not have an "unpaid family worker" response category.

unpaid family worker (for male respondents) or who are themselves unpaid family workers (for female respondents). As this table indicates, roughly the same proportion of Japanese women capitalists are independents as in the United States and the United Kingdom, but a much lower proportion of Japanese women employers and petty bourgeois are independent than in any of the other countries. While two-thirds of American women small employers are independent, and between a third and a half of women employers in Sweden, Norway, Canada and the UK are independent, there were no independent women small employers in Japan; 33% of the fifteen Japanese women small employers in the sample were married to small employers and the remaining 67% classified themselves as unpaid workers in a family business. In no other country did more than 20% of such women classify themselves in this way. A similar, if somewhat less extreme, contrast between Japan and the other countries is found among women in the petty bourgeoisie.

What these results suggest is that small firms in Japan appear to be much more dominated by traditional, family enterprises than in North America and Europe. Such family enterprises are typically organized in a highly patriarchal manner in which the male head of household effectively controls the operation of the firm and fulfills the functions of owner and employer. It is therefore somewhat misleading to classify women unpaid family workers in such small firms as "employers."[15]

2.3 Class and race

Of the six countries included in this chapter, race is a salient feature of the social structure only in the United States. Table 2.6 presents the class by race by gender distributions for the US. The results in the table indicate quite complex interactions between race and gender in affecting class distributions. For the various categories of self-employment, the racial differences are generally much bigger than the gender differences. In our sample, at least, there are no black capitalists, only one black small employer (a woman) and only a handful of black petty bourgeois (all men). Among white women, in contrast, 5.6% are either capitalists or small employers and nearly 9% are petty bourgeois. In terms of access to property ownership, racial inequality appears to make a much bigger difference than gender inequality.

The situation is quite different when we look at the expert-manager class location. In this case it appears that black men are somewhat advantaged relative to white women: 5.1% of all black men (in the employed labor force) are in expert-manager positions compared to only 2.8% of white women and no black women (in our sample). For the extended expert-manager category the figures are 8.4% for black men, 6.9% for white women and 1.7% for black women. White men, of course, are unambiguously the most privileged, with 18.5% being in the extended expert-manager category.

If we combine these findings by defining a category of "privileged

---

[15] It should also be noted that the small size of the Japanese sample may mean that the figures for women capitalists are simply the results of sampling fluctuation.

Table 2.6. *Class by race by gender distributions in the United States*

| | Class distribution within race and gender categories | | | | Race-gender distributions within class categories | | | | |
| | Whites | | Blacks | | Whites | | Blacks | | All others |
	Males	Females	Males	Females	Males	Females	Males	Females	
1 Capitalists	3.0	0.7	0.0	0.0	80.6	16.4	0.0	0.0	3.1
2 Small employers	8.2	4.9	0.0	1.3	63.1	30.3	0.0	1.3	5.4
3 Petty bourgeoisie	6.4	8.8	3.6	0.0	44.6	49.4	2.7	0.0	3.2
Total self-employed	17.6	14.4	3.6	1.3	56.6	37.5	1.3	0.5	4.2
4 Expert managers	8.5	2.8	5.1	0.0	72.2	19.3	4.7	0.0	3.9
5 Skilled managers	5.7	2.4	2.0	0.0	72.0	24.2	2.7	0.0	2.7
6 Nonskilled managers	2.3	3.9	1.0	6.3	35.6	49.2	1.6	12.0	1.5
7 Expert supervisors	4.2	1.7	1.3	1.7	64.8	20.9	2.2	3.2	8.8
8 Skilled supervisors	7.9	4.3	7.5	2.0	58.6	25.8	6.1	1.8	7.8
9 Nonskilled supervisors	5.0	9.3	4.6	7.7	32.4	48.8	3.3	6.1	9.4
10 Experts	3.2	3.5	2.9	1.8	47.9	42.8	4.7	3.2	1.4
11 Skilled workers	17.4	7.7	24.3	10.9	60.3	21.6	9.2	4.6	4.3
12 Nonskilled workers	28.2	50.0	47.7	68.4	33.3	47.6	6.1	9.9	3.1
Extended expert managers (4, 5, 7)	18.5	6.9	8.4	1.7	70.3	21.2	3.5	0.8	4.3
Extended working class (9, 11, 12)	50.6	67.0	76.6	86.9	39.2	42.0	6.5	8.3	4.1
Total sample					47.0	37.9	5.1	5.8	4.2
N					648	524	70	80	58

class locations" that includes capitalists, small employers and the extended expert-manager category, then just under 30% of white men occupy privileged class locations, compared to 12.5% of white women, 8.4% of black men and 3% of black women. In terms of proletarianization, nearly 87% of black women, 77% of black men and 67% of white women in the employed labor force are in the extended working class, compared to only about 51% of white men. Even excluding the problem of the so-called "underclass" – the chronically poor segment of the population outside of the formal labor force – race therefore seems to have a bigger overall effect on access to privileged class locations than does gender.[16]

When most people think of "the working class," the image that comes to mind is the white male industrial worker. When we define the working class in terms of individuals occupying positions within the social relations of production, this image is clearly grossly inaccurate. Only 33% of the people in the working class and 39% in the extended working class are white males. By a large margin, the American working class now predominantly consists of women and racial minorities.

2.4 Type of employing organization

No capitalist society consists entirely of capitalist organizations. In particular, a significant proportion of the labor force in every capitalist country is employed directly by the state. Even if one believes that state employment in capitalist societies is heavily shaped by the fact that state organizations recruit their labor force through a capitalist labor market and interact in various ways with capitalist firms, nevertheless, state organizations are not capitalist firms. A complete picture of the class structure of capitalist societies, therefore, should distinguish between class locations in the private capitalist sector and class locations inside of the state.

Furthermore, even within the private market sector of the economy, there are important variations in the nature of the capitalist firms

---

[16] If anything these results understate the contrast between racial and gender differences in access to privileged class locations, since many white women will have indirect access to privileged class locations via their husbands (i.e. their "mediated" class location will be to a relatively privileged class even if their direct class location is not).

Table 2.7. *Distribution of type of employing organization within employee class locations*

	Size of private sector firms			
	Small (<50)	Medium (51–1000)	Large (>1,000)	State
United States				
Public and private sectors				
Extended expert managers	13.3	25.4	38.7	22.1
Extended working class	20.2	25.1	31.3	23.5
Working class	21.2	27.2	34.1	17.4
Total employee labor force	20.5	24.4	33.4	21.5
Private sector only				
Extended expert managers	17.3	32.9	49.8	
Extended working class	26.5	32.7	40.8	
Working class	25.7	32.9	41.4	
Total private sector employees	26.2	31.1	42.7	
Sweden				
Public and private sectors				
Extended expert managers	7.0	10.5	29.6	53.4
Extended working class	15.1	14.7	23.2	47.0
Working class	17.6	14.6	25.6	42.2
Total employee labor force	13.6	14.0	23.0	49.4
Private sector only				
Extended expert managers	15.0	22.5	62.5	
Extended working class	28.5	27.7	43.8	
Working class	30.5	25.3	44.2	
Total private sector employees	27.0	27.6	45.4	
Norway				
Public and private sectors				
Extended expert managers	15.5	22.8	8.3	53.4
Extended working class	24.5	18.6	12.0	44.9
Working class	29.8	21.8	13.7	34.7
Total employee labor force	23.0	19.5	11.3	46.1
Private sector only				
Extended expert managers	33.3	48.9	17.8	
Extended working class	44.5	33.7	21.7	
Working class	45.5	33.4	21.0	
Total private sector employees	42.8	36.3	20.9	

Table 2.7. (*continued*)

	Size of private sector firms			
	Small (<50)	Medium (51–1000)	Large (>1,000)	State
Canada				
Public and private sectors				
Extended expert managers	21.8	18.3	23.4	36.5
Extended working class	21.3	20.1	23.7	35.0
Working class	23.8	22.3	27.1	26.8
Total employee labor force	20.6	19.2	23.2	36.9
Private sector only				
Extended expert managers	34.4	28.8	36.8	
Extended working class	32.7	30.9	36.4	
Working class	32.6	30.4	37.0	
Total private sector employees	32.7	30.4	36.9	
United Kingdom				
Public and private sectors				
Extended expert managers	13.1	11.5	26.2	49.2
Extended working class	19.5	14.1	25.9	40.6
Working class	19.4	15.4	29.2	35.9
Total employee labor force	17.5	12.8	25.8	44.0
Private sector only				
Extended expert managers	25.8	22.6	51.6	
Extended working class	32.8	23.7	43.5	
Working class	30.3	24.0	45.7	
Total private sector employees	31.2	22.8	46.0	
Japan				
Public and private sectors				
Extended expert managers	22.5	33.9	33.9	9.7
Extended working class	31.2	31.9	29.2	7.7
Working class	33.1	31.3	32.7	2.8
Total employee labor force	30.1	32.6	29.9	7.1
Private sector only				
Extended expert managers	25.0	37.5	37.5	
Extended working class	33.8	34.5	31.6	
Working class	34.1	32.2	33.7	
Total private sector employees	32.5	35.2	32.3	

within which people work. The petty bourgeoisie, of course, works in noncapitalist, market-oriented "firms." Some capitalist firms are small, locally-based enterprises operating in highly competitive markets; others are large corporations employing thousands of people spanning the globe in both their organization of production and their markets. In understanding the variations in class structure across countries, therefore, it is important to know how different classes are distributed across these different kinds of sectors. These distributions are presented in Table 2.7.

First let's look at the issue of state employment. In every country, a higher proportion of the extended expert-manager category than of the working class is employed by the state. In three countries (the UK, Sweden and Norway), around 50% of the extended expert-manager category is employed directly by the state, while in no country is more than 42% of the working class employed by the state. More generally, the middle class (all wage-earners outside of the extended working-class category) is much more tied to state employment than is the working class. As we will see in Chapter 14, these differential ties to the state have complex implications for the forms of class consciousness typically found among workers and the middle class.

Within the private sector in every country except Canada, a higher proportion of people in the extended working-class category than in the extended expert-manager category is employed in small firms (under fifty employees), and, in every country except Canada and Norway, a higher proportion of people in the extended expert-manager category than in the extended working-class category is in large firms (over 1,000 employees). This difference in employment settings for different classes is especially marked in Sweden: within the Swedish private sector, 15% of the extended expert-manager category is employed in small firms compared to 28.5% of the extended working class; and 62.5% is employed in firms of over 1,000 employees compared to only 43.8% of the extended working class. In other countries the contrast between workers and expert managers is less marked, but generally still present.

Overall, then, as a general characterization, in most countries the middle class tends to be more closely tied to large corporations and the state than is the working class. Compared to the working class, people in the middle class are thus relatively advantaged not merely with respect to their generally stronger position in the labor market and their location within the authority hierarchies of employing organizations, but also in terms of their employment in the most secure and economically dominant sectors of the economy.

2.5 A summing up

This chapter has descriptively explored a wide range of properties of the class structures of advanced capitalist societies. Several broad generalizations stand out.

The working class, even if defined narrowly, remains the largest class location in the class structure of developed capitalist countries, and if it is extended to include those contradictory locations closest to it, then it constitutes a substantial majority of the labor force. While, as we will see in the next chapter, the working class has declined somewhat in recent years, if the working class is defined in relational terms it is hardly the case that the working class has largely disappeared, as some commentators have suggested.

Not only is the working class the largest class location in all of the countries we have examined, among employees taken separately there is relatively little variation in class distributions across these countries. The only partial exception to this is Sweden, which has a larger working-class and smaller expert-manager category than the other countries. This difference in Sweden may be due to the political specificity of the Swedish "class compromise" which may have somewhat reduced the need for intensive supervision and surveillance in the labor process. Still, even including Sweden, the variations in class distributions among employees across these countries are fairly muted.

In contrast to the relatively small variation across countries in class distributions among employees, there is significant variation in the size of the petty bourgeoisie. With the exception of the Japanese case, the differences in the size of the petty bourgeoisie across these countries is mainly due to properties of the sectoral structure of their economies: having a large state sector depresses the size of the petty bourgeoisie; having a large agricultural sector expands it. In the case of Japan, there is higher self-employment in all sectors. This indicates the stronger persistence of traditional, very small family businesses in Japanese society.

Compared to the relatively modest differences across countries in overall class distributions, there are very sharp differences between genders in class distributions within countries. In all countries, women are much more proletarianized than men and are particularly excluded from the expert-manager class locations. While these gender differences are considerably more exaggerated in Japan than in the other countries, the basic pattern is the same across all countries. In terms of the probabilities of a person being in a given class location, one's gender matters more than one's country.

Methodological appendix

The samples

The precise definitions of the samples and the specific procedures for interviewing respondents vary somewhat from country to country. All of the samples include employed people in the labor force, but some countries also include the unemployed and some include housewives as well. In some countries the sample excludes people over 65 years of age; in others there is no age restriction. The surveys in some countries were administered through face-to-face interviews, in others exclusively through telephone interviews, and in still others through combinations of mailed questionnaires and personal interviews. The surveys in all countries except Japan were national random samples; in Japan the sample was drawn from Tokyo and the surrounding hinterland. In order to insure as much comparability as possible, in the data analysis of this chapter we have restricted the samples in all countries to adults in the labor force who are currently employed. The attributes of the different national surveys are presented in Appendix Table 2.1.

Operationalization of class structure variable

The operationalization of the class structure variable used in this and most other chapters in this book is presented in Appendix Table 2.2. Two comments on these operationalizations are necessary. First, we have combined "unpaid workers in a family business or farm" with the petty bourgeoisie, small employers and capitalists depending upon how many people are employed in the family business. Many different kinds of social relations are packaged under the rubric "unpaid family worker." Sometimes this simply reflects cultural conventions about which family member is the "real" owner. In other cases it reflects age and gender-based hierarchies within family units. However, in general this expression does not designate a distinctive class location, and thus we are treating unpaid family workers as self-employed.

Appendix Table 2.1. *Properties of the sample*

Country	Interview method	Sample size	Date
United States	Telephone	1,498	1980
Australia	Personal	1,195	1986
United Kingdom	Personal	1,770	1984
Canada	Personal	2,577	1982
Sweden	Telephone/mail	1,145	1980
Norway	Personal	2,532	1982
Japan[a]	Personal	823	1987

a. The Japanese sample is for Tokyo and environs and covers approximately 40% of the Japanese population.

Second, the intermediary categories on each of the three dimensions of the class structure – supervisors on the authority dimension, skilled employees on the skill/expertise dimension, and small employers on the ownership dimension – represent a combination of two sorts of cases: people whose objective situation is *marginal* with respect to the theoretical logic of the dimension, and people for whom our measures of their objective situation are *ambiguous*. The category "supervisor," for example, combines people who really are in an intermediary location on the manager/nonmanager distinction, and people who are probably really managers or really workers, but for whom our measures do not give us unambiguous information. The effect of including the intermediary categories in the matrix, therefore, is to improve our confidence that the people in the corners of the table – expert managers, nonskilled managers, nonmanagerial experts and workers – are properly classified. This is especially important for analyses later in the book when we are interested in such things as the ideological differences between workers and managers. In such analyses we are more concerned that people we classify as workers are really workers and the people we classify as managers are really managers than with the possibility that some workers and managers have been incorrectly placed in the adjacent intermediary categories.

Reliability of estimates of distributions compared to official statistics

It is difficult to compare our estimates of class distributions with other statistics in order to evaluate the reliability of our estimates, since few

Appendix Table 2.2. *Operationalization of class structure*

	Self-employed or unpaid family worker	Number of employees	Position in authority structure[a]	Position in labor market (occupation)
1 Capitalists	yes	10 or more		
2 Small employers	yes	2-9		
3 Petty bourgeoisie	yes	0-1		
4 Expert managers	no		Manager	Professional and managerial occupations[b]
5 Expert supervisors	no		Supervisor	Professional and managerial occupations
6 Expert nonmanagers	no		Nonmanagement	Professional and managerial occupations
7 Skilled managers	no		Manager	Technical, semi-professional, crafts
8 Skilled supervisors	no		Supervisor	Technical, semi-professional, crafts
9 Skilled workers	no		Nonmanagement	Technical, semi-professional, crafts
10 Nonskilled managers	no		Manager	All other occupations
11 Nonskilled supervisors	no		Supervisor	All other occupations
12 Nonskilled workers	no		Nonmanagement	All other occupations

a. The threefold distinction in position in authority hierarchy is constructed on the basis of three groups of items from the surveys: 1. direct participation in a wide range of policy decisions in the workplace (*decisionmaking authority*); 2. ability to impose rewards and punishments on subordinates (*sanctioning authority*); and 3. position in the formal hierarchical structure of the organization (nonmanagement, supervisor, lower manager, middle manager, upper manager, top manager). These items are combined as indicated for the intermediate operationalization (Auth-2) in Appendix Figure 2.1. For a detailed discussion of how these clusters of items are aggregated into the authority dimension of the class structure, see Wright (1985, Appendix II, pp. 303-317).

b. Managerial occupations should not be confused with managerial positions within the authority structure. Many people are in jobs that are designated managerial occupations without having real managerial authority, and many people have significant levels of managerial authority without being in managerial occupations.

76

Appendix Table 2.3. *Comparison of selfemployment estimates from the Comparative Project and from published data*

	Estimate from the Comparative Project	Estimate from from OECD published figures	Ratio of Project estimates to OECD estimates
United States (1980)	14.7	9.4	1.56
Sweden (1980)	10.7	8.0	1.34
Norway (1983)	14.0	13.2	1.06
Canada (1983)	17.7	10.4	1.70
UK (1982)	14.0	9.2	1.52
Japan (1986)[a]	31.0	19.2	1.61

Source: *Labor Force Statistics, 1970–1990* (OECD, Paris: 1992)

a. The figures for Japan are for the nonagricultural sector, since the Japanese sample contains almost no one from agriculture. The official estimate for Japan comes from the Japanese Ministry of Labor, *Yearbook of Labor Statistics* (1986). The OECD figures for self-employment in the total Japanese labor force is 24.9% for 1986.

other data sources contain the specific questions about authority or the number of employees of self-employed people. Official government labor force statistics, however, do contain information about self-employment and thus we can compare our estimates on this dimension with other sources. Appendix Table 2.3 presents government statistics assembled by the OECD on self-employment rates among the employed civilian labor force in the six countries we are examining. As this table indicates, in every country in our sample except for Norway, our estimates of self-employment are 30–70% higher than these official government statistics. In the United States, for example, our estimate is that 14.7% of the employed labor force is self-employed, whereas the data in the OECD report (derived from US Current Population Surveys) indicates that only 9.4% were self-employed.

The question, then, is this: should we believe the government estimates or the estimates from the Comparative Project? I do not have a firm explanation for these divergences in estimates of self-employment. One possibility, of course, is that there is a sample bias in favor of self-employment in the Comparative Project surveys. However, given that we have weighted the US data to match the 1980 occupation-by-education distributions in the US Census, the discrepancy of these two estimates is unlikely to be the result of some kind of peculiar sample bias. It is hard to imagine how we could oversample the self-employed without also oversampling the high self-employment occupational groups. It is also striking that the order of magnitude of the divergence between the sample estimates and the official statistics is fairly similar in most of the countries, in spite of the substantial differences in sample design and interview procedures. This again suggests that the difference in estimates between the surveys and government statistics is probably not the result of oversampling of self-employed people.

A second possible source of divergence of estimates between our surveys and government statistics may be differences in the wording of the questions asked. For example, the Japanese figures in the official statistics in Table 2.3 refer exclusively to self-employed people in *unincorporated* businesses, whereas the Comparative Project's definition of self-employment includes self-employed people who incorporate their business. In the United States, roughly 22% of all self-employed people were incorporated in 1980, and, if there are similar proportions in other countries, this would certainly generate a divergence between ⌐.⌐r estimates of self-employment and government statistics.[17]

A third possible explanation of the divergence in estimates is simply that a higher proportion of people *claim* to be self-employed in the Comparative Project's interviews in most countries than in the interviews conducted by official government agencies. This could occur because some respondents are worried about such things as tax liabilities when they are interviewed by government agencies. It is also possible that higher responses of self-employment in the Comparative Project may be because the interviewers in the Comparative Project were told to probe respondents to be sure to get accurate information on this issue. Census surveys are often self-administered and this can lead to systematic response errors. In the US case, for example, the census figures are based on a self-administered questionnaire in which the response categories in the relevant question are listed as follows: "(1) employee of a private company, business, or of an individual, for

---

[17] There was no documentation in the OECD report to indicate how incorporated self-employed are treated in each country. In the case of Japan, the Japanese Ministry of Labor figures (which exclude incorporated) are identical to the OECD figures, thus indicating that the OECD figures also exclude incorporated self-employed for Japan. This may not, however, be consistent across countries.

wages, salary or commissions; (2) federal government employee; (3) state government employee; (4) local government employee; (5) self-employed in own business, professional practice or farm; (6) own business not incorporated; (7) own business incorporated; (8) working w/o pay in family business or farm." It is possible that a certain proportion of self-employed people who work for individual clients of one sort or another might give the first response in a self-administered questionnaire. If this interpretation is correct, then it may well be the case that our estimates are more accurate than those published in official sources. In any case, the discrepancy in estimates exists and should be kept in mind as we examine the results.

Cross-national comparability of measurements

Comparative survey research is always bedeviled with problems of comparability of measurements. Even with careful translations of items and back-translations to the original language to identify potential slippages, it is very difficult to insure that the questionnaire items have the same substantive meanings across different cultural contexts.[18] The problem of comparability of meaning of questions, therefore, is a point of vulnerability to virtually everything discussed in this book.

In the present chapter the skill/expertise dimension of the class-structure matrix is particularly vulnerable to problems of noncomparability across countries. This dimension relies on the coding of occupational titles and descriptions, and since the national conventions for occupational classifications vary, it is difficult to be completely certain that the criteria are being specified in exactly the same way across countries. It would, of course, have been desirable for all countries to use a common set of international occupation codes, but this was not done.[19] While the directors of the projects in all of the countries agreed

[18] This problem of shifting cultural meanings to formally equivalent items, of course, is not unique to cross-national survey research. Within a given country people in different classes, with different levels of education and with different personal histories, may understand a given question in quite different ways. Even with the most rigorous pretesting it is impossible to eliminate such potential divergence of interpretation within even a modestly heterogeneous set of respondents.

[19] A number of the countries (including the United States in a 1991 replication of the survey) did use the International Labor Organization's international occupational coding scheme (ISCO codes), but even when identical coding categories are used it is still difficult to insure strictly comparable practices in going from nationally specific occupational titles and descriptions in the questionnaires to these common categories. For example, it appears to be the case that in Great Britain when a job

to aggregate their detailed occupational codes into a common set of twenty-seven occupational categories, the national differences in the disaggregated codes may undermine the strict comparability of the resulting aggregations.

At various times I have experimented with strategies for increasing the reliability of the comparative measures of the skill/expertise dimension by explicitly including educational credentials and job autonomy as additional criteria for specifying the distinctions between experts, skilled employees and nonskilled employees. In some of the analyses in Part III and IV of the book, in which only the United States and Sweden are being compared, these more refined criteria will be used. In the end, however, these refinements were unworkable when more countries were included in the analysis because of the difficulty in treating educational credentials in a comparable way across different education systems and because of the absence of the autonomy questions from some of the national datasets. As a result, in this chapter we use a simple occupational criterion for the skill/expertise dimension, recognizing that this does not provide us with strict cross-national comparability.

The problem of operational arbitrariness

All social research faces the problem of the relationship between abstract concepts and concrete measures, and inevitably there is a certain arbitrariness in the relationship between the two. Measures are always underdetermined by concepts. In the present instance we have an abstract class-structure concept built around three dimensions – property relations, authority relations and skills. Two kinds of measurement problems intervene between this abstract conceptual map and concrete research:

1 What indicators are to be used to measure each of these dimensions? To measure the authority dimension, for example, there are many possibilities: formal positions within authority hierarchies as indicated by organizational charts; the nature of the decisions which the individual makes in the workplace; the kinds

description includes a professional designation (e.g. engineer) and a managerial designation (e.g. manager in charge of an engineering department), the convention is to use the professional occupational code, whereas in the United States the convention seems to be to use the appropriate managerial code.

of powers the individual has over subordinates; the kinds of powers other people have over the individual. And, each of these possible indicators of "authority" could themselves be measured in many different ways.

2 How should these indicators be combined to generate operational variables? Even after a set of specific observations are made relevant to each dimension of the class-structure typology, there is the problem of aggregating these data into usable variables. In the Comparative Class Analysis Project we have dozens of questions tapping various aspects of authority. Respondents were asked about their participation in eight different kinds of decisions, and for each of these they have four options for describing the form of their participation. They were asked about their responsibilities with respect to several different kinds of tasks performed by their subordinates, as well as a series of questions over the kinds of rewards and punishments they could impose on their subordinates. And for each of these rewards and punishments, they were asked detailed questions about the relationship between their control of these sanctions and higher ups in the organization. The problem, then, is to take this mass of data and deploy it in a way that operationalizes the class map we have been using in this chapter.

In the Comparative Project, the basic strategy for dealing with the first of these measurement problems was to include a wide variety of indicators in the survey instrument. The hope was that by building in lots of redundancy and alternatives we would be able to improve the accuracy with which we could construct maps of the class structure.

Unfortunately, increasing the number of indicators only intensifies the second problem – how to aggregate these many observations into usable variables. Appendix Table 2.4 indicates three different ways of aggregating occupations into categories on the skill dimension, and Appendix Figure 2.1 indicates three alternative operationalizations of the authority dimension. These alternatives differ in how restrictive or expansive are the criteria used to define the thresholds for the lines of demarcation on the skill and authority dimensions of the class structure; all of them are logically compatible with the abstract concept. In skill-1 and auth-1, the thresholds are set in such a way as to produce the smallest working-class and the largest expert-manager category. That is, on the skill dimension the criteria for being an expert or being skilled are

Appendix Table 2.4. *Alternative operationalizations of skill dimension*

| | | Different skill dimension variables | | |
| | | Skill-1 | Skill-2 | Skill-3 |
Occupation		Restrictive nonskilled & expansive expert criteria	Intermed- iate criteria	Expansive nonskilled & restrictive expert criteria
1	Physicians and dentists	expert	expert	expert
2	Other medical & paramedical	expert	skilled	skilled
3	Accountants, auditors	expert	expert	expert
4	Techers, elementary & secondary	expert	skilled	skilled
5	Teachers: university	expert	expert	expert
6	Engineers, scientists	expert	expert	expert
7	Technicians	expert	skilled	skilled
8	Public advisors	expert	skilled	skilled
9	Judges and lawyers	expert	expert	expert
10	Creative, entertainment	expert	skilled	skilled
11	Managers in public sector	expert	expert	skilled
12	Managers in corporattions	expert	expert	skilled
13	Managers, other	expert	skilled	skilled
14	Secretaries	nonskilled	nonskilled	nonskilled
15	Other clerical	nonskilled	nonskilled	nonskilled
16a	Sales: retail	nonskilled	nonskilled	nonskilled
16b	Sales: wholesale	skilled	nonskilled	nonskilled
17	Foremen	skilled	skilled	nonskilled
18	Crafts	skilled	skilled	nonskilled
19	Government protective workers	skilled	skilled	nonskilled
20	Transportation workers	nonskilled	nonskilled	nonskilled
21	Operatives except transport	nonskilled	nonskilled	nonskilled
22	Laborers except farm	nonskilled	nonskilled	nonskilled
23	Farm laborers and foremen	nonskilled	nonskilled	nonskilled
24	White collar services	skilled	nonskilled	nonskilled
25	Skilled manual services	skilled	skilled	nonskilled
26	Unskilled services	nonskilled	nonskilled	nonskilled
27	Farmers	skilled	skilled	nonskilled

set fairly expansively so that skilled employees are placed in the expert category, and certain skilled service workers are placed in the skilled category. Similarly, on the authority dimension, anyone with virtually any indicator showing that they might be a manager is placed in the manager category, and anyone with even nominal supervisory responsibilities is considered a supervisor. In skill-3 and auth-3, the opposite strategy is adopted: very restrictive criteria are deployed for defining experts, skilled employees, managers and supervisors. The result is a very small expert-manager category and a large working class. Skill-2 and auth-2 constitute a compromise between the two extremes.

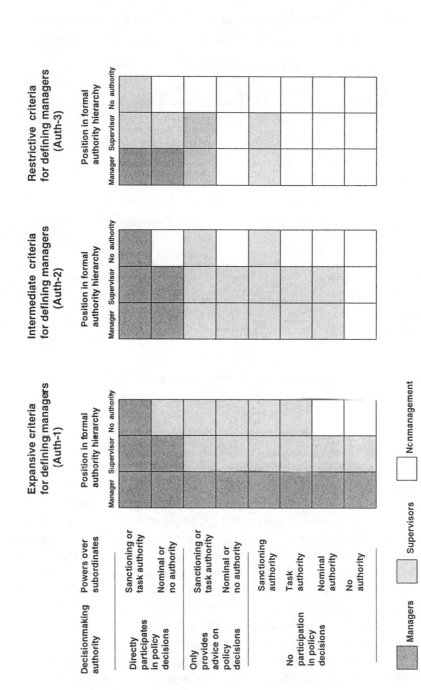

Appendix Figure 2.1 *Alternative operationalizations of managerial authority*

Appendix Table 2.5. *Distributions of respondents according to different criteria*

I. % of employees in different categories using different criteria for skill[a]

	United States			Sweden		
	skill-1	skill-2	skill-3	skill-1	skill-2	skill-3
Experts	25.4	13.5	6.5	26.4	8.2	4.9
Skilled	19.2	27.2	18.8	19.8	29.7	21.5
Nonskilled	55.3	59.3	74.6	53.8	62.3	73.6

II. % of employees in different categories using different criteria for authority[b]

	United States			Sweden		
	auth-1	auth-2	auth-3	auth-1	auth-2	auth-3
Managers	23.3	17.3	9.0	14.3	10.0	5.2
Supervisors	30.1	20.7	19.8	20.2	11.0	10.0
No authority	46.6	62.0	71.2	65.0	72.1	84.4

a. These different skill variables are operationalized in Appendix Table 2.4.

b. These different authority variables are operationalized in Appendix Figure 2.1.

Appendix Table 2.5 indicates the distribution of respondents into the different skill and authority categories using these different constructs for the United States and Sweden, and Appendix Figure 2.2 indicates what the resulting overall class distributions would look like in the two countries. These results clearly demonstrate that these choices make a substantial difference in the overall picture of class distributions in the two countries. Using skill-1 and auth-1, the expert manager category is nearly 10% of the labor force in the US and 7.6% in Sweden, while using skill-3 and auth-3 this category shrinks to less than 1% in each country. The working class, on the other hand, is 53.3% of the labor force in the United States and 60% in Sweden using skill-3 and auth-3, but only 32% and 37.4% using skill-1 and auth-1.

The basic conclusion from this exercise is that *estimates of the distribution of the labor force into class locations are quite sensitive to relatively arbitrary operational choices* even within a single conceptual framework. There are several general implications of this conclusion:

RELATION TO THE MEANS OF PRODUCTION

	OWNER		EMPLOYEES			
10+	Capitalists		Expert managers	Skilled managers	Nonskilled managers	Manager
2-9	Small employers		Expert supervisors	Skilled supervisors	Nonskilled supervisors	Supervisor
0-1	Petty bourgeoisie		Experts	Skilled workers	Nonskilled workers	No authority

NUMBER OF EMPLOYEES (vertical axis, left)
RELATION TO AUTHORITY (vertical axis, right)

Expert   Skilled   Nonskilled
RELATION TO SCARCE SKILLS

OPERATIONAL CRITERIA FOR AUTHORITY AND SKILL DIMENSIONS

United States (n = 1,493)   **Sweden (n = 1,074)**

Skill (skill-1): restrictive criteria for nonskilled & expansive criteria for experts

1.8	9.9	2.6	3.9		0.7	7.6	2.2	3.0
6.0	6.9	6.7	11.4		4.7	6.8	3.7	7.6

Authority (auth-1): restrictive criteria for no authority & expansive for managers

6.9	4.8	7.1	32.0		5.4	9.1	11.7	37.4

Skill (skill-2): Intermediary criteria for nonskilled and experts

1.0	5.5	3.7	2.8		0.7	3.2	4.1	2.3
6.0	3.1	6.3	7.2		4.7	1.3	5.0	4.2

Authority (auth-2): intermediary criteria for no authority and for managers

6.8	2.9	13.1	40.6		5.4	2.7	17.4	49.1

Skill (skill-3): expansive criteria for nonskilled & restrictive criteria for experts

1.8	0.7	2.6	1.3		0.7	0.7	2.6	1.3
6.0	1.8	4.3	9.2		4.7	0.8	3.6	4.5

Authority (auth-3): expansive criteria for no authority & restrictive for managers

6.8	3.1	7.7	53.3		5.4	2.8	12.9	60.0

Appendix Figure 2.2 *Class distributions in the United States and Sweden using different operationalizations*

1 All of the results we explore throughout the book must be viewed with a certain caution, since it is always possible that with alternative specifications of the variables different conclusions would be drawn.

2 Operational arbitrariness is a particularly important threat to attempts at drawing *inductive* generalizations from data analysis. Tests of deductively driven hypotheses are generally less vulnerable since there is no particular reason to believe that the arbitrariness of the operational choices would increase the likelihood of specific substantive hypotheses being supported by the data (unless, of course, one tries many different operationalizations and then selects the one which is most consistent with one's hypotheses!).

3 The operational arbitrariness also has bigger effects in noncomparative descriptions than in comparative ones. In Figure 2.2, there is much more instability in the estimates for particular class locations within countries than in the estimates of the differences between countries. Thus, for example, the size of the working class in the US is 21.3 percentage points higher in using skill-3 and auth-3 than in using skill-1 and auth-1, and in Sweden the difference is 22.6 percentage points. The difference between the two countries, however, is 5.4 percentage points in the first constructs and 6.7 in the third. Generally speaking, therefore, we will have more confidence in the descriptions of differences between countries than in the absolute values of the results for any country.

4 Finally, this kind of operational arbitrariness seriously undermines one of the favorite sports of class analysts – comparing alternative class concepts. The problem is that if one demonstrates that class concept X is "better" by some criterion than class concept Y (e.g. it has a higher R^2 in a regression equation or generates fewer anomalous classifications), it is difficult to prove that this is because it is a better concept rather than because the operationalization of concept X is better than the operationalization of Y. Precisely because concepts underdetermine operationalizations, the empirical comparison of operationalizations of different concepts bears a problematic relation to a comparison of the underlying concepts.

A good example of this difficulty in drawing inferences about the relative coherence of contending concepts directly from empirical observations derived from operationalizations of those concepts is found in the book *Classes in Modern Britain* by Marshall, Newby, Rose and Vogler (1988). This book, written by members of the British research group in the Comparative Class Analysis Project, partially revolves around a series of careful comparisons of my class structural concept with that developed by John Goldthorpe. While there is a great deal that is of interest in this book, it suffers from inattention to the difference between problems in the relative merits of alternative operational choices and problems in the underlying concepts themselves. Thus, for example, they criticize my conceptual map of classes on the grounds that I have allocated certain people – such as a skilled machinist with a subordinate apprentice – into "managerial" class locations who should properly be classified as workers (as such people were in Goldthorpe's framework). This may be a valid criticism, but it is simply a criticism of an operational criterion adopted in my research, not of the conceptual issues differentiating the two approaches. In terms of managerial authority, Goldthorpe and I share virtually the same conceptual criterion: in both cases the issue is real (not merely nominal) participation in making significant organizational policy decisions and having significant power over subordinates. A skilled machinist with one subordinate apprentice, therefore, is probably misclassified if placed into a managerial class location by my operational criteria. However, in my empirical work, because of my specific analytical objectives, I am especially concerned with avoiding incorrectly describing a manager as a worker (i.e. I want to create a relatively "pure" working-class category) and thus I deliberately adopt a "generous" set of operational criteria for defining managerial locations. This may well be an unsatisfactory operational decision for the analytical objectives of other scholars, or even for my own work. But the anomalies in the classification of certain people which result from these operational criteria should not be attributed to conceptual differences between my approach and Goldthorpe's.

How to measure class structure with relatively few questionnaire items

The strategy for measuring class structure adopted in this book involved asking dozens of time consuming questions on many diverse aspects of work and authority. For many people interested in including

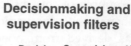

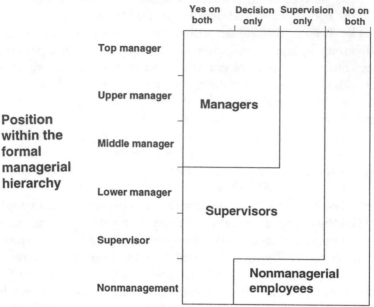

Appendix Figure 2.3 *Operationalization of authority dimension using only three items*

class concepts in their research, it is impossible to include such a broad battery of items. The question, then, is how good a job will a smaller subset of questionnaire items do in approximating the class map generated by the full inventory. In practice, this is mainly an issue of simplifying the measurement of the authority dimension of the class typology, since the skill dimension is based primarily on occupation and secondarily, in some analyses, on education, both of which are routinely gathered in most surveys anyway.

Suppose you could only ask three questions: (1) the formal hierarchical position variable; (2) the filter question used for a battery of supervision items; and (3) the filter question used for the set of decisionmaking items. Appendix Figure 2.3 indicates one way of aggregating these three items to generate a variable measuring the authority dimension of the class typology. Appendix Table 2.6 presents a cross-tabulation of this fairly simple construction and the trichotomy used in this chapter. It also presents the even simpler cross-tabulation

Appendix Table 2.6. *Comparison of simple and complex operationalizations of authority*

		Relation to authority using formal position in hierarchy as only criterion[a]		
		Manager	Supervisor	Nonmanagerial employees
Relation to authority using complex operationalization	Manager	67.1 (7.3)[b]	0.0 (0.0)	0.0 (0.0)
	Supervisor	25.3 (2.8)	85.7 (17.5)	10.8 (7.4)
	Nonmanagerial employee	7.6 (0.8)	14.3 (2.9)	89.2 (61.2)
Total %		100.0	100.0	100.0
N		137	254	855

		Relation to authority using formal hierarchical position, supervision filter and decisionmaking filter[c]		
		Manager	Supervisor	Nonmanagerial employee
Relation to authority using complex operationalization	Manager	81.2 (7.3)	0.0 (0.0)	0.0 (0.0)
	Supervisor	17.8 (1.6)	95.0 (22.5)	5.4 (3.6)
	Nonmanagerial employee	1.0 (0.1)	5.0 (1.2)	94.6 (63.6)
Total %		100.0	100.0	100.0
N		113	294	836

a. Top managers, upper managers and middle managers on the formal hierarchical position question are classified as "managers"; lower managers and supervisors are classified as "supervisors."

b. Figures in parentheses are the percentages of the total table that fall into a given cell.

c. See Appendix Figure 2.2 for construction of this variable.

of a three-category version of the formal hierarchy variable by itself and the complex authority variable.

The punchline of this exercise is that you can do pretty well with very few questions. With the simple three-level version of the formal hierarchy variable, 86% of the respondents are classified in the same three categories of authority as they were with the complex operationalization in Appendix Table 2.2 and Appendix Figure 2.1. The biggest classification problem when simply using the formal hierarchy variable occurs for managers: a third of the managers according to the more complex operationalization are classified as supervisors or nonmanagerial employees according to the formal hierarchy variable. When we add the two simple filter questions in the manner indicated in Appendix Figure 2.2, however, the classification improves considerably. Now almost 94% of the cases are "correctly" classified, and 81% of the people classified as managers by the simpler criteria were also classified as managers by the more complex operationalization.

Given the time and expense of asking so many detailed questions about supervision and decisionmaking, in retrospect I wish that in the Comparative Class Analysis Project we had adopted this much simpler set of measures. This would have introduced some additional error in our measurements, at least if one is willing to assume that the greater information in our current operationalization reduces error. But it would have opened more space in the survey for other questions which we were unable to ask because of time constraints. In any case, for people interested in pursuing this line of research in the future, there is relatively little loss in using the more limited set of questions in Appendix Figure 2.2.

3 The transformation of the American class structure, 1960–1990

Two opposed images have dominated discussions of the transformation of class structures in developed capitalist societies.[1] The first of these is associated with the idea that contemporary technological changes are producing a massive transformation of social and economic structures that are moving us toward what is variously called a "post-industrial society" (Bell 1973), a "programmed society" (Touraine 1971), a "service society" (Singelmann 1978; Fuchs 1968) or some similar designation. The second image, rooted in classical Marxist visions of social change, argues that in spite of these transformations of the "forces of production," we remain a capitalist society and the changes in that class structure thus continue to be driven by the fundamental "laws of motion" of capitalism.

The post-industrial scenario of social change generally envisions the class structure becoming increasingly less proletarianized, requiring higher and higher proportions of workers with technical expertise and demanding less mindless routine and more responsibility and knowledge. For some of these theorists, the central process underwriting this tendency is the shift from an economy centered on industrial production to one based on services. Thus, Fuchs (1968: 189), in a relatively early statement of the service society perspective, contrasted industrialization with the service society by arguing that

> industrialization has alienated the worker from his work, that the individual has no final contact with the fruit of his labor and that the transfer from a craft society to one of mass production has

---

[1] Not all of these discussions explicitly talk about "class structure." I am thus translating into the terms of class analysis certain discussions which talk about the occupational structure or related categories.

> resulted in the loss of personal identification with work ...
> [whereas] the direct confrontation between consumer and worker
> that occurs frequently in services creates the possibility of a more
> completely human and satisfactory work experience.

Other theorists have placed greater stress on the emancipatory effects of the technical-scientific revolution within material production itself. This position was forcefully elaborated by Radovan Richta and his associates. Automation, Richta et al. (1969: 112–114), argue,

> relieves [the worker] of his role as a mere cog in the machine
> system and offers him the position of inspirer, creator, master of
> the technological system, able to stand apart from the immediate
> manufacturing process ... We may assume that the advance of the
> scientific and technological revolution will first engulf the opera-
> tive type of work involving manual machine-minding and later the
> less sophisticated regulatory and control activities – in a word, the
> traditional simple industrial work, insofar as man does not need it
> and it is enforced by external necessity, or will cut it down to a
> degree not exceeding people's need for movement. Then, when
> man stops doing the things that things can do for him, he is offered
> the prospect of creative activity as the normal occupation through
> which he can exercise all his powers – activity imbued with
> scientific elements, discovery, invention, pioneering and culti-
> vating human powers.

Although Richta and his associates argued that such tendencies cannot reach full realization with the constraints of capitalist social relations, they nevertheless feel that changes in this direction are already characteristic of the transformations of work within capitalism itself. The result is a trajectory of changes that undermines the material basis of alienation within production by giving employees progressively greater control over their conditions of work and freedom within work. In class terms, this augurs a decline in the working class and an expansion of various kinds of expert and managerial class locations.

The early statements of post-industrial theory tended to paint a very rosy picture of the future trajectory of class relations. Some more recent expressions of this general view tend to express more ambivalence. Robert Reich (1991), for example, sees the potential for a deeply polarized society emerging, consisting of a highly educated, pros-perous class of "symbolic analysts" and an increasingly poor class of "routine production workers" and "in-person servers." In his most pessimistic scenario, the symbolic analysts virtually secede from the national community, abandoning most public services in favor of private education, private parks and private police, and leaving the bottom four-fifths or so of the population to lives of desperation.

The classical Marxist image of transformation of class relations in capitalism is almost the negative of post-industrial theory: work is becoming more proletarianized; technical expertise is being confined to a smaller and smaller proportion of the labor force; routinization of activity is becoming more and more pervasive, spreading to technical and even professional occupations; and responsibilities within work are becoming less meaningful. This argument was most clearly laid out in Braverman's (1974) influential book, *Labor and Monopoly Capitalism*. The basic argument runs something like this: because the capitalist labor process is a process of exploitation and domination and not simply a technical process of production, capital is always faced with the problem of extracting labor effort from workers. In the arsenal of strategies of social control available to the capitalist class, one of the key weapons is the degradation of work, that is, the removal of skills and discretion from direct producers. The result is a general tendency for the proletarianized character of the labor process to intensify over time. In terms of class structure, this implies that the working class will tend to expand, skilled employees and experts decline, and supervisory labor increase as the demands of social control intensify.

This chapter attempts to use quantitative data on the changes in distributions of people in the American class structure from 1960 to 1991 as a way of intervening in this debate. In section 3.1 I will lay out a series of alternative hypotheses about the expected changes in different class locations based on the arguments of post-industrial theory and traditional Marxist theory. Section 3.2 will explain the empirical strategy we will adopt. Section 3.3 will then present the basic results.

3.1 Contrasting expectations of post-industrial and Marxist theory

The debate between post-industrial and Marxist conceptions of social change can be seen as a set of competing claims about the relative expansion and contraction of different locations within the class structure.

The classical Marxist theory of capitalist development, especially the theories of the proletarianization of labor and the concentration and centralization of capital, posits three trends which directly affect the class distribution of the labor force. First, the expansion of capitalism tends to destroy independent, self-employed producers. In the nineteenth century and the first half of the twentieth century this process massively affected self-employed farmers in the agricultural sector, but the process is a general one affecting all sectors of the economy. This yields the prediction of a steadily declining petty bourgeoisie. Second, the dynamics of capital accumulation tend to generate increasing concentration and centralization of capital as small capitalist firms are destroyed and larger firms grow. This trend yields the prediction of a decline in small employers and an expansion of managers, especially expert managers, to staff the administrative bureaucracies of corporations. Third, as noted above, in order to increase control over the labor force and the extraction of labor effort, capitalists have an incentive to reduce the autonomy of skilled labor and, where possible, replace skilled with unskilled labor. This, in turn, requires an expansion of the social control apparatus within production to monitor and supervise workers increasingly deprived of knowledge about production. The appropriation by management of knowledge from skilled workers should also lead to the expansion of the expert-manager category. These trends of intensified proletarianization in the labor process generate the prediction of an expansion of the working class, an expansion of supervisors, managers and expert managers, and a decline of (nonmanagerial) experts and skilled workers.

Post-industrial theory does not contain as systematic a set of hypotheses about transformations of the different locations in the class structure of capitalist society. It is especially unclear what post-industrial theorists would predict about the two categories of self-employed. On the one hand, in line with Weberian ideas about bureaucratization and centralization of power, some post-industrial theorists might share the Marxist expectation of a decline of the petty bourgeoisie and small employers. On the other hand, the lower capital intensity in many services, especially those for which human capital is particularly important, might be viewed as opening up new market niches for self-employed consultants and other knowledge-centered small businesses. Because these issues are not central to the preoccupations of post-industrial theory, I will not impute formal predictions for these categories.

The expectations for the changes in various categories of employees can be more clearly derived from the logic of post-industrialism. The expectation in post-industrial theory of a world of work with much more self-direction and autonomy than industrial capitalism, suggests the prediction of a relative decline in purely supervisory labor (i.e. positions of social control within work which are not part of the managerial decisionmaking apparatus). On the other hand, managerial positions would be expected to increase as the complexity of organizations and decisionmaking increases.

Where post-industrial theory differs most sharply from the Marxist arguments outlined above is in the predictions about experts, skilled workers and workers. As a concomitant of the move to a knowledge- and service-based economy, post-industrial theorists would generally expect a pervasive expansion of jobs requiring high levels of expertise and autonomy. This implies a process of gradual *de*proletarianization of labor in which there was steady expansion of the expert and expert-manager class location and a corresponding decline of the core working class. Insofar as manual labor is still required, it would have an increasingly skilled and technical character to it, and thus the numbers of highly skilled workers should also expand. The basic hypotheses of Marxist and post-industrial perspectives are summarized in Table 3.1.

3.2 Methodological strategy

The analytical technique used in this chapter is sometimes referred to as "shift-share" analysis.[2] This procedure divides overall changes (shifts) over time in the class composition of the labor force into three components: a "sector shift" component, a "class shift" component and an interaction component. The first of these identifies the contribution to changes in the class structure that comes from the changing distribution of the labor force across economic sectors. For example, historically the agricultural sector has had an especially high concentration of the petty bourgeoisie in the form of small farmers. A decline in the relative size of the agricultural sector would thus, all other things being equal, have an adverse effect on the relative size of the petty bourgeoisie. In our analysis this would appear as a "negative sector shift" for the petty bourgeoisie. The "class shift" refers to

---

[2] The procedure described here is quite similar to Kitagawa's (1955) approach to decomposing changes in rates into different components. For other uses of this approach see Browning and Singelmann 1975; Gnanasekaran 1966; Huff 1967; Palmer and Miller 1949; Perloff, et al. 1960. For an exposition of the technique using numerical examples, see Wright and Singelmann (1982: 202–205).

Table 3.1. *Hypotheses for transformations of the American class structure*

Class location	Predicted changes in class distributions	
	Traditional Marxist prediction	Post-industrial theory prediction
Class locations for which the two theories make different predictions		
Workers	increase	decrease
Skilled workers	decrease	increase
Supervisors	increase	decrease
Experts (nonmanager)	small decrease	big increase
Class locations for which the two theories have similar predictions		
Managers	increase	increase
Expert managers	increase	big increase
Class locations for which there is not a clear divergence of predictions		
Petty bourgeoisie	decrease	no prediction
Small employers	decrease	no prediction

changes in the class structure that result from a changing class composition *within* economic sectors, independent of changes in the relative size of these sectors. For example, the gradual replacement of Mom and Pop grocery stores by chain supermarkets would be reflected in a negative class shift for the petty bourgeoisie and small employers within the retail trade sector and a positive class shift for managers and supervisors within that sector. Finally, some changes in the class structure cannot be uniquely attributed either to changes within sectors or to changes in the sectoral composition of the labor force. Rather, they result from the interaction of these two forces. This contribution to the overall change in class distributions is thus referred to as the interaction component.

The shift-share technique relies on the construction of counterfactual class-by-sector tables and the comparison of the overall class distribution they imply with the actual class distributions that occur. Thus, to calculate the "sector shift" between 1960 and 1970 we first assume that the class distribution *within* sectors remained unchanged during the decade, but that the distribution of the workforce *across* sectors changed as it actually did. We then construct a class-by-sector table on this assumption using the actual size of the workforce in 1970. We then compare this counterfactual estimate of the size of a given class with the actual size of the class. The difference between these two figures is the "sector shift component." In a similar way the "class-shift component" is calculated by constructing a hypothetical class-by-sector table for 1970 on the assumption that class distributions within sectors changed as they did between the two dates, but the sector distribution remained the same. The "interaction component" is then the remaining unaccounted for change in the size of each class.

3.3 Results

Because of limitations of sample size, for the analyses of this chapter the twelve categories of the class structure matrix have been collapsed into a simpler, eight-category model as indicated in Figure 3.1: employers, petty bourgeoisie, managers, supervisors, expert managers, experts, skilled workers and workers.[3] We will also examine the results for workers and skilled workers combined. This eight-category typology drops the distinction between nonskilled and skilled within the two categories in the authority hierarchy, and the distinction between nonmanagers and supervisors within the expert category. The method for estimating these class distributions within economic sectors for the period 1960–1990 is discussed in the methodological appendix to this chapter.

Throughout the analysis which follows our focus will be primarily on the various class categories among wage-earners rather than on

---

[3]   It should be noted that our analysis will not address the question of whether or not the conditions of work, wages, security and so on *within* the working class has changed over time. Nor will we examine the problem of the "relative surplus population" or the "underclass" – people outside of the paid labor force. Both of these sets of issues are bound up with the problem of transformations of class structure, but, because of data constraints, they fall outside of the purview of the data analysis in this chapter.

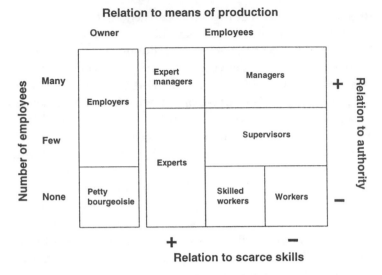

Figure 3.1 *Class categories used in the analysis of transformations of the class structure*

employers and the petty bourgeoisie. This does not imply that the changes affecting these self-employed class categories are uninteresting or unimportant, but simply that they are not theoretical objects of contention in the debate over proletarianization. The problem of the historical trajectory of self-employment in the United States will be examined in Chapter 4.

The basic time series data for class distributions between 1960 and 1990 appear in Table 3.2. The results for the shift-share analysis appear in Table 3.3 and, for selected class locations, in Figure 3.2. The numbers in Table 3.3 are presented as decompositions of the decade *rates of change* in the distribution of people in each class location attributable to each component of the shift-share decomposition. As an example, consider the manager class location for the decade 1980–1990. In 1980 7.95% of the labor force were (nonexpert) managers. This increased to 8.25% in 1990. This represents a 3.76% rate of change over the decade (i.e. 8.25 minus 7.95 divided by 7.95).[4] Of this rate of expansion, 1.88 percentage points are attributable to the class-shift component (which means that on average, the proportion of managers *within* each of the thirty-eight economic sectors increased at a rate of 1.88% over the

---

[4]   Because of rounding, the rates of change do not exactly correspond to the rates which would be calculated from the distributions in Table 3.3.

Table 3.2. *Class distributions in the United States, 1960–1990*

Class location	1960	1970	1980	1990
Nonowners				
1 Managers	7.50	7.57	7.95	8.25
2 Supervisors	13.66	14.86	15.23	14.82
3 Expert managers	3.87	4.41	5.06	5.99
4 Experts	3.53	4.53	5.49	6.90
5 Skilled workers	13.46	14.08	12.92	12.77
6 Workers	44.59	45.13	44.05	41.38
All workers (5, 6)	58.05	59.21	56.97	54.15
Owners				
7 Petty bourgeoisie	5.54	4.09	4.53	5.19
8 Employers	7.86	5.33	4.77	4.71

decade) and 1.58 percentage points are attributable to a shift of the labor force into those sectors within which managers are most heavily represented. The remainder (0.30 percentage points) constitutes the residual interaction component.

The 1960s

The results for the 1960s provide some support for both Marxist and post-industrial perspectives. As both perspectives would predict, managers and expert managers expanded during the decade, and also as both would predict, both of the class locations among the self-employed declined. Other results, however, provide inconsistent support for both perspectives. Thus, as the postindustrial theory would predict, the expert class location expanded rapidly in the 1960s, because of both changing class composition within sectors and changing distribution of the labor force across sectors. On the other hand, contrary to post-industrial theory, but in keeping with Marxist expectations, there was an expansion of both the working class and supervisor class locations during the decade. The results for skilled workers are not entirely comfortable with either set of predictions: while this class

Table 3.3. *Decomposition of rates of change in class structure, 1960–1970, 1970–1980, 1980–1990 (%)*

Class location	Class effect	Economic sector effect	Interaction effect	Total effect
1960–1970				
1 Managers	3.23[a]	-1.76	-0.87	0.60
2 Supervisors	5.19	3.37	-0.81	7.75
3 Expert managers	7.94	6.47	-0.50	13.91
4 Experts	14.36	13.73	0.14	28.22
5 Skilled workers	-0.78	7.64	-0.91	5.95
6 Workers	1.55	-0.55	0.21	1.21
All workers (5, 6)	1.01	1.35	-0.05	2.31
7 Petty bourgeoisie	-15.42	-12.55	1.83	-26.14
8 Small employers	-19.04	-14.67	1.50	32.21
1970–1980				
1 Managers	3.57	0.71	0.71	4.99
2 Supervisors	0.38	2.09	0.03	2.50
3 Expert managers	13.93	0.54	0.19	14.66
4 Experts	15.90	4.02	1.34	21.26
5 Skilled workers	-9.22	0.63	0.32	-8.27
6 Workers	-0.75	-1.37	-0.28	-2.40
All workers (5, 6)	-2.76	-0.90	-0.13	-3.79
7 Petty bourgeoisie	11.69	-0.18	-0.58	10.93
8 Small employers	-9.41	0.37	-1.44	-10.48
1980–1990				
1 Managers	1.88	1.58	0.30	3.76
2 Supervisors	-2.45	-0.38	0.14	-2.69
3 Expert managers	22.04	-1.96	-1.69	18.39
4 Experts	24.71	1.41	-0.50	25.62
5 Skilled workers	1.63	-2.38	-0.45	-1.20
6 Workers	-5.17	-1.20	0.32	-6.05
All workers (5, 6)	-3.63	-1.47	0.15	-4.95
7 Petty bourgeoisie	4.58	8.56	1.32	14.46
8 Small employers	-8.17	8.41	-1.57	-1.33

a. The entries in the table give the three components of the overall rate of change of the percentage of people in a given class location over the decade. These entries can be interpreted as the rate of change per decade of the relative size of the class location attributable to the class effect, the economic sector effect, and the interaction effect.

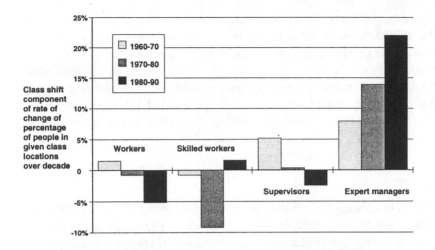

Note: Figures indicate the rate of change in the percentage of people in given class locations which are attributable to changes in class distributions within economic sectors.

Figure 3.2 *Class-shift components of decade rates of change in class
distributions for selected class locations*

location does expand overall (increasing by nearly 6%), as suggested
by post-industrial theory, there was a small *negative* class-shift component (indicating that within economic sectors the proportion of
skilled workers declined), as would be predicted by Marxist theories of
the degradation of labor. Overall, then, the 1960s provide mixed
results, although on balance perhaps more supportive of the expectations of post-industrial theory than of classical Marxism.

The 1970s

The results for the 1970s are somewhat less ambiguous. The relative
size of expert managers, experts and managers continue expanding in
the 1970s. While supervisors also expand, they do so at a much lower
rate than in the 1960s. In particular, the class-shift component for
supervisors which was 5.19 in the 1960s drops to near zero in the
1970s. This is in line with post-industrial thinking, but not Marxist
expectations. Furthermore, the working class declines in the 1970s,
both because of changes within sectors (a negative class-shift component) and because of changes in the distribution of people across
sectors. The only result which might be thought of as supporting

Marxist expectations over post-industrial theory for the 1970s concerns the skilled worker category, which declines fairly sharply in this decade. As predicted by the degradation of labor thesis, this decline is particularly concentrated in the class-shift component (again indicating a relative decline of skilled workers within sectors). However, since this decline in skilled workers is complemented by an expansion of experts rather than of the core working class, even this result is more in line with the arguments of post-industrial theory.

The 1980s

Whatever ambiguity in the results may have been present for the 1970s disappears in the 1980s, for in this decade we get almost exactly the pattern of changes predicted by post-industrial theory for the various wage-earner class locations.[5] The overall rate of decline of working-class locations is even greater in the 1980s than in the 1970s, but even more significantly, the magnitude of the negative class-shift component is considerably greater (−5.17% in the 1980s compared to −0.75% in the 1970s). As predicted by post-industrial theory, skilled workers now have a positive class-shift component, and supervisors have a negative class-shift component. The only slightly surprising result of importance for post-industrial theory is the small negative sector-shift component for expert-managers, but this is completely swamped by the very large class-shift component which generates a large overall rate of expansion of this class location.

Could these results be spurious?

Overall, then, the main thrust of these results run directly *counter* to the principal expectations of classical Marxism as formalized as hypotheses in Table 3.1. What is more, given that the 1970s and 1980s were a period of relative economic stagnation compared to the 1960s, classical Marxism would have predicted that the pressures toward degradation of labor would have intensified. The evidence in these results indicates that, if anything, there was an acceleration in the trend of *de*proletarianization in the 1970s and 1980s. While these results hardly indicate

---

[5]   The results are not as predicted for the petty bourgeoisie or employers, but the expectations for these two class locations are not in dispute between Marxist and post-industrial theory, and in any case are less central to the theoretical preoccupations of post-industrial theory.

that the working class is in the process of dissolution – the core working class remains over 40% of the labor force in 1990, and when combined with skilled workers, the extended working class is 54% of the labor force – nevertheless, the trajectory of change is more in keeping with the expectations of post-industrial theory than traditional Marxism.

Since these results ran so consistently counter to my theoretical expectations, I explored a number of possible ways in which they might be spurious. First, I examined whether alternative operationalizations of some of the class distinctions might affect the results. They did not.

Second, I checked to see if the failure of the predictions might be a consequence of the reliance on formal skill level as a way of tapping proletarianization. Braverman's concept centers more on the issue of *autonomy* within the labor process than on credentials and marketable skills as such. In my earliest class analysis I had represented this idea by introducing the category "semi-autonomous employee" into the concept of class structure. It might be the case therefore that the apparent deproletarianization we have observed might disappear if the category "experts" were replaced with "semi-autonomous employees." Again, the substance of the results are for all practical purposes identical using both approaches for the comparisons of the 1960s and 1970s (Wright and Martin 1987: 17).

Finally, I examined the possibility that the results might be an artifact of changes in rates of unemployment. If the rates of unemployment are dramatically different across classes, and if these rates change substantially across decades, then what might appear to be a decline in the working class might simply be a shift in the proportion of workers who are employed versus unemployed. It is certainly the case that there were higher levels of unemployment in 1980 and 1990 than in 1970 and 1960, and this could conceivably account for some or all of the patterns in Table 3.3. I explored the possible effects of unemployment in two ways for the comparison of the 1960s and 1970s: first, I classified the unemployed in terms of the class and sector location of their previous jobs (thus unemployed workers were included in the working class); second, I included the unemployed as a distinct category in the analysis. Again, while there are some differences in the details of the results, the basic patterns remain unchanged from Table 3.3 (Wright and Martin 1987: 18). The implication of these analyses, then, is unmistakable: the results are more consistent with what I construed to be the "post-industrial society" thesis than the traditional Marxist "proletarianization" thesis.

Refined sectoral analysis

One final step in the data analysis is needed, however, to add force to this conclusion. So far we have only examined the aggregate class and sector shifts for various class locations. It is important to know whether or not these effects are largely contained within particular sectors or are diffused throughout the economy, since this might affect the overall interpretation of the results. Table 3.4 disaggregates the class and sector shifts in Table 3.3 into six different aggregated sectors: extractive, transformative, distributive, business services, personal services and social-political services.[6] There is a great deal of complexity in the results presented in Table 3.4, and I will not attempt to explore fully their implications. Several general observations, however, are relevant to our present concerns.

First, for the working class, the negative class-shift component in the 1970s and 1980s – the deproletarianization process within economic sectors – is observed in four of the six aggregate sectors; it is not simply a result of a massive change in one sector. In both decades, the biggest contributor to the negative class shift for the working class is the transformative sector (manufacturing and processing). This is also the one sector in the 1960s within which there was a negative class shift for workers. Thus, while overall the direction of the class-shift component for the working class changes from the 1960s to the 1970s and 1980s from positive (proletarianization) to negative (deproletarianization), in the case of the transformative sector the 1970s and 1980s represent a continuation and acceleration of a deproletarianization process already in place in the 1960s.

Second, the positive class-shift component for experts and for expert managers occurs within nearly all of these broad sectors. The only consistent exception is for the distributive services sector in which there is a negative component for expert managers in all three decades. The expansion of class locations involving significant credentials and expertise, therefore, is pervasive across sectors in keeping with post-industrial theory.

---

[6] The sector and class shifts in Table 3.4 are based on the full thirty-eight-sector variable for 1970–1990 and the thirty-seven-sector variable for 1960–1970. These detailed sectors are then aggregated under these six rubrics.

Table 3.4. *Disaggregation by sector of class-shift and sector-shift components of changes in US class distribution, 1960–1990*[a]

Class location	Extractive services	Transformative services	Distributive services	Business services	Social-political services	Personal services	Total[b]
1960–1970							
1 Managers							
Sector component	-2.73	-1.38	0.25	1.32	8.99	-8.19	-1.76
Class component	1.38	0.75	0.79	0.77	-1.34	0.88	3.23
2 Supervisors							
Sector component	-2.01	-2.83	0.63	1.91	5.70	-0.03	3.37
Class component	1.52	1.92	1.40	0.46	-0.63	0.51	5.19
3 Expert managers							
Sector component	-0.33	-2.78	1.66	2.96	5.20	-0.24	6.47
Class component	.56	4.25	-1.01	0.05	4.15	-0.08	7.94
4 Experts							
Sector component	-0.45	-1.97	0.58	4.12	11.54	-0.09	13.72
Class component	0.91	4.87	1.20	1.12	6.41	-0.14	14.36
5 Skilled workers							
Sector component	-0.32	-2.93	0.07	0.51	10.36	-0.05	7.64
Class component	0.40	-0.12	1.00	0.13	-2.54	0.34	-0.78
6 Workers							
Sector component	-1.71	-3.16	0.50	1.45	3.85	-1.48	-0.55
Class component	0.37	-1.03	0.70	0.12	0.77	0.62	1.55
All workers (5, 6)							
Sector component	-1.39	-3.10	0.40	1.23	5.36	-1.15	1.35
Class component	0.38	-0.82	0.77	0.12	0.00	0.56	1.01
7 Petty bourgeoisie							
Sector component	-14.87	-1.10	0.44	2.46	1.06	-0.54	-12.55
Class component	-3.86	-0.92	-3.38	-2.24	-2.92	-2.12	-15.42
8 Employers							
Sector component	-16.89	-1.05	0.92	1.69	0.19	0.46	-14.67
Class component	-4.73	-1.03	-6.54	-1.37	-0.51	-4.25	-19.04

Table 3.4. (Continued)

Class	Extractive services	Transformative services	Distributive services	Business services	Social-political services	Personal services	Total
1970–1980							
1 Managers							
Sector component	-0.54	-1.47	-0.51	2.28	3.75	-2.79	0.71
Class component	0.05	2.61	-0.08	-0.19	-0.66	1.84	3.57
2 Supervisors							
Sector component	-0.25	-2.52	-0.68	2.65	1.87	1.01	2.09
Class component	0.65	1.00	0.38	-0.75	-1.39	0.48	0.38
3 Expert managers							
Sector component	0.17	-3.40	-0.55	3.22	1.06	0.04	0.54
Class component	0.51	8.62	-3.08	1.19	6.07	0.63	13.93
4 Experts							
Sector component	0.27	-1.92	-0.15	3.52	2.24	0.06	4.02
Class component	0.74	2.18	-0.58	5.97	7.29	0.30	15.90
5 Skilled workers							
Sector component	0.23	-2.83	-0.38	0.77	2.34	0.50	0.63
Class component	0.56	-5.41	-0.46	-0.52	-3.17	-0.23	-9.22
6 Workers							
Sector component	-0.13	-3.81	-0.97	2.07	1.43	0.03	-1.37
Class component	-0.20	-0.76	0.58	-0.42	0.42	-0.38	-0.75
All workers (5, 6)							
Sector component	-0.04	-3.58	-0.83	1.76	1.65	0.14	-0.90
Class component	-0.01	-1.86	0.33	-0.44	-0.43	-0.34	-2.76
7 Petty bourgeoisie							
Sector component	-3.79	-0.57	-1.25	4.35	1.04	0.05	-0.18
Class component	-0.84	4.44	5.51	1.31	-0.69	1.97	11.69
8 Employers							
Sector component	-4.64	-0.42	-1.08	2.94	1.69	1.88	0.37
Class component	-2.14	1.82	-5.83	0.25	-1.08	-2.43	-9.41

Table 3.4. *(Continued)*

Class	Extractive services	Transformative services	Distributive services	Business services	Social-political services	Personal services	Total
1980–1990							
1 Managers							
Sector component	-0.54	-2.60	0.18	1.93	1.12	1.49	1.58
Class component	0.25	-0.42	-0.08	-0.12	0.68	1.58	1.88
2 Supervisors							
Sector component	-0.72	-4.16	0.31	2.31	0.44	1.45	-0.38
Class component	0.41	-0.80	-0.88	-0.06	-1.46	0.34	-2.45
3 Expert managers							
Sector component	-0.43	-6.62	0.31	3.13	0.82	0.83	-1.96
Class component	0.82	14.21	-3.62	2.67	7.32	0.64	22.04
4 Experts							
Sector component	-0.59	-3.78	0.05	4.78	0.58	0.37	1.41
Class component	0.78	8.92	1.80	3.01	9.57	0.62	24.71
5 Skilled workers							
Sector component	-0.86	-4.58	0.11	0.55	1.19	1.21	-2.38
Class component	-0.17	2.17	-0.33	0.22	0.18	-0.45	1.63
6 Workers							
Sector component	-0.43	-5.50	0.49	1.94	0.85	1.45	-1.20
Class component	0.19	-3.58	0.93	-0.91	-1.48	-0.32	-5.17
All Workers							
Sector component	-0.53	-5.29	0.40	1.63	0.92	1.40	-1.47
Class component	0.11	-2.27	0.65	-0.66	-1.10	-0.35	-3.63
7 Petty bourgeoisie							
Sector component	-1.34	-0.26	0.64	4.26	1.23	4.03	8.56
Class component	-1.40	2.97	0.21	1.34	-0.66	2.11	4.58
8 Employers							
Sector component	-1.93	-0.35	0.47	3.78	3.28	3.20	8.41
Class component	-3.47	2.22	-3.22	0.70	-1.45	-2.95	-8.17

a. The entries in the table give the contribution of each economic sector to the class and economic sector components of the total rate of change for each class over the decade. These entries may be interpreted as the contribution of each economic sector to the decade rate of change of the relative size of the class attributable to the class shift and the economic sector shift.

b. This column is the sum of the components from each economic sector; its entries correspond to those in Table 3.4. Any deviations from the sum of the entries for each economic sector are due to rounding.

Third, the pattern of sectoral shifts is also broadly consistent with the expectations of post-industrial theory: the expansion of managers, experts, and expert managers is most closely linked to the expansion of social and political services in the 1960s and the expansion of business services in the 1970s and 1980s, while the decline of the working class, skilled workers and supervisors throughout these decades is most linked to the decline of employment in the transformative sector.

Finally, the specific pattern of sectoral and class shifts for experts and expert managers is consistent with the expectations of those post-industrial theorists who emphasize the increasing importance of knowledge and information in post-industrial economies. In the 1960s the expansion of experts and expert managers in the class structure was driven almost equally by sectoral shifts in the employment structure centered on the expansion of social-political services (especially medical services) and the expansion of these class locations within sectors. In contrast, by the 1980s the relative expansion of these class locations was almost entirely a product of changes in the class composition within sectors, especially in the transformative sector and the social-political service sector. This is in keeping with the idea of the increasing centrality of knowledge and information within the production processes of post-industrial society even within the manufacturing sectors of the economy.

3.4 Interpretations and implications

The results presented in this chapter pose a real challenge to traditional Marxist expectations about the trajectory of development of the class structure of advanced capitalist societies in general and particularly about the process of intensive proletarianization. Contrary to the traditional Marxist expectation, the working class in the United States has declined over the past three decades, and this decline appears, if anything, to be accelerating. What is especially noteworthy is that this decline is not simply a question of the shift of employment from manufacturing to services; the decline is accelerating within the transformative sector itself. While it may also be true in recent decades that *within* the working class itself working conditions may have deteriorated and exploitation may have increased as real wages have declined, nevertheless within the class structure as a whole the evidence does not support the prediction of increasing and deepening proletarianization.

One response to this challenge is to question the validity of the results themselves by arguing that they are artifacts of the measurements employed. The procedure of imputing class structures in 1960 and 1970 on the basis of class-by-occupation distributions within sectors in 1980 is certainly open to question. The underlying assumption of the procedure is that among wage-earners there has been no significant change in the class distributions *within* specific occupation-by-sector categories. If, however, there has been a dramatic process of proletarianization within such detailed categories, then our results could be quite distorted. Such proletarianization within occupation-sector categories would mean that we are significantly *overestimating* the proportion of workers in these categories in 1970 and even more so in 1960, and underestimating the proportion of workers in 1990. If these over and underestimations were serious enough, then, depending upon how the labor force distribution across occupations and sectors shifted in the three decades, it could happen that this method indicated a decline in the size of the working class whereas in fact it had actually increased.[7] This possibility cannot be dismissed out of hand. Nevertheless, in the absence of specific evidence that measurement biases exist in sufficient magnitude to alter significantly our estimates, the results remain a sharp challenge to traditional Marxist expectations of continuing proletarianization.

A second line of response is to accept the results, but to argue that the transnational character of capitalism in the world today makes it inappropriate to study transformations of class distributions within single national units. The last twenty-five years have certainly witnessed a significant growth of multinational corporate industrial investment in the third world and an accompanying expansion of the industrial working class in third world countries (see Froebel et al. 1980; Nash and Fernandez-Kelly 1983; Warren 1980). Much of the discussion of "deindustrialization" in the United States has been coupled with arguments about capital flight to the third world, border industries, industrial export enclaves and other forms of industrial development in the third world (Bluestone and Harrison 1982; Nash 1983). The Marxist theory of proletarianization is a theory about the trajectory of changes in class structures in capitalism as such, not in

---

[7] It should be noted that whatever the distortions in this method of measurement, it is an improvement over simply using the occupational titles as such as the basis for defining "classes," since such a procedure completely ignores the problem of class heterogeneity within occupations.

national units of capitalism. In a period of rapid internationalization of capital, therefore, national statistics are likely to give a distorted image of transformations of capitalist class structures.

If these arguments are correct, then one would expect that changes in the class structure of world capitalism would be unevenly distributed globally. In particular, there should be at least some tendency for managerial class locations and expert class locations to expand more rapidly in the core capitalist countries and proletarian positions to expand more rapidly in the third world. The fact that in the disaggregated decompositions for the 1970s and 1980s in Table 3.4 the biggest positive class-shift component for expert managers is in the transformative sector, which also has the most negative sector shifts for expert managers in the 1970s and 1980s, is consistent with the hypothesis that these transformations reflect a general process of globalization of capital. Similarly, the class shift for experts is particularly large in the transformative sector in the 1980s (second only to social and political services). It could thus be the case that if it were possible to measure the global class structure of multinational capitalism, the decades of the 1970s and 1980s would have been a period of proletarianization worldwide.

A final line of response to these results is to acknowlege that capitalist class relations are changing in ways unexpected by the traditional Marxist theory of deepening proletarianization. While the problem of extracting labor effort from workers remains an issue within class relations, under conditions of highly developed forces of production this no longer generates an inherent tendency toward the degradation of labor. Instead, as Piore and Sabel (1984) have argued, we may be in the midst of a "second industrial divide" which requires labor with much higher levels of technical training and work autonomy than characterized "Fordist" production, training which makes workers capable of flexibly adapting to rapid changes in technology and the organization of work. The positive class shift for skilled employees within the transformative sector in the 1980s (+2.17), reversing the considerable negative class shift (−5.41) in that sector for this category in the 1970s, is consistent with this account.

These trends do not imply that "post-Fordist" capitalism is any less capitalistic than its predecessors; surplus is still appropriated by capitalists; investments are still allocated on the basis of profit-maximizing in capitalist markets; workers are still excluded from control over the overall process of production. And they also do not imply the imminent demise of the working class. In spite of the decline we have observed, the working class remains around 40% of the labor force in 1990, and when skilled workers are added, the extended working class is still over 50%. What these results do suggest, however, is a trajectory of change within developed capitalist societies toward an expansion, rather than a decline, of contradictory locations within class relations. Unless these trends are a temporary detour, it thus appears that the class structure of capitalism continues to become increasingly complex rather than simplified around a single, polarized class antagonism.

Methodological appendix

Operationalization of economic sector variable

Economic sector is measured by a fairly refined, thirty-eight-category variable. This economic sector typology is derived from the typology used in Wright and Singelmann (1982), which in turn is based on the work of Browning and Singelmann (1978). There is one modification from these earlier typologies. Before 1990, most people engaged in home-based childcare were classified in the hotels and lodging sector. In 1990 a new sector, "family childcare services," was introduced. Since virtually 100% of the people in family childcare services are self-employed, unless a childcare service sector were created for earlier years the large expansion of such services in the 1980s would appear as a change in the class structure *within* the hotels and lodging sector rather than a change in the distribution of self-employed people across *sectors*. I thus created a childcare services sector for 1970 and 1980 by taking all people whose *occupations* were childcare workers (regardless of their sectoral classification) and combining them into a childcare services sector. This could not be done with the 1960 data because childcare occupations were not separately identified in that year. Childcare services is thus a separate sector only for the 1970, 1980 and 1990 censuses. In the 1960–1970 analyses, therefore, we only distinguish thirty-seven sectors.

While all of the shift-share decompositions are calculated on the basis of this detailed sector variable, for some purposes these sectors are aggregated under six more general rubrics: extractive, transformative, distributive services, business services, social and political services, and personal services. The list of sectors included under each of these rubrics appears in Appendix Table 3.1.

Appendix Table 3.1. *Economic sector classifications*

I. *Extractive sector*	V. *Social and political services*
1 Agriculture	21 Legal services
2 Mining	22 Medical services
	23 Hospitals
II. *Transformative sector*	24 Education
3 Construction	25 Welfare
4 Food	26 Nonprofit
5 Textiles	27 Postal
6 Metal	28 Government
7 Machinery	29 Childcare services[a]
8 Chemical	30 Misc. social services
9 Miscellaneous manufacturing	
10 Utilities	
III. *Distributive services*	VI. *Personal services*
11 Transportation	31 Domestic services
12 Communications	32 Hotels
13 Wholesale	33 Eating and drinking
14 Retail	34 Repair
	35 Laundry
IV. *Business services*	36 Barber and beauty shop
15 Banking	37 Entertainment
16 Insurance	38 Misc. personal services
17 Real estate	
18 Engineering	
19 Accounting	
20 Miscellaneous	

a. Childcare services are a separate sector only for 1970, 1980 and 1990. The 1960–70 analysis, therefore, is based on only a 37 category classification of sectors.

Measuring class structure

The class structure variable is particularly difficult to measure accurately since there does not exist a satisfactory time series on many of the central criteria in the concept. The analysis thus relies on a strategy of estimating class distributions for the earlier periods by linking the Class Analysis Project's cross-sectional data on class structure gathered in 1980 with 1960, 1970, 1980 and 1990 census data. On the basis of these imputed class distributions, the class-by-sector tables needed for the shift-share analysis can be generated.

The first step in generating these imputed estimates is to generate class-by-occupation distributions within economic sectors from the

1980 American Class Analysis Project data. We then used these distributions from the 1980 class analysis project to estimate the class distributions within sectors for the census public use samples in 1960, 1970, 1980 and 1990. The details of the estimation strategy are given in Wright and Singelmann (1982: 192–193). Basically, we assume that the class distributions *within* the cells of the occupation-by-sector table do not vary significantly across these census periods. Given that assumption, we could thus use the 1980 class analysis project distributions to apportion people in the cells of the census occupation-by-sector tables into classes for the four time points. For example, if 70% of all professionals in durable manufacturing in the 1980 Class Analysis Project data were managers, we would allocate 70% of the individuals in the corresponding cells of each of the census tables into managerial class positions. In effect this procedure reallocates individuals within each of the thirty-eight economic sectors in the census data from occupational categories to class categories on the basis of the actual class-by-occupation distributions within those sectors for the 1980 class structure project data. These reallocations enabled us to produce the necessary class-by-sector tables for the four points in time.

Where the number of cases in a particular occupation-by-sector cell was too small in the Class Structure Project data for the class distribution to be reliably estimated (i.e. when the number of cases fell below ten) the class distribution for this cell was assumed to be the same as that for the broader economic sector to which the detailed sector in question belonged. If the number of cases was still too small (a rare occurrence), then the class distribution across all sectors was used as the appropriate estimate. Throughout these analyses we used the civilian workforce only; members of the armed forces were excluded entirely.

While the census data lacks direct information on managerial or supervisory responsibility and on number of employees for the self-employed (and thus the necessity for the estimation procedure described above), the censuses do contain the basic distinction between self-employed and employee. In estimating the class distributions within sectors for the four censuses, therefore, we constrained these estimates to reproduce the census self-employment distributions within sectors. That is, we performed the procedure of imputing class structures separately for self-employed and for employees in the census data.

4 The fall and rise of the American petty bourgeoisie

Two hundred years ago Thomas Jefferson (1786 [1984: 580]) argued that the prospect of self-employment justified whatever depredations accompanied indentured service and wage labor:

> So desirous are the poor of Europe to get to America, where they may better their condition, that, being unable to pay their passage, they will agree to serve two or three years on their arrival there, rather than not go. During the time of that service they are better fed, better clothed, and have lighter labour than while in Europe. Continuing to work for hire a few years longer, they buy a farm, marry, and enjoy all the sweets of a domestic society of their own.

In the middle of the nineteenth century Abraham Lincoln (1865 [1907: 50]) also saw self-employment as the natural route to individual prosperity: "The prudent penniless beginner in the world labors for wages awhile, saves a surplus with which to buy tools or land for himself, then labors on his own account another while, and at length hires a new beginner to help him." And even in the waning years of the twentieth century, in an era of large corporations and powerful governments, Ronald Reagan (Public Papers of the Presidents of the United States. Ronald Reagan 1983: 689) extols the virtues of self-employment. Speaking at the awards ceremony for the National Small Business Person of the Year, Reagan remarked:

> I am vividly reminded that those shopkeepers and the druggist and the feed store owner and all of those small town business men and women made our town work, building our community, and were also building our nation. In so many ways, you here today and your colleagues across the country represent America's pioneer spirit . . . You also hold the promise of America's future.

It's in your dreams, your aspirations that our future will be molded and shaped.

Being one's own boss, being self-employed, is a deeply held ideal in American culture. As Table 4.1 (column 1) indicates, in the 1980 US Class Analysis Project data, 54% of people in the American working class, and two-thirds of male workers, say that they would like to be self-employed some day. What is more, this ideal is not a complete fantasy: while, depending upon precise definitions and data sources, only about 8–14% of the labor force in the United States was self-employed in 1980, 16% of current employees have been self-employed at some time during their work lives (almost 20% for men), which means that at least a quarter of the labor force and a third of the male labor force either is or has been self-employed. If we go back one generation, about 31% of Americans currently in the labor force come from families within which the head of the household was mainly self-employed when they were growing up, and 46% came from families within which the head of the household was self-employed at least part of the time while they were growing up. Finally, if we ask Americans to describe the jobs of their three best friends, 31% indicate that at least one of their friends is self-employed, and 7% are married to someone who is self-employed. Taking all of these data together, two-thirds of Americans in the labor force have some direct personal linkage to self-employment, by being or having been self-employed themselves, by coming from a family of origin in which the head of household was self-employed, by having a close friend who is self-employed, or by being married to someone who is self-employed. What is more, this density of ties to self-employment varies hardly at all across the different class locations among employees.

This intermeshing of the lives of the petty bourgeoisie and employees is not a unique feature of the United States. Roughly comparable figures are found in the other countries in the Comparative Class Analysis Project. In Sweden, Norway and Canada, about 55% of the labor force has some direct personal tie to self-employment while in Japan the figure is 68% (mainly because of a much higher level of people who are currently self-employed). Where the United States does seem to differ markedly from the other countries is in the aspiration of employees to become self-employed: nearly 58% of US employees say that they would like to be self-employed someday, compared to 49% in Canada, 40% in Sweden, 31% in Japan and only 20% in Norway.

Table 4.1. *Ties to the petty bourgeoisie by current class location*

Class position	(1) Would you like to be self-employed some day[a] (% yes)	(2) Head of family while growing up *ever* self-employed (% yes)	(3) Head of family while growing up *mostly* self-employed (% yes)	(4) Have you ever been self-employed[a] (% yes)	(5) One of three closest friends is self-employed[b] (% yes)	(6) Has a spouse who is self-employed[c] (% yes)	(7) Any tie to the petty bourgeoisie (% yes in 2, 4, 5 or 6)
United States							
Employers	x	66.5	51.3	x	52.1	25.1	83.4
Petty bourgeoisie	x	64.4	51.9	x	59.0	27.7	85.6
Middle class	60.7	43.3	27.5	18.7	27.7	3.5	62.3
Expert managers	65.2	38.9	23.5	19.8	29.9	5.2	59.1
Managers	57.7	47.9	28.2	17.4	28.8	3.5	64.5
Experts	57.6	45.6	31.7	18.1	23.8	1.4	64.6
Working class	54.0	42.1	26.8	13.1	24.1	3.5	59.3
Total	57.6	46.1	30.8	16.0	31.2	6.9	64.3
United States men							
All self-employed	x	64.3	52.3	x	56.7	21.7	82.3
Middle class	66.9	41.1	24.8	20.6	30.8	2.9	61.1
Working class	66.3	34.9	19.8	18.3	32.6	0.7	58.6
Total	66.7	43.1	27.8	19.8	35.6	5.3	64.1

Table 4.1. (Continued)

United States women							
All self-employed	x	67.4	50.6	x	53.3	33.3	87.6
Middle class	49.3	47.5	32.6	15.1	21.4	4.6	63.5
Working class	45.9	46.8	31.3	9.6	22.5	5.3	59.7
Total	47.3	49.7	34.3	11.8	26.0	8.6	64.6
Country Comparisions							
Self-employed							
United States	x	65.5	51.6	x	55.4	26.3	84.4
Sweden	x	57.4	49.5	x	62.9	29.4	85.0
Norway	x	65.2	59.1	x	51.3	18.4	84.9
Canada	x	74.4	70.9	x	65.7^d	24.6	91.0
Japan	x	61.8	n.a.	x	62.7^d	57.4	91.1
Employees							
United States	57.6	42.7	27.2	16.0	27.0	3.5	60.9
Sweden	39.9	36.1	30.6	7.8	24.3	3.1	52.0
Norway	19.9	39.1	34.4	7.4	24.1	3.9	54.5
Canada	48.8	38.9	34.3	14.6	27.9	4.1	59.9
Japan	31.3	44.4	n.a.	9.5	24.8^d	3.6	58.5

a. Asked only for people who are currently wage-earners.

b. Based on class of the three people to whom the respondent feels personally closest.

c. The percentages in this column are for all respondents whether or not the are married.

d. The Japanese figures are based on only two close friends.

Self-employment is thus a central part of both the ideological and social fabric of American life. Yet, remarkably, self-employment has received almost no systematic empirical study by sociologists. When sociologists study stratification, it is rare that self-employment is treated as a distinct problem. The typical class schema for sociological studies goes from upper white-collar to lower blue-collar and farm occupations, with the self-employed being fused with these categories according to their occupational activities.[1] And, while there are many studies of small business and of specific categories of self-employment, especially farmers and various kinds of professionals, there is very little quantitative research on the general problem of self-employment.[2]

The basic objective of this chapter is to analyze the historical trajectory of self-employment in the United States, particularly in the post-World War Two period. The chapter will revolve around a striking feature of the time trend in rates of self-employment in the labor force: on the basis of the best available time series it appears that from the 1940s to about 1973 there was a virtually monotonic annual decline in the rate of self-employment in the United States, from around 20% to under 10%; from 1973 to 1976 the self-employment rate was basically stable, but since then there has been a gradual increase in the rate of self-employment (see Figure 4.1). By the early 1990s that rate was a full 25% higher than it had been in the mid-1970s. What is the explanation for this dramatic change? Does it reflect a response to stagnation in the American economy since the early 1970s? Is it an aspect of the transition to a "post-industrial" economy in which a variety of new kinds of services, often involving relatively little

[1]   One partial exception to this is the work on stratification and social mobility of John Goldthorpe (Goldthorpe 1980; Erikson and Goldthorpe 1993). Goldthorpe makes a point of distinguishing some types of self-employed from wage-laborers in his occupationally-based hierarchy of classes. However, he fuses certain kinds of privileged employees – high-level professionals and managers – with larger proprietors into a single Class I.

[2]   Some of the recent sociological and economic literature on self-employment and the petty bourgeoisie includes Baudelot, Establet and Malemort (1974); Bechhofer and Elliott (1978, 1981, 1985); Becker (1984); Berger (1981); Bögenhold (1985); Bregger (1963); Curran and Burrows (1986); Dale (1986); Daly (1982); Fain (1980); Linder (1983); Mayer (1977); Ray (1975); Van Regemorter (1981); and Weiss (1984). In addition, there are a number of historical studies on the US and Europe dealing with the self-employed in general (i.e., not focused on specific occupations): Crossick (1978); Geiger (1932); Gellately (1974); Haupt (1985); Philips (1962); Volkov (1978); and Winkler (1972).

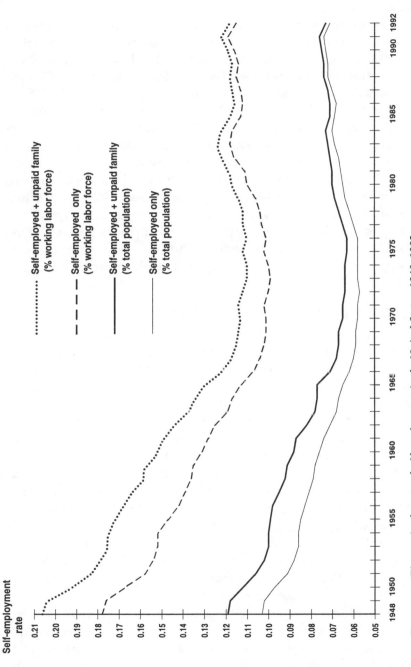

Figure 4.1 *Time series for rate of self-employment in the United States, 1948–1992*

physical capital, are growing? These are the questions which we will explore.

Before we can examine this empirical problem, however, the concept of self-employment requires a more rigorous theoretical elaboration. This will be followed by a discussion of the data we will use and various measurement problems. The empirical investigation will begin with a statistical analysis of the annual time series data for the United States in the post-Second World War period. The central objective of this analysis is to demonstrate that indeed there has been a reversal in the decline of the petty bourgeoisie and that this reversal cannot be seen simply as a reflection of cyclical unemployment during the 1970s and 1980s. Once these trends are firmly established we will decompose by decade the changes in self-employment between 1940 and 1990 into components attributable to changes in self-employment within economic sectors and components due to changes in the distribution of the labor force across economic sectors. This will allow us to pinpoint exactly where the current expansion of self-employment is occurring.

4.1 The theoretical status of self-employment

Self-employment is primarily contrasted to two other conditions: being employed by someone else (i.e. being a wage-earner) or earning an income without working at all (i.e. being a *rentier* of one sort or another who receives an income without working). The category "self-employment" thus describes the intersection of two dimensions of economic relations: first, whether or not one's income depends in part upon one's own labor, and second whether in order to work one has to enter the labor market. In these terms a self-employed person may also be a capitalist – an employer – but would be distinguished from a passive, coupon-clipping *rentier* receiving an income strictly from investments rather than from work. These alternatives are displayed in Table 4.2.

Table 4.2 is a descriptive typology for distinguishing the self-employed from other employment categories, but it does not give the category a firm theoretical status. The traditional way that Marxists have dealt with this issue is by locating self-employment with respect to what is called "simple commodity production."

Simple commodity production is defined as production oriented toward a market in which the direct producers of the commodities own their means of production and thus own the products of labor which they sell on the market. It is thus distinguished both from

Table 4.2. *Theoretical criteria for self-employment*

	Does not work for income	*Works for an income*
Hires labor power	Rentier capitalists	Entrepreneurial capitalists
Neither hires nor sells labor power	Permanently disabled; "the underclass"	Petty bourgeoisie
Sells labor power	Temporarily unemployed	Workers

subsistence production and from *capitalist production*. In subsistence production, the direct producers own their means of production, but products are produced for direct consumption by the producer and his/her primary social group rather than for a market.[3] In capitalist commodity production, production is for the market, but the direct producers of the commodities do not own the means of production and thus, in order to work, must sell their labor power on the labor market for a wage to the owners of the means of production, who consequently own and sell products of labor.

The direct producers in simple commodity production are thus located in a distinctive form of production which should not simply be amalgamated to capitalism as such.[4] Although the direct producers in simple commodity production are frequently called the "petty" bourgeoisie, they should not be understood as "little" capitalists, since they produce under quite different relations of production.[5] Pure petty

---

[3] The concept of subsistence production is not restricted to cases where the producer directly consumes his/her product, but includes cases where this product is consumed by the producer's family or community without the mediation of an exchange relation. Producing a meal for one's family is an example of subsistence production.

[4] There is a debate of sorts among Marxists over whether or not simple commodity production should be treated as a proper "mode" of production, co-equal conceptually to capitalism or feudalism in the Marxist typology of modes of production. I will use the less technical expression "form of production" to sidestep this issue.

[5] Indeed, as John Roemer (1982: ch. 2) has argued, many petty bourgeois may even be exploited by capitalists through unequal exchanges on the market.

bourgeois are distinct from capitalists in that they do not hire and exploit wage laborers; they are distinct from workers in that they own their own means of production and do not sell their labor power on the labor market.

Actual societies, of course, are never made up of pure modes of production, whether capitalist or other. As I have argued elsewhere (Wright 1985: 11), actual societies should be analyzed as specific forms of combination of different kinds of relations of production. In terms of the category "self-employment," this implies that certain self-employed – small employers – combine characteristics of the pure petty bourgeoisie and the capitalist class. Such positions are an example of a "contradictory location within class relations," a location that is simultaneously situated in two distinct forms of class relations. (Since most small employers are indeed very small – in 1980 over 50% of all employers employed less than five employees – Marxists generally assume that the petty bourgeois pole of such contradictory locations is dominant, and thus, typically small employers and the pure petty bourgeoisie are descriptively combined in a more general petty bourgeois class location.)[6] The empirical category "self-employed" thus combines analytically quite distinct kinds of class locations: the pure petty bourgeoisie, small employers and the entrepreneurial capitalist class.

Understood in *historical* terms, simple commodity production is generally regarded by Marxists as a form of *pre*capitalist production, as one of the forms of production that existed within feudal society and which gained particular historical importance in the transition between feudalism and capitalism. Social categories rooted in simple commodity production – peasants, artisans, small shopkeepers, etc. – are therefore generally regarded by Marxists as anachronisms, as categories whose long-term social existence is continually eroded by the dynamic forces of capitalism. Understood in *structural* terms, on the other hand, simple commodity production is simply one distinctive form of social relations constructed within market societies and articulated in various ways to capitalist (and perhaps post-capitalist) relations of production. The historical fact of its precapitalist origins does not preclude the structural fact of its continual reproduction, and under certain circumstances even expansion, within capitalism itself.

---

[6] Throughout this chapter when I wish to refer to the self-employed who employ no wage-labor, I will use the term "*pure* petty bourgeoisie." The unmodified expression will include small employers as well.

Accordingly, contrary to the more historicist Marxist treatments, the social categories rooted in such relations may not be anachronisms at all, but dynamically important elements within contemporary capitalist societies.

Because of the strong identification by Marxists of self-employment with precapitalist relations, classical Marxism predicted the general demise of the petty bourgeoisie. More specifically, Marx identified two long-term causal processes which shape the historical trajectories of the petty bourgeoisie and small employers. First, there is the inherent tendency for the expansion of capitalism to destroy all precapitalist forms of economic relations. At times this destruction takes a violent and political form, as when "bourgeois revolutions" outlaw certain kinds of precapitalist property relations (slavery, feudalism). At times the destruction of precapitalist relations takes the form of the strictly economic erosion of their economic viability, as characteristically occurs in the decline of simple commodity production in agriculture. In either case, the result is that, as capitalism develops, an increasingly greater proportion of economic activity is directly organized within capitalist relations. *If* simple commodity production is viewed as strictly *pre*capitalist, then the advance of capitalism signals the decline of the petty bourgeoisie.

The second long-term causal process which shapes the fate of self-employment is the "concentration and centralization of capital." As capitalism develops, so the story goes, not only does simple commodity production dwindle, but there is a tendency for capitalist units of accumulation to become larger both relatively and asbolutely. Because of increasing returns to scale, capitalist competition tends to destroy small units of production, and thus, over time, the proportion of the labor force that works in small enterprises should decline. This in turn would reduce the proportion of small employers in the population.

Taken together, these two causal processes lead Marx and subsequent Marxists to predict that the petty bourgeoisie (understood as small employers and the pure petty bourgeoisie combined) would gradually wither away under the dual pressure of the destruction of simple commodity production and the concentration/centralization of capital within capitalism. Certainly, on a broad historical scale, this has been one of the most robust of Marx's predictions. As Table 4.3 indicates, in the United States, France and Germany there has been a steady long-term decline in self-employment, from around 40% of the labor force 100 years ago to 10–15% of the labor force today.

Table 4.3. *Long-term trends in self-employment in US, France and Germany*
(*Self-employed + family workers as percentage of total labor force or employed labor force*)

Year[a]	US[b] as % of gainful workers (labor force)	as % of employed	Germany[c] as % of labor force	France[d] as % of labor force	as % of employed
1800					60.0
1866					42.2
1870/75		41.85			39.2
1880/82/81	41.77		38.16		42.2
1890/95/91	37.49		34.58	36.8	
1900/01		34.28		35.7	36.8
1907/10/11	30.58		34.83		39.5
1920/25/21	27.79		33.51	37.8	38.6
1930/33/31	25.47		32.87	36.7	37.5
1939/40/46	20.92	23.50	29.26		38.3
1950/50/55	18.24	19.06	28.45	33.9	34.4
1960	13.14	13.79	22.56	30.1	30.5
1970	9.47	9.85	16.49	20.8	21.3
1976[e]	8.27				
1980	8.80	9.31	12.19	15.5	16.6
1984[f]	9.16		11.77	14.1	15.7

a. In each row, the years to which the figures refer may differ slightly and are indicated in the first column. They follow the same sequence as the countries in the heading (US, Germany, France).

b. Estimates to 1940 from *Historical Statistics of the United States* Part 1 (Washington D.C. 1975). Series D 152–156. Special problems arise with the US figures, as the variable "class of worker" was first reported in the 1940 census (although it was used for coding purposes since the 1910 census; see Conk, 1979). To obtain *minimum* estimates of the number self-employed before 1940, we applied the percentages of self-employed by industry from the 1940 census (with unemployed and employed, since the pre-1940 figures refer to "gainful workers" category) to the absolute labor force in each sector for the 1870–1930 censuses.

c. Sources are Hoffman (1965, pp. 171–209); Statistisches Bundesamt. *Bevölkerung und Wirtschaft 1872–1972* (Stuttgart, 1972), pp. 142–45 for estimated labor force size and total self-employed; and Eurostat (1980 and 1985). The 1950 ff. figures use the most recent updated estimates by the Statistisches Bundesamt.

d. From Toutain (1963, pp. 151 ff), and Eurostat (1980 and 1985). No family workers are included prior to 1955. We have checked Toutain's figures against the original French census material and determined that he has correctly divided the category of so-called "*isolés*" (isolated workers) into estimated self-employed and wage-earning (*ouvriers à façon* and day laborers) portions, and allocated them appropriately. Furthermore, domestic workers are (correctly) not included among the self-employed in these figures, contrary to the common practice in nineteenth-century French statistics. Finally, the unemployed, who *were* counted in French censuses, are not included in numerator, nor are *rentiers* (persons "*vivant exclusivement de leurs revenues*").

e. I have included the year 1976 in this long-term series because it was the year in which self-employment reached its lowest level in the United States. As noted in the text, the CPS estimates for self-employment in every year are always higher than the corresponding census figures. In order for the time series in this table to be consistent, therefore, the 1976 corrected CPS estimates could not simply be inserted. I have thus deflated this 1976 estimate to make it consistent with the overall Census time series by multiplying it by .751, the ratio of the 1980 Census to the corrected 1980 CPS estimates.

f. The 1984 estimate of self-employed was obtained by applying to the 1984 CPS figure the ratio of the 1980 census and the 1980 CPS percentages of self-employed. See footnote e above.

While there is considerable merit in the classical Marxist argument, there are two considerations which suggest that it needs significant modification. First, given the massiveness of capitalist development and the historical transformations of industrial capitalist societies over the past 100 years, one might have expected (given the theoretical claims of the classical Marxist argument) that the petty bourgeoisie should have virtually disappeared by now. Instead of seeing the drop from 40% to 10–15% of the labor force as unequivocal confirmation of the classical argument, perhaps the persistence of as much as 15% of the labor force in self-employment is evidence that the classical argument was deficient. If the tacit prediction of the classical argument is that the expected level of self-employment in the era of multinational monopoly capitalism should be only a few percent of the labor force, then 15% is indeed high.

Second, and perhaps even more tellingly, there are indications that the erosion of self-employment has at least temporarily stopped in many advanced capitalist countries, and perhaps has even been reversed. Table 4.4 presents annual data on self-employment in industry and services for nine European countries (taken from Bechhofer and Elliott 1985: 195). In five of these countries – Italy, the Netherlands, Belgium, UK and Ireland – there was a fairly steady increase in the self-employment rate outside of agriculture between the mid-1970s and the early 1980s. Overall in the nine countries, the self-employment rate was nearly stagnant during the period. While of course this arrest in the historical decline of the petty bourgeoisie may simply be temporary, it does suggest at least that the classical Marxist argument needs to be supplemented by an account of the mechanisms which reproduce, and perhaps even expand, the petty bourgeoisie.

Our goal in this chapter is to begin the task of developing an understanding of these countervailing mechanisms by empirically examining in some detail the historical trajectory of self-employment in the United States in the post-war period. We will do so through two principal strategies of data analysis: first we will do a time series regression analysis of the changes in the annual rate of self-employment since the late 1940s, and second, in a manner similar to our general analysis in Chapter 3 of the overall transformation of the American class structure, we will do a shift-share decomposition of changes in self-employment.

Table 4.4. *Trends in self-employment in Western Europe, 1970-1982*[a]

	Germany	France	Italy	Netherlands	Belgium	Luxemburg	UK	Ireland	Denmark	Total
1970	10.1	12.3	23.7	9.9	14.9	12.2	6.6	10.6	13.1	12.2
1971	9.6	11.9	22.7	10.0	14.3	11.6	7.2	10.4	13.0	11.9
1972	9.5	11.6	22.6	9.7	14.1	11.2	7.2	10.3	11.7	11.8
1973	9.4	11.3	22.2	9.6	13.8	10.4	7.2	10.2	11.8	11.6
1974	9.4	11.0	22.2	9.3	13.5	10.5	7.0	9.9	11.5	11.5
1975	9.4	10.9	21.9	9.0	13.7	10.1	7.1	11.1	12.1	11.5
1976	9.2	10.8	21.8	8.7	13.8	10.1	6.9	11.2	11.7	11.4
1977	9.0	10.7	21.6	8.5	13.8	9.9	6.7	11.0	11.5	11.3
1978	8.8	10.6	22.0	8.5	14.0	9.7	6.7	10.9	11.2	11.3
1979	8.7	10.6	21.7	8.5	13.9	9.5	6.6	10.8	10.7	11.2
1980	8.5	10.6	22.2	8.9	14.0	9.2	7.0	10.7	10.6	11.4
1981	8.4	10.7	22.7	9.2	14.5	9.1	7.8	11.3	9.4	11.7
1982	8.5	10.5	23.2	9.6	14.6	8.9	8.0	11.6	8.6	11.9

Source: Bechhofer and Elliott (1985, p. 195)

a. Non-agricultural self-employed and family workers in industry and services as a percentage of nonagricultural labor force.

4.2 Time series analysis of self-employment in the United States

There are two principal objectives of the time series analysis of self-employment. First, I will show that for the United States the decline in self-employment rates has indeed been reversed in recent years, and that this result is robust across alternative specifications of the self-employment rate. Second, we will examine one important possible explanation for this reversal, namely that it is a direct response to cyclical patterns of unemployment.[7] A certain amount of self-employment is plausibly a response to a lack of good wage-labor employment opportunities. While unemployment insurance and welfare programs may reduce the incentives for the unemployed to seek self-employment, one would nevertheless expect increases in the unemployment rate to generate increases in self-employment. Given the relative economic stagnation in the American economy since the early 1970s, it might be the case that the apparent reversal of the long-term trend in self-employment simply reflects increases in unemployment in the period.

Basic time series results

The annual time series estimates of self-employment rates for the United States from 1947 through 1992 appear in Figure 4.1. Table 4.5 presents the basic time series models both for total self-employed (formally self-employed and unpaid family workers) and for the formal "self-employed" taken separately as a percentage of the adult population.[8] A visual inspection of Figure 4.1 shows the turnaround in self-employment rates in the middle 1970s, regardless of whether unpaid family workers are included or whether the labor force or the adult population is used as the denominator in calculating the rates.

[7] The relationship between unemployment and self-employment rates has often been asserted, but rarely tested empirically. Ray (1975) shows a countercyclical relation between unemployment and self-employment in the United States in the post-war period. Steinmetz (1983: 46, 285) has shown in a study of the economic crisis in France during the 1880s that unemployment was correlated with an increase in the number of small business starts, and with a *decline* in the number of large manufacturing and commercial establishments. This suggests that countercyclical self-employment responses are indeed a micro-level response of jobless workers.

[8] All of the time-series models involve generalized least-squares regression using a maximum-likelihood estimator of Rho as a correction for autocorrelated errors. The method used to estimate Rho is that developed by Beach and McKinnon (1978) and available in the program TSP (Time Series Processor).

Table 4.5 *Time series regressions for self-employment*

Independent variables	Dependent variable: self-employed + unpaid family workers as percentage of adult population		Dependent variable: self-employed as percentage of adult population	
	Model 1 B (t-value)	Model 2 B (t-value)	Model 1 B (t-value)	Model 2 B (t-value)
Time^a	−0.129 (4.3)**	−0.118 (10.8)**	−0.092 (3.3)**	−0.081 (9.3)**
Time squared		0.007 (8.3)**		0.007 (10.1)**
D-W test	0.60	1.27	0.48	1.27
Adjusted R^2	.76	.97	.72	.97
N	37	37	37	37

*p < .05   **p < .01

a. Time goes from 0 to 45 (i.e. year − 1948) and Time squared is measured as (Time − 20)^2. This calibration of time squared maximizes the t-value for the quadratic term.

The results in Table 4.5 confirm that this rise in self-employment since the middle 1970s is statistically significant. Time-squared in these models is measured as $(t-20)^2$, where t goes from 0 to 45.[9] In Model 1 only the simple trend variable, time, appears. In Model 2 the quadratic term is added. A positive coefficient on this term indicates that the time trend follows a basically parabolic curve, first declining and then increasing. Model 2 clearly fits the data much better than does Model 1, both for total self-employment (i.e. including unpaid family workers) and for formal self-employment. The explained variance is considerably higher and the coefficient for the quadratic term highly significant. In results not presented here, this basic quadratic relation also holds if we examine agricultural and nonagricultural self-employment separately, or if we calculate self-employment rates using the labor force rather than the adult population as the denominator.[10] The visual appearance of a reversal in self-employment patterns in Figure 4.1, therefore, is confirmed in the formal statistical analysis.

[9] t-20 rather than t is used for the quadratic term because subtracting this constant in Model (2) yielded the highest t-value. This reflects the fact that the curve in Figure 4.1 reaches its lowest value in the early 1970s. Subtracting a constant from t, of course, does not affect the coefficient for time in Model (1) or the coefficient for time-squared in Model 2.

[10] The results are reported in Steinmetz and Wright (1989: 1011–1013).

The effects of unemployment

Table 4.6 presents the basic results for the relationship between the rates of unemployment and self-employment. In Model 3 the annual average unemployment rate appears as an additive term. In Model 4 it is interacted with time. Two basic results are particularly important in this table. First, including the unemployment rate and the unemployment interaction with time does not reduce the magnitude of the quadratic time term in the models. This suggests that it is unlikely that the reversal in the decline of self-employment in the early 1970s is simply a direct effect of increasing unemployment. Second, in Model 4 there is a significant positive coefficient for unemployment rates and a significant negative coefficient for the time-by-unemployment interaction term. This suggests that while there is a countercyclical character to self-employment – as unemployment rises, self-employment rises – this effect is declining over time.

As in the simple time series analyses, these basic results hold whether or not unpaid family workers are included in the self-employment figures. Furthermore, the patterns are the same when the self-employment rate is measured as a proportion of the labor force rather than the entire adult population, and they are the same for non-agricultural self-employed taken separately (see Steinmetz and Wright 1989: 1011–1012).[11]

From these time series analyses we can draw two basic conclusions: first, there appears to be a significant and sustained reversal of the decline of the petty bourgeoisie in the past two decades in the United States, and second, this reversal does not seem to be a simple, counter-cyclical response to increasing unemployment. While general, long-term stagnation might still be part of the explanation, it would have to work through mechanisms other than the direct linkage between unemployment rates and self-employment.

---

[11] The only analysis in which the pattern in Table 4.6 does not strictly hold is for agricultural self-employed, where the unemployment rate seems to have a much smaller effect than for the nonagricultural sector and the unemployment-by-time interaction term is not statistically significant (see Steinmetz and Wright 1989: 1013). This probably reflects the fact that the start-up costs for agricultural self-employment are sufficiently high to act as a significant barrier to unemployed people becoming self-employed farmers in response to unemployment.

Table 4.6 *Time series regressions for effects of unemployment on self-employment*

Independent Variables	Dependent variable: Self-employed + unpaid family workers as percentage of adult population		Dependent variable: Self-employed as percentage of adult population	
	Model 1 B (t-value)	Model 2 B (t-value)	Model 1 B (t-value)	Model 2 B (t-value)
Time[a]	−0.122 (11.1)**	−0.100 (6.6)**	−0.851 (9.8)**	−0.609 (5.2)**
Time squared	0.007 (8.4)**	0.008 (8.6)**	0.007 (10.4)**	0.008 (11.1)**
Unemployment rate	4.220 (1.2)	14.500 (2.3)*	4.613 (1.6)	16.047 (3.5)**
Unemployment x Time[b]		−0.560 (2.0)*		−0.622 (3.0)**
D-W test	1.31	1.42	1.31	1.44
Adjusted R^2	.97	.97	.98	.98
N	37	37	37	37

*p < .05 ** p < .01

a. Time goes from 0 to 36 (i.e. year−1948) and Time squared is measured as $(Time−20)^2$. This calibration of time squared maximizes the t-value for the quadratic term.

b. Unemployment x Time has the straightforward interpretation as the extent to which the unemployment effects are reduced over time.

4.3 Sectoral decomposition of changes in self-employment

One possible explanation for the reversal of the historical trajectory of the petty bourgeoisie is that expanding opportunities for self-employment are in one way or another bound up with the transition to a so-called "post-industrial" society. One of the hallmarks of post-industrialism, it is often argued, is the importance of knowledge, communications and information. One might hypothesize that the expansion of various kinds of high-tech services opens up greater possibilities for self-employment, since in many instances these services require relatively little physical capital.

We will explore in a preliminary way the plausibility of the post-industrial hypothesis by examining the relationship between changes in the sectoral composition of the employed labor force and self-employment using the sectoral shift-share decomposition procedure.[12]

Table 4.7 presents the decennial changes in self-employment for the period 1940 to 1990, both for the entire employed labor force and for the six broad sectors of the economy. Two things are important to note

[12] As in Chapter 3, all of the shift-share analysis will be done on distributions of the *employed* labor force, rather than the entire labor force, since it is problematic to define the sectoral distribution of the *unemployed* segment of the labor force.

in the overall patterns in this table. First, they indicate that the period 1950–1970 was the period of the most intense decline in self-employment. In the 1950s and 1960s there was a 2.9% *annual* rate of decline of the proportion of the employed labor force that was self-employed, whereas in the 1940s this figure was only 2.1%. Second, the decline in self-employment proportions from the 1940s to the 1960s was a fairly general phenomenon across the entire economy: it occurred within every broad sector (except) the transformative sector in the 1940s. In contrast, in the 1970s and 1980s there was considerable variation across sectors in the trajectory of self-employment. We will look at these variations in detail shortly.

Table 4.8 and Figure 4.2 present the basic shift-share decomposition of the changes in proportion of self-employment by decade from 1940 to 1990. As in the shift-share analysis of Chapter 3, these are all decompositions of the decennial rate of change of the proportion self-employed. The patterns in Table 4.8 and Figure 4.2 indicate that the expansion of self-employment in the 1980s is entirely the result of changes in the distribution of the labor force across sectors. The 1970s is the pivotal decade in these changes: in the 1950s and 1960s both the class-shift component and the sector-shift component were substantial and negative. In the 1970s both the sector-shift component and the class-shift component become negligible. In the 1980s the sector shift becomes fairly large and positive.[13]

In order to get a more fine-grained picture of the economic processes that underwrite these changes, it will be useful to break down the total sector and class shifts for each decade into the contribution of each broad sector of the economy.[14] This appears in Table 4.9. First let's look at the sector shifts. From the 1950s on, there is a steady reduction of the effect of declines in the extractive sector (primarily agriculture) on self-employment. Agriculture is the sector of the economy with the highest

---

[13] It is worth noting here a difference between the results for Table 4.8 and the results reported in Table 3.4 in the previous chapter. In Chapter 3 we distinguished between the petty bourgeoisie and small employers; in this chapter these two class locations are combined in the broader category "self-employed." The results in Table 4.8, therefore, are a weighted average of the results for the two categories in Table 3.4. Thus, in the 1980s there was a positive class-shift component for the petty bourgeoisie of 4.58 and a negative class-shift component for small employers of −8.17. Combining these two class locations into the single self-employed category generates a negative class shift of −0.94 in Table 4.8.

[14] It should be noted that the sector shifts in Table 4.9 are calculated on the basis of the thirty-two sector typology, not these broader six sector categories. These six broad categories are then aggregated from the more disaggregated shift-share calculations.

Table 4.7. *Proportion of the employed labor force self-employed, 1940–1990*

	1940	1950	1960	1970	1980	1990
1 Self-employed as percentage of total employed labor force	23.91	18.72	13.29	9.38	9.30	9.90
2 Change from previous decade		-5.19	-5.43	-3.91	-0.08	0.60
3 Percentage change from previous decade		-21.71	-29.01	-29.42	-0.85	6.45
Percentage self-employed by sector						
Extractive	67.14	65.94	57.91	47.84	40.55	37.57
Transformative	5.49	5.73	5.16	4.70	5.93	7.71
Distributive	20.78	16.97	14.11	10.91	10.46	9.82
Business services	21.18	17.69	16.12	12.71	14.00	15.27
Social & political services	6.58	4.58	4.19	2.87	2.75	2.94
Personal services	20.42	19.77	19.35	17.12	16.34	16.96

Table 4.8. *Decomposition of rates of change of self-employment*

	1940–1950	1950–1960	1960–1970	1970–1980	1980–1990
1 Decade rate of change of proportion of self-employed	-21.71	-29.01	-29.42	-0.85	6.45
2 Class shift	-4.20	-10.56	-17.85	-0.30	-0.94
3 Sector shift	-16.72	-20.29	-12.24	-0.04	7.07
4 Residual	-0.79	1.84	0.67	-0.51	0.32
Percentage of the decade rate of change in self-employment attributable to each component					
5 Class shift	19.35	36.40	60.67	35.29	-9.95
6 Sector shift	77.02	69.94	41.60	4.71	109.61
7 Residual	3.64	-6.34	-2.28	60.00	3.39

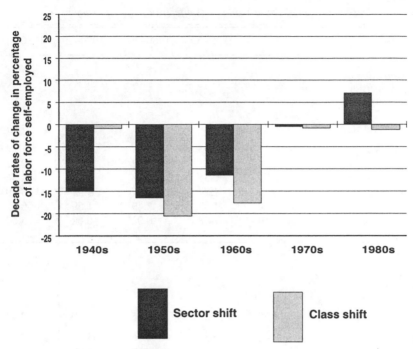

Figure 4.2 *Decomposition of decennial rates of change of self-employment, 1940–1990*

levels of self-employment. Declines in the agricultural sector, therefore, have historically contributed heavily to the sectoral effects on the decline of self-employment. In the 1950s, the decline in the extractive sector reduced self-employment by roughly 22%. This dropped to about 16% in the 1960s, about 4% in the 1970s and less than 2% in the 1980s. As the agricultural sector becomes smaller and smaller, its continuing decline has less impact on the overall class structure of American society. In a complementary manner, the expansion of certain service sectors, especially business services, has an increasingly significant positive effect on self-employment.

The class-shift components also show interesting variations across sectors over time. In the 1940s there was a small expansion of self-employment in the transformative sector which partially countered the decline in self-employment in most other sectors. The result is that the overall class shift was a modest –4.2%. In the 1950s self-employment declined in all but one of the six broad sectors of the economy,

Table 4.9. *Decomposition of sectoral and class effects on self-employment*

	1940–50	1950–60	1960–70	1970–80	1980–90
Decomposition of *sectoral shifts in* *self-employment*[a]					
Total sectoral shift	−16.72	−20.29	−12.24	−0.04	7.07
Extractive	−19.17	−21.93	−15.89	−4.17	−1.64
Transformative	−0.44	0.11	−1.02	−0.54	−0.32
Distributive services	2.03	−0.55	0.68	−1.12	0.56
Business services	0.24	1.77	1.47	3.57	3.89
Social & political services	0.80	1.37	2.49	1.59	0.92
Personal services	−0.19	−1.08	0.02	0.62	3.67
Decomposition of *class shifts in* *self-employment*[b]					
Total class shift	−4.20	−10.65	−17.85	−0.30	−0.94
Extractive	0.08	−5.51	−4.36	−1.56	−2.46
Transformative	1.51	−0.67	−1.28	2.99	2.58
Distributive services	−2.83	−3.65	−5.20	−0.84	−1.55
Business services	−0.52	−0.37	−1.47	0.65	1.03
Social & political services	−0.87	−0.40	−2.20	−1.03	0.04
Personal services	−1.56	0.04	−3.34	−0.52	−0.58

a. The entries are the contribution of changes in relative employment within each sector to the overall sectoral shift component.

b. The entries are the contribution of changes in self-employment rates within each sector to the overall class shift component in the changes in self-employment rates.

generating a considerably larger total class shift. The decline of self-employment within sectors accelerated in the 1960s. During that decade the sectoral contributions to the negative class-shift component were large and fairly evenly distributed across the economy, indicating a very broad pattern of proletarianization.

The decade of the 1970s represents a sharp break in the pattern of the previous two decades. In those sectors which still contributed a negative class-shift component during the 1970s, the negative effects were always smaller than in the 1960s. And in two sectors – the transformative sector and business services – the negative class-shift effect is actually reversed: self-employment increased as a proportion of the labor force in these sectors over the decade. This basic trend in the transformative sector and business services continued in the 1980s.

How do these sector-specific results bear on the question of whether or not self-employment is largely a "post-industrial" phenomenon? In order to get a more nuanced picture of the changes in the 1970s and 1980s it is useful to disaggregate the results in Tables 4.8 and 4.9 into the full thirty-two sector typology. These results are presented in Table 4.10. In this table, the overall contributions of detailed sectors to the change in self-employment rates are rank ordered from the largest positive contribution to the largest negative contribution. In Table 4.11 these sectors are reaggregated into categories reflecting the post-industrial thesis: *post-industrial services* (i.e. services within which post-industrial activities are dominant); *traditional transformative sectors*; *traditional services*, within which high levels of knowledge production and usage are not central; *agriculture*; and a number of miscellaneous sectors.

The results in Tables 4.10 and 4.11 provide some suggestive support for the view that the expansion of self-employment is significantly linked to post-industrialism. In the 1980s, six of the ten sectors which contributed most to the overall expansion of self-employment are dominated by post-industrial activities: business services, medical and health services, professional services (law, engineering, etc.), banking, education and insurance. A seventh sector, childcare services, while not itself an instance of a post-industrial service (since it does not involve high levels of codified knowledge), is nevertheless closely linked to the expansion of the post-industrial sectors of the economy since those sectors have contributed heavily to the expansion of female labor force participation. All of these, except for professional services, contributed positively both to the sectoral shift in self-employment and the class shift. At the other end of the spectrum, eleven of the twelve sectors whose total contribution to self-employment was negative are sectors within which post-industrial activities are generally marginal. This includes traditional services like lodging or retail, core sectors in the industrial economy like metalworking and food processing, and agriculture. These results thus seem to confirm the centrality of post-industrial tendencies in the expansion of self-employment.

However, if we look a little closer at the decomposition of these effects on self-employment, the picture becomes somewhat more complex. As Table 4.11 indicates, in both the 1970s and the 1980s, the

Table 4.10. *Rank ordering of total contribution of different sectors to changes in proportions self-employed, 1970–1980 and 1980–1990*

		Total contribution of sector to:		
		(1)	(2)	(3)
		Overall change in rate of self-employment	Class shift	Sector shift
1970–1980				
1	Business services	2.11	0.42	1.50
2	Construction	1.94	1.63	0.26
3	Real estate	1.21	0.15	0.99
4	Professional service	0.94	0.02	0.91
5	Repair services	0.85	0.15	0.68
6	Childcare services	0.59	0.87	-0.10
7	Transportation	0.53	0.68	-0.12
8	Entertainment	0.50	0.18	0.27
9	Wholesale	0.45	0.17	0.26
10	Misc. manufacturing	0.29	0.94	-0.51
11	Welfare & nonprofit	0.28	0.21	0.05
12	Banking	0.18	0.06	0.11
13	Machine tool	0.14	0.24	-0.08
14	Education	0.13	0.01	0.12
15	Mining	0.10	-0.01	0.11
16	Insurance	0.07	-0.001	0.07
17	Utilities	0.04	0.03	0.01
18	Communications	0.04	0.04	0.002
19	Metal	0.03	0.12	-0.07
20	Textile	0.01	0.07	-0.03
21	Postal services	0	0	0
22	Government	0	0	0
23	Chemical	-0.01	0.01	-0.01
24	Domestic services	-0.06	0.07	-0.10
25	Food	-0.13	-0.04	-0.09
26	Medical & health	-0.18	-1.26	1.41
27	Hotel & lodging	-0.21	-0.28	0.08
28	Laundry	-0.42	0.20	-0.53
29	Eating & drinking	-0.61	-1.53	1.40
30	Misc. personal services	-1.24	-0.19	-1.09
31	Retail	-2.88	-1.73	-1.27
32	Agriculture	-5.52	-1.55	-4.27
Total		-0.85	-0.30	-0.04

Table 4.10. *(Continued)*

		Total contribution of sector to:		
		(1)	(2)	(3)
		Overall change in rate of self-employment	Class shift	Sector shift
1980–1990				
1	Childcare services	2.73	1.52	0.50
2	Business services	2.45	0.66	1.60
3	Construction	1.55	0.66	0.84
4	Medical & health	1.05	0.38	0.62
5	Repair	1.02	−0.20	1.29
6	Real estatate	0.88	0.21	0.63
7	Professional services	0.65	−0.56	1.38
8	Banking	0.59	0.42	0.11
9	Education	0.51	0.38	0.10
10	Insurance	0.50	0.30	0.17
11	Transportation	0.47	0.43	0.04
12	Misc. manufacturing	0.45	1.06	−0.48
13	Misc. personal services	0.42	−0.35	0.84
14	Entertainment	0.27	−0.24	0.60
15	Communications	0.26	0.29	−0.01
16	Machine tools	0.12	0.49	−0.27
17	Utilities	0.01	0.04	−0.02
18	Textiles	0.01	0.08	−0.05
19	Government	0	0	0
20	Postal services	0	0	0
21	Chemical	−0.01	0.04	−0.04
22	Laundry	−0.06	−0.02	−0.04
23	Wholesale	−0.08	−0.15	0.07
24	Food	−0.09	0.003	−0.09
25	Metal	−0.09	0.22	−0.22
26	Domestic services	−0.10	−0.10	−0.03
27	Mining	−0.10	0.13	−0.18
28	Hotel & lodging	−0.22	−0.29	0.12
29	Eating & drinking	−0.60	−0.91	0.40
30	Welfare & nonprofit	−0.66	−0.72	0.20
31	Retail	−1.72	−2.12	0.46
32	Agricuture	−3.82	−2.59	−1.46
Total		6.45	−0.95	7.07

Table 4.11. *Contributions of post-industrial sectors to expansion of self-employment*

	Components of shift-share decomposition		
	Total	Class shift	Sector shift
1970–1980			
Post-industrial services[a]	3.29	−0.71	4.12
Traditional transformative[b]	1.00	2.04	−0.79
Traditional services[c]	−3.26	−2.96	0.01
Agriculture	−5.52	−1.55	−4.27
Miscellaneous:			
Childcare services	0.59	0.87	−0.10
Welfare and nonprofit	0.28	0.21	0.01
Repair and construction	2.79	1.78	0.94
Total	−0.85	−0.30	−0.04
1980–1990			
Post-industrial services	6.01	1.87	3.97
Traditional transformative	1.65	2.70	−0.72
Traditional services	−2.09	−3.60	2.42
Agriculture	−3.82	−2.59	−1.46
Miscellaneous:			
Childcare services	2.73	1.52	0.50
Welfare and nonprofit	−0.66	−0.72	0.20
Repair and construction	2.57	0.46	2.13
Total	6.45	−0.95	7.07

a. *Post-industrial services* = business services, professional services, banking, education, insurance, medical & health, communications.

b. *Traditional transformative* = transportation, miscellaneous manufacturing, machine tools, mining, utilities, metal, food, textile, chemical.

c. *Traditional services* = real estate, entertainment, domestic services, wholesale, hotel & lodging, laundry, eating & drinking, miscellaneous personal services, retail sales.

sector of the economy within which there was the largest, positive *class* shift was the traditional transformative sector. Indeed, in the 1970s, the rate of self-employment *within* post-industrial services actually declined, thus contributing a negative class-shift to the overall self-employment rate, and while the class shift was positive within post-industrial services in the 1980s, it was still smaller than in the transformative sector. What is more, this positive class-shift component within the traditional transformative sector (+2.07) in the 1980s is generated by some of the core subsectors of the industrial economy: miscellaneous manufacturing (1.06), machine tools (0.49) and metal working (0.22). The reason why the overall contribution of the transformative sector to the expansion of self-employment is smaller than the contribution of post-industrial services is thus entirely due to the negative sector effects of the transformative sector.

Taking these results together, it appears that while the sectoral shift toward post-industrial services contributed substantially to the expansion of self-employment in the 1980s, increasing self-employment within specific lines of economic activity was more concentrated within manufacturing and other traditional transformative sectors. If this class shift within the transformative sector had not occurred (and everything else remained the same), the expansion of self-employment would have been roughly 40% less.

It thus appears that while more than half of the expansion of self-employment in the 1980s can be attributed to sectoral change in the economy toward post-industrial services, the expansion of self-employment within manufacturing and other transformative sectors is also a significant factor. Expanding self-employment is thus not simply a post-industrial phenomenon; it also reflects changes in class distributions within the traditional industrial economy.

4.5 Conclusions and unresolved issues

Four general conclusions stand out among the results of the various data analyses presented here:

First, there is strong evidence that the numerical decline of the petty bourgeoisie which has marked the long-term history of American capitalism has at least temporarily stopped and perhaps been modestly reversed.

Second, this reversal of the historical decline of the petty bourgeoisie is not a direct consequence of countercyclical movements of people from unemployment to self-employment. While there is an effect of the rate of unemployment on self-employment, this effect has been declining in the post-war period, and in any case does not account for the increase in self-employment since the mid-1970s.

Third, the growth of post-industrial services does appear to have significantly contributed to the expansion of self-employment, but this is largely through a direct sectoral change effect, not because self-employment is generally increasing rapidly *within* post-industrial sectors.

Fourth, within many of the older, more traditional industrial sectors of the economy, there appears to be a growth in self-employment in recent years. This is especially noticeable in construction and miscellaneous manufacturing, but is also true in machinery, transportation and even metal working. The expansion of self-employment within particular branches of economic activity, therefore, is not exclusively a post-industrial process but a structural feature of more traditional segments of the economy as well.

The data in this chapter do not provide a basis for exploring alternative possible explanations for this expansion of self-employment within these traditional sectors of the industrial economy. Five possibilities seem particularly important. First, it could turn out that the apparent expansion of self-employment is an illusion, that it represents changes in the systems of classification of particular jobs but not a genuine expansion of self-employment properly understood. Dale (1986) has argued, for example, that much apparent "self-employment" is really simply a new way for employers to hire workers under schemes of homework, freelancing, subcontracting, out-working and the like. Marsh, Heady and Matheson (1981) found that a third of the formally self-employed workers in the construction industry worked exclusively for contractors and provided only their own labor. In such cases there is really very little to distinguish them from wage-workers. While for tax purposes and purposes of labor relations it may be advantageous for employers to reclassify part of their labor force as "self-employed," this does not reflect a sociologically meaningful expansion of the "petty bourgeoisie."[15] The fact that, as we saw in Chapter 3, the class-shift component of the changing class distributions for small employers was negative in the 1970s and 1980s, whereas it was positive for the petty bourgeoisie, is consistent with the view that a significant part of the overall expansion of self-employment could be linked to such contract devices within labor markets.

Second, the increase in self-employment within certain traditional sectors of the industrial economy could be at least partially a demographic phenomenon, reflecting the entry of the baby boom generation

[15]   The advantages of such reclassification include exempting employers from paying most benefits and social security taxes.

into the age range of maximum likelihood of self-employment. Self-employment is generally highest in mid to late career stages, after a certain amount of savings has been accumulated. As the baby boom generation enters mid-career, therefore, one might expect a temporary increase in self-employment. If this demographic explanation is correct, then the rate of self-employment should decline again as this generation ages further.

Third, it might be argued that increasing self-employment could be partially an effect of the increasing participation of married women in the labor force. Self-employment generally brings with it more risks than wage-labor employment. If those risks were to decline, one might expect more people to start their own businesses. One mechanism that could reduce risks to a family would be for one member to hold a stable wage-earner job while another attempts self-employment. The increasing prevalence of dual-earner households, therefore, could be partially underwriting the expansion of self-employment.

Fourth, the increase of self-employment within traditional sectors of the industrial economy could reflect the long-term stagnation of the economy. While we have shown that the increase in self-employment in the 1970s and 1980s cannot be attributed to a direct countercyclical response to unemployment rates, it could nevertheless be a structural response to declining opportunities for good jobs in the industrial economy. As many commentators have noted, much of the job expansion in the wage labor force in the 1980s has centered on low-paying service sector jobs, while much of the decline has been in well-paying core industrial jobs. Many people may therefore enter self-employment because of the absence of good job alternatives, not simply because of the absence of jobs as such. If this explanation is correct, then it would be expected that very little of the expansion of self-employment would be among small *employers*, but rather would be concentrated in the individual self-employed petty bourgeoisie. The patterns of class shifts in Chapter 3 lend some support to this interpretation.

Finally, the introduction of information technologies and improvements in transportation and communication may have lowered the barriers to entry in many areas of light manufacturing, thus facilitating the growth in the numbers of smaller businesses. In recent years there has been much talk about the virtues of decentralization, and many larger corporations have both downsized and increased their reliance on a variety of forms of subcontracting to small employers. The expansion of self-employment in the more traditional manufacturing sectors of the economy may partially reflect these technological and organizational developments.

The American class structure appears to be in a period of significant structural reorganization. As we noted in Chapter 3, the rate of decline of the working class appears to have accelerated in recent decades, and in the 1980s the proportion of the labor force that are supervisors also appears to be declining. We also now see that the decline of the petty bourgeoisie that persisted from the nineteenth century has been halted, at least temporarily. Explaining the mechanisms which are generating these changes is essential if we are to understand the trajectory of the American class structure into the next century.

Methodological appendix[16]

Annual time series analysis of self-employment for the United States

Self-employment measures. The time series labor force data for the analysis of self-employment are taken from the Current Population Survey (CPS) statistics, published monthly in *Earnings and Income*. For most purposes, I consider "unpaid family members" part of "total self-employed," but I present the data for the more formally defined self-employed as well.[17] All statistics refer to civilians aged 16 or over.

Estimating the number of self-employed is more complicated after 1967 than for the earlier period due to changes in the way the census and the CPS deal with "incorporated self-employment." Tax laws and liability considerations make it profitable for many businessmen to incorporate and technically become employees of their own corporations.[18] From a sociological point of view, incorporation does not constitute a meaningful change in one's class location, and thus we

---

[16] A much more detailed discussion of the data and methods in the analysis for this chapter can be found in Steinmetz and Wright (1989).

[17] Many small businesses and farms are run as "family" enterprises. In such cases it often makes little sense to describe one member of the family – typically the husband – as "self-employed" and the others – typically wives and adult children – as "unpaid family workers." While such labels may reflect cultural conventions and gender relations, the essential *class* location of these two categories is the same. When I refer to "self-employed" or "petty bourgeoisie," therefore, this includes unpaid family workers unless explicitly stated otherwise. When I wish to refer to the self-employed exclusive of unpaid family workers, I use the expression "formal self-employment."

[18] Some of the advantages of incorporation by the self-employed are discussed in Alston (1978).

would like to treat incorporated and unincorporated self-employed as equivalent categories. Beginning in 1967, unfortunately, the CPS began classifying such persons as wage-earners. To make matters worse, the critical questionnaire item which is used to produce this classification does not appear on the public-release CPS data tapes and thus it is impossible to reclassify the "incorporated self-employed" from the wage-earner to the self-employed category. This results in a serious underestimation of the number of people who according to the socio-logical definition are actually self-employed.

In order to have a meaningful annual time series of self-employment, therefore, I had to correct for these underestimates, for otherwise changes in the nominal self-employment rate might simply reflect changes in the proportion of self-employed who chose, for strategic legal and tax reasons, to incorporate their businesses. Fortunately, I was able to obtain estimates of the proportion of all self-employed who were incorporated for four years: 1967, 1975, 1978 and 1982.[19] On the basis of data for these years, I was able to estimate the intermediate figures with linear interpolation and the figures after 1982 by linear extrapolation.[20]

Unemployment rates. One of the main purposes of the time series analysis of self-employment is to estimate the existence of and historical changes in the effects of unemployment rates on self-employ-ment rates. This raises the issue of what is the appropriate denominator for these "rates" – the total labor force or the total population. The problem with using the labor force as a denominator is that as unemployment increases, the labor force itself tends to decline because of the increase in "discouraged workers." This implies that there will be a tendency for self-employment as a proportion of the labor force to increase under these conditions simply because the denominator declines and not because of any causal relation between unemploy-ment and self-employment as such. Therefore, rather than using unemployment and self-employment as a proportion of the labor force, I use total US adult population as a denominator. I also performed the regressions using labor force ratios, and none of the conclusions were substantively affected.

[19] These data were from articles in the *Monthly Labor Review* published by the US Bureau of Labor Statistics (Becker 1984; Fain 1980; Ray 1975).

[20] For a detailed discussion of these adjustment procedures, see Wright and Martin (1989).

Shift-share decomposition of changes in self-employment

The shift-share analysis of the changes in self-employment by economic sector and by decade between 1940 and 1990 is based on national census data. In general, census estimates of self-employment in the United States tend to be lower than estimates from other sources. For example, in 1970 the census indicated that 9.85% of the labor force were in the categories unincorporated self-employed plus unpaid family members, while the Current Population Survey estimate is 11.30%, and in 1980 the census result is 9.47% while the CPS is 11.70% and the estimate from the class analysis survey over 14%. As mentioned in Chapter 2, this problem in estimates of self-employment is not just an issue in the United States; for nearly all countries in the Comparative Class Analysis Project, estimates from the project surveys are several percentage points above estimates from national censuses.

I know of no research which has carefully investigated the reasons for the chronically lower estimates of self-employed in the census than in sample surveys, but I suspect that it has to do with the self-administered nature of the census questionnaire which may lead to underreporting of self-employment. In any case, unless this problem of underreporting varies dramatically over time and sector, the census data should provide us with a reasonable basis for decomposing *change* in self-employment into components due to changing sectoral composition of the labor force and changing self-employment rates within sectors.

Self-employment measures. The shift-share analysis uses the "class of worker" item from the 1940–1990 decennial US censuses, including the recently released 1940 and 1950 US Census Public Use Microdata Samples (1% files) (Census of the Population 1940, 1950). I generated tables of industrial sector by self-employed/wage-earner using the "class of worker" and industry variables. These data are for all *employed* adults in the labor force 16 years and older. I restrict the analyses in this part of the chapter to *employed* adults (rather than the adult labor force or the entire adult population as in the general time series analyses) because we are interested in the *sectoral* distribution of self-employment. Since unemployment has at best an ambiguous status within economic sectors, it is difficult to define the total labor force of a sector in a meaningful way. The self-employment rates used in the shift-share analysis, therefore, all use employed adults in sectors as the denominator.

The class of worker variable used by the census bureau was transformed into its current form only after the 1940 census.[21] In the 1940 census, the self-employed were distributed among the categories "own account" worker and "employer." Census enumerators were instructed to exclude persons working for wages from the "own account" status (US Department of Commerce 1940: 69). However, some wage-workers without steady employment, for example day laborers, may also have been entered in this category.[22]

Unpaid family workers are included along with the traditionally defined self-employed in the shift-share analyses, as with the time series. The difficulty we encountered in the annual CPS data with estimating the incorporated self-employed does not arise with the 1970–1990 census data, because these cases are identified as a separate category in the Public Use Samples and can thus be merged with unincorporated self-employed. The analysis of the 1940–1990 data exclude the currently unemployed and all persons under 16 years of age.[23]

Economic sector. For the economic sector classification, I use a modified form of the thirty-eight-sector industry scheme discussed in Chapter 3. Because the industry codes used in the 1940 and 1950 censuses were not as detailed as in later censuses, it was necessary to collapse some of the categories as indicated in Appendix Table 4.1. Also, because the childcare services sector was impossible to specify for 1960 and before, this sector is included only for the analyses of the period 1970–1990.

---

[21] Jenkins (1985: 63). The 1910 census was the first to differentiate among occupations on the basis of social class (Conk 1979: 25).

[22] Margo Conk, an historian who has written extensively on the Census Bureau, suggested in a personal communication that these kinds of misclassifications were likely to have occurred.

[23] The 1950 data are weighted according to the weight p10–13–BRWT; the 1940 data are unweighted, because only persons from the self-weighting sample were selected.

Appendix Table 4.1. *Sector classification categories for shift-share analysis*

Sector[a]	Categories for analysis of petty bourgeoisie	Categories used in analysis of class distributions in chapter 3
1 *Extractive*		
Agriculture, forestry, fishing	1	1
Mining	2	2
2 *Transformative*		
Construction	3	3
Food	4	4
Textiles	5	5
Metal	6	6
Machinery	7	7
Chemical	8	8
Misc. manufacturing	9	9
Utilities	10	10
3 *Distributive*		
Transportation	11	11
Communication	12	12
Wholesale	13	13
Retail	14	14
4 *Business services*		
Banking	15	15
Insurance	16	16
Real estate	17	17
Professional services (law, engineering, etc.)	18	18, 21
Business services	19	19, 20
5 *Social and political services*		
Medical and health sevices	20	22, 23
Education	21	24
Welfare and nonprofit	22	25, 26, 29
Postal services	23	27
Government	24	28
Childcare services	25[a]	
6 *Personal services*		
Domestic services	26	30
Hotels and lodging	27	31
Eating and drinking	28	32
Repair (auto, misc.)	29	33
Laundry	30	34
Entertainment	31	36
Misc. personal services	32	35,37

a. Military and the unemployed are excluded from the analysis.

b. Before 1990, most people engaged in home-based childcare were classified in the hotels and lodging sector. In 1990 a new sector, "Family childcare services," was introduced. Since virtually 100% of the people in family childcare services are self-employed, the large expansion of such services in the 1980s would appear as an increase in self-employment in hotels and lodging unless a childcare service sector were created for earlier years. We have done this by taking all people whose *occupations* were childcare workers (regardless of their sectoral classification) and combining them into a childcare services sector.

Part II

The permeability of class boundaries

5 Class-boundary permeability: concepts and methodological issues

Class structures differ not only in the distribution of people across the various locations in that structure, but also in the extent to which people's lives are bounded by specific class locations. At the micro-level, class is explanatory because it shapes the *interests, strategic capacities* and *experiences* of people, and each of these effects depends not simply on the static location of individuals in a job-class structure but also on the complex ways in which their lives are linked to various classes through careers, mobility, voluntary associations and social ties.[1] In some class structures, friendships, marriages, churches and sports clubs are largely homogeneous with respect to class. In such cases, class boundaries can be thought of as highly impermeable. In other class structures, these social processes frequently bring together people in different class locations. When this happens, class boundaries become relatively permeable.

In this chapter I will give some precision to the concept of the permeability of class boundaries and propose a general empirical strategy for analyzing permeability. In Chapters 6, 7 and 8 I will apply this method to three kinds of permeability: the formation of friendship ties across class locations, the class composition of families and intergenerational class mobility.

---

[1] For an extended discussion of the relationship of class to interests, experiences and capacities, see Wright (1989a: 278–295). This problem is also discussed in Chapter 13 below.

5.1 Theoretical issues

Permeability in the Marxist and Weberian traditions

The two primary sociological traditions of class analysis – Marxist and Weberian – have given different priorities to class structure and boundary permeability as objects of analysis. In a variety of ways, Marxists (e.g. Carchedi 1977; Poulantzas 1975; Resnick and Wolfe 1988; Szymanski 1983; Wright 1978, 1985, 1989a) generally put the analysis of class structure (or a closely related concept like "relations of production") at center stage and pay relatively little attention to the permeability of class boundaries (for an exception see Bertaux 1977). In contrast, the permeability of class boundaries looms large in the Weberian tradition, whether termed "class structuration" (Anthony Giddens 1973) or "closure" (Parkin 1974, 1979). This is especially clear in the analysis of social mobility, which is largely inspired (if in a somewhat diffuse way) by Weberian conceptions of class rooted in a concern with "life chances." Weberians tend to devote much less attention to the rigorous elaboration of the concept of class structure itself. As Burris (1987) and Wright (1990: 313–323) have argued, sociologists working in the Weberian tradition typically treat locations within class structures as soft categories requiring only loose definitions and relatively casual theoretical defense.

The analyses of class-boundary permeability in the next three chapters, therefore, combine the conceptual apparatus of the Marxist tradition with the substantive focus of the Weberian tradition on the intersection of people's lives with class structures. This marriage of Marxist categories with Weberian questions is motivated by a desire to deepen the micro-analysis of class within the Marxist tradition. My assumption is that the complex ways in which individual lives traverse class boundaries is one of the important factors that shape the ways in which people experience class structures. For example, political coalitions across specific class boundaries should be facilitated to the extent that friendship and family ties cross these boundaries. On the other hand, higher levels of class consciousness would be expected in societies in which friendship ties and biographical trajectories were overwhelmingly confined within the same class rather than diffused across a variety of class locations.

Our focus in these chapters is on the structural patterns of class-boundary permeability rather than on the possible *effects* at the individual level of permeability experience on such things as political behavior or class consciousness. The issue of effects on consciousness of one aspect of permeability, class mobility, will be taken up in Chapter 15.

Static and dynamic permeability

The permeability of class boundaries can be usefully divided into two general forms which we will refer to as *static* permeability and *dynamic* permeability. The static permeability of class boundaries refers to the patterns of social ties between people situated in different locations within a class structure. Examples would include such things as the cross-boundary patterns of neighborhood composition, household composition, memberships in voluntary associations and friendship networks. Dynamic permeability, on the other hand, refers to the ways in which biographical trajectories traverse different locations within class structures. Inter- and intragenerational class mobility would, of course, be prime examples, but life-course patterns of participation in various social networks would also be relevant to the dynamic permeability of class boundaries. For example, different levels of the education system might vary a lot in the extent to which they bring people from very different classes together in the classroom. Pre-school might be more class homogeneous than elementary school, and elementary school classrooms less class segregated than high schools (because of tracking), and high schools less than universities. The biographical trajectory of people through the education system, therefore, can involve moving through a series of settings with more or less permeable class boundaries.

Defined in these terms, the problem of the permeability of social boundaries is by no means restricted to class analysis. International migration, for example, constitutes an aspect of the dynamic permeability of national boundaries, while patterns of membership and participation in international professional associations are an aspect of the static permeability of those boundaries.[2] Interethnic marriages and friendships are aspects of the static permeability of ethnic boundaries, while the problem of "salad-bar ethnicity" and the intergenerational transmission of ethnicity are aspects of the dynamic permeability of those boundaries. Interdisciplinary research institutes and faculty seminars are instances of the static permeability of the boundaries of

---

[2] The expression "boundary" has a literal as well as metaphorical meaning in the case of national boundaries, since the boundaries are legally enforced through citizenship laws and are represented by the territorial borders of the nation-state. More generally, a "boundary" can be viewed as any qualitative line of demarcation between locations – social positions filled by individuals – within a social structure.

academic disciplines, while the pattern of career trajectories through academic specialities is an example of dynamic permeability.

The problem of permeability of social boundaries is sociologically important because it may help us to understand the extent to which various kinds of social cleavages are reinforced or undermined by the social ties and experiences of people within social structures (cf. Blau 1988). It is often argued, for example, that a regime of very high social mobility will tend to generate less bitter interclass conflict than a regime of rigid class boundaries (Blau and Duncan 1967: 440; Sorokin 1927; Westergaard and Resler 1975: 285–286). It would be expected that situations in which there are high degrees of interràcial, inter-ethnic or interreligious marriage and friendship will contribute to (and be fostered by) low levels of conflict across these boundaries (see Blau and Schwartz 1984: ch. 3, for a discussion of this issue for religious groups). Interlocking directorates among firms are generally thought to facilitate cooperation among corporations (Burt 1983). Career trajectories that involve movement from private business to government and back to business probably reduce conflict between the state and private enterprises. In these and other ways, the variable permeability of different kinds of social boundaries can play an important role in bridging or intensifying the fault lines of social structures.

In Chapters 6, 7 and 8 we will explore two aspects of the static permeability of class boundaries – friendships and cross-class families – and one aspect of dynamic permeability – intergenerational mobility. The rest of this chapter will lay out the variables, measures and general analytical strategy we will adopt to study these processes.

5.2 Class-structure variables

Operationalizing class structure

In order to study class-boundary permeability, we have to measure class locations both for the respondents and for various other people: friends, spouses, and the heads of the households in which the respondents lived while growing up. Unfortunately, in the Comparative Class Analysis Project surveys, there were generally less detailed data available for operationalizing class for these other people than for the respondents themselves. In order to have the same criteria for defining class applied to both respondents and these other categories of people, therefore, it was necessary to adopt somewhat different operationalizations of the property and authority dimensions for the analysis of permeability than for most of the other analyses in this book. For theoretical rather than pragmatic reasons, a slightly different operationalization was also adopted for the skill dimension. These operationalizations are summarized in Table 5.1.

The property dimension. No data were available on the number of employees for self-employed friends, spouses, or childhood heads of household. Employers are therefore defined as self-employed persons who have any employees.

The authority dimension. Respondents were asked a single question concerning the authority of friends, spouses, and childhood heads of households: "Was this [the person's job] a management or supervisor position, or a nonmanagement position?" On the basis of this question alone it was only possible to distinguish people in a combined manager-supervisor category from nonmanagers. For the analysis of friends and of spouses, however, it is possible to impute the distinction between managers and supervisors using a method which will be described in chapter 7. This was not possible for the mobility analysis. Thus, for the analysis of the permeability of class boundaries to mobility, the authority dimension is measured by a simpler dichotomy.

The skill dimension. In most of the other analyses in this book, "experts" are defined as people in professional or managerial occupations. The category "managerial occupations" is obviously more heterogeneous with respect to ownership of scarce skills and expertise than the category "professional occupations," particularly since, unlike the professions, in general managerial occupations are not credentialed. For the analysis of class-boundary permeability, therefore, it seemed desirable to adopt a more restrictive definition of "experts" in which this category is limited to people in the professions (i.e. occupations requiring more than a B.A. degree). Managerial occupations are then combined with skilled employee and technical occupations into the intermediate category (referred to as "skilled employee") on the skill dimension of the class-structure variable.

Because of limitations on sample size, we are not able to operationalize all of the combinations of these three dimensions in the analyses of class-boundary permeability. For the friendship and family analyses we can operationalize eight class locations: employers, petty bourgeoisie, expert managers, managers, supervisors, professionals, skilled

Table 5.1. *Operationalization of class structure for permeability analyses*

| Class Location | Property | | Authority | Skill |
	Self-employed	Has employees	Managerial or supervis-ory position[a]	Occupation
Employers	Yes	Yes		
Petty bourgeoisie	Yes	No		
Expert managers	No		Yes	Professional, technical or managerial occupations
Manager/supervisors	No		Yes	Occupation other than professional, technical or managerial occupations
Professionals[b]	No		No	Professional occupations (i.e. occupations that require post-undergraduate education)
Skilled employees	No		No	Technical, managerial or semi-professional occupation
Workers	No		No	Occupation other than ·professional, technical or managerial occupations

a. For *respondents*, but *not* for friends, spouses, or origins, we can distinguish "managers" from "supervisors" on the basis of respondents' report of whether their own job is best described as a "management position" or a "supervisor position."

b. For purposes of the analysis of class boundary permeability, we have defined the expert category more narrowly than in other analyses by restricting experts to credentialled professionals. We thus refer to this category as "professionals" rather than "experts." The intermediary skill category is also different from other analyses since it contains managerial and semi-professional occupations which elsewhere are included in the experts category. We refer to this category as "skilled *employees*" rather than "skilled workers" to differentiate it from the treatment in other analyses.

employee and workers. The delineation of these class locations in terms of the three dimensions is shown in Figure 5.1. In the mobility analysis, managers and supervisors are combined, yielding a total of seven categories.

The permeability-event matrix

On the basis of the categories defined in Figure 5.1 we can construct an 8 x 8 matrix of permeability events (a 7 x 7 matrix in the case of mobility) as illustrated in Figure 5.2. In the analysis of mobility, one

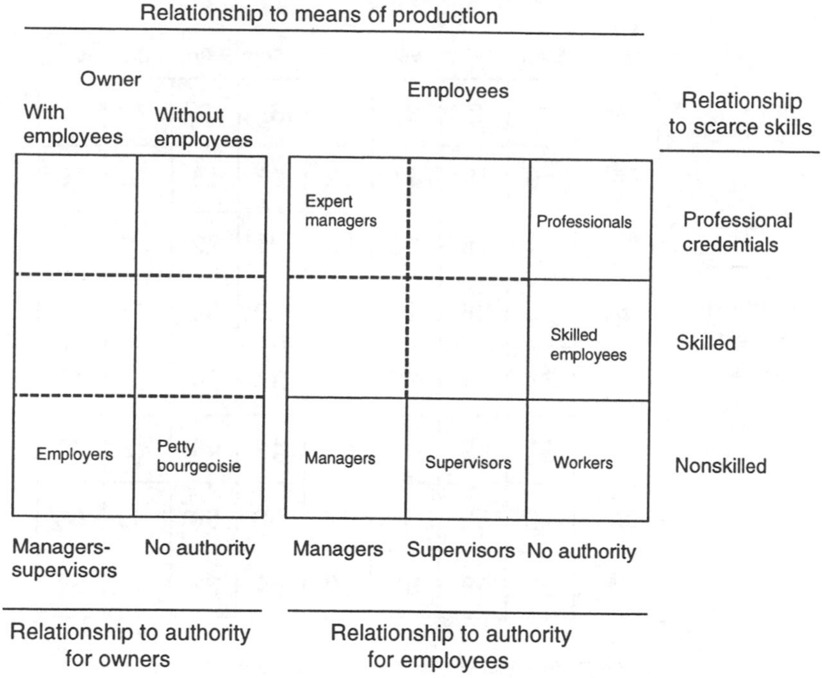

Relationship to means of production

Figure 5.1 *Class categories used in the analysis of permeability of class boundaries*

axis of this matrix represents class origins, the other class destinations. In the analysis of the permeability of the class structure to friendship ties, one axis of this matrix represents the class locations of respondents and the second axis represents the class location of respondents' friends. And, in the analysis of the cross-class families, one axis represents the class location of husbands and the other of wives in

Individual's class location

	Emp	PB	EM	Mgr	Sup	Pro	SE	Wkr
Emp	1	2	3	4	5	6	7	8
PB	9	10	11	12	13	14	15	16
EM	17	18	19	20	21	22	23	24
Mgr	25	26	27	28	29	30	31	32
Sup	33	34	35	36	37	38	39	40
Pro	41	42	43	44	45	46	47	48
SE	49	50	51	52	53	54	55	56
Wkr	57	58	59	60	61	62	63	64

Class location of friend, spouse or parent

Emp = employers; PB = petty bourgeoisie; EM = expert managers; Mgr = managers;
Sup = supervisors; Pro = professionals; SE = skilled employees; Wkr = workers

Figure 5.2 *Permeability event matrix*

two-earner households. The cells in the table thus constitute types of permeability and impermeability events: the off-diagonal cells represent events that cross class locations; the diagonal cells represent events contained within a given class location. Thus, for example, in the mobility analysis, the diagonal cells are different types of immobility and the off-diagonal cells different types of mobility.

Our analytical task is to analyze the relative likelihood of different types of permeability events in this matrix. If, for example, the likelihood of friendship ties linking an employer with an employee is much lower than the likelihood of friendship ties linking a professional with a nonexpert, then we will say that the property boundary is less permeable than the skill boundary. The statistical strategy for modeling differential relative odds of such events is standard loglinear analysis. For readers unfamiliar with loglinear analysis, a brief, nontechnical introduction is presented in the appendix to this chapter.

5.3 Permeability variables

Alternative approaches to analyzing permeability

There are two ways to conceptualize the problem of "boundary permeability" in the class structure. The first strategy sees the class structure as an array of categorically defined locations (cells in a matrix) such as those portrayed in Figure 5.1. A permeability event, therefore, is anything in the life of an individual which links that person to two or more of these locations. Thus, for workers, there would be seven possible boundary-crossing events: worker | employer, worker | petty bourgeois, worker | expert manager, etc. For expert managers, there are six additional boundary-crossing events (since the worker | expert manager boundary has already been counted). Among the eight class locations in Figure 5.1, there are thus twenty-eight boundaries across which permeability events can occur. We will refer to this as *locational* permeability.[3] One approach to studying the permeability of class boundaries, then, would be to measure the relative permeability of each of these twenty-eight locational boundaries and rank order them from highest to lowest degree of permeability.

The second strategy analyzes directly the three underlying mechanisms that generate the locations in the class structure: property, authority and skills/expertise. These mechanisms might be thought of as more fundamental than class location as such, since the concept of class structure is constructed by combining these mechanisms in different ways.[4] Data analysis would then involve assessing the relative densities of permeability events which span the categories defined by these three underlying mechanisms rather than studying the permeability events between pairs of cells of the class-structure matrix. We will refer to this as *dimensional* permeability.

In the empirical investigations of friendships, mobility and family structure in this book I will employ both strategies, although the

---

[3] If we had been able to operationalize all twelve class locations discussed in Chapter 2, locational permeability would be comprised by sixty-six boundary crossing events.

[4] Halaby and Weakliem (1993) argue that the concept of class structure used in the class analysis project should be decomposed into these three "primitive" dimensions and that nothing is gained by the theoretical gestalt class "structure." For a critique of Halaby and Weakliem's argument, see Wright (1993).

emphasis will be on dimensional permeability. The bulk of the analysis revolves around a series of loglinear models of the relative likelihood of permeability events across the property, authority and skill boundaries. Once the basic pattern of dimensional permeability is mapped in terms of these three class boundaries, we will then use the first strategy to analyze in a more fine-grained manner the locational permeability between the working class and other class locations.

The dimensional-permeability variables: PROPERTY, AUTHORITY and SKILL

In order to test the relative permeability of the boundaries constituted by the three exploitation mechanisms in the class structure, three variables are constructed using the permeability matrix in Figure 5.2: PROPERTY (a measure of permeability events across the property boundary); AUTHORITY (a measure of events across the authority boundary); and SKILL (a measure of events across the skill boundary). A convenient way of showing how these variables are constructed is with a device called a "design matrix." The design matrices for constructing these variables are presented in Figure 5.3. The cell entries "1" or "0" in these matrices are codes that indicate whether or not a particular cell in the matrix involves a permeability event across one of the three class boundaries in which we are interested. Thus each of the three boundary-crossing variables – PROPERTY, SKILL and AUTHORITY – is a dichotomous dummy variable, with "1" indicating an event across a class boundary, and "0" otherwise.

In these variables, an event is treated as crossing a boundary on a particular dimension of exploitation if it links the *extreme* categories in the trichotomies on the dimension. Thus, on the PROPERTY variable only events linking employees and employers are treated as crossing the property boundary. Events involving the petty bourgeoisie with either employers or employees are thus treated as *not* crossing the property boundary. On the AUTHORITY variable, events linking managers and nonmanagers are treated as crossing the authority boundary, whereas events between mere supervisors and either managers or nonmanagers are not. And, on the SKILL variable, events linking professionals and nonexperts are treated as crossing the skill boundary, whereas events between skilled employees and either professionals or nonexperts are not. In each case, a boundary-crossing event is thus defined as a event that crosses two "levels" of the relevant dimension.

Permeability events that cross two levels of the property boundary [PROPERTY]

	Emp	PB	EM	Mgr	Sup	Pro	SE	Wkr
Emp	0	0	1	1	1	1	1	1
PB	0	0	0	0	0	0	0	0
EM	1	0	0	0	0	0	0	0
Mgr	1	0	0	0	0	0	0	0
Sup	1	0	0	0	0	0	0	0
Pro	1	0	0	0	0	0	0	0
SE	1	0	0	0	0	0	0	0
Wkr	1	0	0	0	0	0	0	0

Permeability events that cross two levels of the authority boundary [AUTHORITY]

	Emp	PB	EM	Mgr	Sup	Pro	SE	Wkr
Emp	0	1	0	0	0	1	1	1
PB	1	0	1	1	0	0	0	0
EM	0	1	0	0	0	1	1	1
Mgr	0	1	0	0	0	1	1	1
Sup	0	0	0	0	0	0	0	0
Pro	1	0	1	1	0	0	0	0
SE	1	0	1	1	0	0	0	0
Wkr	1	0	1	1	0	0	0	0

Permeability events that cross two levels of the skill boundary [SKILL]

	Emp	PB	EM	Mgr	Sup	Pro	SE	Wkr
Emp	0	0	1	0	0	1	0	0
PB	0	0	1	0	0	1	0	0
EM	1	1	0	1	1	0	0	1
Mgr	0	0	1	0	0	1	0	0
Sup	0	0	1	0	0	1	0	0
Pro	1	1	0	1	1	0	0	1
SE	0	0	0	0	0	0	0	0
Wkr	0	0	1	0	0	1	0	0

Permeability events that link the working class with other class locations [WORKER]

	Emp	PB	EM	Mgr	Sup	Pro	SE	Wkr
Emp	0	0	0	0	0	0	0	1
PB	0	0	0	0	0	0	0	2
EM	0	0	0	0	0	0	0	3
Mgr	0	0	0	0	0	0	0	4
Sup	0	0	0	0	0	0	0	5
Pro	0	0	0	0	0	0	0	6
SE	0	0	0	0	0	0	0	7
Wkr	1	2	3	4	5	6	7	0

Within-class events: quasi-independence matrix [QI]

	Emp	PB	EM	Mgr	Sup	Pro	SE	Wkr
Emp	1	0	0	0	0	0	0	0
PB	0	2	0	0	0	0	0	0
EM	0	0	3	0	0	0	0	0
Mgr	0	0	0	4	0	0	0	0
Sup	0	0	0	0	5	0	0	0
Pro	0	0	0	0	0	6	0	0
SE	0	0	0	0	0	0	7	0
Wkr	0	0	0	0	0	0	0	8

1	Crosses two levels of a class boundary
0	Does *not* cross two levels of boundary
[0]	Crosses only one level of boundary
Emp	Employers
PB	Petty Bourgeois
EM	Expert managers
Mgr	Managers
Sup	Supervisors
Pro	Professionals
SE	Skilled emplopyees
Wkr	Workers
[NAME]	Name of variable in equations

Figure 5.3 *Design matrices for class-boundary-crossing variables*

Because of limits in sample size, a number of decisions had to be made in operationalizing the three boundary-crossing variables. First, it was impossible to disaggregate the managerial and supervisory locations by the three levels of the skill dimension and still have sufficient cases in every cell of the permeability matrix for the kinds of models used in these analyses. Consequently, I have constructed a broad "expert-manager" class location which combines four categories that are somewhat heterogeneous conceptually (manager professionals, supervisor professionals, manager skilled employees and supervisor skilled employees). This poses a problem in constructing the SKILL and AUTHORITY variables. For example, some friendships between workers and this heterogeneous "expert-manager" category cross only one level of the authority boundary (because the person is actually an expert supervisor) and some cross two levels. For purposes of these analyses, I decided to treat this fused category as if it were composed entirely of manager professionals. Thus, events linking workers and expert managers are treated as crossing both the skill boundary and the authority boundary.

Second, in the AUTHORITY variable, employers are taken as having full managerial authority and are treated as managers, whereas petty bourgeois are treated as having no authority and thus classified as nonmanagers. It could be argued that petty bourgeois make organizational policy decisions and should thus be treated as managers, but, to maintain a sharp conceptual distinction between the property boundary and the authority boundary, we treat the manager value on the authority variable as requiring authority over people, not just things.

Third, the SKILL variable poses problems for the two self-employed categories because we distinguish experts from nonexperts only among employees. Although employers and perhaps the petty bourgeoisie could be considered "experts," we classified all employers and petty bourgeois, regardless of credentials or occupational activities, as nonexperts. In the exploitation-mechanism approach to class analysis, the ownership of scarce skills is a basis of exploitation insofar as it enables actors who sell their labor power on a *labor market* to obtain a "rent" component in their wages. Because employers and petty bourgeois do not sell their labor power, and, with some exceptions, credentials are not required for either position, expertise in the sense we are using it becomes largely irrelevant for shaping their class interests.[5] Nevertheless, it would have been desirable to distinguish experts from nonexperts among employers and petty bourgeois, since the issue is not only how skill shapes exploitation-based *interests*, but also how it shapes life-style and informal interaction opportunities. Our sample size, however, made this impossible. The issue, then, was whether the self-employed should be globally treated as "professionals," "skilled employees" or "nonexperts" in constructing the SKILL variable. On the basis of the *occupational* distinction that we use to define nonexperts for employees, the large majority of both employers and petty bourgeois fall into the nonexpert category (69.8% of employers and 81.4% of petty bourgeois). We thus decided to treat all employers and petty bourgeois as nonexperts throughout this analysis.[6]

The locational-permeability variable: WORKER

The fourth matrix in Figure 5.3, WORKER, captures permeability events between the working class and each other class location. One of the main reasons that Marxists and other class analysts are interested in the permeability of class boundaries is that the fluidity of the class structure might have an impact on the formation of alliances between the working class and other class locations. If, for example, mobility trajectories structurally bind people in some class categories to others and if friendships form freely between these same class locations, then, other things being equal, it would be predicted that the possibility of class alliances between members of those class locations would increase. This argument suggests that we should model permeability events that link specific pairs of class locations – what we have termed "locational permeability" – in addition to events that cross the constituent dimensions of the class typology.

Comprehensively examining the relative permeability of boundaries between all of the class locations in our typology would involve ranking locational boundaries between twenty-eight pairs of class

---

[5]   In our sample, no more than 4% of employers and petty bourgeois were credentialed professionals (doctors, dentists, lawyers, accountants).

[6]   To see if this decision threatened the robustness of our analysis in the case of friendship ties, we merged the data for the four countries into a single matrix and were thus able to make the full set of distinctions in the expertise dimension among employers and petty bourgeois. The distinction did not improve the goodness of fit of the models and so we feel reasonably confident that treating these categories as nonexperts does not seriously undermine our results.

categories. It is impossible to do this simultaneously with estimating the three boundary-crossing coefficients because of internal redundancies among the parameters. Given the theoretical importance of coalitions between the working class and other classes to social change, we therefore focus on the permeability of boundaries between the working class and other class locations. The WORKER variable consists of seven nominal categories whose values index specific boundaries between the working class and other class locations. WORKER specifies a series of contrasts between all of the different permeability events involving the working class. When this variable is included in a loglinear model with the other terms, it takes up any residual cell-specific association between the working class and each of the other categories that has not been accounted for by the variables capturing more general effects.[7]

The diagonal cells: quasi-independence matrix

The final matrix in Figure 5.3 is the standard "quasi-independence" matrix (QI) used in mobility studies. This variable treats all off-diagonal cells, i.e. permeability events that cross any class boundary, as a single category but distinguishes between each cell on the diagonal, i.e. the eight within-class events.[8] While our primary concern is not with such within-class events, proper specification of the boundary-crossing models requires that we include a variable which maps the diagonal of the matrix. When we add QI to models containing the three boundary-crossing variables we purge the coefficients of the permeability variables of any specifically diagonal effects due to within-class events that might otherwise influence both diagonal and off-diagonal cells. This means that coefficients for the boundary-crossing terms are "pure" or "partial" estimates of the

---

[7]   It would be possible to construct other class-specific interaction terms parallel to the WORKER variable. One could, for example, construct a CAPITALIST variable that would differentiate all permeability events between the capitalist class and other classes. However, because of the degrees of freedom required, it is not possible to simultaneously include in a model the three additive boundary permeability terms, the WORKER interaction term and other class-specific interactions. Since the WORKER interaction is of particular theoretical interest, we will therefore only examine the WORKER interaction in our analyses.

[8]   If all within-class events were equally likely, then we would have created a simple variable that had 1s for all cells on the diagonal, 0s elsewhere. However, previous research on occupational mobility suggests this is an implausible assumption (Hollingshead 1949; Laumann 1966; Verbrugge 1977).

inherent permeability of the property, skill and authority boundaries, uncontaminated by anything that is affecting the main diagonal.

The problem of symmetry

As can be seen in Figure 5.3, we operationalize the three boundary-crossing variables *symmetrically* about the main diagonal. In the case of friendships, this poses no conceptual problems because the matrix is logically symmetrical (i.e. the probability of a worker having a friend who is an employer is the same as an employer having a friend who is a worker), so long as the friendships are reciprocal relations.[9] In the case of both mobility and cross-class families, however, symmetry is not logically entailed by the concepts themselves. Most people would predict, for example, that the probability of a female worker being married to a male capitalist is higher than the probability of a female capitalist being married to a male worker. Symmetry thus seems pretty far-fetched.

It turns out, however, that in the models we will be exploring in Chapters 6, 7 and 8, the data are fairly symmetrical around the diagonal. The reason is that, following conventional procedures for loglinear analysis, in all of these models we control for the effects of the marginal distributions of each of the dimensions of the matrix. In the case of the cross-class family analysis, for example, all of our models control for the marginal class distributions of husbands and wives. Thus, while it remains true that the gross probability of a female worker being married to a male capitalist is greater than the probability of a male worker being married to a female capitalist, once we control for the fact that there are many fewer female capitalists than male capitalists (i.e. once we control for the marginal distributions), then the odds of these two events look relatively similar. Global tests of symmetry of the odds ratios around the main diagonal for the matrices we are exploring suggest that the data within each country are characterized by a roughly symmetrical association structure.

5.4 Models

The matrices in Figure 5.3 differentiate distinct kinds of permeability events. In the chapters which follow, we deploy these variables in a

---

[9]   This issue will be discussed at greater length in the chapter on friendships.

baseline model and four primary analytical models for each form of permeability we will be analyzing:

$$\log F_{ijk} = C + D_1 + D_2 + QI + C \times D_1 + C \times D_2 \qquad \text{(Baseline)}$$

$$\log F_{ijk} = \text{Baseline} + \text{PROPERTY} + \text{AUTHORITY} + \text{SKILL} \qquad (1)$$

$$\log F_{ijk} = \text{Model (1)} + \text{WORKER} \qquad (2)$$

$$\log F_{ijk} = \text{Model (1)} + QI \times C \qquad (3)$$

$$\log F_{ijk} = \text{Model (3)} + \text{PROPERTY} \times C + \text{AUTHORITY} \times C + \text{SKILL} \times C \qquad (4)$$

where D_1 and D_2 are the two dimensions of the permeability matrix (e.g. class origins and class destinations in the mobility analysis); C is country; QI is the quasi-independence matrix; PROPERTY, AUTHORITY, SKILL, and WORKER are variables defined by the matrices in Figure 5.3; and F_{ijk} is the expected frequency in the ijk^{th} cell of the 8 x 8 x 4 matrix (7 x 7 x 4 matrix for the mobility analysis) of D_1 by D_2 by country.[10] Our central attention in these models will be primarily on the relative magnitudes of the coefficients of the three dimensional permeability variables, PROPERTY, AUTHORITY and SKILL. The coefficients of each of these variables tells us the log of the odds of a permeability event occurring across the relevant boundary compared to such an event not occurring. The *difference* in these coefficients, therefore, is the log of an odds ratio, a measure of the relative permeability of one kind of boundary compared to another.

Model (1) is the basic additive model of permeability events. In this model, country appears as an additive term and as an interaction term with the marginal distributions on the two dimensions of the perme-

[10] In Model (2) there is a small difference in the design of the QI matrix from the other models, because the quasi-independence variable in Model (2) makes it impossible to estimate all six coefficients in the WORKER variable. One will be mathematically redundant because it is a linear combination of the other WORKER coefficients and the worker diagonal cell in the quasi-independence matrix. Because we are not specifically interested in the coefficients for the Worker I Worker diagonal cell, and because we want to have an explicit coefficient for every boundary between the working class and other class locations in Model (2), we used a modified quasi-independence variable in Model (2) in which the Worker I Worker diagonal cell (category 7 on the original QI variable in Figure 5.2) is assigned to level 0 and thus merged with all of the off-diagonal cells. This has no effect on the goodness of fit of Model (2) or on the values of the additive terms in that model. It also has no effect on the *relative* magnitude of the coefficients for the WORKER variable and thus no effect on the ranking of the permeability of boundaries between the working class and other class locations, but it does make the discussion of the coefficients more straightforward.

ability-event matrix, but there are no country interactions with the permeability variables themselves. In effect, then, this model assumes that the patterns of relative permeability across the three class boundaries are the same in all countries.

Model (2) adds the WORKER interaction variable to the variables in Model (1). This model will enable us to see if the likelihood of a permeability event between the working class and each of the other class locations is greater or smaller than would be predicted on the basis of the additive effects of the three permeability variables.

Models (3) and (4) enable us to examine variations across countries in the patterns of permeability. In Model (3), country interactions with the QI matrix are added to Model (1). Because our analysis is concerned with class-boundary permeability, we will not explicitly examine the QI × C interactions, i.e. differences across countries in *within*-class friendship patterns. Nevertheless, in order to purge our estimates of country interactions with the permeability variables from possible effects of country differences on the diagonal, the QI × C interactions must be in the equations testing country differences in the three boundary-crossing coefficients. The comparison of the goodness of fit of Model (3) with Model (4), therefore, provides the basis for a global test of country differences in class-boundary permeability.

Methodological appendix: a brief introduction to loglinear models

A loglinear model is a particular way of statistically analyzing the data in a table. It is especially useful when the natural way of measuring concepts is in terms of nominal categories rather than continuous variation. In our analyses of permeability the central variables we will be exploring all involve specifications of class locations – locations of respondents, of their class origins, of their friends, and their spouses. These locations are distinct categories, not simply values on a continuous metric scale.

The central idea underlying loglinear analysis is the notion of *odds* and *odds ratios*. When we say that the odds of a horse winning a race is 2:1 what we mean is that it has a 66% chance of winning and a 33% of losing. The ratio of these two percentages is 2. If the horse had a 50% chance of winning, the odds of it winning would be 1.0 (i.e. "even" or 50:50). In practice, we calculate the odds by taking the ratio of the frequency of one kind of outcome to the frequency of another. In more technical terms, we define the odds of event X occurring as the probability that X does occur – $\Pr(X=1)$ – divided by the probability that it does not occur – $1-\Pr(X=1)$. Consider the simple mobility analysis in which 1,000 people are divided into two classes – middle class and working class. Suppose 60% of people from middle-class origins end up in the middle class and 40% end up in the working class, whereas only 20% of people from working-class origins end up in the middle class while 80% end up in the working class. The odds of a person of middle-class origin ending up in the middle class is thus 60:40, or 1.5. The odds of a person of working-class origin ending up in the middle class is 20:80 or .25. If we want to compare these two odds, we then calculate an odds ratio – the ratio of the odds of a person of middle-class origin compared to a person of working-class origin ending up in the middle class. In this case, this odds ratio $(60/40) \div (20/80) = (60 \times 80) \div (40 \times 20) = 6$. (Note that the probability of someone from a middle-class origin ending up in the middle class is only three times greater than the probability of someone from a working-class origin, but the odds of this happening are six times greater.)

Loglinear analysis is built around the investigation of odds and odds ratios of particular kinds of events occurring. In conventional linear regression analysis, a distinction is made between "independent variables" and "dependent variables": the former are thought to predict (and in many instances cause) the dependent variable. In loglinear analysis there are no "independent" and "dependent" variables as such. Rather, there is a table with two or more dimensions, and frequencies within the cells of the table. What a loglinear analysis basically attempts to do is predict the frequencies within these cells on the basis of hypotheses about which cells are theoretically the same and which are different.

Consider the simple mobility matrix in Appendix Table 5.1. Each of the cells in this table represents a kind of event. The upper left hand corner, for example, is the event of coming from a capitalist origin and ending up in a capitalist destination. The frequency of this specific event is designated F_{11}. More generally, then, the frequency of the events in the cells of the table can be designated F_{ij}, where i indicates the row and j indicates the column in the matrix.

Loglinear analysis is a strategy for analyzing the frequencies in the cells of this kind of table. The frequency in any given cell can be represented as a mathematical function of the frequency of each of the marginal distributions of the table – how many people are in each of the rows and columns of the table – and the odds of being in a particular combination of a row and column. Of course, we could

Class origins

		Capitalist class	Petty bourg.	Middle class	Working class
		1	2	3	4
Capitalist class	1	F_{11}	F_{12}	F_{13}	F_{14}
Petty bourg.	2	F_{21}	F_{22}	F_{23}	F_{24}
Middle class	3	F_{31}	F_{32}	F_{33}	F_{34}
Working class	4	F_{41}	F_{42}	F_{43}	F_{44}

Class destination

F_{ij} = The frequency in cell i,j

Appendix Figure 5.1 *Mobility matrix used in loglinear analysis*

predict perfectly the frequency in every cell of the matrix if we specified a sufficient number of these odds. The trick is to see how well you can predict the frequencies in the table by specifying a small number of these odds. This is what the various boundary-crossing variables we have constructed attempt to do.

For technical reasons, in a loglinear analysis of cross-tabulated data, it is necessary to analyze the tables in terms of log transformations of frequencies. The coefficients of the variables in the equations, therefore, predict the *log of the frequencies* in the cells and margins of the tables rather than the frequencies themselves. Let us look at one of the variables we will be using to illustrate this point. The variable PROPERTY defined in Figure 5.3 has a value of 1 when a permeability event crosses the property boundary, and a value of 0 when it does not. In a loglinear model, this variable will have a coefficient which indicates the *difference* between the log of the frequency of cases in cells with a value of 1 on this variable and the log of the frequency in cells with a value of 0. (This is quite analogous to the meaning of a coefficient of a dummy variable in a normal, linear regression: it is the difference between the mean value on the dependent variable for people with a value of 1 on the dummy variable and people with a value of 0.) The antilog of this coefficient, therefore, is the ratio of these frequencies. This, however, is just the odds of being in a cell with a value of 1 on the PROPERTY variable.[11]

Many analysts of loglinear models are mainly concerned with how well the model "fits" the data. A good fit means that the model reproduces the frequency distribution across the cells of the table pretty well. While we will pay some attention to overall fit of the models, we will be more concerned with the relative magnitudes of the coefficients for the three permeability variables. Each of these coefficients represents the log of the odds of a particular kind of permeability event. Our prediction is that all of these permeability coefficients will be negative, indicating that the odds of such events are less than 1. If the coefficient for the PROPERTY variable is significantly more negative than the coefficient for the SKILL variable, therefore, this means that the odds of an event across the property boundary are significantly less than the odds of an event across the skill boundary. Since the antilog of each of these coefficients is the odds of a particular kind of event occurring, the antilog of the *difference* between these coefficients is an odds ratio.

[11] This follows from the elementary mathematics of logarithms in which the log of a ratio equals the difference between the log of the numerator and the log of the denominator: $\text{Log}(X/Y) = \text{Log}\,X - \text{Log}\,Y$. In the case we are discussing, let X = the frequency of cases in cells of the matrix for which PROPERTY = 1, Y = the frequency of cases in cells of the matrix for which PROPERTY = 0, and N = the total number of cases in the matrix. The probability of being in a cell in which PROPERTY = 1 is therefore X/N, and the probability of not being in such a cell is $1 - X/N$, or, equivalently, Y/N. The odds of being in a cell in which PROPERTY = 1 is therefore $(X/N) \div (Y/N) = X/Y$. This is simply the antilog of the coefficient for the PROPERTY variable in the loglinear model.

6 The permeability of class boundaries to intergenerational mobility

One of the core legitimating principles of capitalism is the idea that free markets organized around voluntary exchange constitute the central determinants of income distribution and, by virtue of this, income inequality generated by those exchanges is just. This general principle can be broken down into two more specific claims: (1) that purely competitive processes, free of coercion, generate the allocation of *people* to income-generating *positions*, and (2) that free competition also generates the allocation of *income* to those *positions*. The resulting distributions are thus thought to be just in a double sense: they are just because the way people get into those positions is just, and because the amount of income attached to those positions is just.

The argument that the class structure of capitalism is exploitative is primarily an attack on the second of these claims to justice. In spite of the fact that income is generated through competitive market processes, Marxists claim, the resulting distribution involves exploitative appropriations of surplus. Voluntary exchange is seen as masking an underlying coercive structure embedded in property relations.

The indictment of market-generated income distributions as involving exploitation would be less salient if it were the case that the process by which people ended up in specific class positions was itself free of all coercive elements. Suppose that incomes were given to people on the basis of a tax-based lottery. The system of taxation coercively appropriates surplus from people and then distributes different quantities on the basis of a random drawing. The taxation could thus be seen as a form of exploitation, particularly for those people who objected to lotteries. One might object to such a mechanism on all sorts of grounds, but the objection would be somewhat muted if everyone had a fair and equal chance of getting the prizes. "Fair play" can at least partially mitigate the sense of injustice generated by the absence of "fair shares."[1]

These kinds of normative issues underlie much sociological research on social mobility. *Achievement* is contrasted with *ascription* as processes by which individuals are allocated to social positions. If the fates of individuals – their life chances – are determined by merit and effort, the moral intuition goes, then it does not matter so much how unequal the material conditions of life end up. Inequalities in material conditions are still of normative interest insofar as they may get in the way of the proper functioning of the achievement process, but they would not be normatively salient in their own right. "Equal opportunity" for material gain is the pivotal issue in this line of reasoning, not the degree of inequality in the outcomes themselves.

Within this normative framework, intergenerational class mobility provides one basic index of how close a society really is to an unfettered achievement model. To the extent that the positions occupied by people within the system of social stratification are very similar to those of their parents, doubt is cast on the claim that the market provides an arena of genuinely equal opportunity. These concerns, then, lead naturally to a basic focus on the patterns of class *immobility* – the extent to which the class occupied by parents provides a good predictor of the class occupied by their adult children.

Given this set of normative concerns, it is not surprising that most research on social mobility has been at least loosely linked to a Weberian framework of class analysis. The Weberian concept of class revolves around the problem of common life chances of people within market exchanges. This naturally leads to a concern with the intergenerational transmission of life chances – i.e. the extent to which one's own class location is determined by the class into which one is born and raised.

Marxist class analysis has paid much less systematic attention to the problem of mobility. Although Marxists engaged in qualitative and historical research on problems of class consciousness and class formation frequently allude to the issue of mobility in the context of discussing the development and transmission of class cultures and community solidarities, there are virtually no systematic quantitative investigations of class mobility within a specifically Marxist frame-

---

[1] The contrast between fair play and fair shares as a way of characterizing the normative issues underlying sociological studies of inequality is taken from Ryan (1981).

work. Thus, while we know a great deal about social mobility between categories defined in occupational terms, we know little about the specific patterns of mobility across class boundaries defined explicitly in terms of social relations of production. Exploring such patterns is the basic objective of this chapter.

6.1 Theoretical expectations

Relative permeability of class boundaries

There are two basic reasons why one might expect different class boundaries to have different degrees of permeability to intergenerational mobility. First, the extent to which the parental generation is able to appropriate surplus income through mechanisms of exploitation shapes the material advantages and disadvantages experienced by their children. It would therefore be predicted that the more exploitation is linked to a class boundary, the more that class boundary should be impermeable to mobility. Second, insofar as the cultural resources of the parental generation are linked to different class locations, children from different class origins will have different occupational aspirations and cultural advantages. It would therefore be predicted that the more divergent is the "cultural capital" across class boundaries, the less permeable will be the boundary. The first of these mechanisms is the one most associated with Marxist understanding of class. The second is more closely associated with theorists such as Bourdieu (1984, 1985, 1987) who stress the cultural dimension of class relations. Goldthorpe (1987: 99) combines these arguments when he asserts that the class mobility regime depends on the different material opportunities parents have to shape their children's economic welfare, and the likely preferences of offspring for some jobs rather than others.

Taken together, these arguments imply relatively impermeable boundaries associated with both property and skills, and a more permeable boundary associated with authority.[2] Mobility across the

---

[2] Recall from the discussion in Chapter 5 that permeability across the skill boundary is defined as an event that links people in professional occupations with people in nonskilled occupations (not merely nonprofessional occupations), while permeability across the property boundary is defined as an event that links an employer and an employee (not simply a self-employed person and an employee). The skill boundary and property boundaries are thus being defined in a relatively restrictive way.

property boundary is likely to be limited because, first, financial and physical capital are potentially transferable to the offspring of property owners (Stier and Grusky 1990), and second, capitalist parents are able to finance their children's businesses out of profits or borrowings. Parental property ownership is therefore "insurance" against downward mobility into wage labor for the offspring of capitalists, and the requirement of capital ownership is a barrier to entry to the children of most employees. The rigidity of the property boundary may be further compounded by the preferences of children of property owners for self-employment rather than wage labor. In small businesses, the experience of unpaid family labor may lead the offspring of the self-employed to value self-employment especially strongly (Hout 1989: 79). At the very least, the experience of growing up in a capitalist family of origin presents children with an example of property ownership as a viable form of economic activity that children whose parents are not self-employed may lack.

The material circumstances and lived experiences associated with high levels of skill assets also make for a relatively impermeable mobility boundary on the skill dimension of the class typology. Like financial capital, skills and expertise are potentially transferable to children, and this generates a barrier to entry into expert labor markets. Because of the rent components of their wages, expert parents have significant economic resources to invest in their children's education. In addition, given that the economic welfare of experts depends on the mobilization of institutionalized skills, expert parents may have an especially strong commitment to education as a mechanism of social attainment. Such preferences form part of the cultural capital expert parents are uniquely placed to pass on to their children through familial socialization (Joppke 1986).

Unlike the property and skill boundaries, the mechanisms of inheritance associated with managerial authority are much weaker, and thus our expectation is that the mobility boundary between managers and non-managers would be much more permeable. Organizational control is an attribute of a position in a formal authority hierarchy, and as such is not individually transferable to offspring in the manner of physical capital or expertise. While a limited argument can be made that some intergenerational transmission of authority occurs indirectly because of the specific cultural capital associated with being in a position of responsibility, our expectation is that this mechanism will be much weaker than the transmission of human capital and property that shape the relative impermeability of the skill and property boundaries.

Our first expectation, then, is that the property and skill boundaries will be less permeable than the authority boundary to intergenerational mobility. It is less clear what should be the expectations about the relative mobility permeability of the property boundary compared to the skill boundary. Marxist class analysis assumes that private property in the means of production is fundamental to the distribution of material welfare and control over the surplus product in capitalist societies and thus capitalist property ownership should generate bigger divisions in financial resources available to offspring than either of the other class boundaries. This suggests that the mobility boundary between property owners and nonowners should be especially sharply defined. On the other hand, non-Marxists such as Bourdieu (1987: 733) have argued that the most important source of social power in advanced capitalist societies is the symbolic mobilization of cultural capital, rather than the ownership of means of production. In Bourdieu's account, generalized cultural competencies are symbolically legitimated in formal academic qualifications, and reproduced intergenerationally through class-specific differential educational attainment (Bourdieu and Passeron 1990: 153–164). This view suggests that the skill boundary should be most impermeable to intergenerational mobility.

The above arguments imply two rankings from the least to the most permeable class boundaries to intergenerational mobility: *property, skill, authority* for Marxist class analysis; *skill, property, authority* for Bourdieu's culturally grounded class analysis. Both of these hypotheses rest on assumptions that the capacity to transmit assets to offspring is an integral aspect of property rights in productive resources, and that the impermeability of mobility boundaries associated with these resources is a function of the relative importance of such resources in the distribution of social power.

Cross-national variations

The reasoning in both the Marxist and Bourdieu approaches to class has implications for expected cross-national variations in patterns of class-boundary permeability. Both approaches would argue that the more purely capitalistic is an economy, the more impermeable would be the property boundary relative to other boundaries. To use

Bourdieu's formulation, the more central to a system of power and privilege is a specific "form of capital," the greater will be the concern of those who hold such capital to safeguard its reproduction. In terms of permeability of class boundaries, this means that the more a class structure is dominated by capitalist relations, the greater will be barriers to acquiring capitalist property. In a purely capitalist economy, therefore, Bourdieu would agree with Marxists that the property boundary should be less permeable than the skill boundary.[3] This runs counter to popular mythologies of capitalism, where it is believed that the more open and unfettered is the "free market," the greater will be the opportunity for propertyless individuals to accumulate wealth and thus traverse the class boundary between wage-earners and capitalists.

In this chapter we will analyse data from four countries: the United States, Canada, Sweden and Norway. While all four of these countries have capitalist economies, they differ significantly in terms of the extent to which their economies are dominated by capitalist principles. Within the family of economically developed capitalist economies, the United States is generally considered the most purely capitalistic, both in its institutional structure and in its popular culture, while Sweden is the paradigm of social democratic capitalism, a capitalism in which the state plays a systematic role in countering the inequalities generated by capitalist markets. According to figures cited in Currie and Skolnick (1988: 41–43), next to Japan, the United States has the lowest rate of taxation (29% in 1984), and the lowest rate of government expenditure (38% in 1983) as a proportion of GDP among developed capitalist countries, while Sweden has the highest rate for both of these (taxes are 50.5% and spending is 66% of GDP). Sweden also has the highest level of government expenditure on social welfare of all capitalist countries (Ginsburg 1992: 33). Canada is generally closer to the United States, and Norway closer to Sweden on these and other indicators.

This leads to the following two comparative hypotheses for the four countries in the study: first, the property boundary should be less permeable in the North American countries (especially the United States) than in the Scandinavian countries (especially Sweden), and second, the difference in permeability between the property boundary

---

[3]   In these terms, the disagreement between Bourdieu and most Marxists in the analysis of class structures of advanced capitalism centers on the empirical question of how central capitalist property relations remain in structuring the overall class structures of these societies.

and the skill boundary should be greater in the North American countries than in the Scandinavian countries.

Hypotheses

Taking all of these arguments together yields five general hypotheses about the relative permeability of class boundaries to intergenerational mobility:

> *Hypothesis 1.* The authority boundary should be the most permeable of the three class boundaries.
>
> *Hypothesis 2. Marxist hypothesis.* The rank ordering of class boundaries from least permeable to most permeable will be property, skill, authority.
>
> *Hypothesis 3. Cultural capital hypothesis.* The rank ordering of class boundaries from least permeable to most permeable will be skill, property, authority.
>
> *Hypothesis 4.* The property boundary should be less permeable in North America than in Scandinavia.
>
> *Hypothesis 5.* The difference in permeability between the property and skill boundaries should be greater in North America than in Scandinavia.

The predictions in these hypotheses are vulnerable to a criticism coming from the core of research on occupational mobility. One of the most robust findings in mobility research is the low level of mobility of people from nonfarm origins into the occupation "farmer" and the accompanying high level of self-recruitment among farmers. Since farmers are largely self-employed, it could be the case that whatever differences we observe in the permeability of the property and skill boundaries is a consequence of the low permeability of the farmer occupational boundary. Of course, some of the mechanisms purported to explain the distinctive mobility patterns of farmers – especially the particular heritability of the family farm and preferences for "being one's own boss" – can be interpreted as being linked to the class character of farming. But other factors, such as the specialized skills associated with farm labor and the strong preferences of the offspring of farmers for farm jobs (Grusky and Hauser 1984), have relatively little to do with the specific class dimensions of farming. Thus, it could be the case that the greater impermeability of the property boundary compared to the skill boundary in Hypothesis 2 might really be an artifact of the relative immobility of farmers due to the distinctive occupational, rather than class, character of farming. What appears to be a class barrier, therefore, might really be an occupational barrier.

Because of limitations of sample size, it is not possible with the present data to fully explore this objection by examining models in which we allow the occupation of farmer to interact with the dimensions of the class mobility matrix. What we can do, however, is exclude everyone from the matrix who either is a farmer or has a farm origin. We will then examine the extent to which the results we obtain for the entire sample hold for class boundaries in the nonfarm sector of the economy. This yields a sixth hypothesis:

> Hypothesis 6. The basic patterns of relative permeability of class boundaries will remain the same when people with farmer origins and/or destinations are excluded from the analysis.

Gender and class-boundary permeability to intergenerational mobility

Most research on social mobility has been restricted to the analysis of mobility of men.[4] This may be in part due to sexism on the part of sociological researchers, but, more importantly, this lack of attention to the problem of mobility for women reflects theoretical ambiguities in defining the location of married women in the class structure and thus of specifying their "destination" within a mobility matrix. Two issues are particularly important: First, given that most mobility research defines origins and destinations in terms of labor force occupations, the fact that married women's labor force participation has traditionally been both lower and more erratic than that of married men made it problematic to assign a robust occupational destination to many women. While one could have treated the role of housewife an "occupation," this clearly falls outside the conceptual space of the Weberian concept of common life chances within market exchanges.

[4] For some exceptions, see Chase (1975); Dunton and Featherman (1983); Goldthorpe and Payne (1986); Marshall et al. (1988): ch. 4; Portocarero (1983a, 1983b); Roos (1985): ch. 4; Tyree and Treas (1974). In most of this research, loglinear models are used to examine hypotheses about global similarities and differences in male and female mobility; no attention is generally paid to the specific coefficients in the models (for an exception see Hayes 1990). The lack of attention given to modelling women's relative mobility patterns is indicated by the fact that none of the contributors to a monograph on women's mobility (Abbot and Payne 1990a) addresses this task. In part this reflects a substantive preference for studying absolute rather than relative mobility patterns (Abbot and Payne 1990b: 22).

Second, because of gender inequality in the labor market, the standard of living of most married women, even when they were in paid labor force jobs, has depended more on their husbands' jobs than their own. Again, this makes it conceptually problematic to assign them an unambiguous "destination" in a mobility matrix on the basis of their own occupations. Given these complexities, most researchers have simply sidestepped the issue and studied intergenerational mobility for men only.

While most of this chapter will focus on the mobility permeability of class boundaries for men, I will present an exploratory analysis for women as well. The analysis is exploratory both because I do not have strongly formulated deductive hypotheses about gender differences in permeability, and thus the investigation has a more inductive character, and because the sample size of women in the labor force in the data is quite small, thus making systematic hypothesis testing difficult.

Our objectives in the gender analysis are twofold. First, we want to see whether the patterns of class-boundary permeability observed among men hold for women as well. Marxist class analysis does not have anything specific to say about how class-boundary permeability should differ for men and women. Of course, scholars working in the Marxist tradition might have particular expectations about gender differences, but those expectations would not be derived from Marxist class analysis as such, since there is nothing in the core arguments of Marxist class analysis that suggests that the rank orderings of boundary permeability should apply only to men. By default, therefore, our core hypothesis will be:

> *Hypothesis 7.* The rank ordering of class-boundary permeability to intergenerational mobility among women will be the same as for men.

Our second purpose in examining class-boundary permeability among women is to explore in a preliminary fashion the problem of how to conceptualize the class location – and thus class mobility – of married women in two-earner families. We have already briefly engaged this issue in Chapter 2 and will do so in more detail in Chapter 10. One of the principal arguments advanced by John Goldthorpe and others in favor of treating the family rather than the individual as the unit of class analysis is that relying on women's own economic activity to allocate them to a class produces spuriously high estimates of women's class mobility. Since women typically occupy white-collar clerical and sales jobs, Goldthorpe has argued that mobility into these positions from father-derived blue-collar origins gives a misleading impression of the permeability of the "class" boundary between manual and nonmanual classes.[5]

To explore the problem of the appropriate unit of analysis for defining-class locations we will compare the patterns of boundary permeability for women when their class location is defined in terms of their individual-class location or their family-class location.[6] The basic hypothesis we will examine is:

> *Hypothesis 8. Goldthorpe family-class hypothesis.* The permeability of class boundaries for women should be greater when individuals rather than families are used as the unit of analysis for defining class locations.

6.2 Relationship to prior mobility research[7]

This chapter attempts to contribute to our knowledge of class structures in capitalist societies by analyzing one aspect of the dynamic permeability of class boundaries. The objective is therefore not primarily to contribute to the general literature on social mobility as such. Nevertheless, it will be useful to discuss briefly the relationship between the analytical strategies and objectives of our approach and other mobility research. In the conclusion to the chapter, I will relate our findings to the substantive results of previous mobility studies.

---

[5]   This specific problem of "spurious" mobility holds only if the manual/nonmanual division is accepted as the basis for a class division, as it is in Goldthorpe's early work (e.g. Erikson, Goldthorpe and Portocarero 1979). In our class typology all individuals in nonsupervisory jobs in semi-skilled and unskilled blue- or white-collar occupations are treated as in the working class and consequently movement from a blue-collar origin to a clerical destination would not count as "mobility." Goldthorpe now recognizes this point himself. Later accounts of his class scheme (e.g. Goldthorpe and Payne 1986) argue that nonsupervisory semi and unskilled white-collar work is probably more accurately regarded as working class than middle class.

[6]   "Individual-class" location is defined as the class of the woman's job in the paid labor force, or what we have called her direct class location. "Family-class" location is defined by the class of the woman's husband's job if she is married (i.e. her mediated class location) and by her own job if she is either single or her husband is out of the labor force.

[7]   This section and section 6.4 were written by Mark Western for the previously published article (Western and Wright 1994) on which this chapter is based.

Analytical strategies

Currently two approaches predominate in the study of intergenerational mobility.[8] First are investigations of intergenerational class mobility, generally drawing upon the occupationally based class schema of John Goldthorpe. (See e.g. Erikson and Goldthorpe 1985, 1987a, 1987b, 1993; Erikson, Goldthorpe and Portocarero 1979, 1982, 1983; Goldthorpe 1987; Ishida, Goldthorpe and Erikson 1991; Jones and Davis 1986, 1988a, 1988b.) These analyses conceptualize class structure in terms of the market and work situations of occupations which define nominal class categories (Goldthorpe 1987: 40–43). No consistent hierarchy is believed to underlie the class structure (Erikson and Goldthorpe 1993: 123; Goldthorpe 1987: 43) and no systematic "vertical" gradient accounts for relative mobility chances. The odds of mobility from any origin to any destination are not a continuous function of the metric distance between class categories (cf. Hout and Hauser 1991) but instead reflect distinct mechanisms which promote or impede the likelihood of mobility between origin and destination. Such mechanisms are represented by "topological" models (Hout 1983: 37–51) which map the cells of the mobility matrix into a series of dummy variables according to the way each cell is subject to the mobility mechanism in question.

In Goldthorpe's class mobility framework, three basic principles are usually argued to shape relative mobility chances: the relative desirability of different class positions; the relative advantages of particular class origins; and the barriers associated with particular class destinations (Goldthorpe 1987: 99). In the "model of core fluidity" developed by Erikson and Goldthorpe (1987a, 1992: 121–131), these ideas are operationalized with specific dummy variables to capture social distance effects between classes, excess diagonal immobility, sectoral mobility between agricultural and nonagricultural categories, and residual mobility tendencies.[9]

---

[8] We confine this discussion to empirical work that analyzes the association between origins and destinations that is found in an intergenerational mobility matrix. Status attainment research is not directly relevant to our concerns.

[9] Although the "hierarchy" or "social distance" parameters of the core model tap some notion of vertical mobility, as dummy variables they do not incorporate any information about the metric intervals between classes. In the topological setup, vertical mobility is modeled as a discontinuous (that is, step) function of the number of "levels" between classes, rather than a continuous function of the metric distances between categories (Hout and Hauser 1991).

The second major approach conceptualizes mobility in terms of an underlying vertical dimension. (See e.g. Breen 1987; Breen and Whelan 1985; Ganzeboom, Luijkx and Treiman 1989; Grusky and Hauser 1984; Hauser 1984; Hauser and Grusky, 1988; Hout 1988, 1989 ch. 6; Hout and Hauser 1991; Hout and Jackson 1986; Wong 1990, 1992; Xie 1992; Yamaguchi 1987.) Usually such research focusses upon inter-generational occupational mobility rather than class mobility, but there are some examples of research using Goldthorpe's class categories which nevertheless analyze mobility as vertical movement (in spite of Goldthorpe's explicit rejection of the view that the class structure has an underlying vertical dimension). Vertical mobility describes mobility "up" or "down" the social structure in which the probability of a given movement is (mathematically) functionally related to the interval distances between categories. Such distances may represent occupational differences in socio-economic status, occupational prestige, or some other characteristic. Whatever the basis of the hierarchy, if it is assumed that categories can meaningfully be scored on some metric(s) of socio-economic attributes, then relative mobility patterns should, at least partially, reflect the distances between categories that these scores represent. The research referred to above illustrates this point by using loglinear and logmultiplicative association models which explicitly take category scores into account to model vertical trends in mobility chances. (See Agresti 1984, 1990; Goodman 1979, 1984; Hout 1983: 51–68 for expositions of these models).

The research in this chapter has similarities and differences with both strategies. Like Weberian class mobility research, I argue for a nominal measure of class structure and, consequently, topological loglinear models. The models we will explore are also premised on the view that relative mobility patterns reflect general mechanisms associated with the advantages and disadvantages of class origins, barriers to entry to class destinations, and cultural resources associated with the family of origin. However, Weberian class analysts have not explicitly modeled mobility trajectories across the constituent dimensions of the class structure with a view to determining which mechanisms most strongly restrict or encourage mobility. Indeed, the conceptual heterogeneity of Goldthorpe's Class I, combining as it does large proprietors, high status professionals and top managers, precludes such an analysis.

This research on class-boundary permeability also has a certain affinity to some analyses of vertical mobility. The trichotomous treatment of the property and skill dimensions of the class structure suggests a kind of vertical image of boundary crossing, and even the dichotomous treatment of the authority boundary suggests upward/downward movement. More significantly, there is a similarity between the approach adopted here and one variety of occupational mobility research, the "multidimensional" association models proposed by Hout (1983: 76–80, 1984, 1988, 1989: 62–68), and the "hybrid" model of vertical and nonvertical mobility proposed by Wong (1992). Hout assigns separate scores to occupational categories to reflect levels of occupational status, autonomy, and training, which he believes underlie the stratification hierarchy. Vertical mobility chances, with respect to each of these separate dimensions, can then be determined. Wong develops a new classification of class structure that explicitly incorporates self-employment, in order to examine the argument that restricted mobility flows occur between self-employment and wage labor, net of the effects of hierarchical differences between occupational strata. He then models mobility between self-employment and wage labor simultaneously alongside vertical mobility. Both of these models are thus similar to the attempt here at modeling specific theoretical dimensions of the mobility process through studying the relative permeability of different boundaries within the class structure.

There are, however, some significant differences between analyses of vertical mobility and our analysis of boundary permeability. First, the three-dimensional class typology does not imply any overall vertical hierarchy to class locations. While it may be possible to rank order the boundaries between class locations according to the extent to which mobility between them is common or rare, this does not imply that there is an overall vertical hierarchy to the locations within a class structure. Mobility boundaries between class categories may be more or less well defined, but the locations themselves cannot be arranged on any overarching continuum. Second, while research on vertical mobility has explored multidimensional association models of occupational strata, none of this research has analyzed the relative permeability of the three class boundaries we are examining. The question of differential class-boundary permeability has thus not been pursued systematically in any of the contemporary analyses of intergenerational mobility of which we are aware.

Conceptualizations of class structure

The class analysis framework commonly used in stratification research that is closest to the one used here is that of John Goldthorpe (1987; Erikson and Goldthorpe 1987a, 1987b, 1993; Ishida, Goldthorpe and Erikson 1991; Jones and Davis 1986). As in my class categories, Goldthorpe recognizes the importance of property, expertise and managerial power, and like my schema, he operationally deploys his class framework using different numbers of categories depending upon the availability of data and the analytical context. While these two frameworks have thus considerable affinity (in spite of the fact that one is anchored in the Marxist tradition and the other in the Weberian tradition) there are two differences worth noting. First, as already noted, the framework we are using interprets class relations in terms of exploitation rather than simply "life chances." The central contention is that what most decisively divides classes and constitutes their relations as antagonistic is exploitation, not simply privileges and advantages. Second, in terms of the details of the elaboration of the concept of class structure, Goldthorpe (1987: 39) collapses into a single category, his "Class I," large proprietors, high-level professionals and top officials of large public and private organizations. This effectively collapses the distinctions among our three class boundaries for people commanding the highest levels of assets with respect to any one of these boundaries.[10] This would make it impossible using Goldthorpe's class categories to compare directly the relative permeability of the property, skill and authority boundaries of class structures.

The comparative design

The data analysis will begin by first assuming that the pattern of class-boundary permeability is the same for all four countries. In effect, this

---

[10]   Hout and Hauser (1991) argue that the Goldthorpe class categories are internally heterogeneous with respect to occupational prestige, education and income level, and that the combined classification that Erikson and Goldthorpe (1987a, 1987b, 1993) rely upon collapses categories that show heterogeneous rates of mobility, thereby giving rise to misleading patterns of association. Similar objections, of course, could be raised against our empirical analysis since we are forced to collapse some of our categories into more heterogeneous groupings because of data constraints. Nevertheless, our theoretical model tries to retain a high degree of conceptual homogeneity within categories, and we try to sustain the distinctions as much as possible in the execution of the data analysis.

implies that the mechanisms which generate boundary permeability reflect the general properties of class structures in developed capitalist societies rather than historically specific social and political conditions of different countries. This is the class analysis equivalent to the well-known "FJH hypothesis" in occupational mobility research (Featherman, Jones and Hauser 1975) which argues that the mechanisms generating occupational mobility do not significantly vary across industrial societies.

After we have explored these models that assume cross-national uniformity, we add country interactions. We will interpret cross-national differences in the coefficients of the equations as indicating that there are significant national variations in the causal structure generating mobility across specific class boundaries. This approach differs from previous research that has engaged the FJH hypothesis in that we will test specific *differences* in coefficients measuring relative boundary permeability across countries rather than focussing exclusively either on the global fit of models or on individual coefficients of those models. The comparative design thus provides some validation of any broad conclusions we might draw about the mobility permeability of class boundaries in capitalist societies together with a context for exploring nationally specific patterns of variation.

6.3 Results

We will first explore the results for men for Models (1) and (2) presented at the end of Chapter 5 and then turn to the cross-national comparisons in Models (3) and (4). This will be followed by an examination of Model (1) when people from farm origins and destinations are excluded from the analysis. We will conclude by examining the basic models for women.

The relative permeability of class boundaries among men

Table 6.1 presents the coefficients for the three class-boundary crossing variables for men in Model (1).[11] We will refer to these as "mobility-permeability coefficients" throughout this discussion. Model (1) is clearly an improvement in fit over the baseline model: the likelihood

---

[11] The raw frequencies for the origins by destinations mobility tables on which these loglinear analyses are based are presented in the appendix to Western and Wright (1994: 626–627).

Table 6.1. *Parameter estimates for permeability of class boundaries to mobility:*
men in the labor force in the United States, Canada, Sweden and Norway

Variable	Coefficient (s.e.)	Antilog
Boundary-crossing coefficients[a]		
PROPERTY	−1.10 (.125)***	.33
AUTHORITY	−0.08 (.049)[b]	.92
SKILL	−0.61 (.099)***	.55
Scaled deviance (134 d.f.)	192.2	
Baseline scaled deviance (137 d.f.)[c]	300.6	
Overall improvement in fit (3 d.f.)	108.4***	
Differences in boundary-crossing coefficients		
PROPERTY − AUTHORITY	−1.01 (.118)***	
SKILL − AUTHORITY	−0.52 (.100)***	
PROPERTY − SKILL	−0.49 (.155)**	

Significance levels (two-tailed tests): * p < .05   ** p < .01   *** p < .001

a. The coefficients are calculated from model (1): log f_{ijk} = Country + Origins + Destinations +
   QI + Country x Origins + Country x Destinations + PROPERTY + AUTHORITY + SKILL

b. This coefficient is significant at the .05 level using a one-tailed test which is appropriate given
   the directional character of the hypothesis.

c. Baseline model: log f_{ijk} = Country + Origins + Destinations + QI + Country x Origins +
   Country x Destinations

ratio chi-squared (L^2) declines by about 108 for three degrees of
freedom. The significant, negative coefficients for PROPERTY and for
SKILL indicate that both of these class boundaries generate obstacles to
intergenerational mobility. The authority boundary, in contrast,
appears to be relatively permeable.

The bottom panel of Table 6.1 presents formal tests of the differences
in permeability coefficients. On the basis of these data and variables,
the property boundary is significantly less permeable to mobility than
both the skill boundary and the authority boundary, and the skill
boundary is less permeable than the authority boundary. These results
are broadly in keeping with the expectations of a neo-Marxist approach
(Hypothesis 1 and 2).

It could be objected that the higher level of permeability of the authority boundary in Model (1) is due to the fact that AUTHORITY is more crudely measured than either PROPERTY or SKILL since we were only able to dichotomize the authority dimension whereas we trichotomized the other two dimensions. To see if this objection is plausible, Model (1) was reanalyzed by collapsing employers and petty bourgeois into a more diffuse self-employed category, and professionals and skilled employees into a broader expert category. While this did reduce the coefficients for PROPERTY and SKILL (from −1.09 to −0.51 and from −0.59 to −0.42 respectively), nevertheless both permeability coefficients remained significantly less than 0, and both were significantly less than the authority coefficient.

Mobility across the working-class boundary among men

Table 6.2 presents the results for Model (2), in which the WORKER locational-permeability variable is added to the basic additive boundary-crossing model. The fit of this model is a significant improvement over Model (1), indicating that the likelihood of mobility between the working class and other class locations is not simply an additive function of the average likelihood of mobility across the three class boundaries that define the class structure. What is particularly striking in the results for Model (2) is that the permeability coefficient for class mobility between workers and the petty bourgeoisie (net of the additive effects of the three boundary-crossing variables) is significantly *greater* than 0, while the coefficient for mobility between workers and employers is significantly *less* than 0. Clearly, the socially significant barrier to mobility across the property boundary for people in the working class is not between workers and self-employment as such, but between workers and employers.

On the basis of the results in Table 6.2 it is possible to rank order all of the boundaries between the working class and other specific class locations in terms of their overall degree of permeability by adding up the coefficients which pertain to a given cell in the table. The antilogs of these sums of coefficients for worker I nonworker cells in the mobility matrix give us the relative odds of different mobility trajectories involving the working class (net of other effects in the model). As indicated in Table 6.3, these results indicate that the odds of worker I professional mobility are twice that of worker I employer mobility, while the odds of worker I petty bourgeois mobility are over five times greater.

Table 6.2. *Interactions with mobility across the working-class boundary: men in the labor force in the United States, Canada, Sweden and Norway*

Variable	Coefficient (s.e.)
PROPERTY	−1.05 (.15)***
AUTHORITY	0.18 (.09)
SKILL	−0.40 (.12)***

Mobility between workers and nonworkers:[a]

Level 1[b]	Worker|Employer	−0.52 (.13)***
Level 2	Worker|Petty bourgeois	0.38 (.11)***
Level 3	Worker|Expert manager	−0.33 (.13)**
Level 4	Worker|Manager/supervisor	−0.17 (.11)
Level 5	Worker|Professional	−0.24 (.21)
Level 6	Worker|Skilled employee	−0.15 (.14)

Scaled deviance (129 d.f.)   162.7
Improvement over Model (1)   29.5***

Significance levels (two-tailed tests): * $p < .05$ ** $p < .01$ *** $p < .001$

a. Worker|Nonworker mobility is measured by a series of dummy variables. The coefficients indicate the difference between a given category of Worker|Nonworker mobility and mobility that does *not* cross the worker boundary (i.e. the combination of Worker|Worker immobility and Nonworker|Nonworker immobility).

b. "Level" refers to the categories in the design matrix for the WORKER variable in Figure 5.3. Because of the inability to distinguish managers from supervisors in class origins, levels 4 and 5 in the design matrix in Figure 5.3 have been combined for the analysis of mobility.

Cross-national variations among men

Table 6.4 presents the results for country interactions. In the global test of country interactions (Model (4) vs. Model (3)), there was no significant improvement in the goodness of fit when country interactions with the boundary-crossing variables were added to the equation.[12] It is tempting to conclude from this result that the basic pattern of mobility permeability displayed in Table 6.2 is invariant across the four countries in our sample. This is not, however the case. When we look at the permeability coefficients separately *within* each country (panel II, Table 6.4), a clear pattern of cross-national variation emerges. In the United States and Canada the property boundary is significantly

[12] There was also no significant improvement in goodness of fit when COUNTRY × WORKER interactions were added to Model (4).

Table 6.3. *Rank ordering of boundary impermeability for mobility across the working-class boundary: men in the labor force in the United States, Canada, Sweden and Norway*

Cross-class boundary	Coefficients added to get overall permeability	Sum of coefficients	Antilog of sum of coefficients	Antilog relative to Worker|Employer mobility
1 Worker|Employer	PROPERTY + AUTHORITY + WORKER (level 1)[a]	−1.39	0.25	1.0
2 Worker|Professional	SKILL + WORKER (level 5)	−0.65	0.52	2.1
3 Worker|Expert manager	AUTHORITY + SKILL + WORKER (level 3)	−0.55	0.58	2.3
4 Worker|Skilled employee	WORKER (level 6)	−0.15	0.86	3.4
5 Worker|Mgr/supervisor	AUTHORITY + WORKER (level 4)	0.01	1.00	4.1
6 Worker|Petty bourgeois	WORKER (level 2)	0.38	1.46	5.9

a. "Level" refers to the categories in the design matrix for the WORKER variable in Figure 5.3 and the coefficients reported in Table 6.2. Because of the inability to distinguish managers from supervisors in class origins, levels 4 and 5 in the design matrix have been combined for the analysis of mobility.

Table 6.4. *Cross-national interactions in mobility permeability of class boundaries: men in the labor force in the United States, Canada, Sweden and Norway*

I. *Goodness-of-fit of different models*

Model	d.f.	Scaled deviance
Baseline model	137	300.6
Model (1): PROPERTY + AUTHORITY + SKILL	134	192.2
Model (2): Model (1) + WORKER	129	162.7
Model (3): Model (1) + QI x Country	113	157.5
Model (4): Model (3) + PROPERTY x C + AUTHORITY x C + SKILL x C	104	146.2
Model (5): Model (3) + PROPERTY x NA + SKILL x NA^a	111	151.5
Model (4) vs. Model (3)	9	11.3
Model (5) vs. Model (3)	2	6*

II. *Boundary-permeability coefficients within countries*

	US	Canada	Sweden	Norway
PROPERTY	-1.36 (.28)***	-1.33 (.21)***	-0.67 (.35)*	-0.93 (.23)***
AUTHORITY	-0.03 (.11)	-0.04 (.09)	-0.29 (.12)*	-0.03 (.09)
SKILL	-0.45 (.20)*	-0.54 (.17)***	-0.90 (.27)***	-0.63 (.19)***

Table 6.4. (Continued)

III. Differences between permeability coefficients within countries

	US	Canada	Sweden	Norway
PROPERTY – AUTHORITY	–1.33 (.26)***	–1.29 (.20)***	–0.39 (.33)	–0.90 (.22)***
SKILL – AUTHORITY	–0.43 (.20)*	–0.50 (.17)**	–0.62 (.27)*	–0.60 (.19)***
PROPERTY – SKILL	–0.90 (.33)**	–0.79 (.26)***	+0.23 (.42)	–0.30 (.29)

IV. Differences between North America and Scandinavia in permeability of PROPERTY and SKILL boundaries

PROPERTY	–0.56 (.24)*
SKILL	+0.18 (.20)
PROPERTY – SKILL	–0.74 (.32)*

Significance levels: * p < .05   ** p < .01   *** p < .001

a. NA = North America dummy variable (US and Canada = 1; Sweden and Norway = 0). Since the AUTHORITY coefficients do not vary across countries, we have interacted NA only with PROPERTY and SKILL.

less permeable than the skill boundary; in Sweden and Norway, these two boundaries do not differ significantly. Indeed, in Sweden the skill boundary is nominally (although not statistically significantly) less permeable than the property boundary.

As often happens in analyses of cross-national variations, certain coefficients are significant in some countries and not in others, and yet the cross-country differences in these coefficients are not themselves significant in global tests of country interactions. One of the reasons why the global test of significance may have failed to support the apparent cross-national differences in boundary permeability is that this type of overall test has weak statistical power to detect specific differences of the kind referred to above. In simultaneously testing cross-national variation in three class boundaries over four countries we use up nine degrees of freedom, whereas an inspection of the country-specific mobility tables suggests only two salient cross-national differences: between North America and Scandinavia, with respect to PROPERTY and SKILL. We therefore respecified the country interactions with the following model:

$$\log F_{ijk} = \text{Model (3)} + \text{PROPERTY} \times NA + \text{SKILL} \times NA \qquad (5)$$

where NA is a dummy variable distinguishing the two North American countries from the two Scandinavian countries.[13] The result (panel IV, Table 6.4) indicates that there is a significant cross-national variation in the differential mobility permeability of these two class boundaries: the difference between the property and skill boundaries is 0.74 greater in North America than Scandinavia (significant at the .05 level). This finding is due mainly to a *less* permeable property boundary in North America (−.56 less permeable in North America compared to Scandinavia, significant at the .05 level). The results are thus consistent with Hypotheses 4 and 5, suggesting that the property boundary is less permeable in societies within which capitalist economic relations are less constrained by state interventions.

The problem of farmers

Table 6.5 presents the results for the analyses of class boundary permeability when people who either come from farmer origins or are

[13] There is no main effect of NA because it is fully captured by the additive COUNTRY term. We have not included an AUTHORITY $\times NA$ term since the authority coefficients differ hardly at all across countries.

Table 6.5. *Parameter estimates for permeability of class boundaries to mobility, excluding farmers and people with farmer origins*

Boundary-crossing variable	Boundary-crossing coefficients		
	All countries combined	North America	Scandinavia
PROPERTY	−0.70 (.18)***	−0.83 (.24)***	−0.54 (.28)*
AUTHORITY	−0.02 (.06)	0.08 (.08)	−0.06 (.08)
SKILL	−0.44 (.10)***	−0.34 (.14)*	−0.57 (.16)***
PROPERTY − SKILL	−0.26 (.20)	−0.50 (.26)[a]	0.02 (.32)

	Boundary-crossing coefficients			
	US	Canada	Sweden	Norway
PROPERTY	−0.86 (.41)*	−0.82 (.29)**	−0.49 (.49)	−0.60 (.34)
AUTHORITY	0.09 (.11)	0.09 (.11)	−0.24 (.14)	0.05 (.10)
SKILL	−0.32 (.21)	−0.33 (.18)*	−0.81 (.28)**	−0.45 (.20)*
PROPERTY − SKILL	−0.55 (.45)	−0.49 (.34)	0.32 (.55)	−0.16 (.39)

Significance levels (one tailed tests): * $p < .05$ ** $p < .01$ *** $p < .001$

a. The t-ratio for this coefficient is 1.875 which falls just below the conventional $p < .05$ significance level for a two-tailed test.

currently farmers are excluded from the mobility matrix. This exclusion reduces the sample size for each country by 20–25%. The exclusion of farm origins and destinations from the analysis does affect the magnitudes of the coefficients for both the property boundary and the skill boundary: both boundaries appear to be more permeable (i.e. the coefficients are less negative) when farmers are excluded from the analysis. In the United States sample, for example, the coefficient for the property boundary is −1.36 for the entire sample while only −0.86 in the sample excluding farm origins and distinctions, and the coefficient for the skill boundary is −0.45 in the entire sample and −0.32 in the sample without farmers. As a result, the difference between the degree of impermeability of the property and skill boundaries is smaller when farmers are excluded from the analysis. Some of the aggregate difference in permeability between the property and skill boundaries, therefore, does appear to be linked to the specific mobility patterns of farmers.

Nevertheless, the basic pattern of results we observed in Table 6.4 holds in Table 6.5. In the two North American countries taken together, the property boundary is less permeable (at the p <.06 level, two-tailed test) than the skill boundary, whereas in the two Scandinavian countries there is no statistically significant difference in the degree of permeability of these boundaries in the nonfarm sample.[14] The general pattern of differential class-boundary permeability, therefore, is not merely an artifact of the occupational immobility of farmers.

Gender and class-boundary permeability

There are interesting similarities and differences in the results for women compared to men. Table 6.6 indicates that for women, as for men, both the property boundary and the skill boundary constitute statistically significant obstacles to class mobility. This is true whether individuals or families are used as the unit of analysis for defining women's class locations. Also, as in the results for men, the authority boundary is significantly less permeable than the skill and property boundaries. However, unlike the results for men, the property boundary for women is not significantly less permeable than the skill boundary.

The clearest difference in the patterns for men and women centers on the property boundary: this boundary is significantly *more* permeable for women than it is for men (see Table 6.6, panel III). The permeability coefficient for the property boundary using women's direct class is −0.42 compared to −1.10 for men. Taking antilogs of these coefficients indicates that women have nearly twice the relative odds of mobility across the property boundary as do men. In contrast, the skill and authority permeability coefficients hardly differ at all between men and women. These results do not depend upon the use of individual

---

[14] A two-tailed test is used here since we have been entertaining two alternative hypotheses about the rank ordering of the expertise and property boundaries (the Marxist and cultural capitalist hypotheses). If we used a one-tailed test on these models on the grounds that the tests without farmers are meant to confirm the previous result, then the significance level would, of course, be p <.03. In any case, from a scientific point of view, there is no substantive difference between a .05 significance level and a .06 level.

Table 6.6. *Parameter estimates for permeability of class boundaries to mobility: women compared to men in the labor force in the United States, Canada, Sweden and Norway*

Variable	Coefficients (s.e.)		
I. *Boundary-crossing coefficients*[a]	Women: direct class[b]	Women: mediated/direct	Men: direct class
PROPERTY	-0.42 (.19)***	-0.50 (.17)***	-1.10 (.13)***
AUTHORITY	-0.08 (.06)	-0.15 (.06)**	-0.08 (.05)#
SKILL	-0.61 (.11)***	-0.59 (.10)***	-0.61 (.10)***
Scaled deviance (134 d.f.)	158.6	170.8	192.2
Baseline scaled deviance (137 d.f.)[c]	190.8	208.2	300.6
Overall improvement in fit (3d.f.)	32.2***	37.4***	108.4***
II. *Differences in boundary-crossing coefficients within gender categories*			
PROPERTY - AUTHORITY	-0.34 (.18)#	-0.36 (.16)*	-1.01 (.12)***
SKILL - AUTHORITY	-0.52 (.13)***	-0.44 (.11)***	-0.52 (.10)***
PROPERTY - SKILL	0.18 (.22)	0.08 (.20)	-0.49 (.16)**

III. *Gender differences in boundary-crossing coefficients*	Women direct vs. men direct	Women mediated/direct vs. men direct
PROPERTY	0.67 (.23)**	0.59 (.21)**
AUTHORITY	0.00 (.08)	-0.06 (.08)
SKILL	0.00 (.15)	0.02 (.14)

Significance levels (two tailed tests): # $p < .10$ * $p < .05$ ** $p < .01$ *** $p < .001$

a. The coefficients are calculated from model (1): $\log_{ijk}$ = Country + Origins + Destinations + QI + Country x Origins + Country x Destinations + PROPERTY + AUTHORITY + SKILL.

b. "Direct Class" is defined as the class of the individual's own job; "Mediated/Direct class" is defined as the class of the individual's spouse's job if the individual is married and the class of her own job if she is single.

c. The baseline model is $\log_{ijk}$ = Country + Origins + Destinations + QI + Country x Origins + Country x Destinations.

class or family class as the basis for defining the class location of women.

One possible interpretation of the greater permeability of the property boundary to class mobility for women compared to men is that marriage provides a stronger channel for crossing the property boundary (in both directions) for women than for men. For example, because of the way gender affects career aspirations and class opportunities, it would be expected that when a man from a capitalist origin marries a woman from a noncapitalist origin they are both more likely to end up in capitalist destinations (whether those destinations be defined in the direct or mediated manner) than when a woman with a capitalist origin marries a man from a noncapitalist origin. If this is the case, then the property boundary would be more permeable for women than for men. While we have no way of exploring this hypothesis in the present data, it suggests that the "marriage market" has different effects on the class mobility of men and women, at least as this concerns the property dimensions of class structures.[15]

Table 6.7 presents the results for women's class mobility between the working class and other class locations using the WORKER interaction variable. As in the case for men, the permeability of the worker I employer boundary and the worker I expert-manager boundary is significantly negative for Model (2), indicating that these boundaries are less permeable than is predicted by the additive boundary-crossing model. Again, as in Model (1), there is very little difference in the results for women using individual class or family class as the criterion for current class location.

Table 6.8 presents the results of the cross-national interactions for women. As in the results for men, the goodness of fit of Model (1) is not significantly improved when country interactions are added in Model (3). Also as in the case of men, this absence of global country interactions hides some more fine-grained cross-national variations in specific coefficients. Unlike in the case of men, however, for women the cross-national contrast is not between North America and Scandinavia, but between the United States and the other three countries. As Table 6.8 (panel II) indicates, in the United States, the skill boundary does not constitute a significant barrier to class mobility for women, whereas for the other three countries the coefficients for the skill boundary are significantly negative (and virtually the same as for men in those countries). This difference between the United States and the other three countries combined is itself statistically significant. Taking antilogs of these coefficients indicates that the odds of mobility for American women across the expert boundary are roughly twice that of

[15] For discussions of the marriage market and mobility, see Chase (1975); Goldthorpe and Payne (1986); Tyree and Treas (1974).

Table 6.7. *Interactions with mobility across the working-class boundary: women compared to men in the labor force in the United States, Canada, Sweden and Norway*

Variable	Coefficients (s.e.)		
	Women: direct class[c]	Women: mediated/direct	Men: direct class
PROPERTY	−0.55***	−0.48***	−1.05***
AUTHORITY	−0.05	−0.01	0.18
SKILL	−0.40***	−0.47***	−0.40***
Mobility between workers and nonworkers:			
Level 1[a] Worker|Employer	−0.34 (.14)*	−0.43 (.15)**	−0.52 (.13)**
Level 2 Worker|Petty bourgeois	0.01 (.12)	0.07 (.12)	0.38 (.11)**
Level 3 Worker|Expert manager	−0.40 (.153)*	−0.30 (.14)*	−0.33 (.13)**
Level 4 Worker|Managers/supervisor	−0.11 (.12)	−0.21 (.12)	−0.17 (.11)
Level 5 Worker|Professional	−0.46 (.26)	−0.34 (.23)	−0.24 (.21)
Level 6 Worker|Skilled worker	−0.51 (.14)**	−0.22 (.15)	−0.15 (.14)
Model (3) scaled deviance (129 d.f.)	147.0	162.0	166.0
Model (1) scaled deviance (134 d.f.)	158.6	170.8	196.5
Improvement in fit (5 d.f.)	9.6	8.8	30.5 ***

Significance levels: * $p<.05$ ** $p<.01$ *** $p<.001$

a. "Level" refers to the categories in the design matrix for the WORKER variable in Figure 5.3. Because of the inability to distinguish managers from supervisors in class origins, levels 4 and 5 in the design matrix in Figure 5.3 have been combined in this analysis.

women in the other three countries.[16] I cannot offer a compelling interpretation of these specific patterns of cross-national variation in boundary permeability among women.

6.4 Implications of the results for mobility research

How do these results square with previous research on social mobility? The differences in conceptual frameworks and analytical objectives between this project and previous mobility research make direct comparisons of results difficult. There is no simple correspondence between our categories and the occupational strata of stratification

---

[16] There is also some difference in the property coefficient across the countries for women's *direct* class (it is significantly negative in the US but not elsewhere), but this cross-national difference is not itself significant, and in any case it is not present when we substitute women's family-class location for the direct class of married women.

Table 6.8. *Cross-national interactions in mobility permeability of class boundaries: women compared to men in the labor force in the United States, Canada, Sweden, and Norway*

I. *Goodness-of-fit of different models*

Model	d.f.	Scaled deviance Women: direct	Women: mediated/direct	Men:
Baseline Model	137	190.8	208.0	300.6
Model (1): PROPERTY + AUTHORITY + SKILL	134	158.6	170.8	192.2
Model (2): Model (1) + WORKER	129	147.0	162.0	162.7
Model (3): Model (1) + QI x Country	113	133.9	147.6	157.5
Model (4): Model (3) + PROPERTY x C + AUTHORITY x C + SKILL x C	104	124.0	136.1	146.5
Model (4) vs. Model (3)	9	9.9	11.5	11.3

II. *Boundary-permeability coefficients within countries[a]*

Boundary-crossing coefficients

Variable	US	Canada	Sweden	Norway
Men:				
PROPERTY	-1.36***	-1.33***	-0.67*	-0.93***
AUTHORITY	-0.03	-0.04	-0.29*	-0.03
SKILL	-0.45**	-0.54**	-0.90***	-0.63**
Women, direct class:				
PROPERTY	-0.71*	-0.18	+0.57	-0.57
AUTHORITY	-0.10	-0.02	-0.13	-0.14
SKILL	-0.05	-0.66**	-0.94*	-0.72***

Table 6.8. *(Continued)*

Women, mediated/direct class:

PROPERTY	-0.51	-0.43	-0.48
AUTHORITY	-0.04	-0.28	-0.15
SKILL	-0.77***	-0.74**	-0.67***

III. *Cross-national differences between permeability coefficients among women: US vs. other countries*

	Direct class	Mediated/direct class
PROPERTY	-0.43	-0.09
AUTHORITY	-0.01	-0.04
SKILL	+0.68*	0.85**
PROPERTY – AUTHORITY	-0.42	-0.04
SKILL – AUTHORITY	+0.69*	0.90**
PROPERTY – SKILL	-1.12	-0.94 (t = 1.9)

Significance levels (two tailed tests): * p < .05 ** p < .01 *** p < .001

a. There were no statistically significant differences between boundary-crossing coefficients among women within any country.

research or the class categories associated with most Weberian-inspired research. Furthermore, we are primarily concerned with the specific problem of relative boundary permeability – the analysis involves differences between mobility coefficients, and differences of differences – rather than with the overall contours of a mobility regime as in most mobility research.

Nevertheless, some comparisons with the findings of other research can be made. John Goldthorpe's Weberian-inspired class mobility research suggests, first, that there is disproportionate immobility within the service class and within the farm and the nonfarm petty bourgeoisie, and second, that there are mobility barriers of varying strength throughout the class structure between white- and blue-collar classes, and between agricultural and nonagricultural classes (Erikson and Goldthorpe 1987a, 1993: ch. 4; Erikson, Goldthorpe and Porto-carero 1982; Goldthorpe 1987: ch. 4; Jones and Davis 1986: ch. 3; Kurz and Muller 1987). Occupational mobility research repeatedly affirms the disproportionate immobility of farmers, and the boundaries between farmers and other strata (Ganzeboom et al. 1989; Hout 1984, 1989: ch. 6; Hout and Hauser 1991; Wong 1990). Occupational mobility research also suggests that the odds of mobility between strata diminish as the metric distances between categories increase (Wong 1992). Since most occupational mobility studies either employ or derive scale scores that rank occupations with professionals, managers and proprietors at one extreme, and semi- and unskilled manual workers at the other (e.g. Hauser 1984; Hout and Hauser 1991; Ganzeboom et al. 1989), these results imply a mobility regime domi-nated by a vertical gradation in mobility chances that varies linearly with socio-economic status (Ganzeboom, Treiman and Ultee 1991). This is accompanied by boundaries into and out of farming, and, by implication, proprietorship and self-employment, more generally.

Our findings suggest some elaboration of these results, and some directions for future research. If our results are correct, the stratified pattern of mobility exchanges between blue- and white-collar classes that Weberian class analysis has found is more likely to reflect the relative impermeability of property and skill than the effects of authority. Goldthorpe (1987: 99) argues that relative mobility patterns can be attributed to the differing importance of economic and cultural capital, but given the composition of his class schema he cannot directly investigate this issue. His inferences about the relative im-portance of different kinds of class resources must be drawn indirectly since his classes are heterogeneous with respect to property and skill. Our results suggest that Goldthorpe's assertion about economic and cultural capital is accurate, but that property is a stronger barrier to mobility than cultural capital (at least as reflected in skills and expertise).

Our findings also imply that occupational mobility research should consider property ownership as a discrete dimension of mobility, alongside vertical mobility. Wong (1992) has partially addressed this issue already by incorporating mobility between self-employment and wage labor into his investigation of vertical mobility. However, he argues for the importance of self-employment *per se*, rather than capitalist property ownership, as a determinant of relative mobility. Our findings of excess mobility between workers and the petty bourgeoisie, net of the effect of property, suggest that capitalist property ownership, rather than simple self-employment, is what counts. This is obviously a question for further research.

Finally, our findings are also consistent with the view that social democratic welfare states can influence the operation of capitalist class mechanisms toward greater equality (e.g. Stephens 1979). In the two more "purely" capitalist countries we examine, the property boundary is a more substantial barrier to intergenerational mobility than the skill boundary. In the Scandinavian countries, the effects of property on mobility chances appear attenuated. While we obviously cannot attribute these national differences to differences in welfare state regimes and public policy, our results are consistent with the findings we would expect if social democratic welfare states do ameliorate class inequalities.

6.5 Conclusions

Five general conclusions stand out from these results. First, in North America, the patterns of permeability of class boundaries to mobility among men are broadly consistent with the expectations of neo-Marxist conceptualizations of class: the property boundary is the least permeable, followed by the skill boundary and then the authority boundary. While the specific occupational immobility of farmers contributes to this difference in class-boundary permeability, the difference in permeability of the property and skill boundaries remains significant even when farmers are excluded from the analysis. On the basis of these results, the material resources linked to capitalist property relations appear to constitute a more significant barrier to mobility in the US and Canada than the cultural resources linked to skills.

Second, in Sweden and Norway, the property and skill boundaries do not differ significantly in their degree of permeability to inter-generational mobility among men. This difference from North America is primarily because the property boundary is more permeable in Norway and Sweden. The relative degree of permeability to mobility of different class boundaries, therefore, is not an invariant feature of capitalist class structures. Our results suggest that the more purely capitalistic is an economic structure, the less permeable will be the property boundary to intergenerational mobility.

Third, the permeability patterns suggest that the class structure should not be viewed simply as the "sum" of the three dimensions that underlie it. Halaby and Weakliem (1993) argue that combining these three dimensions into a "class structure" typology is simply a descriptive convenience; the analysis of classes can just as easily be carried out directly on the basis of the three "primitive" dimensions taken one by one. The results of the analysis of the WORKER interaction terms in Model (2) indicate that the additive effects of these three dimensions do not exhaust mobility patterns within this typology, and thus class structures are indeed "wholes" that are not reducible to the "sum of their parts" in the sense that there are distinctive effects of the gestalt as such.

Fourth, the patterns of class-boundary permeability are significantly different for women and for men. For men, the property boundary is significantly less permeable than the skill boundary; for women these two boundaries do not significantly differ. This contrast reflects the weaker barriers women face for mobility across the property boundary which is possibly due to the operation of "marriage markets."

These gender differences in boundary permeability raise interesting questions for both Marxist and non-Marxist understandings of class mobility. The gender difference in mobility regimes is principally because the property boundary is differentially permeable between men and women. Whether the male or female property boundaries better represent the "normal" effect of property on mobility chances is open to debate. However, if capital inheritance and opportunities to marry into the capitalist class vary by gender, then *both* men's and women's relative mobility chances are independently shaped by gender relations that operate through the family and the marriage market, as well as distinctive class mechanisms. To the extent that these class and gender mechanisms are empirically interconnected, future research on patterns of relative boundary permeability should explicitly take gender into account, for men as well as women.

Finally, with some marginal exceptions, the results for women are virtually identical using the individual or the family as the unit of analysis for defining class locations. There is no evidence that using direct class for women's class destination inflates the amount of class mobility attributed to women. While this does not, of course, resolve the conceptual issues raised in the debate over the appropriate unit of class analysis, it does indicate that empirically it does not appear to make much difference, at least for the problem of class mobility.

Methodological appendix

Variables

The basic variables used in this analysis have been described in Chapter 5. In all our mobility tables, the class *origins* variable derives from information about the job of the main breadwinner in the respondent's family of origin. The questionnaire asked respondents to indicate a variety of attributes of the job of their family's "main breadwinner" during the time "when you were growing up." If the respondents said that the main breadwinner had a variety of different kinds of jobs, they were asked for information on the main job during the period when the respondent was growing up. If the respondent said that there was no "main" job, the question was then restricted to the main breadwinner's job when the respondent was 16 years of age. The questions were asked in this somewhat diffuse way – "when you were growing up" – rather than at a specific time in order to get data on the characteristic "class origin" of the respondent during their childhood as a whole, not just at the moment close to when they left home. This person need not be the respondent's father; rather the identity of the primary breadwinner was left up to the respondent. However, overwhelmingly in these data, respondents indicated their fathers as the major breadwinner in the family.

Measurement problems

All of the analyses in this chapter are vulnerable to a variety of measurement problems. It is possible that respondents have less accurate information on the authority aspects of their parents' jobs than on the skill or property dimensions, and thus we may well be measuring authority more poorly than the other two class boundaries. It is also the case, as noted in Chapter 5, that on the authority dimension for respondents' origins we are unable to distinguish between supervisors and proper managers, and again, this weakens the measurement of this dimension of the matrix. Perhaps even more significantly, the implicit metrics on the three dimensions of the class typology are not really commensurable. There is therefore no reason to believe that the "distance" between a small capitalist and an employee is equivalent to the "distance" between a professional and a noncredentialed employee. Thus, if much more restrictive definitions of "nonexperts" (limiting them to completely unskilled labor) and of professionals (limiting them to the highest status professionals) were adopted, it is possible that this boundary would appear much less permeable than it does in the results reported here. The same could be said of the authority dimension. If we restricted "managers" to "top executives" or "CEOs," then it might well be that the case that the redefined authority boundary might become the least permeable. This means that if Hypothesis 2 is confirmed and the property boundary as measured is less permeable than the skill boundary, this could be an artifact of arbitrariness in the classification scheme. For this reason I have defined capitalists in this analysis in an extremely weak manner – a capitalist is any self-employed person with *any* employees – so that it is unlikely that the results will be biased in the direction of our principal hypothesis.

7 Cross-class friendships

Class mobility is not the only issue involved in understanding the permeability of class boundaries. Patterns of intimate social interaction among people within marriages and friendships are also relevant aspects of the permeability of such boundaries. A rigid class structure in which people's lives are tightly bounded within particular class locations is not simply one in which there are few prospects for individual mobility but one in which social networks rarely cross class boundaries. In the popular consciousness, when people argue that social classes are not very important in the United States, part of what they mean is that the social barriers that separate people in different classes are thought to be relatively weak. The extent of cross-class friendships would be one measure of the extent to which this is true.

As in the case of class mobility, it is plausible that the class patterning of friendship interactions is one of the micro-processes that shapes the ways in which people experience the class structure. For example, political coalitions across specific class boundaries should be facilitated to the extent that friendship ties frequently cross these boundaries. All things being equal, higher levels of class consciousness would be expected in societies in which friendship ties were overwhelmingly with others in the same class rather than diffused across a variety of class locations.

In this chapter we will not explore the problem of the subjective effects of the class content of friendship networks. Rather, as in Chapter 6, our focus will be on the class patterning of these networks through an investigation of the relative permeability of different class boundaries to the formation of friendships.

7.1 Orienting hypotheses

This research on friendships was not initially launched to test a series of *a priori* hypotheses. Because the literature in structural class analysis has not systematically examined friendship ties (and certainly not in a comparative framework) there were no well-established hypotheses to test. The objectives, therefore, were largely exploratory and inductive – to discover coherent patterns and to report our confidence in the observations.

Nevertheless, a number of orienting hypotheses can be derived from class analysis and the sociology of friendships to guide our exploration of these patterns. As in Chapter 6, these hypotheses are organized around the rankings of the three class boundaries by degree of *im*permeability (see Table 7.1). The predicted rank order depends upon theoretical expectations of how property, authority and skill generate various obstacles to the formation of intimate interpersonal relations. We explore three ways in which these class mechanisms might generate such obstacles and thereby shape patterns of friendship formation: (1) by structuring the *interests* of actors; (2) by shaping actors' *life-styles*; and (3) by creating differential *opportunities* for informal interpersonal contact. Each of these causal processes suggests different rankings of the three kinds of class boundaries by relative permeability.

Class interests (Marxian variant)

Marxism has relatively little to say about interpersonal relations. Nevertheless, the Marxist approach to class analysis would generally predict that the more antagonistic are two individuals' class interests, the less likely it is that friendships will form between them, i.e. the more *im*permeable will be the corresponding class boundaries. This is clearly the case for friendships between workers and their own employers, since for these actors there is a direct correspondence between their concrete interpersonal relations and their general class interests. Although these antagonistic interests might not inherently block friendship formation between workers and capitalists who were not in a direct employment relation to each other, nevertheless within a broadly Marxist understanding of the relationship between the objective properties of class structures and the subjective states of actors, it would be predicted that such friendships are unlikely. To the extent

Table 7.1. *Rank orderings of relative impermeability of class boundaries to friendship ties in different theoretical perspectives*

	Ranking from most impermeable (1) to most permeable (3)		
Theoretical Perspective	PROPERTY	AUTHORITY	SKILL
Class interests (Marxian variant)[a]	1	2 or 3	3 or 2
Class interests (Dahrendorf variant)	2	1	3
Class habitus (Bourdieu)	2	3	1
Class as opportunity structure[b]	1 or 2	3	2 or 1

a. The Marxian variant of the class interest perspective predicts the property boundary to be the most *im*permeable, but provides no clear basis for rank ordering the authority or skill boundaries.

b. The "opportunity structure" perspective predicts the authority boundary to be the most permeable, but provides no clear basis for rank ordering the property or skill boundaries.

that class interests shape values and ideologies, which in turn affect the likelihood and durability of friendships, Marxists would predict that friendships crossing the property boundary are particularly unlikely, i.e. the property boundary should be the most impermeable.

Because there is considerable disagreement among Marxists about the importance of authority and expertise as bases of class interests and class conflicts, it is unclear how Marxists would rank the relative permeability of the authority and skill boundaries. Insofar as Marxists regard the interests of managers as closely integrated with the interests of capitalists, they would rank the authority boundary as more impermeable than the skill boundary, but this judgment would be tempered by the realization that segmentation of labor markets by credentials is a deep source of conflict in contemporary capitalist societies.

Class interests (Dahrendorf variant)

Ralf Dahrendorf (1959) argued that in contemporary societies authority is the fundamental basis of class antagonism. In early periods of capitalist development, his argument goes, authority and property coincided, and thus social theorists like Marx mistakenly identified property as the fundamental axis of class conflict. In the twentieth century, however, the deepening separation of formal ownership of property from substantive command means that property ownership has declined as a basis for class relations. This perspective would therefore predict that the authority boundary should be the most impermeable. To the extent that property ownership still confers some authority, the property boundary would be expected to have intermediate permeability. Since skill without organizational authority confers little capacity to command, the skill boundary should be the most permeable of the three.

Class habitus (Bourdieu)

As virtually all research on friendship formation has argued, one of the primary mechanisms shaping friendship patterns is common values and life-styles. All other things being equal, individuals who share salient aspects of life-style are more likely to become friends than individuals with highly disparate life-styles. As Pierre Bourdieu (1984, 1985, 1987) has argued in his analysis of "class habitus," a pivotal determinant of life-style is cultural capital. This suggests that the odds of friendship ties between experts and nonexperts should be particularly low since people on either side of the skill boundary are likely to differ sharply in terms of cultural capital. Thus, class habitus theory would predict the skill dimension to be the most impermeable. Furthermore, because wealth and income are generally viewed as crucial bases of life-style (although perhaps less important than cultural capital), the property boundary would be expected to be more impermeable than the authority boundary.

Interaction opportunity

Sociological analyses of friendships decompose the friendship formation process into two consecutive processes, meeting and mating. *Meeting* is the process of strangers being converted into acquaintances; *mating* is the conversion of acquaintances into friends (Verbrugge 1977: 576–577). Although meeting can be simply a matter of chance, typically it is the result of people being in situations that systematically facilitate friendship formation. In part, this is a question of spatial proximity, as in the importance of neighborhood of residence as a factor influencing friendship formation – people often make friends with neighbors of dissimilar social position (Huckfeldt 1983; Nahemow and Lawton 1975). More significant than sheer proximity for our present purposes, certain "foci" of social interaction, to use Feld's (1981) expression, generate sustained joint activities among people and thus enhance the probabilities of people getting to know each other in ways that could lead to friendship.

Worksites are an important instance of such interactional foci. Furthermore, many worksites involve joint activity among people in different class locations, thus creating opportunities for cross-class friendships, particularly between managers and nonmanagers. These opportunities are further enhanced by the fact that many supervisors and even some managers spend significant parts of their careers as nonmanagerial employees. Intracareer authority mobility is undoubtedly much higher than intracareer mobility across either the property or skill boundaries. To the extent that friendships survive promotions, then, this would also enhance the permeability of the authority boundary. The opportunity structure arguments, therefore, would suggest that the authority class boundary should be the most permeable. The opportunity structure perspective, however, makes no clear prediction about relative impermeability of the property or skill boundaries.

The Weberian tradition

I have offered no hypotheses based explicitly on predictions from the Weberian tradition because the Weberian tradition of class analysis is consistent with virtually any ranking. Weberians who speak with a relatively Marxian voice, like Giddens (1973), would likely support the Marxist predictions. Others, like Parkin (1979), who emphasize the role of social closure in labor markets, are likely to predict a ranking like the class habitus perspective. Weberians who are preoccupied with status groups and the formation of symbolic communities would also probably share the predictions of class habitus theory. Dahrendorf is often considered a theorist in the Weberian tradition because of his emphasis on the importance of bureaucratic organization, so his variant of class interest theory could also be considered consistent with a Weberian-inspired approach. In any case, the theoretical predictions portrayed in Table 7.1 are not meant to be tight deductions from first principles, but rather general orienting hypotheses linked to different sociological intuitions that will facilitate the interpretation of our findings.

Relation to previous research

This research differs from previous research on friendships and social stratification in three respects (e.g. Curtis 1963; Hollingshead 1949;

Jackson 1977; Laumann 1966, 1973; Verbrugge 1977, 1979). First, previous research has revolved around status definitions of socio-economic stratification, whether or not the term "class" was used, whereas our research is organized around an economic structural definition of class. Second, within-status friendships have been at the center stage in these earlier studies. Those studies focussed primarily on the extent to which within-status friendships are more likely than cross-status friendships and on the variability of within-status friend-ships across social strata. Less attention has been given to friendships that cross status categories, which is the focus of this chapter. Finally, when cross-status friendships have been studied, systematic attention has not been given to the patterning of such friendships across qualitatively different status boundaries. Previous research has been concerned primarily with the relationship between the degree of status difference and the likelihood of friendship ties, and with status-asymmetries in cross-status friendship choices, i.e. the tendency to identify people of slightly higher status as one's friends (Hauser 1981; Jackson 1977). In contrast, this study of differential permeability of class boundaries concerns the patterns of friendships across the three qualitatively distinct class boundaries.

7.2 Results

The relative permeability of the three class boundaries

Table 7.2 presents the core substantive results for Model (1). The results are presented for two somewhat different specifications of the data: one in which the sample size is defined by the total number of friendships in the data, and the other in which the sample size is defined by the number of respondents. The explanation for these two specifications is presented in the methodological appendix to this chapter. All three boundaries, regardless of how sample size is defined, have statistically significant negative coefficients, indicating that these boundaries do in fact constitute obstacles to the formation of friend-ships.[1] The negative coefficients for the property and expert boundaries are significantly greater than those for the authority boundary. The

---

[1]   The coefficients are slightly different under the different specifications of sample size, since the average number of reported friends with data varies somewhat across countries. This means that the relative weight of the data from different countries in generating the coefficients will be slightly different in the two analyses.

Table 7.2. *Coefficients for permeability of the three exploitation boundaries: adults in the labor force in four countries*

Variable	Sample size defined as number of friendship ties		Sample size defined as number of respondents	
	Coefficient (s.e.)	Antilog	Coefficient (s.e.)	Antilog
Boundary-permeability coefficients				
PROPERTY	−0.99 (.09)***	.37	−0.98 (.14)***	.38
AUTHORITY	−0.32 (.03)***	.73	0.30 (.05)***	.74
SKILL	−0.79 (.04)***	.45	−0.77 (.07)***	.47
Scaled deviance	370.1		139.0	
Degrees of freedom	185		185	
Differences in boundary-permeability coefficients				
PROPERTY − AUTHORITY	−0.67 (.08)***		−0.68 (.14)***	
SKILL − AUTHORITY	−0.47 (.04)***		−0.47 (.09)***	
PROPERTY − SKILL	−0.20 (.10)*		−0.22 (.15)	

Significance levels (two-tailed test): * p < .05   ** p < .01   *** p < .001

authority boundary is thus more permeable than the property or the skill boundary. Taking the antilog of these coefficients, the odds of a friendship across the authority boundary are nearly 100% greater than the odds of a friendship across the property boundary and 60% greater than a friendship across the skill boundary.

The comparison of the permeability of the property and skill boundaries is slightly less clear. If the number of respondents rather than the number of friendship ties is used as the sample size, the property-boundary coefficient does not differ significantly from the skill-boundary coefficient. When sample size is the full number of friendship ties, however, the coefficient of the property boundary is significantly different from that of the skill boundary.[2] Taking the antilog of these coefficients indicates that the odds of friendships

---

[2] See the methodological appendix to this chapter for a discussion of the problem of sample size in the analysis of friendship ties.

crossing the skill boundary are about 20% greater than the odds of friendships crossing the property boundary.

The relative permeability of boundaries between working-class and nonworking-class locations

Model (1) gives information about the relative permeability of boundaries defined by the three underlying dimensions of the class structure. In Model (2), the WORKER interaction matrix is added to measure what we call locational permeability in Chapter 5. This matrix distinguishes friendships between the working class and each of the other class locations. If none of the coefficients for the dummy variables generated by this matrix are significant, then the likelihood of friendships between workers and other class locations is simply a function of the overall additive effects of crossing various combinations of the three exploitation boundaries we are considering.

A significant improvement in fit of Model (2) over Model (1) implies that the differential permeability of boundaries between the working class and the other class locations is not fully captured by the additive effects of the three underlying class-boundary variables, i.e interaction effects across specific class locations are also present. The WORKER variable also enables us to construct an overall ranking of the permeability of the boundaries between the working class and the other class locations by adding up, for each worker I nonworker friendship tie, the corresponding coefficients for the PROPERTY, AUTHORITY, SKILL and WORKER variables as indicated in Table 7.4. The individual coefficients in the equation for Model (2) are logs of odds ratios. The antilog of the sum of the coefficients corresponding to each cell thus gives the relative odds of a friendship tie occurring in that cell, given the constraints of Model (2).

Table 7.3 gives estimates of the coefficients for Model (2) for the three additive exploitation variables and the seven cross-class friendship ties involving the working class. The goodness of fit of Model (2) is a significant improvement over Model (1), indicating that there are significant friendship-tie-specific interactions between the working class and other class locations. With the exception of worker I manager and worker I supervisor friendships, friendships between workers and nonworkers are significantly less likely than would be predicted by the additive model. Furthermore, the coefficients for the worker I manager and worker I supervisor boundaries are both significantly *greater* than

Table 7.3.   *Coefficients for worker\nonworker boundary permeability: adults in the labor force in four countries*

Variable	Sample size defined as number of friendship ties Coefficient (s.e.)	Sample size defined as number of respondents Coefficient (s.e.)
Boundary-permeability coefficients		
PROPERTY	−0.95 (.11)***	−0.96 (.16)***
AUTHORITY	−0.40 (.06)***	−0.34 (.09)***
SKILL	−0.72 (.06)***	−0.67 (.10)***
Worker\nonworker ties:[a]		
Level 1[b] Worker|Employer	−0.17 (.08)*	0.20 (.12)
Level 2 Worker|Petty bourgeois	−0.30 (.07)***	−0.26 (.11)*
Level 3 Worker|Expert manager	−0.18 (.07)*	−0.23 (.11)*
Level 4 Worker|Manager	0.06 (.08)	−0.06 (.13)
Level 5 Worker|Supervisor	0.06 (.06)	0.07 (.09)
Level 6 Worker|Professional	−0.36 (.11)***	−0.38 (.16)*
Level 7 Worker|Skilled employee	−0.31 (.06)***	−0.33 (.09)***
Scaled deviance	337.2	126.11
Degrees of freedom	179	179
Improvement of scaled deviance over model (1)	32.0***	12.89*
Degrees of freedom	6	6

a. These coefficients indicate the difference between a given category of Worker|Nonworker ties and all friendships that do not cross the worker boundary (i.e. Worker|Worker and Nonworker|Nonworker ties).

b. "Level" refers to the categories in the design matrix for the WORKER variable in Figure 5.3.

those for any other categories, indicating that for workers the authority boundary is more permeable relative to other boundaries than it is for the labor force as a whole.

As was also indicated in the mobility permeability analysis, the results in Table 7.3 have an important conceptual implication for class-structure analysis. The presence of significant tie-specific interactions supports the view that the class structure cannot be understood simply as a sum of the three underlying exploitation dimensions. If there were

Table 7.4. *Rank ordering of boundary impermeability for friendship ties between workers and other class locations*

Cross-class boundary	Coefficients added to estimate overall permeability	Sum of coefficients[a]	Antilog of sum of coefficients	Relative to worker|employer friendship tie
1 Worker|Employer	PROPERTY + AUTHORITY + WORKER (level 1)[b]	−1.52	0.22	1.0
2 Worker|Expert manager	AUTHORITY + SKILL + WORKER (level 3)	−1.30	0.27	1.3
3 Worker|Professional	SKILL + WORKER (level 6)	−1.07	0.34	1.6
4 Worker|Manager	AUTHORITY + WORKER (level 4)	−0.34	0.71	3.2
5 Worker|Skilled employee	WORKER (level 7)	−0.31	0.74	3.4
6 Worker|Petty bourgeois	WORKER (level 2)	−0.30	0.74	3.4
7 Worker|Supervisor	WORKER (level 5)	0.06	1.06	4.9

a. Sample size is the number of friendship ties.

b. "Level" refers to the categories in the design matrix for the WORKER variable in Figure 5.3 and the coefficients reported in Table 7.3.

no tie-specific interactions, then the concept of "class structure," formed through the combination of the three "primitive terms," would simply be a heuristic convenience. Nothing would be lost by simply talking serially about the effects of property ownership, the effects of skill and the effects of authority, and ignoring the effects of specific locations in the class structure. "Location" gets its analytical bite from the synergetic consequences of the specific combinations of dimensions that generate a given location. To use a cliché, "the whole is greater than the sum of the parts,"[3] and the presence of tie-specific interactions captures this.

The additive and interaction terms in Model (2) generate the ranking of the likelihood of the various worker I nonworker friendships presented in Table 7.4. Of the seven boundaries, the WORKER I EMPLOYER boundary is the least permeable, while the WORKER I SUPERVISOR boundary is the most permeable: workers have nearly five times the odds of a friendship with a supervisor than with an employer. The second and third ranks in impermeability are the worker I expert manager and worker I professional boundaries. As defined in Model (2), both of these ties cross two "levels" of the skill dimension. The next three boundaries – worker I manager, worker I skilled employee, and worker I petty bourgeois – are of roughly equal permeability. In the structure of Model (2), the last two of these cross only one "level" of their respective exploitation dimension – worker I skilled employee crosses one level on skill and no levels on property or authority; worker I petty bourgeois crosses one level on property and no levels on authority or skill. Thus, worker I manager friendships, which cross *two* levels of the authority dimension (but cross no levels on the property or skill dimensions) are about as likely as friendships that cross only one level of the skill or property boundary. This affirms the relatively high permeability of the authority boundary. As in the previous results for mobility, the results for the worker I petty bourgeois boundary indicate that the salient issue for the property boundary is not self-employment as such, but capitalist property relations. The odds of friendship ties between workers and petty bourgeois are over three times greater than those between workers and employers.[4]

---

[3]   The same point can be made about the claim that the "class structure" as a whole has effects that cannot be reduced to the separate additive effects of the dimensions that constitute it.

[4]   Arguably, the relative permeability of the worker I petty bourgeois boundary has

Country interactions

Models (1) and (2) assume that the relative permeabilities of boundaries are the same in each of the four countries. The presence of intercountry differences in the permeability coefficients in Model (1) is tested by comparing the goodness of fit of Model (3) and Model (4) and by examining the patterns of within-country coefficients. These results are reported in Table 7.5.

In the global test for country interactions in Model (4), there is no statistically significant improvement in goodness of fit over Model (3), even when we use the number of friendship ties as the sample size.[5] Furthermore, a pairwise examination of all possible differences across countries in boundary coefficients (a total of eighteen pairwise tests) revealed no statistically significant differences. On the basis of such direct tests, therefore, one would conclude that the pattern of class-boundary permeability was relatively invariant across countries.

This cross-national invariance is confirmed by most of the patterns we observe when we look at the models separately within each country. Specifically, within all four countries, the permeability coefficients for the three class boundaries are significantly negative, and the authority boundary is significantly more permeable than either the property or skill boundary. And, in three of the four countries – the United States, Canada and Norway – the rank order of the relative permeabilities of the three boundaries is the same: property, skill, authority. Finally, while only in the United States is the property boundary significantly less permeable than the skill boundary, if we combine the data for Norway and Canada, thus reducing the standard error in our estimates of coefficients, then the difference between the property and the skill-boundary coefficients is significant at the .05 level on a one-tailed test for these countries as well.[6]

---

historically facilitated various forms of populism, which frequently involve political and ideological alliances between workers and small property owners, e.g. in the US in the late nineteenth century.

[5]   There is also no improvement in the fit of the models if we drop the $QI \times C$ terms from Model (4) and compare it directly with Model (1). However, Model (3) itself is a significant improvement in fit over Model (1), indicating that there are significant $QI \times C$ interactions. While class-boundary *permeability* does not vary significantly across countries, the likelihood of *within-class* friendships does.

[6]   Given that the purpose of the within-country analysis is to test whether or not the earlier results are confirmed within countries, a one-tailed test is arguably appropriate.

Table 7.5. *Cross-national interaction in permeability of class boundaries to friendships*

I. *Goodness-of-fit of different models (sample size = number of friendship ties)*

Model	d.f.	Scaled Deviance
Baseline model	188	783.9
Model (1): PROPERTY + AUTHORITY + SKILL	185	370.1
Model (2): Model (1) + WORKER	179	337.2
Model (3): Model (1) + QI x Country	161	318.7
Model (4): Model (3) + PROPERTY x C + AUTHORITY x C + SKILL x C	152	313.9
Model (4) vs. Model (3)	9	5.2

II. *Boundary-permeability coefficients within countries*

	US	Canada	Sweden	Norway
PROPERTY	-1.11 (.16)***	-1.06 (.19)***	-0.67 (.22)***	-1.03 (.15)***
AUTHORITY	-0.23 (.06)***	-0.33 (.08)***	-0.29 (.07)***	-0.35 (.06)***
SKILL	-0.72 (.09)***	-0.85 (.10)***	-0.81 (.10)***	-0.80 (.07)***

III. *Differences in permeability coefficients within countries*[a]

	US	Canada	Sweden	Norway	Canada & Norway
PROPERTY – AUTHORITY	0.83 (.15)***	0.73 (.18)***	0.42 (.21)*	0.68 (.15)***	0.70 (.11)***
SKILL – AUTHORITY	0.44 (.09)***	0.52 (.10)***	0.52 (.10)***	0.45 (.07)***	0.47 (.06)***
PROPERTY – SKILL	0.39 (.17)*	0.21 (.20)	-0.14 (.23)	0.23 (.16)	0.23 (.13)#

Significance levels (two-tailed test): # < .10 * p < .05 ** p < .01 *** p < .001

a. There were no statistically significant differences in permeability coefficients across countries.

These results are similar to those in the mobility analysis, except that in this case Canada seems more like Norway than the US. Also, as in the mobility analysis, the nominal pattern of coefficients in Sweden seems especially different from those in the US, since in Sweden the skill boundary is nominally (but not statistically significantly) less permeable than the property boundary. Unlike in the case of the mobility results, however, none of the tests of differences in coefficients between the United States and other countries are statistically significant, even when other countries are combined. As is often the case in comparative analyses, because the standard errors of interaction terms tend to be quite large, it is possible for there to appear striking descriptive differences in patterns of association across countries – as in the case of significant differences in the property- and skill-boundary coefficients for the United States but not for Sweden – and yet for the difference across countries in these coefficient differences not to be themselves statistically significant. Our general conclusion, therefore, is that these patterns are relatively invariant across the countries we are examining, with the probable exception of Sweden.

7.3 Conclusions

Overall, the results in this chapter indicate that, with the possible exception of Sweden, the property boundary is the most impermeable to the formation of friendships, followed by the skill boundary, with the authority boundary being the most permeable. This rank order is most sharply inconsistent with perspectives based on class interests, such as Dahrendorf's, which are built exclusively around the authority axis. Not only is authority the most permeable of the three boundaries in relative terms, it is also quite permeable in absolute terms.

What about the three other theoretical perspectives discussed in section 7.1? Marxist theory predicts that the property boundary should be the most impermeable, and this is supported by the analysis. The results for the skill and authority boundaries, however, are not entirely what most Marxists would expect: the skill boundary is less permeable and the authority boundary is more permeable than would be expected on the basis of a theory of exploitation, domination and common interests alone. While the Marxist concern with exploitation and class interests may be consistent with the finding that the skill boundary is less permeable than the authority boundary, Marxist class analysis would not expect the relative magnitude of these two permeability coefficients to be so sharply different.

The findings for the skill and authority boundaries, therefore, seem more consistent with the class habitus and opportunity structure perspectives. On the one hand, the relatively high impermeability of the skill boundary is consistent with theories of cultural capital, even if such theories tend to minimize the continuing importance of property as a basis for structuring class practices. On the other hand, the high relative permeability of the authority boundary is best predicted by the opportunity structure perspective on friendships. In many workplaces there are diverse opportunities for informal interaction between workers and supervisors, and even between workers and managers. This density of interactional possibilities, combined with relatively high levels of career mobility across authority boundaries compared to the property and expert boundaries, may account for the relatively high permeability of the authority boundary.

The analysis thus suggests that the causal mechanisms identified by theories of class interests (at least the Marxist variant), class habitus and opportunity structure probably all operate to create obstacles and opportunities for friendship formation across class boundaries. The result of the joint operation of these three clusters of causes is that the boundary Marxists predict to be the least permeable is indeed the least permeable. This might imply that the property-exploitation-interest mechanism is a more powerful structuring mechanism than are the class habitus or opportunity mechanisms. Such a conclusion, however, is vulnerable to criticism on two scores.[7] First, claims about the relative potency of causal processes are always vulnerable to measurement issues. Our conclusion about the relatively high permeability of the authority boundary might change if we adopted a more restrictive definition of authority, e.g. limiting "managers" to high-level execu-tives. Also, if we distinguished among professionals between highly credentialed professionals and other professionals, the skill boundary might become the "least" permeable. While such conjectured results could potentially be countered with a comparable respecification of the property-boundary, this would only reaffirm the sensitivity of claims about relative causal potency to measurement choices.[8] Second, even if

---

[7] For a general philosophical discussion of the problem of assessing the relative causal potency of different causes in a multicausal process, see Wright, Levine and Sober (1992).

[8] In a separate analysis of employers with more than ten employees (not reported

a more fine-grained inspection revealed that our core results were robust across alternative specifications of these boundaries, there is still the problem of ascribing this impermeability to "exploitation interests" rather than class habitus or opportunity structure. Employers certainly live different life-styles from most nonproperty owners, and the physical opportunities for informal interaction between most employees and employers are few. Therefore, while our data are consistent with the claim that property-based interests have stronger effects on friendship formation than either opportunity structure or class habitus, they cannot effectively refute counterclaims.

Methodological appendix

The friendship-ties matrix

Respondents were asked to think of the three people – friends or relatives, but not immediate family members – to whom they felt "personally closest." (I refer to these people as "friends" even though some of them are relatives. The sample size was too small to separately analyze relatives.) Respondents were then asked a series of questions about the jobs of each of these friends. The friends' class locations were coded using nearly the same criteria used for respondents, except for the authority dimension of class structure (see below). Friends not in the labor force were excluded from the analysis. As explained in Chapter 5, I then collapsed these class locations into eight categories.

Once all of the friends had been allocated to class locations, I then transformed the data so that friendship ties would be the unit of analysis. In the US sample, for example, 1,363 respondents provided data on at least one friend for a total of 3,114 friends. Thus we have a sample of 3,114 friendship ties, each tie characterized by two values – the class of the respondent and of the respondent's friend. The data analysis, then, was carried out on an 8 x 8 friendship-ties matrix.

Objections to the structure of the data

There are several possible objections to the structure of the data. First, the decision to exclude friends who are not in the labor force could bias

here) we found that the likelihood of these employers having friendships with employees was significantly lower than for smaller employers.

our results if our primary interest was a comprehensive social structural analysis of friendship patterns. However, because our interest is
in certain properties of the class structure – namely, the differential
permeability of class boundaries – the relevant data are friendship ties
that link people occupying locations in that class structure. In any
event, the respondents' data are from a labor force sample in most
countries and introducing friends from outside the labor force (housewives, unemployed, retirees) into the analysis would create an asymmetry in the matrices.

Second, restricting the analysis to *three* friends rather than a comprehensive list of friends may introduce distortions in the results. Holland
and Leinhardt (1973) have argued that this kind of fixed-choice
procedure for studying friendship patterns may introduce severe
measurement error in sociometry because it forces people with more
friends than the fixed number to arbitrarily omit some friends and
forces people with fewer than the fixed number to arbitrarily include
some nonfriends. I believe this problem is unlikely to seriously distort
the results. Unlike the sociometric work reported by Holland and
Leinhardt, we are not studying within-group sociograms such as the
patterns of friendships among children in a classroom. In examining
social ties across class boundaries, we are not interested in the patterns
of reciprocity, closure, asymmetry, etc. among a particular group of
individuals, but rather the likelihood of close friendships among
individuals with particular class attributes. It is not clear that the kinds
of distortions Holland and Leinhardt reported in the shape of sociograms apply to our analytical context.[9]

Finally, it could be objected that by looking at "close" friends we are
ignoring the important problem of the "strength of weak ties" (Granovetter 1973). It is possible that certain class boundaries are more
permeable by casual friendships than by intimate interpersonal relations. Restricting attention to close friends may understate the overall
permeability of boundaries to interpersonal relations. However, ours
is not a comprehensive analysis of all dimensions of the permeability
of boundaries. Such an analysis would include marriage patterns,

---

[9] Furthermore, even in their own analytical context Holland and Leinhardt (1973)
stated that "a gross structural feature like sex-cleavage in children's groups will not
be affected by fixed-choice errors if there are more children of both sexes than
allowed choices..." (p. 103). Our analysis of class-boundary permeability resembles
an analysis of a structural feature like sex-cleavage more than it resembles the fine-
grained analysis of sociometric terms.

mobility, neighborhood interactions, and participation in voluntary associations as well as casual friendships. Our analysis is a reasonable first step in examining one particular type of social interaction that crosses class boundaries – intimate friendships – and for this it is appropriate to restrict the data to the "three people with whom one is personally closest."

The problem of asymmetric friendships

As in the case of the mobility analysis, I treat the friendship ties matrix symmetrically. That is, I assume that the probability of a worker respondent reporting having a manager friend is the same as the probability of a manager respondent reporting having a worker friend. There are various reasons why one might expect asymmetrical responses. In particular, if there are status issues involved in reporting having "friends in high places," then one would predict that workers are more likely to claim that they have friends who are experts, managers or capitalists than are people in these categories likely to claim that they have friends who are workers. This distortion could be either because of incorrect attributions of job characteristics to a real friend of the respondent, or incorrect claims that a particular person is in fact a friend. It is also possible, of course, that there are real asymmetries in friendship patterns: it could be the case that workers actually are more likely to have manager friends than vice versa, since it need not be the case that all friendships are fully bilateral.[10]

To test whether the data roughly fit this assumption, I conducted a test of global asymmetries around the diagonal of the friendship matrix by comparing the goodness of fit for the quasi-independence model (all off-diagonal cells are treated as a single category while each cell on the diagonal is differentiated) with a model that differentiates

---

[10] Nonreciprocity in friendships is especially possible given the restriction of the questionnaire to three closest friends. Imagine the following hypothetical situation:

1   All mangers have six friends, three of whom they consider really close friendships and three of whom they consider somewhat less intimate.

2   All workers also have six friends, three of whom they consider really close friendships and three of whom they consider somewhat less intimate.

3   The three closest friends reported by both managers and by workers are all managers.

In such a configuration, there would be a deep asymmetry in the data, since the worker respondents would report 100% of their friends were managers whereas the manager respondents would report 0% of their friends were workers.

cells above the diagonal from cells below the diagonal. The model that differentiated the off-diagonal cells in this way did not significantly improve the fit and thus the hypothesis that the data were roughly symmetrical above and below the diagonal could not be rejected.

The problem of sample size

The number of friendship ties is obviously considerably larger than the number of respondents in the original sample – the total number of respondents for whom we have appropriate data in the four countries is 4,896, whereas the number of friendship ties is 11,782. It is not obvious what sample size should be used in the calculation of standard errors for the various coefficients in our models. The most conservative choice is to use the number of original respondents. This, however, treats the data as if we had a sample of only one friend per respondent and would therefore understate our confidence in whatever patterns we observe. The least conservative choice is to treat the number of friendship ties as the sample size. However, because these friendship ties are not independent of each other, they are not a random sample of ties. I do not know of any definitive statistical rationale for deciding where in this range to set the sample size. I therefore report results using both sample sizes. Because there are slightly different numbers of friends per respondent in different countries, the actual coefficients vary slightly in the analyses using the two different sample size figures.

Distinguishing supervisors from managers for friends' class locations

The authority dimension of class relations poses a problem because there is more refined data for respondents than for their friends. Respondents are asked: "Which of the following best describes the position which you hold within the business or organization in which you work? Would it be a managerial position, a supervisory position or a nonmanagement position?" Those in a nonmanagement position are classified as "nonmanagers." To distinguish managers from supervisors, I then utilize the detailed information about participation in decisionmaking, supervisory responsibilities, as well as formal position in the managerial hierarchy as discussed in Chapter 2. A respondent is defined as a "manager" if he/she participates directly in making workplace policy decisions *and* is *either* in a position that is formally called a "managerial" position (as opposed to a supervisory position) *or* has the power to impose sanctions on subordinates. All others who said they were in managerial or supervisory positions are classified as "supervisors."

For friends, respondents were asked: "Does [this friend] occupy a management or supervisor position at the place where he/she works?" A "no" response was classified as "nonmanager." Unfortunately, the data on friends lacked the information needed to distinguish managers from supervisors. Because the classification of individuals along these three dimensions was used to create the eight class locations for the subsequent friendship-ties matrix and because we wanted a symmetrical 8×8 matrix, a strategy was needed to estimate the number of managers and supervisors among friends for each category of the respondents class location. Since in the friendship-tie models we do not differentiate managers from supervisors among *experts* for either respondents or friends (because of sample size constraints), I only had to make these estimates for nonexpert friends.

The estimation procedure I adopted assumes that the friendship-tie matrix is roughly symmetrical around the diagonal. For each class location of *friends*, we know the ratio of nonexpert managers to nonexpert supervisors among *respondents*. Each such ratio is then used for the corresponding respondent class location to divide the undifferentiated nonexpert managers and supervisors among friends into separate components. For example, the ratio of nonexpert managers to nonexpert supervisors among the friends of respondent workers, is assumed to be the same as the known ratio of nonexpert-manager respondents with worker friends to nonexpert-supervisor respondents with worker friends. This enables us to estimate the frequency of nonexpert supervisor friends of respondent workers and nonexpert-manager friends of respondent workers. In this way the full 8×8 friendship-tie matrix was constructed.

8 Cross-class families

The third form of class-boundary permeability we will explore occurs when husbands and wives in dual-earner families occupy jobs in different classes. As already noted in the discussion of class mobility for women in Chapter 6, there is considerable controversy over how best to conceptualize such "cross-class families." Should the class character of the family in such cases be viewed as in some sense internally heterogeneous, or should the class of the family be identified strictly with the class of the principal breadwinner? If individuals are treated as the central units of analysis in class structures, then such families clearly have a mixed class character and constitute the sites of class-boundary permeability. If the family is the fundamental unit of class analysis and all members of a family are treated as necessarily having the same family-class, then it is less clear that this is properly an example of boundary permeability. What looks superficially like an instance of a *cross*-class family when a secretary is married to a capitalist would not really constitute an instance of permeability, since the female secretary would really be "in" the capitalist class by virtue of being the wife in a capitalist class family.

We will defer until Chapter 10 a detailed examination of the various arguments in the debate over how to understand the class character of families. In this chapter we will take individuals as the unit of analysis and examine the extent to which marriage ties in two-earner households cross specific class boundaries.

8.1 Theoretical issues

The patterns of homogeneity and heterogeneity of class compositions within families is the result of three interconnected processes:

1 The process of what sociologists call "assortative mating" by which men and women from different class origins and occupying different job-classes before marriage make marriage choices in the first place. To the extent that class origins affect class destinations as well as marriage partners, the class composition of families will be affected by assortative mating.

2 The process within marriages which determine if and when the wife enters the labor force. Unless one regards the role of "housewife" as having a distinctive class character in its own right, the problem of cross-class families is only generated when wives enter the labor force. If labor force participation rates of wives vary significantly by the class of husbands, then this could affect the patterns of cross-class families among two-earner households.

3 The processes which determine the job-class occupied by husbands and wives given their class origins and the decisions about labor force participation.

With the available data we cannot even begin to sort out the separate contributions of these three processes. What we can do, in a manner parallel to the exploration of permeability of class boundaries to friendships and mobility, is map out the static patterns of class-boundary permeability within families that result from the interactions of assortative mating, labor force participation decisions and job acquisition.

I do not have any predictions about these patterns within families which reflect the distinctive character of processes of family formation and decisionmaking. There may be reasons to believe, for example, that class plays a different role in "marriage markets" than in friendship formation, especially for propertied classes where issues of inheritance of wealth are salient. Given the sex segregation of many workplaces, worksites may be a less important venue for the selection of potential marriages partners than of friendships, and this could have implications for the patterns of class-boundary permeability in cross-class families. While such complexities may exist, I do not have a deep enough understanding of the process of family formation to generate nuanced hypotheses. Furthermore, the existing sociological literature is also not particularly helpful in this regard. While there is a literature on the ways in which socio-economic background, race, religion and education affect assortative mating (the first process above), there is very little systematic quantitative research on the class composition of the resulting families, and none which explicitly explores the permeability of class boundaries within dual-earner families.[1] It is therefore not possible to derive a set of contrasting predictions about class-boundary permeability within families directly from the existing literature.

By default, therefore, I will simply apply the same models and predictions of Chapters 6 and 7 to the study of cross-class families. That is, I will take the core predictions from a Marxist class analysis to be that the property boundary will be the least permeable to cross-class families, whereas a class analysis that emphasizes issues of cultural capital would predict that the skill boundary would be the least permeable.

8.2 Results

Patterns of cross-class families

Before looking at our statistical models of class-boundary permeability for cross-class families, it will be useful to get some sense of the overall distribution of cross-class families. Figure 8.1 presents the distribution of people within dual-earner marriages into families of different class compositions in the four countries we are examining. The details of how this table was constructed are given in the methodological appendix. The diagonal cells in these matrices represent families which are homogeneous in terms of class composition. The unshaded cells in the matrices constitute families within which the spouses occupy class locations that span two levels on at least one of the three dimensions of the class-structure typology. The lightly shaded cells are cases in which there is marginal heterogeneity of class composition.

Several things are worth noting in these tables. First of all, in all of these countries most of the possible forms of cross-class families exist. In all countries there are instances of employer husbands and working-class wives, and except for the case of Sweden, there are even employer wives married to husbands in working-class jobs.

---

[1] The closest piece of research to that reported in this chapter is Hout's (1982) study of the association of occupational statuses of husbands and wives in two-earner families, but his study looks strictly an occupational status, not class. There is some recent literature on cross-class families, but mostly these studies simply document the proportion of families within which husbands and wives are in jobs of different classes; no effort at fine-grained modeling of the class composition of families is made. For a good example see McRae (1986).

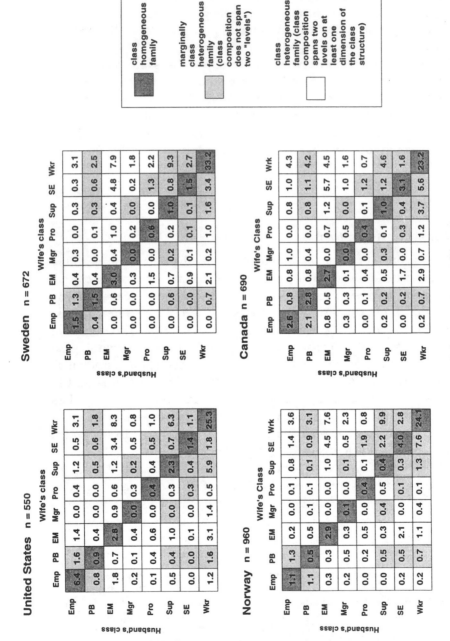

Emp = employers; PB = petty bourgeoisie; EM = expert managers; Mgr = managers;
Sup = supervisors; Pro = professionals; SE = skilled employees; Wkr = workers

Figure 8.1 Class composition of dual-earner families

Second, cross-class families are not a rare occurrence. In roughly 30–35% of dual-earner families in these four countries, the husbands and wives occupy jobs in clearly different class locations. Roughly half of these families consists of one spouse in the working class and one who is an employer, an expert manager, a manager or a professional. Since in the early 1980s when these data were gathered roughly 40% of all people lived in dual-earner households in these countries, this means that about 12% or so of the population live in cross-class families.[2] While it is still the case that most people live in class-homogeneous households, cross-class families are a reality in developed capitalism.

Third, as would be expected, it is much more common in cross-class families for the husband to be in a more privileged class location than the wife. In the United States, for example, about 10% of all dual-earner marriages consist of a manager or professional husband and a working-class wife, but only 5% consist of a manager or professional wife and a working-class husband. In Sweden and Norway this contrast is even greater: 10–12% of dual-earner households have manager/professional husbands and worker wives, but only 2–3% have manager/professional wives and working-class husbands. Still, even though this expected gender difference occurs, there are a significant number of households, especially in the United States and Canada, in which the wife's job is in a more privileged class location than is the husband's.

The relative permeability of the three class boundaries

Table 8.1 presents the results for the additive model without country interactions (Model (1)). The coefficients for all three class boundaries indicate some degree of impermeability. The property boundary is clearly the least permeable and the authority boundary the most permeable for cross-class marriages. Taking the antilogs of the coefficients indicates that the odds of a cross-class family across the property boundary is less than one-sixth the odds of one across the authority boundary and one-third the odds of one across the skill boundary. These results are strongly consistent with expectations of Marxist class analysis.

[2] Non dual-earner households include households headed by single adults, households in which no one is in the labor force and families with a single person in the labor force.

Table 8.1. *Permeability of class boundaries to cross-class families in dual-earner households*

Variable	Coefficient (s.e.)	Antilog
Boundary-crossing coefficients[a]		
PROPERTY	-1.96 (.18)***	.14
AUTHORITY	-0.17 (.09)	.85
SKILL	-0.86 (.09)***	.42
Scaled deviance (185 d.f.)	295.63	
Baseline scaled deviance (186 d.f.)[b]	500.29	
Overall improvement in fit (3d.f.)	204.66	
Differences in boundary-crossing coefficients		
PROPERTY − AUTHORITY	-1.79 (.18)***	
SKILL − AUTHORITY	-0.70 (.10)***	
PROPERTY − SKILL	-1.09 (.19)**	

Significance levels (two-tailed tests): * p < .05   ** p < .01   *** p < .001

a. The coefficients are calculated from model (1): log f_{ijk} = Country + H-Class + W-Class + QI + Country x H-Class + Country x W-Class + PROPERTY + AUTHORITY + SKILL, where H-Class is the husband's class and W-Class is the wife's class.

b. The baseline model is log f_{ijk} = Country + H-Class + W-Class + QI + Country x H-Class + Country x W-Class

The relative permeability of boundaries between working-class and nonworking-class locations

As in the prior analysis of mobility and friendships, the WORKER interaction matrix differentiates each of the cross-class family types involving the working class. A significant improvement in the fit of the equation when this variable is added (Model (2) compared to Model (1)) indicates that the degree of permeability of class boundaries between the working class and other class locations is significantly different from what would be predicted from the simple additive model. If the WORKER interaction is significant, then we can use the coefficients from this model to rank the differential locational permeability between the working class and the other seven class locations.

Table 8.2 presents the results for Model (2). The WORKER interaction

Table 8.2. *Permeability of class boundaries within dual-earner families which cross the working-class boundary*

Variable	Coefficient (s.e.)
PROPERTY	−1.79 (.22)***
AUTHORITY	−0.23 (.13)
SKILL	−0.75 (.14)***

Cross-class families across the working-class boundary:[a]

Level 1[b]	Worker|Employer	−0.31 (.17)
Level 2	Worker|Petty bourgeois	−0.41 (.15)**
Level 3	Worker|Expert manager	−0.21 (.16)
Level 4	Worker|Manager	−0.27 (.20)
Level 5	Worker|Supervisor	0.25 (.11)*
Level 6	Worker|Professional	−0.43 (.22)*
Level 7	Worker|Skilled employee	−0.37 (.11)***
Scaled deviance (179 d.f.)		273.49
Improvement over model (1)		22.14***
Degree of freedom		6

Significance levels (one-tailed tests): * $p < .05$ ** $p < .01$ *** $p < .001$

a. Worker|Non-worker family-class composition is measured by a series of dummy variables. The coefficients indicate the difference between a given category of Worker|Non-worker family and a family composition that does not span the worker boundary (Worker|Worker and Non-worker|Non-worker family-class composition). See Figure 5.3 for definition of this variable.

b. "Level" refers to the categories in the design matrix for the WORKER variable in Figure 5.3.

variable significantly improves the fit of the model. As in the previous analyses, therefore, the simple additive model does not fully capture the class-boundary permeability involving the working class. Also as in the analyses of friendships and mobility, when we aggregate the additive and interactive coefficients in Table 8.3, the odds of a worker|employer cross-class family are much lower than any other combination. The odds ratio for a worker|expert-manager family is three times greater than for a worker|employer family, for a worker|petty bourgeois family almost seven times greater, and for a worker|supervisor family thirteen times greater. These results again confirm the relatively high permeability of the authority boundary, the impermeability of the property boundary, and the fact that the salient aspect of the property boundary is not self-employment as such, but capitalist class relations.

Country interactions

Table 8.4 presents the results for tests of cross-national variations in patterns of permeability. There is very little indication in these results that the patterns of permeability of class boundaries within dual-earner families vary significantly across these countries. In the global test for country interactions, Model (4) is not a significant improvement over Model (3). Furthermore, even when we look at contrasts between pairs of countries or groups of countries, there are no significant differences at all between any of the coefficients.[3] While there are a number of nominal differences between the countries which might turn out to be significant if we had larger samples – the coefficient for skill seems smaller (i.e. less negative) in the US and the coefficient for property seems somewhat larger in Sweden – nevertheless, with the present data none of these approaches the conventional levels of statistical significance. We can thus conclude that the patterns of permeability of class boundaries within cross-class families appear relatively invariant across countries.

8.3 Comparing the three forms of class-boundary permeability

Figure 8.2 compares the odds (the antilogs of the permeability co-efficients) for the three aspects of class-boundary permeability we have been exploring. Considering how much friendships, family structure and mobility differ as social phenomena, the patterns of boundary permeability within countries are quite similar across these three social phenomena.[4] In all four countries, the authority boundary is the most permeable for all three of these social phenomena, although in the United States the authority and skill boundaries are not significantly different for cross-class families. In the United States, Canada and Norway, the rank order of permeability is the same for each of the

---

[3] The only instance where there is a nominal difference across countries in the patterns of coefficients is that in the United States the skill and authority coefficients are not significantly different, whereas they are in the other three countries. This difference between the US and the other countries, however, is not itself statistically significant.

[4] It is problematic to directly compare the magnitudes of these coefficients across the three phenomena since the samples differ. For mobility, the sample is restricted to men; for marriages, the sample was restricted to men and women in dual-earner households; and for friendships, the sample includes all adult men and women in the labor force.

Table 8.3. *Rank ordering of boundary-impermeability for the working class boundary in dual-earner families*

Cross-class boundary	Coefficients added to get overall permeability	Sum of coefficients	Antilog of sum of coefficients	Relative to worker|employer mobility
1 Worker|Employer	PROPERTY + AUTHORITY + WORKER (level 1)[a]	-2.33	0.10	1.00
2 Worker|Expert manager	AUTHORITY + SKILL + WORKER (level 3)	-1.18	0.31	3.18
3 Worker|Professional	SKILL + WORKER (level 6)	-1.17	0.31	3.19
4 Worker|Manager	AUTHORITY + WORKER (level 4)	-0.50	0.61	6.26
5 Worker|Petty bourgeois	WORKER (level 2)	-0.41	0.67	6.87
6 Worker|Skilled employee	WORKER (level 7)	-0.37	0.69	7.14
7 Worker|Supervisor	WORKER (level 5)	0.25	1.28	13.18

a. "Level" refers to the categories in the design matrix for the WORKER variable in Figure 5.3 and the coefficients in Figure 8.2.

Table 8.4. *Cross-national interactions in permeability of class boundaries to cross-class families*

I. Goodness-of-fit of different models

Model	d.f.	L^2
Baseline model	188	500.29
Model (1): PROPERTY + AUTHORITY + SKILL	185	295.63
Model (2): Model (1) + WORKER	179	273.49
Model (3): Model (1) + QI x Country	161	260.94
Model (4): Model (3) + PROPERTY x C + AUTHORITY x C + SKILL x C	152	249.88
Model (4) vs. Model (3)	9	11.06

II. Boundary-permeability coefficients within countries

	United States	Canada	Sweden	Norway
PROPERTY	-1.55 (.38)***	-1.82 (.34)***	-2.68 (.45)*	-2.01 (.30)***
AUTHORITY	-0.26 (.18)	-0.14 (.16)	-0.22 (.22)*	.00 (.17)
SKILL	-0.52 (.21)*	-0.92 (.18)***	-1.01 (.18)***	-.91 (.15)***

III. Differences between permeability coefficients within countries[a]

	United States	Canada	Sweden	Norway
PROPERTY – AUTHORITY	-1.29 (.36)***	-1.68 (.31)***	-2.46 (.46)***	-2.01 (.27)***
SKILL – AUTHORITY	-0.26 (.22)	-0.78 (.16)***	-0.79 (.22)***	-.91 (.15)***
PROPERTY – SKILL	-1.03 (.42)*	-0.90 (.36)*	-1.67 (.47)***	-1.11 (.31)***

Significance levels: * p < .05   ** p < .01   *** p < .001

a. There were no statistically significant differences in coefficients between countries.

three phenomena, although there are a few cases in which the coefficients for the property and skill boundaries do not differ significantly within boundaries. Only Sweden exhibits clear differences in the basic patterns for the property boundary across the three phenomena: the property boundary is much less permeable than the skill boundary for the class composition of marriages, while the two boundaries do not differ significantly for mobility or friendships. With the exception of Sweden, therefore, the patterns of boundary permeability are rather consistent across these qualitatively different social phenomena.

Taken together, these results support several general conclusions. First, they lend support to the general expectation in Marxist class analysis that the property dimension of the class structure remains the most fundamental in capitalist societies. While class structures in capitalism cannot adequately be described simply in terms of relationship to the means of production, nevertheless the property boundary appears to be the most rigid. What is more, this relative impermeability of the property boundary is not generated by the division between the self-employed and employees, but rather by capitalist property relations. As the analysis of the locational permeability between the working class and other class locations demonstrates in all three analyses, the boundary between the working class and employers is the least permeable of all boundaries, and much less permeable than the boundary between workers and the petty bourgeoisie.

Second, with the exception of some of the results for Sweden, the cross-national variations in the patterns of class-boundary permeability are quite muted. While in the case of the mobility results, there was some basis for distinguishing the patterns in the social democratic Nordic countries from the more purely capitalistic North America, nevertheless these differences constitute variations on a theme rather than completely different patterns. This suggests that the relative permeability of different class boundaries is shaped more by properties of the class structure itself than by cultural or political processes.

Finally, the results from the analysis of the locational permeability between the working class and other class locations support the view that the class structure is not simply the "sum" of its underlying dimensions. The probabilities that friendships, biographies and marri-

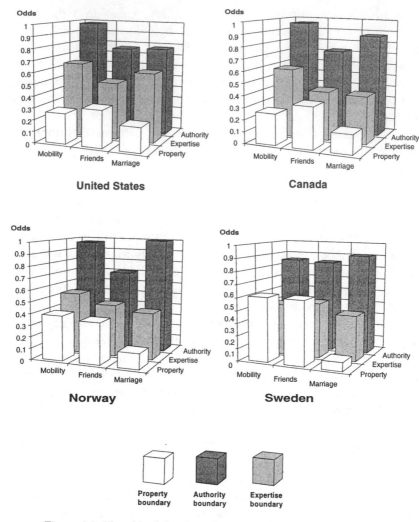

Figure 8.2 *The odds of class-boundary permeability to mobility, friendships and cross-class families in the United States, Canada, Norway and Sweden*

ages cross specific class boundaries are the result of the interactions among these dimensions, not simply their separate effects. If this interpretation of the results is correct, then the concept of "class structure" should not simply be seen as a heuristic convenience for summarizing the three separate underlying dimensions.

Methodological appendix

The family-class composition matrix

As in the case of the analysis of friendships, there are more refined data for respondents than for their spouses. Specifically, for respondents, but not their spouses, we can distinguish mere supervisors from proper managers. This means, following the coding scheme discussed in chapter 5, that we have eight class categories for respondents but only seven for their spouses. However, as in the case of the friendship analysis, it is possible in the family-class composition data to make plausible estimates of the full 8 x 8 husband-by-wife family-class composition matrix. We begin by constructing separate 8 x 7 respondent-by-spouse matrices for the female and male respondents. Among our female respondents we therefore can distinguish managers from supervisors within every class category of their husbands. Similarly, among our male respondents we can distinguish managers from supervisors within every class category of their wives. On the basis of these separate matrices, therefore, we can estimate the ratio of manager:supervisor husbands within every class category of wives and manager:supervisor wives within every class category of husbands. We then use these ratios to construct a symmetrical 8 x 8 family-class composition matrix.[5]

Housewives

A fully developed analysis of the class composition of households would include spouses who are not in the paid labor force. The salience of the existence of cross-class families in the class structure depends not only on the frequency of various combinations of job-classes of husbands and wives, but on the frequency of dual-earner families. If only 10% of households had two earners, then even if it were the case that in most of these families husbands and wives were in different job-classes, this would not profoundly affect the class structure as a

---

[5] There is one complication with this procedure: we cannot use this procedure to make estimates of the diagonal cells – the manager-wife/manager-husband cell and the supervisor-wife/supervisor-husband cell. For these cases we simply assume that the ratio of manager:supervisor respondents within the combined manager-supervisor spouse category is the same as in the separate supervisor and manager categories.

whole. Ideally, then, we would want to map the class character of all households – those of single persons, families with one earner, dual-earner families, and families with no one in the labor force (including retirees, those on welfare, etc.) – and then examine the class distributions of these different kinds of families. The specific investigation of class-boundary permeability could then control for the distribution of family forms.

The data in this study do not allow for such an analysis since the sample in most of the countries is restricted to people in the labor force. This means that none of our respondents are housewives, retirees, on welfare, etc., and thus we cannot construct an adequate estimate of the class distribution of all households. As a result, the analysis is limited to people in dual-earner families.

Part III

Class and gender

9 Conceptualizing the interaction of class and gender

9.1 The debate over class primacy

In many ways the most sustained challenge to class analysis as a central axis of critical social theory in recent years has come from feminists. Class analysts, especially in the Marxist tradition, have often implied that class was a "more important" or "more fundamental" dimension of social structure than gender.[1] While such claims to explanatory primacy have rarely been explicitly defended, the relative inattention to gender in the Marxist tradition is taken by many commentators as a *de facto* denigration of gender as a significant causal factor.

To some extent this suggestion that class is "more important" than gender is simply a by-product of a specific set of theoretical preoccupations. To focus on class as a causal mechanism in social explanations implies bracketing other concerns. As explained in Chapter 1, class analysis is an "independent variable" specialty, and of necessity this means focussing on class and its ramifications and giving relatively less attention to other causal factors. This does not absolve class analysts from the criticism of sometimes overstating the explanatory power of class for certain problems, but it does imply that the sheer fact of focussing on class and its effects is not a legitimate basis for indicting class analysis.

There are times, however, when the claim that class (or closely associated concepts like "mode of production" or "economic struc-

---

[1] The idea that in a multicausal system one factor is "more important" than another is fraught with ambiguities and is very difficult to pin down. For an extended discussion of the problem of causal primacy, see Wright, Levine and Sober (1993: ch. 7).

ture") is "more important" than other factors is a substantive thesis, not a heuristic device. Classical historical materialism is the most elaborated instance of such an argument. As G. A. Cohen (1978) has forcefully demonstrated, the part of historical materialism that is built around the base/superstructure metaphor ascribes explanatory primacy to class through the use of functional explanations: the base (the economic structure conceptualized in class terms) "functionally explains" the superstructure. What does this mean? It means that superstructural phenomena take the form that they do because this form helps to reproduce the existing economic structure. This is quite akin to functional explanations in biology where a given trait of an animal is functionally explained by its effects in helping the animal survive and reproduce. Why are the bones in the wings of birds hollow? Because this helps them to fly. The beneficial effect of hollowness (lighter wings) explains the fact of hollowness. In the social case, the functional explanation embodied in historical materialism means that various social institutions – certain features of the state, certain aspects of ideology, certain kinds of laws and so forth – are explained by the fact that they generate effects which help reproduce the economic structure.[2] Since the economic structure is itself composed of social relations of production which collectively define the class structure, this is a form of class primacy.

At first glance it might seem as though classical historical materialism makes extraordinarily strong and encompassing claims about the centrality of class. But as G. A. Cohen (1988: ch. 9) has also argued, even classical historical materialism does not make the grandiose claim that class is the most important cause of *everything* social. Historical materialism is not a theory of all social phenomena, but only of a specific set of explananda – the historical trajectory of economic structures and their accompanying superstructures.[3] The super-

---

[2] It is important to note that in this kind of functional explanation there is no suggestion that the superstructure is "epiphenomenal" – a mere reflection of the base that has no consequences in its own right. To say that X functionally explains Y implies that Y has significant effects on X. If it is true that the class structure of capitalism functionally explains the form of the state, then this implies that the state must have significant consequences for reproducing the class structure. If the state had no consequences there would be no point to a functional explanation.

[3] There are Marxists, particularly those working within a strongly Hegelian tradition, who insist that Marxist concepts and theory do attempt to explain everything. Shelton and Agger (1993: 36), for example, write, "Marxism is *not* simply a theory of class but a theory of everything, including women." While I do not think that the aspiration for such a totalizing theoretical project should be rejected *a priori*, in

structure, in these terms, is not defined as all social relations and institutions that are not part of the economic base. Rather, the superstructure is limited to those noneconomic social phenomena which have effects on the reproduction of the base; these are the phenomena which are candidates for functional explanations of the sort historical materialism defends. What Cohen aptly calls "restrictive historical materialism" is agnostic about the relative explanatory importance of class for various phenomena which are not part of the economic structure or the superstructure, and this would potentially include many cultural phenomena and possibly significant aspects of gender relations.[4]

The kind of functionalist reasoning in historical materialism has played an important role in Marxist analyses of gender relations. Engels' (1968 [1884]) famous discussion of the origins of male domination, for example, explains the subordination of women in terms of its effects on stabilizing the inheritance of private property. This is an explanation of gender relations in terms of the functional requirements of maintaining a system of private property. In more recent discussions, the functional explanations have shifted to the beneficial effects of gender oppression for capital accumulation.[5] For example, a number of contributors to the "domestic labor debate" of the 1970s (e.g. Gardiner 1975; Secombe 1974) argued that the subordination of women is rooted in the sexual division of labor in the household, and this in turn is to be explained by the fact that the unpaid domestic labor of women raises the rate of profit by lowering the costs of

---

practice Marxism has not been successful in accomplishing this ambition, and the prospects for doing so are not very promising.

4   The contrast to "restrictive" historical materialism is "inclusive" historical materialism, in which the superstructure is defined as everything that is not in the base. Cohen shows that inclusive historical materialism is wildly implausible. Probably no one who really thought systematically about the issues seriously ever really held it.

5   These arguments do not necessarily use the explicit language of functional explanation. Thus, for example, Gardiner (1975: 52) discusses domestic labor in terms of the "essential although changing role" it plays. She asks the question, "Why has domestic labour been maintained?" and answers it by saying: "capitalism developed out of feudalism through workers becoming dependent on the wage system, but has never provided totally for workers' needs through commodity production, instead retaining domestic labor to carry out an important part of the reproduction and maintenance of labor power." The suggestion here is that the explanation for the maintenance of unpaid domestic labor (and the gender relations associated with this labor) is the role played by this labor for capitalism. The word "role" in this context implies a functional explanation.

reproducing labor power (since part of the consumption of workers takes the form of unpaid services of housewives). Others (e.g. Zaretsky 1976) have argued that the central basis for women's oppression in capitalism lies in the ways the gender division of labor helps to reproduce capitalist ideology by strengthening a privatized, consumption-centered vision of family life. In all of these instances, class is accorded explanatory primacy through the use of functional explanations.

Relatively few class analysts, even those still explicitly identifying with the Marxist tradition, strictly adhere to the tenets of classical historical materialism any longer. Virtually no one defends strong functionalist versions of the base/superstructure image of society, even for the specific task of explaining historical trajectories of economic structures. Marxist class analysis is now generally closer to what might be loosely termed "sociological materialism," in which class, because of its linkage to exploitation and the control of economic resources, has a presumptive importance for a broad range of social problems, but is not invariably viewed as the most important determinant. While it remains the case that Marxists generally do try to place class analysis in an historical context, this usually has at best a tenuous relation to a materialist theory of the overall trajectory of human history as such. In practice, then, to be "historical" has generally come to mean "to be historically specific," rather than "to be embedded in a theory *of* history."[6] As a result, the debate over what was once called "class reductionism" or "economic determinism" has waned considerably in recent years.

If one accepts this way of understanding the explanatory project of class analysis, then the central task is to sort out for specific explananda the specific causal interactions between class and gender. Class may indeed turn out to be "more important" than gender for certain problems, but equally, gender may be more important than class for others. Advances in the class analysis of gender *and* the gender analysis of class depend upon research that will clarify these interactions.

9.2 Forms of interconnection of class and gender

As a preliminary task to empirical investigations of class and gender, it is useful to lay out a conceptual menu of the various ways that class

---

[6] For a discussion of the slide from historical materialism toward sociological materialism, see Wright, Levine and Sober (1992: ch. 5).

and gender might be interconnected. This list is not meant to be exhaustive, and it certainly does not constitute a *theory* of class and gender. Rather, it is an agenda of issues that need to be considered within empirical research and theory construction.

Gender as a form of class relations

While the concepts of class and gender are analytically distinct, there are empirical situations in which gender relations themselves are a form of class relation (or, equivalently, that class relations are themselves directly organized through gender relations). Frederick Engels (1968 [1884]: 503), in his classic essay on the family and private property, formulates the relationship between class and gender in early civilizations this way: "The first class antagonism which appears in history coincides with the development of the antagonism between man and woman in monogamian marriage, and the first class oppression with that of the female sex by the male." Gerda Lerner (1986) elaborates a rather different argument about the confluence of class and gender in early civilizations. She argues that one of the earliest forms of male domination consisted of men effectively *owning* women, and by virtue of this appropriating the surplus produced by women. The most important form of this surplus was new people – children – who were a valuable resource in early agrarian civilizations. Control over the capacity of women to produce new labor power was thus a pivotal form of property relations. If this account is correct, then this would constitute a specific form of gendered slavery in which gender and class are melded into a single relation.[7]

Gender relations and class relations as reciprocally affecting each other

Certain kinds of class positions may exist only by virtue of the fact that specific forms of gender relations are present. The classic example is domestic services: gender relations play a crucial role in making possible maid and childcare services (Glenn 1992). It is not just that gender sorts people into these jobs; if gender relations were dramatically more egalitarian, the jobs themselves might not exist. The availability of single, unmarried farm girls in nineteenth-century New

---

[7] This would only strictly be true if it were the case that all women were slaves, which does not seem to be the case in the historical examples cited by Gerda Lerner. The dystopia portrayed by Margaret Atwood (1987) in *A Handmaid's Tale* comes closer to a society within which class and gender are fused into a single relation.

England who were not needed on the farm and who were not in line to inherit the farm was important for the development of the textile industry and the accompanying emergence of the early industrial working class. In many parts of the third world, gender plays a critical role in making available a supply of cheap vulnerable labor employed in various kinds of manufacturing. Again, it is not just that gender distributes people into an independently created set of class positions; the structure of gender relations helps to explain why jobs with particular characteristics are available.

Equally, class relations can have an impact on gender. The physical demands of many blue-collar, industrial working-class jobs put a premium on toughness, which in turn may help to reinforce a macho gender culture among working-class men. The competitive, high pressure career demands of many managerial and professional occupations help to reinforce a specific kind of domestic gender relations in which housewives are available for managing the personal affairs of their husbands. As it is often quipped by women in such careers, what they need is a wife.

One of the most important ways in which class relations and gender relations have shaped each other centers on the problem of the "family wage." Johanna Brenner and Maria Ramas (1984) have argued that the material constraints of working-class life in the nineteenth century were a major force in shaping the development of the working-class family form, and thus gender relations. Because of high infant mortality and the need for high rates of fertility among workers (since having adult surviving children was crucial for old age security for parents), it was in the interests of working-class families for the wife to stay at home and the husband to work in the paid labor force. This was not feasible, however, until the "family wage" was instituted. The family wage, in turn, became a powerful material force for keeping women in the home and reinforcing gender differences in pay. These gender differentials in pay, in turn, made it rational for families to orient their economic strategies around the class and job interests of the "male breadwinner," further marginalizing women's paid work. It is only in the last several decades as the male breadwinner family wage has begun to decline that this system has begun to erode.[8]

[8]   There has been a lively debate over the explanation of the family wage (see, e.g. Barrett 1984; Hartmann 1979b; Humphries, 1977; Lewis 1985). In contrast to Brenner and Ramas's argument that the family wage was in the interests of both male and

Particular class relations may also facilitate the transformation of gender relations in more egalitarian directions. As a professor, I occupy a quite privileged class location as a relatively affluent "expert" with high levels of control over my own work. Of particular importance to many professors is the way in which professorial work confers tremendous control over scheduling and time. Professors may work many hours per week, but they often have considerable discretion over when they put in the hours. Furthermore, at various times I have had grants which enabled me to buy off teaching and thus have even greater flexibility in organizing my time. This has made it possible within my family for me to play a major role in all aspects of parenting from the time when my children were infants. It has also changed the domestic terrain on which struggles over the domestic division of labor have been waged. The result is a relatively egalitarian division of labor around most domestic chores. This does not imply that class determines the gender division of labor. Far from it. As we shall see in Chapter 11, class location does not have a powerful overall impact on the gender division of labor in the home. Nevertheless, the specific properties of class positions transform the *constraints* within which people struggle over gender relations in their own lives, and under certain conditions this facilitates forging more egalitarian gender relations.

Gender as a sorting mechanism into class locations[9]

The way gender sorts people into class locations is probably the most obvious aspect of the interconnection of class and gender. One does

female workers, many feminists have argued that the family wage should primarily be viewed as a victory of men over women, reflecting the strategic interests of men in keeping women in their place. Insofar as it was the gender interests of men that formed the basis for the struggle over the family wage, then this would be another instance of the way in which gender relations shape the class structure. In any case, once the family wage is in place as a specific feature of class relations, it becomes an important material condition constraining transformations of gender relations.

[9] It may also be possible to conceptualize the complementary causal relation: class as a sorting mechanism of people into "gender locations." At first glance this might seem like a bizarre claim since we tend to think of gender categories as dichotomous, polarized and isomorphic with sexual categories – male and female. This image reflects the tendency for most people (including most sociologists) to conflate gender categories with sex categories, in spite of the formal acknowledgment that gender is a social, not biological, category. Once we break from the biological specification of gender *relations*, however, then it is clear that men and women can occupy many different sorts of gender locations, and class may influence where people end up in such relations.

not need to do high-powered research to observe that men and women in the labor force have very different occupational and class distributions, and most people would explain these differences by referring to gender in one way or another. It is less obvious, of course, precisely what gender mechanisms are at work here. Relatively few social scientists now believe that biological differences between men and women are the primary cause of occupational sex segregation, but such views are undoubtedly still common in the general population. Typically in social science discussions of these issues two kinds of factors linked to gender relations are given central stage in explanations of gender differences in occupational and class distributions: (1) gendered socialization processes which shape the occupational aspirations and skills of men and women, and thus affect the kinds of jobs they are likely to get; (2) various forms of inequality, domination and discrimination which either directly affect the access of men and women to various kinds of jobs, or indirectly affect access by affecting their acquisition of relevant resources. As feminists have often noted, inequalities in the sexual division of labor in the household constrain the labor market strategies of many women and thus the kinds of jobs for which they can realistically compete. Discrimination in credit markets may make it more difficult for women to become capitalists. Traditionally, discrimination in admissions to certain kinds of professional schools made it more difficult for women to acquire the credentials necessary to occupy the expert locations within class structures. As we shall see in Chapter 12, gender discrimination in promotions within authority hierarchies directly affects the probabilities of women becoming managers. In each of these instances, the distribution of power and resources within gender relations affects the likelihood of men and women occupying certain kinds of class locations.

Gender as mediated linkage to class location

As we discussed in Chapters 1 and 2, individuals are linked to class structures through a variety of relations other than their direct location in the social relations of production. The class locations of children are derived from the social relations within families that tie them to the class of their parents, not their own "jobs." Gender relations constitute one of the pivotal ways in which such "mediated linkages" to the class structure are organized, especially through marriages. One of the ways in which class and gender are interconnected, then, is via the way gender relations within families and kinship networks link people to various locations within the class structure. These mediated class locations affect both the gender interests of men and women – the interests they have by virtue of the specific gender relations within which they live – and their class interests.

Gender as a causal interaction with class in determining outcomes

Gender and class are interconnected not merely through the various ways they affect each other, but also through their mutual effects on a wide range of social phenomena. Of particular interest are those situations in which class and gender have interaction effects, for the presence of interaction effects indicates that the causal processes represented by the concepts "class" and "gender" are intertwined rather than operating simply as independent mechanisms.

One way of formally representing the interaction of class and gender is with a simple equation of the sort used in multivariate regression analysis. Suppose we were studying the effects of class and gender on political consciousness. The interaction of class and gender could then be represented in the following equation:

Consciousness = a + B_1[Class] + B_2[Gender] + B_3[Class x Gender]

The coefficients B_1, B_2, and B_3 indicate something about the magnitude of the effects of each term in the equation on consciousness. The interaction term, B_3, indicates the extent to which the effects of class vary by gender or, equivalently, the effects of gender vary by class. An example would be a situation in which the ideological difference between capitalists and workers was greater among men than among women.

In a model of this sort, it could turn out that the additive terms were negligible (i.e. B_1 and B_2 would be zero). This would imply that both class and gender only have effects on this dependent variable when they are combined in a particular way. This would be the case, for example, if male and female capitalists and male workers all had indistinguishable attitudes, but female workers were significantly different. In such a situation, the two independent variables in our equation – class and gender – could in practice be replaced by a single variable which would have a value of 1 for female workers and 0 for everyone else. The effects of class and gender would thus function like hydrogen and oxygen in water. When the amount of water given to plants is varied, there is no "additive effect" of the amount of hydrogen and the amount of oxygen on plant growth; the effects are entirely a function of the amount of the "interaction" compound, H_2O. If class and gender behaved this way then perhaps it would be useful to introduce a new concept, "clender," to designate the interaction term itself. In general, however, the claim that class and gender "interact" in generating effects does not imply that there are no additive effects. This means that some of what is consequential about gender occurs independently of class and some of what is consequential about class occurs independently of gender. The task of class analysis, then, is to sort out these various kinds of effects.

In Chapters 10, 11, and 12 we will explore several of these forms of interconnection of class and gender. Chapter 10 discusses the problem of the class location of married women in dual-earner families. It is thus an investigation of the ways in which gender mediates class locations. The chapter also includes an analysis of the effects of the interaction of gender and the class composition of households on class identity. Chapter 11 explores the ways in which class locations might shape one important facet of gender relations – the sexual division of labor in the home. Finally, Chapter 12 looks in detail at one specific aspect of the way gender sorts people into class locations – the differential access of men and women to positions of workplace authority.

10 Individuals, families and class analysis

Consider the following list of households in which family members are engaged in different kinds of jobs:

Employment composition of household

	Wife's job	Husband's job
1	Typist, full time	No husband
2	Typist, full time	Factory worker
3	Typist, full time	Lawyer
4	Typist, part time	Lawyer
5	Lawyer	Lawyer
6	Lawyer	Factory worker
7	Homemaker	Factory worker
8	Homemaker	Lawyer

What is the appropriate way of defining the social class of each of the individuals in this list? For some of the cases, there is no particular difficulty: the women in the first two households and the man in the second would usually be considered working class, while both people in the fifth household would be considered "middle" class. Similarly, the class of the homemakers in cases 7 and 8 would generally be identified with the class of their husbands.[1] The other cases, however,

---

[1] Some feminists would object to deriving the class location of full-time housewives from the class of their husbands. Such critics insist that the social relations of domination within the household should also be treated as a "class relation." One rationale for this claim treats production in the household as a distinctive mode of production, sometimes called the "domestic mode of production." In capitalist societies, it is argued, this mode of production is systematically structured by gender relations of domination and subordination. As a result, within the domestic mode of production, the domestic laborer (the housewife) occupies a distinctive exploited and dominated class position in relation to the nonlaborer (the male "head of

have no uncontroversial solutions. In particular, how should we under-stand the class location of married women in the labor force when their jobs have a different class character from that of their husbands? Intuitively, it seems that a typist married to a factory worker is not in the same class as a typist married to a lawyer, even if the jobs of the two typists are indistinguishable. And yet, simply to say that the second typist is "middle" class seems to relegate her own job to irrelevance in class analysis. In class terms she would become in-distinguishable from the woman lawyer in case 5. And what about the woman lawyer married to a worker? It seems very odd to say that she is in the same class as the typist married to a factory worker. Many feminists have strongly objected to equating a married woman's class with her husband's, arguing, to use Joan Acker's (1973) formulation, that this is an example of "intellectual sexism." And yet, to identify her class position strictly with her own job also poses serious conceptual problems. A typist married to a lawyer is likely to have a very different life-style, and above all very different economic and political interests from a typist married to a factory worker.

Of course, if these kinds of "cross-class" household compositions were rare phenomena, then this issue of classification would not have great empirical importance, even if it still raised interesting theoretical issues. However, as we saw in Chapter 8, the kinds of examples listed above are not rare events: in the United States (in 1980) 32% of all married women employed in expert-manager jobs have husbands in working-class jobs, and 46% of men in such expert-manager jobs whose wives work have wives employed in working-class jobs. Class heterogeneous families are sufficiently prevalent in contemporary capitalism that these problems of classification cannot be ignored in class analysis.

The central purpose of this chapter is to try to provide a coherent conceptual solution to this problem of identifying the class location of married women in the labor force and then to deploy this solution in an empirical analysis of the relationship between class location and subjective class identity in the United States and Sweden. There are two basic reasons why I think solving this problem of classification is

household"). This effectively places housewives in a distinctive class in relation to their husbands. A housewife of a working-class husband is thus not "in" the working class as such, but in what might be termed the "proletarian domestic labor class." One of the best known defenses of this view is by Christine Delphy (1984: 38–39).

important. First, as a practical matter, if one is doing any kind of research in which the class of individuals is viewed as consequential, one is forced to adopt a solution to this conceptual problem if only by default. Survey research on political attitudes, for example, frequently examines the relationship between an individual's class and attitudes. Typically, without providing a defense, attributes of the job of the respondent, whether male or female, are used to define class. Like it or not, this implies a commitment to the view that the class of individuals is appropriately measured by their own jobs regardless of the class composition of their households.

More substantively, this problem of classification raises important issues concerning the underlying explanatory logic of class analysis. By virtue of what is a person's class location explanatory of anything? Is it because class identifies a set of micro-experiences on the job which shape subjectivity? Even though they are not dealing with the problem of class and gender, this is essentially the argument of Melvin Kohn (1969) in his numerous studies of the effects of the complexity of work on cognitive functioning and of Michael Burawoy (1985) in his research on consent and conflict within work. If one adopts this job-centered view of the mechanisms through which class matters, then household class composition becomes a relatively secondary problem in class analysis. On the other hand, if one sees the central explanatory power of class as linked to the ways in which class positions shape material interests then household class composition becomes a more salient issue. Resolving this issue of classification, therefore, is bound up with clarifying the mechanisms through which class is explanatory.

In the next section of this chapter I will briefly review the recent discussion of the problem of defining the class location of married women. In section 10.2 I will elaborate an alternative approach built on the distinction between direct and mediated class relations briefly discussed in Chapter 1. Section 10.3 will then use this distinction to develop a concrete set of predictions about the linkage between class location and class identity in Sweden and the United States. Section 10.4 will present the results of the analysis.

10.1 The debate on women and class

These empirical and theoretical issues on the class analysis of women were crystallized in a debate launched in 1983 by John Goldthorpe's controversial essay, "Women and Class Analysis: in Defense of the

Conventional View." Goldthorpe endorses the conventional view that the class of women is derived from the class of their husbands:

> the family is the unit of stratification primarily because only certain family members, predominantly males, have, as a result of their labour market participation, what might be termed a directly determined position within the class structure. Other family members, including wives, do not typically have equal opportunity for such participation, and their class position is thus indirectly determined: that is to say, it is "derived" from that of the family "head" ...
>
> Moreover, the authors in question [traditional class analysts] would not regard their case as being basically affected by the increase in the numbers of married women engaged in paid employment. They would emphasize that although the degree of women's economic dependence on their husbands may in this way be somewhat mitigated, such employment typically forms part of a family strategy, or at all events, takes place within the possibilities and constraints of the class situation of the family as a whole, in which the husband's employment remains the dominant factor. (Goldthorpe 1983: 468–469)

Goldthorpe's paper sparked a lively, if sometimes overly polemical, series of exchanges. Goldthorpe's critics (e.g. Heath and Brittain 1984; Stanworth 1984) argued that the class character of the jobs of married women in the labor force have significant effects independently of the class of their husbands, and as a result, those families within which husbands and wives occupy different job-classes should be treated as having a dual-class character.

Goldthorpe (1984) replied by arguing that treating families as having a cross-class composition risks undermining the coherence of class analysis and subverts the explanatory capacity of the concept of class. Since class conflicts run between families, not through families, if families are treated as lacking a unitary class character, class structure will no longer provide a systematic basis for explaining class conflicts.

Goldthorpe's argument can be broken down into two primary theses:

1 *Unitary family-class thesis*: Families pool income as units of consumption. This means that all family members benefit from the income-generating capacity of any member.[2] Consequentially, all

---

2   This argument holds for either Weberian or Marxist conceptualizations of the income-generating process – i.e. whether income is viewed simply as the result of market capacities or exploitation. In either case, the household income derived from

family members have the same material – and thus class – interests. As a result, it is in general families, rather than atomized individuals, that are the effective units collectively organized into class formations. Class struggles occur *between* families, not *within* families.

2 *Husband's class derivation thesis*: Because of the gender division of labor in the household and male dominance in the society at large, the economic fate of most families depends much more heavily upon the class character of the husband's job than of the wife's. In family strategies of welfare maximization, therefore, in nearly all cases the class imperatives of the husband's job will overwhelmingly pre-empt strategic considerations involving the wife's job. As a result, the causally effective class of married women (i.e. the class that has any explanatory power) is in general derived from the class location of her husband.

Goldthorpe, of course, does not deny that by and large individuals rather than families fill *jobs* in capitalist economies. What he disputes is the claim that the class structure should be treated as a relational map of the job structure. Instead, classes should be defined as *groups of people who share common material interests*. While it may be the case that the basic material interests of people depend upon their relationship to the system of production, it need not be the case that those interests depend primarily upon their individual position within production (i.e. their "job"). Insofar as families are units of consumption in which incomes from all members are pooled, then all members of the family share the same material interests and thus are in the same class, regardless of their individual jobs. Individual family members would occupy different locations in the class structure only when it is the case that the family ceased to genuinely pool resources and act as a unit of consumption sharing a common fate.

A number of interconnected criticisms can be levied against these theses. First, while it may be true that all family members benefit from income brought into the household, it does not follow from this that they all share a unitary, undifferentiated interest with respect to such income. To claim that wives and husbands have identical interests with respect to the gross income of the family is somewhat like saying

production, in Goldthorpe's view, generates common interests for all household consumers of that income.

that both workers and capitalists have an interest in maximizing the gross revenues of a business – which is frequently true – and therefore they are in the same class – which is false. Families may pool income, but there is evidence that this does not mean that husbands and wives always share equally in the real consumption derived from that income.[3]

Inequality in the consumption of family income by husbands and wives, of course, does not necessarily mean that married women in the labor force have material interests in their own individual earnings as such, and thus distinct individually based class interests in their jobs. It could be the case that they have *gender* interests in a redistribution of power within the household, but that they still lack any autonomous *class* interest in their own earnings independently of the family income as a whole. There are, however, two reasons why it is plausible to see married women as having individual class interests linked to their own earnings. First, the high rates of divorce in contemporary capitalist societies mean that the jobs of many women in the labor force constitute for them a kind of "shadow class" – the class they would occupy in the face of marital dissolution. Given the relatively high probability of such events, married women have personal class interests in the earnings capacities they derive from their individual jobs.[4] Second, there is evidence that the proportion of the family budget brought in by the wife affects her bargaining power within the family.[5] Even if the family pools income, therefore, married women would have some autonomous personal interests in their own earning capacity in their paid jobs.

[3] Annemette Sorensen and Sara McLanahan (1987) cite a number of studies demonstrating that families often do not pool all of their income: Edwards (1982), Taylor-Gooby (1985) and Pahl (1983). See also Amartya Sen (1984) who presents data showing that there are often great inequalities in food distribution within families under conditions of poverty, again suggesting that the family should not be treated as a homogeneous unit of undifferentiated material interests.

[4] For a discussion of the consequences of divorce for the income of women, see Duncan and Hoffman (1985), and McLanahan, Sorensen and Watson (1986). Duncan and Hoffman estimate that on average divorce results in a 30% decline in the real income of wives and practically no change for husbands.

[5] Research which supports the claim that a wife's economic contribution to the family shapes her bargaining power include Hood (1983), Blumstein and Schwartz (1984), Coverman (1985), and Sorensen and McLanahan (1987). In the research on housework reported in Chapter 11 below, we find that the proportion of family income generated by the wife's job predicts the husband's level of housework in Sweden, but not in the United States.

A second general criticism of Goldthorpe's argument concerns his very narrow understanding of class interests. The unitary family-class thesis rests on the claim that since husbands and wives pool income, they have identical interests with respect to overall family earnings capacity and thus identical class interests. The interests that are tied to classes, however, are not simply income-based interests. At least if one adopts a broadly Marxist concept of class, issues of autonomy, the expenditure of effort, and domination within work are also systematically linked to class. These kinds of interests are at the heart of what Burawoy (1985) has called the "politics of production" and center much more directly on individuals as job holders than as members of household units of consumption. Even if married couples share a unitary family consumption-class, the potential differences in their job-classes could still generate differences in their class interests.

Third, contrary to Goldthorpe's view, it is not inherently the case that families rather than individuals are mobilized into class struggles. While this may generally be the case, especially in situations where families are class homogeneous, it is possible to imagine circumstances in which a wife is a union member engaged in union struggles of various sorts and her husband is a manager or petty bourgeois generally opposed to unions.[6] Particularly if class interests are seen as broader than simply interests in income, one can imagine husbands and wives in different job-classes, involved in organizations supporting quite different kinds of class interests. To be sure, it is highly unlikely that husbands and wives would be actively on opposite sides of the barricade in a given class struggle – for the husband to be a top manager or employer in a firm in which his wife was on strike. But this does not imply that in other contexts they could not be involved in quite distinct and even opposing kinds of class formations.

Finally, Goldthorpe argues that because the economic fate of the family is *more dependent* upon income from the husband's job than the wife's, the class location of the family should be *exclusively* identified with his job. This assumes that in the strategic choices made within families over labor market participation and job choices, there is minimal struggle, negotiation and bargaining, and as a result the

---

[6] Costello (1991) cites a number of examples of this type in her analysis of union mobilization among clerical workers in the insurance industry. To be sure, such differences in class formation within families were a source of tension in these families, but nevertheless they did occur and were important for understanding the dilemmas of mobilization she studied.

interests linked to the husband's job always pre-empt those of the wife's job. Family strategy, then, is not some kind of negotiated weighted average of the class-based imperatives linked to each spouse's job, but uniquely determined by the class imperatives of the male breadwinner.

This claim by Goldthorpe is simply asserted on his part, unbacked by either theoretical argument or empirical evidence. Of course, there are many cases where a story of this sort has considerable face validity. There are undoubtedly families in which the husband is in a well-paying managerial or professional job with a systematic career structure while the wife holds part-time flexible work to which she has little commitment. In such situations it might well be the case that whenever there is a trade-off between interests tied to the wife's job and to the husband's job, *both* parties agree to adopt a strategy supporting the husband's interests. In such a situation it may be reasonable, at least as a first approximation, to identify the family-class exclusively with the husband's job. But there is no reason to assume that this particular situation is universal. It is much more plausible to suppose that there is systematic variation across families in such strategic balances of interests and power, and thus that the relative weight of different spouse's job-classes in shaping the class character of the family as a whole is a variable, not a constant.

In 1980, in roughly 10% of all two-earner families in the United States the wife earns 40–49% of the family income and in 25% of all two-earner married couples she contributes 50% or more of the total family income. In Sweden the figure is even higher: 45% of respondents in two-earner families report that the wife contributes "about 50%" of the income and 10% report that she brings in 75% or more of the income.[7] Certainly, in

---

[7] The wording of the question asked in the US and Swedish surveys was slightly different in generating these data. In the US respondents were asked to estimate what proportion of the total family income was earned by their spouse. In Sweden they were asked whether their spouse contributed "less than 25%," "about 25%," "about 50%," "about 75%" or "more than 75%" of the family income. The American estimate of wife contribution is very close to the figure reported by Annemette Sorensen and Sara McLanahan (1987). By their estimates, in 1980, wives contributed 50% or more of the family income in 22% of all two-earner white couples and in 33% of all two-earner nonwhite couples. It should be noted that this represents a *decline* in the proportion of family income contributed by wives *in two-earner households* since 1950. In 1950, in two-earner families, wives contributed half or more of the family income in 36% of white couples and 35% of nonwhite couples. Thus, while it is true that by virtue of the massive increase in married women in the labor force, there are many fewer wives who contribute no income to the family income (a

such families, even from a narrow economic point of view, the family strategies should be affected by the class character of both spouses' jobs. Furthermore, even when it is the case that in decisive zero-sum trade-off situations, interests derived from the husband's job usually pre-empt those of the wife's, it does not follow from this that in other situations the interests linked to the wife's job are irrelevant and do not shape family income maximization strategies. Even where the wife contributes less than the husband, therefore, the class character of her paid work could systematically shape family strategies, and thus the class character of the family unit.

If these criticisms are correct, then one is unjustified in simply equating the class location of married working women with the job-class of their husbands. But it also seems unsatisfactory to treat their class as simply based on their own immediate work. Some other conceptual solution to defining their class must be found.

10.2 An alternative approach: direct and mediated class locations

Most class concepts view class structures as a set of rooms in a hotel filled by guests. The dwellers may be individuals or families, and they may change rooms from time to time, but the image is of "empty places" being filled by people. There is, however, an alternative general way of understanding class structure: instead of a set of rooms, class structures can be understood as a particular kind of complex network of social relations. What defines this network of relations as a *class* structure is the way it determines the access of people to the basic productive resources of a society and the processes of exploitation, and thus shapes their material interests.[8] A "location," then, is not a "room" in a building, but a node in a network of relations.

In a highly simplified model of the world we can reduce such a

decline from about 68% of all wives in 1950 to only about 30% of wives in 1980), among wives in the labor force the degree of economic dependency on husbands in the United States has actually increased.

[8] To speak about a "social *relation*" which links a person to resources means that this relation simultaneously interconnects the person with other people. A physical relation may define the link between a farmer and the soil in the labor process; the social property relation which defines the farmer's link to the land, however, simultaneously defines his or her relation to other people as buyers of farm produce, lenders of credit, competitors in the market, etc. The traditional Marxist definition of classes in terms of the (social) relation of people to the means of production is equivalent to defining classes in terms of the social relation between owners and nonowners of the means of production.

network of social relations to a single link between individuals and productive resources constituted by their direct, personal control or ownership of such resources. This is the abstraction characteristic of most Marxist class analysis. But there is no reason to restrict class analysis to such simplifications. The material interests of real, flesh and blood individuals are shaped not simply by such direct personal relations to productive resources, but by a variety of other relations which link them to the system of production. In contemporary capitalist societies these include, above all, relations to other family members (both within a single generation and intergenerationally) and relations to the state.[9] I will refer to these kinds of indirect links between individuals and productive resources as "mediated" relations, in contrast to the "direct" relations embodied in the individual's immediate job and personal ownership of productive resources.

For certain categories of people in contemporary capitalism, location in the class structure is entirely constituted by mediated relations. This is most clearly the case for children. To say that children in a working-class family are "in" the working class is to make a claim about the ways in which their class interests are shaped by their mediated relations (through their families) to the system of production. Mediated class relations also loom large in understanding the class interests of housewives, the unemployed, pensioners, students. In each of these cases an adequate picture of their class interests cannot be derived simply from examining their direct participation in the relations of production.

The class structure, then, should be understood as consisting of the totality of direct and mediated class relations. This implies that two class structures with identical patterns of direct class relations but differing mediated relations should be considered different kinds of structures. Consider the following rather extreme contrast for purposes of illustration:

> *Class structure I.* In 66% of all households, both husband and wife are employed in working-class jobs and in 33% of

---

[9] It is because relations to the state can constitute an important mechanism through which individuals are linked to productive resources that Philippe Van Parijs (1986) has argued that "welfare capitalism" is a distinct "mode of production" from pure capitalism, not simply a variant of capitalism. The redistributive and regulative aspects of the welfare state, in his view, constitute a basic transformation of the broadly defined "social relations of production," since it creates links between nonproperty owners and the means of production that do not exist in capitalism.

households both husband and wife are co-owners of small businesses employing the workers from the other households.

Class structure II. 33% of the households are pure working-class households, 33% have a working-class husband and a small employer wife and 33% have a small employer husband and a working-class wife.

For a strict adherent of the view that class structures are constituted by the individual's direct relation to the means of production, these two class structures are the same: 66% working class, 33% small employers. Also, ironically perhaps, for a strict adherent of Goldthorpe's husband-based family class approach, the two class structures are identical: 66% working class, 33% small employers. If, however, class structures are defined in terms of the *combination* of direct and mediated class locations, then the two structures look quite different: in the first structure, two-thirds of the population is fully proletarianized (i.e. both their direct and mediated class locations are working class); in the second structure, only one third of the population is fully proletarianized.[10]

Once the distinction between direct and mediated class locations is introduced into the conceptual repertoire of class analysis, it becomes possible to ask the question: what determines the relative weight of these two kinds of linkages to productive resources for particular categories of actors? To say that the class structure is constituted by the totality of such relations is not to imply that class interests are equally determined by direct and mediated relations. Indeed, there may be variations both within and across class structures in the relative importance of these different mechanisms that link people to productive resources. One can imagine a class structure in which mediated relations loom very large for certain people and not for others in shaping their material interests, and thus their overall position in the class structure.

The problem of women in the class structure can now be recast in terms of the relative salience of direct and mediated class relations in determining their class interests. Goldthorpe takes a rather extreme

---

[10] Examples like this are not entirely fanciful. It is quite conceivable that in a third world country one could have two communities in which the same proportions of the labor force were engaged in proletarianized wage labor activities and in self-employed subsistence peasant agriculture, but in which these corresponded to entirely different patterns of household proletarianization.

position on this question for contemporary industrial capitalist societies: with few exceptions, the mediated class location of married women completely overrides any systematic relevance of their direct class location. Implicit in his argument, however, is the acknowledgment that under appropriate conditions this would not be the case. If, for example, there was a dramatic erosion of the sexual division of labor in the household and gender differences in power and in labor market opportunities, then the direct class location of married women would begin to matter more both for their class location and for that of their husbands.[11]

The theoretical task, then, for understanding the location of women in the class structure, consists of trying to identify causal processes which shape the relative salience of direct and mediated class relations. We will explore this problem in the context of an empirical comparison of the relationship between the class composition of families and class identity in Sweden and the United States.

10.3 A strategy for studying the effects of direct and mediated class locations

There are two general empirical strategies that could be adopted to explore these arguments about direct and mediated class locations. If one had adequate longitudinal micro-level household data, one could actually measure the extent to which the material interests of married working women in the United States and in Sweden depend upon their own direct class location or the class location of their husbands, and one could assess the extent to which these direct and mediated class interests impact on individual and collective family strategies. Alternatively, we could consider something which an individual's class location is meant at least partially to explain – such as class consciousness, class identity, participation in class conflict, etc. – and examine the relative "explanatory power" of the direct and mediated class locations of individuals. The only reason for introducing the distinction between direct and mediated class locations is because we believe that an individual's location in a class structure is consequential and that this distinction provides a better specification of this con-

---

[11] In the logic of Goldthorpe's analysis, under such conditions the class location of the family would begin to have an amalgamated character, combining the job-class of both spouses. All members of the family, however, would continue to have the same class location.

sequence producing process. Variations in the relative salience of direct and mediated class locations, therefore, should be reflected in the effects of these two dimensions of class on whatever it is that class locations ought to explain.

In this chapter I will adopt this second strategy. More specifically, we will examine the relationship between class locations (direct and mediated) and the probability of having a working-class identity, i.e. subjectively considering oneself in the working class. Subjective class identity is not, perhaps, the most subtle indicator of the subjective effects of class location. However, of all dimensions of "class conscious-ness" it is probably the one most directly reflecting the subjective understanding of one's place in the class structure. Class identity is thus the indicator most closely tied to the theoretical questions of this chapter. The premise of the analysis is that to the extent direct class relations more powerfully determine a person's class location than do mediated relations they will also be more strongly associated with the probability of having a particular class identity.

Underlying the empirical investigation is the simple theoretical model presented in Figure 10.1. Direct and mediated class locations are associated with different causal pathways that affect class iden-tity. Direct class locations affect class identity both because a person's job affects a range of class experiences within work and because direct class locations shape material interests. Mediated class loca-tions, on the other hand, only affect class identity via material interests. The relative weight of direct and mediated class locations on class identity, therefore will depend upon two kinds of factors: (1) the relative weight of direct and mediated class locations on material interests, and (2) the relative salience of production-centered class experiences and consumption-centered class experiences in shaping class identity.

Hypotheses

The following simple linear equations will form the basis for the data analysis:

Probability of wife having working-class identity =
  H_w [Husband's job-class] + W_w [Wife's job-class)

Probability of husband having working-class identity =
  H_h [Husband's job-class] + W_h [Wife's job-class]

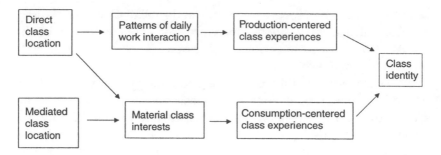

Figure 10.1 *A general model of the effects of direct and mediated class locations on class identity*

where H_w is the effect of husband's job-class on wife's identity, W_w is the effect of wife's job-class on wife's identity, H_h is the effect of husband's job-class on husband's identity, and W_h is the effect of wife's job-class on husband's identity.[12]

Goldthorpe predicts that for both men and women the H coefficients will be substantially greater than the W coefficients. Indeed, in the most extreme formulation of his position, W_w and W_h should be zero – the unitary class of the family is entirely derived from the husband's class and therefore the effects of the wife's job-class on class identity should be negligible.

In contrast, the view that a person's class location should be viewed as a combination of direct and mediated class relations suggests that the relative magnitudes of H and W should be variable across families, across genders and across countries depending upon the relative salience of the individual's direct class location and their mediated location via their family ties. Because of the economic dependency of married women on their husband's jobs, it would generally be expected that family mediated class locations would be more salient for women than for men. That is, H_w should be greater than W_h. But, unlike in Goldthorpe's approach, there is no general expectation that W_w or W_h will be negligible.

We will examine the above equations for married couples with two earners in the United States and Sweden. There are a variety of reasons why one might expect the relative salience of direct and mediated class locations for married women to vary between Sweden and the United

---

[12] In the actual equations job-classes for both husbands and wives will be measured by a series of dummy variables rather than by a single variable.

States: greater parity in wages between men and women in Sweden means that Swedish wives are less economically dependent upon their husbands' jobs than American wives, and thus their economic welfare depends less upon their mediated class location; the strong redistributive policies of the state mean that Swedes in general – both men and women – are less dependent than Americans upon their family's earnings for their standard of living; the higher degree of class organization within work in Sweden means that an individual's own job is likely to be more salient in shaping their consciousness. This line of reasoning suggests that the ratio W_w/H_w should be greater in Sweden than in the United States.

The empirical analysis which follows, therefore, will revolve around the following contrasting hypotheses for predicting the probability of a subjective working-class identification:[13]

Goldthorpe hypotheses
(1.1) $H > W$ for both men and women (i.e. the husband's job-class is more important than the wife's job-class in predicting the identity of both husbands and wives).
(1.2) W_w and W_h will always be insignificant (i.e. the wife's direct class will not affect either her own or her husband's class identity).

Mediated and direct class locations hypotheses
(2.1) $H_w > W_h$ (i.e. mediated class locations will have greater salience for wives than for husbands).
(2.2) W_w/H_w will be greater in Sweden than in the United States (i.e. the direct class location of married women will have greater salience relative to their mediated class location in Sweden than in the United States).

10.4 Results

The results will be presented in two steps. First, we will examine the effects of direct and mediated class locations on class identity for wives and for husbands. This will provide the primary basis for examining the core hypotheses. Second, we will add a number of control variables to the equations in order to test the robustness of the initial findings.

---

[13] All of the coefficients in these hypotheses are for the working-class dummy variables in the equations.

Because, as described in the methodological appendix to the chapter, the dependent variable in the analysis is a dichotomy (in which 1 = having a working-class class identity) the analysis will be based on logistic regressions rather than OLS regressions.[14]

The effects of class composition on class identity

Table 10.1 and Figure 10.2 indicate the percentage of men and the percentage of women who subjectively identify with the working class in each cell of the family-class typology in the United States and Sweden. Table 10.2 presents the logistic regression equations used to model the patterns observed in Table 10.1. Because so few people fall into the cells of Table 10.1 with petty bourgeois family members, the discussion which follows will generally concentrate on those families in Table 10.1 within which both husband and wife are wage-earners (that is, the four cells in the lower right hand corner of each subtable).[15]

In the United States, for wage-earning families, the class character of the wife's job seems to have no effect on the class identification of either men or women. Among women, roughly 20% of women wage-earners married to men with middle-class jobs and roughly 50% of women wage-earners married to men with working-class jobs subjectively identify with the working class, regardless of the class character of the woman's own job. Among men the pattern is essentially the same (although the percentages are somewhat different): 20% of men in middle-class jobs and just over 35% of men in working-class jobs subjectively identify with the working class, regardless of the class character of their wife's job.[16]

---

[14] In a logistic regression, the coefficients of the independent variables are the logs of odds ratios. See the appendix to Chapter 5 for a brief discussion.

[15] One comment about the results for the petty bourgeoisie is needed. In both the United States and Sweden a high proportion of men in homogeneous petty bourgeois families (i.e. both spouses hold petty bourgeois jobs) subjectively identify with the working class. Indeed, in the United States this is considerably higher than the proportion of men in homogeneous working-class families (62.5% vs. 39%). Because of the relatively small numbers involved we cannot rigorously explore this category empirically. I suspect, however, that this high subjective identification of petty bourgeois men with the working class reflects a traditional populist meaning of the expression "working class" as the working people (to be contrasted to "parasites" – bankers, speculators, etc.).

[16] I cannot offer an explanation for why working-class identification is higher for women married to working-class men (about 50%) than for the working-class men themselves (under 40%).

Table 10.1. *Percentage of people who say they are in the working class in families with different class compositions (dual-earner households only)*

United States

Male respondents (N=268)

		Wife's job-defined class		
		Petty bourgeoisie	Middle class	Working class
Husband's	Petty bourgeoisie	62.5[a]	(24.7)[b]	(43.7)
job-defined	Middle class	(18.4)	20.9	23.4
class	Working class	(0.0)	35.7	38.9

Female respondents (N=273)

		Wife's job-defined class		
		Petty bourgeoisie	Middle class	Working class
Husband's	Petty bourgeoisie	16.2	(8.5)	(26.5)
job-defined	Middle class	(43.4)	20.0	22.9
class	Working class	(23.0)	51.0	53.0

Sweden

Male respondents (N=318)

		Wife's job-defined class		
		Petty bourgeoisie	Middle class	Working class
Husband's	Petty bourgeoisic	41.2	(18.2)	47.8
job-defined	Middle class	(40.0)	19.0	37.8
class	Working class	(100.0)	64.0	71.8

Female respondents (N=297)

		Wife's job-defined class		
		Petty bourgeoisie	Middle class	Working class
Husband's	Petty bourgeoisie	(22.2)	(37.5)	(41.7)
job-defined	Middle class	(66.7)	11.6	39.7
class	Working class	(100.0)	44.8	71.7

a. Entries are the percentage of respondents in a cell who state they are in the working class.

b. ( ) indicates that the number of cases in the cell is less than 15.

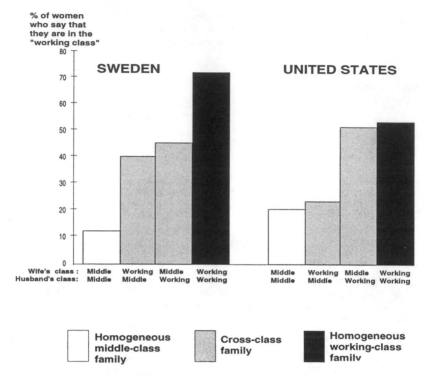

Figure 10.2 *Percentage of women who say they are "working class" in dual-earner families with different class compositions*

These observations are statistically confirmed in the logistic regressions in Table 10.2. For American wives in two-earner households, only the coefficients for the husband's class are significant predictors of their class identity. For American husbands, on the other hand, their wives' class location appears to have no effects at all on their identity. Mediated class locations, therefore, have a strong effect on the class identity of women, but none at all on the class identity of men. In short, in the United States, once you know the class position of husbands, your ability to predict class identification for either husbands or wives does not improve by adding information on the wife's class position.

When we turn to the Swedish data, however, we get a very different picture. In Sweden, for both men and women, there are consistent effects of both husband's and wife's job-class on the subjective class identification of respondents. For Swedish women, about 12% of the

Table 10.2. *The effects of household class composition on class identity (logistic regression)*

Variables	Women		Men	
	United States	Sweden	United States	Sweden
Respondent's class:[a]				
Petty bourgeoisie	0.01[b]	1.11	1.01**	0.24
(s.e.)	(.43)	(.64)	(.38)	(.38)
Working class	0.29	1.23**	0.73*	1.61**
(s.e.)	(.31)	(.30)	(.31)	(.27)
Spouse's class:				
Petty bourgeoisie	−0.38	0.17	0.59	0.87
(s.e.)	(.45)	(.47)	(.44)	(.53)
Working class	1.07**	1.46**	0.27	0.78**
(s.e.)	(.31)	(.28)	(.31)	(.28)
Scaled deviance	310.2	348.1	329.5	384.4
Degrees of freedom	249	265	275	313

Significance levels (two-tailed tests):   * $p < .05$ ** $p < .01$

a. The left-out category for both respondent's class and spouse's class is "middle class." The coefficients for these variables, therefore, equal the difference between these dummy variable class categories and the middle class. The constant term has been left out of the table.

b. The logit coefficients and standard errors come from logistic regressions predicting working-class identification for the category of people defined by the column heading.

respondents in homogeneously middle-class families subjectively identify with the working class compared to nearly 72% in homogeneously working-class families. Women in class heterogeneous families – women in middle-class jobs married to husbands in working-class jobs or women in working-class jobs married to husbands in middle-class jobs – have an intermediate likelihood of working-class identification, around 40%. A similar, if attenuated, pattern occurs for Swedish men: 19% of the men in homogeneous middle-class families and 72% of the men in homogeneous working-class families subjectively identify with the working class, compared to about 38% of middle-class men married to working-class wives and 64% of working-class men married to middle-class wives.

These observations are also statistically confirmed in the logistic regressions in Table 10.2. The coefficient for the working-class dummy variables are statistically significant for the class location of both respondents and spouses for both men and women. The ratio W_w/H_w for Swedish women (for the working-class dummy variables) is 0.84, indicating that the effects of their direct class on class identity is nearly as great as their mediated class. Unlike in the United States, the class identity of both husbands and wives in Sweden are significantly affected by the class character of the wife's job as well as the husband's job.[17]

Multivariate results

In order for the results in Table 10.2 to constitute plausible tests of the hypotheses about direct and mediated class locations in Sweden and the United States, the observed linkage between class locations and class identity displayed in these results must be attributable to class as such rather than to some other variable. For example, imagine that it were in fact the case that class identity was basically a result of family income, not of structurally determined class locations of either husbands or wives. Furthermore, let us suppose that family income were linked to the class composition of households in different ways in Sweden and the United States (because of different wage structures). It could happen under such circumstances that the relationship between family composition and class identity would look quite different in the two countries even though the relation between family income and identity – the real causal mechanism – was the same in both countries.

What we want to find out, therefore, is whether or not the patterns in Table 10.2 remain largely the same when various controls are added to the equation. We will not be particularly concerned with the values of the coefficients for these controls as such, but rather in the impact of

[17] An overall test of the relative explanatory power of direct and mediated class locations for Swedish and American men and women can be conducted by examining the reduction in "scaled deviance" in models containing only respondent's class or spouse's class with the model containing both class locations. In Sweden, the reduction in scaled deviance for husbands is 38.7 when the respondent's class is added to the spouse's class equation, whereas it is only 8.2 when spouse's class is added to respondent's class equation. For Swedish women, on the other hand, the two effects are of roughly equal magnitude: 30.8 when spouse's class is added and 22.3 when respondent's class is added. All of these improvements in fit of the models are statistically significant. There is no improvement in the United States models when the wife's class is added to the model containing the husband's class for either men or women.

their inclusion in the equation on the values of the coefficients for respondent's class and spouse's class.

Four basic control variables will be included in the analysis: number of hours worked per week by the respondent, percentage of total family income contributed by the wife (wife's economic contribution), total family income and age of respondent. The equations containing these variables are given in Table 10.3.

With one exception, the inclusion of the control variables in Table 10.3 does not alter the basic patterns reported in Table 10.2. In the United States it is still the case that for women the coefficients for respondent's class are insignificant while the coefficients for working-class spouse are quite significant, whereas for men the reverse is the case. In Sweden, as in Table 10.2, among women the effects of wife's class and husband's class are of nearly equal magnitude even when the four controls are added. The one case where the controls do change the pattern from Table 10.2 is for Swedish men: their spouse's class no longer has a significant effect (at the .05 significance level) on their class identity once the control variables are added to the equation. Nevertheless, the basic conclusions from the initial analysis hold: compared to American women, the direct class of married working Swedish women has greater salience relative to their mediated class in predicting their class identities.

10.5 Implications

One simple way of characterizing the results we have been discussing is that the predictions from the "conventional wisdom" of Goldthorpe's model are reasonably accurate for the United States, but not for Sweden. In the former, no predictive power is lost by defining the class location of married women in the labor force by the class of their husbands, whereas in the latter this is not the case.

How can these different causal structures in Sweden and the United States be explained? There are a range of interpretations which might be pursued. The different patterns we have observed could directly reflect different cultural conventions for the meaning of class identity for men and women in the two countries. Alternatively, they could be effects of strategies by political parties or unions in treating men and women differently in the forging of collective solidarities. Or, perhaps, the results we have been discussing could be artifacts of measurement problems in one or more of the variables in the analysis. All of these

Table 10.3. *The effects of household class composition on class identity
with various controls (logistic regression)[a]*

Variables	Women		Men	
	United States	Sweden	United States	Sweden
Respondent's class:[b]				
Petty bourgeoisie (s.e.)	0.20 (.47)	0.68 (.73)	1.08 (.43)*	0.23 (.43)
Working class (s.e.)	0.09 (.34)	1.16 (.32)**	0.75 (.31)*	1.61 (.31)**
Spouse's class:				
Petty bourgeoisie (s.e.)	-0.48 (.49)	0.16 (.51)	0.63 (.56)	0.52 (.59)
Working class (s.e.)	0.99 (.33)**	1.31 (.31)**	0.23 (.31)	0.53 (.31)
Control variables:				
Hours worked/wk (s.e.)	-0.00 (.01)	0.03 (.01)**	0.01 (.01)	-0.02 (.02)
Wife's economic contribution (s.e.)	-0.01 (.01)	0.01 (.01)	-0.01 (.01)	0.01 (.01)
Family income: $1,000s (s.e.)	-0.41 (.15)**	-0.40 (.18)*	-0.25 (.11)*	-0.47 (.15)**
Age (s.e.)	-0.01 (.01)	0.04 (.01)**	-0.01 (.01)	0.04 (.01)**
Scaled deviance	294.9	324.3	316.6	360.6
Degrees of freedom[c]	241	258	268	306

Significance levels: * $p < .05$ ** $p < .01$

a. The coefficients in this equation are calculated in an equation in which missing data for each of
the control variables is included in the equation in the form of a dummy variable which = 1 for
cases with missing data on that variable and 0 for cases with values on the variable. In only one
case (family income for US men) was the coefficient for these missing data dummy variables
even close to statistical significance (i.e. there is no indication that the presence of missing data
in general biases the estimates of coefficients). Since in general these coefficients were not
statistically significant, these missing data dummy variables are not included in the presentation
of results in this table. The constant term has also been left out of the table.

b. The left-out category for both respondent's class and spouse's class is "middle class." The
coefficients for these variables, therefore, equal the difference between these dummy variable
class categories and the middle class.

c. The degrees of freedom in these equations include the missing data dummy variables referred
to in footnote a above.

arguments have some plausibility. In the present context, however, I
will limit the discussion to two alternative class-centered explanations
since these most directly bear on the theoretical agenda of direct and
mediated class relations.

There are two somewhat different ways that the basic differences we have been discussing between Sweden and the United States can be described. First, we could look at the ratio W_w/H_w – that is, the ratio of the effect of wife's class on wife's consciousness to the effect of husband's class on wife's consciousness – and say that for women in Sweden there is rough parity in the effects of direct and mediated class locations on their class identity, whereas in the United States there is a much stronger effect of mediated class than of direct class. Or, alternatively, we could say that in both countries there is roughly the same effect of mediated class for women; what differs between the countries is simply that direct class location has a much bigger effect on identity in Sweden than in the United States for *both* men and women.[18] In the first description we are focussing on the *relative* salience of direct and mediated relations; in the second, on the *absolute* magnitudes of each of them.

These two descriptions suggest different possible class-centered explanations of the differences between the Swedish and American patterns. The first description corresponds to an emphasis on the ways the economic dependency of wives on husbands shapes the construction of class interests and thus class identity (the causal pathway from class location through class interests to class identity in Figure 10.1). The reasoning, as suggested earlier, is that the less dependent a wife's material welfare is on her husband's job, the less will her class interests be derived from his direct class, and thus the greater the relative weight of her own direct class location. In Sweden a higher proportion of family income in two-earner families is contributed by wives than in the United States. It is also the case that the welfare and redistributive policies of the Swedish state make the individual economic interests of married women less dependent upon their husbands. In this line of reasoning, then, the greater relative impact of a married woman's own job on her class identity in Sweden than in the United States is seen as a consequence of the lower degree of economic dependence of wives on husbands in Sweden. In terms of the model in Figure 10.1, this implies that relative to women in Sweden, for women in the United States the causal path between direct class location and material interests is much weaker than the path from mediated location and interests.

[18] It is worth noting that in the model with the various control variables the effect of mediated class for *men* in both countries is also roughly the same (and not significantly different from zero).

The second description, in contrast, corresponds to the view that class locations are explanatory not simply because they determine a set of material interests, but because they deeply shape patterns of daily lived experiences, above all within work.[19] Instead of focussing on variations of material dependency of wives on husbands, such work experience-centered views of class would direct the inquiry toward a different type of explanation of the patterns we have observed. Michael Burawoy suggested, in an informal discussion of these results, that a central contrast between Sweden and the United States might be between a society within which class has its effects primarily through work and a society within which class has its effects primarily through consumption. This general view of the effects of class emphasizes the production-centered causal path in Figure 10.1. In terms of this model, then, the United States would be characterized as a society within which the causal effects of class – both direct and mediated – work primarily through the material interests/consumption path, whereas Sweden is a society within which both causal paths play an important role.

The explanation of this difference between the two countries (if this characterization is correct) could lie in a range of possible institutional and historical factors: the nature of the politics of production within the two societies, the forms of articulation between "global politics" and shop floor politics, the degree of collective organization of workers as workers through unions, etc. For example, it might be the case that the specific forms of corporatist, centralized unionism in Sweden have the effect of reducing competition between workers in different labor markets (both external and internal). This in turn could mean that the daily experiences within work tend to reinforce class-based solidarities, which in turn strengthen working-class identity. But whatever the specific historical and institutional explanation might be, the result is that in Sweden subjective class identification is forged much more systematically through experiences within work than in the United States, whereas, in the United States, class identity is formed primarily within consumption and community.

This line of argument, then, suggests that the reason the direct class

---

[19] Johanna Brenner (1989) makes this argument explicitly in the context of a critique of my own exploitation-centered concept of class structure. Such a view also underlies Melvin Kohn's (1969) investigations of the effects of class on cognitive complexity, Michael Burawoy's (1985) analysis of class and the labor process, and E. P. Thompson's (1968) concept of class as lived experience.

of married women does not matter very much for predicting class identity in the United States is precisely because in the United States classes are primarily constituted within consumption on the basis of material interests alone, and in terms of consumption a married woman's mediated class location is generally much more causally important than her own direct class. *If* in Sweden classes were similarly constituted primarily in the realm of consumption, then in spite of the weaker economic dependence of women on their husbands, their direct class would still not have a particularly powerful impact on their identity. The greater predictive power of married Swedish women's direct class on their identity comes from the greater salience of class experiences within work on the lives of workers in general in Sweden.[20] In this alternative approach to the issues, then, Goldthorpe's predictions about married women work reasonably well in the United States because the central presupposition of his conceptualization of class – that classes consist of families as units of common material interests/consumption – is much more appropriate for the class structure of the United States than of Sweden.

The data in the present analysis do not lend themselves to a direct assessment of these alternative types of explanations. To explore the issues properly we would need two other cases: one which was rather like Sweden in the degree of economic autonomy of women, but shared with the United States a consumption-based (family based) constitution of classes, and one which shared with Sweden the pro-duction-centered salience of class, but had the American pattern of economic dependency. Parallel data for such cases are not available.

There are indirect pieces of evidence in the data, however, which are supportive of the interpretation which emphasizes both causal path-ways in Figure 10.1. If the material interest dependency argument was correct, then it would be expected that the wife's economic contribu-tion variable in in Table 10.3 should have a systematic effect on class identity. This effect might be a direct one – the greater the wife's contribution, the higher the probability of a working-class identity – or it might be an interactive one – the greater the wife's contribution, the stronger the relationship between her direct class and her identity (or the weaker the relationship between her spouse's class and her identity). In no equation was this variable ever statistically signifi-

---

[20] It should be noted in this context that the coefficients for the working-class dummy variable for Swedish women's direct class in all equations are greater than the corresponding dummy variable for *men* in the United States.

cant.[21] Thus, while it is the case that Swedish married women contribute proportionately more to the total family income than do American married women, there is no evidence that the class identity of either American or Swedish women is affected by the variation across households in such contributions.

A second piece of evidence consistent with the emphasis on workplace experience rather than simply material interests concerns the Hours Worked variable in Table 10.3. This variable is very significant for Swedish women, but not for American women, indicating that the more hours a Swedish woman works on the job, the higher the probability of a working-class identification. If we assume that class experiences at the workplace become more salient as one works longer hours, then this result for Swedish women is consistent with the view that what is distinctive in Sweden is the greater salience of workplace-centered class experiences in constituting classes.

These results, it should be stressed, do *not* indicate that it is incorrect to conceptualize classes in terms of common material interests. The consistent explanatory power of women's mediated class locations for their identity in both the United States and Sweden and the strong negative coefficient for the family income variable for men and women in both countries are consistent with the view that class structure is explanatory at least in part because of the material interests it generates. What the data do not support is the view that *differences* in the class-based configurations of material interests for women in the two countries explain the *differences* in the patterns we have observed. The reason why direct class relations have greater salience relative to mediated class relations among Swedish women, therefore, seems largely due to causal processes which intensify the importance of workplace class experiences in the constitution of class in Swedish society in general, rather than to mechanisms which affect the relative contribution to material interests of direct and mediated relations.

---

[21] I tried a variety of interaction models, thinking that perhaps the economic contribution variable would only have a positive effect on identity within the working class, but none of these interactions was significant either. The lack of significant coefficients for wife's income contribution could, of course, simply be the result of poor measurement of this concept. Or it could be the case that this concept is a poor indicator of economic dependency: dependency may be a function of what a married woman *could* earn counterfactually if she needed to, rather than what she actually does earn. Nevertheless, the more straightforward interpretation of these results is that they run counter to the expectations of the dependency interpretation.

10.6 Conclusions

At the core of much Marxian class analysis is the claim that class structure is a fundamental determinant of social conflict and social change. In trying to defend and deepen this intuition, contemporary Marxist theorists have been torn between two theoretical impulses. The first impulse is to keep the concept of class structure as simple as possible, perhaps even accepting a simple polarized vision of the class structure of capitalism, and then to remedy the explanatory deficiencies of such a simple concept by introducing into the analysis a range of other explanatory principles (e.g. divisions within classes or between sectors, the relationship between work and community, the role of the state or ideology in shaping the collective organization of classes, etc.). The second impulse is to gradually increase the complexity of the class structural concept itself in the hope that such complexity will more powerfully capture the explanatory mechanisms embedded in class relations. Basically, these alternative impulses place different bets on how much explanatory work the concept of class structure itself should do: the first strategy takes a minimalist position, seeing class structure as at most shaping broad constraints on action and change; the second takes a maximalist position, seeing class structure as a potent and systematic determinant of individual action and social development.

My work on class has pursued this second strategy. In my theoretical discussions of class structure I have been preoccupied with the problem of the "middle class," with elaborating a class structure concept that would give a coherent and systematic theoretical status to nonproletarian employees in the class structure. This led to the introduction of the concept of "contradictory locations within class relations," and subsequently, to the reformulation of that concept in terms of a multidimensional view of exploitation.

In this chapter I have tried to elaborate a second kind of complexity in the problem of class structure: a complexity derived from the fact that people are tied to the class structure not simply through their own personal jobs and property but through a variety of other kinds of social relations. Above all, in the present context, social relations within families constitute an important mechanism through which people are indirectly linked to the class structure. Since families are units of consumption, the class interests of actors are derived in part from the total material resources controlled by the members of a family and not simply by themselves. Social relations within families thus constitute a crucial source of what I have termed "mediated class relations."

The risk in adding this kind of complexity to class analysis is that the concept of class structure becomes more and more unwieldy. The simple, polarized image of class structure contained in Marx's theoretical writings has enormous polemical power and conceptual clarity. A concept of class structure that posits contradictory class locations and complex combinations of direct and mediated class relations may, in the end, add more confusion than analytical power.

For the moment, however, I think that this is a line of theoretical elaboration that is worth pursuing. In particular, the couplet direct/ mediated class relations offers a specific way of linking a Marxist class analysis to an analysis of gender relations without simply subsuming the latter under the former. When the concept of class structure is built exclusively around direct class locations it seems reasonable to treat class relations and gender relations as having a strictly *external* relationship to each other. Gender relations may help to explain how people are *sorted* into class positions, and they may even have specific effects on the overall distribution of class positions (i.e. particular gender patterns may shape the availability of certain kinds of labor power and thus the potential for expansion of certain kinds of class positions), but the two kinds of relations – gender and class – do not combine to form a system of internal relations.[22]

When mediated class relations are added to a class-structure analysis, this strict dualism of external relations becomes unsatisfactory. Gender mechanisms do not simply sort people into mediated class locations whose properties are definable independently of gender. Rather, gender relations are constitutive of mediated class relations as such. Such mediated class relations through the family are inherently gendered since the gender relations between husbands and wives are the very basis for their respective mediated class locations. The concept of mediated class relations, therefore, makes it possible to move away from a view of class and gender in which these two kinds of relations

[22] The contrast between X and Y being linked by *external* relations and *internal* relations is rather similar to the distinction between a liquid in which two elements are in suspension and a liquid in which two elements have combined to form a compound. In the former case, X and Y act independently of each other producing effects; in the latter they constitute a gestalt formed by the internal relations, and some of their effects come from the operation of these internal relations.

are treated as entirely distinct, separate structures. And yet it does not move all the way toward the view that class and gender constitute a unitary, undifferentiated system. Mediated class relations therefore provides a basis for conceptualizing one form of interaction of class and gender without collapsing the distinction itself.

We began this chapter by asking a question about the class location of husbands and wives in a number of "cross-class" families. The theoretical and empirical analyses of this chapter suggest that this question needs to be re-posed in a somewhat different way. Rather than asking "in what class is person X," we should ask, "what is the location of person X within a network of direct and mediated class relations." While the question is rather inelegant, nevertheless it identifies a critical dimension of complexity of the class structures of contemporary capitalism.

Methodological appendix

Variables

Class location. Because of sample size limitations and because of the less detailed data available for spouse's direct class, for most of the analysis in this chapter we have to collapse the categories in the class typology into broader groups. In particular, there are two important departures from the more nuanced typology. First, it is necessary to combine all self-employed into a single category, thus ignoring the distinction between the petty bourgeoisie and small capitalists. Since the large majority of individuals in this combined category are either strict petty bourgeois employing no wage-earners, or employers with fewer than five employees, I will generally refer to this category as the "petty bourgeoisie" in the discussion. Secondly, the categories of "contradictory class locations" among wage-earners will be combined into a single and rather heterogeneous "middle class." The analysis will therefore revolve around three basic class categories (see Wright 1985: Table 6.13: 226, for details of the operationalizations used for this analysis):

petty bourgeoisie = all self-employed

middle class = all wage-earners occupying managerial or supervisory authority positions or in professional, managerial or technical occupations

working class = all wage-earners in nonsupervisory jobs and
occupations other than professional, managerial and technical

Class identity. Throughout this analysis we focus on *working-class
subjective identification* as the dependent variable. All respondents were
asked whether or not they thought of themselves as belonging to a
social class. If they responded "yes," they were asked to name the
class; if they answered "no," they were asked whether they would
consider themselves to be working class, middle class or upper middle
class if they had to make a choice. For the present analysis all working-
class responses have been combined to form a simple dichotomy:
1 = working-class identification; 0 = all others. The class identity
variable is available only for respondents, not for their spouses.

Wife's economic contribution. Respondents with spouses in the labor
force were asked to estimate the proportion of the total family income
contributed by their spouses. For women respondents, this is the
proportion of family income coming from the husband; for men it is
the proportion coming from the wife. By subtracting the figure for
female respondents from 100, the variable is converted into a wife's
economic contribution variable.

Assumptions underlying the empirical strategy

Any empirical investigation presupposes a set of premises about the
measurement of concepts which are not directly subjected to empirical
tests in the research. Since some of these may affect the data analysis
and interpretation, it is important to make them as explicit as possible.

1 *The formal criteria for class location are the same for men and women.*
   Throughout the analysis we use exactly the same formal criteria –
   authority position, occupational credentials, property ownership
   – for defining and operationalizing the class location of the jobs of
   men and women. This may be problematic. If, for example, the
   same formal position in authority hierarchies confers radically
   different powers on men and women, or the same occupational
   credentials confers different potentials for "skill exploitation,"
   then different formal criteria should be used for men and women.
   It is always possible, therefore, that what appears to be different
   effects of direct and mediated class relations on the class identities

of men and women might simply be a result of the gender-specific problems of measurement of class.

2 *Responses to a direct question about class identification is an appropriate way of measuring class identity.* Measuring any aspect of subjectivity poses familiar and pervasive methodological problems. There is no need here to review the specific difficulties in using an attitude survey as an instrument for measuring class identity. The premise of the analysis is *not* that the measures we use are unbiased, but rather that whatever biases and problems occur in these measurements of class identity are not systematically related to the problem of the relative importance of direct and mediated class relations among men and women. If this assumption is correct, then even if we do not have confidence in the actual *levels* of working-class identification we observe, we would have reasonable confidence in the *patterns of association* of working-class identification with other variables.

3 *Working-class identity has basically the same meaning in Sweden and the United States.* The practical problems in measuring dimensions of subjectivity are dramatically augmented in comparative research. If the term "working class" has a dramatically different meaning in two countries, then any different patterns of association with "independent variables" that one observes could simply reflect the fact that the operational dependent variables are tapping substantively different aspects of subjectivity. Suppose, for example, that the words "working class" mean "manual laborer" in one country, "nonsupervisory labor" in another, and "hard-working people" (as opposed to "social parasites") in a third. It would be expected that different objective characteristics of jobs would predict "working-class identity" in these three countries, simply because the words are being used differently. To be sure, such linguistic differences might be of considerable sociological interest and could themselves be closely bound up with different historical patterns of class struggle, but such variations in the cultural meaning of terms should not be confused with differences in the causal structures of the same categories of subjective class identification.

4 *The relative salience of direct and mediated class relations in the constitution of class locations will be reflected in their respective*

associations with subjective class identity. We are using the correlations between class locations (direct and mediated) and subjective class identity as a criterion for assessing arguments about the relative salience of direct and mediated class relations. This whole enterprise hinges on the untested assumption that when direct class locations are more salient than mediated class relations, they will also have a stronger association with subjective class identity. If that premise is incorrect, or if it is correct for one gender or country and not another, then the conclusions we draw from that premise will also be incorrect. One reason that one might doubt this assumption is that class itself may have significantly different meanings for men and women. Gender may not simply shape the relative salience of direct and mediated class locations; it may also shape what it is about those locations that is causally salient. Using the same indicators for men and women, therefore, would significantly distort the interpretation of the results.

We are not able to systematically address any of these possible sources of bias and distortion in the data analyses of this chapter. Any one of them could seriously undermine the interpretations of results I elaborate. It is important to remember, however, that, in and of itself, a measurement bias does not inherently negate the value of a given set of results, since biases can as easily randomize results as support a particular hypothesis. For example, the possible problems in measurement of class location specified in assumption (1) above would have to be consistent not merely with the observed lower explanatory power of class (as measured) for women than for men, but also for the particular differences in gender patterns between the United States and Sweden. Simply pointing out measurement biases is insufficient to challenge the meaningfulness of a given interpretation of the patterns of results. The burden of a skeptic, therefore, is to show how a particular measurement bias actually generates the observed patterns, and thus renders them spurious.

11 The noneffects of class on the gendered division of labor in the home

The central objective of this chapter is to explore systematically the empirical relationship between *the location of households in the class structure* and *gender inequalities in performance of housework*. Since the middle of the 1970s, class analysts interested in gender, particularly those rooted in the Marxist tradition, have placed domestic labor at the center of analysis. In a variety of different ways, they have argued that the linkage between the system of production, analyzed in class terms, and the domestic division of labor, analyzed in gender terms, was at the heart of understanding the social processes through which gender relations were themselves reproduced (or perhaps even generated) in capitalist societies. Sometimes this argument took a rather reductionist form, particularly when the performance of unpaid domestic labor by women in the home was explained by the functional requirements of capital accumulation.[1] In other cases, the argument was less reductionist, emphasizing the nature of the class-generated constraints imposed on strategies of men and women as they negotiated gender relations within the household rather than the functional fit between capitalism and patriarchy.[2] And in still other analyses, the possibilities

[1] The debate over the functional relationship between capitalist exploitation and unpaid domestic labor by housewives came to be known as the "domestic labor debate" in the 1970s. The essential argument of the class-functionalist position was: (1) that unpaid domestic labor had the effect of lowering the costs of producing labor power; (2) that this had the effect of increasing the rate of capitalist exploitation since capitalists could pay lower wages; (3) that in an indirect way, therefore, capitalists exploited housewives; and (4) that the basic explanation for the subordination of women – or at least, for the reproduction of that subordination – lay in the ways such domestic production fulfilled functions for capitalism. For a review of this debate see Molyneux (1979). Some of the main contributors to the discussion were Gardiner (1975), Secombe (1973), Hartmann (1981) and Barrett (1980).

[2] For a particularly cogent elaboration of this approach, see Brenner and Ramas (1984).

of systematic contradictions between the logics of capitalist class domination and patriarchal male domination were entertained.[3] In all of these analyses, in spite of the differences in theoretical argument, the role of domestic labor in the linkage between class relations and gender relations was a central theme.

With this theoretical preoccupation, it might have been expected that there would have developed a substantial body of research exploring the empirical relationship between the domestic division of labor and classes. This has not happened. While there are historical and qualitative case studies which examine the domestic division of labor and a few of these attempt to explore the class variations in such patterns, there is almost no research that tries to map out in a systematic quantitative manner the relationship between class and the gender division of labor in the household.[4]

A number of reasons might explain the lack of such research. Quantitatively oriented sociologists who have engaged with the problem of housework have not been particularly interested in class analysis or the dialogue between Marxism and feminism. At most, class enters the analysis in the form of occupation as one variable among many rather than as the central focus of investigation.[5] Marxists, who are centrally concerned with class and its effects, have generally posed the problem of class and gender at the abstract macro-structural level of analysis as the relationship between "capitalism" and "patriarchy." This tends to push offstage more micro-level problems concerned with the relationship between variations in class location and gender relations. Feminists, who are often deeply committed to the investigation of concrete, micro-level processes, have generally not taken class very seriously. And both Marxists and feminists have generally been quite hostile to quantitative research.

The basic objective of this chapter, then, is to explore empirically the relationship between class and the gendered domestic division of labor. More specifically, we will examine how the proportionate contribution by husbands to housework in dual-earner families varies

---

[3]   The possibility of such contradictions between capitalism and patriarchy plays an important role in Heidi Hartman's (1979a) influential essay, "The Unhappy Marriage of Marxism and Feminism."

[4]   For examples of the historical perspective on the gendered division of labor in the household, see Cowan (1983) and Strasser (1982).

[5]   Limited treatments of the relationship between occupationally defined class categories and the domestic division of labor can be found in Pahl (1984: 270–272), Berk (1985), Presser and Cain (1983), Coverman (1985).

across households with different class compositions. We will not attempt to develop a comprehensive multivariate explanatory model of gender inequalities in housework. Our object of explanation, therefore, is not strictly speaking the gender division of housework as such, but the relation between class and the gender division of labor. While it would be desirable to situate the problem of class and its effects on housework within such a comprehensive model, the data we will use in this analysis lack a number of critical variables needed for such an endeavor. In any case, before worrying about how class might be linked in a complex multivariate relationship to the various other determinants of gender inequalities in housework, it is important to establish as systematically as possible the class effects themselves. This is the task of the present analysis.

11.1 Theoretical expectations

As in Chapter 10, because of limitations of available data for spouses' class and because of limitations in sample size, the empirical investigations of this chapter will rely on a class concept which distinguishes only three categories: the self-employed (consisting of employers and petty bourgeois), "middle class" (employees who occupy a managerial or supervisory position within authority structures and/or are employed in a professional, managerial or technical occupation) and working class (all other employees). This simple three-category class variable in principle yields nine family-class locations. Unfortunately, again because of the relatively small sample size, there were two few people in family-class locations involving the self-employed to be able to differentiate all five of these categories. As a result, for families involving self-employment we will not distinguish between the husband and wife being self-employed. The resulting family-class categories are presented in Table 11.1. Our empirical task, then, is to explore how inequality between husbands and wives in housework varies across the categories of this family-class composition typology.

While neither Marxism nor feminism has a well-developed body of theory about the *variability* of the domestic division of labor across households with different class compositions, nevertheless there are some general expectations within class analysis and feminism that point toward certain broad hypotheses about this relationship. We will explore five such hypotheses.

Table 11.1. *Family-class composition matrix*

		Husband's job class		
		Self-employed	Middle class	Working class
Wife's job class	Self-employed	1	2	3
	Middle class	2	4	5
	Working class	3	6	7

Categories which we will distinguish in the family class composition matrix:

1 = pure self-employed family
2 = self-employment + middle class
3 = self-employment + working class
4 = pure middle-class family
5 = middle-class wife + working-class husband
6 = working-class wife + middle-class husband
7 = pure working-class family

Proletarianization and gender equality

The best-known discussion of the gender division of labor in classical Marxism is found in Frederick Engels' study, *The Origins of the Family, Private Property and the State* (Engels 1968 [1884]). Engels argued that male domination within the family was rooted in male control of private property. The pivot of this linkage was the desire by men to ensure that their property was inherited by their children. To accomplish this, men needed to control the fertility of women. Given the power and status they had by virtue of controlling property, men were able to translate this desire into practice. The broad institutions of male domination, Engels argued, are built upon this foundation.

On the basis of this reasoning, Engels argued that male domination would wither away in the households of porpertyless proletarians:

Here, there is a complete absence of all property, for the safe-guarding and inheritance of which monogamy and male domination were established. Therefore, there is no stimulus whatever here to assert male domination ... Moreover, since large scale industry has transferred the woman from house to the labour market and the factory, and makes her, often enough, the bread-winner of the family, the last remnants of male domination in the proletarian home have lost all foundation ... (Engels 1968 [1891]:508)

Engels' reasoning leads to two basic hypotheses:

Hypothesis 1. Working-class egalitarianism. The more proletarianized is a household, the more housework will tend to be equally divided between husbands and wives. The homogeneous working-class family, therefore, should have the most egalitarian distribution of housework.

Hypothesis 2. Petty bourgeois inegalitarianism. Households within which private ownership of the means of production remains salient will have a more inegalitarian division of housework. The homogeneous petty bourgeois household should therefore have the least egalitarian distribution of housework.

Sexism and class cultures

One of the persistent images in popular culture is the contrast between the middle-class husband with an apron helping in the kitchen, and the working-class husband tinkering with the car or drinking in a bar with his friends. There are many possible mechanisms which might under-write this contrast. The premium placed on physical toughness and male solidarity in manual labor may constitute a material basis for an exaggerated masculine identity in the working class. In line with the arguments of Melvin Kohn (1969) about the relationship between work and values, the greater cognitive complexity of middle-class jobs may encourage a more flexible and open set of attitudes toward gender roles. Regardless of the specific mechanism, this image leads to a specific prediction about class and the gender division of labor:

Hypothesis 3. Class cultures. Working-class men will, in general, do proportionately less housework than middle-class men. Homogeneous working-class households should therefore have the most inegalitarian distribution of housework, while homogeneous middle-class households should be the most egalitarian.

Class and power within the family

An important theme in the sociology of gender is the problem of bargaining power between men and women within households. Particularly in an era in which gender roles are being challenged, the division of labor in the household should not be viewed as simply the result of a script being followed by highly socialized men and women. Rather, the amount of housework done by husbands should be viewed as at least in part an outcome of a process of contestation, conflict and bargaining.

The class location of husbands and wives bears on their respective power in the household in two ways. First, as in any bargaining situation, the resources people bring to household bargaining affect their relative power. In these terms, class inequalities between men and women would be expected to be translated into power differentials within the household. The more economically dependent a wife is on her husband, the weaker will be her bargaining position within the household and thus the more inegalitarian the gender division of labor is expected to be.[6] This would imply that when wives are in more advantaged class locations than their husbands, housework should be more equally divided. Second, quite apart from sheer material resources, status differentials are likely to play a role in bargaining situations (Coverman 1985). To the extent that wives occupy lower status in the labor force than their husbands, they are thus also likely to be in a weaker bargaining position within the household. Taking these two issues together leads to the following hypothesis:

> *Hypothesis 4. Class bargaining power.* In households in which the wife is in a more privileged class location than her husband she will have greater relative bargaining power and thus her husband is likely to do more housework. Households with middle-class wives and working-class husbands are thus likely to be the most egalitarian.

---

[6] Examples of this kind of argument can be found in Blumstein and Schwartz (1984) and Hood (1983). Becker (1981) also argues that women will specialize in housework because of the wage gap between men and women, but he does not see this as affecting housework because of the implications of wage differentials for power within the family. Instead, he sees this simply as a rational allocation of labor time given that male leisure time is more valuable for the economic welfare of the family as a whole.

Autonomy of gender relations

One of the core feminist theses about gender relations in capitalist society is that they have a certain degree of real autonomy with respect to other causal processes. On the one hand, this means that gender is socially constructed rather than a mere expression of biological processes. On the other hand, it means that in the social processes within which this construction takes place, gender is not reducible to any other social phenomenon, particularly class or the economy. While there may be important causal interactions between class and gender, gender relations are not mere functions of class or anything else, and in this sense they have some genuine autonomy.

An implication of relatively strong versions of the gender autonomy thesis is that the amount of housework men do will be primarily determined by the nature of gender relations and gender struggles, not by such things as class. While this does not mean that class would have no effects at all, these effects should be fairly muted. This suggests the following hypothesis:

> *Hypothesis 5. Gender autonomy.* The degree of equality in the gender division of labor will not vary very much across households with different class compositions.

11.2 Results

As in Chapter 10, we will explore this problem comparatively in Sweden and the United States.[7] Sweden and the United States are almost at opposite poles among developed capitalist countries in terms of economic inequalities in general and the gender dimension of inequality in particular. The Swedish state has poured much greater resources into public childcare, paid parental leaves and other programs which might impact on the gender division of labor within families.[8] A comparison of inequalities in housework in the two countries, therefore, may give some insight into the extent to which

---

[7] There have been few cross-national comparisons of housework, and those which do exist have not discussed class. For other comparative analyses of housework see Robinson, Andreyenkov and Patrushev (1988) and Szalai (1966a, 1966b; Szalai et al. 1972).

[8] For a discussion of these family policies in Sweden, see Moen (1989: 24–28) and Ruggie (1984).

this egalitarianism in the public sphere is reflected in greater egalitarianism in the private sphere.

We will present the results in three steps. First, we will examine briefly the overall distributions of housework in the two countries. This is mainly to provide a background context for the rest of our analysis. Second, we will examine the overall patterns of class variation in husbands' performance of housework. Finally, we will examine how these patterns are affected when various other variables are included in the analysis. In particular, we will be concerned to examine the effect of including education in the equation, since it might be thought that what at first looks like class differences in housework performance could in fact be education differences.

Overall distributions

Table 11.2 presents the basic distributions of husbands' percentage contribution to housework as reported by the male and female respondents to the surveys in the United States and in Sweden. There are a number of features of these distributions worth noting.

First of all, the basic contours of the distributions in Table 11.2 are similar to those reported in other studies. Most research indicates that in families within which both husbands and wives are in the paid labor force, men do between 20% and 30% of housework. This is roughly what we find here.[9]

Second, it is also worth noting that while the reports of husbands' contributions to housework are consistently higher by our male respondents than by our female respondents, the rank orders of husbands' contributions to different tasks based on male and female reports are identical in the US and nearly identical in Sweden. For routine housework tasks, in both countries husbands make the least contribution to laundry and the most contribution to grocery shopping.

Third, overall, Swedish husbands in two-earner households appear to do a somewhat greater proportion of housework than their American counterparts.[10] On the basis of the female reports of husbands'

---

[9]　The proportion of housework men do is reported in other studies as follows: Pleck (1985; 30–31): 20.3%, and over 30% where childcare is included; Berk (1985; 66): 27%; Walker and Woods (1976): 21.6%, and with childcare, 20.7%; Robinson (1977; 63): 17.5%, and 20.7% with childcare; Meissner et al. (1975): 20.7% including childcare.

[10]　This finding is consistent with the findings of Haas (1981) that Swedish households involved a more egalitarian gender distribution of labor than American households.

contribution, with the exception of childcare, Swedish men contribute more to housework than American men on every household task. Taking all of these tasks together, Swedish men in two-earner families do on average just over 25% of the housework whereas American men only do about 20%.

If anything, this is an underestimate of the real difference between the two countries in gender inequality in housework, since a much higher proportion of Swedish married women in the labor force than of American married women are part-time employees. The average number of hours worked per week by the wives in our sample is 30.9 in Sweden and 39.9 in the United States. If we adjust for differences in hours of paid labor force participation, then the difference in husbands' contribution to housework between the two countries is even more striking. A Tobit[11] regression of wife's hours of paid labor force work on husband's percentage contribution to housework generates following equations for Sweden and the United States:

Sweden: Husband's contribution = 16.01 + 0.563 [Wife's hours]
US: Husband's contribution = 3.32 + 0.418 [Wife's hours]

On the basis of these equations, in two-earner families in which the wife works 40 hours a week, her husband would be expected to do about 20% of the housework in the United States, whereas in a comparable family in Sweden, the husband would be expected to do over 38% of the housework.[12] While the data do indicate that housework remains unevenly divided in both countries, the degree of gender inequality in the household is clearly greater in the United States than in Sweden.[13]

Variations in husbands' housework across class locations

The dependent variable in our analyses of the relationship between class and housework is the variable "total housework" in column 8 of

---

[11] For technical reasons, it is preferable to use Tobit regressions rather than OLS regressions in the analysis of housework because of the large number of zero values on the dependent variable. The rationale for this technique is presented in the methodological appendix.

[12] These estimates are basically the same if OLS regressions are used instead of Tobit regressions.

[13] Of course, the fact that wives are more likely than husbands to be part-time workers in Sweden is itself a result of qualitative aspects of the gender division of labor. Swedish policies which facilitate part time work and more flexible career structures (through parental leave and other arrangements), therefore, may not by themselves challenge gendered divisions of labor as such, but they do appear to underwrite less gender inegalitarianism within the domestic sphere of work itself.

Table 11.2. *Distribution of husband's contribution to housework in the United States and Sweden*

Percentage of housework done by husband	1 Routine cleaning	2 Cooking	3 Meal cleanup	4 Grocery shopping	5 Laundry	6 Total routine housework[a]	7 Childcare	8 Total housework[b]
United States								
Women's reports								
0%	43.7	46.1	44.0	42.3	68.9	19.8	5.1	12.1
1–10%	9.1	18.4	12.2	10.4	8.3	23.5	1.5	23.5
11–30%	17.6	14.2	13.2	10.0	7.0	37.4	32.3	42.5
31–49%	6.3	3.1	2.0	3.8	1.9	13.1	18.7	15.4
50% or more	23.2	18.2	28.5	33.6	13.9	6.2	42.4	6.5
Mean	20.8	17.0	21.7	24.7	11.3	18.9	37.8	20.5
Weighted N	276	279	273	278	276	281	133	281
Men's reports								
0%	26.2	34.4	22.6	31.9	50.0	11.6	0.0	3.9
1–10%	12.3	21.5	18.0	12.3	10.3	17.8	2.1	21.7
11–30%	27.1	17.1	15.0	12.9	14.0	36.2	26.6	37.8
31–49%	6.6	4.9	10.3	4.6	3.8	24.4	23.9	26.8
50% or more	27.9	22.1	34.1	38.4	21.9	10.0	47.4	9.8
Mean	25.9	21.8	28.5	30.0	20.1	24.6	41.0	26.2
Weighted N	259	266	259	264	261	266	149	266
Ratio of women's mean to men's mean	0.80	0.78	0.76	0.82	0.56	0.76	0.92	0.78

Table 11.2. (Continued)

Sweden

Women's reports

0%	29.4	21.8	31.0	14.2	52.0	4.3	16.9	3.7
1-10%	11.7	27.3	14.8	16.3	9.5	20.7	15.8	18.7
11-30%	22.4	22.2	20.7	20.4	15.6	40.5	24.3	44.5
31-49%	7.4	3.8	2.1	9.2	3.1	25.1	9.0	24.1
50% or more	29.1	24.9	31.4	40.0	19.7	9.4	33.9	9.0
Mean	26.2	23.1	24.5	32.4	17.1	24.6	28.2	25.1
N	299	293	290	240	294	299	177	299

Men's reports

0%	19.0	13.5	29.7	8.5	39.0	3.4	6.6	3.2
1-10%	15.8	27.4	14.8	11.3	23.3	14.9	22.3	13.2
11-30%	22.1	22.8	20.1	23.9	13.7	40.4	29.9	42.4
31-49%	7.2	6.9	5.5	8.9	4.4	29.2	9.5	30.7
50% or more	35.9	29.4	29.9	47.4	19.8	12.0	31.8	10.6
Mean	30.5	27.6	25.7	37.4	19.1	28.2	30.8	28.5
N	348	347	344	293	344	349	211	349

Ratio of women's mean to men's mean	0.86	0.84	0.95	0.86	0.90	0.87	0.92	0.88

a. "Total routine housework" is a weighted sum of columns 1 through 5. The weights are: routine cleaning = 0.27; cooking = 0.32; cleaning up after meals = 0.14; groceries = 0.12; laundry = 0.15.

b. "Total housework" is equal to "total routine housework" for people without children under 16 living in the household, and is a weighted sum of columns 6 and 7 for people with children. The weights are: 0.84 for routine housework and 0.16 for childcare.

Table 11.2. The details for the construction of this variable are presented in the methodological appendix to this chapter. This scale is available for both our male and female respondents. We will present the results for all respondents combined and for the women respondents taken separately.[14]

Table 11.3 presents the mean amounts of housework performed by husbands within families of different class compositions. Table 11.4 then presents the Tobit regressions corresponding to Table 11.3. In these regressions, the pure middle-class household is the omitted dummy variable. The coefficients in the equation are thus differences between a given family-class location and the pure middle-class family.[15]

Before looking at specific class differences, it is worth looking at the overall analytical power of these equations. As Table 11.4 indicates, the R^2 from the OLS regressions corresponding to the Tobit equations is very low in both countries: for the women respondents' equations, only about 0.02 in the US and 0.04 in Sweden. This is not simply because the dependent variable is measured badly, for in the second equation reported in Table 11.5 the R^2 for the equation for Swedish women increases to 0.28 and for US women to 0.18. What the low R^2 in Table 11.4 therefore indicates is that very little of the variation across households in the relative contributions of husbands to housework is attributable to the class composition of the household in either country.

Class differences might not matter a great deal for the entire population, and yet certain contrasts across classes could still be quite large. Let us look first at the households within which both spouses are employees (i.e. cells 4–7 in Table 11.3). Two general results stand out: first, there are generally bigger class differences across these locations in Sweden than in the United States, and second, even in Sweden the class differences are not very striking. For the women respondents, in

---

[14] For reasons explained in the methodological appendix, the reports of wives about the proportion of housework done by their husbands are probably more accurate than the reports given by husbands about the proportion of housework they themselves do. For this reason, we will generally not discuss the separate results for the male respondents. These results are presented at the end of the methodological appendix.

[15] One technical note on interpreting these results: since the equations in Table 11.4 are based on Tobit regressions (rather than OLS regressions), the coefficients in these equations are not precisely the same as the differences in means between cells in Table 11.3.

the United States the proportion of housework done by husbands is virtually indistinguishable across the four employee class locations, whereas in Sweden, husbands in the pure middle-class household do a significantly greater proportion of the housework than do husbands in any of the other employee households (5.0–7.6 percentage points more than other family-class locations in Table 11.3). In terms of the actual numbers in Sweden and the United States in Table 11.3, the big difference between the two countries occurs in the pure middle-class households: Swedish middle-class husbands in pure middle-class households do nearly 10 percentage points more housework than their American counterparts (30.4% compared to 21.0%), whereas the differences between the United States and Sweden in the three other employee family-class locations are only a few percentage points.

Turning to the self-employed categories, we find that there are significant class differences in both countries, although again we find that in Sweden the class differences are larger than in the US. In the United States, husbands in families consisting of one self-employed member and one working-class member do less housework than in any other family-class location (only about 13% of total housework in Table 11.3, compared to around 21% in most other locations). In the results for the full sample, husbands in the pure self-employed household also do significantly less housework than in other class locations.[16] In Sweden, women in both of these family-class locations (households with both spouses self-employed and households with one self-employed and one worker) report that their husbands perform less housework than husbands in any other class location – less than two-thirds the contribution of husbands in the pure middle-class family. In both countries, therefore, it appears that in what might be thought of as traditional petty bourgeois households a more traditional form of patriarchy exists.

Multivariate equations

Table 11.5 presents the Tobit equations for class effects controlling for various other variables. In the first panel, only education is added to the equation; in the second panel, a number of other variables generally included in analyses of housework are included. Since many of these

[16] In the male only data, men in this kind of family report that they do an average of 14% of the housework which is actually less than reported by women in comparable families. The number of cases, however, is quite small.

Table 11.3. *Mean levels of husband's percentage contribution to total housework[a] by family-class composition (dual earner households only)*

All respondents

United States (N = 537)

		Husband's job-class		
		Self-employed	Middle class	Working class
Wife's job class	Self-employed	[1][b] 17.1	[2] 22.8	[3] 16.1
	Middle class	[2] 22.8	[4] 23.9	[5] 25.5
	Working class	[3] 16.1	[6] 22.3	[7] 27.1

Sweden (N = 641)

		Husband's job-class		
		Self-employed	Middle class	Working class
Wife's job class	Self-employed	[1] 16.0	[2] 25.1	[3] 19.6
	Middle class	[2] 25.1	[4] 32.4	[5] 27.8
	Working class	[3] 19.6	[6] 25.1	[7] 28.1

Women respondents

United States (N= 267)

	Husband's job-class		
	Self-employed	Middle class	Working class
Wife's job — Self-employed	[1] 19.8	[2] 22.4	[3] 13.1
Wife's job — Middle class	[2] 22.5	[4] 21.0	[5] 20.0
Wife's job — Working class	[3] 13.1	[6] 21.3	[7] 22.1

Sweden (N= 297)

	Husband's job-class		
	Self-employed	Middle class	Working class
Wife's job class — Self-employed	[1] 17.9	[2] 22.8	[3] 19.3
Wife's job class — Middle class	[2] 22.8	[4] 30.4	[5] 22.9
Wife's job class — Working class	[3] 19.3	[6] 24.3	[7] 25.4

a. "Total Housework" is a weighted average of the five housework tasks and childcare (for families with children under 16 living in the household) and simply of the five housework tasks for families without children at home. The weights are given in Table 11.2.

b. The numbers in square brackets refer to the categories listed in Table 11.1

Table 11.4. *Tobit regressions of family-class compositions on husband's housework*

	Men and Women (p)[a]		Women only (p)	

United States

Class categories[b]

1 Self-employed household	−7.5	(.03)	−2.4	(.60)
2 Self-employed + middle	−1.4	(.69)	1.1	(.83)
3 Self-employed + worker	−8.7	(.02)	−9.9	(.04)
5 Wife middle + husband worker	1.0	(.75)	−1.8	(.68)
6 Wife worker + husband middle	−2.0	(.48)	−0.6	(.89)
7 Wife worker + husband worker	3.6[c]	(.17)	1.8	(.62)
R^2 from corresponding OLS regression	.03		.02	
N	537		267	

Sweden

Class categories

1 Self-employed household	−17.9	(.00)	−13.8	(.01)
2 Self-employed + middle	−8.3	(.02)	−8.9	(.11)
3 Self-employed + worker	−13.3	(.00)	−11.0	(.02)
5 Wife middle + husband worker	−4.8	(.09)	−7.7	(.05)
6 Wife worker + husband middle	−7.4	(.00)	−6.2	(.04)
7 Wife worker + husband worker	−4.4	(.03)	−5.1	(.07)
R^2 from corresponding OLS regression	.06		.04	
N	641		297	

a. (p) is the statistical significance level using a t-test on the Tobit coefficient.

b. The pure middle-class household is the left-out category. All coefficients are therefore the difference between a given family class and the pure middle class.

c. There is a statistically significant difference (p < .03) between categories (7) and (6) – the pure working–class family and the wife worker/husband middle family – in this equation for all respondents taken together but not for the women only equation.

variables are measured only at the individual (rather than family unit) level of analysis, we have not included the regression for the male and female combined sample in these results.

The inclusion of education in the equation serves an important analytical purpose. In most concepts of class structure, education levels vary systematically across classes. In the conceptual approach we have adopted, education is intimately linked to one of the three assets which

Table 11.5. *Tobit regressions for family-class composition and selected other variables on husband's housework*

	United States	Sweden
	Women respondents (p)[a]	Women respondents (p)
Class categories[b]		
1 Self-employed household	-1.4 (.77)	-9.5 (.10)
2 Self-employed + middle	0.9 (.86)	-7.7 (.17)
3 Self-employed + worker	-8.9 (.06)	-7.5 (.14)
5 Wife middle + husband worker	-0.6 (.89)	-5.0 (.22)
6 Wife worker + husband middle	-0.3 (.93)	-2.9 (.39)
7 Wife worker + husband worker	2.5 (.52)	-0.8 (.82)
Respondent's education	1.0 (.40)	1.8 (.03)
R^2 from corresponding OLS regression	.03	.06
N	267	297
Class categories		
1 Self-employed household	0.5 (.91)	-10.5 (.04)
2 Self-employed + middle	1.7 (.71)	-8.8 (.08)
3 Self-employed + worker	-1.4 (.77)	-5.0 (.29)
5 Wife middle + husband worker	-3.3 (.46)	-5.9 (.11)
6 Wife worker + husband middle	-0.8 (.83)	-2.4 (.42)
7 Wife worker + husband worker	4.3 (.26)	-2.6 (.41)
Respondent's education	-0.2 (.86)	0.5 (.55)
Respondent's hours of paid work	0.4 (.00)	0.4 (.00)
Wife's income contribution	0.5 (.78)	3.7 (.002)
Total family income ($ x 10^{-4})	0.5 (.51)	0.8 (.28)
Respondent's gender ideology	1.2 (.06)	0.9 (.09)
Age	-0.3 (.03)	-0.2 (.02)
Kids under 16 in household (0-1)	-1.4 (.57)	-4.5 (.02)
R^2 from corresponding OLS regression	.18	.28
N	267	297

a. (p) is the statistical significance level using a t-test on the Tobit coefficient.

b. The pure middle-class household is the left-out category. All coefficients are therefore the difference between a given family class and the pure middle class.

underlie class relations – ownership of skills. It could well be, therefore, that what might at first blush look like class differences in husbands' performance of housework might turn out to be strictly education differences as such, reflecting the cultural effects of educational attainment rather than the class effects linked to the control of educational assets. The problem here is that the category "education" embodies two quite distinct kinds of mechanisms – a class-exploitation mechanism linked to labor markets and work relations and a cultural-cognitive mechanism. An association of wife's education with husband's performance of housework could be generated by either of these causal processes. Such a possibility is not terribly relevant for the US results, since there were such meager class effects in the first place, but it is clearly relevant for the Swedish case since in Table 11.4 husbands in the pure middle-class households do perform significantly more housework than husbands in other class locations.

As Table 11.5 illustrates, the class differences between the pure middle-class household and other households in Sweden are considerably reduced when education is included in the equation. Only one contrast remains statistically significant (at the marginal .10 level of significance), that between the pure middle-class household and the pure self-employed household. None of the differences across employee households are now statistically significant. Indeed, for one of these contrasts – the pure middle-class compared to the pure working-class family – the absolute magnitude of the difference in husband's contribution declines from 5.1 to 0.8. Basically all of the initial difference between these two family-class locations is associated with the differences in education of the wives in the two classes.

How should this education effect be interpreted? Can it be interpreted as bound up with the class-exploitation nexus? Table 11.6 indicates what happens to the value of the education coefficient when other variables are added to the equation in the top panel of Table 11.5. This table indicates that what is probably lurking behind the education effect is age: when age is included in the equation, the education coefficient is cut in half and its level of statistical significance drops from .03 to .29. Regardless of how one might want to interpret this age effect in its own right, its effect on the education coefficient indicates that the education effect itself cannot plausibly be considered an indirect form of class effects.[17]

---

[17] The coefficient for age in Table 11.6 and in the more complex multivariate equation

Table 11.6.   *Tobit regression coefficients for education on husband's housework controlling for various other variables (Swedish women only)*

	Education coefficient (p)[a]	Coefficient for added control variable (p)
Education + class dummies only	1.79 (.03)	
Education + class + age	0.89 (.29)	−0.30 (.001)
Education + class + ideology	1.35 (.10)	1.49 (.010)
Education + class + wife's income contribution	1.33 (.09)	6.24 (.000)
Education + class + wife hours in labor force	1.76 (.02)	0.58 (.000)
Education + class + kids under 16 in household	1.78 (.03)	−7.00 (.001)

a. (p) is the statistical significance level using a t-test on the Tobit coefficient.

The bottom panel of Table 11.5 presents the more complex multi-variate equation. Since our interest is primarily on class effects as such, we will not explore the coefficients in these equations in any detail. A number of things are worth noting.

First of all, in Sweden, but not in the United States, the contrast between the first two categories of self-employed households and middle-class households is, if anything, slightly more pronounced in the more complex multivariate equation than it was in the equation containing only class and education. In the United States there are absolutely no significant class contrasts in the multivariate equation.

Second, overall family income has no effect in either country, but the wife's proportionate contribution to family income has a considerable effect in Sweden (but not in the United States).[18] This indicates that while direct class effects on male housework are not very strong in Sweden, the economic status of the wife within the household is a significant determinant.

Third, the biggest single contributor to the increased R^2 between the top and bottom panels of Table 11.5 in both countries is the number of

in Table 11.5 probably reflects more of a cohort-cultural process than simply a life-cycle process, since the age affect remains highly significant even when the presence of children in the household is included in the equation.

[18] Other research has reported quite inconsistent results on the effects of relative earnings on the household division of labor. In no research has relative earnings been shown to be a powerful determinant of husbands' contribution to housework, although in some research it has some effect (e.g. Farkas 1976; Huber and Spitze 1983). For a review of this literature, see Coverman (1985).

hours worked in the paid labor force per week by the wife. The R^2 for this variable alone is .14 in Sweden and .07 in the US. This is consistent with the finding of much other research which indicates that because of a simple scarcity of time, as women increase their labor force participation, less housework gets done and thus inequality in housework time is reduced. The result is also consistent with the argument that when women work longer hours in the paid labor force they have more leverage in internal family bargaining to get their husbands to do more housework.[19]

Finally, the gender ideology of the wife has a modest effect in both countries. As might be expected, in the parallel equations for male respondents (see Appendix Table 11.5 in the methodological appendix) the gender ideology coefficient is much larger. This is particularly striking in the United States.[20] Since it is likely that the age variable (understood as measuring cultural-historical cohorts) also partially taps cultural dimensions of gender relations, these data indicate that gender ideologies vary across households in ways that are consequential for household gender practices.

11.3 Implications

Overall, the basic implication of these results is that location within the class structure is not a very powerful or systematic determinant of variations in the gender division of labor across households. This is most consistent with Hypothesis 5, the gender-autonomy hypothesis. This is decidedly not what I had expected when I began the analysis. Indeed, as part of my general agenda of class analysis, I was initially quite bent on demonstrating that class was a significant part of the explanation of variations in gender practices. When I initially encountered such marginal class effects, I therefore tried many alternative ways of operationalizing the details of the class variable and aggregating the class distinctions. I examined the separate effects of husband's and wife's class rather than simply family-class composition. I

---

[19] For a recent study which systematically explores the interactions between hours of paid work by women and domestic work, see Kalleberg and Rosenfeld (1990).

[20] It must be remembered that in the husbands' equations, the number of hours worked by the wife is not included as an independent variable. To the extent that husbands' ideology has effects on time allocated to the paid labor force of the wife, then it is not possible to unequivocally compare the coefficients for ideology in the male and female equations.

changed the boundaries of the sample, restricting it to two-earner families with two full-time workers, or two-earner families with and without children. I even explored the possibility that class was linked to the tails of the distribution of housework – to the contrast between highly egalitarian and inegalitarian households – rather than to the distribution as a whole. None of these manipulations of the data changed the essential contours of the results: class location is simply not a powerful determinant of the amount of housework husbands perform.

This does not mean that class has no relevance whatsoever for the analysis. In Sweden, at least, husbands in property-owning households (especially the purely self-employed households) seem to do significantly less housework than husbands in employee households, even after controlling for the range of variables in Table 11.5. This difference was equally strong in the equations for our male respondents taken separately (see Appendix Table 11.5). These results therefore provide some modest support for part of Engels' classic argument about property ownership and male domination. Still, while this specific class effect does seem robust, it nevertheless is not at the center stage of the process by which variations in gender relations are produced and negotiated within families. And, in any case, there are no consistent, significant class effects on housework in the United States data. On balance, therefore, there is no support in the data at all for Hypotheses 1, 3 and 4 – the working-class egalitarianism hypothesis, the class culture hypothesis and the class bargaining power hypothesis – and at best very limited support in Sweden for Hypothesis 2, the petty bourgeois inegalitarianism hypothesis.

There are possible responses to these results that a staunch defender of class analysis might propose. First of all, we have restricted the analysis to two-earner families. It could certainly be the case that class plays an important role in determining the basic decisions within households concerning wives' labor force participation in the first place, and as all research on the topic indicates, this certainly affects the relative (but not necessarily absolute) amount of housework done by husbands. There is, however, little empirical support for this response. The labor force participation rates of wives do not vary dramatically across husbands' class location either in the United States or in Sweden (see Table 11.7). Also, while husbands in all classes do a higher proportion of housework when their wives are in the labor force, the pattern of variation across classes does not itself differ very

Table 11.7   *Wives' labor force participation rates and husband's contribution to housework by husband's class*

Husband's class location	Labor force partici- pation rates of wives	Husband's percentage of contribution to total housework	
		Wife in paid labor force	Wife not in paid labor force
United States			
Capitalist class	54.3	20.1	17.0
Petty bourgeoisie	55.8	16.9	13.0
Middle class	51.6	25.2	19.8
Working class	50.4	30.8	21.7
N		266	247
Sweden			
Capitalist class	78.6	18.2	13.3
Petty bourgeoisie	86.0	19.0	10.6
Middle class	83.4	29.6	20.0
Working class	74.6	31.3	25.7
N		348	89

much between two-earner and single-earner households in either Sweden or the US.[21]

A more promising defense of class analysis shifts the focus from the problem of variations across households, to the more institutional issue of the relationship between the political mobilization of classes on the one hand and gender relations on the other. One might argue that the degree of housework egalitarianism in the society as a whole depends, in part, on processes of class politics which reduce or increase overall economic inequality. The greater egalitarianism of the gender division of labor within Swedish households is plausibly linked to the greater

[21] It also might be thought that class could be implicated in the husband's performance of housework via its effect on the number of hours of paid labor performed by wives. As we noted in the discussion of Table 11.5, the amount of hours worked in the labor force is a highly significant predictor of husbands' relative contribution to housework in two-earner households. However, this variable is itself only weakly linked to the class composition of households. Among two-earner employee households, in the United States the range across family-class locations in average hours of paid labor by wives is from 37 to 43 hours, and in Sweden from 29 to 32.

societal egalitarianism produced by the combined effects of Swedish social democracy and the labor movement.

While I would not want to minimize the importance of class politics in the formation of the Swedish welfare state, nevertheless it is problematic to attribute Swedish gender politics entirely to the logic of political class formation. Swedish social democracy has not merely produced an amorphous economic egalitarianism driven by working-class progressive politics; it has also supported a specific agenda of gender egalitarianism rooted in the political involvement of women. As Moen (1989) indicates, particularly in the 1970s, the Social Democratic government enacted a series of reforms specifically designed to transform the relationship between work, gender and family life: in 1971 separate income tax assessments were made mandatory for husbands and wives (which established the principle that each partner should be economically independent); in 1974 parental leave was established giving both mothers and fathers the right to share paid leave after the birth of a child; in 1978 paid leave was extended to 270 days and in 1980 to 360 days; in 1989 parents of infants became legally entitled to six-hour days, thus encouraging the expansion of opportunities for shorter work weeks. Furthermore, as reported by Haas (1981: 958), a specific objective of cultural policy in Swedish education is to encourage gender equality in childcare and, to a lesser extent, domestic chores. It seems likely that the greater egalitarianism within Swedish households has as much to do with these specific family-work policies and educational practices as it does with the more general class-based egalitarianism of Swedish society. To be sure, the class politics of social democracy helped to sustain a set of political and social values favorable to the enactment of such policies; but it seems unlikely that such policies can themselves be primarily explained in class terms.

One final line of response of class theorists to this research could be to shift the problem from the relationship between family-class location and gender to the relationship between class structure as such and gender. Instead of asking how the gender division of labor within families varies across locations within a class structure, the focus of analysis would be on how the gender division of labor varies across different kinds of class structures. Such an investigation could be posed either at the mode of production level of analysis, involving comparisons of capitalist class structures with different kinds of noncapitalist class structures, or at a more concrete level of analysis, involving comparisons across capitalist class structures at different stages of development. It is certainly possible that the central dynamics of capitalism as a specific kind of class system of production provide the most important explanations for the changing forms and degrees of labor force participation of women over the past century in Western capitalist countries, and these changing forms of labor force participation in turn provide the central structural basis for transformations of gender relations within families, reflected in changes in husbands' participation in housework. The trajectory of development of the class structure of capitalism, therefore, might explain much of the trajectory of changes in gender relations even if gender relations do not vary systematically across different locations within a given class structure. For the moment, however, such arguments must remain speculative hypotheses. Much additional research is needed to validate or modify such claims.

Where does this leave us? Feminists have long argued for the autonomy of gender mechanisms in explaining the production and reproduction of male domination. While Marxist class analysis has generally come to acknowledge this autonomy, nevertheless there has remained a tendency for Marxists to see class as imposing systematic limits within which such autonomous gender mechanisms operate. The data analysis in this chapter indicate that, at least in terms of the micro-analysis of variations in gender relations within housework across households, there is basically no support for the view that class plays a pervasive role. The class effects are extremly weak – virtually nonexistent in the United States, and largely confined to the effects of self-employment in Sweden. While *economic* factors do seem quite relevant – the number of hours worked by wives in the labor force is a relatively strong determinant of variations in housework as is the wife's contribution to household income (at least in Sweden) – the relevance of these economic factors is not closely linked to class as such.

Methodological appendix

1 Variables

Gender division of labor in the household
The gender division of labor within households has both a qualitative and quantitative aspect. Qualitatively, the concept concerns the alloca-

tion of different sorts of tasks and responsibilities to husbands and wives; quantitatively it concerns the amount of time each spouse devotes to housework relative to other kinds of activities (including leisure). As all research on the topic has indicated, in most families men not only do different household tasks from their wives, but spend much less total time on housework as well.[22] While both of these dimensions are of general interest, we focus primarily on the quantitative aspects of the domestic division of labor in this chapter. That is, we are concerned with seeing if the degree of gender inequality in time contributions to housework varies across families in different locations in the class structure.

It is an arduous affair to measure fully the division of labor in the household. The most elaborate studies have involved complex time budget diaries in which household members carefully record the time at which they start and stop every activity during a particular period of time.[23] We rely on a much simpler kind of data. In the surveys we use, respondents were asked to estimate roughly what percentage of each task on a list of common household tasks they did themselves and what percentage was done by their spouses. Five tasks were included in the list: routine housecleaning, cooking, cleaning up after meals,

[22] Most research also indicates that, at least in dual-earner households, husbands in general spend less total time on all forms of "work" – paid work + domestic work. Walker (1970) finds for dual-earner households that women who do at least 15 hours of paid work per week do an average of 70 hours combined paid work and housework per week, compared to 63 hours for men. In a later study, Walker together with Woods (1976) found that in dual-earner families wives did a daily total of 10.1 hours of paid and unpaid labor, and husbands did 7.9. Robinson (1977) reports that husbands in dual-earner households do 6.9 hours of total work/day while wives do 9.3 hours. Similar findings are reported by Meissner et al. (1975) who calculates husbands working 7.7 hours total work per day and wives 9.0 hours. Pleck (1985) is one of the few analysts who has shown some skepticism toward the magnitudes of these differences in total hours of work of husbands and wives in dual-earner households. He analyzes data from two surveys, one which finds that employed wives work slightly longer in combined paid work and housework (0.2 hours/day more) and a second which finds that employed wives have substantially longer work days (paid and housework combined) than their husbands (2.2 hours/day more). The differences in the results of these two studies reflect, to a significant degree, different definitions of what constitutes "work" within the household, particularly whether *all* childcare time is counted as work, or whether some of this is considered "play."

[23] Studies which have employed time budget approaches are: Berk (1979, 1985), Berk and Berk (1979), Geerken and Gove (1983), Meissner et al. (1975), Morgan et al. (1971), Pleck (1985), Robinson (1977), Robinson, Andreyenkov and Patrushev (1988), Szalai et al. (1972).

grocery shopping and laundry. A similar question was also asked for childcare for those families with children under 16 in the household. The percentages for each of these tasks were then combined into two aggregate housework scales:

1 a simple additive scale (the unweighted mean of the components);
2 a weighted scale, in which the components were weighted by the relative amount of time these tasks typically take (based on published time-budget research).

Initially this scale was constructed only for the routine housework tasks. For people with children, this scale was then combined with the childcare tasks to produce an overall domestic labor contribution scale, to be referred to as "Total Housework Contribution." As it turned out, none of the results differ substantively for any of these scales, so throughout this chapter the analysis is restricted to the weighted total housework contribution scale. The weights used in constructing this scale are as follows:[24]

> *Routine Housework scale =*
>   0.32 [cooking meals] + 0.12 [cleaning up after meals]
>   + 0.15 [laundry] + 0.27 [general housecleaning] + 0.14 [groceries].
> *Total Housework scale =*
>   0.84 [routine housework] + 0.16 [childcare].

The resulting variable, therefore, is a measure of the percentage, from 0 to 100, of the total housework performed by the respondent. For people with children under 16 years of age in the home this includes childcare; for people without children it does not. In order to facilitate the data analysis, I converted this scale into a *husband's* housework contribution variable.[25] A figure around 50, therefore, means that husbands and wives contribute more or less equally to housework.

It should be noted that relative equality in housework contributions

---

[24] The sources for the routine housework weights were the findings in Robinson (1977: 148–149) and Meissner et al. (1975: 432) and for the childcare weights, Meissner, et al. (1975: 432).

[25] Because not all the percentages reported for respondents and spouses added up to 100, I first proportionately balanced the reported shares. Then for male respondents, I took the respondents' reports for their own share of housework, and for the female respondents, I took the proportion they reported for their spouses. When there was missing data from some of these elements of the scale, I adjusted the weights accordingly and calculated the total housework contribution variable

can be achieved through two routes: either men can do more house-work, or women can do less. Other research has indicated that when women enter the labor force there is, at best, a modest increase in the absolute amount of time husbands spend on housework, whereas wives reduce the amount of time considerably.[26] Less housework is done, and that which is done is done more intensively. The result is less inequality in housework contributions, but not primarily because of more housework on the part of husbands.[27] We cannot in the present study address this issue at all. Our analysis will be entirely focussed on the degree of inegalitarianism in the gender distribution of housework time, not on the amount of housework actually performed.

Problems of biases in the housework measures
It is important to stress that the measures of husbands' performance of housework we are using are all based on subjective estimates; we have no independent way of checking the reliability of our respondents' reports. It might therefore be reasonably expected that there are biases in these estimates. In particular, one might expect men to exaggerate their relative contribution to housework. This expectation is confirmed by the fact that the mean values of husbands' housework contribution for each of the components of the scale (and thus for the aggregate scale itself) are significantly lower when reported by the wives in the sample than by the husbands (see Table 11.2). This is particularly striking in the United States data where the reports by women of their

for the available data (as long as there were reports on at least two of the household tasks).

[26] No difference in the absolute amount of housework men do when their wives enter the labor force is reported by Meissner et al. (1975), Walker (1970); and Walker and Woods (1976), while an increase of between 4 and 6 minutes per day is reported by Robinson (1977), Berk (1985) and Pleck (1985). The decrease in the amount of housework women do when they enter the workforce is reported as follows: Robinson (1977): 3.5 hours per day decrease; Walker and Woods (1976): 3.3 hours/ day; Walker (1970): 1 hour/day less when the wife works less than 15 hours weekly, 2 hrs/day less when she works between 15 and 19 hours per week, and 3 hours less when she works more than 30 hours in a week; Pleck (1985): 3 hours/day less; Vanek (1974): 4 hrs/day.

[27] If the changes in the *intensity* at which women do housework is sufficiently great because there are simply fewer hours available for such work, then the apparently greater egalitarianism in housework contributions could be entirely an illusion. The disparities in the actual *amount of work*, measured not in units of time but in units of time weighted by effort or intensity, could remain constant, or even increase. No research of which I am aware has even broached this problem, let alone attempted to empirically engage it.

husbands' contributions to housework are generally about 75% of the men's reports of their own contributions, whereas in Sweden the women's reports are closer to 90% of the men's.

Since we are mainly interested in the *variability* of husbands' housework contribution across class location and not with estimating the absolute levels of gender inequality within families, these kinds of biases would only undermine the usefulness of these data if they were significantly correlated with class. Unfortunately, there is some indication that this may be the case. If the gender bias in measures of housework were unrelated to class, then the patterns of *differences* in husbands' housework across the cells in the family-class matrix should be basically the same for data based on the reports of wives and of husbands. That is, all of the variables in such an analysis are derived from family-level data: the class composition of the family and the husbands' proportion of total family housework. Given that we have restricted the sample to two-earner families, there is no *substantive* reason why the patterns of differences across family-class categories of the table for data reported by men and by women should differ.

But they do. To give just one example, the average of husbands' housework contribution reported by Swedish women in the pure middle-class family is 30.4%, while the average of reports by men in the same kind of household is 33.9%. Those are reasonably close estimates. In households in which the husband is in a working-class job and the wife is in a middle-class job, on the other hand, the reports are quite divergent: 22.9% for female respondents compared to 32.6% for male respondents. The differences *across* these family-class locations, therefore, are 7.5% as reported by women but only 1.3% as reported by men. On the basis of the male responses we would conclude that there were no family-class composition effects, whereas on the basis of the female responses we might conclude the opposite. Whatever might be the root cause of the measurement problems, these discrepancies indicate that not merely is it the case that men may overestimate the amount of housework that they do, but that these overestimates vary from class to class and thus potentially undermine our attempt at a class analysis of housework.

What should be done in these circumstances?[28] There are two

---

[28] We have been unable to find any research on housework which systematically explored the degree of biases in reports of housework contributions. Berk and Shih (1980) do extensively explore the patterns of the discrepancies of reports by husbands and wives, but do not attempt to actually assess which estimates are less

plausible strategies. In the first strategy of analysis it is assumed that reports of both men and women are biased, but in different directions. Each spouse overestimates his or her *own* contribution, and since our data are proportions, this necessarily means that they underestimate their partners' contribution. Thus, the most accurate measure of housework is likely to come from combining the data from men and women into a single analysis. This calls for analyzing the relationship between class location and housework for the total sample of respondents in two-earner families, ignoring the respondent's gender. In the second strategy, it is assumed that women will have a more accurate view, both because they have so much more general *responsibility* for these tasks and because their contributions to housework are often less visible than their husbands' and thus are more likely to go unnoticed by their spouses. If one accepts this assumption, then it would make more sense to rely exclusively on the data for women. In neither strategy is there much value in analyzing the men's responses separately.

In the statistical analysis in section 11.2 we therefore focus almost entirely on the data from the women respondents, and secondarily on the results for the total sample. For readers skeptical of the justification for this strategy for contending with the biases in the data, the results based on the male data taken separately are presented at the end of this appendix.

There is one other relevant source of bias in the housework data. The list of tasks included in the analysis consists entirely of stereotypically female tasks within the traditional gender division of labor. I have not included characteristically male tasks such as home repairs, lawn mowing, etc. If there were households in which such male-stereotyped tasks took up great amounts of time, then conceivably in those households our scale would not be an accurate measure of the degree of gender inequality in the total time spent on domestic labor. But again, unless this measurement problem were strongly linked to class, it would not undermine the objectives of this chapter. And, in any case, all of the research on housework that raises the issue indicates that male household tasks are less routine and take up much less total time than female tasks.

biased. Berk (1985: 77) notes that for every household task in her study, "wives reported a smaller contribution for husbands than husbands reported for themselves." She, however, does not pass judgment as to whose reports are more accurate: "It seemed useless to spend time wondering whose version represented the 'true' report of who did what and how often" (Berk 1985: 55).

Other variables
A number of other variables are included in the analysis. Three of these describe attributes of the family: total annual family income, wife's percentage contribution to family income, and presence of children under 16 years of age in the household. The rest describe attributes of the respondent alone: hours worked by respondent, respondent's gender ideology, respondent's education and age. A few of these variables need brief explanation:

Wife's percentage contribution to family income. Respondents were asked to estimate the proportion of total household income brought in by their spouse. These responses were then converted into a "wife's percentage contribution" variable so that its meaning is homogeneous for our male and female respondents.

Gender ideology. I constructed a gender-ideology typology based on four Likert type (agree/disagree) questions on gender attitudes:

1 It is better for the family if the husband is the principal bread-winner outside of the home and the wife has primary responsibility for the home and children.
2 If both husband and wife work, they should share equally in the housework and childcare.
3 There are not enough women in responsible positions in government and private business.
4 Ideally, there should be as many women as men in important positions in government and business.

Items 1 and 2 were first combined into a variable tapping attitudes toward the sexual division of labor in the family (Family-Gender Attitude scale), and items 3 and 4 into a variable tapping attitudes toward gender and public authority (Gender-Authority Attitude scale). Each of these constructed variables has three values: 1 = sexist response pattern; 2 = mixed response; 3 = egalitarian response pattern. The coding scheme for each of these intermediate constructed variables is given in Appendix Table 11.1. These two intermediate variables were then combined into a seven-level ordinal gender-ideology variable, as illustrated in Appendix Table 11.2. Since a much smaller proportion of the sample took the extreme sexist position on the family-gender attitude variable than on the gender-authority variable, I treated the sexist pole of the gender-family variable as measuring a more extreme

Appendix Table 11.1.   *Constructing family-gender attitude variable and authority-gender attitude variable*

1. *Gender-family attitudes*

		Item 2		
		Sexist response	Egalitarian response	Missing data
	Sexist response	1	2	2
Item 1	Egalitarian response	2	3	3
	Missing data	1	3	missing

2. *Gender-authority attitudes*

		Item 4		
		Sexist response	Egalitarian response	Missing data
	Sexist response	1	3	1
Item 3	Egalitarian response	2	3	3
	Missing data	1	3	missing

Definitions of items:

1. It is better for the family if the husband is the principal breadwinner outside of the home and the wife has primary responsibilities for the home and children.

2. If both husband and wife work, they should share equally in the housework and childcare.

3. There are not enough women in responsible positions in government and private business.

4. Ideally, there should be as many women as men in important positions in government and business.

form of sexism than the gender-authority variable. When the two variables were combined, therefore, the gender-family variable was treated as defining the sexist end of the gender-ideology scale and the gender-authority variable was used to differentiate levels within the

Appendix Table 11.2. *Constructing the gender ideology scale*

		Gender authority attitudes variable			
		Sexist	Mixed	Egalitarian	Missing
	Sexist	1	1	1	1
Gender family attitudes variable	Mixed	2	3	4	4
	Egalitarian	5	6	7	7
	Missing	5	6	7	missing

mixed and egalitarian regions of the scale. After constructing this variable, I examined a variety of other ways of aggregating the original four items. *None* of the results in this chapter were substantively affected by alternative forms of the gender ideology variable.

Education. Education is measured by the highest *level* of education attained by the respondent. Because the education systems differ in the United States and Sweden, the actual steps on this scale are not identical in the two countries. The American variable has the following levels: 1 = primary school or less; 2 = some secondary school; 3 = completed high school; 4 = some post-high-school education; 5 = college degree or more. The Swedish variable is coded as follows: 1 = primary school or less; 2 = vocational training without high school degree; 3 = terminal high school degree; 4 = *arbitur* high school exam or some education beyond high school; 5 = college degree or more.

Family income. Family income is measured as total family income from all sources, including unearned income. The Swedish data have been converted into dollars at the rate of exchange at the time of the surveys (1980).

2 Data, methods and analytical strategy

Sample
For the purposes of the present analysis, the sample is restricted to cases in which respondents are living with partners (married or unmarried) and in which both people are in the paid labor force. This

yields an effective sample of 271 men and 268 women in the United States and 349 men and 299 women in Sweden. Since in the population, there are exactly the same number of men as women living in two-earner households, there should be roughly the same number of men and women respondents who satisfy this criterion in the sample. This is the case in the United States, but not in Sweden, where there are fifty more men than women. I have not been able to discover the source of this difference in sample size. It could have been due to slightly different criteria being used to define being "in the labor force" for respondents and for spouses, but as far as I can tell, this is not the case.

This restriction is not meant to imply that the question of the relationship between class and gender relations is only relevant in cases where both partners are in the labor force. Clearly, the issue of the interaction of class and gender may bear on the decision of married women to enter the labor force, and, even in households with full-time housewives, class might still bear on the gender domestic division of labor. Nevertheless, for the present purposes the analysis is restricted to two-earner families for three reasons: first, the Swedish data excludes housewives from the sample of respondents, and thus there would only be data reported by men for such households; second, the problem of equality in the division of labor in housework is more acutely posed when both spouses are in the labor force; and third, if class location has effects on the division of labor in the household and not simply on the labor supply decisions of men and women, these effects are most likely to be apparent for two-earner households.

Limitations in the data
Two significant problems with these data need to be acknowledged. First of all, only one person in each family was interviewed, and thus there are no data on the ideological orientations of the respondent's spouse. Since it would be expected that the attitudes of both parties bear on the gender practices within the family, this is a significant limitation on the kinds of models we can explore. Second, the surveys inadvertently failed to ask respondents questions about the number of hours worked in the paid labor force by their spouses, or about spouses' education. Thus both of these variables are also available only for respondents. The absence of data on number of hours worked in the paid labor force by the wives of the male respondents is a particu-

larly serious liability, since this is clearly one of the important determinants of inequalities in housework.

These limitations in the data would matter more if the objective of this chapter were to provide empirical support for a general explanation of gender inequalities in housework. This is not, however, the goal. Rather, as already stated, the objective is narrower, focussing specifically on the relationship between class and housework rather than more broadly on housework as such.

Analytical strategy

The basic analytical strategy of this chapter is to examine the differences in the amount of housework husbands do across the cells of the family-class composition matrix in Table 11.1. The conventional way for exploring such differences would be to run ordinary least squares regression equations predicting housework with class entered as a series of categorical variables (0–1 dummies). The problem with such an approach is that the housework variable has a peculiar distribution that violates the assumptions of OLS regression, namely it has vastly more zero values (i.e. husbands doing no housework) than could occur in a normal distribution. In formal statistical terms, the distribution is "censored" at 0. Truncating a regression equation in this way on the dependent variable potentially introduces serious distortions in the slopes of the independent variables and in any statistical tests one might want to conduct on the coefficients in the equation.

We will deal with this technical problem by using Tobit regressions rather than OLS regressions. The statistical logic and rationale for this procedure is discussed in Maddala (1983) and Mare (1986). The coefficients in a Tobit regression can be treated in essentially the same way as ordinary regressions, so this should not cause any difficulties in interpreting the results. I also ran all of the equations in OLS regression, and none of the results were substantively different. The only disadvantage with Tobit regressions is that they do not generate a simple R^2 statistic, which many people find a particularly useful summary statistic for the analytical power of an equation. Given that in the present analysis the OLS and Tobit regressions do not differ substantively, I will therefore report the R^2 for OLS equations that correspond to the Tobit analyses to give readers a sense of the relative overall analytical power of the equations.

3 Results for male respondents taken separately

Appendix Table 11.3. *Mean levels of husbands' percentage contribution to total housework for dual-earner families with different family-class compositions: reports of male respondents only*

UNITED STATES

		Husband's job-class		
		Self-employed	Middle class	Working class
Wife's job-class	Self-employed	[1] 14.1	[2] 23.2	[3] 23.1
	Middle class	[2] 23.2	[4] 27.8	[5] 30.7
	Working class	[3] 23.1	[6] 23.4	[7] 30.9

SWEDEN

		Husband's job-class		
		Self-employed	Middle class	Working class
Wife's job-class	Self-employed	[1] 14.6	[2] 26.3	[3] 19.7
	Middle class	[2] 26.3	[4] 33.9	[5] 32.6
	Working class	[3] 19.7	[6] 25.8	[7] 30.8

Appendix Table 11.4. *Tobit regressions for family-class compositions on husband's housework: male respondents only*

	United States	Sweden
Class categories[a]		
1 Self-employed household	−13.8***	−21.0***
2 Self-employed + middle	−4.7	−8.4*
3 Self-employed + worker	−4.8	−15.1***
5 Wife middle + husband worker	2.4	−1.6
6 Wife worker + husband middle	−4.3	−8.2**
7 Wife worker + husband worker	3.2[b]	−3.2
R^2 from corresponding OLS regression	.07	.09
N	270	344

Significance levels: * $p < .10$ ** $p < .05$ *** $p < .01$

a. The pure middle-class household is the left-out category. All coefficients are therefore the difference between a given class and the pure middle class.

b. There is a statistically significant difference ($p < .05$) between categories 7 and 6 – the pure working-class family and the wife worker/husband middle family.

Appendix Table 11.5. *Tobit regressions for family-class composition and selected other variables on husband's housework: male respondents only*

	United States	Sweden
Class categories[a]		
1 Self-employed household	−2.8	−10.2*
2 Self-employed + middle	−1.9	−2.0
3 Self-employed + worker	−0.4	−6.2
5 Wife middle + husband worker	−0.6	−1.8
6 Wife worker + husband middle	−2.0	−4.1
7 Wife worker + husband worker	5.7	−0.5
Respondent's education	−0.71	0.95
Respondent's hours of paid work	−0.21**	−0.46***
Wife's income contribution	3.5**	2.48**
Total family income ($ x 10^{-4})	0.20	0.75
Respondent's gender ideology	3.0***	1.32**
Age	−0.15	−0.22**
Kids under 16 in household (0-1)	1.2	−2.0
R^2 from corresponding OLS regression	0.2	0.2
N	270	344

Significance levels: * $p < .10$ ** $p < .05$ *** $p < .01$

a. The pure middle-class household is the left-out category. All coefficients are therefore the difference between a given class and the pure middle class.

12 The gender gap in workplace authority

In this chapter we will explore the intersection of gender inequality and one specific dimension of class relations – the authority structure within workplaces. Authority is of particular interest for the analysis of gender inequality in three principal ways. First, authority is itself a valued attribute of jobs, both because it confers status on a person and because the responsibilities it involves may be intrinsically rewarding. Second, authority is one of the central ways in which the financial rewards of work are allocated. (Halaby 1979; Jaffee 1989; Reskin and Padavic 1994: 85; Reskin and Roos 1992; Robinson and Kelley 1979; Roos 1981; Spaeth 1985; Wright 1979). As is often noted, employees get connected to jobs, and thus to earnings, through basically two mechanisms – recruitment through external labor markets and promotions within internal labor markets. Internal promotions to better paying jobs frequently involve movement up authority hierarchies.[1] Third, and perhaps most significantly, because of the real power associated with positions in authority hierarchies, gender inequalities in authority may constitute one of the key mechanisms which helps to sustain gender inequalities in workplace outcomes in general. The under-

---

[1] There are a variety of possible reasons why increases in authority are associated with increases in pay: hierarchical position may be associated with increases in job experience and other forms of human capital, and thus pay differentials across levels of authority may partially reflect human capital differences of job holders across levels; the added responsibilities and stress of supervisory and managerial jobs may require added financial compensation to induce people to take these jobs; and pay differentials may be needed as part of a process of social control to insure diligent performance of managerial responsibilities. The use of pay differentials as a strategy of social control has been theorized in terms of efficiency wage theory (Akerlof and Yellen 1986), employment rents within contested exchanges (Bowles and Gintis 1990), and loyalty rents within structures of exploitation (Wright 1985).

318

representation of women in positions of authority, especially in higher levels of management, is not simply itself an *instance* of gender inequality; it is likely to be a significant *cause* of gender inequality. If, as Kanter (1977) suggests in her classic study of gender and management, male managers in a male-dominated hierarchy are likely to act in ways which preserve male privileges and advantages, then gender inequality in workplace authority becomes a key institutional element in the reproduction of gender inequality throughout work organizations.

No one, of course, is surprised by the general fact that workplace authority is unequally distributed between men and women in all of the countries we examine. What might be surprising to most people, however, is the pattern of cross-national variation in the gender gap in authority. To take just one example, in the United States the probability of a man in the labor force occupying an "upper" or "top" management position is 1.8 times greater than the probability of a woman occupying such a position, whereas in Sweden, the probability for men is 4.2 times greater than for women. These results may seem counter-intuitive, since in many respects gender relations are more egalitarian in Sweden than in the United States: the wage differential between men and women is much lower in Sweden;[2] husbands, on average, perform a somewhat higher proportion of housework;[3] and gender attitudes are significantly more egalitarian in Sweden than in the United States.[4] Nevertheless, the gender gap in workplace authority is considerably greater in Sweden than in the United States.

The objective of this chapter is to document and to attempt to explain these kinds of cross-national variations in gender inequality in workplace authority in seven developed capitalist countries – the United States, Canada, the United Kingdom, Australia, Sweden, Norway and Japan.[5] While there exists some limited research on

[2] In Sweden, in the late 1980s, women's hourly earnings were roughly 91% those of men, whereas in the United States the figure was about 65% (National Committee on Pay Equity 1988).

[3] See section 11.2 above.

[4] On the basis of the Comparative Class Analysis Project data used in this book, 57.1% of Americans compared to 74.1% of Swedes agree (somewhat or strongly) with the statement, "Ideally there should be as many women as men in important positions in government and business." For a discussion of differences in gender attitudes between Sweden and the United States, see Baxter and Kane (1994).

[5] The specific set of countries in this chapter was chosen largely because of availability of strictly comparable micro-level data on workplace authority rather than on *a priori* theoretical grounds. Nevertheless, they are sufficiently diverse politically and

gender inequalities in the distribution of authority (Diprete and Soule 1988; Grandjean 1981; Hill 1980; Jacobs 1992; Jaffee 1989; McGuire and Reskin 1993; Reskin and Roos 1992; Rosenbaum 1984; Wolf and Fligstein 1979a), I know of no quantitative research which systematically explores this problem in a broad comparative context. The objective of this chapter is to begin to fill this gap in the literature.

12.1 Analytical strategy for studying the "gender gap"

Several familiar factors may make women less likely than men to occupy workplace positions involving authority. Gender differences in aspirations and occupational preferences, partially a result of socialization processes and partially of adaptive preference formation, may lead women to select themselves out of the running for authority positions. Gender differences in various kinds of individual attributes, especially specialized training and labor market experience, may make women less qualified for many managerial jobs. Gender differences in employment settings – sectors, size of employing organization, state versus private employers, part-time work – may affect the opportunities for promotion into positions of authority. And, of course, active gender discrimination may simply make it harder for qualified women to be promoted. The beliefs and motives of actors engaged in discrimination can take many different forms: a commitment to norms barring women from exercising authority over men (Bergman 1986; Kanter 1977); stereotyped beliefs that women are too emotional to be effective managers (Kanter 1977; Reskin and Hartman 1986); belief in the efficiency of "statistical discrimination" (Bielby and Baron 1986; Wolf and Fligstein 1979a); or simply the desire to preserve men's power and privileges (Acker 1990; Reskin 1988). Regardless of the underlying motives, discrimination affects the relative chances of men and women to occupy positions of authority, either because it affects access to the social networks and personal interactions that facilitate promotions, or because people in positions of higher authority directly discriminate against women in their allocation of people to positions of authority.

The ideal data for analyzing gender discrimination in access to authority would include direct observations of the discriminatory acts

culturally to provide a good empirical context for studying variations in the gender gap in authority among economically developed capitalist democracies.

that cumulatively shape the outcomes. Since such data are never available in systematic, quantifiable form, research on gender inequalities in labor market outcomes typically relies on indirect methods of assessing discrimination. Two principal strategies have been adopted. In the first, which can be called the "net gender gap" approach, a multivariate equation predicting workplace authority is estimated in which the independent variables include gender plus a series of control variables thought to represent various nondiscrimination effects on authority (for example, education or job experience). A significant coefficient for the gender variable in this equation is then taken as an indicator of the degree of likely discrimination in the *direct* allocation of workplace authority. Active, direct discrimination in the allocation of authority is thus treated as the "residual explanation" when other nondiscrimination explanations (represented in the control variables in the equation) fail to fully account for gender differences in authority.[6] Of course, even if the gender coefficient were zero, this would not prove that discrimination is absent from the social processes generating overall gender differences in authority, since discrimination could systematically affect the control variables themselves.[7] The net gender gap strategy, therefore, is effective only in assessing the extent to which discrimination operates *directly* in the process of allocating authority within organizations.

The net gender gap strategy of analysis is always vulnerable, either because of possible misspecifications of the equation (important nondiscrimination causes of the gender gap are excluded from the analysis) or because of poor measurement of some of the variables. What looks like a residual "discrimination" gap, therefore, may simply reflect limitations in the data analysis. Nevertheless, if the gender gap in authority remains large after controlling for a variety of plausible factors, then this adds credibility to the claim that direct discrimination

[6] This approach resembles the strategy frequently used to study racial discrimination (Beck, Horan and Tolbert 1978; Featherman and Hauser 1978)) or gender discrimination in earnings (Treiman and Roos 1983; Rosenfeld and Kalleberg 1990).

[7] For example, suppose that the coefficient for gender in a multivariate equation predicting authority were to become zero when sector of employment and job seniority were included in the equation. This would indicate that men and women in the same sector of employment and with the same seniority had the same probabilities of having authority. The gross gender differences in authority, therefore, could plausibly be attributed to the fact that women were concentrated in sectors with few managers and had lower average job seniority than men. It could still be the case, however, that gender discrimination could explain why women were concentrated in those sectors and why they had less seniority.

exists in the process by which authority is allocated. Versions of this approach to analyzing the gender gap in authority were adopted by Jaffe (1989), and Reskin and Roos (1992) and Wolf and Fligstein (1979b). In all of these studies, a significant net gender gap in authority remains after extensive sets of controls were included in the equation.[8]

The second strategy for indirectly assessing the role of discrimination in generating gender differences in authority can be called the "gender-interaction approach." In this strategy, separate multivariate equations predicting authority are estimated for men and women. Gender differences in the slopes of key variables are then interpreted as reflecting likely discrimination. The key idea here is that discrimination does not simply have additive effects on outcomes; it also affects the relative success with which women can convert various relevant individual attributes into authority. Thus, for example, Wolf and Fligstein (1979a), in the earliest quantitative modeling of gender differences in authority, observe that men get significantly higher authority returns to education than do women, even after controlling for variables such as age and work experience. This difference in slopes, they argue, is more likely to be attributable to the behaviors of employers than to the attitudes and behaviors of women and thus probably reflects discrimination in the authority promotion process. In general, research using this strategy has found that more of the overall difference in authority between men and women can be attributed to differences in the authority returns to such things as education or experience than to differences in the means between men and women on these determinants of authority. (See also Halaby 1979, Hill 1980 and McGuire and Reskin 1993).

The research in this chapter will rely mainly on the net gender gap strategy. Since our main concern is with cross-national comparisons, the gender-interaction approach to studying discrimination would involve the analysis of three-way interaction terms (country x gender x independent-variables). Because of relatively small sample sizes in our

---

[8] Wolf and Fligstein (1979b) control for education, experience, and tenure; Jaffe (1989) controls for socio-economic status, education, marital status, children, work experience, race, age, and the sex composition of three-digit-code occupations; Reskin and Roos (1992), predicting the number of arenas of final decision-making among managers, control for education, firm tenure, hours worked, self-employment, organization size, managerial level, supervisory authority, percentage female in occupations and census-designated managerial occupation.

data, the standard errors of three-way interaction coefficients are typically large even when there appears to be quite substantial nominal differences across countries in the size of two-way interactions. In all of the dozens of possible country contrasts in gender interactions in our data, there were only a few scattered three-way interactions that even approached conventional criteria for statistical significance. Furthermore, even apart from such statistical considerations, with seven countries and a large array of independent variables, the gender-interaction approach quickly gets extremely complicated conceptually. Since this is the first cross-national analysis of the gender gap in authority, it seemed desirable to adopt the simpler, net gender-gap approach, even though the interaction approach is a more realistic way of understanding the process of discrimination.

12.2 Empirical agenda

The data analysis in this chapter revolves around four main tasks: documenting the cross-national variations in the gender gap in authority; diagnosing the proximate causes of the gender gap in having authority within countries; diagnosing the gender gaps in the *amount* of authority within countries; exploring a variety of possible explanations of the cross-national variations in net gender gaps.

The extent and cross-national patterning of the gender-authority gap

Since there is little publicly available documentation about gender differences in authority, let alone cross-national variations in these differences, before we attempt to explore explanations of cross-national variations it is important to document as precisely as possible what needs explaining. To do this, we use three different primary measures of authority: *Sanctioning Authority* (the ability to impose positive or negative sanctions on subordinates); *Decisionmaking Authority* (direct participation in policymaking decisions within the employing organization); and *Formal Position in the authority hierarchy*. We also construct two aggregated measures: *Overall Authority dichotomy* (a dummy variable with a value of 1 if a person has at least two of the three primary forms of authority), and *Amount of Authority scale* (a 10-level variable combining the three primary forms of authority). These variables are described in the methodological appendix to this chapter.

Explaining the gender gap in having authority within countries

The core idea of the "net gender gap" approach is to specify plausible explanations of gender differences in authority that do not involve direct discrimination in promotions and then to see if the authority gap disappears when these nondiscrimination factors are held constant in an equation predicting authority. We will explore two explanations of this sort of the gender gap in authority: (1) the gender gap is due to gender differences in various personal attributes of men and women and their employment settings; (2) the gender gap is due to the self-selection of women.

1 *Compositional Factors.* If managers and employers make promotion decisions in a largely gender-neutral manner in response to various observable attributes of potential candidates, then the underrepresentation of women in hierarchies will be largely the result of their under-representation in the pool of potential candidates or their possessing less adequate qualifications than men. For example, because it is more efficient for organizations to employ full-time managers than part-time managers, part-time employees are less likely to be in the pool of candidates for vertical promotions.[9] Since a higher proportion of women than of men work part time, it could therefore be the case that the overall gender differences in authority might in part be the result of the different gender distributions of part-time employment. Or, to take another example, because of labor force interruptions, women have on average less labor market experience than men and thus, while they may be in the pool of potential candidates for promotions, they are, on average, less qualified. Of course, it could be the case that both of these facts may themselves be partially attributable to gender discrimination of various sorts. Nevertheless, if the gender gap in authority disappears once we control for such compositional factors, then we would say that the gap is unlikely to be due to discrimination in the *direct allocation* of authority to individuals within the employment setting.

We will explore three clusters of such compositional factors: *firm attributes* (industrial sector, state employment, firm size), *job attributes* (occupation, part-time employment, job tenure) and *personal attributes*

---

[9] In principle, of course, if an organization needs a given number of hours of managerial labor a week, instead of hiring full-time managers it could employ twice as many half-time managers. In most work settings this would be organizationally less efficient because of the complexity of coordination of responsibilities and decisionmaking tasks among a greater number of part-time employees.

(age, education, labor force interruptions).[10] To the extent that women are concentrated in sectors with a lower proportion of managers, or have various job and personal attributes associated with low probabilities of managerial promotions, then, once we control for these factors, the authority gap between men and women should be reduced and perhaps even disappear.

It could be objected that some of these compositional factors are in part consequences of discrimination in promotions rather than indirect causes of the gender gap. It could be the case, for example, that one of the reasons women are more likely to work part time is precisely because they are excluded from promotions to managerial positions. Or, women could have shorter average job tenure because they have less attachment to a given employer due to exclusion from promotion possibilities. It certainly could be the case that women have a higher probability of being in a lower white-collar occupation because they are not promoted into positions of authority, since at least some of the time such promotion brings with it a change in formal occupational title from lower white collar to upper white collar.[11] Exclusion from positions of authority could thus explain some of these compositional factors rather than vice versa. We have no way in the present data analysis to investigate this possibility. Nevertheless, if the inclusion of these diverse controls does *not* significantly reduce the gender gap in authority, this would add considerable weight to the claim that the gap is to a significant extent the result of direct discrimination in the allocation of authority positions.

2 *Self-selection because of family responsibilities.* For various reasons, it might be argued, women in similar employment situations and with similar personal attributes to men may simply not want to be promoted into positions of authority as frequently as men, particularly

---

[10] One notable variable is absent from this list – total labor force experience. This variable was not available for most of the countries in the sample. However, we have included job tenure with current employer, age and labor force interruptions which, together, would be highly correlated with total labor force experience, so it seems unlikely that the omission of this variable would seriously compromise the results.

[11] It should be noted that the definition of *authority* used here is largely independent of the formal "occupation" in which a person is employed. There are plenty of people in lower white-collar occupations who nevertheless have significant amounts of authority, when authority is measured directly in terms of the powers people exercise on the job. Only a minority of people with even high levels of authority are in jobs which bear the occupational title "manager" (and not all people in jobs that are called "manager" have authority by our criteria).

because of family responsibilities. Given the array of feasible alternatives, women may actually prefer the "mommy track" within a career because of the reduced pressures and time commitment this entails even though it also results in lowered career prospects, especially for vertical promotion. Again, this is not to deny that such preferences may themselves reflect the operation of oppressive gender practices in the society. The gender division of labor in the household or the absence of affordable high quality childcare, for example, may serve to block the options women feel they realistically can choose in the workplace. Nevertheless, self-selection of this sort is a very different mechanism from direct discrimination by managers and employers in promotion practices.

Self-selection is an especially difficult process to measure. Unless direct data on the micro-details of promotion practices of employers and the career strategies and preferences of employees are available, it is hard to rule out self-selection as part of the process that generates gender differences in outcomes. Nevertheless, we can get some purchase on this problem by examining the interactions between gender and certain variables likely to be closely linked to self-selection.

The most often-cited form of gender self-selection centers around the choices women make with respect to family responsibilities and work responsibilities. We can therefore treat the presence of such responsibilities as additional "compositional factors." However, unlike in the simple compositional arguments which are based on additive models of compositional effects, the arguments for self-selection require an *interactive* model. For example, the self-selection hypothesis claims that the presence of children in the household leads women to select themselves out of competition for authority promotions whereas it does not for men. This means that in a model predicting authority, the coefficient for a variable measuring the presence of children would be negative for women but zero, or perhaps even positive, for men, if the presence of children increases the incentives for men to seek promotions because of increasing financial needs of the family. To assess the presence of such self-selection, therefore, we have to estimate a model that includes gender-interactions with the self-selection variables (as well as the additive compositional effects), and then assess the gender gap in authority at appropriate values for the interacting independent variables. For this purpose, we include three variables which are plausibly linked to self-selection: marital status, the presence of children in the household and the percentage of housework performed by the husband.

Two objections to this strategy for exploring self-selection can be raised. First, what might look like *self*-selection may really just be another form of discrimination and exclusion. The presence of children, for example, may constitute a criterion that employers use to assign women to a "mommy track" rather than a situation which leads women to choose not to compete energetically for promotions. We cannot, in the present data, rule out these possibilities. *If* the authority gap is significantly reduced when we control for these alleged self-selection indicators, therefore, we may simply be tapping mechanisms through which employers deny women promotions. However, if controlling for these indicators has little effect on the authority gap, this would be strongly suggestive evidence against the self-selection hypothesis.

Second, as in the case of the additive compositional controls, some of these family-responsibility variables may be partially the *result* of the relationship of women to authority rather than causes of that relation. For example, women in positions of authority might, as a result of increased work pressures, do less housework and thus have a more egalitarian division of labor in the home. Living in an *in*egalitarian household may therefore not be an explanation for why women do not have authority, but rather the result of their not having authority. We have no way of exploring such reciprocal effects and thus our interpretation of these interaction terms must be viewed as tentative.

The gender gap in the amount of authority

One of the most striking metaphors linked to the efforts of women to gain equality with men in the workplace is the "glass ceiling." The expression has been used in government hearings, reports and legislation as well as in the popular press.[12] The image is that while women may have gained entry through the front door of managerial hierarchies, at some point they hit an invisible barrier which blocks their further ascent up the managerial highrise. In one of the earliest studies

---

[12] See, for example, the hearing before the Senate subcommittee on employment and productivity of the committee on labor and human relations, "Women and the Workplace: the glass ceiling", October 23, 1991; US Department of Labor, "A Report on the Glass Ceiling Initiative," 1991; State of Wisconsin Task Force on the Glass Ceiling Initiative, 1993; the US Federal "Glass Ceiling Act of 1991." For a discussion of the glass ceiling in the mass media, see Garland (1991).

of the problem, Morrison et al. (1987: 13) define the glass ceiling as "a transparent barrier that kept women from rising above a certain level in corporations ... it applies to women as a group who are kept from advancing higher *because they are women*."[13]

The glass ceiling metaphor therefore suggests not simply that women face disadvantages and discrimination within work settings and managerial hierarchies, but that these disadvantages relative to men *increase* as women move up the hierarchy.[14] Employers and top managers may be willing to let women become supervisors, perhaps even lower to middle-level managers, but – the story goes – they are very reluctant to let women assume positions of "real" power and thus women are blocked from promotions to the upper levels of management in corporations and other work organizations. This may be due to sexist ideas or more subtle discriminatory practices, but in any case the glass ceiling hypothesis argues that the relative disadvantages women face in getting jobs and promotions are greater in the upper levels of managerial hierarchies than at the bottom.

Casual observation seems to confirm this argument. There is, after all, a much higher proportion of bottom supervisors than of chief executive officers who are women. In the class analysis project data, at the bottom of managerial hierarchies perhaps 20–25% of lower level supervisors are women in the United States. In contrast, at most a few percent of top executives and CEOs in large corporations are women.[15] Reviewing the data on what they call the "promotion gap," Reskin and Padavic (1994: 84) report that "although women held half of all federal government jobs in 1992 and made up 86% of the government's clerical workers, they were only a quarter of supervisors and only a tenth of senior executives." Reskin and Padavic report similar findings for other countries: in Denmark women were 14.5% of all managers and administrators, but only between 1 and 5% of top managers; in Japan

---

[13] A similar definition is used in Catalyst (1990), the US Department of Labor (1991) and Scandura (1992).

[14] Sometimes the expression "glass ceiling" seems to be used simply to designate the general presence of discrimination throughout managerial hierarchies rather than the specific claim of increasing discrimination at higher levels of organizations. Such a usage, however, does not conform to the image suggested by the metaphor, and in any case, most commentators who refer to the glass ceiling are making the more complex claim about heightened barriers to women at the top of hierarchies.

[15] According to Fierman (1990) fewer than .5% of the 4,012 highest paid managers in top companies were women, while fewer than 5% of senior management in the Fortune 500 corporations were women and minorities.

women were 7.5% of all administrators and managers but only 0.3% of top management in the private sector. The report of the State of Wisconsin Task Force on the Glass Ceiling Initiative (1993: 9), states that while 47% of supervisors and 42% of middle management in Wisconsin were women, only 34% of upper management and 18% of executives were women. Similar findings are reported in the 1991 US Department of Labor "Report on the Glass Ceiling Initiative" (p. 6): in 94 randomly sampled reviews of corporate headquarters of Fortune 1000 sized companies between 1989 and 1991, women were found to represent 37.2% of all employees of these companies, yet only 16.9% of all levels of management and 6.6% of managers at the executive level. It is hardly surprising with such distributions that it is commonly believed by those working for gender equality that a glass ceiling exists in the American workplace.

However, things may not be what they seem. A simple arithmetic example will demonstrate the point. Suppose, as illustrated in Table 12.1, there is a managerial hierarchy with six levels. In the first example in this illustration, 50% of men but only 25% of women get promoted at each level (i.e. men have twice the probability of being promoted than women at every level of the hierarchy). In this situation, if roughly 25% of line supervisors are women, only 1% of top managers will be women. In the second example, the ratio of the probabilities of men getting promoted to women getting promoted becomes steadily more egalitarian as you move up the hierarchy. This ratio is 2:1 for promotions from nonmanagement to supervisor positions, but only 1.16:1 for promotions to the top manager position. Yet, even in this situation the proportion of top managers who are women is drastically less than the proportion of supervisors who are women: 6% compared to about 25%.[16]

---

[16] This hypothetical example roughly corresponds to some available organization-level data. In data from a court case, *Marshall et al.* v. *Alpha Beta*, concerning gender distributions at different levels of a managerial hierarchy in a grocery chain (reported in Reskin and Padavic 1994:89), 49.9% of grocery department clerks were female, 16.8% of assistant grocery department managers were female, 7.6% of grocery department managers were female and 3.1% of store managers were female. The relative chances of a man compared to a woman being an assistant manager instead of a clerk was roughly 5:1, whereas the relative chances of a man compared to a woman being a department manager instead of an assistant manager was only 2.4:1, and the relative chances of a man compared to a women being a store manager instead of a department manager was 2.5:1. While women face significant barriers to promotions at all levels of this organization, these barriers appear, if anything, to be stronger at the bottom than at the top.

Table 12.1 *How there can be very few women top managers and gender discrimination without a "glass ceiling"*

Managerial level	Number of people in level			Promotion rates to next hierarchy level		
	Men	Women	% Women	Men	Women	Ratio
Constant intensity of discrimination up the hierarchy						
Top managers	100	1	1			
Manager level 4	200	4	2	50%	25%	2:1
Manager level 3	400	16	4	50%	25%	2:1
Manager level 2	800	64	7.5	50%	25%	2:1
Manager level 1	600	256	14	50%	25%	2:1
Line supervisor	3,000	1,024	24	50%	25%	2:1
Nonmanagement	6,400	4,096	42	50%	25%	2:1
Declining intensity of discrimination up the hierarchy						
Top managers	100	6	6			
Manager level 4	200	14	6.5	50%	43%	1.16:1
Manager level 3	400	36	8.3	50%	40%	1.25:1
Manager level 2	800	98	11	50%	37%	1.35:1
Manager level 1	600	297	15.7	50%	33%	1.52:1
Line supervisor	3,200	1,024	24	50%	29%	1.72:1
Nonmanagement	6,400	4,096	42	50%	25%	2.00:1

Neither of these two examples fits the story of the "glass ceiling." According to the glass ceiling hypothesis, the obstacles to women getting managerial positions are supposed to increase as they move up the hierarchy. This could either take the form of a dramatic step function – at some level recruitment and promotion chances for women relative to men plummet to near zero – or it could be a gradual deterioration of the chances of women relative to men. In either case, the glass ceiling hypothesis implies that it becomes increasingly difficult for women, relative to men, to get managerial jobs as they move toward the top. In the two examples just reviewed, the disadvantages women face relative to men are either constant as they move up the hierarchy (case 1) or they actually decrease (case 2). And yet, in both cases there are almost no women top managers.

What these examples illustrate is that the existence of a glass ceiling cannot be inferred simply from the sheer fact that there are many fewer people at the top echelons of organizations who are women than at the bottom levels. The *cumulative* effect of *declining* discrimination can still produce an *increasing* "gender gap in authority" as you move to the top of organizational hierarchies.

The Comparative Class Analysis Project data do not allow us to conduct a fine-grained test of the glass ceiling hypothesis. Nevertheless, I will make a first cut at the problem with two empirical strategies. First of all, we examine the net gender gap in the 10-point *amount of authority scale* in a manner parallel to the way we examined the net gap in the probability of having authority. If there is a glass ceiling, then the gender gap in the amount of authority should be considerably greater than the gender gap in simply having authority.

Second, we will explore a weak form of the glass ceiling hypothesis more directly by examining the gender gap in authority separately for those people who have made it into the authority hierarchy. If we find that the gender gap in amount of authority for people in the hierarchy is the same or smaller than for the sample as a whole, then this undermines the glass ceiling hypothesis that gender discrimination is weaker at the port of entry into the hierarchy than in promotions within it. This would not imply that gender discrimination was absent in vertical promotions within authority hierarchies, only that such discrimination was not more intense than the discrimination that affects entry into the hierarchy. Of course, the glass ceiling could take the form of an abrupt step function in which intensified discrimination only occurs at the very apex of organizations. If this were the case, then we will not be able to observe a glass ceiling in our analysis because of limitations of sample size. If, however, the glass ceiling takes the form of gradually increasing discrimination with higher levels of authority, then the gender gap in how much authority people have, conditional upon them having any authority, should be greater than the gender gap in simply having authority.[17]

---

[17] A more refined strategy for studying the gender gap conditional on being in the hierarchy would have been to construct a formal two-stage sample selection model in which we simultaneously predicted whether a person was in the hierarchy at all and how much authority they had if they were in the hierarchy. This would allow us to correct the estimates of the coefficients in the latter equation for the effects of variables on selection into the equation. Recent methodological discussions (Manski 1989; Stolzenberg and Relles 1990), however, indicate that such models are quite problematic and that the "corrections" to the coefficients that they generate can just

Explaining cross-national variations

We will pursue two different strategies for exploring possible explanations for the cross-national variations in the gender gap in authority. First, we will compare the differences across countries in the *gross* gender gaps in authority (i.e. the country-specific gender gaps not controlling for any compositional effects) with the differences across countries *net* of the various compositional factors. If a significant portion of the gender gap within countries is explained by such compositional factors, then these factors may also account for much of the difference across countries in the gender gap. For example, in Sweden women are much more likely to be employed in part-time work than in the United States, and, as already noted, employees in part-time work are much less likely to have workplace authority. It could thus be the case that the larger gross gender gap in authority in Sweden compared to the United States was mainly due to this difference in employment patterns. In the extreme case, if all of the gender gaps within countries were explained by these compositional controls, thus indicating that direct discrimination in promotions was probably not a significant part of the within-country explanation of the gender gap, then it would also be the case that these compositional controls would explain the differences in the gross gender gap across countries.

Second, if significant differences across countries in the gender authority gap remain after controlling for all of the compositional factors, we then examine in a somewhat less formal way a number of possible macro-social explanations by comparing the rank ordering of the seven countries on the net gender gap in authority with the rank ordering on the following variables:

1 *Gender ideology.* One of the obvious cultural factors which might shape the gender gap in workplace authority is gender ideology. All things being equal one would expect a smaller gender gap in workplace authority in societies with relatively egalitarian gender ideologies compared to societies with less egalitarian ideologies.

2 *Women's reproductive and sexual rights.* Developed capitalist societies differ in the array of rights backed by the state in support of gender equality. While in all democratic capitalist states women now have equal voting rights to men, countries differ on a range of other issues

as easily increase the biases in the estimates as reduce them. For this reason we will restrict our analysis of the glass ceiling to single equations of the authority gap for people already in the hierarchy.

which bear on the rights of women with respect to sexual and reproductive issues, such as rights to abortion, rights to paid pregnancy and maternity leaves from work, and laws concerning sexual violence, abuse and harassment. While such state-backed rights and provisions may not directly prevent discriminatory practices in promotions, they may contribute to the political climate in ways that indirectly affect the degree of inequality in promotions and thus in workplace authority. It would therefore be predicted that societies with strong provisions of these rights would have a smaller gender gap in authority than societies with a weaker support for these rights.

3 *Gender earnings gap.* In addition to gender ideology and legal rights, the gender-authority gap could be related to various institutional arrangements for gender equality in labor market outcomes. In particular, it might be expected that in societies in which there was a relatively small gender gap in earnings, the gender gap in workplace authority would also be relatively small. The argument is not that greater equality in earning capacity between men and women is a *cause* of a smaller authority gap (if anything, a smaller gender gap in authority could itself contribute to narrowing the gender earnings gap), but rather that a society that fosters low levels of income inequality between men and women is also likely to foster low levels of authority inequality as well. Low gender differences in earnings would therefore be taken as an indicator of an underlying institutional commitment to gender equality as such.

4 *Occupational sex segregation.* The logical relationship between occupational sex segregation and gender inequalities in workplace authority is complex. Clearly, the probability of acquiring authority varies from occupation to occupation, and thus occupational sex segregation can reasonably be viewed as one likely cause of inequalities in authority. However, if norms against women supervising men are strong, then, in a limited way, occupational sex segregation might actually open up managerial positions for women insofar as it increases the chances of women being able to supervise only women. Furthermore, promotions into positions of authority often entail changes in occupational titles. This is particularly true for occupations that are formally called "managerial occupations." Barriers to acquiring workplace authority for women, therefore, are also likely to be a cause of occupational sex segregation. In examining variations across countries in occupational sex segregation, we are thus not suggesting that this variation is itself a direct cause of variation in the net gender

gap in authority. Rather, as in the case of the earnings gap, we will treat occupational sex segregation as an indicator of underlying processes that shape gender inequalities in the society. Since the sex segregation of occupations arguably is the result of many of the same causal processes that affect the gender gap in authority – different socialization of boys and girls, different patterns of human capital acquisition and various forms of discrimination – it would be expected that countries with relatively high levels of occupational sex segregation would also have large gender gaps in authority.

5   *The proportion of the labor force with authority.* There are two reasons for expecting the gender gap in authority to be greater in countries in which a relatively small proportion of the labor force held positions of authority than in countries in which there are many authority positions. First, it is more difficult for employers and top executives adequately to fill the positions with men in countries in which a high proportion of the employees of organizations have authority. In simple supply and demand terms, therefore, employers have an incentive to fill a higher proportion of authority positions with women in a country with a large proportion of managerial and supervisory positions in the job structure. Such recruitment, in turn, means that women will begin to develop the kinds of networks that facilitate subsequent recruitment and promotion of women (Kanter 1977). In particular, over time more women are likely to be in positions themselves to hire and promote.

Second, if as some scholars argue (e.g. Acker 1990; Bergman 1986; Reskin 1988), the gender-authority gap is at least partially the result of the interests of men in maintaining male predominance in the authority hierarchy, then the incentive for them to try to do so would be stronger when there were relatively few such positions to go around. This need not imply a coordinated conspiracy of men. Rather, when authority is a scarce good, individual male managers will be concerned with protecting their networks and reducing competition for managerial positions, and one by-product of this will be the exclusion of women. A large managerial population, therefore, increases the incentives for the heads of organizations to recruit women into managerial positions and it reduces the incentives for male managers to engage in restrictive practices to protect their positions.

6   *The organized women's movement and political culture.* If sex discrimination plays a significant role in the exclusion of women from positions of responsibility and power within the workplace, then it would be expected that one of the determinants of the erosion of such sexist

practices would be the extent and forms of women's organized challenge to these practices. Two issues in this respect would seem especially important. First, the *overall strength* of the women's movement is crucial for its ability to challenge the gender gap in workplace authority. Second, and perhaps less obviously, the specific *ideological orientation* of the women's movement may shape the extent to which it directs its energies toward problems of workplace discrimination. Broadly speaking, we can distinguish women's movements that are primarily concerned with directly improving women's economic and social welfare and women's movements that are more concerned with equalizing women's and men's access to positions of social power through which welfare is distributed. The former kind of movement, often linked to social democratic politics, focusses on the provision of services and benefits of interest to women; the latter kind of movement, more associated with liberal democratic politics, focusses on questions of rights, opportunities and discrimination. This reasoning suggests the prediction that, all things being equal, the gender gap in authority would be lower in countries with a strong liberal rights-oriented women's movement than in those with a social democratic women's movement.

12.3 Results

Most of the formal statistical analysis in this chapter revolves around equations predicting whether or not an individual has various kinds of workplace authority. The basic strategy we will use for analyzing such dichotomous dependent variables is logistic regression.[18] To determine the gross gender gap in authority – the gender gap without any control variables – we first estimate, for each country, logistic regressions in which gender is the only independent variable:

$$\text{Log } [\text{Pr}(A=1)/\text{Pr}(A=0)] = a + B_1\text{Female} \tag{1}$$

where $\text{Pr}(A=1)$ is the probability of a person having authority as defined by our various measures, $\text{Pr}(A=0)$ is the probability of a person not having authority, and Female is a dummy variable. The significance level of coefficient B_1 in this model is a test of whether men and women differ significantly in their chances of having managerial authority.

To evaluate the "net gender gap," we add the compositional control variables to test whether the bivariate relationship between gender and

---

[18] In analyzing the *amount of authority scale*, we use cumulative logistic regressions. See the methodological appendix for an explanation.

authority reflects other factors that are correlated with gender and managerial authority:

$$\text{Log } [\Pr(A=1)/\Pr(A=0)] = a + B_1\text{Female} + \Sigma_i B_i X_i \tag{2}$$

where the X_i are the firm attribute, job attribute and person attribute compositional variables listed in Appendix Table 12.1.

In interpreting these logistic regressions we focus specifically on the gender coefficients from the bivariate and multivariate equations. Since gender is a dummy variable (1=female), the coefficient indicates the difference between women's and men's logged odds of having managerial authority. Taking the antilog of this coefficient then yields an odds ratio.[19] This indicates a woman's odds of having managerial authority compared to a man's odds of having authority. For example, if the antilog of the gender coefficient is 0.9 then a woman's odds of having managerial authority are 90% those of a man's, net of the other factors in the equation. The "gender gap" can then be defined as 1 minus the antilog of the logit coefficient for the Female dummy variable: when this is 0, there is no gender gap in authority; when it is 1, there are no women at all with authority. In Model (1) we will refer to this as the "gross gender gap" and in Model (2) as the "net gender gap" in workplace authority.

Gross gender differences in having authority

Table 12.2 presents the basic descriptive cross-tabulations of gender-by-authority for the seven countries in this study. Figure 12.1 presents in graphic form the gender authority gaps (1–antilogs of the gender coefficients) for the overall authority dichotomy variable. Table 12.3 presents the results for the logistic regression analysis of gross gender differences in each of our measures of authority using Model (1).[20] Several results are striking.

[19] If $X = \text{Log}(Y) - \text{Log}(Z)$, then the antilog of $X = Y \div Z$. In the above logistic equation, $B_1 = \log$ (odds of women having authority) $-\log$ (odds men having authority). The antilog of B_1 thus $=$ (odds of women having authority) $\div$ (odds men having authority), which is an odds ratio. See the methodological appendix to Chapter 5 for a discussion of odds and odds ratios.

[20] Significance tests for country differences are only presented for the aggregate authority measures. The tests for country differences in the gender coefficients for models predicting sanctioning authority and formal position are virtually identical to the results for the overall authority dichotomy. In general, there are fewer statistically significant country differences in the gender coefficients predicting the decisionmaking variable.

Table 12.2. *Distributions of authority within gender categories: seven countries*

	Decisionmaking (% yes)		Sanctioning authority (% yes)		Formal position (% yes)		Overall authority dichotomy (% yes)		N	
	Men	Women	Men	Women	Men	Women	Men	Women	Men	Women
United States	22.3	13.1	32.1	20.5	37.6	25.9	29.9	18.7	629	549
Australia	37.0	29.9	37.9	23.4	50.4	39.9	40.3	27.4	543	463
United Kingdom	24.0	12.3	27.9	10.9	38.7	22.4	29.5	13.6	594	457
Canada	26.1	14.3	25.0	10.2	35.4	18.8	26.6	11.1	785	639
Sweden	19.7	10.8	17.4	4.7	34.1	16.3	21.9	5.3	549	436
Norway	26.6	12.7	23.3	4.1	39.4	10.7	29.4	5.4	827	588
Japan	28.5	3.5	34.0	2.9	47.0	3.5	38.3	1.7	253	173

	Top manager		Upper manager		Middle manager		Lower manager		Supervisor		Nonmanagement		N	
	Men %	Women %	Men %	Women %	Men %	Women %	Men %	Women %	Men %	Women %	Men %	Women %	Men	Women
United States	3.3	2.8	4.5	1.5	5.7	3.6	3.3	2.2	20.7	15.9	62.4	74.1	622	539
Australia	3.0	1.9	5.9	2.1	8.7	4.1	2.4	2.6	30.3	29.1	49.6	60.1	492	419
United Kingdom	3.9	0.9	1.2	0.2	8.6	1.8	4.9	1.1	20.2	18.4	61.3	77.6	594	456
Canada	3.7	0.9	5.2	0.9	5.4	3.0	2.3	2.0	18.9	11.9	64.6	81.2	785	639
Sweden	1.9	1.0	2.3	0	6.2	1.7	4.9	2.6	18.8	11.1	65.9	83.7	531	416
Norway	5.0	0.9	5.5	0.9	5.1	0.5	0.5	0.2	23.4	8.3	60.6	89.3	822	581
Japan	1.2	0	4.3	0	2.8	0	1.6	0	37.2	3.5	53.0	96.5	253	173

Table 12.3. *Gender coefficients from logistic regression analyses of the odds of women having work authority relative to men in seven countries: model with no controls*

| | Specific dimensions of authority | | | | | | Aggregate measures of authority | | | |
| | Decisionmaking | | Sanctioning authority | | Formal position | | Overall authority dichotomy | | Amount of authority (0-9 ordinal scale) | |
Country (N)[a]	b^b (s.e.)	Gender gap 1−Exp(b)	b (s.e.)	Gender gap 1−Exp(b)	b (s.e.)	Gender gap 1−Exp(b)	b (s.e.)	Gender gap 1−Exp(b)	b^c (s.e.)	Gender gap 1−Exp(b)
United States (1,178)	−0.64 (.16)	.47	−0.60 (.14)	.45	−0.54 (.13)	.42	−0.62 (.14)	.46	−0.63 (.14)	.47
Australia (1,006)	−0.32 (.14)	.27	−0.70 (.14)	.50	−0.43 (.14)	.35	−0.58 (.14)	.44	−0.64 (.13)	.47
United Kingdom (1,051)	−0.82 (.17)	.56	−1.15 (.18)	.68	−0.79 (.14)	.55	−0.98 (.16)	.62	−1.06 (.16)	.65
Canada (1,424)	−0.75 (.14)	.53	−1.08 (.16)	.66	−0.86 (.13)	.58	−1.07 (.15)	.66	−1.10 (.15)	.67
Sweden (985)	−0.70 (.20)	.50	−1.46 (.26)	.77	−0.97 (.16)	.62	−1.61 (.24)	.80	−1.57 (.24)	.79
Norway (1,415)	−0.91 (.15)	.60	−1.95 (.22)	.86	−1.70 (.15)	.82	−1.98 (.20)	.86	−1.98 (.20)	.86
Japan (426)	−2.40 (.44)	.91	−2.85 (.47)	.94	−3.21 (.43)	.96	−3.56 (.60)	.97	−3.58 (.60)	.97

Table 12.3. *(Continued)*

a. The Ns reported here are from the aggregate authority model. Ns for the other models may differ slightly.

b. Logit coefficient for gender effect in model 1: $\text{Log}[\text{Pr}(A=1)/\text{Pr}(A=0)] = a + B_1 \text{Female}$.

c. Coefficient for cumulative logit (ordered logit) model.

Significance levels for differences (two-tailed test) between rank-ordered countries on aggregate authority measures:

	[.03]
Overall authority dichotomy [p value of differences in logits between countries]	Australia [.85] US [.09] UK [.69] Canada [.05] Sweden [.24] Norway [.01] Japan
	[.06]
	[.001]
Amount-of-authority scale [p value of differences in cumulative logits between countries]	US [.92] Australia [.03] UK [.76] Canada [.10] Sweden [.19] Norway [.02] Japan

Explanation: The countries are ranked from small to large gender gaps in authority. The numbers in square brackets represent the p values for the differences between adjacent rank-ordered countries in their gender coefficients. In situations in which the p value does not fall below the .05 threshold for adjacent countries in the rank order, the closest pair of countries whose coefficients differ at the .05 level is indicated above or below the list of countries. In all cases the significance levels are internally consistent across rank orders.

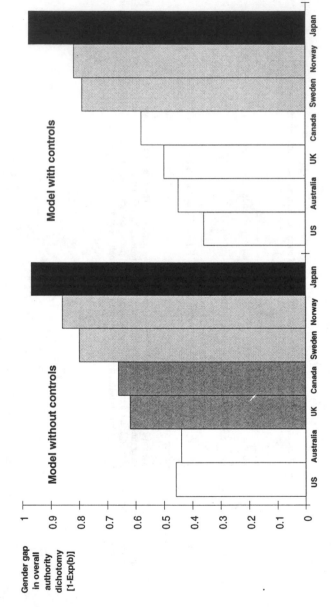

Bars of different shades indicate differences significant at p <.05 or better, with two exceptions: in the model without controls, the UK and Australia differ at the p <.06 level and the UK and the United States differ at the p <.09 level.

Figure 12.1 *The gender gap in authority in seven countries*

First, in every country, for every measure of authority, there is a significant gender gap. Women are less likely than men to be in the formal authority hierarchy, to have sanctioning power over subordinates and to participate in organizational policy decisions.

Second, there are statistically significant cross-national variations in the degree of gender inequality in authority. On all of the measures of authority, the United States and Australia have the smallest gender gap, and Japan has by far the largest gap.[21] On the basis of the exponentiated gender gap coefficients, in Japan the odds of a woman having authority are only between 3% and 9% the odds of a man having authority (depending upon the measure) whereas the odds of a woman in the United States and Australia having authority are generally around 50% to 60% that of a man. The other two English speaking countries – Canada and the United Kingdom – tend to have significantly greater gender-authority gaps than does the United States and Australia, but, perhaps surprisingly, smaller gaps than the two Scandinavian countries, Sweden and Norway. While, as already noted, in many respects the Scandinavian countries are among the most egalitarian in the world both in terms of class and of gender relations, with respect to the distribution of authority in the workplace, they are clearly less egalitarian than the four English-speaking countries in our analysis.

Third, while the gender gap appears in all of our measures of authority, it is generally somewhat more muted for the decisionmaking measure than for sanctioning authority and position in the formal hierarchy. In all countries except for the United States, the gender gap is considerably smaller for decisionmaking participation than for the other two measures, and the cross-national variations are less significant. While this may reflect a weakness in our measure of decisionmaking, it may also indicate that the most salient issue in gender inequalities of authority centers on direct power over people rather than organizational responsibilities as such.

Net gender differences in authority with compositional controls

Table 12.4 presents the coefficients for gender in Model (2). These coefficients tell us the size in the gender gap in authority net of any

---

[21] The magnitude of the gender gap in authority in Japan as estimated by our direct measures of authority is even greater than the 9:1 ratio estimated by Brinton (1988:311) using managerial occupations as the criterion.

Table 12.4. *Logistic regression analyses of the odds of women having work authority relative to men in seven countries: model with controls[a]*

Country (N)[b]	Specific dimensions of authority						Aggregate measures of authority				Percentage of gap in "overall authority" closed by adding controls to Model 1[e]
	Decision-making		Sanctioning authority		Formal position		Overall authority dichotomy		Amount of authority (0-9)		
	b[c] (s.e.)	Gap 1-Exp(b)	b (s.e.)	Gap 1-Exp(b)	b (s.e.)	Gap 1-Exp(b)	b (s.e.)	Gap 1-Exp(b)	b[d] (s.e.)	Gap 1-Exp(b)	
United States (1,178)	-0.55 (.19)	.42	-0.51 (.17)	.40	-0.48 (.17)	.38	-0.45 (.18)	.36	-0.51 (.17)	.40	22
Australia (1,006)	-0.51 (.17)	.40	-0.66 (.17)	.48	-0.44 (.17)	.35	-0.60 (.17)	.45	-0.70 (.16)	.50	-1
United Kingdom (1,051)	-0.72 (.22)	.51	-0.96 (.22)	.62	-0.59 (.20)	.44	-0.70 (.21)	.50	-1.02 (.21)	.64	19
Canada (1,424)	-0.84 (.17)	.57	-0.80 (.18)	.55	-0.77 (.16)	.54	-0.87 (.18)	.58	-0.93 (.17)	.61	12
Sweden (985)	-0.85 (.24)	.57	-1.24 (.29)	.71	-0.98 (.21)	.62	-1.54 (.27)	.79	-1.51 (.27)	.78	1
Norway (1,415)	-0.95 (.18)	.61	-1.53 (.25)	.78	-1.44 (.18)	.76	-1.70 (.22)	.82	-1.68 (.22)	.81	5
Japan (426)	-2.12 (.52)	.88	-2.51 (.52)	.92	-3.29 (.53)	.96	-3.73 (.76)	.98	-3.65 (.75)	.97	-1

Table 12.4. (*Continued*)

a. The compositional controls are industry, state, occupation, part time, education and age (only variables available in all countries are included).

b. The Ns reported here are from the aggregate authority model. Ns for the other models may differ slightly.

c. Logit coefficient for sex effect in model 2: Log [Pr (A=1)/Pr (A=0)] = a + B₁Female + ∑iBiXi.

c. Logit coefficient for sex effect in model 2: $\text{Log} [\text{Pr} (A=1)/\text{Pr} (A=0)] = a + B_1\text{Female} + \sum_i B_i X_i$.

d. Coefficient for cumulative logit (ordered logits).

e. Percentage of gap closed = (Gap in model 1 – Gap in model 2) ÷ (Gap in model 1).

Significance levels for differences (two-tailed test) between rank-ordered countries on aggregate authority measures:

Overall authority dichotomy [p-value of differences in logits between countries]	US [.54] Australia [.71] U.K. [.55] Canada [.04] Sweden [.65] Norway [.01] Japan				

[.005]

Amount-of-authority scale [p-value of differences in cumulative logits between countries]	US [.82] Australia [.22] U.K. [.87] Canada [.09] Sweden [.59] Norway [.03] Japan				

Explanation: The countries are ranked from small to large gender gaps in authority. The numbers in square brackets represent the p-values for the differences between adjacent rank-ordered countries in their gender coefficients in the relevant equation. In situations in which the p-value does not fall below the .05 threshold for adjacent countries in the rank order, the closest pair of countries whose coefficients differ at the .05 level is indicated above the list of countries. In all cases the significance levels are internally consistent across rank orders.

compositional differences between men and women on the other
variables in the equation.

The results in Table 12.4 and Figure 12.1 clearly demonstrate that
relatively little of the overall differences in authority among men and
women in any country can be attributed to gender differences in these
control variables.[22] The biggest compositional effects seem to be in the
United States and the United Kingdom, where roughly 20% of the total
gender authority gap is closed when the controls are added.[23] In the
other countries the figures range from less than 1% in Japan to 12% in
Canada. In both the US and the UK, virtually all of this modest
reduction in the gender gap in authority comes from the two job
attribute variables (occupation and full time); the inclusion of the
personal attribute variables in the equation has almost no effect on the
authority gap.

The results in Table 12.4 also show that while the significance level
of some of the cross-national differences declines in the equations
controlling for compositional effects, the basic patterns of the results
are essentially the same as in the equations for gross gender differences. In particular, in the equations predicting the overall authority
dichotomy, the only change between the model without compositional
effects and the model with compositional effects is that in the latter the
gender coefficients among the four English-speaking countries no
longer differ significantly. For the net gender gap, therefore, we have a
very clear grouping of our seven countries: the four English-speaking
countries have the smallest net gender gaps in authority, the two
Scandinavian countries have significantly larger net gender gaps, and
Japan has by far the largest.

While it is always possible that we have omitted some crucial
compositional variable from the analysis which might affect the
results, nevertheless, these results are strongly supportive of the claim
that gender differences in authority, and cross-national patterns of

[22] The results reported in Table 12.4 are from the *uniform* equations, i.e. the equations
containing exactly the same variables for all countries. When we estimate the results
using the nonuniform equations in which we include all of the variables available
for each country, the results are virtually identical.

[23] If the compositional factors accounted for all of the gender gap, then the gender gap
– 1 minus the exponentiated gender coefficient – would be 0 in model 2 in Table
12.4. In the United States results, the gender gap for the aggregate authority
measure is 0.46 in the model with no controls (Table 12.3). The gender gap in the
model with controls in Table 12.5 is 0.36. The difference in these coefficients – 0.10 –
is 21.7% of 0.46, the gender gap from model 1.

such differences, are not primarily the result of differences in the distributions of relevant attributes of men and women and their employment situations. This adds credibility to the claim that direct discrimination or self-selection in the promotion process itself are likely to be important.

Self-selection models

The self-selection hypothesis states that because of family responsibilities, women voluntarily make themselves less available for promotion into positions of authority in the workplace. We will explore this hypothesis through the following interaction model:

$$\text{Log } [Pr(A=1)/Pr(A=0)] = a + B_1\text{Female} + B_2\text{Married} + B_3\text{Kids} + B_4[\text{Husband's Housework}] + B_5[\text{Female x Married}] + B_6[\text{Female x Kids}] + B_7[\text{Female x Husband's Housework}] + \Sigma_i B_i X_i \quad (3)$$

where the X_i are those compositional variables in Model (2) which are available in all countries. If self-selection is a powerful force in shaping the gender gap in authority, then the interactive terms in these equations should be statistically significant.

Table 12.5 presents the interaction coefficients for Model (3) using the overall authority dichotomy as the dependent variable.[24] The results indicate that in the United States, Sweden and Australia, none of the interactions are significant in Model (3). In Norway and Canada, however, the interactions of Female with Husband's Housework are significant, and in Canada the Female x Married interaction term approaches the .05 level of significance and becomes statistically significant when the Female x Kids interaction term is dropped.[25] In

---

[24] These models could not be estimated for Japan and the UK because they lacked data on the division of labor in the household. The interaction terms in a simpler model without this variable were not significant for these two countries.

[25] The Female x Married coefficient in Canada is -1.20 with a standard error of 0.48 in equation 3 when the Female x Kids interaction term is dropped. In no other country is this interaction term significant. However, if the X_i compositional terms are also excluded (but not the self-selection variables), the Female x Married interaction also is significant in Norway. The coefficient for this interaction indicates that married women have a significantly lower probability of having authority than married men; it does not say that married women have a lower probability of having authority than single women. It turns out that there is no significant difference in the likelihood of authority between married and single women. The significant Married x Female interaction comes from the fact that married *men* have a significantly *higher* likelihood of having authority than single men. When age is added as a compositional control in Model (3),

Table 12.5. *Testing the "self-selection" hypothesis: analysis of the odds of women having authority relative to men in model which includes interactions with marital status and husband's housework*

| | | Logit coefficients[a] | | | | Gender gap in authority at selected values of self-selection indicators[b] | | |
		Female	Female × married	Female × kids	Female × husband's housework	Unmarried (weak self-selection pressures)	Married in relatively egalitarian households without children (intermediate self-selection pressures)[c]	Married in relatively *inegalitarian* households with children (maximum self-selection pressures)[d]
United States	b	−0.46	−0.32	0.21	0.009	.37	.33	.38
	(s.e.)	(.27)	(.43)	(.35)	(.010)			
Australia	b	−0.31	−0.21	−0.01	−0.004	.27	.49	.44
	(s.e.)	(.29)	(.49)	(.35)	(.01)			
Canada	b	−0.13	−0.94	−0.49	0.020*	.13	.23	.82
	(s.e.)	(.36)	(.52)	(.38)	(.010)			
Sweden	b	−1.61*	−0.36	0.18	0.009	.80	.80	.82
	(s.e.)	(.54)	(.84)	(.58)	(.02)			
Norway	b	−1.42*	−0.84	−0.22	0.025*	.76	.71	.89
	(s.e.)	(.52)	(.71)	(.47)	(.0125)			

Significance levels: * p < .05

a. Logit coefficients are from model with compositional controls predicting overall authority dichotomy: $\text{Log}[\text{Pr}(A=1)/\text{Pr}(A=0)] = a + B_1\text{Female} + B_2\text{Married} + B_3\text{kids} + B_4\text{Husband's housework} + B_5\text{Female} \times \text{Married} + B_6\text{Female} \times \text{Kids} + B_7\text{Female} \times \text{husband's housework} + \sum_i B_i X_i$, where the X_i are industry, state, occupation, part time, education and age.

b. Gender gap = 1−Exp(b). This gap is evaluated at specific values of the interactive terms. For example, the gender gap in the United States for married people (married =1) with children (kids=1) in inegalitarian households (husband's housework = 10) = 1 − Exp [(−.46) + (−.32) + (.21) + (.009 x 10)] = 1 − Exp (−.48) = 1 − .62 = .38.

c. Egalitarian households are defined as those in which husbands do 40% of housework.

d. *Inegalitarian* households are defined as those in which husbands do 10% of housework.

these two countries, as the proportion of housework done by their husbands increases, the likelihood of married women having workplace authority also increases. Only in Canada, however, does this interaction term generate a substantively large effect on the gender gap in authority. As Table 12.5 indicates, the gender gap in authority for married women without children in the home, living in a relatively egalitarian household (a household in which husbands do 40% of the housework) is 0.23, whereas the gap for married women with children in the home living in an *in*egalitarian household (in which husbands do only 10% of the housework) is 0.82, comparable to the levels in Sweden and Norway. I can offer no explanation for why the patterns in Canada are so different from the other countries. For Canada, therefore, these interactions are consistent with the claims of the self-selection hypothesis that when women have high levels of domestic responsibility they frequently select themselves out of the running for positions of authority.[26] There is little or no support for the self-selection hypothesis, however, for the other countries in the study.

The gender gap in the amount of authority

So far we have only discussed the differential likelihood of men and women *having* authority, but not the *amount* of authority that they have. We will examine the amount of authority in two ways, first by estimating cumulative logits in Model (2) with the 10-point authority scale as the dependent variable, and second, by looking at the amount of authority of men and women conditional upon having some authority. This second analysis will provide a way of exploring the glass ceiling hypothesis.

As Tables 12.3 and 12.4 indicate, the pattern of gender gaps in the amount of authority as measured by the cumulative logits are

the coefficient for the Married × Female interaction term is considerably reduced and ceases to be statistically significant in Norway.

[26] While these results lend support to the self-selection hypothesis for Canada, and to a lesser extent for Norway, it should be noted that the negative association between housework inequality and women's workplace authority in Canada and Norway could partially reflect a causal impact of having authority on housework rather than of housework on the likelihood of getting authority. Managerial and supervisory women may on average do less housework because of the demands of their jobs, and thus the gender distribution of housework in their homes will be less unequal. If this is the case, then the positive interaction between gender and husband's housework in Table 12.5 would not indicate self-selection.

generally quite similar to the results for the dichotomous authority variables. As in the previous analysis, the addition of the compositional control variables has, at best, a very modest effect on the gender gap. Also, the rank order of countries in the gender gap in the amount of authority is almost identical to the rank order in the odds of having authority.

The strategy for evaluating the glass ceiling hypothesis involves restricting the analysis to respondents in the authority hierarchy and then examining gender gaps in authority within this subsample. To do this, we used the formal position in the authority-hierarchy variable as the criterion for restricting the sample: all persons who say that they are at least a supervisor on this question will be treated as in the hierarchy. On this restricted sample, we then run Model (2) for three dependent variables: sanctioning authority; middle manager or above in the formal hierarchy; and the amount-of-authority scale.[27] The results are presented in Table 12.6.

The most striking thing in Table 12.6 is the sharp difference between the United States and other countries. In all countries except the United States, the gender gap in sanctioning authority, hierarchical position and the amount of authority remain large and statistically significant when we restrict the sample to people in the hierarchy.[28] In contrast, in the United States, the gender gap ceases to be statistically significant for all three of these variables.[29] This is not because the standard errors of the gender coefficients become large in the United States (they are among the smallest of any of the countries), but because the absolute value of the gender gap coefficients become relatively small. On the bases of these data, in the United States the net gender gap in sanctioning authority among people in the authority hierarchy is only about 0.08 (i.e. the odds of a woman in the hierarchy having sanction-

---

[27] Two notes concerning this analysis: First, there were no women in the Japanese sample who were in middle manager or above positions, and thus we cannot estimate equations for this dependent variable on the Japanese sample. Second, as noted in the discussion of Tables 12.3 and 12.4, the decisionmaking variable seems to be a weaker indicator of real authority than the other measures we are using. We are therefore not including this dependent variable in the analysis of the glass ceiling hypothesis.

[28] In the analysis of the decisionmaking dependent variable (not shown), the gender gaps for the UK and Norway also cease to be statistically significant in the model with compositional controls.

[29] The gender coefficient was also statistically insignificant in the United States in the bivariate equations (not presented here) for the gross gender gap when the sample was restricted to people in the hierarchy.

Table 12.6. *Testing the glass ceiling hypothesis: logistic regression analyses of the odds of women having different kinds of work authority relative to men in seven countries (sample restricted to people in the formal hierarchy)*

	Model (2) with controls[a]					
	Sanctioning authority		Middle manager or above in formal hierarchy		Amount of authority (0–9 scale)[b]	
Country (N)[c]	b (s.e.)	Gap 1−Exp(b)	b (s.e.)	Gap 1−Exp(b)	b (s.e.)	Gap 1−Exp(b)
United States (373)	−0.08 (.27)	.08	−0.36 (.28)	.30	−0.28 (.23)	.24
Australia (414)	−0.65 (.25)	.48	−0.55 (.27)	.42	−0.64 (.21)	.47
United Kingdom (332)	−0.80 (.31)	.55	−1.08 (.39)	.66	−1.03 (.27)	.64
Canada (398)	−0.44 (.26)	.35	−0.71 (.29)	.51	−0.72 (.23)	.51
Sweden (248)	−0.61 (.36)	.46	−0.91 (.43)	.60	−0.91 (.32)	.60
Norway (376)	−0.93 (.35)	.61	−0.98 (.38)	.63	−1.06	.65
Japan (125)	−2.37 (1.26)	.91	n.a.[d]	1.0	−1.21 (1.05)	.70

a. Logit coefficients for sex effect in Model (2): $\text{Log}[Pr(A=1)/Pr(A=0)] = a + B_1 \text{Female} + \sum_i B_i X_i$. The compositional controls are: industry, state, occupation, part time, education and age (only variables available in all countries are included).

b. Coefficient for cumulative logit (ordered logit) models corresponding to Model (2).

c. The Ns reported here are from the sanctioning-authority model. Ns for the other models may differ slightly.

d. There are no women in the Japanese sample in middle-management positions or above. Hence these models are not calculated for Japan, but we assume that women's odds of having work authority relative to men are close to zero.

ing authority are about 8% less than those of a man, controlling for the other variables in the equation), while the gender gap in being at least a middle manager is only 0.30 and the gender gap in the amount of authority as measured by the cumulative logit is 0.24. In other countries, the gender authority gaps conditional on being in the hierarchy are generally 0.50 and above.[30]

What do these results mean for the "glass ceiling hypothesis"? The glass ceiling hypothesis states that the barriers women face, relative to men, for promotions up the authority hierarchy are generally greater than the barriers they face getting into the hierarchy itself. If this hypothesis were correct, then the gender gap in authority should generally be greater among people inside the authority hierarchy (Table 12.6) than for the labor force as a whole (Table 12.5). With only two exceptions, the coefficients in these tables are not consistent with this prediction. For sanctioning authority and for the amount-of-authority scale, the gender coefficients for people in the hierarchy are, in every country, either the same as or smaller than the gender coefficients for the sample as whole. The only cases in which the results are in line with the expectations of the glass ceiling hypothesis are for the formal position variable in the UK and Australia.[31] With these limited exceptions, therefore, these results do not lend support to the glass ceiling hypothesis. Especially in the United States, it does not appear that once women are in the hierarchy, the barriers they face to promotion relative to men at least into the middle range of the hierarchy are greater than the barriers they faced in getting into the hierarchy in the first place.

It is important to stress that these results do not demonstrate that there is no gender discrimination in promotions for people already in authority hierarchies. Indeed, in all countries except for the United States the gender gap in authority for people already within the hierarchy is statistically significant, and with a larger sample, the gap

---

[30] Because of the small sample size in these analyses, it is not possible to test the differences between the coefficients for the United States and each of the other countries taken separately. If, for the restricted sample of people in the hierarchy, we compare the United States to all of the other countries taken together except for Japan (Japan was dropped because it has such large standard errors), then we find that in model 1 for sanctioning authority the coefficient for the United States is 0.43 smaller than the other countries combined (p <.08) and the coefficient for being a middle manager or above in the formal hierarchy is 0.54 smaller in the United States (p <.02). In the parallel results for Model (2), the magnitude of the differences in coefficients is virtually the same, but the standard errors increase so the significance level drops to p < .13.

[31] For those people already in the hierarchy, the odds of a woman being at least a middle manager are 66% less than for men in the UK and 42% less than for men in Australia, whereas the odds of a woman simply being in the hierarchy are only 44% less than for men in the UK and 35% less than for men in Australia.

in the American data would almost certainly be statistically significant as well. But the glass ceiling hypothesis is stronger than simply a claim about the existence of discrimination within hierarchies; it is a claim that such discrimination *increases* as one moves up the hierarchy, and the comparative data we have examined does not lend support to this view. Of course, these data do not speak to the issue of whether or not there is a significant glass ceiling at the highest levels in authority hierarchies in the largest firms. In a random sample of this sort we certainly do not have sufficient data on CEOs or even top executives of large corporations to examine whether significant barriers exist at the top of hierarchies.[32] Nevertheless, while a gender gap in the level of authority among people in the hierarchy probably does exist in the United States, our data indicate that it is weaker than in other countries in this study and that it is not properly described as constituting a glass ceiling, at least in the middle ranges of organizational hierarchies.

Explaining cross-national variations

We have already examined, and rejected, one possible explanation for the differences across countries in the gender gap in workplace authority. These differences cannot be attributed to differences in the various compositional factors included in Model (2). As already pointed out (see Figure 12.1), the basic pattern of intercountry differences is the same in Model (1) and Model (2) for each of the measures of authority we have been examining.

We will now explore somewhat less formally a number of general macro-social and cultural factors which might help explain the variations across countries in the gender gap. The results are presented in Table 12.7.

1 Gender ideology. The Comparative Project on Class Structure and Class Consciousness contains a limited number of attitude items on

---

[32] The item which measures position within the formal hierarchy, however, does distinguish between top and upper managers on the one hand, and middle managers on the other, although the number of cases gets so small that in most countries we cannot make reliable estimates of the gender gap in authority at this level of the hierarchy. Nevertheless, the same basic pattern occurs with top/upper manager being the dependent variable: in the United States the gender gap in being an upper or top manager, conditional upon being in the hierarchy, is about 0.25, whereas in other countries the figures are all between 0.47 and 0.67.

Table 12.7. *Rank ordering of countries from more to less egalitarian by the gender gap in authority and other relevant variables*

Net gender gap in having authority (model 2)		Gender attitudes[c]		Legal gender egalitarianism[d]	
Rank order of countries[a]	Gender gap[b]	Rank order of countries	Mean score	Rank order of countries	Mean score
US	.36	Sweden	1.77	Norway	1.83
Australia	.45	Norway	1.82	Sweden	1.17
UK	.50	Canada	2.01	US	1.17
Canada	.58	Australia	2.05	Canada	-.48
Sweden	.79	US	2.17	UK	-.48
Norway	.82	Japan	2.43	Australia	-1.02
Japan	.98			Japan	-1.02

Gender earnings gap[e]		Occupational sex segregation (Index of dissimilarity)[f]	
Rank order of countries	Women's hourly earnings as percentage of men's	Rank order of countries	Mean score
Sweden	91.0	Japan	22.2
Norway	81.9	Australia	31.9
Australia	81.7	US	36.6
UK	74.0	Canada	41.0
Canada	66.0	Sweden	41.8
US	65.0	UK	44.4
Japan	51.8	Norway	47.2

Occupational sex segregation ("Ratio index of sex segregation")[g]		Proportion of the labor force in official managerial positions[h]	
Rank order of countries	Mean score	Rank order of countries	Proportion of labor force (%)
US	.65	Australia	15.8
Japan	.72	US	13.7
Canada	.75	Canada	12.2
UK	.92	UK	12.2
Australia	.95	Sweden	10.9
Sweden	.96	Norway	10.4
Norway	.99	Japan	5.9

Table 12.7. *(Continued)*

a. As indicated in Figure 12.1, the rank ordering of countries is virtually the same for the gross gender gap and the net gender gap (Models 1 and 2).

b. The gender gap in workplace authority is defined as $1-\text{Exp(b)}$, where b is the coefficient for gender in the logistic regression predicting the overall authority dichotomy in Model 2.

c. This is a simple index based on three Likert items concerning sex role attitudes. The lower the score the more egalitarian. The scores range from 1 to 4. The variable was not available for the United Kingdom.

d. This is a simple factor analytic scale of three legal rights for women: rights to abortion; rights to at least 12 weeks paid pregnancy leave; marital rape is a crime. See Charles (1992: 491-2).

e. Sources. Sweden, Norway, Australia, UK, Canada, US: National Committee on Pay Equity, "Closing the Wage Gap: an international perspective" (Washington, DC: National Committee on Pay Equity, 1988), pp. 10-14. *Japan: The Yearbook of Labor Statistics* (Geneva: International Labor Organization, 51st edn, 1992), pp. 798-804. There are some differences in the definitions for each country: Australia (1985), full time, average weekly earnings; Canada (1986), not specified; Japan (1984), average monthly earnings; Norway (1980), average hourly earnings in manufacturing; Sweden (1985), average monthly earnings, industry; United Kingdom (1985), average hourly earnings; United States (1987), median annual earnings.

f. Blau and Ferber (1990) .

g. Charles (1992: 489).

h. This is defined as people in jobs which are described as "managerial positions" (but not supervisory positions) in the formal hierarchy variable.

gender equality. Respondents were asked whether they strongly agreed, somewhat agreed, somewhat disagreed or strongly disagreed with each of the following statements:

1 Ideally, there should be as many women as men in important positions in government and business.
2 If both husband and wife work, they should share equally in the housework and childcare.
3 It is better for the family if the husband is the principal bread-winner outside the home and the wife has primary responsibility for the home and children.

A gender-ideology scale was constructed by rescaling item 3 so that the egalitarian response was in the same direction as the other two questions, and then adding the responses to each item and averaging over the number of valid items. The scale ranges from 1 indicating a consistently strong egalitarian attitude toward gender roles to 4, indicating a consistently strong conservative attitude.

As can be seen from column 2 in Table 12.7, the rank ordering of countries in terms of their degree of ideological gender egalitarianism does not at all parallel the rank ordering for the gender gap in workplace authority. Sweden and Norway are the most ideologically egalitarian but have among the largest gender gaps in authority; the United States is exceeded only by Japan in the level of inegalitarianism ideologically, yet it has the smallest gender gap in authority. The overall level of ideological beliefs in gender equality in these societies, therefore, does not seem to be closely linked to the relative magnitudes of the gender gaps in workplace authority.

2 *Sexual and reproductive rights.* Maria Charles (1992) has constructed an index of legally enforced gender egalitarianism based on a principal components analysis, single factor solution of three dummy variables: (1) abortions available on request; (2) marital rape is a crime; and (3) women are guaranteed at least twelve weeks of paid pregnancy leave from work. The scale values range from 1.83 to −1.02, where positive scores indicate more rights. As can be seen from column 3 in Table 12.7, the rank order among the seven countries on this variable is both quite different from the rank order for gender attitudes and the rank order for the net gender gap in having authority.

3 *Gender earnings gap.* While cross-national variation in ideological gender egalitarianism does not seem closely linked to the variation in the gender-authority gap, it might still be the case that the gender-authority gap could be related to broader institutional arrangements for gender equality within work. The gender gap in earnings is one possible indicator of this. Contrary to this expectation, however, the data in Table 12.7 indicate that there is no association between the level of the gender gap in hourly earnings and the gender gap in authority. Japan and the United States both have relatively large gender differences in earnings, yet the United States has a small gender gap in authority while Japan has the largest gender gap; Sweden and Norway are both relatively egalitarian in terms of gender differences in earnings, yet they both have relatively large gender gaps in authority.[33]

4 *Occupational sex segregation.* As in the case of the gender gap in income, the expectation that the rank order of countries in sex segregation of occupations should roughly mirror the gender gap in

---

[33] The figures for the earnings gap in Table 12.7 are not strictly comparable from country to country. In some countries the figures are for the gap in hourly earnings, in others for monthly or annual earnings. Nevertheless, the rough rank ordering of these particular countries is unlikely to be significantly altered if hourly earnings were available for all countries.

authority is not supported by the available data. Based on the data of two comparative studies of occupational sex segregation, Blau and Ferber (1990) and Charles (1992), the rank ordering of our seven countries in terms of overall occupational sex segregation is not the same as the rank ordering in terms of the gender gap in authority.[34] As shown in Table 12.7, columns 5 and 6, Japan has among the lowest levels of sex segregation in occupations, while, depending upon the measure of sex segregation used, the United Kingdom and Australia have among the highest levels of occupational sex segregation. While it is possible that with a more fine-grained analysis of occupational sex segregation this rank ordering might change, Brinton and Ngo (1991) have shown that even with an 89-category classification, the United States has a higher index of dissimilarity than Japan (55.6 compared to 49.8).[35] It thus seems unlikely that a more refined analysis would support the view that variations across countries in the gender-authority gap are simply a reflection of variations in broader processes in the association of gender and occupation.

5 *The proportion of the labor force with authority.* Table 12.7, column 7, presents the rank ordering of the countries in our sample by the proportion of the labor force in managerial positions (as measured by the formal hierarchy variable). The results indicate that the rank ordering for the size of the managerial category quite closely mirrors the rank ordering of the gender gap in authority: the four English-speaking countries have the largest proportion of their labor forces in managerial positions, followed by the two Nordic countries and then, with a much smaller figure, Japan.[36] It does appear therefore that the

[34] Blau and Ferber (1990) use a seven category occupational classification to compute a standard index of dissimilarity. Charles uses a six category occupational classification to compute what she calls a "ratio index of sex segregation."

[35] Brinton and Ngo (1991) demonstrate that the lower overall occupational sex segregation in Japan than in the United States occurs because there is lower occupational sex segregation among low-status occupations in Japan compared to the United States, but higher sex segregation among high-status occupations. They propose an alternative measure which weights the index by the prestige of occupations. This weighting procedure considerably increases the index of dissimilarity for Japan and modestly reduces it for the United States, with the result that the (prestige-adjusted) occupational sex segregation in Japan is higher than in the United States. Such a more refined set of occupational sex segregation measures are not available for the other countries in our analysis, but given the relative cultural similarity among these countries it seems unlikely that such prestige adjustments would produce as large a shift in the index of dissimilarity as it does in Japan.

[36] When the rank ordering is based on people who occupy *either* manager *or* supervisor positions in the formal hierarchy variable, the authority rank ordering

aggregate availability of managerial positions in the society may influence the size of the gender gap in the allocation of authority.

6 *The organized women's movement and political culture.* I know of no comparative research which systematically assesses women's movements in different countries either in terms of their organizational and political strength or in terms of the details of their ideological stance. Our analysis of these issues, therefore, will have to remain at a relatively impressionistic level.

In terms of the political strength of the women's movement one thing seems particularly clear: the women's movement in Japan is far weaker than in any other country. It is less obvious how to judge the relative strength of women's movements in the other six countries, although it seems clear that the politically organized women's movement in the United States would be among the strongest. Katzenstein (1987: 12) writes, "Mainstream feminism in the United States, liberal in its political tenets, is the only movement of those described in this volume[37] with a mass-based national organization run by a paid, professional staff. In no country in Western Europe is there a national organization analogous to the National Organization for Women (NOW)." She further notes that, while in Sweden feminist consciousness is fairly highly diffused in the population (in contrast to Britain where she feels it is less developed) and has had a major impact on social policies of the Swedish Social Democratic welfare state, "In Sweden policy success is won at the price of organizational weakness [of the women's movement]" (Katzenstein 1987:16). This image of a relatively weakly mobilized women's movement in Sweden is echoed

---

differs somewhat from the gender gap rank ordering. In particular, Japan, which is at the bottom of the rank ordering of the gender-authority gap, is in the middle of the rank ordering of proportion of labor force in supervisor or manager positions. However, since the supervisor category is the category most likely to include people with only nominal authority, the somewhat more restrictive definition is more appropriate for present purposes. It should also be noted that when the other two dimensions of authority we have been examining – decisionmaking and sanctioning authority – are used as the basis for the rank ordering of the size of the authority-holding population, the rank ordering does not correspond so neatly to the rank ordering of the gender gap. If we regard the formal hierarchy variable as a measure of authority *positions* and the sanctioning and decisionmaking variables as measures of authority *functions* or *responsibilities*, then it appears that the critical "scarce resource" that differentiates our countries is the availability of positions, not simply the availability of responsibilities.

[37] The volume discusses the women's movements in the United States, Britain, Sweden, the Netherlands, France, Italy and Germany.

by Mary Ruggie (1988: 187) who writes, "Swedish women themselves are not greatly mobilized for change at present, either in autonomous groups or in workplace organizations." While this evidence is impressionistic, it seems fairly safe to say that the politically organized women's movement is probably weakest in Japan and strongest in the United States, with the other countries falling somewhere in between.

It is somewhat easier to make some judgments about the ideological orientations of different women's movements, at least if we are willing to assume that these women's movements are likely to reflect to a significant extent the broader political culture of their societies. Esping-Anderson (1990) classified capitalist democracies along a variety of dimensions characterizing the ideological principles within their welfare states. These are presented in Table 12.8. With the exception of the placement of Japan within these rank orderings, these political orderings closely parallel the rank ordering of the gender gap. Specifically, the four English-speaking countries score low on what Esping-Anderson terms "decommodification" (i.e. welfare state policies which reduce the dependency of workers on the market) and high on liberalism of regime characteristics, whereas Norway and Sweden score high on decommodification and extremely low on liberalism.

How does this relate to the problem of the gender gap in authority? Liberalism is a doctrine which argues that markets are a legitimate and efficient means of distributing welfare so long as they are "fair." Eliminating ascriptive barriers to individual achievement in labor markets and employment relations is therefore a central objective of liberal politics. A women's movement animated by a liberal political culture, therefore, would be particularly concerned with equal rights and the elimination of such barriers. In keeping with this expectation, Goldberg and Kremen (1990: 28–30) have emphasized the relatively strong forms of anti-discrimination laws that have been passed in the United States and their relative effectiveness, at least compared to many other countries.

Social democracy, in contrast, questions the legitimacy of market-determined inequalities regardless of the equality of opportunity and seeks to render human welfare at least partially independent of market mechanisms. A women's movement embedded in a social democratic political culture would be expected to be much less concerned with labor market mechanisms as such, and more concerned with state interventions which directly provide services and resources which enhance the welfare of women. Policy initiatives would therefore concentrate on such things as parental leaves, maternal health care,

Table 12.8 *Rank ordering of countries' political culture and institutions from liberal/ commodified to socialist/decommodified*

Degree of "decommodification" in the welfare state[a]		Degree of liberalism in regime attributes[b]		Degree of socialism in regime attributes	
Rank order	Score	Rank order	Score	Rank order	Score
Australia	13.0	United States	12	United States	0
United States	13.8	Canada	12	Japan	2
Canada	22.0	Australia	10	Australia	4
U K	23.4	Japan	10	U K	4
Japan	27.1	U K	6	Canada	4
Norway	38.3	Norway	0	Norway	8
Sweden	39.1	Sweden	0	Sweden	8

a From Esping-Anderson (1990: 52). This score is a measure of the extent to which the welfare state neutralizes the effects of the market through its welfare policies.

b. From Esping-Anderson (1990:74). The score indexes the extent to which welfare state interventions follow the principles of classical liberalism. The socialism score indexes the extent to which the regime follows socialist principles. Because in Esping-Anderson's analysis there is a third form of regime, "classical conservatism," the rank ordering for socialism is not necessarily simply the inverse of the rank ordering for liberalism.

childcare services and child allowances. Women would certainly benefit in many ways from such strategies, as many commentators on Scandinavian social democracy have stressed (Goldberg and Uremen 1990: 141–144; Moen 1989), but these priorities would not directly impact on barriers to authority promotions in the workplace. Commenting on the contrast between American liberal feminism and European social democratic feminism, Nancy Fraser (1993) argues that the former adopt a "universal breadwinner" model of gender equality which emphasizes employment rights, whereas the latter adopt a "caregiver parity" model which stresses the provision of services and resources to equalize the conditions of life of women engaged primarily in domestic responsibilities. The relatively large gender gap in workplace authority in the social democratic Nordic countries, therefore, may in part be a by-product of the relatively lower priority placed on liberal goals of individual competition and achievement relative to more communal benefits.

These various arguments suggest that the variations across countries in the size of the gender gap in workplace authority are the result of the interaction between the relative scarcity or abundance of authority positions on the one hand and the capacity and interest of the politically organized women's movement to challenge the barriers to women being promoted into those positions on the other. Where there are relatively few managerial positions in the first place and the women's movement is particularly weak, as in Japan, the gender gap in authority will be very large. Where there are somewhat more managerial positions, but the women's movement is oriented toward collective goods and decommodified social provisions, the gender gap will still be relatively large. Where there are relatively abundant managerial positions in the job structure and where the women's movement is relatively strong and oriented toward liberal individualist goals, the gender gap will be most effectively challenged. The evidence in support of these interpretations is rather sketchy, especially because we do not have cases of countries with a high proportion of the labor force in managerial positions combined with a weak women's movement, or countries with a strong, liberal women's movement and relatively few manager positions. Such cases would be needed to tease out the relative importance of these two factors and the nature of their interactions. Considerably more research is needed about the impact of women's struggles and the process by which the gender gap in authority changes over time within and across countries before these interpretations could be affirmed with confidence.

12.4 Conclusions

This chapter has examined gender inequality in workplace authority in a range of countries and has provided an empirical assessment of a number of competing explanations concerning the continued persistence of gender differences in men's and women's attainment of authority. We have directly tested the impact of three broad sets of nondiscrimination factors – gender differences in aspirations (self-selection), gender differences in individual attributes and gender differences in employment settings – and indirectly examined the effect of active discrimination, on the gender gap in authority. Finally we have examined cross-national differences in the degree of authority men and women have, as well as cross-national differences in the factors affecting attainment of workplace authority.

Several conclusions emerge from this research. First, while a gender gap in authority exists in all of the countries we have studied, there is considerable cross-national variation in the magnitude of this gap: it is smaller in the English-speaking countries, especially in the United States and Australia, relatively large in the Scandinavian countries, and huge in Japan. These results appear quite robust across a variety of measures. While the results for Japan are perhaps the least surprising, the difference between the English-speaking countries and the Scandinavian countries might be unexpected to many people. Sweden, and to a lesser extent Norway, are both countries with a long history of commitment to social democratic programs aimed at achieving gender equality, and on many indicators, notably the gender gap in earnings, taxation policies, childcare programs and welfare rights, considerable progress has been made. However, our data show that gender inequality in access to workplace authority in Scandinavia lags a considerable way behind less "progressive" countries such as the United States, Australia, Canada and the United Kingdom. These findings thus raise serious questions about the most effective means of reducing gender inequality in the workplace. While a general commitment toward gender equality and decommodified social provisions may go some way toward reducing gender inequality, it appears that this must also be combined with other initiatives, in particular a strong, politically organized women's movement which directly confronts the barriers women face in the labor market and work settings.

Second, the gender gap in authority within countries and the pattern of cross-national variations do not appear to be significantly the result of compositional factors among men and women in the labor force. Even when we control for a range of attributes of firms, jobs and individuals, the gap within every country and the basic pattern of cross-national differences remain. This implies that a significant proportion of the differences in men's and women's attainment of authority is attributable to discrimination. While it appears that some of the gender gap in authority in some countries (especially Canada) may be due to self-selection by women, our data analysis does not support the view that this is generally a major determinant of gender inequality in authority, and in most of the countries we have studied it appears to be of relatively small importance. Much of the gender gap in workplace authority in the countries we have studied can thus provisionally be attributed to various forms of discrimination, particularly in the promotion process.

Third, the glass ceiling hypothesis (at least in the relatively weak form we were able to investigate) is not supported in most of the countries in the study. While a gender gap in authority generally continues to exist when we restrict the analysis to people already in the authority hierarchy, this gap does not appear to be greater than the gap in acquiring authority in the first place. The commonly held view that the women's movement has been more successful in opening up positions at the bottom of the organizational hierarchy for women, and less successful in moving women up the corporate ladder is not supported by these data. Interestingly, in terms of the country differences on this issue, in the United States promotional possibilities among women already in the authority hierarchy appear to be significantly less obstructed than in any of the other countries in the study. While in many other respects the United States is far from a leader in egalitarian policies, on gender issues in workplace hierarchies, the United States does appear to have made considerable progress relative to most other countries.

Finally, and more tentatively, we have examined data which suggest that the variations in the gender gap across countries may be the result of the interaction between variations in the relative abundance of authority positions and the effectiveness of different women's movements in challenging barriers women face in moving into those positions. Both political and economic factors thus seem to be important in explaining variability in gender inequality in workplace authority, whereas cultural variations more specifically linked to gender ideology seem less significant.

Methodological appendix

Variables used in logit models

The operational criteria for the variables we use in this chapter are presented in Appendix Table 12.1. Some of the variables in this table need some clarification.

Formal hierarchical position. The simplest of the measures of authority is formal position in the authority hierarchy in which respondents classify themselves into nonmanagement, supervisor, lower manager, middle manager, upper manager or top manager positions. Since the meaning of these different "levels" varies from organization to organization depending upon the size of the organization and the conventions used to designate different positions, for most of the analysis we will not use this variable as a continuous measure of hierarchical

Appendix Table 12.1. *Variables used in the analysis*

I. Dichotomous authority variables

Variable	*Definition*
1. Sanctioning authority	Has direct influence on pay, promotions or punishments of subordinates (yes/no)
2. Decisionmaking authority	Directly participates in making policy decisions in the workplace (not just provides advice)
3. Formal position	Occupies a position in the formal authority structure of the workplace: supervisor, lower manager, middle manager, upper manager or top manager
4. Overall authority dichotomy	A positive response to any two of the three dimensions of authority

II. Amount-of-authority scale

Amount-of-authority scale	Overall authority dichotomy variable	Sanctioning authority	Position in formal hierarchy
0	no		
1	yes	yes	0 = nonmanagement
2	yes	no	1 = supervisor
3	yes	yes	1 = supervisor
4	yes	no	2 = lower manager
5	yes	yes	2 = lower manager
6	yes	no	3 = middle manager
7	yes	yes	3 = middle manager
8	yes	no	4, 5 = upper or top manager
9	yes	yes	4, 5 = upper or top manager

III. Control variables	Descriptions	Excluded countries
1. Firm attributes		
1.1 Industry	Dummy variables distinguishing in a conventional manner extractive, trans-formative (manufacturing, transportation, utilities) and service sectors. Contrast category is the transformative sector.	*none*
1.2 State	Dummy variable distinguishing public and private sector employees (1 = private)	*none*
1.3 Firm size	Continuous variable measuring respondent's estimate of the number of employees in the firm (not the establishment) in which the respondent is employed (for private sector only)	*Australia*

Appendix Table 12.1.   *(continued)*

2. Job attributes		
2.1 Occupation	Four dummy variables for standard occupational distinctions: upper white-collar, lower white-collar, upper manual, lower manual occupations. Contrast category is lower manual.	*none*
2.2 Full time	Dummy variable, 1 = works at least 30 hours per week, 0 = less than 30 hours per week	*none*
3. Personal attributes		
3.1 Education	Years of education	*none*
3.2 Age	Age in years	*none*
3.3 Labor force break	Dummy variable, 0 = interrupted labor force history, 1 = continuous labor force participation since first full-time job after completing education	*Australia, Japan, Sweden*
3.4 Tenure	Length of time in years employed at current employer	*Sweden, UK*
4. Household attributes		
4.1 Kids	Dummy variable, 1 = children present in the home, 0 = no children living in the home	*none*
4.2 Married	Dummy variable, 1 = married, 0 = not married	*none*
4.3 Housework	Husband's contribution to five housework tasks measured by the respondent's report of the percentage of total time for each task performed by the husband. (See chapter 11 for details.)	*Japan, UK*

position. Instead, the variable *Formal Position* is defined as a dichotomy with a value of 1 if a person is at least a supervisor in the formal hierarchy and 0 if person is in a nonmanagement position. At certain places in the analysis other more restrictive, variables are created on the basis of these items.

Sanctioning authority. This variable refers to the capacity of individuals to impose sanctions of various sorts – positive rewards or punishments – on subordinates. Respondents will be considered to have sanctioning authority if they say that they have any direct influence on any of three forms of sanctioning of subordinates: granting a pay raise or promotion to a subordinate; preventing a subordinate from getting a pay raise or promotion because of poor work or misbehavior; firing or temporarily suspending a subordinate. In the United States sample, just over 37% of people who said that they did supervise other employees on the job do *not* appear to have any sanctioning authority. The variable *Sanction* is given a value of 1 if the respondent has such powers and 0 if the respondent does not.

Decisionmaking responsibility. This variable concerns the direct participation of respondents in organizational policymaking decisions. The variable *Decisionmaker* will have a value of 1 for respondents who directly participate in making any of the following six workplace decisions and 0 for those only provide advice for these decisions or do not participate at all: policy decisions to increase or decrease the total number of people employed in the place where you work; policy decisions to significantly change the products, programs or services delivered by the organization; policy decisions to significantly change the basic methods or procedures of work used in a major part of the workplace; policy decisions concerning the size or distribution of the budget at the place where you work.

Sanctioning authority and decisionmaking authority are not equivalent to the formal hierarchy question above. It is entirely possible for a person to have authority by the sanctioning criterion or the decisionmaking criterion and yet not be in the "formal" authority hierarchy or, alternatively, to be in the formal hierarchy without having sanctioning or decisionmaking authority. Appendix Table 12.2 presents the cross tabulation of the formal hierarchy position variable by the sanctioning-authority variable and by the decisionmaking variable for the seven countries in the sample.

Authority-dichotomy constructed variable. This variable has a value of 1 if the respondent has a value of 1 *on any two of the three dimensions*, and 0 otherwise. In effect, it treats the three separate aspects of authority as multiple indicators of true authority and distinguishes between those individuals who we are quite confident have authority and those who almost certainly do not.

Amount-of-authority scale. This variable attempts to tap variation in the "amount" of authority controlled by the respondent. The idea of authority varying in degree is complex, since what it means to have high, middle or low "levels" of authority depends significantly upon the details of different organizational settings. The number of distinct kinds of decisions in which a person is involved, for example, may not be a good indicator of how much authority a person has, since certain kinds of decisions may be more or less important in different kinds of organizations and the division of

Appendix Table 12.2. *Relationship between formal position in authority hierarchy and ability to impose sanctions and participate in decisionmaking for men and women in seven countries*

Position in formal hierarchy	Percentage who have sanctioning authority		Percentage who are decisionmakers		Percentage at each hierarchical level	
	Men	Women	Men	Women	Men	Women
United States						
Top manager	84.3	68.9	90.4	63.4	4.4	3.4
Upper manager	85.0	[69.6][a]	72.8	[56.1]	5.8	1.9
Middle manager	71.3	80.0	60.0	43.4	7.7	4.1
Lower manager	59.2	40.9	33.2	[41.2]	3.8	2.8
Supervisor	64.4	59.1	28.9	20.4	21.8	15.3
Nonmanagerial employee	9.5	6.1	8.5	6.4	56.7	72.5
N	622	539	618	537	639	535
Sweden						
Top manager	[70.0]	[50.0]	[62.5]	[50.0]	1.9	1.0
Upper manager	[75.0]	–[b]	[83.3]	–	2.3	0.0
Middle manager	66.7	[85.7]	72.4	[66.7]	6.2	1.7
Lower manager	[36.0]	[36.4]	38.5	[57.1]	4.9	2.6
Supervisor	40.0	15.2	38.2	9.1	18.8	11.1
Nonmanagerial employee	0.9	0.03	5.1	8.2	65.9	83.7
N	519	410	497	390	531	416
Norway						
Top manager	56.1	[40.0]	75.6	[40.0]	5.0	0.9
Upper manager	81.0	[00.0]	75.0	[40.0]	5.5	0.9
Middle manager	56.1	[66.7]	42.9	[66.7]	5.1	0.5
Lower manager	[66.7]	[00.0]	[50.0]	[00.0]	0.5	0.2
Supervisor	50.0	25.5	42.6	40.4	23.4	8.3
Nonmanagerial employee	2.4	1.6	10.7	9.5	60.6	89.3
N	807	572	817	577	822	581
Canada						
Top manager	86.2	[83.3]	96.6	[66.7]	3.7	0.9
Upper manager	85.4	[66.7]	87.2	[80.0]	5.2	0.9
Middle manager	71.4	[42.1]	61.0	[42.1]	5.4	3.0
Lower manager	[44.4]	[30.8]	[44.4]	[30.8]	2.3	2.0
Supervisor	50.7	44.7	37.2	30.3	18.9	11.9
Nonmanagerial employee	4.5	1.9	10.7	9.2	64.6	81.2
N	785	639	782	638	785	639

Appendix Table 12.2 *(continued)*

United Kingdom

Top manager	95.7	[75.0]	82.6	[75.0]	3.9	0.9
Upper manager	[100.0]	[00.0]	[71.4]	[00.0]	1.2	0.2
Middle manager	88.2	[75.0]	62.7	[87.5]	8.6	1.8
Lower manager	79.3	[60.0]	55.2	[60.0]	4.9	1.1
Supervisor	55.0	42.9	30.8	31.0	20.2	18.4
Nonmanagerial employee	[0.8]	0.6	9.1	4.8	61.3	77.6
N	594	456	592	456	594	456

Australia

Top manager	86.7	[87.5]	92.9	[100.0]	3.0	1.9
Upper manager	86.2	[66.7]	96.4	[88.9]	5.9	2.1
Middle manager	81.4	[58.8]	79.1	[64.7]	8.7	4.1
Lower manager	[58.3]	[27.3]	[75.0]	[54.5]	2.4	2.6
Supervisor	71.1	53.7	48.6	43.0	30.3	29.1
Nonmanagerial employee	4.9	4.4	18.4	21.1	49.6	60.1
N	492	418	489	417	492	419

Japan

Top manager	[100.0]	–	[100.0]	–	1.2	0.0
Upper manager	[81.8]	–	[100.0]	–	4.3	0.0
Middle manager	[100.0]	–	[71.4]	–	2.8	0.0
Lower manager	[75.0]	–	[75.0]	–	1.6	0.0
Supervisor	60.6	[16.7]	43.6	[33.3]	37.2	3.5
Nonmanagerial employee	5.2	2.4	6.7	2.4	53.0	96.5
N	253	173	253	173	253	173

a   Square brackets indicate that the N on which the percentages are calculated for that cell is less than twenty cases.

b. There are no women in the sample for this country in this stratum of the managerial structure.

labor among managers will be significantly affected by such things as organizational size.

The measure in our data which is most clearly linked to the degree of authority is formal hierarchical position since, *within a given hierarchy*, the ability to issue binding orders generally increases as one moves from bottom to top. It is much less clear, of course, whether someone who is an "upper manager" in one organization has more or less authority than someone who is a middle manager in a different organization, since this will depend upon such factors as the size and internal structure of the two organizations. Does a top manager in a small firm have more or less authority than a middle manager in

General Motors? This difficulty in assuming equivalence in meanings across organizations will certainly introduce some error into our measures since it would be expected that the people in our sample who claim to be "top" or "upper" managers are likely to be employed on average in smaller organizations than those who claim to be middle or lower managers. Nevertheless, this is the variable which most directly taps the idea of different levels of authority, and thus the *amount-of-authority scale* relies more heavily on the formal hierarchical position measure than the other two dimensions of authority. Respondents who receive a 0 on the overall authority dichotomy variable also get a 0 on the amount-of-authority variable. Respondents who are deemed to have authority on the dichotomy are then assigned values of 1–9 on the amount-of-authority scale depending primarily on the formal position in the hierarchy and secondarily on their possession of sanctioning authority.

Control variables. Four groups of control variables will be used to explore the possibility that gender differences in authority are the result of gender differences in other variables: firm attributes, job attributes, personal attributes and household attributes. Most of these variables are available in an identical form for all seven countries in our analysis, but as indicated in Appendix Table 12.1 there are a few which are missing from certain countries. In exploring the extent to which the gender gap in authority can be explained by these control variables we therefore always conduct two separate analyses – one containing only variables which are present in every country, and one including all the available variables for each country. Since the results for these two analyses are virtually identical, we will only report the coefficients for the analysis of common variables.

Comments on two of these control variables are needed. First, we are using part-time vs. full-time employment as a dichotomous 0/1 variable rather than total hours worked, since extended work hours beyond normal full time is in part a consequence of being a manager rather than a determinant of the chances of becoming a manager. The part-time/full-time distinction therefore better captures the idea that the lower incidence of authority among women might be because they are disproportionately in employment settings in which they are not available for promotion. Second, we are using a relatively crude four-category occupational classification to avoid problems of circularity that are introduced if a more refined set of categories were used. A higher level of disaggregation of occupations would involve a category such as "managerial occupations" which is too closely tied conceptually to the dependent variable to be treated as a compositional control in the present analysis.

The problem of cross-national comparability of authority measures

Although identical questions were asked about authority in each of the national surveys, it is always possible that the *meaning* of the questions differs significantly cross-culturally. As a result, what look like cross-national differences in the gender gap in authority might to a significant extent reflect cross-national differences in the meaning of the terms in the questionnaire item. For example, it could be the case that in some countries the label "supervisor" in the formal hierarchy question is frequently used as a largely honorific title implying no real powers, whereas in other countries it is used only where real powers are present. There are certainly many jobs that are formally called "supervisor" in the United States in which the supervisor has at best nominal powers over other workers or workplace decisions. If it should also happen that women were more likely than men to get the honorific supervisor title, then it might appear that the gender gap in authority was smaller in the country with honorific supervisor titles than in the one where the term "supervisor" was used more restrictively.

While we cannot be certain that our results are not affected by such shifts in the meaning of questions, there are three reasons why we feel this is not a significant problem in our analyses. First, two of the three measures of authority we use (sanctioning and decisionmaking) ask respondents what they can actually do on their jobs, not what formal labels are used to describe their jobs. These questions should be less vulnerable to such problems of meaning. Second, in the aggregate measures of authority we use, a person must satisfy at least two of the three authority criteria, which means that the bias would have to work in the same direction on two of the measures in order to create a biased overall measure. Finally, if you look at the distributions in Appendix Table 12.2, it is clear that it is *not* the case that the countries with the *smallest* gender gap are the countries within which there is any indication that the formal hierarchy titles have the *least* substantive content. The United States and Australia are both countries with relatively small gender authority gaps compared to the other countries, yet over 50% of the women in supervisor positions within the formal hierarchy variable say that they have sanctioning authority in these countries, whereas in Norway and Sweden – countries with significantly larger gender gaps in authority – the figures are only 25% and 15% respectively. If anything, then, the formal title "supervisor" appears to have a more honorific meaning in countries with a large gender authority gap than in countries with a small gender gap. In any event, the measures of authority which we will use in this analysis are more comparable across countries than any others of which we know, and thus this is a plausible set of data within which to begin the exploration of cross-national variations in gender patterns in workplace authority.

Sample restrictions

Throughout the analysis we are restricting the national samples to employees in the labor force, thus excluding all people who are self-employed, unemployed and outside of the labor force. Self-employed people with employees – employers – could be considered to have authority within the workplace, but since the causal processes surrounding gender differences in authority among employees are quite distinct from gender differences in property ownership, we are excluding the self employed from this analysis.

Method of analysis for the amount-of-authority scale

In the analysis of the *amount-of-authority* scale we will use cumulative logistic (also called ordered logistic) regressions. This has an advantage over OLS regression of not assuming equal intervals between the levels in the dependent variable and of generating a gender coefficient which is conceptually analogous to the coefficients in the logistic regressions for the authority-dichotomy variable. The cumulative logit for a dependent variable with J ordered categories is defined as:

$$L_j = \log \left[(\Sigma_j P_j) / (\Sigma_j P_{j+1}) \right]$$

where $j = 1 \ldots J\text{-}1$ and P_j is the probability of being in category j of the dependent variable (Agresti 1990: 321). The multivariate model for the net differences in the amount of authority for men and women is then estimated according to:

$$L_j = a_j + B_1\text{Female} + \Sigma_i B_i x_i \tag{2a}$$

where $j = 1 . . . . . J$-1. Each logit is thus a function of a separate intercept and a common set of slope coefficients. The coefficient of the gender dummy variable in equation 2a is thus like a weighted average of the gender coefficients in a series of separately calculated logit regressions in equation 2 in which the dependent variable – the amount-of-authority scale in this case – had been successively dichotomized at each possible point.

Since in this chapter we are only interested in the gender coefficients, the coefficients of the control variables are not presented, except in the analysis of self-selection where some of these coefficients are important for the interpretation of the results.

Part IV

Class structure and class consciousness

13 A general framework for studying class consciousness and class formation

In one way or another, most class analysts believe that at the core of class analysis is a relatively simple causal structure that looks something like the diagram in Figure 13.1. There is, of course, much disagreement about precisely how to conceptualize the arrows in this causal stream. Do they mean "determines" or "shapes" or "imposes limits upon"? Is there a clear sense in which the horizontal causal stream in this structure is "more important" or "more fundamental" than the unspecified "other causes"? At one extreme, orthodox historical materialism claimed that one can broadly read off patterns of class struggle directly from the class structure, and these, in turn, determine the fundamental course of history; in the long run, at least, class structures are thought to determine class struggle and class struggles (in conjunction with the development of the forces of production) to determine trajectories of social change. At the other extreme, most non-Marxist class analysts as well as some Marxists view the class structure as at most providing us with the vocabulary for identifying potential actors in class struggles; class structure does not, however, necessarily have a more powerful role in determining actual patterns of class struggle than many other mechanisms (ideology, the state, ethnicity, etc.), and class struggles are only one among a host of change-producing factors.

In this chapter we will explore the elements on the left hand side of Figure 13.1: "Class structure → class struggle." I will propose a general model of the relationship between class structure and class struggle which captures both the core traditional Marxist intuition that class structures are in some sense the fundamental determinant of class struggles, but nevertheless allows other causal factors considerable potential weight in explaining concrete variations across time and

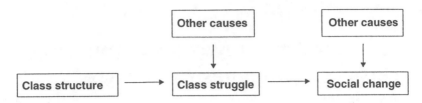

Figure 13.1 *Simple core model of class analysis*

place. The core of the model is an attempt to link a micro-conception of the relationship between class *location* and class *consciousness* with a more macro-level understanding of the relationship between class *structure* and class *formation*.

In section 13.1 of this chapter we will set the stage for this model by briefly elaborating the contrast between micro- and macro-levels of analysis. Section 13.2 will discuss the definitions of a number of the core concepts which we will use, especially class formation and class consciousness. This will be followed in section 11.3 by a discussion of the micro-model, the macro-model and their interconnection.

13.1 Micro- and macro-levels of analysis

The contrast between micro- and macro-levels of analysis is often invoked in sociology, and much is made about the necessity of "moving" back and forth between these levels, but frequently the precise conceptual status of the distinction is muddled. I will use the terms to designate different units of analysis, in which macro-levels of analysis are always to be understood as "aggregations" of relevant micro-units of analysis. The paradigm for this usage is biology: organisms are aggregations of interconnected organs; organs are aggregations of interconnected cells; cells are aggregations of interconnected cellular structures; cellular structures are aggregations of interconnected molecules. The expression "are aggregations of" in these statements, of course, does not simply mean, "haphazard collections of," but rather "structurally interconnected sets of." A given macro-level always consists of *relations* among the relevant constituent micro-units.

What precisely do we mean by "relations" among micro-units? This term is often imbued with arcane meanings. I will use it in a fairly straightforward way to designate any systematic pattern of interactions among the micro-units. Relations can thus be strong, well ordered and systematic, involving intensive and repeated interactions among constituent micro-elements, or weak and rather chaotic, involving few and erratic interactions among those elements. To analyze any unit of analysis, therefore, is to investigate the nature and consequences of these relations among its subunits.

In specifying any hierarchy of nested micro- to macro-levels, therefore, we need to define the relevant sub-units and the nature of the relations among them. One way of understanding the hierarchy of units of analysis in sociology is represented in Table 13.1 and Figure 13.2.

The micro-level of sociological analysis consists of the study of the relations among individuals. Individuals are the constituent elements within these relations, but it is the relations as such that are the object of study of micro-level sociological analysis. The study of interactions among siblings or between bosses and workers are thus both micro-level social phenomena.

The individuals within these relations, of course, can also be considered "units of analysis," and the relations among *their* constituent "parts" can also be studied. The study of such *intra*-individual relations is the proper object of human biology and psychology. The analysis of individuals-qua-individuals is thus at the interface between sociology – in which the individual is the unit within micro-relations – and psychology – in which the individual is the macro-level within which relations of various sorts are studied.

The meso-level of social analysis consists of the investigation of relations among inter-individual relations. The units characteristic of such relations-among-relations are normally what we call "organizations," although looser units such as social networks would also constitute a meso-level of analysis. The macro-social level of analysis, then, consists of relations among organizations and other forms of meso-level units. At the most macro-level, the "world system" consists of relations among nations and economic regions.

Dividing up the units of sociological analysis in this way is, of course, highly stylized and oversimplified. Depending upon one's theoretical purposes, one can add many intermediate levels of analysis to this simple schema. Organizations, for example, can be analyzed in terms of the relations among a series of suborganizational units – offices, branches, departments – and each of these, in turn, can be analyzed in terms of the relations among sets of inter-individual relations.

Table 13.1. *Logic of micro- and macro-levels of social analysis*

Level of analysis	Constitutent sub-units	Nature of relations	Examples of relations
Micro-social level	individuals	inter-individual relations	friendships, point-of-production class relations
Meso-social level	inter-individual relations	bounded organizations and networks (relations among inter-individual relations)	firms, families, unions, schools
Macro-social level	organizations	relations among organizations	nations, economies

The micro–macro distinction understood in this way should not be confused with the abstract–concrete distinction. While it often seems that micro-analysis is more concrete than macro-analysis – since it deals with apparently concrete entities, "individuals" – one can perfectly well develop very abstract concepts for dealing with micro-analyses (as is often done in rational-actor models) or quite concrete concepts for dealing with macro-analyses (as occurs in many historical analyses of institutional development). Individuals are not inherently more concrete than firms or societies, any more than cells are more concrete than organisms.

In terms of class analysis, the concept of "class location" is a preeminently micro-level concept. Individuals are the units that occupy the class locations defined by class structures.[1] The "capitalist-class location" and the "working-class location" are defined by the social relations of production that link individuals in these locations together. The micro-analysis of class *locations*, therefore, should not be

---

[1] There are class structures in which an entire family occupies the "locations" within the relations that make up that structure. This would simply shift the micro/meso/macro hierarchy, but would not change the logic of the hierarchy as a nested set of relations among units which are themselves constituted by relations. In any case, for present purposes, it is not necessary to add this complication.

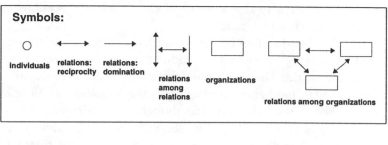

MICRO-LEVEL

MESO-LEVEL

MACRO-LEVEL

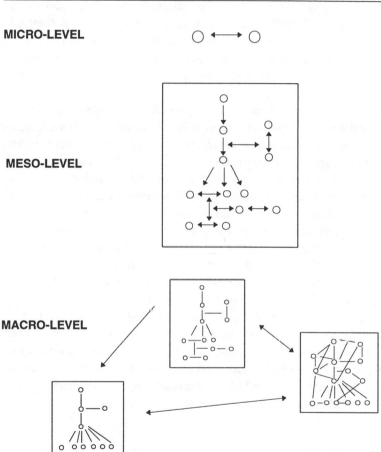

Figure 13.2 *Micro, meso and macro-units of analysis*

seen as an alternative to the analysis of class *relations*: locations are always specified within relations.

To be "in" a class location is to be subjected to a set of mechanisms that impinge directly on the lives of individuals as they make choices and act in the world. There is some debate over what is most salient about these micro-mechanisms attached to the locations within class structures: should they primarily be thought of as determining the material interests of individuals? or shaping their subjective under-standings of the world? or determining the basic resources they have available to pursue their interests? In any event, to develop a concept of class at the micro-level of analysis is to elaborate the concept in terms of the mechanisms that directly affect individuals within class locations.

The term "class structure," then, is the way of designating the set of class relations and locations within different units of analysis. One can speak, for example, of the class structure of a firm. Some firms are run by a single capitalist entrepreneur who hires a few managers and a homogeneous set of workers. Such a firm has a quite different class structure from a large corporation, with a hierarchically differentiated managerial structure, an external board of directors representing rentier capitalist stockholders and a segmented working class. One can also speak of the class structure of a society as a whole, or even, perhaps, of the class structure of the world capitalist system. Some capitalist societies, for example, will have a huge middle class, others a small middle class. The size of the middle class is an attribute of the society itself and depends upon the specific way in which all of the firms of that society are organized and interconnected. All capitalist societies will have state apparatuses and private firms, and among private firms some will be small and some large. The size of the middle class in the society as a whole will depend upon the specific mix of these kinds of meso-level employment organizations.

13.2 Basic concepts

The models we will be discussing revolve around a number of interconnected concepts of class analysis: class structure, class location, class interests, class experiences, class consciousness, class formation, class practices and class struggles. Some of these concepts, especially class structure, have been given considerable discussion in previous chapters, so we will not discuss all of them in detail here.

Class structure and class location

I will use the term "class location" as a micro-level concept referring to the location of individuals (and sometimes families) within the structure of class relations, whereas I will use the term "class structure" as concept referring to the overall organization of class relations in some more macro-level of analysis, typically an entire society. To say that someone is "in" a managerial class location is to claim that they are embedded in a set of inter-individual interactions (relations) in which they are empowered to give various kinds of commands either directly to their subordinates (i.e. supervisory powers) or indirectly via their control over production decisions. Class structures are aggregations of all of the relations among these micro-level class locations at some more macro-level of analysis.

Class formation

I will use the expression "class formation" either to designate a process (the process of class formation) or an outcome (*a* class formation). In both cases the expression refers to the formation of *collectively organized social forces within class structures in pursuit of class interests.* If class structures are defined by the *antagonistic* social relations *between* class locations, class formations are defined by *cooperative* social relations *within* class structures. Strong, solidaristic relations in which individuals are prepared to make significant sacrifices for collective goals would be one form of class formation, but class formation can also be more narrowly instrumental, without strong solidarities binding people together.[2]

Class formations are important because they constitute a crucial link between class structure and class struggles. Of course, class struggles may also involve various kinds of conflict between people acting strictly as individuals in uncoordinated ways, but since the capacity of individuals, especially those in exploited classes, to pursue their class interests is so weak when they act alone, people constantly attempt to forge various kinds of collectivities to enhance their capacity for struggle. In these terms, class *formations* are important above all

---

[2] The conception of class solidarity in terms of the willingness of individuals to make sacrifices for the welfare of others has been elaborated by Jon Elster (1985).

because of the ways in which they shape class *capacities* and thus the balance of power within class struggles.

Understood in this way, the contrast between class structure and class formation is similar to the traditional Marxist distinction between a class *in itself* and a class *for itself*. The class in itself/for itself distinction, however, was linked to a teleological notion of the inevitable trajectory of class struggle within capitalism toward the full, revolutionary formation of the proletariat. The expression "class formation," in contrast, does not imply that the collectively organized social forces within a class structure have any inherent tendency to develop toward revolutionary organization around "fundamental" class interests. "Class formation" is thus a descriptive category which encompasses a wide range of potential variations. For any given class or group of class locations one can speak of "strong" or "weak" class formations; unitary or fragmented class formations; revolutionary, counterrevolutionary or reformist class formations.

Typically, class formations involve creating *formal* organizations (especially political parties and unions) which link together the people within and across different locations in a class structure, but class formation is by no means limited to formal organization. Any form of collectively constituted social relations which facilitate solidaristic action in pursuit of class interests are instances of class formation. Informal social networks, social clubs, neighborhood associations, even churches, could under appropriate circumstances be elements of class formations. The extensive research on the role of social clubs in coordinating the interests of the ruling class, for example, should be regarded as documenting one aspect of bourgeois class formation.[3]

Class formations should not be thought of simply in terms of the forming of social relations among people within homogeneous class locations in a class structure. The forging of solidaristic relations *across* the boundaries of the locations within a class structure are equally instances of the formation of collectively organized social forces within class structures. Class formation thus includes the formation of class *alliances* as well as the internal organization of classes as such.[4] For

---

[3]   For an illustrative example of research on the informal networks of ruling class formation, see G. William Domhoff (1971).

[4]   This usage of the concept of class formation represents a slight shift from my earlier treatment in Wright (1978: 97–108) in which I restrictively defined class formations as the formation of social relations within classes. Class alliances were thus not included as a type of class formation.

example, "populism," to the extent that it provides a context for the pursuit of certain class interests, can be viewed as a form of class formation that forges solidaristic ties between the working class and certain other class locations, typically the petty bourgeoisie (especially small farmers in the American case).

This definition of "class formation" and the corresponding distinction between "class structure" and "class formation" is not universally adopted by class analysts. Sometimes the expression "class formation" is used to describe the extent of biographical continuity linked to particular kinds of class locations. Thus, for example, Goldthorpe (1983: 467) writes:

> For any structure of positions, the empirical question can then be raised of how far classes have in fact formed within it, in the sense of specific social collectivities; that is, collectivities that are identifiable through the degree of continuity with which, in consequence of patterns of class mobility and immobility, their members are associated with particular sets of positions over time.

Marshall et al. (1988: 22) refer to this as "demographic class formation." This usage of the term "class formation" is also quite close to Giddens' (1973) expression "class structuration," referring to the ways in which the lives of people are effectively bounded within given class locations.

There are also instances in which authors use the unmodified term "class" to mean what I am calling "class formation." Przeworski (1985: 47), for example, writes "Classes must thus be viewed as effects of struggles structured by objective conditions that are simultaneously economic, political and ideological." What I am calling "class structure" constitutes part of what Przeworski is calling "objective conditions;" what he is calling "classes" is what I am calling "class formations."

Class practices

Class practices are activities engaged in by members of a class using class capacities in order to realize at least some of their class interests. "Practice" in these terms implies that the activity is *intentional* (i.e. it has a conscious goal); "class" practices implies that the goal is the realization of class-based interests. Class practices include such mundane activities as a worker selling labor on a labor market, a foreman disciplining a worker for poor performance or a stockholder voting in a stockholders' meeting. But class practices also include such things as participating in a strike or busting a union.

Class struggle

The term "class struggle" refers to organized forms of *antagonistic* class practices, i.e. practices that are directed against each other. While in the limiting case one might refer to a class struggle involving a single worker and a single capitalist, more generally class struggles involve collectivities of various sorts. Class formations, not atomized individuals, are the characteristic vehicles for class struggles. Class struggles, therefore, generally refer to macro-phenomena. Given the antagonistic nature of the interests determined by class structures, class practices of individuals will have a strong tendency to develop into collective class struggles since the realization of the interests of members of one class generally implies confrontation against the interests of members of other classes.

Class consciousness[5]

I will use the concept of class consciousness to refer to particular aspects of the subjectivity of individuals. Consciousness will thus be used as a strictly micro-concept. When it figures in macro-social explanations it does so by virtue of the ways it helps to explain individual choices and actions. Collectivities, in particular class formations, do not "have" consciousness in the literal sense, since they are not the kind of entities which have minds, which think, weigh alternatives, have preferences, etc. When the term "class consciousness" is applied to collectivities or organizations, therefore, it either refers to the patterned distribution of individual consciousnesses within the relevant aggregate, or it is a way of characterizing central tendencies. This is not to imply, of course, that supra-individual social mechanisms are unimportant, but simply that they should not be conceptualized within the category "consciousness." And it is also not to imply that the actual distribution of individual consciousnesses in a

---

[5] Some of the text in this section and the next is adapted from my earlier book, *Classes* (Wright 1985: 243–251).

society is not of social significance and causal importance. It may well be; but a distribution of consciousnesses is not "consciousness."[6]

Understood in this way, to study "consciousness" is to study a particular aspect of the mental life of individuals, namely, those elements of a person's subjectivity which are *discursively accessible to the individual's own awareness*. Consciousness is thus counterposed to "unconsciousness" – the discursively inaccessible aspects of mental life. The elements of consciousness – beliefs, ideas, observations, information, theories, preferences – may not continually be in a person's awareness, but they are accessible to that awareness.[7]

This conceptualization of consciousness is closely bound up with the problem of *will* and *intentionality*. To say that something is discursively accessible is to say that by an act of will the person can make themselves aware of it. When people make choices over alternative courses of action, the resulting action is, at least in part, to be explained by the particular conscious elements that entered into the intentions of the actor making the choice. While the problem of consciousness is not reducible to the problem of intentionality, from the point of view of social theory one of the most important ways in which consciousness figures in social explanations is via the way it is implicated in the intentions and resulting choices of actions by actors.

This is not to suggest, of course, that the only way *subjectivity* is consequential is via intentional choices. A wide range of psychological mechanisms may directly influence behavior without passing through conscious intentions. Nor does the linkage of consciousness to intentionality and choice imply that in every social situation the most important determinants of outcomes operate through consciousness; it may well be that the crucial determinants are to be found in the processes which determine the range of possible courses of action open to actors rather than the conscious processes implicated in the choice among those alternatives. What is being claimed is that in order to fully understand the real mechanisms that link social structures to

---

6 This is by no means the only way that class consciousness has been understood in the Marxist tradition. In particular, Lukacs (1971 [1922]) seems to attribute the category "class consciousness" to the class of workers as a collectivity, not to the empirical individuals who make up that class. For a discussion of Lukacs' views on this see Wright (1985: 242).

7 To be accessible to awareness also does not mean that the individual is capable of articulately verbalizing to others the elements of consciousness. While capacity for communication is closely bound up with consciousness, communicating beliefs and having beliefs are not identical.

social practices, the subjective basis of the intentional choices made by the actors who live within those structures and engage in those practices must be investigated, and this implies studying consciousness.

Given this definition of "consciousness," "class" consciousness can be viewed as those aspects of consciousness *which have a distinctive class character*. To speak of the class "character" of consciousness implies two things. First, it means that the beliefs in question have a substantive class *content* – in one way or another, the beliefs are about class issues. For example, private ownership of means of production is a distinctive structural feature of capitalist class relations; the belief in the desirability of private ownership, therefore, could be viewed as having a class content. Second, the class character of consciousness refers to those aspects of consciousness which have effects on how individuals actually operate within a given structure of class relations and effects on those relations themselves. The class dimensions of consciousness are implicated in the intentions, choices and practices which have what might be termed "class-pertinent effects" in the world.

Both of these aspects of the "class character" of consciousness – the content of the beliefs and the effects of beliefs – are necessary to speak of class consciousness. Beliefs about gender relations, for example, could have class-pertinent effects if, for example, stereotypical beliefs about masculinity undermined solidarity between men and women in class struggles. Yet it would not be useful to describe gender ideologies as *aspects* of class consciousness, although they might certainly be relevant for explaining aspects of class consciousness and class struggle. To count as an aspect of class consciousness, then, the belief in question must both have a class content and have class-pertinent effects.[8] If class structure is understood as a terrain of social relations that determine objective material interests of actors, and class struggle is understood as the forms of social practices which attempt to realize those interests, then class consciousness can be understood as the subjective processes with a class content that shape intentional choices with respect to those interests and struggles.

A potential point of terminological confusion needs to be clarified at

[8]   In an earlier work (Wright 1985: 246) I identified class consciousness only with the idea of class-pertinent effects of beliefs. This is unsatisfactory since it allows for all sorts of beliefs that do not have anything inherently to do with class relations to be considered aspects of class consciousness.

this point. It is common in Marxist discussions to distinguish between workers who "are class conscious" from those who "are not class conscious." The generic expression "class consciousness" in such usage is being identified with a particular *type* of class consciousness. In the usage of the term I am proposing, this would be a form of class consciousness in which individuals have a relatively "true" and "consistent" understanding of their class interests. I am thus using the term class consciousness in a more general way to designate all forms of class-pertinent consciousness regardless of its faithfulness to real or objective interests. In order to specifically indicate the presence of a particular type of class consciousness, therefore, it will be necessary to employ suitable adjectives: proworking-class consciousness, anticapitalist class consciousness, revolutionary working-class consciousness, and so forth. When I use the unmodified expression "class consciousness" it will always refer to the general domain of consciousness with a class content relevant to class practices. There will be no implication that such consciousness can always be evaluated as "true" or "false."

This way of understanding class consciousness suggests that the concept can be decomposed into several elements. Whenever people make conscious choices, three dimensions of subjectivity are implicated:[9]

1 *Perceptions and observations.* In one way or another, conscious choice involves processing information about the world. "Facts," however, are always filtered through categories and beliefs about "what exists." Some workers believe that their employers worry about the welfare of employees, while others believe that employers are only interested in their own profits. Such beliefs about the motivations of employers are an aspect of class consciousness because they are implicated in the way workers are likely to respond to various kinds of class practices of their employers. "Class consciousness," in these terms, involves the ways in which the perceptions of the facts of a situation have a class content and are thus consequential for class actions.

2 *Theories of consequences.* Perceptions of the facts by themselves are insufficient to allow people to make choices; people also must

---

[9] These three dimensions of class consciousness correspond roughly to the three-fold distinction Goran Therborn (1982) makes between three "modes of ideological interpellation" in terms of answers to the questions: what exists? what is possible? what is good?

have some understanding of the expected consequences of given choices of action. This implies that choices involve theories. These may be "practical" theories rather than abstractly formalized theories; they may have the character of "rules of thumb" rather than explanatory principles. One particularly important aspect of such theories is conceptions of what is possible. Workers may decide that there is no point in struggling to establish a union because it is impossible for such a struggle to succeed. "Impossible" does not mean, of course, that one couldn't try to form a union, but simply that the consequence of such an attempt would not be the desired outcome. Historically, working-class rejections of socialism and communism have as much to do with the belief that such radical alternatives to capitalism would never work or that they are unachievable because of the power of the dominant classes, as with the belief that alternatives to capitalism are undesirable.

3 *Preferences.* Knowing a person's perceptions and theories is still not enough to explain a particular conscious choice; in addition, of course, it is necessary to know their preferences, that is, their evaluation of the desirability of those consequences. "Desirability," in this context, can mean desirable in terms of the material benefits to the person, but there is no necessary restriction of preferences to selfish or egotistical evaluations. Preferences can also involve deep commitment to the welfare of others based on a sense of shared identity and meaning. "Class identity" may therefore figure as a salient aspect of class consciousness insofar as it shapes the extent to which an individual's preferences include a concern for the well-being of other members of a class.[10]

With this understanding of class consciousness, one can begin to develop fairly complex typologies of qualitatively distinct forms of class consciousness in terms of the ways in which perceptions, theories and preferences held by individuals advance or impede the pursuit of

---

[10] There are discussions in which class identity is viewed as the central core of class consciousness. Class consciousness thus becomes almost equivalent to consciousness of one's membership in a class. While I think that class identity may indeed be quite important, it does not exhaust class-pertinent aspects of consciousness, since the ways in which a strong class identity will lead to action will still depend upon one's perception of alternative courses of action and one's theories of the consequences of different choices.

class interests. It is possible, for example, to distinguish between "hegemonic," "reformist," "oppositional" and "revolutionary" working-class consciousness in terms of particular combinations of perceptions, theories and preferences. This is essentially what the more sophisticated typologies of class consciousness developed in recent years have tried to do.

In the present study I will not attempt to elaborate a nuanced typology of forms of class consciousness. The data that we will employ could potentially be stretched to operationalize such typologies, but my general feeling is that the limitations of survey research methodology make it preferable to adopt relatively simple and straightforward variables. The measures of class consciousness which we will use, therefore, are designed to tap in a general way the extent to which individuals have attitudes that are consistent with working-class or capitalist-class interests.

Limitation, selection and transformation

In elaborating a micro-model of class consciousness and a macro-model of class formation we will describe the causal relations among the various elements of the models in terms of three different "modes of determination": limitation, selection and transformation. Let me first explain limitation and transformation.

Figure 13.3 illustrates the general abstract relation between limitation and transformation: structures impose limits on practices; practices transform the structures that so limit them. *Limits*, in this context, does not simply mean that given the existence of the social structure in question certain practices are absolutely impossible, i.e. they are "outside" of the limits. In the extreme case, certain forms of practice may become virtually impossible given the existence of a particular structure, but the concept of limits is meant to refer to the effects of the structure on the probabilities of all types of relevant practices occurring. The substantive claim being made when it is said that "structures —*limit*→ practices" is that the structures impose on the actors within those structures various kinds of obstacles and facilitations, sanctions and incentives, risky options and easy opportunities, which make certain kinds of practices much more likely and sustainable than others, and some simply impossible.

Transformation refers to the impact of practices on structures. Structures are objects of human intervention. Precisely because they limit action, people try either to change or to maintain them depending

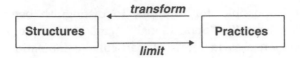

Figure 13.3 *The dialectic of structure and practice*

upon the effects of those structures on their interests. The structures in question may be embedded in the most macro-settings of social life such as the state or the more micro-settings of families and work-places. The feminist aphorism "the personal is political" is precisely a claim that practices can transform structures in the mundane, micro-arenas of everyday life.

The reciprocal effects "structures —*limit*→ practices" and "practices —*transform*→ structures" is one way of understanding the basic "dialectic" of structure and agency. To paraphrase Marx, human beings make history (practices transform structures), but not just as they please (structures limit practices). This way of thinking about structure and agency is thus neither a form of structuralism that marginalizes the human agent, nor a form of voluntarism that margin-alizes structural constraints. The limits of social structures are real, but they are transformable by the conscious action of human agents.

What about "selection," the third mode of determination? Selection should be understood as "limits within limits." Selection enters the analysis when we are concerned with the interaction of more than one kind of structure with practices. This is illustrated in a general, abstract form in Figure 13.4. We now have two structures, X and Y. Structure X imposes *limits* on practices while structure Y *selects* practices within those limits. In the extreme case, structure Y may narrow the alter-natives to the point where only one type of practice is possible. In such a case, we can say that structure Y *determines* the practice within the limits established by structure X. More typically, selection refers to a narrowing of possibilities. With these concepts in hand, we can turn to the problem of the causal models of class consciousness and class formation.

13.3 The micro-model

If class consciousness is understood in terms of the content of the perceptions, theories and preferences that shape intentional choices relevant to class interests, then the explanatory problem in the analysis

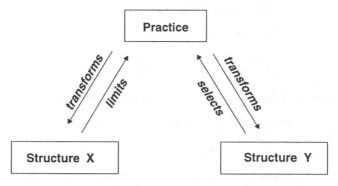

Figure 13.4 *Forms of determination: limits, selects, transforms*

of class consciousness is to elaborate the processes which shape the variability in the class content of consciousness. The theory of commodity fetishism in classical Marxism is precisely such a theory: it is an account of how the perceptions and theories of actors are imbued with a particular class content by virtue of the operation of commodity relations. The immediate lived experience of producers in a commodity producing society, the story goes, represents the social relations between people as relations between things (commodities), and this in turn generates the mental structures characterized as "fetishized consciousness." Such consciousness in turn, it is argued, plays an important role in conveying a sense of the permanence and naturalness of capitalism, thus impeding revolutionary projects for the transformation of capitalist society.

The micro-causal model of consciousness formation which we will discuss in this chapter is deliberately simple. Its purpose is to try to capture the most pervasive and systematic determinants at work, rather than to map the full range of complexities that may enter into the class consciousness formation process of any given individual. This bare-bones model is illustrated in Figure 13.5. The model should be read as follows: class locations impose limits on the consciousness of individuals within those locations and on their class practices. Class consciousness, in turn, selects specific forms of practice within the limits imposed by class locations. Class practices, then, transform both class consciousness and class locations. Let me explain each of these causal connections:

1   **Class locations** —*limits*→ **class consciousness**. Incumbency in a given class location renders certain forms of class consciousness much

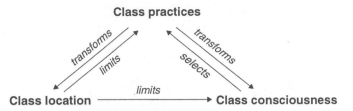

Figure 13.5 *Micro-model of class location, class consciousness and class practice*

more likely than others. In the extreme case, certain forms of consciousness may become virtually impossible to sustain for individuals in certain class locations, but the concept of limits need not imply any absolute barrier to any form of consciousness. Capitalists are much more likely to believe in the virtues of unfettered capitalism than are workers, but some capitalists (Frederick Engels, for example) do become revolutionary communists; industrial workers are more likely than capitalists to believe in the desirability of strong unions and workplace participation of workers in management decisions, but some workers believe that nonmanagement employees have no business interfering with the functioning of free markets and the powers of employers. Living within a given class location increases the probability that certain perceptions, certain theories of how society works and certain values will seem more immediately credible than others, but a wide range of other causal factors can intervene to counter these probabilities. Forms of consciousness which seem unlikely by virtue of the "class location — *limits*→ class consciousness" relation may thus become much more likely because of the presence of other, contingent, causal processes.

2   **Class locations** —*limits*→ **individual class practices**. In a fairly straightforward way, class locations significantly shape the feasible set of what individuals in those locations can do to satisfy their material interests. The crucial mechanism through which being in a class location limits the feasible set of practices is through access to the resources needed to pursue specific courses of action. Being in a working-class location, and thus being deprived of the ownership of means of production, means that in order to obtain subsistence both in the present and in the future it is generally necessary to look for paid employment. Certain other options may be relatively easy, at least for some people in working-class locations in some countries. Criminal activities may be an option, or living off welfare. Other options may be more difficult, but still not absolutely impossible. It is generally quite

difficult for a worker to get loans to start a business, and most workers are not in a position to save sufficient income to be able to acquire future subsistence in the form of returns on investments, but both of the options are possible under unusual circumstances. More frequently, some workers can invest in various kinds of training which has the potential of enhancing their material interests. And of course, workers may have the option of joining unions and engaging in various kinds of collective practices in pursuit of class interests. The relative ease and difficulty of these alternative courses of action is what is meant by "limits" in the expression: class location —*limits*→ class practices.

3   **Class consciousness** —*selects*→ **individual class practices**. While class locations may shape the feasible set of class practices, the actual choice of specific practices still depends upon the perceptions, theories and values of individuals. In this sense class consciousness selects practices within limits imposed by class locations.

4   **Individual class practices** —*transforms*→ **class locations**. The most obvious sense in which an individual's class practices can transform that individual's class location is through class mobility. But class practices can also transform various concrete class-pertinent features of jobs – the degree of authority, autonomy, pay – without generating class mobility in the usual sense. When an individual worker engages in various forms of resistance to the domination of a boss, that worker transforms aspects of his or her class location. When employers introduce new technologies and work organization which enhance their capacity to monitor the labor process and extract labor effort from workers, they have engaged in a class practice which transforms a specific aspect of the class relation to their employees.

5   **Individual class practices** —*transforms*→ **class consciousness**. One of the classic themes in Marxist theories of consciousness is the idea that in the capitalist labor process workers are constantly producing themselves while they are producing commodities. This is one of the central themes of Michael Burawoy's numerous studies of workers on the shopfloor (Burawoy 1979, 1985, 1992; Burawoy and Wright 1990). The norms and values of workers, he argues, are not mainly the result of deep socialization outside of the sphere of work, but are generated within production by the practices workers adopt in their efforts to cope with the dilemmas of their situation. Of particular salience in these terms are the ways in which individual participation in class struggles of various sorts contributes to the formation of solidaristic

preferences. More generally the claim is that the perceptions of alternatives, theories and values held by individuals situated in different class locations are not just shaped by where they are but by what they do.

Our empirical objectives in the next several chapters are particularly concerned with the relationship between class location and class consciousness. In this micro-model, class location affects class consciousness through two routes: one via the direct impact of being in a class location on consciousness, and the other via the way class locations affect class practices which in turn affect consciousness. One way of thinking about these two causal streams is that the former concerns things that *happen to people* and the latter concerns things *people do*.

By virtue of being in a class location (understood both as direct and mediated locations in the sense discussed in Chapter 10) a person is subjected to certain experiences with greater or lesser probability. Insofar as class location determines access to material resources, being in a class location shapes the mundane material conditions of existence – how comfortable is daily life, how physically and mentally taxing is work, how hungry one is. Class location significantly determines the probability of being the victim of different kinds of crime. Class locations shape the kind of neighborhood one is likely to live in and the nature of the social networks in which one is embedded, and all of these may have an impact on class consciousness. Above all, class locations impose on people a set of trade-offs and dilemmas they face in the pursuit of their material interests. Capitalists have to worry about challenges from competitors, how to extract the maximum labor from their employees, and alternative uses of their investment resources. Workers have to worry about finding a job, about unemployment and job security, about skill obsolescence and job injury, about making ends meet with a paycheck. To say that members of a class share common class interests means that they objectively face similar strategic choices for advancing their material welfare. Such a strategic environment continually generates experiences which shape a person's beliefs about the world.[11]

People do not, however, simply live in a strategic environment; they also adopt specific strategies. And what they actually do also shapes their consciousness. Managers do not simply confront the

[11] See Wright (1989a: 280–288) for an extended discussion of the idea that what it means to talk about "common class interests" is a common set of strategic trade-offs and dilemmas for advancing material interests.

problems of eliciting work effort from subordinates and impressing their superiors. They also issue orders, discipline subordinates and suck up to higher management and owners. Workers do not simply face the strategic problem of individually competing with fellow workers or solidaristically struggling for higher wages; they also join unions, cross picket lines and quit jobs to find better work. Class consciousness, then, is shaped on the one hand by the material conditions and *choices people face* (class location —*limits*→ consciousness) and on the other by the *choices people actually make* (class location —*limits*→ practices —*transform*→ consciousness). Consciousness shapes choices; choices change consciousness.

Both of these causal paths have a crucial temporal dimension. Class consciousness is not the instantaneous product of one's present class location and class practices. At any given point in time, consciousness about anything is the result of a life-time history of things that happen to people and things they do, of both choices faced and choices made, of interests and experiences. Most obviously, there is the life-time biographical trajectory of the individual's locations within the class structure (the classical sociological problem of inter and intragenerational class mobility), but other experiences such as unemployment or strikes are also relevant.

A fully developed theory of consciousness formation would also include an account of the psychological mechanisms through which interests and experiences actually shape perceptions of alternatives, theories and preferences. It is not enough to identify a salient set of experiences and interests through which class locations limit class consciousness; it is also necessary to understand how these limits work through psychological processes within the individual. Jon Elster's (1985: ch. 8) accounts of such cognitive mechanisms as wishful thinking and adaptive preference formation (cognitive dissonance) would be examples.

I will not attempt to elaborate an account of these psychological mechanisms; they will thus remain largely a "black box." Implicitly in my arguments, however, is a fairly naïve form of learning theory which underlies most sociological accounts of the effects of social conditions on consciousness. The basic assumption is that the probability that people will hold beliefs congruent with their class location depends upon the extent to which their life experiences reinforce or undermine such beliefs. All other things being equal, the more a person's life is bound up with a single, coherent set of class experiences, the more likely it is that this person's consciousness will be imbued with a corresponding class content. Perceptions, theories and preferences are the result of learning from experiences, and to the extent that one's class experiences all push in the same direction, class consciousness will tend to develop a coherent class content.[12]

It might be objected, however, that a set of class experiences, no matter how consistent, is not enough to predict a form of consciousness. Experiences are not translated directly into consciousness; they must first be *interpreted*, and interpretations always presuppose some kind of political and cultural context. The same micro-class experiences and interests with the same psychological mechanisms could generate different forms of consciousness depending upon the broader historical context of politics and culture. To understand these issues we must now turn to the macro-model and then to the interaction between the macro- and micro-levels of analysis.

13.4 The macro-model

In the macro-model our object of investigation is no longer individual class consciousness as such, but collective forms of class formation and class struggle. The model is illustrated in Figure 13.6. As in the micro-model, the causal logic revolves around the way structures impose limits on practices and practices in turn transform structures. In the macro-model class structures impose limits on class formations and class struggles. Within those limits, class formations select specific forms of class struggle. Class struggles transform both class formations and class structures. Let us look at each of these connections.

1   **Class structure** —*limits*→ **class formation**. To say that class structures impose limits on class formations means that the class structure

---

[12] This implicit learning theory of the black box of consciousness formation is quite similar to Therborn's (1980) view that "ideological interpellation" is the result of the patterns of subjection and qualification which an individual experiences by virtue of the affirmations and sanctions connected to different social positions. It is also close to Bourdieu's (1985) view that daily lived experiences constitute a set of common conditions that generate common conditionings, although Bourdieu is more concerned with the formation of *non*conscious dimensions of subjectivity ("dispositions") than consciousness as such. Bourdieu's concept of *class habitus* is meant to encompass the full range of nonconscious subjective effects on actors that result from such common conditionings/experiences. A class habitus is defined as a common set of dispositions to act in particular ways that are shaped by a common set of conditionings (subject-forming experiences) rooted in a class structure.

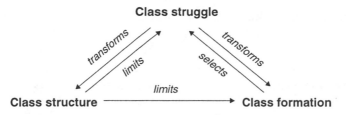

Figure 13.6 *Macro-model of class structure, class formation and class struggle*

imposes obstacles and opportunities with which any agent attempting to forge class formations must contend. Within any given class structure, certain class formations will thus be relatively easy to create and are likely to be stable once created, others will be more difficult and unstable, and certain class formations may be virtually impossible.[13] As Przeworski (1985: 47) puts it: "Processes of formation of workers into a class are inextricably fused with the processes of organization of surplus labor. As a result, a number of alternative organizations of classes is possible at any moment of history."

Three kinds of mechanisms are central to this limiting process: (1) the nature of the *material interests* generated by class structures; (2) the patterns of *identities* that emerge from the lived experiences of people in different locations in the class structure; and (3) the nature of the resources distributed in the class structure which make certain potential alliances across locations in the class structure more or less attractive. The first two of these are closely tied to the micro-analysis of class locations while the third is more strictly macro in character.

Material interests. The argument about material interests is the most straightforward. The central thesis of the Marxist theory of class structure is that the underlying mechanisms of exploitation in an economic structure powerfully shape the material interests of people in that structure. Consider the matrix of locations within the class structure which we have adopted in this book. This matrix can be

---

[13] To claim that a particular kind of class formation is virtually impossible is not to claim that the *attempt* to forge such a class formation will never occur, but simply that such attempts have a low probability of success, and if they were to succeed because of highly contingent conditions, they would have a very low probability of surviving over time.

viewed as a map of the degree of inherent antagonism of material interests of people located in different places in the structure: locations relatively "close" to each other will have relatively overlapping material interests whereas more distant locations will have more antagonistic interests. All things being equal, class formations that link locations with relatively similar material interests are thus easier to create than class formations that link locations with quite disparate interests. From the vantage point of working-class locations in the class structure (the lower right hand corner of the matrix), as you move toward the upper left hand corner of the matrix (expert managers among employees, and capitalists among property owners) class interests become progressively more antagonistic, and thus class formations joining workers with such locations more and more difficult to forge. This does not mean, it must be emphasized, that material interests alone determine class formations; but they do define a set of obstacles with which parties, unions and other agents of class formation have to contend in their efforts to consolidate and reproduce particular patterns of class formation.

Identities. The second mechanism through which class structures shape the possibilities of class formations centers on the ways class affects the class identities of people, the ways people define who is similar to and who is different from themselves, who are their potential friends and potential enemies within the economic system. As in the case of material interests, it would be expected that class formations that attempt to bind people together with similar identities are likely to be easier to accomplish and more stable than class formations which combine highly disparate and potentially conflicting identities. All things being equal, it would be predicted that class identities would more or less follow the same contours as class interests, and thus common identity would reinforce common interests as a basis for forging class formations.

However, it is rarely the case that all things are equal. Class identities are heavily shaped by idiosyncrasies of personal biographies and by historical patterns of struggles, as well as by the intersection of class with other forms of social collectivity (ethnicity, religion, language, region, etc.). Thus, while it is plausible to argue that there should be some rough association between the objectively given material interests of actors and the kinds of class identities they develop, there is no reason for these two aspects of class to be isomorphic. Class interests and class identities, therefore, may not reinforce each other in linking class structures to class formations.

Resources. The third mechanism that underlies the ways in which class structures limit class formations centers on the effects of the macro-attributes of class structures, in particular the distribution of resources across classes which are relevant for class formations and class struggles. For working-class formations, probably the most important resource is sheer numbers of people, although organizational and financial resources may also be important. As Przeworski (1985, ch. 3) and Przeworski and Sprague (1986) have stressed, in deciding which potential alliances to nourish, the leadership of working-class electoral parties pay particular attention to the potential gains in electoral strength posed by forging different sorts of alliances. The attractiveness of worker–peasant alliances in revolutionary movements in third world countries or of worker–petty bourgeois alliances in nineteenth-century North American populism is significantly shaped by the power of numbers.

Numbers, however, are not the whole story. Financial resources may also be crucial to the strategies of actors attempting to build class formations. The financial resources available to the middle class give them considerable leverage in forging particular kinds of alliances and coalitions. One of the reasons why working-class parties may put more energy into attracting progressive elements of the middle class than in mobilizing the poorest and most marginalized segments of the population is that the former can potentially make greater contributions.

The combination of these three class-based mechanisms – exploitation → material interests; lived experiences in a class struc-ture → class identities; distribution of class resources → attractiveness of potential alliances – determines the underlying probabilities that different potential class formations will occur. Figure 13.7 illustrates a range of possible class formations that might be constructed on the same basic class structure. The first two of these follow the contours of the central tendencies generated by the class structure itself: class formations directly mirror the exploitation-generated interest config-uration. In Model 1, a middle-class formation is a buffer between working-class and bourgeois class formations; in Model 2, a pure polarization exists between two "camps." In Model 3, the structural division between workers and contradictory locations has been se-verely muted in the process of class formation: workers have been

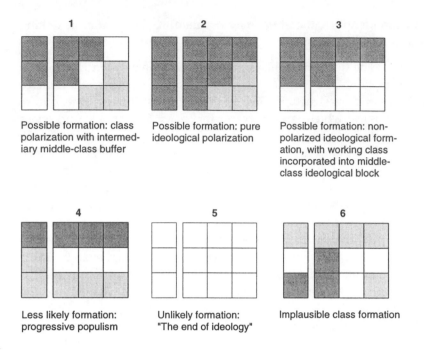

Possible formation: class polarization with intermediary middle-class buffer

Possible formation: pure ideological polarization

Possible formation: non-polarized ideological formation, with working class incorporated into middle-class ideological block

Less likely formation: progressive populism

Unlikely formation: "The end of ideology"

Implausible class formation

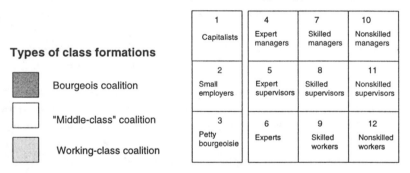

Basic class typology

Types of class formations

Bourgeois coalition	■
"Middle-class" coalition	□
Working-class coalition	▨

1	4	7	10
Capitalists	Expert managers	Skilled managers	Nonskilled managers
2	5	8	11
Small employers	Expert supervisors	Skilled supervisors	Nonskilled supervisors
3	6	9	12
Petty bourgeoisie	Experts	Skilled workers	Nonskilled workers

Figure 13.7 Formable and unformable class formations

incorporated into a middle-class ideological block. The Models 4 and 5 are perhaps less likely, but still consistent with the underlying class structure: in Model 4 one class formation of capitalists and managers confronts a "populist coalition" of workers, intellectuals (nonmanagerial experts and semi-experts) and petty bourgeois, with a weak intermediary formation; in Model 5 a broad cross-class ideological consensus has been forged in which no clear ideological class coalitions appear. Finally, Model 6 represents a structurally very improbable class formation: workers, managers and capitalists collectively organized into a working-class coalition while experts and petty bourgeois are organized into a bourgeois coalition.

2   **Class structure** —*limits*→ **class struggle.**[14] The simplest sense in which class structure limits class struggles is that without the existence of certain kinds of class relations, the relevant actors for certain kinds of class struggles simply do not exist. You cannot have struggles between workers and capitalists without the existence of capitalist class relations. But class structures shape the probabilities of different forms of class struggles in more subtle ways as well. As we discussed in Chapters 3–5 above, different class structures are characterized by different degrees of permeability of class boundaries, and this will affect the plausibility to people in exploited classes of individualistic strategies for pursuing material interests. Where individualistic strategies are closed off (i.e. boundaries are highly impermeable), collective organization and collective struggle become more likely. Class structures also vary in the degree of polarization of material conditions associated with the various dimensions of exploitation. Again, it would be expected that militant forms of struggle are more likely under relatively polarized material conditions than under relatively egalitarian conditions. In these and other ways class structures limit class struggles.

3   **Class formation** —*selects*→ **class struggle.** Class structures may set limits on class struggles via the ways in which class structures determine the interests and opportunities of actors, but actual struggles depend heavily upon the collective organizations available for contending actors. It is a telling fact about repressive right-wing political

---

[14] In earlier works (Wright 1985) I have argued that class formation (rather than class structure) imposes the basic *limits* on class struggles, whereas class structure merely *selects* specific forms of struggle from within those limits. I argued that without a particular kind of class formation, a particular kind of class struggle could not occur and it was for this reason that class formation should be seen as imposing the basic limits on class struggle. It now seems to me more reasonable to argue that since the class structure determines the basic antagonistic interests over which class struggles occur, that class structures should be seen as determining the basic probability-limits for class struggles. In any case, as I have argued extensively elsewhere (see Wright, Levine and Sober, 1992: ch. 7), to claim that class structure imposes the basic limits on class struggle while class formations select forms of struggle within those limits is not to claim that class structure is more *important* for explaining the relevant variations in class struggles.

regimes that they are concerned above all with repressing collective organization, especially unions and parties. When such organizations are destroyed, struggles of all sorts are themselves much more easily controlled. It is not, however, merely the sheer existence of organizations of class formation that matter; the specific form of those organization also has systematic effects on patterns of class struggle. As Joel Rogers (1990) has argued, the degree of centralization or decentralization, unity or fragmentation of the organizational structures of the labor movement has profound consequences for the kinds of working-class struggles in capitalist societies.

4   **Class struggles** —*transforms*→ **class structure**. One of the central objects of class struggle is the class structure itself. In the extreme case, this constitutes an object of revolutionary transformation, when particular forms of class relations are destroyed. More commonly, class struggles transform class structures by transforming particular properties of class relations – the degree of exploitation and polarization of material conditions, the range of powers freely exercised by owners and managers and the barriers to permeability of boundaries, to name only a few examples. Struggles over the redistributive practices of the state, over the right of capitalists to pollute, or over the representation of workers on the boards of directors of firms are, in this sense, struggles to transform class structures since they bear on the class powers of capitalists and workers.

4   **Class struggles** —*transforms*→ **class formations**. Class struggles are not simply over the material interests rooted in class structures. Class struggles are also directed at the organizational and political conditions which facilitate or impede the struggles themselves. This is the central theme of Przeworski's (1985: 71) analysis of classes when he writes:

> (1) classes are formed as an effect of struggles; (2) the process of class formation is a perpetual one: classes are continually organized, disorganized, and reorganized; (3) class formation is an effect of the totality of struggles in which multiple historical actors attempt to organize the same people as class members, as members of collectivities defined in other terms, sometimes simply as members of "the society."

Worker struggles to organize unions and state repression of the labor movement are both instances of class struggles transforming class formations.

13.5 Putting the micro- and macro-models together

At several points we have already touched on the interconnection between the micro- and macro-levels of analysis. The claim that class structure limits class formation, for example, depends in part on the arguments about how the material interests and experiences of individuals are shaped at the micro-level by their class locations. Equally, the micro-level claim that class locations limit class practices depends in part on the argument that individuals in different locations face different opportunities and dilemmas in deciding how best to pursue their material interests. Opportunities and dilemmas, however, are not strictly micro-concepts; they depend crucially on properties of the social structure as a whole.

There is a tradition in social theory, sometimes marching under the banner of "methodological individualism," that insists that macro-phenomena are *reducible* to micro-phenomena. Elster (1985:11) defends this claim explicitly when he defines methodological individualism as "the doctrine that all social phenomena – their structure and their change – are in principle explicable in ways that only involve individuals – their properties, their goals, their beliefs and their actions. To go from social institutions and aggregate patterns of behavior to individuals is the same kind of operation as going from cells to molecules." While it may be necessary for pragmatic reasons to continue to use macro-concepts like "class structure," in principle, methodological individualists believe, these could be replaced with purely micro-concepts.[15]

Most sociologists reject this kind of reductionism, preferring instead to talk loosely of the "interaction" of macro- and micro-levels of analysis. Macro-social phenomena are seen as imposing real constraints of various sorts on individuals, constraints which cannot be simply dissolved into the actions of individuals; but individuals are seen as nevertheless making real choices that have real consequences, including consequences for the stability and transformation of the macro-phenomena themselves.

One way of thinking about this micro-macro interaction is illustrated in Figure 13.8: micro-level processes constitute what can be called the

---

[15] For an evaluation and critique of the micro-reductionist program, see Wright, Levine and Sober (1992: ch. 6).

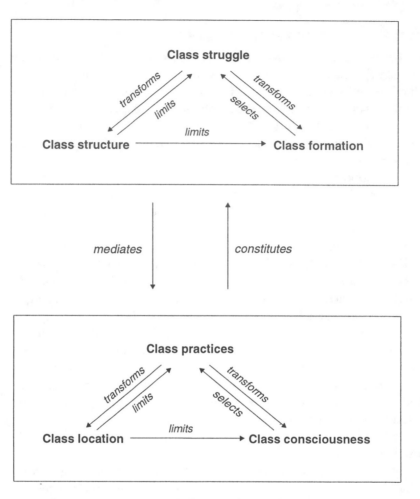

Figure 13.8 Macro-micro linkage in class analysis

micro-foundations of the macro phenomena while macro-level processes *mediate* the micro-processes.

One of the standard ways in which social theorists defend holism against attempts at individualistic reductionism is to state that "the whole is greater than the sum of the parts." The whole, sociologists are fond of saying, has "emergent properties" which cannot be identified with the parts taken one by one and added up. If this were not true, then an adequate description of each part taken separately would be sufficient to generate an adequate description of the whole. Yet it is also true that without the parts, there would be no whole, and this suggests that in some sense the parts taken together do constitute the whole. These two observations – that the whole is greater than the *sum* of the parts and yet the parts *collectively constitute* the whole – can be reconciled by stating that "the whole equals the sum of the parts *plus* all of the interactions among the parts." The "emergent properties" of the whole can then be identified as properties resulting from the interaction of the parts, not simply their serially aggregated individual properties.

To study the micro-foundations of macro-phenomena is thus to study the ways in which wholes are constituted by the sum and interactions of their parts. Consider class structure. Class structures are constituted by individuals in class locations and all of the interactions among those individuals by virtue of the locations they occupy. To study the micro-foundations of the class structure, therefore, is to explore the ways in which attributes of individuals, their choices and actions, help explain the nature of these locations and interconnections. Workers do not own means of production and thus seek employment in order to obtain subsistence; capitalists own means of production and thus seek employees to use those means of production in order to obtain profits. The class relation between worker and capitalist is constituted by the actions of individuals with these attributes (owning only labor power and owning capital) and these preferences (seeking subsistence and seeking profits). The totality of such relations, resulting from these interconnected individual attributes and choices, constitutes the macro-phenomenon we call "class structure."

In a similar way, class formations are constituted by the participation of individuals with varying forms of class consciousness in collective associations organized to realize class interests. Studying the micro-foundations of such collective organization involves understanding the process by which solidarities, built around different forms of con-sciousness, are forged among individuals, and the ways in which this facilitates their cooperation in the collective pursuit of class interests. Different kinds of class formations are grounded in different forms of individual consciousness and solidaristic interdependency.

Finally, to study the micro-foundations of class struggles is to explore the ways in which the attributes, choices and actions of individuals, occupying specific class locations and participating in specific class formations, constitute the collective actions that are the hallmark of class struggle. Take a prototypical example of a class struggle, a strike by a union. The search for micro-foundations insists that it is never satisfactory to restrict the analysis to the "union" as a collective entity making choices and engaging in practices directed at "capitalists" or "management." Since the union as an organized social force (an instance of class formation) is constituted by its members and their interactions, to understand the actions of a union – the decision to call a strike for example – we must understand the attributes, choices and interactions of the individuals constituting that union. This would involve discussions of such things as the free rider problem within unions, the conditions for solidarity to emerge within the membership, the relationship between rank-and-file members and leadership in shaping the decisions of the union, and so on.[16] Class struggles can thus be said to be constituted by the class practices of the individuals within class formations and class structures and all of the interactions among those class practices.

Exploring the micro-foundations of macro-phenomena is only one half of the micro-macro linkage in Figure 13.8. The other half consists of the ways in which macro-phenomena can be said to mediate the effects of micro-processes. To say that the macro mediates the micro means that the specific effects of micro-processes depend upon the macro-setting within which they take place. For example, at the core of the micro-model of consciousness formation in Figure 13.5 is the claim that the class consciousness of individuals is shaped by their class location. These micro-level effects, however, are significantly shaped in various ways by macro-level conditions and processes. Occupying a working-class location in a class structure within which the working class is collectively disorganized has different consequences for the likely consciousness of individuals than occupying the same class location under conditions of the cohesive political formation of the class. This is more than the simple claim that macro-conditions of class formation themselves have effects on consciousness; it implies that the causal impact of individual class location on consciousness is enhanced or weakened depending upon the macro-conditions.

In formal terms, this means that the model argues for the interactive effects of micro-and macro-factors rather than simply additive effects.

---

[16] For a useful discussion of the micro-foundations of class struggle specifically engaging Marxist class analysis, see Elster (1985: pp. 344ff.). Elster characterizes the emergence of solidarity within unions as a shift from a prisoner's dilemma to an assurance game in which conditional altruism defines the central preference ordering of members with respect to shared sacrifice and struggle.

Suppose, for example, we wanted to represent in a simple equation the effects of class location and class formation on class consciousness. The simple additive model would look like this:

$$\text{Consciousness} = a + B_1[\text{Class location}] + B_2[\text{Class formation}]$$

where B_1 and B_2 are coefficients which measure the linear effects of these variables on consciousness. The interactive model – the model of macro-mediation of the micro – adds a multiplicative term:

$$\text{Consciousness} = a + B_1[\text{Class location}] + B_2[\text{Class formation}]$$
$$+ B_3[\text{Location x formation}]$$

where B_3 indicates the extent to which the effects of class locations vary under different macro-conditions of class formation.[17] It could happen, of course, in a specific empirical setting that B_3 is insignificant, indicating that the effects of class location are invariant under different forms of class formation. Indeed, although less plausible, B_1 and B_2 could also be insignificant, indicating that variations in class formation and variations in class location have no consequences for individual consciousness.

13.6 Using the models in empirical research

The model laid out in Figure 13.8 is incomplete in a variety of ways. First, the model is highly underelaborated in terms of the specification of the relevant range of variation of some of the elements in the model. Thus, while I have proposed a detailed account of the variations in "class locations" in the micro-model that are relevant for explaining class consciousness, the discussions of the relevant range of variation of "individual class practices" in the micro-model or of "class formation" or even "class structure" in the macro-model are quite underdeveloped. Even more significantly, there is no specification of the actual magnitudes of the causal relations included in the model. For example, class location is said to impose "limits" on individual class

---

[17] Technically, of course, the interactive term is symmetrical, and B_3 could be said to indicate the extent to which the macro-effects of class formation vary for different class locations. That is, the extent to which the working class is cohesively organized has different effects for people in different class locations, and also, the effects of being in a working-class location have different effects depending upon the degree to which the class is cohesively organized.

consciousness, but the model itself leaves open the nature and scope of these limits. The macro-processes of class formation are said to mediate the micro-processes of consciousness formation, yet the model is silent on the precise form and magnitude of these interactive effects. There is thus nothing in the model which would indicate what the relative probabilities of procapitalist or anticapitalist consciousness would be for people in different class locations, nor how these probabilities would themselves vary under different macro-conditions of class formation. Finally, the model is incomplete because it restricts itself to class-related determinants of the elements in the model. A complete theory of class consciousness and class formation would have to include a wide range of other causal processes – from the nature of various nonclass forms of social division (race, ethnicity, gender), to religion, to geopolitics.

Given these limitations, these models should not be seen as defining a general *theory* of class consciousness and class formation, but rather as a *framework for defining an agenda* of problems for empirical research within class analysis. In the multivariate empirical studies of class consciousness and class formation in Chapters 14–16, therefore, we will not directly "test" the models as such. The models constitute a framework within which a range of alternative hypotheses can be formulated and tested, but the framework itself will not be subjected to any direct tests.

14 Class consciousness and class formation in Sweden, the United States and Japan

This chapter will try to apply some of the elements of the models elaborated in the previous chapter to the empirical study of class formation and class consciousness in three developed capitalist countries – the United States, Sweden and Japan. More specifically, the investigation has three main objectives: first, to examine the extent to which the overall relationship between class locations and class consciousness is broadly consistent with the logic of the class structure analysis we have been using throughout this book; second, to compare the patterns of class formation in the three countries; and, third, to examine the ways in which the micro, multivariate models of consciousness formation vary across the three countries. The first of these tasks centers on exploring the "class location —*limits*→ class consciousness" segment of the model, the second focusses on the "class structure —*limits*→ class formation" segment, and the third centers on the "macro —*mediates*→ micro" aspect of the model.

In the next section we will discuss the strategy we will deploy for measuring class consciousness. This will be followed in section 14.2 with a more detailed discussion of the empirical agenda and the strategies of data analysis. Sections 14.3 to 14.5 will then present the results of the data analysis.

14.1 Measuring class consciousness[1]

Class consciousness is notoriously hard to measure. The concept is meant to denote subjective properties which impinge on conscious choosing activity which has a class content. The question then arises

---

[1] This section is largely drawn from an earlier discussion (Wright 1985: 252–253).

whether or not the subjective states which the concept taps are really only "activated" under conditions of meaningful choice situations, which in the case of class consciousness would imply above all situations of class struggle. There is no necessary reason to assume that these subjective states will be the same when respondents are engaged in the kind of conscious choosing that occurs in an interview. Choosing responses on a survey is a different practice from choosing how to relate to a shopfloor conflict, and the forms of subjectivity which come into play can be quite different. The interview setting is itself, after all, a social relation, and this relation may influence the responses of respondents out of deference, or hostility or some other reaction. Furthermore, it is always possible that there is not simply slippage between the way people respond to the artificial choices of a survey and the real choices of social practices, but that there is a systematic inversion of responses. As a result, it has been argued that there is little value in even attempting to measure class consciousness through survey instruments.[2]

These problems are serious ones, and potentially undermine the value of questionnaire studies of class consciousness. My assumption, however, is that there is at least some stability in the cognitive processes of people across the artificial setting of an interview and the real life setting of class struggle, and that in spite of the possible distortions of structured interviews, social surveys can potentially measure these stable elements. While the ability of a survey may be very limited in predicting for any given individual the way they would behave in a "real life setting," surveys may be able to provide a broad image of how class structure is linked to likely class behaviors.

Deciding to use a questionnaire to tap class consciousness, of course, leaves open precisely what kinds of questionnaire items best measure this concept. Here again there is a crucial choice to be made: should questionnaires be built mainly around open-ended questions or pre-formatted, fixed option questions. Good arguments can be made that open-ended questions provide a more subtle window on individuals' real cognitive processes. When you ask a person, "What do you think are the main causes of poverty in America?" individuals are more likely to reveal their real understandings of the problem than when you ask the fixed-option question, "Do you strongly agree, somewhat

[2] For a critique of attitudes as a way of measuring class consciousness from one of the members of the British research team in the Comparative Class Analysis Project, see Marshall (1983).

agree, somewhat disagree or strongly disagree with the statement 'One of the main reasons for poverty is that some people are lazy and unmotivated to work hard.'" Fixed-option questions risk putting words into people's mouths, giving them alternatives which have no real salience for them.

On the other hand, open-ended questions often pose severe problems in consistent coding and data analysis. There have been innumerable sociological surveys with ambitious open-ended questions which have never been systematically analyzed because the coding problems proved insurmountable. Open-ended responses often are used primarily anecdotally to add illustrative richness to an analysis, but they frequently are abandoned in the quantitative analysis itself.

The problems with coding open-ended questionnaire responses are greatly compounded in cross-national comparative research. Even if one could somehow devise a common coding protocol for open-ended questions in different languages and cultural contexts, it would be virtually impossible to insure that the coding procedures were applied in a rigorously comparable manner across countries. This has proven exceedingly difficult even in the case of coding occupational descriptions into internationally agreed upon categories. It would be much more difficult for open-ended responses to attitude questions. In the Comparative Class Analysis Project we found it hard enough to get the projects in different countries to stick to a common questionnaire. It would be virtually impossible to enforce acceptable standards of comparability to the coding of open-ended questions.[3]

Thus, while it is probably the case that open-ended questions provide a deeper understanding of an individual's consciousness, for pragmatic reasons our analysis will be restricted to closed questions. In general, in research of this kind, systematic superficiality is preferable to chaotic depth.

The survey used in this research contains a wide variety of attitude items, ranging from questions dealing directly with political issues, to normative issues on equal opportunity for women, to explanations for various kinds of social problems. Many of these items can be inter-

---

[3]   There were a series of open-ended attitude questions included in the questionnaire, dealing with explanations and solutions for poverty and crime. Our original intention was to combine these open-ended questions with the parallel set of closed option questions. To my knowledge there is not a single publication from any of the countries in the project which use the open-ended version of the questions in a systematic manner.

preted as indicators of class consciousness, but for most of them the specific class-content of the items is indirect and presupposes fairly strong theoretical assumptions. For example, Marxists often argue that the distinction between explaining social problems in individualist terms ("the poor are poor because they are lazy") instead of social structural terms ("the poor are poor because of the lack of jobs and education") is an aspect of class consciousness. While this claim may be plausible, it does require a fairly strong set of assumptions to interpret the second of these explanations of poverty as an aspect of anticapitalist consciousness. For the purposes of this investigation, therefore, it seemed advisable to focus on those items with the most direct class implications, and to aggregate these questions into a fairly simple, transparent class consciousness scale.

Five attitude items from the questionnaire will be used to construct the scale.[4] These items are all Likert-type questions in which respondents were asked whether they strongly agreed, agreed, disagreed or strongly disagreed with each of the following statements:

1 Corporations benefit owners at the expense of workers and consumers.
2 During a strike, management should be prohibited by law from hiring workers to take the place of strikers.
3 Many people in this country receive much less income than they deserve.

---

[4]   In the previously published research on Sweden and the United States that is the ancestor of this chapter (Wright, Howe and Cho 1989) a sixth item was included in the analysis:

"In a protracted strike over wages and working conditions, which outcome would you like to see happen:
(a)   workers win most of their demands;
(b)   workers win some of their demands and make some significant concessions
(c)   workers win only a few of their demands
(d)   workers go back to work without winning any of their demands."

Even though this item revealed very interesting differences between Sweden and the United States, it had to be dropped in the current three-country comparison because in the Japanese survey the wording was inadvertently changed. Instead of asking "which outcome *would you like to see* happen" the Japanese question read "which outcome *do you think is mostly likely* to happen." We were alerted to the fact that something was amiss with the Japanese question wording when we observed that a much higher proportion of Japanese respondents gave answer (c) than in any other country. In any case, none of the results for the United States and Sweden are in any substantive way affected by dropping this item.

4 Large corporations have too much power in American/Swedish/Japanese society today.

5 The nonmanagement employees in your place of work could run things effectively without bosses.

The responses to each question are given a value of -2 for the strong procapitalist response, -1 for the somewhat procapitalist response, 0 for "Don't know," $+1$ for the somewhat anticapitalist response and $+2$ for the strong anticapitalist response.[5] The scores on these individual items were combined to construct a simple additive scale going from -10 (procapitalist extreme value) to $+10$ (anticapitalist extreme value). If respondents had missing data on some of these items, the mean value for the valid items was calculated and this mean was then multiplied by 5, thus yielding the same range of possible values. A number of methodological issues connected with this scale are discussed in the methodological appendix to this chapter.

14.2 The empirical agenda

Class locations and class consciousness

Before we engage in the detailed discussion of the patterns of class formation and the multivariate models of class consciousness, it will be useful to examine the extent to which the overall relationship between class locations and class consciousness is consistent with the basic logic of the concept of class structure we have been exploring. To recapitulate the basic idea, class structures in capitalist societies can be analyzed in terms of the intersection of three ways people are linked to the process of material exploitation: through the ownership of property, through positions within authority hierarchies, and through possession of skills and expertise. If class locations defined in this way systematically shape the material interests and lived experiences of individuals, and if these interests and experiences in turn shape class consciousness, then there should be a systematic relationship between class location and class consciousness. Underlying this chain of reasoning is the assumption that, all things being equal, there will be at least a weak tendency for incumbents in class locations to develop forms of class consciousness consistent with the material interests

---

[5] "Don't know" was not an explicit response category in the interview, but interviewers indicated this response if the respondent gave it.

linked to those locations. The perceptions of those interests may be partial and incomplete, but, in general, distorted perceptions of interests will take the form of deviations from a full understanding of interests, and thus on average there should be a systematic empirical association of class location and consciousness of interests.

In terms of the empirical indicators of class consciousness we are using in this chapter, this argument about the link between class location and consciousness suggests that as one moves from exploiter to exploited along each of the dimensions of the class structure matrix, the ideological orientation of individuals should become more critical of capitalist institutions. If we also assume that these effects are cumulative (i.e. being exploited on two dimensions will tend to make one more anticapitalist than being exploited on only one), then we can form a rather ambitious empirical hypothesis:

> Along each of the rows and columns of the class structure matrix, there should be a monotonic relationship between the values on the anticapitalism scale and class location.

In terms of the 12–location class structure matrix with which we have been working, we will explore three more specific hypotheses:

Hypothesis 1. The working-class location in the matrix should be the most anticapitalist, the capitalist class location the most procapitalist.

Hypothesis 2. Within the owner portion of the matrix, the attitudes should monotonically become more procapitalist as you move from the petty bourgeoisie to the capitalist class.

Hypothesis 3. Within the employee portion of the matrix attitudes should become monotonically more procapitalist as you move from the working-class corner of the matrix to the expert-manager corner table along both the rows and the columns.

Hypothesis 3 applies especially to the four categories at the corners of the employee portion of the matrix – expert managers, nonmanagerial experts, nonexpert managers and workers. As explained in chapter 2, the intermediary categories on each dimension – supervisors and skilled employees – combine various kinds of measurement errors with genuinely intermediary values, and thus predictions about these categories are necessarily less certain.

The exploitation-centered class concept does not generate clear hypotheses about the class consciousness of the petty bourgeoisie compared to the contradictory class locations among employees. There is no clear reason to believe that the petty bourgeoisie should be more or less procapitalist than those wage-earners who occupy a contradictory relationship to the process of exploitation, i.e. managers and experts. On the one hand, petty bourgeois are owners of the means of production and thus have a clear stake in private property; on the other hand they are often threatened and dominated by capitalist firms in both commodity markets and credit markets, and this can generate quite a lot of hostility. Given that the questions we are using in the class consciousness scale deal with attitudes toward capitalism and capitalists, not private property in general, there may be many petty bourgeois who take a quite anticapitalist stance. In any case, I make no predictions about whether they will be more or less anticapitalist than the "middle class" (i.e. contradictory class locations among employees).

Class formation

In the previous chapter we defined class formation in terms of solidaristic social relations within class structures. Individuals occupy locations in class structures which impose on them a set of constraints and opportunities on how they can pursue their material interests. In the course of pursuing those interests, collectivities of varying degree of coherence and durability are forged. The study of class formation involves the investigation of such collectivities – of their compositions, their strategies, their organizational forms, etc.

The research on class formation reported in this chapter is quite limited and focusses entirely on the problem of the class composition of what I will call "ideological class formations." Our approach will be largely inductive and descriptive. The central task will be to map out for the United States, Sweden and Japan the ways in which the various locations in the class structure become grouped into more or less ideologically homogeneous blocks.

The research is thus, at best, an indirect approach to the proper study of class formation itself. Ideally, to chart out variations in class formations across countries we would want to study the ways in which various kinds of solidaristic organizations – especially such things as unions and political parties – link people together within and across class locations. A map of the ways in which class-linked organizations of different ideological and political profiles penetrate different parts of the class structure would provide a basic description of the pattern of class formation. Data on the class composition of formal membership and informal affiliation in parties and unions would provide one empirical way of approaching this.

The data used in this project are not really amenable to a refined analysis of the organizational foundations of class formation. I will therefore use a more indirect strategy for analyzing the contours of class formation in these three countries. Instead of examining organizational affiliations, we will use the variation across the class structure in ideological orientation toward class interests as a way of mapping out the patterns of solidarity and antagonism.

This strategy of analysis may generate misleading results for two reasons. First, the assumption that the class mapping of attitudes will roughly correspond to the class mapping of organized collective solidarities is certainly open to question. Even though people in different class locations may share very similar attitudes, nevertheless they have different vulnerabilities, control different resources and face different alternative courses of action – this is in fact what it means to say that they are in different "locations" – and this could generate very different tendencies to actually participate in the collective actions of class formation.

Second, the method we are using to measure ideological class coalitions is vulnerable to all of the problems that bedevil comparative survey research. It is always possible that apparently identical questionnaire items might actually mean quite different things in different cultural contexts, regardless of how good the translation might be. A good example in our questionnaire is the following Likert-type question: "Do you strongly agree, somewhat agree, somewhat disagree or strongly disagree with this statement: Workers in a strike are justified in physically preventing strike-breakers from entering the place of work." The problem with this question is that in the Swedish context there is not a well-established tradition of strikes using picket lines to bar entrance to a place of work. As a result, the expression "physically prevent" suggests a much higher level of potential violence to a Swedish respondent than it does to an American. For a Swede to agree with the question, in effect, they must feel it is legitimate for workers to assault a strikebreaker. For this reason, although this item appears in the survey we have not included it in this analysis.[6]

---

[6]   We were alerted to the fact that this question had culturally noncomparable

This problem of cultural incommensurability of questionnaire items might mean that cross-national differences in patterns of ideological class formation might simply be artifacts of slippages in the meaning of questions. My hope is that with enough discussion among researchers from each of the countries involved and enough pretesting of the questionnaire items, it is possible to develop a set of items that are relatively comparable (or at least that the researchers from each country believe mean the same things).[7] In any event, the precise wording of the items is a matter of record which should facilitate challenges to the comparability of the meanings by skeptics.

Our empirical strategy, then, is to treat the class distribution of class-relevant attitudes held by individuals as an indicator of the patterns of ideological coalitions within class formations. Where individuals in different class locations on average share similar class-relevant attitudes, we will say that these class locations constitute an ideological coalition within the structure of class formations. By using attitudes as an indicator of solidarity and antagonism in this way I am not implying that class formations can be reduced to the attitudes people hold in their heads about class interests. The claim is simply that the formation of ideological configurations contributes to and reflects solidaristic collectivities and is therefore an appropriate empirical indicator for studying the relationship between class structure and class formation.

The specific methodology we will use to distinguish ideological class coalitions is explained in detail in the methodological appendix to this chapter. The basic idea is to ask, for each of the twelve locations in the class structure matrix whether the average person in that location is ideologically closer to the working class, the capitalist class or an ideologically neutral position between these two poles. Locations that are closer to the neutral position will be referred to as part of the

---

meanings in the US and Sweden because the distribution of responses in Sweden were so disjoint with other questions in the survey. On all other class conflict items, Swedish workers took a much more proworker stance than American workers, but not on this item.

[7] The questionnaire used in these comparisons was developed in a series of very intensive and detailed discussions involving the American and Swedish researchers (among others). Many items were dropped from the survey or had their wordings modified because of problems of equivalence of cultural meanings. Unfortunately, the Japanese project did not exist at that time and thus they were not involved at all in the initial design of the questionnaire. They were forced, therefore, to accept the questions without modification and this may mean that there is more cultural slippage in the Japanese survey than in the other two.

middle-class ideological coalition, whereas those closer to the polarized class locations will be referred to as part of the working-class coalition or the bourgeois coalition. The basic objective of this part of the analysis is to examine how these ideological class coalitions differ in the United States, Sweden and Japan.

Class consciousness

Our analysis of class formation revolves around examining differences and similarities in ideological orientation across locations in the class-structure matrix. In the analysis of class consciousness the unit of analysis shifts to the individual. Here the task is to construct a multi-variate model of variations in individual consciousness, measured using the same anticapitalism scale, and see how these models vary across countries.

These models contain five clusters of variables: *class location* (11 dummy variables); *past class experiences* (dummy variables for working-class origin, capitalist origin, previously self-employed, previously supervisor and previously unemployed); *current class experiences and material conditions* (union member, home owner, unearned income dummy variable, personal income, density of ties to the capitalist class, density of ties to the working class); *demographic variables* (age and gender); and *country* (two dummy variables). The precise definitions of these variables are presented in the methodological appendix. The data analysis will be built around five equations predicting values on the anticapitalism scale:

Equation 1. *Class location only*
Equation 2. *Class location + Past class experiences + Current class experiences + Union membership + Demographics*
Equation 3. *Country only*
Equation 4. *Class location + Country*
Equation 5. *Equation (2) + Country*

We will first merge the three national samples into a single dataset in which we treat nationality simply like any other variable. This will enable us to answer the following question: which is more important for predicting individuals' class consciousness, the country in which they live or their class location and class experiences? We will then break the data into the three national samples and estimate equation 1 and 2 separately for each country. Here we will be particularly interested in comparing the explanatory power of different groups of variables across countries.

14.3 Results: The overall relationship between locations in the class structure and class consciousness

The results for the overall linkage between class location and class consciousness in Sweden, the United States and Japan are presented in Figure 14.1. With some wrinkles, these results are broadly consistent with each of the three broad hypotheses discussed above. In all three countries the working-class location in the class structure matrix is either the most anticapitalist or is virtually identical to the location which is the most anticapitalist.[8] Also in all three countries, the capitalist class is either the most procapitalist or has a value which is not significantly different from the most procapitalist location.[9] These results are thus consistent with Hypothesis 1.

The results also support Hypothesis 2 for all three countries. In each case there is a sharp ideological gradient among owners: the capitalist class is 3–4 points more procapitalist than the petty bourgeoisie, with small employers falling somewhere in between.

Hypothesis 3 is strongly supported by the results for Sweden and the United States, and somewhat more ambiguously supported by the results for Japan. In Sweden, the results nearly exactly follow the predictions of the hypothesis: as you move from the working-class corner of the matrix to the expert-manager corner, the values on the scale declines in a perfectly monotonic manner, whether you move along the rows of the table, the columns of the table, or even the diagonal.[10] Indeed, in the Swedish data the monotonicity extends across the property boundary as well. In the United States the results are only slightly less monotonic: in the employee portion of the matrix,

---

[8] In the US and Sweden the working-class location is virtually indistinguishable from the skilled nonmanagerial employee location; in Japan it is indistinguishable from the petty bourgeoisie.

[9] In the United States the value for the expert-manager location is −2.62 and for the capitalist location, −2.17. These values do not differ significantly at the 0.05 level. It should also be noted that what we are calling "capitalists" are generally quite small capitalist employers, since the cut-off point between capitalists and small employers is only ten employees. This may help to explain why the capitalists in the United States sample are not more procapitalist than expert managers.

[10] The only minor qualification to this description is that there is no real difference between nonskilled workers and skilled workers. This does not, however, undermine the substantive point of the hypothesis.

SWEDEN

	Owner	Employee		
Capitalist	-3.41	-2.36	0.60	1.05	Manager
Small employer	-0.70	0.56	2.07	3.50	Supervisor
Petty bourgeoisie	0.87	1.98	4.60	4.61	Non-management
		Expert	Skilled	Nonskilled

UNITED STATES

	Owner	Employee		
Capitalist	-2.17	-2.62	-0.68	-1.09	Manager
Small employer	0.35	-0.73	1.30	2.28	Supervisor
Petty bourgeoisie	1.08	0.16	2.67	2.66	Non-management
		Expert	Skilled	Nonskilled

JAPAN

	Owner	Employee		
Capitalist	0.17	0.32	2.10	1.83	Manager
Small employer	0.76	0.68	2.68	1.57	Supervisor
Petty bourgeoisie	3.08	1.09	2.61	3.07	Non-management
		Expert	Skilled	Nonskilled

The numbers in the cells of the class structure matrix are values on the anti-capitalism attitude scale (range, -10 to +10), in which negative values indicate a procapitalist orientation and positive values a proworking class orientation.

Figure 14.1 *Class structure and class consciousness in Sweden, the United States and Japan*

skilled managers are slightly less anticapitalist than unskilled managers. In all other respects, the US data behave in the predicted monotonic manner.

The pattern for Japan is somewhat less consistent. If we look only at the four corners of the employee portion of the matrix, then the predicted monotonicity holds. The deviations from Hypothesis 3 come with some of the intermediary values. In particular, skilled supervisors in Japan appear to be considerably more anticapitalist than unskilled supervisors. The number of cases in these locations is, however, quite small (25 and 19 respectively), and the difference in anticapitalism scores between these categories is not statistically significant at even the .20 level. The other deviations from pure monotonicity in the Japanese class structure matrix are even less statistically significant. The results for Japan thus do not strongly contradict the predictions of Hypothesis 3, although they remain less consistent than those of Sweden and the United States.

Overall, then, these results for the three countries suggest that the patterns of variation across the locations of the class structure in class consciousness, as measured by the anticapitalism scale, are quite consistent with the theoretical predictions derived from the multi-dimensional, exploitation concept of class structure. While empirical consistency by itself cannot definitively prove the validity of a concept, nevertheless it does add credibility to the conceptual foundations that underlie the class analysis of this book.

14.4 Results: The macro-analysis of class formation

The basic patterns of ideological class formation will be presented in three different visual formats, since each of these helps to reveal different properties of the results. Figure 14.2 presents the results in terms of a one-dimensional ideological spectrum on which the values for the different class locations are indicated in a manner similar to Appendix Figure 14.1. Figure 14.3 represents the patterns as two-dimensional coalition maps as discussed in Chapter 13, Figure 13.7. Figure 14.4 presents these same results as three-dimensional graphs of the relationship between values on the anticapitalism scale and location within the class structure matrix. (Note that in these three-dimensional graphs, the ordering of the categories in the class-structure matrix – the horizontal plane in the graph – has been changed from the ordering in Figure 14.3 and elsewhere so that none of the bars on the graph would be hidden.) The numerical data on which these figures are based are presented in Figure 14.1.

Before turning to the rather striking contrasts in patterns of class formation between these three countries, there are two similarities

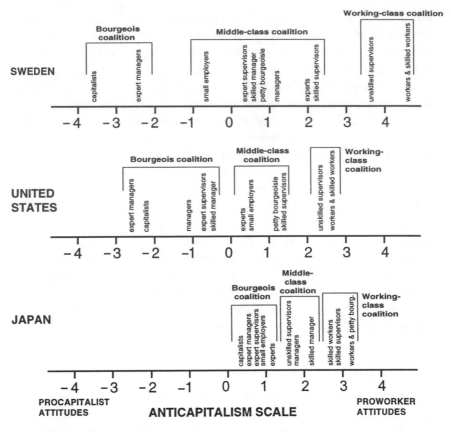

Figure 14.2 *Class and the ideological spectrum in Sweden, the United States and Japan*

which are worth noting. First, in all three countries skilled workers are in the working-class ideological coalition and have virtually identical scores on the anticapitalism scale as nonskilled workers. This finding supports the common practice of treating skilled and nonskilled workers as constituting "the working class." Second, in all three countries, in spite of the quite different overall configurations of the bourgeois ideological coalition, expert managers are part of this coalition. The most exploitative and dominating contradictory class location among employees (expert managers) is thus consistently part of the capitalist class formation, while the least exploitative and dominating contradictory location (skilled workers) is part of the working-class formation.

SWEDEN

Capitalists	Expert managers	Skilled managers	Nonskilled managers
Small employers	Expert supervisors	Skilled supervisors	Nonskilled supervisors
Petty bourgeoisie	Experts	Skilled workers	Nonskilled workers

UNITED STATES

Capitalists	Expert managers	Skilled managers	Nonskilled managers
Small employers	Expert supervisors	Skilled supervisors	Nonskilled supervisors
Petty bourgeoisie	Experts	Skilled workers	Nonskilled workers

JAPAN

Capitalists	Expert managers	Skilled managers	Nonskilled managers
Small employers	Expert supervisors	Skilled supervisors	Nonskilled supervisors
Petty bourgeoisie	Experts	Skilled workers	Nonskilled workers

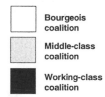

Bourgeois coalition

Middle-class coalition

Working-class coalition

Figure 14.3 *Patterns of ideological class formation*

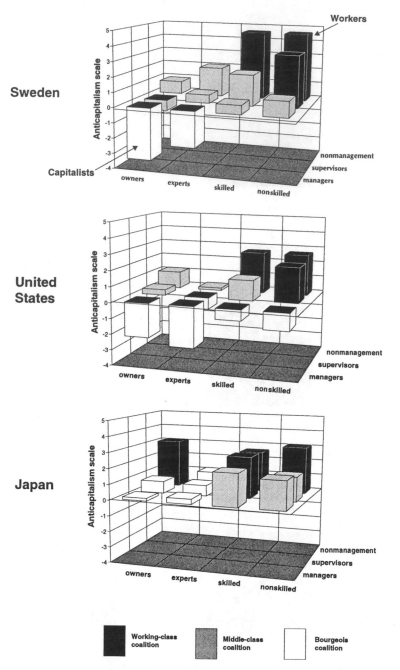

Figure 14.4 *Three-dimensional representation of patterns of ideological class formation*

In other respects, the three countries we are considering present very different patterns. Let us look at each of them in turn.

Sweden

As indicated in Figure 14.2, the ideological spectrum across the locations of the class structure is larger in Sweden than in the other two countries, spanning a total of over 8 points on the anticapitalism scale.[11] On this ideological terrain, the three ideological class coalitions are well defined and clearly differentiated from each other. The mean values on the anticapitalism scale for each of the coalitions differ from each other at less than the .001 significance level.

The working-class coalition contains three class locations: the working class plus the two class locations adjacent to the working class – skilled workers and nonskilled supervisors. This coalition is quite clearly demarcated ideologically from the middle-class coalition. The value on the anticapitalism scale of the category in the working-class coalition with the *lowest* value on the scale, nonskilled supervisors (3.50), is significantly greater (at the .05 level of significance) than the value of the category within the middle-class coalition with the *highest* value, skilled supervisors (2.07).

The bourgeois coalition is sharply polarized ideologically with respect to the working-class coalition. It consists of capitalists and only one contradictory class location, expert managers. Like the working-class coalition, the bourgeois coalition is clearly demarcated from the middle-class coalition: expert managers are 1.66 points more procapitalist than the category in the middle-class coalition with the most procapitalist attitudes, small employers.[12] While the numbers of capitalists in the Swedish sample is very small (8), it is striking that they hold stronger procapitalist views than the capitalist class in either the United States or Japan. Social democracy may have become a stable ideological framework for Swedish politics in general, affecting the

---

[11] The maximum possible difference between class locations on the scale is 20 points, but of course because of internal ideological heterogeneity within any social category, the average value on the scale for a category could never approach this theoretical extreme. A difference of over 8 points is therefore quite large.

[12] Because of the small number of cases in these class locations, the significance level of this difference (.06) falls just below the conventional .05 threshold of significance. Nevertheless, the absolute magnitude of the demarcation between bourgeois and middle-class coalition (1.66) is actually greater than the distance between the middle-class coalition and the working-class coalition (1.43).

policy profiles of even conservative parties, but the Swedish capitalist class remains staunchly procapitalist.

The middle-class coalition in Sweden is quite broad and encompasses most of the employee contradictory locations within class relations as well as the petty bourgeoisie and small employers. This coalition is much more heterogeneous ideologically than either of the other two coalitions. Three of the categories in this middle-class formation fell into "marginal zones" of the middle-class ideological segment (see the discussion in the methodological appendix, section 2 for the strategy for constructing boundaries of class formations), and the values on the anticapitalism scale of the locations within this coalition span nearly 3 points on the anticapitalism scale (from −0.7 to +2.07) in contrast to just over 1 point within the capitalist and working-class coalitions.[13]

The United States

The ideological class formations constructed on the American class structure are somewhat less ideologically polarized than the Swedish. In particular, the American working-class coalition is clearly less anticapitalist than the Swedish working-class coalition. The unweighted mean of the American working-class coalition is 2.53 compared to 4.24 in Sweden. American capitalists and expert managers (the two locations that are in both the US and Swedish bourgeois coalitions) are only slightly less procapitalist than their Swedish counterpart, −2.40 compared to −2.89.[14] The way to characterize the overall contrast between the ideological spectra in the two countries is thus that the working-class coalition in the US moves significantly toward the center compared to Sweden while the core of the bourgeois coalitions (capitalists and expert managers) are equally on the right (i.e. procapitalist). Nevertheless, in spite of this somewhat lower level of polariza-

[13] The greater ideological heterogeneity of the middle-class coalition is not an artifact of the analytical strategy used to define ideological class coalitions. There is nothing in the method which will tend to generate greater heterogeneity within the middle-class coalition compared to the other coalitions. Indeed, in the United States, the bourgeois ideological coalition is more heterogeneous than the middle-class coalition.

[14] The weighted mean of these two categories combined is −2.4 in the US and −2.59 in Sweden. This difference is not even marginally statistically significant (the t-value is 0.21), while the difference in the means between the working-class coalitions in the two countries is significant at the .001 level.

tion, the three ideological class coalitions all still differ from each other at better than the .001 significance level.

The American working-class coalition includes the same three categories as in Sweden. While it is clearly less radical than the Swedish working-class coalition, it is almost as well demarcated from the middle-class coalition. The value on the anticapitalism scale of the category in the working-class coalition with the lowest value on the scale, nonskilled supervisors (2.28), is significantly greater (at the .05 level of significance) than the value of the category within the middle-class coalition with the highest value, skilled supervisors (1.30).

The bourgeois coalition in the United States extends much deeper into the contradictory class locations than in Sweden (see especially Figures 14.3 and 14.4). All three managerial class locations as well as expert supervisors are part of the American bourgeois ideological class formation. Unlike in Sweden, therefore, management is firmly integrated into the bourgeois ideological coalition.[15]

The middle-class coalition is somewhat attenuated in the US compared to Sweden reflecting the fact that a part of the contradictory class locations among employees in the US has been integrated ideologically into the bourgeois coalition. The middle-class coalition is also somewhat less sharply demarcated from the bourgeois coalition than it is from the working-class coalition. Although the overall means of the middle-class coalition and the bourgeois coalition differ significantly (at the p<.001 significance level), the two categories nearest the "boundaries" of these two coalitions (experts in the middle-class coalition and skilled managers in the bourgeois coalition) do not differ significantly.

Japan

The patterns of ideological class formation in Japan present a sharp contrast to both the United States and Sweden. To begin with, the

---

[15] Two of these categories, skilled managers and expert supervisors, fell into the "marginal zone" of the capitalist ideological segment, but were included in this coalition because their values on the anticapitalism scale were closer to the nearest class location in the core zone of the capitalist segment, nonskilled managers, than they were to the nearest class location in the core of the middle-class coalition, nonmanagerial experts. This contributes to the relatively wide range of values on the anticapitalism scale within the American bourgeois coalition, from −0.68 for skilled managers to −2.62 for expert managers, compared to the other two coalitions (a range of just over 1 point on the scale for the middle-class coalition and less than half a point for the working-class coalition).

entire ideological spectrum is much more compressed in Japan than in the other two countries. What is particularly striking is that the capitalist class and expert managers have moved to the center of the anticapitalism scale. These two categories combined are significantly less anticapitalist (at the .01 significance level) than the same categories in Sweden and the United States (whereas, as already noted, these categories do not differ between Sweden and the United States). In fact, the values on the anticapitalism scale for the bourgeois coalition in Japan fall entirely within the range for the middle-class coalitions in the other two countries. The Japanese working-class coalition, in contrast, does not differ significantly on the anticapitalism from the American working-class coalition. The conventional image of Japanese society as lacking highly antagonistic class formations is thus broadly supported by these data. While the mean values on the anticapitalism scale for the three ideological coalitions still do differ significantly,[16] the lines of demarcation between these coalitions are much less sharply drawn than in the other two countries.

Not only is the overall degree of ideological polarization of the class structure much less in Japan than in Sweden and the United States, but the pattern of class formation reflected in these ideological cleavages is also quite different. Specifically, in Japan the line of ideological cleavage among employees is much more pronounced between experts and nonexperts than it is along the authority dimension. In Sweden and the United States, in contrast, the cleavages along these two dimensions are of roughly comparable magnitude.

These contrasts are revealed in an especially stark manner in the three-dimensional graphs in Figure 14.4. In Japan the cleavages along the authority dimension are quite subdued compared to the other two countries. This is especially clear among experts and among skilled employees. In Japan there are no statistically significant differences on the anticapitalism scale across levels of authority for these two categories, whereas in both Sweden and the United States there are sharp and statistically significant differences. For example, consider skilled employees. In Japan the values on the anticapitalism scale for managers, supervisors and nonmanagers among skilled employees are 2.1, 2.68 and 2.61 respectively. In the United States the corresponding values are −0.68, 1.30 and 2.67, while in Sweden they are 0.6, 2.07 and

---

[16] The significance levels are as follows: bourgeois coalition vs. middle-class coalition, p=.03; middle-class coalition vs. working-class coalition, p=.008.

4.60. The differences between managers and workers among skilled employees are thus 0.5 in Japan, 3.3 in the US and 4 in Sweden. With the single exception of the contrast between nonskilled supervisors (anticapitalism score, 1.57) and nonskilled workers (anticapitalism score, 3.07), there are no statistically significant differences across authority levels in Japan.

In contrast to these patterns for authority, Japan is less deviant from Sweden and the United States in the ideological differences between experts and skilled employees *within* levels of authority. The difference in anticapitalism between expert managers and skilled managers is 3 points in Sweden, 1.9 points in the US and 1.8 points in Japan. Among supervisors the corresponding figures for the three countries are 1.5, 2.0 and 2.0, and among nonmanagerial employees, 2.6, 2.5 and 1.5.

These differences in patterns of ideological cleavage generate very different patterns of class formation in Japan as seen in Figure 14.3. First, consider the bourgeois coalition: in Japan, experts at all levels of the authority hierarchy are part of the bourgeois ideological coalition, whereas skilled and nonskilled managers are not. This contrasts sharply with the United States in which managers of all skill levels are part of the bourgeois coalition, and Sweden, in which only expert managers were part of that coalition. In Japan therefore, it appears that credentials more than organizational position constitute the basis for ideological linkage to the bourgeoise.

The working-class coalition in Japan, as measured by our procedures, has a rather odd shape, consisting of skilled and nonskilled workers, and skilled supervisors, but not nonskilled supervisors. These results are puzzling, since within the conceptual framework of contradictory class locations one would normally think that in comparison with *skilled* supervisors, *nonskilled* supervisors would have interests more like those of workers and thus would have a stronger tendency to be part of the working-class ideological coalition. This is certainly the case for Sweden and the United States. I cannot offer a plausible explanation for these specific results. They may reflect some significant measurement problems in operationalizing the distinction between skilled and nonskilled for Japan. But it is also possible that these results reflect some complicated interaction of class location with such things as variations in employment situation, sector of employment, age or some other factor. Unfortunately, because the number of cases in these categories is so small, we cannot empirically explore possible explanations for this apparent anomaly. In any case, as already noted, the difference between skilled and nonskilled supervisors in Japan is not statistically significant even at the .10 level.

One final contrast between Japan and the other two countries concerns the petty bourgeoisie. In Japan the petty bourgeoisie is just as anticapitalist as is the working class and is firmly part of the working-class ideological coalition. In both Sweden and the United States, the petty bourgeoisie is part of the middle-class coalition and has an anticapitalist score that is significantly lower than that of the working class. In these terms, the Japanese pattern looks rather like the populism of several generations ago in the United States in which labor–farm coalitions were politically organized against capitalists. Japan continues to have a relatively large petty bourgeoisie and it appears to have an ideological profile that ties it relatively closely to the working class.[17]

Summary of the comparisons of the three countries

Taking all of these results for the macro-analysis of class formation together, three contrasts among the countries we have examined stand out:

1   The degree of ideological polarization across class formations differs significantly in the three cases: Sweden is the most polarized, Japan the least, and the United States is in between. These variations in the degree of polarization do not come from a symmetrical decline in the range of ideological variation across classes. Compared to Sweden, in the United States the working-class coalition is significantly less anticapitalist, but there is little difference between the two countries in the procapitalist attitudes of the core of the capitalist coalition. In Japan, in contrast, both the capitalist-class coalition and the working-class coalition are ideologically less extreme than their Swedish counterparts.

2   While expert managers can be considered the core coalition partner of the capitalist class in all three countries, the overall shape of the bourgeois coalitions varies sharply in the three cases. In Sweden, the bourgeois coalition is confined to this core. In both Japan and the United States the coalition extends fairly deeply into contradictory class locations among employees, but in quite different ways. In Japan contradictory class locations are integrated into the bourgeois class

---

[17] Since the Japanese sample is largely an urban sample, there are virtually no farmers in the Japanese petty bourgeoisie, so these attitudes do not reflect agrarian anticapitalism.

formation more systematically through credentials than through authority, whereas the reverse is true in the United States. Authority hierarchy thus plays a more central role in processes of bourgeois class formation in the United States than in the other two countries, and credentials a more central role in Japan.

3   Overall, Sweden and the United States are much more like each other than they are like Japan. The shape of the working-class formation is identical in the US and Sweden and is clearly differentiated ideologically from the middle-class coalition, and even though the bourgeois coalition penetrates more deeply into employee locations in the United States, it does so in a way that is entirely consistent with the underlying patterns in Sweden. Japan, in these terms, is quite different. The working-class formation has a more populist character because of the presence of the petty bourgeoisie and is much less differentiated ideologically from the middle class. The middle-class coalition also looks entirely different from that in the other two countries. Furthermore, whereas, in Sweden and the United States, both the skill and authority dimensions among employees are sources of systematic ideological cleavage, in Japan only the contrast between credentialed experts and nonexperts constitutes a consistent source of cleavage among employees.

14.5 Explaining the differences in class formations

It is beyond the capacity of the data in this project to test systematically alternative explanations of the cross-national patterns of class formation we have been mapping out. Ultimately this would require constructing an account of the historical trajectory in each country of class struggles and institution building, especially of unions, parties and states. But we can get some suggestive ideas about explanations by looking at some of the proximate institutional factors that might underpin the ideological configurations that we have been examining. We will first focus on the contrast between the US and Sweden and then turn to the problem of Japan.

The overall differences in patterns of class formation between Sweden and the United States can be summarized in terms of two contrasts: first, the bourgeois class formation penetrates the middle class to a much greater extent in the United States than in Sweden, and second, the working-class formation is ideologically more polarized with the capitalist-class formation in Sweden than in the United States.

In the conceptual framework for the analysis of class formation laid out in Chapter 13, class formations were seen as the result of two clusters of causal factors, one linked to the effects of class structure on class formation and the other of class struggle on class formation. Class structure was seen as shaping class formations via the ways in which it influenced the material interests, identities and resources of people; class struggle was seen as shaping class formations by affecting the organizations of collective action. Different patterns of class formation would therefore be expected in cases where the linkage between class location and material interests was quite different or situations in which the linkage between class location and organizational capacities was quite different. We will explore two specific mechanisms reflecting these factors: state employment and unionization.

State employment

State employment might be expected to be particularly important for insulating the middle class from the bourgeois coalition. Within the capitalist corporation, through mechanisms of career ladders, vertical promotions, job security, and in the case of higher level managers, stock bonuses of various sorts, the material interests of managers and experts tend to be closely tied to the profitability of the corporation itself, and thus the general class interests of the middle-class employed in private corporations tend to be closely tied to those of the bourgeoisie.[18] Within the state, however, this link between middle-class interests and bourgeois interests is much less direct. While, in the long run, the salaries of state employees depend upon state revenues, and state revenues depend upon a healthy capitalist economy and thus upon profits, there is in general no direct dependency of the material interests of state employees on the interests of any particular capitalist. State employment, therefore, could potentially constitute a material basis for the middle class to develop a sense of its own class interests

18 Of course, to some extent the same might be said for the working class since the immediate material interests of workers are also tied to the profitability of the firms within which they work. All things being equal, workers are better off when the profits of a firm are strong than when they are feeble. Nevertheless, because of generally lower levels of job security and more limited career ladders among workers, and because of the short-term trade-off between workers' wages and profits, it would be expected that the immediate interests of managers and experts within corporations will be more closely tied to the interests of capitalists than will be the interests of workers.

relatively differentiated from those of the capitalist class. All things being equal, in a society with a large state sector, therefore, it would be expected that the middle class would be more autonomous ideologically from the bourgeoisie than in a society with a relatively small state sector.

In the United States, the material fate of the middle class is much more directly tied to the fortunes of corporate capitalism than in Sweden. In the United States only about 18% of the labor force as a whole is employed by the state, and while the figures are generally higher for those middle-class locations which are not in the working-class coalition (about 23% are employed in the state) it is still the case that most middle-class jobs are in the private sector. In Sweden, in contrast, 38% of the entire labor force, and nearly 50% of the middle-class contradictory locations are directly employed by the state. This makes middle-class interests in Sweden less immediately tied to those of the capitalist class, and thus creates greater possibilities for the formation of a distinctive middle-class ideological coalition.

Some evidence in support of this interpretation is presented in Table 14.1. In the United States, "middle-class" wage-earners (i.e. those that are outside of the working-class ideological coalition) in the state sector have, on average, a significantly less procapitalist ideological orientation than middle-class wage-earners in the private sector. This contrast is especially sharp among expert managers, the contradictory class location most closely allied with the capitalist class. Expert managers in the state have a value on the anticapitalism scale of -0.04 whereas those in the private sector have a value of -3.59 (difference significant at the $p < .05$ level). Furthermore, US middle-class employees in the state sector do not differ significantly from Swedish middle-class state employees on the anticapitalism scale (1.37 compared to 1.56).[19] The significantly more conservative profile of the US middle class in the United States, therefore, is largely concentrated in the private sector of the US economy. In Sweden, the difference between state and private sector middle-class employees is in the same direction as in the United States, but is not statistically significant. This suggests, perhaps, that under conditions of a large state sector, the middle class as a whole has greater ideological autonomy from the bourgeoisie, not simply those middle class actually employed by the state. The much greater role of

[19] If expert managers are excluded from these figures the comparison is 1.89 for Sweden compared to 1.52 for the United States.

Table 14.1. *Values on the anti-capitalism scale for class categories within state and private sectors*

	United States		Sweden		Japan[a]	
	State (N)	Private (N)	State (N)	Private (N)	State (N)	Private (N)
Categories in bourgeois or middle-class coalition						
Expert manager	-0.04 (8)	-3.59 (23)	-2.00 (10)	-2.55 (19)		
Expert supervisor	-0.05 (13)	-0.92 (47)	0.61 (18)	0.51 (17)		
Expert worker	0.62 (10)	-0.01 (26)	1.88 (25)	2.06 (29)		
Skilled manager	-2.13 (5)	-0.52 (44)	1.50 (8)	-0.42 (7)		
Skilled supervisor	2.56 (44)	0.85 (119)	2.29 (53)	1.78 (41)		
Nonskilled manager	4.00 (1)	-1.37 (12)	8.00 (1)	0.19 (8)		
Total	1.37 (80)	-0.23 (271)	1.56 (115)	0.76 (121)	1.92 (9)	1.44 (106)
Significance level of difference between state and private sectors (one-tailed test)[b]	$p < .005$		$p < .10$		$p < .35$	
Categories in working-class coalition						
Nonskilled supervisors	2.56 (14)	2.25 (112)	4.50 (20)	2.93 (35)		
Skilled workers	2.73 (69)	2.63 (127)	3.52 (106)	5.62 (112)		
Nonskilled workers	3.07 (96)	2.58 (485)	4.52 (174)	4.67 (287)		
Total	2.89 (179)	2.53 (724)	4.16 (300)	4.77 (434)	4.31 (21)	2.74 (283)
Significance level of difference between state and private sectors (two-tailed test)	$p < .15$		$p < .07$		$p < .04$	

Table 14.1. *(Continued)*

a. Because there were only 30 state employees in the Japanese sample it was not possible to make meaningful estimates of the differences in attitudes between state and private sectors within specific class locations.

b. Since the hypothesis for ideological differences between state and private sectors within the middle class has a specific direction, a one-tailed significance test is appropriate. For the working-class coalition, a two-tailed test is used since we do not have a directional hypothesis.

state employment in the Swedish class structure, therefore, may be one of the reasons why the Swedish bourgeois coalition is restricted to expert managers within the middle class whereas the American bourgeois coalition penetrates much deeper into managerial class locations. We will explore these issues in greater depth in chapter 15.

Unionization

A second proximate mechanism for consolidating the boundaries of a class formation is collective organization, of which unionization is probably the most important for the working-class formation. Where unions are broad-based and organizationally autonomous from the capitalist class, it would be expected that the working-class coalition would be more ideologically polarized with the capitalist class coalition than in cases where unions were weak and lacked real autonomy

Sweden and the United States offer clear contrasts in the nature of their respective union movements. While in both countries unions are relatively autonomous organizationally from the capitalist class – company unions are not significant features in either case – the Swedish labor movement has a much broader base than its American counterpart. In the American working-class coalition, 24.4% are union members compared to 82.6% in Sweden. What is even more striking, perhaps, is that in Sweden there is a high rate of unionization among middle-class contradictory class locations as well: 83.9% of the people in middle-class contradictory locations outside of the working-class coalition belong to unions in Sweden compared to only 10.3% in the United States. The low American figures partially reflect the overall weakness of the American labor movement, but, more significantly, they reflect legal barriers to unionization among people who are formally part of "management." This is reflected in the minuscule unionization rates among people in managerial class locations (expert managers, skilled managers and nonskilled managers): in the US out of ninety-two people in such positions in our sample there were only two union members for a rate of 2.2%, whereas in Sweden out of fifty-three people in managerial class locations, 60.4% belonged to unions.[20]

To what extent, then, does this higher level of unionization in Sweden help to explain the greater ideological polarization between working class and bourgeois class formations in Sweden than in the United States? Table 14.2 indicates that in both the United States and Sweden there are sharp ideological differences between union members and nonmembers within all class locations. These ideological differences are especially striking in Sweden among the various locations in the middle class. For most contradictory class locations in the middle class in Sweden, the difference between union members and nonmembers on the anticapitalism scale is between 4 and 5 points.[21] The result is that the difference between unionized workers and nonunionized expert managers is nearly 11 points on the scale.

For our present concerns, what is particularly relevant in these results is that within the working-class coalitions in Sweden and the United States, *non*union members in the two countries do not differ significantly on the anticapitalism scale. The mean value for the nonunion segment of the working-class coalition in the United States is 2.24 while in Sweden it is 2.41. The mean values for the unionized segments, on the other hand, do differ significantly (p <.001): 4.97 in Sweden and 3.72 in the United States.

The overall greater anticapitalism of the Swedish working-class coalition is thus partially due to the fact that Swedish union members are more anticapitalist than American union members and partially to the fact that the Swedish working-class coalition has a much higher rate of unionization. We can estimate the rough magnitudes of these components by playing a kind of counterfactual game in which we ask two questions:

[20] In the United States 80% of the unionized people in the middle-class coalition were in skilled supervisor positions. Looking more closely at these people, 65.5% of them are teachers or skilled craftsmen compared to only 24.6% of the nonunionized skilled supervisors. In terms of the overall structural properties of their class location it may well be the case that these people would better be classified with skilled workers rather than with other skilled supervisors. In any event, as Table 14.2 indicates, unionized skilled supervisors do not differ at all ideologically from unionized skilled workers, whereas nonunionized skilled supervisors do differ substantially from nonunionized skilled workers.

[21] The only exception is among nonskilled managers where the difference is only about 2 points.

Table 14.2. *Values on the anticapitalism scale for union members and nonmembers within class categories*

	United States		Sweden		Japan	
	Union member (N)	Nonunion member (N)	Union member (N)	Nonunion member (N)	Union member (N)	Nonunion member (N)
Categories in bourgeois or middle-class coalition						
Expert manager	-0.03 (1)	-2.74 (30)	-0.84 (20)	-5.75 (9)	0.67 (3)	0.26 (19)
Expert supervisor	2.59 (3)	-0.89 (58)	1.41 (29)	-3.5 (6)	0.56 (4)	0.71 (14)
Expert worker	1.45 (2)	0.08 (33)	2.36 (48)	-1.0 (6)	1.17 (6)	1.00 (5)
Skilled manager	5.0 (1)	-0.76 (48)	3.00 (8)	-2.14 (7)	2.25 (4)	2.06 (17)
Skilled supervisor	4.06 (29)	0.71 (134)	2.30 (89)	-2.0 (5)	3.71 (7)	2.08 (12)
Nonskilled manager	(0)	-1.09 (12)	2.25 (4)	0.10 (5)	3.60 (5)	1.37 (19)
Total	3.65 (36)	-.27 (315)	1.89 (198)	-2.72 (38)	2.21 (29)	1.23 (86)
Significance level of difference between union members and nonmembers (one-tailed test)[a]	p < .001		p < .001		not significant	
Total excluding expert managers	3.75	-0.01	2.19	-1.78	2.31	1.50
Significance level of difference between union members and nonmembers (one-tailed test)	p <.001		p <.001		not significant	

Table 14.2. (Continued)

	United States		Sweden		Japan	
	Union member (N)	Nonunion member (N)	Union member (N)	Nonunion member (N)	Union member (N)	Nonunion member (N)
Categories in US and Swedish working-class coalition						
Nonskilled supervisors	4.37 (19)	1.90 (107)	4.44 (45)	-0.73 (10)	1.62 (8)	1.54 (17)
Skilled workers	3.56 (59)	2.27 (136)	5.04 (189)	1.77 (29)	2.43 (27)	2.74 (39)
Nonskilled workers	3.71 (143)	2.32 (439)	5.00 (372)	2.97 (89)	3.13 (73)	3.03 (140)
Total	3.72 (222)	2.24 (681)	4.97 (606)	2.41 (128)	2.85 (108)	2.84 (196)
Significance level of difference between union and nonunion members (one-tailed test)	$p < .001$		$p < .001$		Not significant	
Total for Japanese working-class coalition (skilled supervisors, skilled workers, nonskilled workers)					3.00 (107)	2.91 (191)
Significance level of difference					Not significant	

a. Since the hypothesis for ideological differences between union and nonunion members has a specific direction, a one-tailed significance test is appropriate.

1 What would the mean value on the anticapitalism scale be for the US working-class coalition if (a) it had the unionization rate of the Swedish working-class coalition but (b) union members and nonmembers in the United States working-class coalition still had the same values on the scale that they currently have?

2 What would the mean value on the anticapitalism scale be for the US working-class coalition if (a) it had the unionization rate that it actually has, but (b) union members and nonmembers in the United States working-class coalition each had the values on the scale of their Swedish counterparts?

The first question imputes a mean value on the scale to the US working-class coalition under the assumption that all that changes is the unionization rate in the United States; the second question assumes that all that changes is ideology.

On the basis of these two questions we can decompose the total difference in values on the anticapitalism scale between the working-class coalitions in the two countries into three components: a component reflecting the differences in unionization rates (the distribution effect), a component reflecting the differences in ideologies, and an interaction component. The interaction term is a mathematical residual that occurs when the sum of the first two effects does not equal the total difference between the two countries. The results are presented in Table 14.3.

In this counterfactual game, just under 45% of the total difference in the anticapitalism scale between the American and Swedish working-class coalitions is attributable to the higher rate of unionization in Sweden, about 20% is attributable to the fact that Swedish union members are more radical than their American counterparts, and about 35% is attributable to the interaction between these two effects. The sheer fact of higher levels of unionization, therefore, contributes substantially to the greater ideological polarization between the Swedish working-class formation and bourgeois formation.[22]

This analysis, of course, is entirely static in character. The counterfactual is completely unrealistic as a dynamic proposition since the

[22] One other property of these results is worth noting: with only minor exceptions, the monotonic relationship between class location and anticapitalist consciousness holds in Sweden for both unionized and nonunionized employees. In the United States there are so few union members among locations in the middle class that we cannot evaluate monotonicity.

Table 14.3. *Decomposition of ideological difference between US and Swedish working-class coalitions*

Actual mean ideology scores within countries

(1)	US mean ideology score for working-class coalition	2.60
(2)	Sweden mean ideology score for working-class coalition	4.52
(3)	Total difference between US and Sweden mean ideology scores	1.92

Counterfactual ideology scores

(4)	US mean ideology score if US had Swedish union membership distribution + US union and nonunion mean ideology scores	3.40
(5)	US mean ideology score if US had Swedish union and nonunion mean ideology scores + US union membership distribution	3.04

Decomposition of actual national differences into components

(6)	Distribution effect (4)–(1)	0.86
(7)	Ideology effect (5)–(1)	0.44
(8)	Interaction effect (3)–(6)–(7)	0.62
(9)	Percentage of total difference between countries attributable to distribution effect (6) ÷ (3)	44.8%
(10)	Percentage of total difference between countries attributable to ideology effect (7) ÷ (3)	19.8%
(11)	Percentage of total difference between countries attributable to distribution effect (8) ÷ (3)	35.4%

degree of ideological polarization enters into the explanation of changes in the rate of unionization. In the dynamic micro-macro model elaborated in the previous chapter, class struggles transform class formations, but those class struggles are themselves constituted by the class practices of individuals with specific forms of consciousness. The greater ideological anticapitalism of union members in the working-class coalition in Sweden compared to the United States is thus both a consequence of the strength of the Swedish labor movement (and of the associated Social Democratic political party) and also part of the historical explanation for the strength of that movement. In the present research there is no way of sorting out these two sides of the dynamic process.[23]

[23]   To do so would require an historical-comparative framework in which we tracked changes in anticapitalist consciousness and unionization over time. In an ideal dataset of this sort we would have measures of anticapitalist attitudes of US and Swedish union members and nonmembers since before the period of the rapid expansion of unionization in Sweden. Such data, needless to say, do not exist.

Japan

Two features of the Japanese case which differentiate it from both the United States and Sweden need to be explained: first, the much lower degree of overall ideological polarization compared to the other two countries, and second, the absence of significant forms of ideological cleavage along the managerial dimension of the class structure.

The conventional image of Japan is of a society in which firms are organized on a relatively cooperative basis, with high levels of loyalty on the part of most workers, not just managers, and low levels of conflict. Managers in many firms spend significant time on the shop floor doing the work of ordinary workers prior to assuming their managerial responsibilities, which further mutes the sense of vertical antagonism. The pay-off, many observers have argued, is that Japanese firms are able to achieve large productivity gains because relatively little human energy is wasted in destructive conflict.[24]

As numerous commentators have noted, this popular image of Japan is misleading in several important respects. While it is true that general labor–management relations are relatively harmonious by international standards, these high levels of cooperation and loyalty mainly apply to workers in the core of the corporate economy with life-time employment security; the large number of part-time and temporary workers in the core firms, and the workers in the numerous small firms reap few of the benefits of this system (Chalmers 1989; Gordon 1985; Tsuda 1973). Furthermore, as various critical observers of the Japanese factory have stressed, these apparently harmonious relations are combined with intense competition among workers and pervasive surveillance and social control of work performance (Dohse, Jurgens and Malsch 1985; Kamata 1982).

The results for ideological differences between union members and nonmembers in Table 14.2 give us some clue about the underlying processes at work in the Japanese case. The most striking feature of the Japanese data is the virtual absence of ideological differences between union members and nonmembers, especially within the working-class coalition (regardless of whether we use the Japanese or the Swedish/American specifications of this coalition). Whereas in Sweden and the United States union members in the working-class coalition were

---

[24] For discussions of Japanese firms as embodying highly cooperative relations between managers and workers, see Dore (1987), Vogel (1979) and OECD (1977).

between 1.5 and 2 points more anticapitalist than nonmembers, in Japan these groups differ by only 0.09 points (using the Japanese specification of the working-class coalition). The contrast is equally striking for the middle class: in Sweden and the United States union members in the middle-class coalition were roughly 4 points more anticapitalist than nonmembers, whereas in Japan the figure is only about 0.8 points.

These results indicate that in Japan unions are not an organizational basis for formulating and representing distinctive class interests. As critics often note, Japanese unions function basically like company unions, being oriented toward serving corporate interests rather than defending the interests of workers. Without an autonomous organizational basis for the articulation of class interests, class formations become ideologically fuzzy, with diffuse boundaries and weak antagonisms. The result is a pattern of class formation with low levels of polarization that is especially muted along the authority dimension of class relations.

As in the explanation of the differences between Sweden and the United States, this is a purely static explanation: given the existence of company unions and the absence of any autonomous organizational basis for a working class formation, class formations in Japan will be relatively nonpolarized and poorly demarcated. Dynamically, of course, these ideological configurations themselves contribute to the absence of autonomous working-class organizations and act as obstacles to any strategies for transforming Japanese class formations. In these terms it is worth noting that Japanese class formations were not always so nonantagonistic and unpolarized. The early 1950s were a period of intense labor conflicts and mobilization, with militant unions and periodic widespread strikes. It was really only after the defeat and repression of these movements that the current pattern of quasi-company unions was consolidated and integrated with the current forms of "cooperative" labor–management relations.[25]

14.5 The micro-analysis of class consciousness

So far we have focussed on macro-patterns of class formation, using ideology as a criterion for mapping the boundaries of class formations.

---

[25] For discussions of the origins of the Japanese labor relations system in the post-World War II era, see Gordon (1985) and Fujita (1973).

Of course, the process by which individuals acquire their consciousness was implicated in this analysis, both because our measures were all based on responses by individuals to questionnaire items and because it is impossible to talk about the differences between groups without alluding to the differences in the interests and experiences of the individuals that make up those groups. Nevertheless, in the discussion so far we were not interested in explaining variation across individuals as such. It is to this issue that we now turn.

As discussed in section 14.2, we will engage in two different kinds of analyses of individual class consciousness. In the first, we will merge the data from all three countries into a single dataset and test the relative explanatory power of nationality compared to class. In the second we will investigate the differences in coefficients in more complex multivariate equations estimated separately for each country.

Additive country effects

Table 14.4 presents the standardized coefficients for the regression equations (described in section 14.2) in which the three national samples are merged into a single dataset. Equation 1 includes only class location, while Equation 2 adds to this past class experiences, age, sex, current class experiences and current material conditions. Since the three national samples are combined in these equations, the coefficients should be interpreted as averages of the coefficients within each country, weighted by the sample size from each country. In this combined sample, class location alone explains about 10% of the variance in values on the anticapitalism scale. This increases to about 17% when past class experiences, age, sex, current class experiences and current material conditions are added to the regression in Equation 2.

Equation 3 includes only the two country dummy variables. Together they account for only about 2% of the variance in the anti-capitalism scale. Equation 4 includes the country dummy variables along with class, and Equation 5 includes country with the other variables in Equation 2. Equation 5a presents the coefficients for Equation 5 in consolidated form in which a single coefficient is used to represent the combined effect of each group of variables in the original equation. These equations clearly indicate that country is a less important determinant of individuals' scores on the anticapitalism scale than is class location. Indeed, in Equation 5a the beta coefficient

Table 14.4. *Class determinants of class consciousness: three countries combined*

	B	s.e.	beta
Equation (1): Class only			
Class location[a]	1.00	.05	.32***
Adj. R² = .10			
Equation (2): Class + past class experiences + demographics + current class correlates			
Class location	1.00	.10	.20***
Working-class origins	.16	.17	.02
Capitalist origins	-.46	.20	-.04*
Previously self-employed	-.27	.26	-.02
Previously supervisor	-.24	.22	-.02
Previously unemployed	.93	.17	.10***
Gender (female = 1)	.20	.17	.02
Age	-.016	.006	-.05**
Personal income	-.14	.04	-.07***
Unearned income (dummy)	-.14	.17	-.01
Capitalist network	-.25	.08	-.06**
Working-class network	.07	.05	.02
Home owner	-.57	.17	-.07***
Union member	2.04	.17	.22***
Adj. R² = .17			
Equation (3): Country only			
Japan (0/1)	-0.81	.22	-.07***
US (0/1)	-1.59	.18	-.17***
Adj. R² =.02			
Equation (4): Class and country			
Class location	1.0	.05	.32***
Japan (0/1)	-0.45	.22	-.04*
US (0/1)	-1.41	.18	-.15***
Adj. R² =.12			

Table 14.4. *(Contined)*

	B	s.e.	Beta

Equation (5): Class + past class experiences + demographics + Current class correlates + country

	B	s.e.	Beta
Class location	1.00	.11	.18***
Working-class origins	.26	.17	.03
Capitalist origins	−.50	.20	−.05**
Previously self-employed	−.10	.26	−.01
Previously supervisor	.07	.23	.01
Previously unemployed	1.04	.17	.11***
Gender (female = 1)	.16	.17	.02
Age	−.016	.006	−.05**
Personal income	−.20	.04	−.10***
Unearned income (dummy)	−.09	.17	−.01
Capitalist network	−.18	.085	−.04*
Working-class network	.10	.05	.04*
Home owner	−.55	.17	−.06***
Union member	2.00	.20	.22***
Japan (0/1)	.89	.25	.08***
US (0/1)	−.43	.21	−.05*
Adj. R^2 = .18			

Equation (5a): Equation (5) with consolidated variables[b]

	Beta
Class location	.18***
Past class experiences	.13***
Demographics	.05**
Current class correlates	.15***
Union member	.22***
Nation	.11***
Adj. R^2 = .18	

Significance levels (one-tailed tests since predictions for most coefficients are directional):
*** $p < .001$ ** $p < .01$ * $p < .05$

a. Since in this equation the separate coefficients for each of the eleven dummy variables used to measure class location are not of interest, the dummy variables are replaced with an aggregate class variable with a single coefficient representing the total relationship between class location and consciousness. See Chapter 14 methodological appendix, section 4, for details. The aggregate class location variable always has an unstandardized coefficient of 1.0. The standardized (beta) coefficient for this variable indicates its relative explanatory power compared to the other variables in the equation.

b. The aggregated clusters of variables – past class experiences, demographics and current class correlates – are constructed in the same manner as the aggregated class location variable described in footnote *a* above. See methodological appendix, section 4.

for country is smaller than any of the class related variables, and in Equation 4, the R^2 for country is a fifth of the R^2 for class location alone in Equation 1. At least within this sample of countries, if you want to predict an individual's class consciousness, therefore, it is more important to know what class they are in than to know what country they are from.

Cross-national comparisons of micro-equations

In Table 14.4, country is treated simply as an additive variable. Needless to say, from what we already know about the cross-national variations in class formation, this is an unsatisfactory way of modeling the effects of nation on individual consciousness. A more appropriate model involves country interactions in which we estimate the regression equations separately within each national sample and examine cross-national differences in coefficients. The results are presented in Table 14.5.

There are several striking contrasts in these equations across the three countries. First, the overall predictive power of the equation is strongest in Sweden and, by a considerable margin, weakest in Japan. In Sweden, Equation 2 explains 24% of the variance in the anticapitalism scale, which is quite a respectable R^2 for an attitudinal dependent variable. Since a good part of the observed variance in attitude scales is always due to measurement problems and random variation across individuals, the "explainable" variance is much less than the total variance.[26] Accounting for a quarter of the total variance in an attitude variable thus indicates that this dependent variable is quite closely associated with the independent variables in the equation. The 16% R^2 in the American equation is also fairly characteristic of regressions on attitude variables. The 8% explained variance for Japan, however, is rather low, indicating that these variables for Japan do not account for much of the variance on the anticapitalism scale.

Second, each of the blocks of variables closely linked to class predicts consciousness more strongly in Sweden than in the other two coun-

---

[26] By "random variation" I mean responses that are affected by such things as inattention during the interview and by purely idiosyncratic responses to particular words in items. It is of course impossible to distinguish empirically "explainable" from "unexplainable" variance in a variable, but it is important to remember that the ratio between these two itself varies across different kinds of variables in survey research.

Table 14.5. *Class location and class consciousness in Sweden, the United States and Japan (beta coefficients)*

	Sweden	United States	Japan
Equation (1)			
Class location[a]	.41***	.31***	.26***
Adjusted R^2	.16	.09	.05
Equation (2)			
Class location	.27***	.16***	.13**
Past class experiences			
Working-class origin (0/1)	.04	-.01	.07*
Capitalist origin (0/1)	-.06*	-.05	-.02
Previously self-employed (0/1)	-.06*	.00	.07
Previously supervisor (0/1)	-.06*	.05	-.01
Unemployment experience (0/1)	.13***	.09***	.04
Current class experiences			
Capitalist network	-.07*	-.04	.01
Working-class network	.06*	.02	-.02
Union member (0/1)	.23***	.17***	.07
Consumption			
Personal income	-.05	-.13***	-.19***
Unearned income (0/1)	.01	-.02	.03
Home owner (0/1)	-.07**	-.05*	-.01
Demographics			
Gender (female = 1)	-.02	.02	.06
Age	.02	-.12***	.00
Adjusted R^2	.24	.16	.08
Equation (2a) with aggregated clusters of variables[b]			
Class	.27***	.16***	.13**
Past class experiences	.18***	.11***	.12**
Current class experiences	.11***	.05*	.03
Union member	.23***	.17***	.07
Consumption	.09***	.15***	.20***
Demographics	.03	.12***	.06
(N)	(1,089)	(1,471)	(608)

Significance levels (one-tailed test since predictions of most coefficients are directional):

***p < .001   **p < .01   *p < .05

a. See footnote a, Table 14.4 and methodological appendix, section 4 for explanation.

b. See footnote b, Table 14.4 and methodological appendix, section 4 for explanation.

tries; nearly every variable closely tied to class is more strongly related to consciousness in Sweden than in the US and, especially, Japan. The set of class dummy variables by themselves explains 16% of the variance in the attitude scale in Sweden, compared to 9% in the US and 5% in Japan. In the multivariate equation (Equation 2), the coefficient for the aggregated block of class location dummy variables is 0.27 in Sweden, 0.16 in the US and 0.13 in Japan. Similar differences occur for past class experiences, current class experiences and union membership. Class location and class experiences, therefore, seem to shape consciousness most pervasively in Sweden and least pervasively in Japan.

Third, those variables which tap into consumption rather than directly into class are better predictors in the United States and Japan than in Sweden. Taken as a group, the coefficient for the consumption variables is 0.09 in Sweden compared to 0.15 in the US and 0.20 in Japan. This is consistent with the interpretation of the results in chapter 10 concerning the class identities of married women in the labor force in Sweden and the United States: relative to Sweden, class in the US appears to be structured subjectively more around the sphere of consumption than the sphere of production. At least on the basis of the results for the anticapitalism scale, this appears to be even more strongly the case for Japan.

Finally, in no country is gender a significant determinant of class consciousness in the multivariate equation, and only in the United States does age have a significant effect. I do not have a specific interpretation of the age coefficient for the US. Most likely this reflects an effect of historical cohorts in which the younger cohorts of Americans, perhaps especially the "60s generation," are more critical of capitalism than older cohorts. If this is the correct interpretation of the age coefficient, then such generational cleavages in ideology appear stronger in the US than in the other two countries, perhaps indicating that the experience of the civil rights and antiwar movements of the 1960s constituted a greater discontinuity in American political life than has occurred in either of the other two countries.

14.7 A brief note on class, race, gender and consciousness

Because of the constraints of sample size, it is impossible with the Comparative Class Analysis Project data to explore systematically the ways class, race and gender interact in the formation of class consciousness. Nevertheless, it is worth looking briefly at the overall pattern of variation in consciousness across race, gender and class categories in the United States since these results are quite suggestive and pose interesting questions for further research.

Figure 14.5 presents the mean values on the anticapitalism scale for black and white males and females in the "extended" working class and the "middle" class.[27] The most striking feature of these results is that within classes (especially within the working class), racial differences in class consciousness are much greater than gender differences. Within the working class, there are virtually no differences in the values on the anticapitalism scale between white men (2.41) and white women (2.38) or between black men (3.8) and black women (3.5), whereas there are sharp differences between blacks and whites. Indeed, the differences between black and white workers within the US is of the same order of magnitude as the difference between American and Swedish workers.

It is always possible that the explanation of why these racial divisions in consciousness within the working class are greater than gender differences is simply a result of the internal heterogeneity of the class categories. Within the broad category "extended working class" in Figure 14.5, black men and women tend to be concentrated in the most proletarianized and exploited segments. The more anticapitalist value for black workers, therefore, could simply be an artifact of the racial differences in composition of this category. These compositional effects would be much more muted between men and women within racial categories because of the effects of household class compositions on class consciousness.[28]

A more interesting explanation centers on the linkage between different forms of oppression in people's lives. A good argument can be made that racial inequality is much more closely linked to class oppression than is gender inequality. In its earliest forms in the United States, racial oppression was virtually equivalent to a specific class relation, slavery. While the race–class linkage has weakened over the

---

[27] The "extended" working class consists of nonskilled workers, skilled workers and nonskilled supervisors. The middle class consists of all types of managers and experts plus skilled supervisors.

[28] In the case of racial differences in the degree of proletarianization within the extended working class, household compositions will tend to reinforce the effects of individual class locations, whereas for gender differences, household compositions will tend to neutralize these effects.

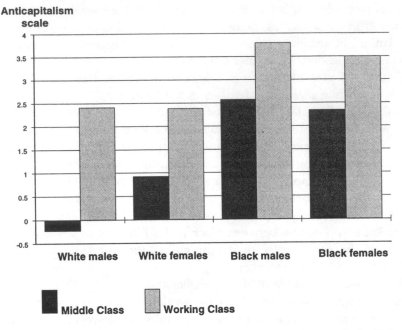

Figure 14.5 *Race and gender differences in class consciousness in the United States*

past 100 years, it is still the case that the content of the disadvantages racially oppressed groups experience are deeply linked to class.[29] Because of this intimate link to class, racial oppression itself may tend to generate a heightened critical consciousness around issues of class. Gender inequality is less closely linked to class, and thus the experience of gender oppression is less immediately translated into a critical consciousness of class inequality. This may help explain why men and women within the working class have similar levels of class consciousness, whereas black workers are more anticapitalist than white workers.

One other aspect of the results in Figure 14.5 should be noted: class differences between the working class and the middle class are considerably greater among white men than among white women or

---

[29] This does not mean that racial oppression is simply a form of class oppression; racial inequality, like gender inequality, is reproduced by a set of distinctive mechanisms that are not reducible to class. Nevertheless, the characteristic form of racial subordination is the allocation of people from racially oppressed groups to particularly exploited class locations.

blacks. Among black men and women, workers score on average about 1.2 points more on the anticapitalism scale than do people in the middle class. Among white women the figure is about 1.5 points higher. Among white men, in contrast, workers score 2.6 points higher than the middle class. As in the results for racial differences within classes, these results could be generated in part by compositional differences in class distributions within groups: among white men a higher proportion of the "middle-class" category consists of expert managers than is the case for any of the other groups, and this could account for the sharper ideological difference between the working class and the aggregated "middle class" among white males. But these results could also suggest that, at least in the United States, the class model which we have been using works better among white men than other categories. When class intersects other forms of oppression in the lives of people, its effects on consciousness may be confounded by the effects of these other relations. In order to pursue these conjectures, research on much larger samples will be needed.

14.8 Conclusions

The relationship between class structure and class formation at the macro-level of analysis and between class location and class consciousness at the micro-level are at the core of class analysis. The Marxist claim that class has pervasive consequences for social conflict and social change crucially hinges on the ways in which class structures shape class formations and class locations shape class consciousness. In these terms, the most important general conclusion from the analysis in this chapter is the high degree of variability in these relationships across highly developed capitalist economies. While in very general terms one can say that there is a certain commonality in the patterns of class formation and in the association of class location to class consciousness in the three countries we have examined, what is equally striking is the extent to which these countries vary.

At one end of the spectrum is Sweden. At the macro-level Sweden is characterized by a pattern of class formation which is both quite polarized and in which there are clear demarcations between the three class coalitions we examined. At the micro-level, class location and class experiences, past and present, appear to strongly shape the attitudes of individuals toward class issues. Class thus appears to powerfully impinge on the lives and subjectivities of people in Swedish society.

At the other extreme is Japan. At the macro-level, class formations are neither very polarized ideologically, nor sharply demarcated. At the micro-level, although class remains significantly associated with consciousness, the effects are much weaker and mainly confined to the indirect effects of class via the sphere of consumption. While the class character of Japanese society may be of great importance for understanding the rhythm of its economic development, the constraints on state policies, the nature of political parties and so on, at the micro-level, variation in class location and class experiences does not appear to pervasively shape variations in class consciousness.

The United States falls somewhere between these two cases, probably somewhat closer to Sweden than to Japan. The patterns of class formation are rather like those in Sweden, only more muted, with a broader bourgeois class coalition and a working-class coalition that is closer to the middle class. At the micro-level, class location and experiences do systematically shape consciousness, but less strongly than in Sweden and with a greater relative impact of the sphere of consumption.

Methodological appendix

1 Methodological issues in constructing the class-consciousness scale

Coding strength of agreement/disagreement

In coding the responses to the attitude questions used in constructing the anticapitalism scale a decision had to be made about whether or not to code the *strength* of agreement or disagreement. In other analyses using these data involving only Sweden and the United States, I simply dichotomized the responses on the grounds that there was no reason to assume that one person's "somewhat" in fact constituted a weaker response than another person's "strongly." The contrast in apparent strength of opinion could simply reflect personality characteristics of the respondents, some people being more tentative in their public display of opinions than others. In this chapter, however, I decided to use the full range of responses to the questions. There were two reasons for this decision. First, because of the inclusion of Japan in the analysis of this chapter, there were fewer attitude items available than in the analyses involving only the

United States and Sweden and this reduced the variance in the scale constructed on the basis of these items. Differentiating values on the basis of strength of agreement/disagreement increases the variance somewhat. Secondly, as an empirical matter, the explained variances in the micro-level equations were somewhat higher, especially in Japan, when the distinction between "strongly" and "somewhat" was coded.

Yea-saying biases

One potential problem with these items is that all of them are worded in the same ideological direction: agreeing with the item reflects an anticapitalist view, disagreeing with them a procapitalist view. It clearly would have been desirable for the items to have been balanced in positive and negative wording to avoid any possible biases due to "yea saying," the tendency for some individuals to agree with every question regardless of content. Methodological research on questionnaire design has indicated that "yea saying" seems to be somewhat more of an issue among relatively less educated people, and since education is correlated with class location, it is possible that there are yea-saying biases linked to location in the class structure.[30] This could potentially affect our analyses of class differences in forms of class consciousness. In the larger set of attitude items in the survey such balance exists, but it just happened that in the subset of questions which were common to all three of these countries and which dealt with the specific problem of pro and anticapitalist attitudes, all of the items were worded in the anticapitalist direction. Since there is no reason to believe that yea-saying biases are a bigger problem in one country than in another, this problem should not distort our comparative analyses, but nevertheless it remains a potential source of distortion in our results.

Simple additive scales vs. complex factor analytic scales

In earlier research on these same data (Wright, Howe and Cho 1989) comparing only the United States and Sweden, a variety of more complex scales were also constructed using confirmatory factor analytic measurement models (LISREL IV). There are analytical and interpretative advantages and disadvantages to each of these measurement

---

[30] See Watson (1990) for a review of the relevant methodological literature on yea-saying biases and a specific discussion of the problem of yea-saying in the US data in this project.

strategies. The advantage of the simple additive scale is that the absolute values on the scale have the same direct, *prima facie* interpretation across countries. If the mean value for workers in the United States is much lower than in Sweden, for example, we can conclude that on average they take the anticapitalist ideological position on fewer of these items than do their Swedish counterparts. The metric is the same in both countries and the interpretation of magnitudes in the results straightforward. In the confirmatory factor analytic scales, the metric is different in each country which makes it problematic to compare scale values across countries. The disadvantage of such simple additive scales is that, unlike scales generated by confirmatory factor analysis, they obliterate potential multidimensionality of the attitudes we are studying and are insensitive to the different measurement properties in the various countries of the relationship between item responses and underlying conceptual variables.

The present analysis relies exclusively on the simple additive scale. Since our interest is primarily comparative, the noncomparability of the metrics in the LISREL scales is a significant disadvantage. It could also be argued that even if the confirmatory factor analysis demonstrated that our indicators of ideology tap conceptually distinct dimensions in measurement models of the attitude structure of individuals, it is nevertheless appropriate to map out ideological coalitions using all of the indicators in a one-dimensional scale. The working-class coalition is precisely the coalition of *positions* that are basically similar in overall ideological orientations across these dimensions. Ideological coalitions are socially constituted *collectivities* that somehow transcend the cognitive multidimensionality of the ideological orientations of the *individuals* within such coalitions. This kind of ideological coalition may thus be better measured by the simple additive scale than by the more technically sophisticated LISREL variables. In any case, in the earlier analysis using these complex scales for Sweden and the United States, none of the substantive conclusions were different using the more complex measurement strategy (see Wright, Howe and Cho 1989 for a presentation of the data from both kinds of scales). Rather than encumber the present discussion with a variety of different scales that are tapping essentially the same concepts, the analysis is restricted to the simpler, more transparent variable, the additive anticapitalism scale.

2 Strategy for measuring ideological class formations

In order to use class-relevant attitudes as a way of identifying the patterns of class formation within a class structure we need to develop an analytical strategy that enables us to group the various locations in the class typology into ideological clusters. The strategy we will use is illustrated in Appendix Figure 14.1:

1 The means on the anticapitalism scale are calculated for each of the twelve locations in the class structure matrix.

2 The range between the means for the working-class location of the matrix and the capitalist location of the matrix is divided into three equal segments. These segments are called the working-class ideological segment, the middle-class ideological segment and the capitalist-class ideological segment.

3 Every location in the matrix can then be located in one of these three segments.

4 On this basis three potential coalitions are constructed: a working-class coalition, a bourgeois coalition and a middle-class coalition. It is possible, of course, that there will be no locations in the third of these if the class structure is highly polarized between the extreme values.

There may be situations in which this procedure generates an unrealistic picture. For example, in the pattern of values across the locations of the matrix illustrated in Figure 14.1, the working-class location has a mean value on the anticapitalism scale of +7 and the capitalist class location, −5. This yields a bourgeois ideological segment of values between −5 and −1, a middle-class segment between −1 and +3 and a working-class segment between +3 and +7. If we mechanically apply the procedure specified above, then class locations F and G would be in the middle-class coalition, location D would be in the bourgeois coalition, and category E would be indeterminate (because it is on the dividing point between the capitalist and middle-class segments). A more realistic characterization of these data, however, would treat categories D, E, F and G as constituting the middle-class ideological coalition, since categories D and E are so much closer to the actual values of the two locations in the middle-class ideological segment. To allow for this kind of situation, an additional procedure has been added to the strategy:

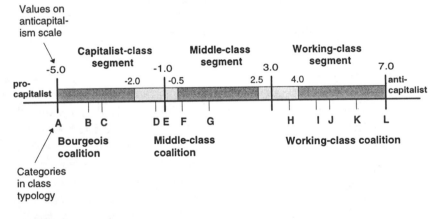

Figure Appendix 14.1 *Example illustrating method for constructing map of ideological class coalition.*

5 The range within an ideological segment is divided into a "core" zone consisting of 75% of the range and a "marginal" zone consisting of 25% of the range. (For the middle-class ideological segment, this 25% is equally split between the two boundaries of the segment.) If a class location falls into a marginal zone, then the distance between that location and the nearest locations in the core zones of each adjacent segment is calculated. The marginal location is then considered part of the coalition with the nearest location in a core zone.

In Figure 14.1, three locations, D, E and H, fall into marginal zones. For categories D and E we then compare the distances between each of them and, on the one hand, category C (the closest category in the core zone of the capitalist ideological segment), and, on the other hand, category F (the closest category in the core zone of the middle-class ideological segment). Since they are both closer to F, we treat these categories as part of the middle-class ideological coalition. Similarly, since category H is closer to I (in the core zone of the working-class segment) than it is to category G, we place it in the working-class segment.

It is important, of course, not to reify this kind of procedure. The underlying logic is that class formations exist "in reality," but that our observations only give us indirect indicators. Inevitably, then, the procedures we adopt for aggregating these observations contain an element of arbitrariness. If we adopted different formal criteria we could certainly generate different apparent configurations of coalitions. The resulting categories, therefore, should not be confused with the reality they attempt to tap. All interpretations of the resulting patterns, therefore, must be attentive to the problem of slippage between the real patterns of class formation and our formalized map of ideological coalitions.

In this strategy of analysis, a class coalition is defined as the set of *locations* that fall within a given segment of the ideological spectrum between capitalists and workers. Within every class location, of course, there will be individuals who differ radically from this norm. There are individual capitalists whose own ideological orientation would firmly place them within the working-class coalition. Our interest here, however, is not with the ideological profiles of individuals as such, but with the contours of class formations as reflected in the ideological orientations characteristic of different class locations.

It would obviously be desirable to conduct formal statistical tests of confidence intervals for these descriptions. Suppose that in the data for one of the countries the score for the working-class location was +4.0 and for the capitalist location was −2.0. The cut-off points for three ideological segments would thus be +2.0 and 0. A location whose value was 2.5 would then fall in the working-class ideological coalition, whereas a location that was at 1.5 would fall into the middle-class coalition. How confident should we be that the observed value of 2.5 is in fact greater than the criterion threshold of 2.0? It turns out that with a relatively small sample, the estimates of the standard errors for this kind of test are almost invariably quite large. The problem is that we are not simply testing the difference between two sample means – i.e. the difference in the mean values for two locations in the matrix. We are examining the difference between the mean in one location and a value – the criterion value that distinguishes coalitions – that is itself estimated from the means of two other locations. The standard error of this difference is thus derived from the standard errors of the estimates for three locations, one of which (the capitalist location) has a relatively small sample size and thus a relatively large standard error.[31]

Because of these difficulties, I do not attempt to calculate confidence intervals for our descriptive claims and, accordingly, treat the results with some caution.

3 Variables used in multivariate models

1. *Class location*. This variable is measured by eleven dummy variables representing the twelve categories in the class structure matrix.

---

[31] An earlier published version of this analysis (Wright, Howe and Cho, 1989) adopted a somewhat different strategy for estimating confidence intervals. For each cell in the matrix we simply asked whether or not it differed significantly from the polarized cell to which it was closest. If it did not, then it was considered a partner in that ideological coalition. This way of carving up the matrix is inadequate because it makes the descriptive picture of the boundaries of class formations too sensitive to sample size. With a big enough sample which would make small differences "significant," no two cells would be in the same coalition. This strategy thus confuses the problem of the confidence level one has in a given descriptive result with the task of producing the descriptions themselves. In the current procedure, the descriptive map of class formations is generated independently of sample size, simply on the basis of assessing how close a given cell is to the three test values. With a large sample our confidence that this map was not due to chance would be greater, but the map itself would not be affected by sample size.

2. *Past class experiences.* These variables tap different aspects of a person's class biography:

   (a) *Working-class origin*: dummy variable, 1 = head of household at age 16 was in a working-class job.
   (b) *Capitalist origin*: dummy variable, 1 = head of household at age 16 was an employer.
   (c) *Previously self-employed*: dummy variable, 1 = self-employed in some previous job.
   (d) *Previously supervisor*: dummy variable, 1 = supervisor in some previous job.
   (e) *Previously unemployed*: dummy variable, 1 = involuntarily unemployed at some point in the past.

3. *Current class experiences and material conditions.* These variable tap aspects of current class experience not directly measured by current class location.

   (a) *Capitalist class network*: a five-point scale measuring the density of interpersonal ties to the capitalist class as measured by the class of three closest friends and spouse class. 0 = no friend or spouse is an employer; 4 = 100% of friends and spouse are employers.
   (b) *Working-class network*: a five-point scale measuring the density of interpersonal ties to the working class as measured by the class of three closest friends and spouse. 0 = no friend or spouse is in the working class; 4 = 100% of friends and spouse are in the working class.
   (c) *Union member*: dummy variable, 1 = union member.
   (d) *Personal annual income*: personal earnings plus income from all other sources.
   (e) *Home owner*: dummy variable, 1 = owns home.
   (f) *Unearned income from investments*: dummy variable, 1 = earns some income from investments other than bank savings.

4. *Demographic variables*

   (a) *Gender*: 1 = female
   (b) *Age*

5. *Country.* Two dummy variables (Japan, US) representing the three countries.

4 Generating single coefficients for groups of variables

In the micro-level equations predicting individual consciousness we are not interested in the separate values of the coefficients for each of the class location dummy variables (which measure the difference between that class location and the left-out category), but rather with the overall effect of class location as a variable (i.e. with the effects represented by the entire set of class location dummy variables). In the presentation of the results, therefore, the eleven individual coefficients are replaced with a single standardized regression coefficient representing the combined effect of class location. This substitution is accomplished by estimating the OLS regression equation with the eleven dummy variables representing class location in the standard way and then constructing a new variable which is the weighted sum of the unstandardized coefficients multiplied by each of the class dummy variables. This variable is then substituted for the original set of dummy variables in the equation and a new equation estimated. In this new equation the aggregate class location variable will always have an unstandardized coefficient of 1.0. The standardized (beta) coefficient for this variable indicates its relative explanatory power compared to the other variables in the equation. The R^2 for this equation is exactly the same as in the original equation with the eleven dummy variables.

A similar procedure is adopted to generate single standardized regression coefficients of the joint effect for the variables within each of the broad groups of variables used in equation 2: *past class experiences; current class experiences and material conditions; demographic variables; country*. These consolidated coefficients facilitate comparisons of relative explanatory power across groups of variables, both within countries and across countries.

15 Class, state employment and consciousness

In Chapter 14, I argued that one of the crucial factors underlying the different patterns of class formation in the United States and Sweden was state employment. More specifically, I argued that state employment may help to explain the greater ideological demarcation between the middle class and the capitalist class in Sweden by reducing the material dependency of a significant segment of the middle class from the capitalist class. In this chapter we will pursue these issues in much greater detail by examining a broader range of indicators of consciousness and a more differentiated account of state employment.

As many commentators have noted, one of the most striking developments in modern societies is the growth of the state. Whether measured by the proportion of GNP that is appropriated by the state in taxation, by the range of social and economic activities in which the state plays a significant role, or by the size of state employment, the state in every industrial society has grown enormously over the past 100 years.

Given this massive growth of the state, one might have thought that the empirical study of the attitudes and ideological orientations of state employees, and especially the differences between attitudes of state and private sector employees, would have become a significant focus of sociological research. This simply has not occurred, at least in the American literature. There are, of course, numerous case studies of the practices and ideologies of people in specific state agencies (schools, police, the military, the courts, etc.). There are countless studies of such things as the transformations of state institutions, the social and economic impacts of state policies, the decisionmaking processes within the state, and the relative autonomy or nonautonomy of state "elites" from manipulation by outside forces. There is a veritable

459

industry of "bringing the state back in" which argues that the institutional properties of state apparatuses and the strategies of state managers are central determinants of state policies. And while there is much historical and sociological writing that discusses interests and ideologies of people in the top political directorate of the state, the research that explores these issues for ordinary state employees and compares them to comparable employees in the private sector is extremely limited.[1]

This lack of sustained attention to the mass of state employees reflects, I suspect, the common tendency among political sociologists to regard the state either as an organization instrumentally controlled by directing elites (whether that elite be viewed as top level state managers, professional politicians or a ruling class outside of the state itself) or as a matrix of apparatuses with a particular institutional structure. However, "the state" is no more simply made up of elites and apparatuses than capitalism is made up solely of capitalists and firms. Just as it is essential to understand the forms of consciousness and strategies of workers and managers in order to understand the dynamics of capitalist firms, so too it is important to understand the ideologies and strategies of the mass of state employees and officials in order to understand the internal dynamics of states. Because of their role in the practical implementation of state policies, this is especially important for the case of what I will call the "state middle class" – the broad ranks of experts and bureaucrats in the state between routinized state workers and state "elites."[2] Any comprehensive sociology of the

[1]   There are a few studies which compare ideological orientations of state and private sector employees in the context of some other agenda of analysis. In particular, some empirical studies of the "New Class" (e.g. Brint 1984; Ladd 1979; Wuthnow and Schrum 1983) have included some marginal analyses of attitudinal correlates of state employment or occupational "government dependence" (to use Wuthnow and Schrum's expression). These studies, however, did not systematically explore differences between state employees and private sector employees outside of the New Class, and even the discussion of state employment differences within the New Class was quite cursory. The few studies directly on the topic of state/private comparisons have quite narrow empirical focusses and are generally on very restricted samples (for example, Bennett and Orzechowski 1983; Gramlich and Rubinfeld 1980; Rainey, Traut and Blunt 1986; and the qualitative interview study by Reinerman, 1987). I found no studies which systematically explore a general array of attitudinal differences between employees in the state and private sectors and no research at all which explores the interaction of class and state employment, let alone research that has looked at these issues cross-nationally.

[2]   I will use the rather vague term "state elite" to designate the top directorate of state institutions. By using this term I am not taking a theoretical stand on the question of

state must attempt to understand the interests, strategies and ideologies of the state employees who actually do the work of the state.

The overarching empirical question which we will address in this chapter is quite simple: are there systematic ideological differences within and across classes between the state and private sectors of employment? More specifically, we will examine two clusters of attitudes – attitudes in support of increasing state intervention to solve various social and economic problems (to be referred to as "prostatist consciousness") and attitudes in support of workers in conflicts with employers and critical of existing economic institutions (to be referred to as "anticapitalist consciousness"). The statistical task of the research is to see how these two clusters of attitudes vary (1) across state and private sectors of employment; (2) across class locations within state and within private sectors; and (3) across sectors within classes.

The next section will briefly explore the concept of "the state" as it bears on the problem of the interests and consciousness of state employees. Section 15.2 will then lay out a series of orienting hypotheses which will guide the empirical investigation. Sections 15.3 and 15.4 will then present and interpret the results of the data analysis.

15.1 Conceptualizing state employment

In the general model of class structure and class consciousness in Chapter 13, class consciousness was seen as shaped by the material interests and lived experiences of individuals by virtue of their class locations. Here we are exploring one additional set of material conditions which impact on lived experience and interests: the nature of the employing organization in which people work. There are many ways in which one could differentiate employing organizations: large corporations vs. small firms, firms in different economic sectors, etc. In this chapter we will focus on only one theoretically salient distinction: state vs. private sectors of employment. The underlying assumption is that individuals employed by the state potentially have different material interests and lived experiences from individuals in the private capitalist sector even when, in other respects, they might be thought of as in the same class location.

whether or not this elite constitutes a "class," a "fraction" of a class, or an elite outside of class relations. Such questions can be bracketed in this chapter since our empirical focus is exclusively on the working class and the "middle" class in the state and private sectors.

The simplest way of approaching this problem would be to treat state employment itself as a unitary category. There are, after all, certain things which nearly all state employees have in common simply by virtue of being employed by the state. Above all, their wages are largely paid out of taxes, and thus they have a different relationship to private profits and public taxation than employees of capitalist firms. In many cases state employees also enjoy various forms of legally backed job security unavailable in the private sector. One might expect, therefore, that the crude distinction between public and private employment by itself could constitute a significant division of material interests and, correspondingly, consciousness.

A more complex perspective sees the state itself as internally divided into apparatuses which have quite different functional relationships to the capitalist economy. Specifically, instead of treating "state employment" as a unitary category, "the state" can be divided into two broad kinds of apparatuses: the *capitalist political superstructure*, and *decommodified state services*. The first of these sectors consists of those state institutions within which the "function" of reproducing capitalist social relations is particularly important.[3] This includes such apparatuses as the police, the courts, the administrative organs of government, the military, the legislature, etc. This does not imply that the sole function of these institutions is sustaining capitalism, or even that in every situation capitalist reproduction is their primary function. What is claimed, however, is that under most conditions the functional relation between the state and capitalist social relations in these institutions is particularly important.

In classical Marxism, the entire state apparatus was viewed as constituting such a superstructure. Indeed, in the most extreme interpretations, this was the only important function of the state. Most contemporary theorists in the Marxist tradition no longer analyze the state in such stark, unitary functionalist terms. The state is seen as fragmented in various ways, with different types of apparatuses organized around different principles. In particular, it is possible to identify a subset of state apparatuses which are sites for the direct

---

[3] The use of functional language to describe properties and activities of the state is fraught with difficulties. I am not suggesting here that there is any homeostatic mechanism which guarantees that these specific apparatuses of the state will effectively perform these functions. All that is being claimed is that in addition to whatever else they do, these apparatuses generally play a particularly important role in sustaining capitalist social relations.

production of use values – goods and services which meet people's needs of various sorts. State apparatuses which specialize in such "decommodified" (i.e. nonmarket) production would include, above all, such things as public health, education, publicly owned utilities, public recreation. Rather than being viewed as exclusively part of the *political superstructure* of capitalism, such institutions should be regarded as also constituting elements of an *embryonic postcapitalist mode of production* located within the state.[4]

Of course, many state institutions combine both "functions" – contributing to the reproduction of capitalist social relations and satisfying human needs of various sorts by producing decommodified goods and services. For example, Marxists have often argued that education is, in certain respects, part of the ideological superstructure of capitalism insofar as it tends to propagate ideological orientations compatible with capitalism. Social welfare agencies may simultaneously provide real services to satisfy people's needs and reproduce capitalism by blocking alternatives. Nevertheless, it is possible to loosely distinguish between those state apparatuses within which the superstructural aspects are particularly strong and those within which the production of goods and services that satisfy people's needs is particularly central.[5] The latter we will refer to as *the state service sector*, the former as *the state political sector*.

---

4   These institutions are *post*-capitalist because the production of the goods and services in question follow a distinctively noncommodified, noncapitalist logic. The production is not oriented toward exchange or profit maximization, but toward the direct satisfaction of needs. This means that the quantity and quality of the products and services are determined through a fundamentally *political* process of contestation rather than through a market. To be sure, within a capitalist *society* such production will be highly constrained by capitalist institutions, and thus it is appropriate to call this an *embryonic* state mode of production rather than a fully developed one existing alongside capitalism. Nevertheless, to be constrained by a capitalist logic is not the same as having a capitalist logic, and it is for this reason that state-centered politically mediated production can be viewed as postcapitalist. For a further discussion of these arguments, see Wright (1994: ch. 6). A similar, although not identical, distinction between different types of state institutions has been made by Hoff (1985). This distinction, however, is quite different from that of Louis Althusser (1971) in his famous essay "Ideology and Ideological State Apparatuses." In Althusser's analysis both the "repressive apparatuses of the state" and the "ideological apparatuses of the state" are characterized exclusively as serving the function of reproducing capitalist relations.

5   The distinction between these two "functions" performed by state apparatuses – superstructural functions (reproducing capitalist relations) and productive functions (producing use-values) – is not identical to another common functional distinction Marxists sometimes make in discussions of the state: the *legitimation* function and

The core data analysis in this chapter revolves around the interaction of state employment and class location in shaping consciousness. Within each of the two subsectors of the state it is possible, in principle, to define the same matrix of class locations as we have been exploring among employees in the private sector. Unfortunately, because of the relatively small sample size of state employees, especially in the American data, for the data analyses here we had to combine all of the "contradictory locations" within class relations into a single "middle-class" category. The resulting set of categories we will use in the chapter are presented in Table 15.1.

15.2 Orienting hypotheses

This research on state employees was not initially orchestrated as a "test" of precisely formulated contending hypotheses about how ideological orientations should vary by class and employment in state and private sectors. Given the lack of sustained attention to the subject in the literature, the research was basically exploratory and inductive rather than driven by an attempt at adjudicating between well-established rival theories. Nevertheless, it will be helpful to lay out the broad outlines of what might be termed "orienting hypotheses" derived from the conceptual framework that informs the analysis.

The central empirical objective of the research is to map out ideological differences between incumbents in the categories within Table 15.1 on the two dimensions of ideology we are considering, prostatist consciousness and anticapitalist consciousness. Of particular importance are the bottom two rows in the table, since for these categories we can explore both class differences within sectors and sector differences within classes.

There are many reasons why one might anticipate ideological differences to occur across the categories of these tables. People in different class-by-sector categories could have very different interests (material as well as nonmaterial interests) by virtue of the constraints

the *accumulation* function (e.g. Offe 1984; O'Connor 1973). Some productive functions may not serve any particular needs of accumulation as such – for example, public provision of recreation facilities; and many state practices subsumed under the rubric "legitimation functions" may involve substantial production of use-values by the state. These are thus cross-cutting functional descriptions used for different analytical purposes.

Table 15.1. *Social structure locations used in analysis of class and state*

Class location	Private sector	State sector	
		Political superstructure	Decommodified services
Capitalist class	Capitalist class		
Petty bourgeoise	Petty bourgeoisie		
Middle class	Private sector middle class	State political middle class	State service middle class
Working class	Private sector working class	State political working class	State service working class

and possibilities they confront, and these interests could in turn underwrite different ideological orientations. Or, people who end up in different categories could have been subjected to different forms of indoctrination during their upbringing and education. Different employment settings could be characterized by conditions encouraging different degrees of cognitive complexity or generating various forms of cognitive dissonance which in turn would affect ideological dispositions. More broadly, the "lived experience" within different kinds of work settings shape ideology. It could be the case, for example, that the experience of "alienation" in the work setting is systematically different for the working class and the middle class in state and in private employment, and that this difference in alienation experiences underwrites different ideological orientations. For all these reasons one might expect attitudes toward the state and classes to vary across the class-by-sector categories we are exploring.

Because of their heterogeneity and complexity, it would be difficult to generate a set of *a priori* predictions from this broad set of causes. We will therefore limit ourselves to one specific causal connection, that between the material interests of actors and their ideologies. This need not imply a mechanical theory of ideology in which consciousness is derived simply from such material interests – many other causes can intervene to break this relation – but it does suggest that one should not be surprised when such correspondences exist.

In terms of the categories in Table 15.1, the problem is thus to figure out how material interests of actors vary across the class-by-sector categories and how this might impact on ideological orientations. The interpretation of our empirical findings will revolve around three propositions concerning the linkage between location, interests and ideology:

Hypothesis 1. Within each sector, people in the working class should both hold more prostatist and more anticapitalist attitudes than will people in the middle class. Workers are more vulnerable to the vagaries of the capitalist labor market and thus in general should be more supportive than the middle class of an expansive role of the state in society. Also, because the material interests of workers are more sharply polarized with those of capital than are the interests of the middle class, one would expect workers to be more supportive of working-class struggles and more hostile to the capitalist class than are people in the middle class. While the degree of such polarization might be greater in the private sector, within each sector for both of these ideological issues we would thus expect workers to be to the left of the middle class.

Hypothesis 2. Within the middle class, people employed in state services will hold more prostatist attitudes and more anticapitalist attitudes than will people in either the private sector or the state political superstructure. The argument for a division in interests between the middle class in state services and the private sector is fairly simple: since the interests of the private sector middle class are more closely tied to those of the capitalist class than are those of the middle class in state services, we would expect the private sector middle class to be more procapitalist. In a complementary way, because of their dependency on state employment, we would expect the middle class in state services to be more prostatist. But what about the middle class in the state political superstructure? Why should they differ ideologically from middle-class employees in state services? The argument here centers on the *functional* linkage between the state superstructure and capitalist interests. The middle class in state superstructural apparatuses plays an active role in managing the programs in the agencies within which they work. To varying degrees this involves limited forms of policy-making and planning as well as authoritative roles in implementing policies. If we are willing to assume that to at least some extent functional roles are causally linked to ideological orientation, then because of their role as managers and experts in apparatuses functionally important for capitalist relations, we would expect the middle class in the state political superstructure to be more procapitalist and less prostatist than the middle class in state services.[6]

Hypothesis 3. The working class in the state sector (either in the state superstructure or in state services) will be more prostatist than in the private sector, whereas the working class in the private sector will be more anticapitalist than in the state sector. By virtue of their employment in the state, the interests of state sector workers confront the interests of capitalists in a less directly polarized manner, and thus they would have less reason to be anticapitalist. On the other hand, because their welfare directly depends upon the vitality of state employment, they would tend to be more prostatist. Unlike in the case of middle-class state employees, because state sector workers have no role in controlling the policies and programs within the agencies in which they work, there would be no particular reason to predict strong ideological divisions among workers within the state.

The overall expectation of the variant of neo-Marxist theory adopted here, therefore, is that (1) workers will be more statist and more anticapitalist than the middle class within all sectors; (2) the middle class will be ideologically divided across the two subsectors of the state whereas the working class will not; (3) the working class will be ideologically divided between the private sector and the state sector as a whole, whereas the middle class in the private sector and the state political superstructure will not differ ideologically. These expectations generate the rank orderings of expected levels of prostatist consciousness and anticapitalist consciousness in Table 15.2.

It could be objected that while these predictions may be reasonable, the explanatory principles behind them are quite wrong-headed since many of the people who end up in these various sectors already held these general ideological orientations *before* entering their specific jobs. It is certainly plausible, for example, that people seek out employment in state services as teachers or welfare workers because they already hold certain kinds of statist and/or anticapitalist values (whether for

---

[6]   There are a variety of causal mechanisms that might link functional roles to ideological orientation. The mechanism might be one of recruitment: only those people whose ideologies are compatible with the mission of a superstructural apparatus will be allowed to enter the apparatus or be retained once in. Or the mechanism might be rooted in simple material interests: the material interests of actors depend upon the extent to which an apparatus adequately fulfills its functional responsibilities, and ideological orientations tend to adjust to such material interests. On either grounds one would predict ideological divisions between state managers and experts in the political superstructure and in state services.

Table 15.2. *Orienting hypotheses of relationship between class, state and ideology*[a]

Rank ordering for prostatism attitudes[b]

Sector of employment

Class	Capitalist private sector	Political superstructure	Decommodified state services
Middle class	4	4	3
Working class	2	1	1

Rank ordering for proworker/anticapitalism attitudes[c]

Sector of employment

Class	Capitalist private sector	Political superstructure	Decommodified state services
Middle class	4	4	3
Working class	1	2	2

a. Entries are predicted rank orderings of particular categories on the two dimensions of ideology. A rank order of 1 implies the strongest degree of support for the ideological element in question. When two categories are given the same rank ordering, this implies that there is no expectation that they will differ on the ideological element.

b. *Prostatism* = attitudes in support of increasing state intervention to solve various social and economic problems.

c. *Proworker/ Anticapitalism* = attitudes in support of workers in conflicts with employers and critical of existing economic institutions.

reasons adduced by New Class theory, neo-Weberian theory or neo-Marxist theory). Instead of employment settings shaping consciousness, forms of consciousness may explain a process of self-selection of people into employment settings.

We will not, in the empirical explorations of this chapter, be able to sort out the micro-biographical issue of how individuals come to hold the attitudes they hold. This does not, however, undermine the arguments about the linkage between interests embedded in different kinds of structural locations occupied by individuals and those individuals' ideological orientation. Whether people are recruited into those locations because they value those interests already, or the locations engender a given set of attitudes by virtue of the interests linked to the location, specific patterns of ideological differences across classes and sectors would be associated with the interests tied to these social locations.

Suppose we observe that managers in state services are much more statist than managers of private business corporations, and further that they were more statist even before they entered these jobs. It would nevertheless be a mistake to conclude from this that the contrast in ideological orientations associated with the two sites of employment is simply the result of attributes of individuals alone (i.e. a "selection" effect of what kinds of people end up in given jobs). Even if middle-class people in state services were prostatist before entering state employment, the attributes of state service employment (and the interests linked to those attributes) would still be a central part of the explanation for why there are aggregate ideological differences between the middle class in state services and the private sector, since if state services did not institutionally embody these particular interests they would "select" people with different ideological orientations.[7] Although important in its own right, it is thus not necessary to solve the problem of selection in order to explore ideological differences across social structural locations of the sort we are studying. Our empirical task, then, is to carefully map out the patterns of these ideological differences across classes and sectors and see the extent to which they conform to the various orienting hypotheses we have examined.

Hypothesis 4. The ideological division within the working class between the two state subsectors should be greater in Sweden than in the United States.

---

[7] Selection in this context can operate through a variety of concrete mechanisms. It can operate directly in recruitment criteria by the hiring authorities at ports of entry to apparatuses. Or, if someone whose ideological orientation is incompatible manages to get hired, they might find their careers blocked by higher-ups in the apparatus. However, even if such screening mechanisms are weak or absent, voluntary self-selection can still accomplish a correspondence between ideological orientation of individuals and institutionally grounded interests.

Since in Sweden the postcapitalist decommodified sector of production (state services) is much more developed than in the United States, and thus constitutes a stronger material basis for distinctive interests of the middle class in that sector, it would be predicted that the ideological division *within* the state between the two subsectors of the middle class should be *greater* in Sweden than in the US. The two countries should not differ, however, in the ideological profiles of the middle class in the political superstructure compared to the private sector: in both countries there should be relatively little ideological division here.

Hypothesis 5. Ideological divisions across sectors within the working class should be weaker in Sweden than in the United States. The model of class formation in Chapter 13 suggests that when the working class is politically and organizationally weak, there will generally be more ideological divisions linked to divisions of *immediate* material interests than when the working class is strong. In the case of the US/Swedish contrast, this suggests that whatever ideological divisions do occur within the working class between the state and private sectors should be greater in the United States than in Sweden since the American working class lacks the kind of class-wide organization which would dampen such divisions. Hypotheses 4 and 5 together thus suggest an interesting pair of contrasts between Sweden and the United States: Sweden should have deeper ideological divisions within the middle class (between subsectors within the state) than the United States, whereas the United States should have deeper ideological divisions within the working class (between the state as a whole and the private sector).

15.3 Results

Our analysis revolves around two clusters of attitudes, "prostatist consciousness" and "anticapitalist consciousness." *Prostatism*, in the context of this research, refers to positive attitudes toward the expansion of interventionist activities of the state. *Anticapitalism* refers to attitudes toward class issues, especially class conflicts and the distribution of power and resources across classes in capitalist society. These are by no means the only kinds of attitudes which would be relevant to an analysis of ideological orientations. However, since we are particularly interested in the effects of state employment and class position on ideology, these two dimensions seemed particularly relevant. The specific questions used to operationalize these two variables are presented in the methodological appendix to this chapter.

The essential task of the empirical analysis of this chapter is to see in what ways ideological orientations vary across the eight social structural locations in Table 15.1, and then to compare these patterns for the United States and Sweden. This involves conducting a large number of statistical tests of specific differences across the cells of the table. More specifically, we want to explore the following contrasts:

1 Within the *columns* in Table 15.2 (i.e. within the private sector, the state political superstructure and the state-service sector) are there significant differences in the ideological orientations of people in different class locations?

2 Within the *rows* of the table (i.e. within the different classes) are there significant differences in ideological orientations across different sites of employment?

3 Do these patterns of differences vary significantly between the United States and Sweden (i.e. are there significant differences between the two countries in the magnitudes of the within-sector class contrasts and the within-class sector contrasts)?

Table 15.3 presents the mean values on the ideology scales we are considering for the various class locations in the private sector, the aggregate state sector and in the two subsectors of the state (the state service sector and the state political superstructure) in Sweden and the United States. Table 15.4 presents a summary of the statistical tests of differences across class categories within sectors, and across sectors within classes for both of the dependent variables. Finally, Table 15.5 presents the tests for the differences between Sweden and the United States for a number of the contrasts presented in Table 15.4.

Two preliminary comments before looking at the substantive findings: first, while some passing reference will be made to the ideological orientation of capitalists and the petty bourgeoisie, because of the theoretical objectives of this chapter we will focus nearly all of our attention on the contrasts involving the working class and the middle class – i.e. those class locations found within both the private and state sectors. Second, the samples are relatively small for the state political superstructure categories: eighty-four in the United States (about 34%

Table 15.3. *Ideological orientation within class-by-sector categories in the United States and Sweden*

I. *United States*

I.1. *Number of cases in each class-by-sector category (weighted Ns)*

	Sector of employment				
			Subsectors within state		
Class	Private	State	Political	Services	Row Ns
Capitalist class	112				112
Petty bourgeoisie	110				110
Middle class	291	89	36	53	281
Working class	680	159	48	111	839
Column Ns	1184	248	84	164	1432

I.2. *Prostatism (cell entries = means on prostatism scale; range -3 to $+3$)*

	Sector of employment				
			Subsectors within state		
Class	Private	State	Political	Services	Row means
Capitalist class	0.85				0.85
Petty bourgeoisie	0.84				0.84
Middle class	1.03	1.26	1.05	1.40	1.08
Working class	1.64	1.30	1.26	1.32	1.58
Column means	1.35	1.29	1.17	1.35	1.34

I.3. *Anticapitalism (cell entries = means on anticapitalism scale; range -6 to $+6$)*

	Sector of employment				
			Subsectors within state		
Class	Private	State	Political	Services	Row means
Capitalists	−0.16				−0.16
Petty bourgeoisie	0.54				0.54
Middle class	0.09	1.04	1.14	0.96	0.31
Working class	1.68	1.75	0.98	2.08	1.69
Column means	1.02	1.49	1.05	1.72	1.10

Table 15.3. *(Continued)*

II. *Sweden*

II.1. *Number of cases in each class-by-sector category (weighted Ns)*

	Sector of employment				
			Subsectors within state		
Class	Private	State	Political	Services	Row Ns
Capitalists	61				61
Petty bourgeoisie	58				58
Middle class	123	149	22	127	272
Working class	405	309	33	276	714
Column Ns	647	458	54	404	1106

II.2. *Prostatism (cell entries = means on prostatism scale; range −3 to +3)*

	Sector of employment				
			Subsectors within state		
Class	Private	State	Political	Services	Row means
Capitalists	1.08				1.08
Petty bourgeoisie	1.54				1.54
Middle class	1.14	1.53	1.16	1.59	1.35
Working class	2.02	2.02	1.84	2.05	2.02
Column Means	1.72	1.86	1.57	1.90	1.78

II.3. *Anticapitalism (cell entries = means on anticapitalism scale; range −6 to +6)*

	Sector of employment				
			Subsectors within state		
Class	Private	State	Political	Services	Row means
Capitalists	−0.35				−0.35
Petty bourgeoisie	0.98				0.98
Middle class	1.01	1.66	−0.29	1.99	1.37
Working class	3.47	3.17	3.41	3.14	3.34
Column means	2.42	2.68	1.94	2.78	2.52

Table 15.4. *Tests of differences between classes within sectors and between sectors within classes*

I. *Working class vs. middle class: significance of class differences within each sector*

	Working class vs. middle class in			
	Private sector	State political	State service	Total state
United States				
Prostatism	$>^a$	=	=	=
Anticapitalism	>	=	>	(>)
Sweden				
Prostatism	>	(>)	>	>
Anticapitalism	>	>	>	>

II. *Capitalist class vs. middle class: significance of class differences within sectors*

	Capitalist class vs. middle class in			
	Private sector	State political	State service	Total state
United States				
Prostatism	=	=	<	(<)
Anticapitalism	=	<	<	<
Sweden				
Prostatism	=	=	<	<
Anticapitalism	<	=	<	<

III. *Working class: significance of differences across sectors within the working class*

	State service vs. political	State service vs. private	State political vs. private	Total state vs. private
United States				
Prostatism	=	(<)	=	<
Anticapitalism	>	=	(<)	=
Sweden				
Prostatism	=	=	=	=
Anticapitalism	=	=	=	=

Table 15.4. *(Continued)*

IV. *Middle class: significance of differences across sectors within the middle class*

	State service vs. political	State service vs. private	State political vs. private	Total state vs. private
United States				
Prostatism	=	=	=	=
Anticapitalism	=	(>)	>	>
Sweden				
Prostatism	=	>	=	>
Anticapitalism	>	>	(<)	=

a. Entries in table:

> mean for first category significantly greater than the second category (p < .05, 2–tailed test)
< mean for first category significantly smaller than the second category (p < .05, 2–tailed test)
(>) mean for first category marginally significantly greater than the second category (p < .10, 2-tailed test)
(<) mean for first category marginally significantly smaller than the second category (p < .10, 2-tailed test)
= mean for two categories do not differ significantly (p > .10, 2-tailed test)

of all state employees) and fifty-four in Sweden (about 13% of all state employees).[8] This means that for contrasts involving the middle class within the political superstructure the number of cases gets very small indeed in both countries (thirty-six in the US and twenty-two in Sweden), which makes formal statistical tests quite problematic. For comparisons involving these cases, therefore, I will adopt a fairly loose criterion for statistical significance, while of course regarding the findings as necessarily tentative.

Class differences within sectors

A number of findings concerning class differences within sectors are particularly striking. First, *within the private sector* in both the United States and Sweden there are consistent, significant ideological differences between the working class and the middle class on both the prostatism and anticapitalism scales: in both countries on average

[8] It is worth noting that although the proportion of state employees in the political superstructure is much higher in the US than in Sweden, the proportion of the total labor force that is employed in the state political superstructure is quite similar in the two countries. This reflects the fact that the much larger overall state employment in Sweden is entirely the result of the expansion of decommodified state services.

Table 15.5.   *Test of differences between the United States and Sweden in contrasts across class-sector categories*

I. *Differences between countries in working-class (WC) vs. middle-class (MC) contrasts within each sector[a]*

	Prostatism scale	p[b]	Anticapitalism scale	p
I.1 Private sector: WC vs. MC	0.27	<.10	0.87	<.01
I.2 State political: WC vs. MC	0.46	ns	3.87	<.01
I.3 State services: WC vs. MC	0.53	<.05	0.03	ns
I.4 Total state: WC vs. MC	0.45	<.05	0.80	<.10

II. *Differences between countries in contrasts across sectors within the working class*

	Difference between countries	p
II.1 Prostatism: WC in private vs. total state	−0.34	<.05
II.2 Prostatism: WC in private vs. state service	−0.35	<.05
II.3 Anticapitalism: WC in state service vs. state political	−1.37	<.05
II.4 Anticapitalism: WC in private vs. state political	−0.64	ns

III. *Differences between countries in contrasts across sectors within the middle class*

	Difference between countries	p
III.1 Prostatism: MC in total state vs. private	0.16	ns
III.2 Anticapitalism: MC in total state vs. private	−0.30	ns
III.3 Prostatism: MC in state services vs. private	0.08	ns
III.4 Anticapitalism: MC in state services vs. private	0.10	ns
III.5 Anticapitalism: MC in state political vs. private	−2.36	<.01
III.6 Anticapitalism: MC in state services vs. state political	2.47	<.01

a. Differences are calculated as Sweden − United States.
b. One-tailed test.

workers are more positive about state intervention and are more anticapitalist than are people in the middle class.[9]

Second, for the anticapitalism scale (but only marginally for the prostatism scale), these class differences within the private sector are significantly stronger in Sweden than in the United States (see Table 15.5, line I.1): the ideological difference between private sector workers and middle class on the anticapitalism scale is nearly 2.5 points in Sweden but only 1.6 points in the United States. This is consistent with the findings in Chapter 14, where we did not distinguish state and private sectors, that overall the Swedish class structure is more polarized ideologically than is the American class structure.

Third, in the United States *within the two subsectors of the state* – the state political superstructure and the state service sector – there are no statistically significant ideological differences for *statism* between the middle class and the working class. In Sweden, in contrast, there are significant differences on the prostatism measures between workers and middle class in the state service sector, and marginally significant differences in the state political sector.[10] Furthermore, as indicated in Table 15.5, line I.3, the class difference within the state service sector in Sweden is significantly larger than the corresponding difference in the United States.

Fourth, in terms of the *anticapitalism* scale, there are strong class differences within both subsectors of the state in Sweden, whereas, in the United States, such differences only occur within the state service sector, not the state political superstructure. The class differences in anticapitalist class consciousness in Sweden are significantly greater than in the United States within the state political superstructure (line I.2 in Table 15.5).[11]

---

[9] In keeping with the results for the entire labor force as analyzed in chapter 14, it should be noted that in Sweden there is a significant ideological difference between capitalists and the private sector middle class on the anticapitalism scale, whereas in the United States the private sector middle class does not significantly differ from capitalists on this scale. In neither country do capitalists and private sector middle class differ on statism. The American middle class in the private sector is thus ideologically closer to the capitalist class than is its Swedish counterpart.

[10] The actual magnitude of the difference in Sweden between middle class and working class is larger in the political sector than in the state service sector, but because the sample size is smaller, the class difference within the political sector is only marginally statistically significant.

[11] As explained in the methodological appendix, all of these comparisons were made both with the simple additive scale reported here and with more complex LISREL factor scales. There is only one instance where these scales yield different results in the analysis

Taking these various findings together leads to the following characterization of the class differences within sectors in the two countries. While generally speaking in Sweden there is a higher level of ideological polarization between classes in most sectors than in the United States, *in both countries, there is a higher level of class polarization in the private sector than within the state service sector*. To take one of the clearest examples, in the United States on the prostatism scale, the difference between the middle class and the working class within state services in only 0.08 on the scale (1.40 vs. 1.32), whereas the difference within the private sector is 0.6 (1.03 vs. 1.64). Similarly, to take an example from Sweden, the class difference within the state service sector is 1.2 on the anticapitalism scale compared to 2.5 for the private sector. The results for the state political superstructure are somewhat less clear on this score: in Sweden, particularly for anticapitalism, the state political superstructure is at least as ideologically polarized as the private sector; in the United States this is not the case.[12] In any event, state superstructural employment in both countries is a minority of total state employment (about a third in the US and an eighth in Sweden), so *within the state as a whole in both countries there is clearly less ideological polarization between classes than in the private sector*. These findings are broadly consistent with the expectations in Table 15.2.

Sector differences within classes

Now let us turn to the central question of this chapter, sectoral differences within classes. Two patterns stand out. First, the working class is much more homogeneous across sectors in Sweden than in the United States. In Table 15.4, panel III, there are no significant sectoral

of class differences within sectors: in the United States, within the state service sector, while the middle class and working class significantly differ on the additive anticapitalism scale (as indicated in Table 15.4), they do *not* significantly differ on the prounion factor scale, one of the two LISREL factors generated by the items used in the anticapitalism additive scale. In no other result of class differences within sectors are there any discrepancies across the various analytical strategies we explored.

12   The relatively high level of "progressive" attitudes by the political sector middle class in the US compared to Sweden (especially for the anticapitalism scale) seems to be partially the result of the attitudes of supervisors in state protective services in the US who on average hold relatively prounion and anticapitalist attitudes (as measured by our questions). In terms of the class typology, these individuals are classified as skilled supervisors (marginal skill assets and marginal organizational assets) and thus were placed in the "middle class." The numbers, of course, are relatively small, so it was impossible to systematically analyze these respondents separately.

differences among workers in Sweden, whereas in the United States there are numerous cases in which sectoral differences are significant within the working class.[13] To cite one example, on the anticapitalism scale, US workers in the political superstructure have a score of 0.98 compared to 2.08 in the state service sector and 1.68 in the private sector, whereas in Sweden the three values are 3.41, 3.14 and 3.47. As Table 15.5, line II.3, indicates, the difference between the US and Sweden for contrasts across subsectors of the state within the working class is statistically significant. The Swedish working class is thus more unified ideologically across economic-political sectors than is the American working class.

Second, when we look at the middle classes in the two countries, we get quite a different picture. In the United States within the middle class there are no statistically significant ideological differences between the two state subsectors. The American middle class thus seems to be ideologically divided between the private sector (quite conservative) and a somewhat more progressive, and relatively unified, state sector middle class. In Sweden, on the other hand, the state political superstructural middle class is not ideologically different from the private sector middle class (if anything it is marginally more conservative, as indicated by the anticapitalism scale), whereas the state service sector middle class is much more progressive than the private sector on both the prostatism and anticapitalism scales. The result is that there is considerable ideological division within the middle class *inside* of the Swedish state, particularly in terms of anticapitalism.[14] Overall, then, the American middle class is more

---

[13] There were two instances where the results using the more complex LISREL measurement strategy (see methodological appendix) differed from the results using the simple additive consciousness scale reported here: (1) In Sweden, workers in state services have a lower average score on the anticorporate capitalism factor than workers in the private sector, whereas in the additive scale these two groups of workers do not differ significantly; (2) in the US, workers in the state service sector had a significantly *higher* value on the anticorporate capitalism factor than workers in the private sector, whereas on the additive anticapitalism scale these two groups also did not differ. Nevertheless, the general observation still holds, that the working class is ideologically more homogeneous in Sweden than in the US across these sectors.

[14] As in the results for the working class, there are some slight differences between the results using the LISREL factors (see methodological appendix) and the results using the simple additive scale: (1) in the United States, the middle class in the political superstructure has a higher value than the private sector middle class on the additive anticapitalism scale, but does not differ from the private sector middle class on the prounionism LISREL factor; (2) the Swedish state service sector middle class

ideologically homogeneous across sectors than the Swedish middle class. Particularly for ideological prostatism, there are no divisions at all within the US middle class, whereas the Swedish state service sector middle class is clearly to the left of the private sector middle class.

Taking the patterns for the working class and the middle class together, we can say that in the United States both the working class and the middle class are ideologically divided across sectors, but in different ways. In the US, the division between private sector, political superstructure and state services constitutes a basis for real ideological divisions within classes. In Sweden, on the other hand, this is only true for the middle class, within which there is a fairly sharp ideological division within the state and between the state and private sectors. The Swedish working class, in contrast, remains fairly strongly united ideologically across all of these sectoral divisions.

In terms of the expectations elaborated in Table 15.2, the Swedish picture is consistent with the prediction of significant ideological divisions across sectors within the middle class and only marginal divisions within the working class. The American results, however, are not fully consistent with these predictions. In particular, we did not predict that private sector workers would be *more* prostatist than state sector workers or that state service sector workers would be so strongly more anticapitalist than state superstructural workers.

Sector differences within classes controlling for attributes of individuals

A skeptic might challenge these descriptive results by pointing out that the differences across sectors within classes observed in Table 15.3 and tested in Table 15.4 could simply be artifacts of various kinds of compositional differences across these categories. For example, as Table 15.6 indicates, there are striking differences in gender composition across class-by-sector categories: in both the US and Sweden, 47% of the middle class in the state service sector are women, a much higher figure than in either the state political middle class or private sector middle class. Furthermore, there are big differences between Sweden and the United States in the gender composition of these latter two sectors: women constitute only 10% of the state political middle class in the US but 34% in Sweden, whereas they constitute 33% of the

has a higher value than the political superstructure middle class on the overall additive anticapitalism scale, but not on the prounion LISREL factor. Again, these discrepancies in results do not affect the overall picture.

Table 15.6. *Percentage of women within class-by-sector categories*

Class	Sector of employment		Subsectors within state	
	Private	State	Political	Services
United States				
Capitalists	29.2			
Petty bourgeoisie	49.8			
Middle class	32.8	32.3	9.7	47.6
Working class	50.7	59.9	61.5	59.2
Column means	44.2	49.9	39.1	55.5
Sweden				
Capitalists	17.2			
Petty bourgeoisie	23.7			
Middle class	18.0	45.2	33.6	47.2
Working class	38.3	68.6	67.7	68.7
Column means	31.1	61.0	54.1	61.9

private sector middle class in the US compared to only 18% in Sweden. These are quite large differences across countries, and *if* much of the sectoral differences in ideology within classes within each country were attributable to (for example) gender composition, then this might also explain the differing patterns across countries.

In order to rule out this kind of spurious relationship between class-by-sector categories and ideology, I ran multiple regressions controlling for several variables which might generate such compositional effects: age, gender, education and income.[15] It might seem that a fifth composition variable, union membership, would also be appropriate to include as a control. After all, union membership does vary across sectors and union members are ideologically different from

---

[15] Income is measured as the natural log of personal earnings from the respondent's job. Education is measured as years of schooling in the United States and as level of education (a six-level ordinal scale) in Sweden.

nonmembers. It might thus be argued that the observed sector differences in ideology within classes could simply reflect differences in union membership. I have not, however, included union membership as a control variable in this analysis since union membership is just as plausibly a *consequence* of the ideological orientations of people in different sectors as a cause of such orientations, particularly in the United States. That is, the compositional differences in union membership across sectors are likely to be partially caused by our dependent variables (ideological orientations), and thus it is inappropriate to treat union membership as a control variable for testing the robustness of sector difference in ideology.[16]

The strategy for each equation was to create three dummy variables for the class-by-sector categories – two for the categories being compared and a third for everyone else. We then examined whether the difference between the categories of interest became statistically insignificant when the various controls were added to the equation. We are not, in these analyses, interested in the coefficients for the control variables as such; our only interest is in seeing whether or not the patterns reported in Table 15.4 remain intact when these controls are included in the equations. The results are given in Table 15.7.

The controls seem to affect the patterns for prostatism more than for anticapitalism. When the controls are added, the marginally significant differences between workers in state services and in the private sector in the United States disappear (see line I.1.2 in Table 15.7). For the middle class in the United States, significant differences emerge between state services and the private sector which were not present in the analyses without the control variables (see line II.1.2 in Table 15.7). The result of these two changes in patterns is that once the controls are added to the analysis, the across-sector patterns for the prostatism measures within both the working class and the middle class are virtually identical in Sweden and the United States.

In the case of the anticapitalism scale, in contrast, the controls, if anything, slightly *strengthen* the differences between the United States

---

[16] When union membership is included as a compositional control in the multivariate equations, some, but not all, of the sector differences within classes are reduced. However, even when union membership is included, the basic substantive conclusion of the results reported above – that the US working class is ideologically divided across sectors while the Swedish is not, and the Swedish middle class is divided within the state while the US middle class is not – remains supported by the data.

Table 15.7. *Tests for significance of sectoral differences within classes controlling for age, sex, education and income*

	United States		Sweden	
	Direction and significance of difference between categories		Direction and significance of difference between categories	
	as reported in Table 15.4	controlling for age, sex education and income	as reported in Table 15.4	controlling for age, sex education and income
I. Working class				
1. Prostatism				
1.1 State service vs. state political	=	=	=	=
1.2 State service vs. private	(<)	=	=	=
1.3 State political vs. private	=	=	=	=
1.4 Total state vs. private	<	=	=	=
2. Anticapitalism				
2.1 State service vs. state political	>	>	=	=
2.2 State service vs. private	=	>	=	=
2.3 State political vs. private	(<)	=	=	=
2.4 Total state vs. private	=	=	=	=
II. Middle class				
1. Prostatism				
1.1 State service vs. state political	=	=	=	=
1.2 State service vs. private	=	>	>	>
1.3 State political vs. private	=	=	=	=
1.4 Total state vs. private	=	(>)	>	>
2. Anticapitalism				
2.1 State service vs. state political	=	=	>	>
2.2 State service vs. private	(>)	>	>	>
2.3 State political vs. private	>	>	(<)	=
2.4 Total state vs. private	>	>	=	(>)

See Table 15.4 for explanation of entries in table.

and Sweden observed in Table 15.4. For the American data, there is a stronger indication of ideological divisions in anticapitalist consciousness across sectors within the working class after the controls are added; for the Swedes the homogeneity within the working class is unaffected by the addition of controls. Within the middle class, adding the control variables increased the statistical significance of the contrast between state services and private sector for the United States (line II.2.2), while, again, the results for Sweden were basically unchanged. The central findings for the initial analysis of the middle class are thus confirmed: the Swedish middle class is ideologically divided between the political and service sectors of the state, whereas the American middle class is ideologically divided between the state as a whole and the private sector.

Overall, then, it does not seem plausible that the basic conclusions derived from Tables 15.3 and 15.4 are simply artifacts of the composition of the various class-by-sector categories. Even when controls for education, gender, age and personal income are included in the analysis, the Swedish working class appears to be more ideologically unified across these sectors than the American working class, and the Swedish middle class seems to be more ideologically divided within the state than does the American middle class.

15.4 Implications

While the data analysis in this chapter was not initially framed as a direct test of the hypotheses presented in Table 15.2, nevertheless the results are broadly consistent with these expectations. Table 15.8 reorganizes the results from Table 15.4 in terms of the rank orderings of different cells in our class-by-sector typology in a manner parallel to Table 15.2. The results for the middle class, especially for the anti-capitalism scale, lend some support to the distinction between those state apparatuses which constitute the political superstructure of capitalism and those which embody elements of a decommodified postcapitalist form of social production. If this distinction designates different institutional functions and associated interests within the state, then it would be expected that employees in postcapitalist state services would be more progressive politically than employees in the political superstructure, and that at least middle-class state service sector employees would be more progressive than their private sector counterparts. These expectations are strongly supported for Sweden,

Table 15.8. *Rank orderings of ideological orientation within class-by-sector categories in the United States and Sweden*

I. *United States*

Two sector model | Three sector model

I.1 *Prostatism*

	Private	Total state		Private	State political	State services
Middle class	2^a	2		2	2	2
Working class	1	2		1	$(2)^b$	2

I.2 *Anticapitalism*

	Private	Total state		Private	State political	State services
Middle class	3	2		3	2	2
Working class	1	1		1	2	1

II. *Sweden*

II.1 *Prostatism*

	Private	Total state		Private	State political	State services
Middle class	3	2		3	3	2
Working class	1	1		1	1	1

II.2 *Anticapitalism*

	Private	Total state		Private	State political	State services
Middle class	3	2		4	3	2
Working class	1	1		1	1	1

a. Entries are the actual rank ordering of particular categories on the two dimensions of ideology corresponding to the predictions in Table 2. A rank order of 1 implies the strongest degree of support for the ideological element in question. When two categories do not significantly differ at the .10 level of significance, they are given the same rank ordering.

b. In this instance, the category did not differ significantly from any of the other cells in the table. Since the absolute magnitude of the value in this cell (1.26) is virtually identical to that in some of the other cells in rank 2, it seems appropriate to consider it a rank 2 category.

and at least partially supported for the United States. While in both countries the state service sector middle class is consistently more progressive than the private sector middle class on the anticapitalism scale, the state service middle class is sharply different ideologically from the political superstructure middle class only in Sweden. For the United States, therefore, the results for the middle class conform more to what might be considered a neo-Weberian expectation of an ideological division between state managers and experts *as a whole* and private sector managers and experts, whereas for Sweden, the results are consistent with the neo-Marxist expectation that there will be ideological differences within the state between the middle class in apparatuses which are primarily part of the political superstructure of capitalism and apparatuses which embody decommodified postcapitalist forms of production.

The results for the working class are also broadly consistent with the expectations of the variant of neo-Marxist class analysis we have been considering. In both countries, as expected, the working class is almost always significantly to the left of the middle class within sectors, and there is less ideological division across sectors in the working class than in the middle class. Furthermore, this relative ideological homogeneity is stronger in Sweden than in the United States. In every capitalist society a range of concrete circumstances of different categories of workers generates pressures toward variability in forms of consciousness within the working class. Among other potential divisions, the differences of interests of workers employed in the sectors we have investigated constitute one basis for such variability. In Sweden, the strength of the class-wide political and economic organization of the working class acts to at least mute, if not completely eliminate, such tendencies toward ideological divisions. In the United States, where class formation within the working class is exceptionally weak, there is much more scope for the development of distinctive ideological profiles based on differences of immediate interests tied to different sectors of employment.[17]

---

[17] As has often been noted, the political conditions for working-class formation differ sharply in the two countries. Unlike in Sweden, there has never been a successful class-wide working-class political party in the United States. For a variety of familiar reasons – a much less favorable set of laws around unionization, the weakness of social democratic political tendencies, higher levels of geographical and social division within the working class, etc. – the working class in the United States is also vastly less unionized than in Sweden, and where unionization has occurred it has often served to increase divisions within the working class rather than mitigate

The state has been brought firmly "back in" to the agenda of sociological analyses of public policy, social conflict and social change. It still largely remains, however, outside the concerns of micro-level research in political sociology, social stratification and class analysis. The results of this chapter suggest, to use a favorite expression of neo-Weberian state-centered theorists, that "the state matters," but it matters in different ways for different classes under different historical conditions.

Methodological appendix

1 Dependent variables: prostatism and anticapitalism

Three items were used to measure prostatist consciousness:

1 In order to reduce crime, education and job opportunities for the poor need to be increased. (Do you strongly agree, somewhat agree, somewhat disagree or strongly disagree?)[18]
2 The energy crisis will not be fully solved until the government controls the major energy companies. (Do you strongly agree, etc.?)
3 Do you think that the government should be spending a great deal more on education and health, somewhat more, the present amount, somewhat less, or a great deal less?

Anticapitalist consciousness was measured by the five items used in the anticapitalism scale in Chapter 14 plus one additional item:

> Imagine that workers in a major industry are out on strike over working conditions and wages. Which of the following outcomes would you like to see occur:
> (a) The workers win their most important demands.
> (b) The workers win some of their demands and make some concessions.

---

them. Furthermore, the underdevelopment of the American welfare state means that many sources of individual welfare are tied to specific sites of employment rather than universalized by state provision. This again creates divisions of interests among workers with respect to the state.

[18] While this question does not directly call for state intervention to increase education and job opportunities, I assume that most people who believe that increasing education and jobs would significantly reduce crime would support state intervention to accomplish this.

(c) The workers win only a few of their demands and make major concessions.

(d) The workers go back to work without winning any of their demands.

As in chapter 14, I experimented with a variety of simple and complex strategies of aggregating these items into analytically useful scales: constructing simple additive scales of the items; using ordinal probit analysis to assign magnitudes to the levels in the scales; constructing scales on the basis of confirmatory factor analysis using LISREL IV.[19] It turns out that virtually all of the results are the same regardless of which technique was used and none of the substantive conclusions are affected by different techniques. I have thus decided to use the least complex of the scale construction techniques for this chapter, that is, simply counting the number of items on which a person takes a prostatist position or anticapitalist position. (I have indicated in footnotes the few instances in which a difference in the results would occur if one of the more complex analytical techniques were used.)

To construct the two scales, all of these items were trichotomized, with a value of +1 indicating the anticapitalism or prostatism response, −1 the procapitalism or antistatism response, and 0 the "neutral" response (generally, "don't know"). In the items with agree/disagree responses, we collapsed the "somewhat" and "strong" categories in each question in order to construct these trichotomies. The variable construction therefore differs from the strategy in chapter 14 in which each item was coded on a five-point scale from −2 to +2. Item 3 above was trichotomized by treating the middle response – "government should spend the present amount on health and education " – as the statism-neutral category of 0. In the item on strike outcomes, response category (b) – workers should win some demands and make some concessions – was considered to be a class-neutral answer, and thus

---

[19] In the confirmatory factor analysis, the anticapitalism items were differentiated into two factors – a prounion factor (item 2 in the list in the methodological appendix in chapter 14 and the above strike outcome item) and an anti-corporate capital factor (items 1, 4 and 5 in chapter 14). Item 3 in the list in chapter 14 behaved quite inconsistently across the two countries and was thus dropped from the LISREL-generated scales. In the factor analytic treatment of the data, therefore, we investigated three different scales: prostatism, prounionism and anti-corporate capitalism. The technical details of the LISREL analysis are discussed in Wright, Howe and Cho (1989).

was given 0; the first category was given a value of +1; the third and fourth categories were combined as -1.

The scales were then constructed by summing the three prostatism items to form the prostatism scale (with values from -3 to +3) and summing the items listed in Chapter 14.1 and the strike outcome item to form the anticapitalism scale (with values from -6 to +6). When there were missing values for some of the items used to construct these simple scales, we calculated the mean value of the items for which we had valid responses and then multiplied this by 3 (for the prostatism scale) and 6 (for the anticapitalism scale). We thus replace missing values by the best available estimate based on the mean value of valid responses.

2 Independent variables

1 *Class location.* The "middle class" will be defined as everyone who is a manager, an expert or a skilled supervisor. All other employees are considered in the working class. The "working class" in this analysis thus includes the pure working class plus those "contradictory class locations" with the strongest working-class characteristics – nonskilled supervisors, and nonsupervisory skilled workers. This corresponds to those locations in the class structure which constitute the core of the "working-class ideological coalition" in Chapter 14.

2 *State sector vs. private sector.* All respondents who said that they "worked for someone else" (rather than being self-employed) were asked whether they worked for a government agency, a nonprofit organization or a profitmaking business. In Sweden they were given one additional response category, "government industry." State employees are operationalized as all respondents who say that they worked either for a government agency or government industry.

3 *State political superstructure vs. state services.* The distinction between those apparatuses in the state which constitute the "political superstructure" of capitalism and those which constitute the "service sector" of statist production was operationalized using detailed SIC (standard industry classification) codes. The political superstructure includes defense, government protection services, courts, tax administration and what is generically called "public administration." The state service sector includes a variety of social and related services done within the state sector: education, health, research, communication and

postal services. In addition to those categories, the state service sector also contains employees in government industry.[20]

There are some employment categories in the state which are ambiguous with respect to the theoretical distinction we are making. Welfare agencies, for example, often combine social control functions (part of the political superstructure) with genuine social service functions (providing services for people with disabilities, for example). For the purposes of this analysis we have classified welfare as an aspect of the service sector, since the socio-political *interests* of the people who work in such agencies seem more like those in health and education than like those in defense and the courts.

3 Statistical tests

The data analysis revolves primarily around two kinds of statistical investigations: (1) comparisons of the mean values on the dependent variables between pairs of class-by-sector categories *within* countries, and (2) comparisons *across* countries of the magnitude of these differences in class-by-sector means. The formal statistical tests for the first of these tasks consists of standard *t*-tests on differences in means between two categories. In the analysis of the differences between United States and Sweden, the formal statistical test consists of *t*-tests of differences between the class-by-sector contrasts in the two countries.

It is worth pointing out the familiar technical point that it is possible for a difference between categories to be statistically significant in country A and not statistically significant in country B, and yet for the difference of these differences to not be statistically significant (i.e. the difference in country A minus the difference in B is not significantly greater than zero by standard *t*-tests). In comparing two sets of differences each of which is in the same direction, the *t*-value of the contrast between differences will be lower than the *t*-value of the initial differences. This is because the standard error of the difference of differences (the denominator of the *t*-test) will always be larger than in

---

[20] In general, what we call the political superstructural sector corresponds to what Louis Althusser (1971) refers to as the "RSA," the repressive state apparatuses, and the service branch refers to what he called the "ISA," the ideological state apparatuses. Within Claus Offe's (1984) framework for studying the state, the state service branch consists of those social services which are *decommodified* by the intervention of the state in socio-economic activities.

the separate differences, while the numerator will always be smaller than at least one of the initial differences. It will thus usually be harder to establish a high level of statistical confidence in an observed difference between differences than in the initial within-country differences taken separately.

16 Temporality, class structure and class consciousness

The exploitation-centered concept of class which we have used in this book is part of what is sometimes referred to as a *structural* approach to class analysis.[1] Structural approaches treat class as a matrix of relationally defined empty places filled by individuals. Positions and people are conceptually distinguished: individuals are conceived as moving into and out of these places, but the places themselves are treated as definable independently of such movements of people. While I have emphasized in various places the ways in which incumbency in such "locations" generates various kinds of life experiences which in turn shape forms of consciousness, nevertheless, the analysis is clearly anchored in a structural conception.

There is an alternative general way of thinking about class which is especially influential among those class analysts who focus on problems of subjectivity. In contrast to the structuralist focus on the social relations which constrain the actions of people, what can be termed *processual* views see classes as constituted above all by the lived experiences of people. Classes exist only insofar as the biographies of individuals are organized in such a way that they share a set of experiences over time which define their lives in class terms. E. P. Thompson's (1968: 9) famous definition of class reflects such a perspective: "class happens when some men, as a result of common experiences (inherited or shared), feel and articulate the identity of their interests as between themselves and as against those whose interests are different from (and usually opposed to) theirs." Individual locations within production relations may matter as one of the mechanisms

---

[1] Other examples would include the work of Poulantzas (1975), Carchedi (1977), Cohen (1978).

that generate such a trajectory of experiences, but they are not intrinsically more important than forms of community, family structure or culture in constituting individual biographies in class terms.

In this chapter we will examine the implications for the problem of class consciousness of these two broad approaches to class analysis.

16.1 Structural and processual approaches to class and consciousness

The salient differences between structural and processual approaches to class are summarized in Table 16.1. At the core of this contrast are two different intuitions about what most systematically makes class explanatory of social conflict and social change. Processual approaches see class as explanatory because of the way it determines the *subjective conditions* of conflict, above all the identities and meanings of the various actors engaged in conflict. Structural approaches, in contrast, see the central explanatory power of class coming from the way it determines the *objective conditions* facing different actors, both by determining the material interests of individual actors, and by shaping the various resources actors can collectively deploy in the pursuit of these material interests. To use the language of rational actor models, structural theories center on explaining the feasible set of actions that exist independently of the motivations of the actors while processual theories focus on the preference orderings of actors themselves. In this sense, processual theories are rooted in what can be called *agent-centered* theories of action, whereas structural concepts of class deploy *relations-centered* approaches.

It is easy in discussing these two approaches to slide into caricatures of each. Instead of describing processual approaches as agent-*centered*, defenders of more structural approaches often describe them as voluntaristic and idealist. For their part, supporters of more processual approaches to class often characterize structural approaches as economistic or deterministic. To be sure, it is possible to find examples of such extreme positions.[2] But in general these two approaches are more

---

[2]   For example, Althusser (1971) sees individuals as "bearers" of roles who more or less automatically embody the central subjective properties functionally required by those roles. The objective conditions tied to structural positions are seen as so powerful and pervasive that they essentially impose a set of subjectivities on the actors in those positions. At the other extreme, Laclau and Mouffe (1985) argue that it is meaningless to talk about objective constraints and determinants; subjectivities

Table 16.1. *Alternative general approaches to class analysis*

	Processual	*Structural*
Conditions of conflict explained by class	subjective	objective
Theory of action	agent-centered	relation-centered
Central dimension of class consciousness	identity	interests
Temporality of class	past	future

matters of emphasis than polar opposites: few structural class analysts completely ignore subjectivity and agency, and few processual theorists treat agents as acting without relational constraints. Each of these approaches taps different aspects of the "dialectic" of structure and agency, and depending upon the specific problems being studied, one or the other may be a more effective starting point of analysis. The goal of class analysis, then, is to understand how to conceptualize the relationship between these two modalities of a theory of action rather than to fix exclusively on one or the other.

One way of approaching this task of integrating processual and structural approaches is by linking them to what can be called the *temporal aspects* of class analysis. Processual approaches to class revolve around the problem of *learning*. The central preoccupation is understanding how people come to learn to be class members with the accompanying identities, worldviews, life-styles and meanings. At any given moment, what we have learned is explained by the trajectory of experiences that have accumulated in our lives.[3] This trajectory is both a question of individual biography and collective history. The institutional and cultural legacies of victories and defeats in past class struggles matter just as much as the accumulation of life events in an individual biography. The temporality of class analysis in processual

are forged entirely through culture and discourses. Interests lack any "objective" basis: the actions of individuals-in-classes are to be explained above all by their trajectory of culturally constructed experiences in the past, not by the objective possibilities facing them for the future.

[3] By "experience" in this context, I do not mean "raw experience" unmediated by existing interpretations and meanings, but experiences as they become integrated into subjectivity.

approaches, therefore, is primarily backward looking: *class is an embodiment of the past in the present.*

Structural approaches to class, in contrast, revolve around the objective *choices* facing actors.[4] The feasible set of objective alternatives facing actors within a class structure defines a range of possible future states that are available to them. History may matter insofar as it helps to explain why the class structure is the way it is, but it is not conceptually constitutive of the concept of class itself. The temporality of class analysis in structural approaches, therefore, is primarily future looking: *class is an embodiment of possible futures in the present.* The explanation of *actual* futures, of the specific alternatives that are actually chosen by real actors, then, is the result of the intersection of these two temporalities – of the embodied past that shapes subjectivities and the structurally constrained futures that determine alternatives.

Given these temporalities implicit in class analysis, it is easy to see why the conceptualization of class *consciousness* differs between processual and structural approaches. Processual approaches are preoccupied, above all, with the problem of *identity*, structural approaches with the problem of *interests*.

Class identity refers to the ways in which people consider themselves "members" of different classes.[5] As such, it constitutes one of many ways in which people define what is salient about their lives and what differentiates them from others. "Identity" has both a cognitive and affective component. Cognitively, identity simply defines the ways people place themselves into different systems of formal classification. Affectively, identity refers to the kinds of classifications that are subjectively salient in a person's system of meanings. When asked, a person may classify him or herself as a Democrat rather than a Republican, but this may have little emotional salience and thus not constitute a significant aspect of identity. This affective aspect of "identity" is formed through the individual's biography of experiences in communities and social interactions within which particular identities are culturally salient. It is because meanings are not formed and

---

[4] The distinction between analysis based on *learning* and *choosing* comes from the insightful analysis of Bowles and Gintis (1986).

[5] Subjective class identity is perhaps the aspect of class consciousness most studied by sociologists. For a comprehensive discussion of the problem of class identity, see Jackman and Jackman (1983). The classic early study on class identity is by Centers (1949).

reformed instantaneously as a person moves into new class locations that class identity can be viewed as a "backward-looking" concept: it is rooted in one's personal history and in the ways in which that personal history is tied to the history of communities and social groups.

Consciousness structured around interests, on the other hand, refers to anticipations about the future and can thus be thought of as "forward looking."[6] When Marxists say that workers have particular class interests, the presumption is that the individuals involved are likely to remain workers sufficiently long so that their individual interests can be identified with their position as workers. If a particular worker knows that he or she is likely to exit the working class in the near future – for example, if they are the children of wealthy parents and know that they will inherit substantial funds, or if they are working at McDonald's while attending university and are confident that they will get "middle-class" jobs upon graduation – then their individual interests will be only weakly tied to their current class position. Consciousness of class interests, therefore, is oriented toward the future, reflecting the time horizons in terms of which individuals understand their relationship to the class structure.

Processual understanding of class can thus be seen as providing an analytical framework for understanding the ways in which class biographies generate trajectories of class experiences that are embodied in different forms of class identity, while structural approaches to class provide a way of understanding how class structures impose opportunities and constraints on people which shape their possibilities of action and thus their interests. The goal of the empirical investigations of this chapter is to combine these two approaches in order to understand different dimensions of class subjectivity.

16.2 A model of trajectory, structure and consciousness

One can imagine special cases in which a purely structural account of class or a purely processual account would be adequate. If, for example, the structural constraints on action were so narrow that the feasible set of choices was reduced to a single option, then it really would not matter very much how classes were culturally constituted, or what identities and preferences characterized actors in class posi-

---

[6] Subjective interests refer to the goals of *intentional* action. By "intentional action" we mean, following Elster (1985: 8ff.), action in which anticipated future states provide part of the explanation of the action itself.

tions. Alternatively, if a class structure was characterized by such high levels of mobility and openness that every individual could effectively choose their own class and thus class membership was almost entirely a matter of the formation of preferences for particular ways of living, then structural approaches to class would have little explanatory power.

Real class societies, however, are far from either of these special cases, and thus class analysis should attempt to combine the analytical strategies of processual and structural approaches. In particular, we need to bring the two temporalities of structural and processual approaches to class together to understand how the trajectory of experiences in the past intersects the objective possibilities for the future in explaining the practices and struggles in the present.[7]

In this chapter we will attempt to link the temporalities of processual and structural approaches to class in an empirical analysis of class consciousness. The model will be built round four basic hypotheses:

Hypothesis 1: Basic Structural Hypothesis. The subjective awareness of class interests will be more systematically shaped by a person's class location than by their class trajectory. This follows from the central arguments of structural approaches to class. Class locations determine the *objective* class interests of actors. All things being equal, therefore, there will be a tendency for subjective perceptions of interests to be closely tied to incumbency in a class location. A person's class biography – where they came from, what kinds of class experiences they have had in the past – should matter for individuals' subjective understanding of class interests only to the extent that it gives incumbents of class positions a clearer perception of their class interests.

Underlying Hypothesis 1 is the assumption that the objective interests determined by class structures are tied to class locations of incumbents. The validity of this assumption is contingent upon the

---

[7] In a quite different idiom, Pierre Bourdieu's attempt at developing a theory of class *position* and class *habitus* can be viewed trying to join structural and processual aspects of class (see Bourdieu 1985). The approach we are pursuing here differs from Bourdieu's in two principal respects: first, Bourdieu places explanatory emphasis on the concept of class habitus whereas I assign explanatory primacy to structural concepts of class. Secondly, Bourdieu's concept of class is framed in terms of the social construction of interest-based groups in general; there is no necessary *content* to those interests at all, and certainly no restriction of "class" interests to material exploitation. My usage of class follows more traditional Marxian lines of identifying the concept specifically with exploitation and material interests. For a discussion of Bourdieu's work in these terms, see Brubaker (1985).

time horizons of movements of individuals into and out of class locations. At one extreme is a class structure in which the incumbents of given class locations and their children stay in those class locations permanently; at the other extreme is a structure in which incumbents have a very high probability of being able to move into different locations at will. The objective interests tied to locations are different in these two structures even if the description of the "empty places" themselves is identical. Interests are always claims about desired states in the future (since they take time to accomplish), and therefore if one's future class location is likely to be different from one's present location, one's present interests are affected. At a minimum, therefore, high rates of individual mobility generate some uncertainty or indeterminacy in the relationship between locations and interests. Hypothesis 1, therefore, presupposes that on average there is sufficient stability in class membership that current class location is a pretty good predictor of most people's future class location.

Hypothesis 2: Basic Processual Hypothesis. The subjective class identity of individuals will be more systematically shaped by their class trajectory than by their current class location. Identities are formed over time; they are learned. Whether a given individual has a working-class identity will depend more upon their entire biography of class-based experiences than simply upon their current location within the class structure.

Hypothesis 3: Interaction of processual and structural dimensions of class. The class identity of people will have an effect on their perception of their class interests net of the effect of their current location within the class structure. Class structures define a set of objective interests of incumbents in class locations and this, in and of itself, creates a tendency for subjective perceptions of interests to vary by class location (Hypothesis 1). Subjective perceptions of interests, however, are never a simple, unmediated reflection of "raw sense data," and, if processual theorists of class are correct, one of the central determinants of how people understand their interests is their identity. It is therefore to be expected that identity will shape perceptions of interests even after controlling for the individual's class location.

Hypothesis 4: Class Formation Hypothesis. The strength of the relationships at the micro-level between class location and subjective class interests and between class trajectory and class identity will vary with the degree of the collective formation of classes. Hypotheses 1–3 are all micro-propositions

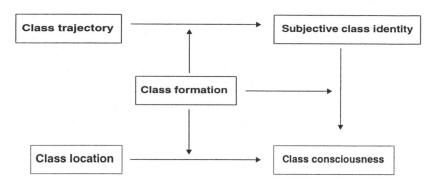

Figure 16.1 *Basic causal model of class identity and subjective interests*

in that each is a claim about how some attribute or state of individuals generates tendencies for them to have particular forms of consciousness. However, as was emphasized in Chapter 13, such tendencies are mediated by the macro-historical context within which these micro-processes take place. Under historical conditions of class formation in which classes are highly organized economically and politically, it would be expected that these micro-tendencies would be much stronger than under conditions in which class formations were highly atomized and fragmented. The "efficiency" with which a particular class location at the micro-level generates subjective perceptions of corresponding class interests, or a given class trajectory generates particular class identities, therefore, will increase as the collective institutions of class formation are stronger. If we were to compare a country with relatively weak and disorganized forms of working-class formations (such as the United States) with a country with relatively strong forms of working-class formation (such as Sweden), we would therefore expect the correlations posited in Hypotheses 1–3 to be weaker in the former than in the latter.

Taking these four hypotheses together we get the simple causal model presented in Figure 16.1. This model will form the basis of the empirical investigation in this chapter of class location, class trajectory and class consciousness in Sweden and the United States.

16.3 Conceptualizing and measuring class trajectory

Ideally, to fully measure class trajectories we would need complete class biographies of individuals, biographies which would include data on the class character of such things as: the individual's family of origin, the various communities the individual has lived in, the class character of schooling experiences, all previous jobs and the length of time within each, and a range of other class-pertinent experiences (unemployment, strikes, etc.). This complex, multidimensional space of class experiences over time could then be collapsed into a smaller number of theoretically coherent types of lives (lives completely embedded in the working class; lives which move back and forth between the working class and the petty bourgeoisie; lives with increasing distance from the working class; etc.).

We do not have this kind of comprehensive data on the class dimensions of biographies and experiences. What we do have is data on class *origins* and current class *locations*. These data enable us to create a simple 4×4 class mobility matrix.[8] Our strategy, then, will be to use the *cells* in this origins-by-destinations class mobility matrix as a first approximation map of possible class trajectories.

Advocates of processual theories of class may object that this is an inappropriate way of specifying a processual view of trajectories for two reasons. First, it does not directly measure "lived experiences" as such, but simply the structural context within which such experiences occur. In order to treat a class mobility trajectory as a variable reflecting a *processual* approach to class analysis, we have to assume that particular biographical movements through the class structure are closely tied to a trajectory of actual class experiences. Treating the link between structure and experience as unproblematic, it could be argued, is precisely what processual theorists object to in structural approaches. Second, mobility trajectory taps a relatively limited aspect

[8]   As in several of the previous chapters, in these analyses all contradictory class locations among employees are combined into a single "middle-class" location. We will therefore be working with four class categories for both origins and current class locations: capitalists, petty bourgeois, middle class and working class. Because of limitations in the available data for class origins, I use a somewhat simpler set of criteria for defining class categories than we have in some of the previous analyses. Specifically, the middle class will be defined as anyone (a) whose job is formally included in the managerial/supervisory hierarchy and/or (b) is in a professional, managerial or technical occupation. Criterion (a) is less refined than the criteria we have used to define authority in most of the previous analyses. The class origins variable is operationalized through a series of questions about the work of the person "who provided most of the financial support for your family while you were growing up." These questions were not pegged to a specific age of the respondent, but to the typical work of the head of household while the respondent was growing up. The actual criteria are the same as for the respondent's own class location.

of overall class trajectory – the link between class origins and destinations – rather than the broad inventory of class-constituting processes discussed by processual theorists. Even aside from the problem of the relationship between a structural biography and a trajectory of experiences, a mobility trajectory may be too thin a basis for tapping processual approaches to class analysis.

These are pertinent objections and they should be kept in mind as we explore the results of the empirical investigation. Nevertheless, I feel that class mobility trajectories are a sufficiently salient aspect of overall class biographies that they are an appropriate preliminary way of empirically mapping this conceptual space. And, further, I believe that the experiences linked to mobility are sufficiently consistent that it is reasonable to interpret the empirical effects of mobility patterns on consciousness as reflecting the kinds of experiential mechanisms postulated within processual views of class. In any case, with the present data these are the best measures of class trajectory we have.

Using a mobility matrix to measure class trajectory in this way, it should be noted, is quite different from the use of such matrices in the conventional study of "mobility effects." In mobility-effects research the typical analytical strategy is to begin by examining an additive model in which social origins and destinations are used to predict the outcome in question. Only after this model has been specified are the effects of "mobility" as such, understood as the *interactions* of origins and destinations, included in the analysis.[9] In the conventional wisdom, origins and destinations are treated as having a logical priority over mobility patterns (i.e. the patterns which link origins and destinations) in the analysis. Indeed, mobility effects are treated as a kind of residual – that part of the consequences of origins and destinations that cannot attributed either to origins or destinations as such. For the purposes of defining class trajectories in our analysis, however, origins and destinations are simply our best available way of

---

[9]   Good examples of this kind of logic would include Duncan (1966), Knoke (1973), Jackman (1972). Much research on the effects of mobility, particularly research before the late 1960s, did not consistently distinguish between the additive effects of origins and destinations on an outcome of interest, and interactive effects as such. Thus, for example, the observation that mobile individuals have ideologies intermediary between the ideologies of immobile individuals of lower and higher statuses has been taken to indicate that mobility matters (e.g. Thompson, 1971), whereas in fact this is the result one would expect if origins and destinations simply affect ideology in an additive manner. See Knoke (1973) for a clear exposition of the different logics of the additive and interactive models.

Table 16.2. *Possible biographical trajectories in a class mobility matrix*

	Class destinations			
Class origins	Capitalist class	Petty bourgeoisie	Middle class	Working class
Capitalist class	1	2	3	4
Petty bourgeoisie	5	6	7	8
Middle class	9	10	11	12
Working class	13	14	15	16

distinguishing different types of lives in class terms; the model of additive effects of origins and destinations is not analytically privileged over an "interactive" model.

To illustrate this logic, consider the simple mobility matrix in Table 16.2. Sixteen different kinds of biographical trajectories are defined in this matrix. Rather than treating these as interactions between two variables – origins and destinations – the cells in this table can be viewed as values in a single sixteen-category typological variable of class trajectories. If we had sufficient data we could, of course, deploy this entire sixteen-category typology in the form of fifteen dummy variables in an analysis of trajectory effects. This would not, however, in general be the most interesting strategy theoretically, since not all of the distinctions among these cells are of equal theoretical interest. An alternative, therefore, is to collapse the cells of this typology in a variety of different ways depending upon one's theoretical and empirical objectives. Some of the possibilities are illustrated in Table 16.3.

These models should be read as follows. Cells which are assigned the same number are treated as conceptually equivalent. The ordering of the numbers has no inherent significance – they designate qualitatively distinct types, not an ordinal ranking. Where all the cells of the table are assigned only two numbers as in Models C and D, this implies that the original sixteeen-value typological variable is being

Table 16.3. *Examples of aggregations of full biographical trajectory typology*

A. Origins model

Destinations

		C	P	M	W[a]
	C	1[b]	1	1	1
Origins	P	2	2	2	2
	M	3	3	3	3
	W	4	4	4	4

B. Current location model

Destinations

		C	P	M	W
	C	1	2	3	4
Origins	P	1	2	3	4
	M	1	2	3	4
	W	1	2	3	4

C. Privilege model

Destinations

		C	P	M	W
	C	1	2	1	2
Origins	P	2	2	2	2
	M	1	2	1	2
	W	2	2	2	2

1 = entire life privileged owner (C) or privileged wage-earner (M)
2 = trajectory touches popular classes (P,W)

D. Underprivilege model

Destinations

		C	P	M	W
	C	1	1	1	1
Origins	P	1	2	1	2
	M	1	1	1	1
	W	1	2	1	2

1 = trajectory touches privileged classes (C or M)
2 = entire life in popular classes (P or W)

E. Privilege, underprivilege, mover model

Destinations

		C	P	M	W
	C	1	2	1	2
Origins	P	2	3	2	3
	M	1	2	1	2
	W	2	3	2	3

1 = always in privileged classes
2 = mixed trajectory
3 = always in popular classes

F. Privilege, underprivilege, upward, downward model

Destinations

		C	P	M	W
	C	1	3	1	3
Origins	P	2	4	2	4
	M	1	3	1	3
	W	2	4	2	4

1 = always in privileged classes
2 = mobile into privilege
3 = mobile into popular classes
4 = always in popular classes

Table 16.3. *(Continued)*

G. *Upward, downward model*[c]

		Destinations			
		C	P	M	W
	C	1	3	3	3
Origins	P	2	1	2	3
	M	2	3	1	3
	W	2	2	2	1

1= immobile
2= upward
3= downward

a. C = Capitalist class, P = Petty bourgeoisie, M = Middle class, W = working class

b. The numbers in the cells are used to identify which cells are being treated as belonging to the same conceptual category; they do not represent any kind of scale.

c. This model assumes that movement between middle class wage earners and the petty bourgeoisie is downward mobility.

collapsed into a single dichotomous variable which distinguishes only two kinds of lives.

Models A and B in Table 16.3 represent the simple class origins model and current class location (or "destinations") model. By collapsing the full typology along the rows in Model A we say, in effect, that in class biographies all that matters is origins; for any given origin, all destinations are conceptually equivalent. Model B, on the other hand, collapses the table along the columns, implying that all that matters is where people end up.

Models C through G represent different kinds of class trajectory models; C and D are the simplest, each distinguishing only two kinds of lives. In Model C all people who have lived their entire lives in what could be termed the "privileged classes" – capitalists among owning classes and the "middle class" among wage-earning classes – are distinguished from everyone else; in Model D, people who have lived their entire lives in the "popular classes" – the petty bourgeoisie and the working class – are distinguished from people whose lives have touched privilege at some time. Models E and F, then, combine Models C and D in different ways: Model E distinguishes a life of privilege (1), a life entirely in popular classes (3) and a mixed life (2); Model F differentiates this mixed category into an "upward" (popular to privileged) and "downward" (privileged to popular) component.

Finally, Model G collapses the various "immobile" categories – the diagonal of the original mobility matrix – into a single category. The result is a conventional upward, downward, stable classification of mobility experiences. Each of these models, therefore, can be viewed as a theoretical hypothesis about what kinds of biographies should be treated as essentially equivalent and what kinds should be distinguished.

It is important to note that the concepts of class trajectory and current class location are not logically independent: class location provides one of the pieces of data used to construct the class trajectory variable. The contrast between "Trajectory" and "Location" is therefore *not* equivalent to the distinction between the "past" and the "present"; trajectory is meant to capture a person's entire biography, which includes the present location. In the data analysis, therefore, it does not make much sense to include both trajectory and location simultaneously in a multivariate equation.[10] When we compare the explanatory power of trajectory and location in Hypotheses 1 and 2, therefore, we will not examine their relative explanatory power within a multivariate equation containing both variables, but their individual explanatory powers in separate equations.

16.4 Results

The empirical analysis will center on two aspects of the class content of consciousness: subjective class *identity*, and attitudes toward the *interests* of workers and capitalists. The overarching hypothesis is that these two dimensions of consciousness reflect different temporalities and thus are likely to be related to the problem of biographical trajectories and class locations in quite different ways.

Class identity is measured by a fairly conventional sociological question about class membership. Respondents were first asked whether or not they thought of themselves as belonging to a social class. If they responded "yes," they were asked to name the class. If they answered "no," they were asked the following: "Many people say they belong to the working class, the middle class or the upper middle

---

10 This is not a problem of multicollinearity, but of logical construction. Imagine that you created a four category race-by-sex typology. It would be mathematically senseless to include this typology in a regression (in the form of three dummy variables) along with sex or race. The categories in the trajectory models are like the categories in the race-sex typology.

class. If you had to make a choice, which class would you say you belonged to?" We are thus able to distinguish between people who spontaneously say that they are in the working class from people who only say that they are in the working class after being prodded into making a choice. If we assume that the spontaneous responses indicate greater salience of class identity than the forced choice, then this enables us to create a working-class identity variable which reflects both the cognitive and affective aspects of identity.[11] It has the following values:

2 = spontaneous working-class identification
1 = forced choice working-class identification
0 = no class identity even when asked to choose
−1 = forced choice nonworking-class identitification
−2 = spontaneous nonworking-class identification

Class interest consciousness is measured by a simple additive scale consisting of those questionnaire items that most closely tap perceptions of class interests.[12]

---

[11] In principle, one would want to know two things about an individual's identity with respect to class: first, how important or salient class identity was to the person relative to other possible identities – ethnic, national, religious, regional, sexual, etc.; and second, with which class the individual identifies. People may say that they are in the working class, but class identity may have no salience at all to them; their identity as Catholics, Irish, football fans or men may matter more to them than their identity as workers. A full analysis of identity formation, therefore, has to contend with the issue of salience as well as class content. The variable we are using only weakly deals with this problem of salience.

[12] Of the items measuring class consciousness in Chapters 14 and 15, three are narrowly concerned with perceptions of class interest: item 1 ("corporations benefit owners at the expense of workers and consumers") and 2 ("during a strike, management should be prohibited by law from hiring workers to take the place of strikers") in section 14.1, plus the item about strike outcomes discussed in the methodological appendix of chapter 15. Each item was coded 1 for a proworking class interest response (strongly agree or somewhat agree on the Likert items and response category 1 on the strike outcome question), −1 for a procapitalist response, and 0 for a class-neutral response (don't know on the Likert items and category 2 on the third variable). These items are summed to form a scale in which + 3 = pure proworking-class interest consciousness and − 3 = pure antiworking-class interest consciousness. In the previously published work on which this chapter is based (Wright and Shin 1988), a second scale was constructed involving a factor analysis of the six items used in chapter 15. None of the substantive results reported here are affected by the use of this more complex variable.

Class interest consciousness

Table 16.4 presents the R^2's for the various models predicting class-interest consciousness. There is considerable variation across categories of actors (the columns in the table) in how well any of the models fit. In general, the models fit much better for Swedish men than for any other category, and roughly equally well for American men and Swedish women. Among American women none of the models fit the data very well at all.

For men in both countries and for Swedish women, the current location model (Model B) is a better predictor of class-interest consciousness than is any of the trajectory models. For Swedish men, the best trajectory model – Model F (the privilege, underprivilege, upward, downward model) – explains about 12% of the variance in class interest consciousness, whereas the class locations model (Model B) explains about 18% of the variance. While the explained variances are smaller for American men and especially for Swedish women for both of these variables, the patterns are essentially the same. For American women, on the other hand, neither class location nor any of the trajectory models have any meaningful explanatory power. At least for men, then, current location has a somewhat stronger impact on class-interest consciousness than does biographical class trajectory. This is consistent with the claims of Hypothesis 1.

Class identity

Table 16.5 presents the percentage of respondents with a subjective working-class identity (i.e. a value of 1 or 2 on the working-class identity scale) within each of the cells in the full 4×4 class mobility matrix for Sweden and the United States. This table reveals strong class trajectory effects on class identity among Swedish men and possibly Swedish women, but not American men and women. Among Swedish men, for people currently in working-class locations, class origins do not matter very much for class identity: about 70% of the people from working-class, petty bourgeois and middle-class origins and 63% of those from capitalist origins identify with the working class. For people in current petty bourgeois and middle-class locations, on the other hand, class origins matter quite a lot. For example, while 48% of Swedish middle-class men from working-class origins subjectively identify with the working class, only 20% of those from middle-class

Table 16.4 *Explained variances (adjusted R^2) of the trajectory models predicting class-interest consciousness*

Models (d.f.)[a]	US		Sweden	
	Male	Female	Male	Female
A Origin (3)	.01	.00	.03***	.05***
B Current location (3)	.08***	.01	.18***	.05***
C Privilege (1)	.03***	.00	.04***	.02***
D Underprivilege (1)	.03***	.00	.10***	.02***
E Privilege, underprivilege, mixed (2)	.04***	.00	.10***	.03**
F Privilege, underprivilege, up, down (3)	.06***	.00	.12***	.03**
G Upward, downward, immobile (2)	.02**	.00	.03***	.00
Model B+E or B+F (5)[b]	.08***	.00	.18***	.06***
Model A+B (6)[c]	.08***	.00	.18***	.09***

Significance levels: * p < .05   ** p < .01   *** p < .001

a. The letters for different models correspond to the models displayed in Table 16.3.

b. The Model B+F has only 5 degrees of freedom because the distinction between category 2 and 3 within model F disappears in the B+F model (i.e. the model B+E and B+F are mathematically equivalent).

c. The model A+B is the conventional additive origin + destinations model.

origins have this class identity. The results for Swedish women are somewhat less striking, but still show such interactions. Within Sweden, therefore, class trajectory appears to systematically affect class identity.

The comparison of the explained variances of class identity for various models of class trajectory and for class location is presented in Table 16.6. As in the results for class-interest consciousness, for American women none of the models in Table 16.6 explains more than about 1% of the variance in class identity. In the more detailed analyses of different models which follows, therefore, the discussion will be restricted to American men and the Swedish sample.

Among the biographical trajectory models, Models E and F are clearly the best for these data. Both of these models provide distinctions between three kinds of biographies: (1) people who have lived their entire lives within the "popular" classes (workers and petty bourgeois); (2) people who have lived their entire lives in the privileged classes (middle-class wage-earners and capitalists); and (3) people whose biographies involve movement between these two. Model F

Table 16.5 *Percentage of males and females with working-class identification by class origin and current class location in the United States and Sweden*

Class origin (parent's class)	Current class location (respondent's class)			
	Capitalist class	Petty bourgeoisie	Middle class	Working class
Unoted States				
Males				
Capitalist class	.16 (19)[a]	.10 (10)	.12 (42)	.42 (26)
Petty bourgeoisie	.43 (21)	.58 (12)	.20 (30)	.53 (32)
Middle class	.21 (19)	.50 (4)	.20 (106)	.37 (86)
Working class	.13 (8)	.60 (10)	.25 (106)	.36 (118)
Females				
Capitalist class	.17 (6)	.38 (16)	.26 (38)	.33 (36)
Petty bourgeoisie	.33 (6)	.50 (12)	.25 (28)	.44 (57)
Middle class	.22 (9)	.14 (14)	.23 (61)	.39 (66)
Working class	.25 (8)	.40 (5)	.33 (69)	.34 (116)
Sweden				
Males				
Capitalist class	.27 (11)	.20 (5)	.24 (25)	.62 (13)
Petty bourgeoisie	.38 (13)	.58 (12)	.49 (35)	.71 (75)
Middle class	.17 (6)	.50 (6)	.20 (71)	.70 (53)
Working class	.33 (9)	.67 (15)	.48 (77)	.73 (129)
Females				
Capitalist class	.00 (1)	.00 (0)	.08 (13)	.40 (20)
Petty bourgeoisie	.50 (2)	.20 (5)	.32 (25)	.68 (65)
Middle class	.50 (2)	.00 (2)	.16 (56)	.43 (49)
Working class	.33 (3)	.40 (5)	.47 (46)	.58 (133)

a. Entries are the percentage of individuals in the cell who say that they are in the working class. The number of cases is in parentheses.

provides a further distinction within the mixed biographies between those who have moved from popular classes to exploiting classes, and those who have moved from exploiting classes to popular classes. Model F performs slightly better than Model E for Swedish men, whereas there is no difference between these models for Swedish women and American men.

Table 16.6. *Explained variances (adjusted R^2) of the trajectory models predicting working-class identity*

Models (d.f.)[a]	United States		Sweden	
	Male	Female	Male	Female
A Origin (3)	.01*	.00	.05***	.06***
B Current location (3)	.04***	.01	.12***	.08***
C Privilege (1)	.03***	.01*	.11***	.07***
D Underprivilege (1)	.03***	.00*	.08***	.07***
E Privilege, underprivilege, mixed (2)	.04***	.01*	.13***	.10***
F Privilege, underprivilege, up, down (3)	.04***	.01*	.14***	.10***
G Upward, downward, immobile (2)	.00	.00	.01*	.00
Model B+E or B+F (5)[b]	.04***	.01	.15***	.11***
Model A+B (6)[c]	.04***	.01	.14***	.11***

Significance levels: * p < .05   ** p < .01   *** p < .001

a. The letters for different models correspond to the models displayed in Table 16.3.

b. The Model B+F has only 5 degrees of freedom because the distinction between category 2 and 3 within model F disappears in the B+F model (i.e. the model B+E and B+F are mathematically equivalent).

c. The model A+B is the conventional additive origin + destinations model.

How do these trajectory models compare to the location model (Model B)? The adjusted R^2 for the current locations model is 12% for Swedish men and 8% for Swedish women. This increases to 14% for model F for Swedish men and 10% for Model E or F for Swedish women. This suggests that the trajectory variable has modestly greater explanatory power compared to the current location variable. For American men the difference in explained variance between the location model and the best of the trajectory models is negligible, and in any case is not very large. Overall, then, the evidence modestly supports Hypothesis 2 for Sweden, but not for the United States: in Sweden class trajectories have a moderately stronger effect on class identity than does current class location.

Class identity effects on class interests

Table 16.7 presents the results for the multivariate regressions of class location and class identity on class-interest consciousness. In each of

Table 16.7. *The effects of class location and class identity on class interest consciousness (unstandardized regression coefficients)*

	United States		Sweden	
	Men	Women	Men	Women
Class identity only	0.46**	0.29*	0.77**	0.49**
Adjusted R^2	0.01	0.01	0.16	0.08
Class location only[a]				
Worker vs. capitalist	1.34**	0.08	2.48**	0.92[b]
Worker vs. petty bourgeoisie	0.96**	0.56*	1.34**	1.71**
Worker vs. middle class	0.85**	0.23	1.20**	0.47**
Middle vs. capitalist	0.50*	−0.15	1.28**	0.46
Middle vs. petty bourgeoisie	0.11	0.33	0.14	1.25**
Petty bourgeoisie vs. capitalist	0.39	−0.48	1.14**	−0.78
Adjusted R^2	0.08	0.01	0.18	0.05
Class identity	0.31*	0.28*	1.12**	0.78*
Class location				
Worker vs. capitalist	1.31**	0.04	2.04**	0.87
Worker vs. petty bourgeoisie	0.97**	0.55*	1.17**	1.47**
Worker vs. middle class	0.79**	0.20	0.81**	0.24
Middle vs. capitalist	0.52*	−0.16	1.23**	0.63
Middle vs. petty bourgeoisie	0.18	0.35	0.36	1.23**
Petty bourgeoisie vs. capitalist	0.34	−0.51	0.87*	−0.60
Adjusted R^2	0.08	0.01	0.26	0.10

Significance levels: * $p < .05$ ** $p < .01$

a. These coefficients are calculated from three separate regression equations with different left out categories. With four dummy variables there are thus six possible contrasts.

b. There are only five Swedish women capitalists in the sample, so the standard errors for these contrasts are quite large.

the equations, class identity significantly predicts subjective class interests. Again, the results are particularly striking for Swedish men: class location and working-class identity alone account for 18% and 16% of the variance in working-class interest consciousness respectively; when combined they account for 26% of the variance. For such a simple multivariate model, this is a high R^2 for a regression on attitudes. The explained variances are lower for Swedish women, but it is still the case that class identity predicts class interests net of class location. For the American equations the effects of class identity on interests, while still statistically significant for both men and women, are much weaker than in Sweden, adding at most a marginal increment in explained variance.

Comparing Sweden and the United States

Hypothesis 4 argues that the effects postulated in Hypotheses 1, 2 and 3 should be stronger under macro-social conditions in which social and political institutions are systematically organized along class lines. Given the greater salience of working-class-centered ideology in the Swedish Social Democratic party than in the US Democratic Party, and given the organizational strength of the labor movement in Sweden, this hypothesis would lead us to expect considerably stronger patterns of results in Sweden than in the United States.

As Tables 16.4 and 16.6 indicate, the overall explanatory power of the various models tends to be much greater in Sweden, especially for Swedish men, than in the United States. For the class identity variable, all of the models have higher R^2 for both Swedish men and women than for American men. The models have little or no explanatory power for American women. For the class-interest consciousness variable, the models for Swedish men all explain more variance than the models for American men. Class location (Model B in Table 16.4) explains 18% of the variance in class-interest consciousness among Swedish men, but only about 8% of the variance among American men. Finally, the unstandardized coefficients for the working-class identity variable in the multivariate equations predicting class-interest consciousness are considerably larger in Sweden than in the United States: 1.12 for Swedish men and 0.78 for Swedish women, but only 0.31 for American men and 0.28 for American women.

Taking these various results together, it is reasonable to conclude that both class location and class trajectory are more powerful determinants of class consciousness in Sweden than in the United States. The results are thus strongly supportive of Hypothesis 4.

Table 16.8 *Summary of gender contrasts across countries: explained variances (R^2) in equations predicting interests and identity*

	US Men	Swedish Men	US Women	Swedish Women
Dependent variable = identity				
1 Origin → identity	.01	.05	.00	.06
2 Location → identity	.04	.12	.01	.08
3 Trajectory → identity	.04	.14	.01	.10
Dependent variable = interests				
4 Origins → interests	.01	.03	.00	.05
5 Location → interests	.08	.18	.01	.05
6 Trajectory → interests	.06	.12	.00	.03
7 Identity → interests	.01	.16	.01	.08
8 Location + identity → interests	.08	.26	.01	.10
Patterns of effects predicting interest consciousness and class identity from class location and class origins	Location has a much stronger effect than does origins in predicting both identity and interests		Neither location nor origins has significant effects on either identity or interests	Origins and locations have about the same effects on both identity and interests

Class and gender in national differences in consciousness

The original objectives of the data analysis in this chapter did not include exploring gender interactions in shaping class identity and subjective class interests. Nevertheless, the effects of gender are sufficiently striking in these results to warrant some comment. Most obviously, within both countries the explanatory power of the equations is much lower for women than for men. More subtly, the pattern of explained variances across models also differs by gender. These contrasts are summarized in Table 16.8.

The explained variances in the basic models we have investigated are typically in the 4–8% range for American men but generally 1% or less for American women, and in the 15–25% range for Swedish men but only 6–10% for Swedish women. At least as measured with the variables and models in this study, both class location and class trajectory are more systematically linked to dimensions of class consciousness among men than among women.

The gender contrasts in the *pattern* of effects across equations is equally striking. If we examine men separately, the basic pattern of coefficients in the models tends to be quite similar in both countries, in spite of the fact that the coefficients are generally much larger in Sweden than in the United States and the explanatory power of the Swedish models considerably greater. For men in both countries, class location matters much more than origins in determining both interest consciousness and class identity. For Swedish women, in contrast, class origins and class locations have roughly equal explanatory power for both of these dimensions of class subjectivity, and for American women, neither has much effect.

There are two possible lines of reasoning for explaining these gender differences. First, the lower causal efficacy of class origins and class location among women could primarily be a measurement problem. Perhaps the same formal criteria for class divisions have a different class content among men than for women. It could be, for example, that because of gender discrimination, the productive assets of "middle-class" women (skills/credentials) are devalued and are thus unable to be converted into exploitation. This would imply that the distinction between working class and middle class among women is a weaker class division than among men. This, in turn, would both reduce the explanatory power of class-centered variables (both location and origins) and potentially change the patterning of their effects.

An alternative approach to explaining these patterns of results is to search for some other mechanism that acts to block the effectivity of these variables among women (or enhance their effectivity among men). One likely candidate for this is the relationship between gender, family structure and class. As discussed in Chapter 10, because of gender inequality both in the home and in the labor market, the material interests of married women are generally more tied to the economic fate of their husbands than are the material interests of married men tied to the economic fate of their wives. To the extent that this is true, then the class interests of married women will be determined less by the class of their own job and more by the class of their husbands. Furthermore, over time this will also mean that their class identity will depend more on their family-class trajectory than simply on their individual-class trajectory. Individual class location will therefore tend to have lower explanatory power among women than among men for both class identity and class interests.

16.5 Conclusions

This chapter has attempted to join structural and processual approaches within class analysis. Much of the analysis is certainly open to criticism. Processual approaches are generally built around a fairly rich inventory of class constitutive experiences in communities, workplaces, schools, etc. Our use of processual approaches, in contrast, is based on a fairly impoverished operationalization of class trajectory, relying entirely on the linkage between class origins and class location. Similarly, contemporary structural approaches to class generally move beyond simple working-class vs. middle-class divisions among wage-earners, but because of the limitations in our data and sample size, we had to rely on this fairly crude class model. What is more, as our results for gender reveal, even within this simple class structural model, our results may be significantly affected by ignoring the problem of the location of families within the class structure.

In spite of these limitations, I believe that the data we have examined provide some support for the general orienting propositions of this chapter. In particular, the following general conclusions should be stressed:

First, class locations are more important than class trajectories for shaping narrowly interest-centered consciousness, whereas class trajectories (at least in Sweden) seem to be somewhat more important than class locations in shaping the more cultural dimensions of class consciousness. The magnitudes of the observed differences in explanatory power of these variables are not enormous, but still these results are in keeping with the view that class-interest consciousness depends more upon the perceptions of one's future class situation than on one's past, whereas class identity is more heavily shaped by one's biography in class-based communities, social networks and interactions. There is some justification in our analysis, therefore, for the focus of structural and processual approaches to class on different dimensions of consciousness.

Second, the perception of class interests is shaped at least as much by class identities as it is by class locations. While structural approaches to class may be correct in positing a set of material interests tied to class structures which create tendencies toward class-interest consciousness, the actual perception of those interests depends as much or more upon class identity as upon class location itself. Indeed, among Swedish men, the case in which class location has the strongest effects on class-interest consciousness, class identity (net of class location) also has the strongest effects on interest consciousness. Processual theorists are thus correct in emphasizing the importance of biographical trajectories of class experience in explaining empirical variations in class consciousness and class behavior. There remains, of course, a *conceptual* primacy of structural over processual class concepts since it is impossible to define the class content of biographical trajectories, communities, workplace experiences, etc. without having a prior elaboration of a structural class concept. But this conceptual primacy does not imply explanatory primacy in the lives of individuals.

Third, as we saw in Chapter 14 as well, all of these micro-mechanisms of consciousness formation are heavily mediated by the macrosocial context in which they operate. Where political and economic conflicts are heavily organized along class lines, these micro-mechanisms are likely to be reinforced; where class has been marginalized in institutional forms of collective organization, then the micro-mechanisms will be weaker. Again, this reflects a fundamental insight of processual theorists of class: the effectivity of the individual experiences that are constitutive of class depends upon the historical context within which those experiences occur.

Finally, and not as part of the original agenda of this chapter, all of the results we have observed of both a processual and structural nature vary sharply by gender. While this does not mean that class mechanisms are inherently *gendered* in the sense of having no independent effectivity in their own right, it does mean that the empirical investigation of the effects of both class location and class trajectory must include an analysis of interactions with gender.

Part V

Conclusion

17 Confirmations, surprises and theoretical reconstructions

Class analysis, in the Marxist tradition, stands at the center of a sweeping analysis of the dilemmas of contemporary society and the aspirations for an egalitarian and democratic future for humanity. Class is a normatively charged concept, rooted in ideas of oppression, exploitation and domination. This concept underwrites both an emancipatory vision of a classless society and an explanatory theory of conflicts, institutions and social change rooted in intrinsically antagonistic interests. The ultimate ambition of this kind of class analysis is to link the explanatory theory to the emancipatory vision in such a way as to contribute to the political project of transforming the world in the direction of those ideals. Marxist empirical research of whatever kind – whether ethnographic case studies, historical investigations or statistical analyses of survey data – should further this ambition.

At first glance it may seem that the empirical studies in this book have little to do with such grand visions. The topics we have explored have revolved around narrowly focussed properties of contemporary capitalist societies rather than the epochal contradictions which dynamically shape social change. While I have invoked the themes of transformative struggles, only a pale reflection of "class struggle" has appeared in the actual empirical analyses in the form of attitudes of individuals. And while the concept of class we have been exploring is conceptualized in terms of exploitation, none of the empirical research directly explores the problem of exploitation as such. In what ways, then, can the masses of coefficients, tables and graphs in this book be said to push forward the central themes and ideas of the Marxist agenda?

Research pushes social theory forward in two basic ways. Where there is a controversy between contending theoretical claims about some problem, research potentially can provide a basis for adjudicating between the alternatives. The more focussed and well defined is the problem, and particularly, the more there is agreement among contending views on the precise specification of what needs to be explained, the more likely it is that research can play this role. Our explorations of alternative expectations about the transformations of the class structure or the permeability of class boundaries are in this spirit. Where successful, the results of research can be said to provisionally "confirm" a particular set of expectations linked to a theoretical perspective.[1] While, at least in social science, such adjudication and confirmation rarely bear directly on the adequacy of broader theoretical perspectives, the cumulative effect of such research can contribute to the erosion of some perspectives and the strengthening of others.

Adjudication and confirmation are at the core of the standard "hypothesis testing" strategies of contemporary sociology.[2] There is, however, a second modality through which research pushes theory forward: the goal of research can be to find interesting surprises, anomalous empirical results that go against the expectations of a theory and thus provoke rethinking. It is all well and good to do research that confirms what one already believes, but the advance of knowledge depends much more on generating observations that challenge one's existing ideas, that are counterintuitive with respect to received wisdom.

Surprises of this sort may be the by-product of the adjudication between rival hypotheses. After all, what is "surprising" within one theoretical framework may be "commonsense" within another. The accelerating decline of the working class is certainly a surprise within Marxism; it is hardly surprising for postindustrial theorists. Research which seems to confirm the expectations of one's theoretical rivals thus provides crucial raw material for efforts at theory reconstruction.

Empirical anomalies may also occur in research that is not explicitly directed at adjudicating between rival hypotheses. The surprises in my

---

1   In this context "confirmation" does not mean "definitively prove" a theoretical claim, but rather "add significantly to the credibility" of that claim. Confirming a theoretical claim is always relative to rival claims and always provisional subject to further research, not a process of establishing absolute "truth."

2   The standard rhetoric is "rejecting the null hypothesis" rather than "adjudicating between rival hypotheses." Nevertheless, the underlying logic of inquiry is using evidence to add credibility to a set of expectations derived from one theory versus alternatives.

research on housework, for example, grew out of an exploration of the implications of class analysis for gender relations rather than a direct confrontation between alternative theories of housework. In any case, empirical surprises force the reconstruction of theory, and it is through such reconstruction that social theory moves forward.[3]

"Reconstructions" of theory in the light of empirical surprises, of course, may be purely defensive operations, patching up a sinking ship that is sailing in the wrong direction. There is no guarantee that reconstructions constitute "progressive" developments within a theoretical framework rather than degenerate branches of a research program, to use Imre Lakatos's formulation. Nevertheless, it is through such reconstructions that theoretical knowledge advances.[4]

The research in this book involves both of these modalities for linking theory and research. Some of the research was primarily concerned with empirically comparing the expectations of a Marxist class analysis with expectations derived from other theoretical perspectives. Other studies were less focussed on adjudicating between well-formulated rival expectations than simply exploring the implications of the Marxist approach itself.[5] Much of this research provides confirmation for what I believed before doing the research, but there were also many surprises, at least some of which may contribute to the ongoing reconstruction of Marxist class analysis.

It is mainly on these surprises that I want to focus in this chapter. In what follows, for each of the major themes in the book I will first present a stylized account of what might be termed the "conventional wisdom" within Marxism. This is not always an easy task, for on some of the topics we have explored Marxists have not had a great deal to say, and in any case there are many Marxisms from which to choose the "traditional view." My characterization of the "traditional under-

---

[3] For a systematic discussion of the reconstructionist logic of theory building as it applies to Marxism, see Michael Burawoy (1990, 1993).

[4] The perspective on social theory presented here sees knowledge advancing through the ways theories are reconstructed in the face of empirical challenge. An alternative view sees theories as simply being "tested" by "data" and falsified when the data contradicts the predictions of the theory. If social scientists rejected theories whenever the data contradicted them, we would have no theories left with which to guide our research.

[5] For the record, some projects began as straightforward explorations of the ramifications of Marxist class analysis for some problem but were eventually transformed into adjudications of alternative expectations in response to criticisms from referees in sociology journals who complained that I was not properly "testing" rival hypotheses.

standing," therefore, is bound to be disputed. My intention is not to give an authoritative account of "what Marx really said," but to capture a set of theoretical intuitions shared by many – perhaps most – Marxists. This account of the traditional understanding will serve as the benchmark for assessing the ways in which the results of the various research projects provide confirmations of these conventional expectations or surprises. The inventory of surprises, in turn, will provide the basis for exploring some of the directions in which Marxist class analysis might be reconstructed in light of the research.

These issues will be explored for five broad themes in class analysis which we have explored in this book: (1) the problem of conceptualizing "locations" within the class structure; (2) the variability and transformation of class structure of advanced capitalist societies; (3) the intersection of the lives of individuals and class structures; (4) the effects of class on class consciousness and class formation; and (5) the relationship between class and other forms of oppression, especially gender.

17.1 Conceptualizing "locations" in the class structure

More than any other issue, this research has revolved around the problem of what it means to "locate" a person in the class structure. If we are to link micro- and macro-levels of class analysis by exploring the impact of class on the lives and consciousness of individuals, some sort of solution to this issue is essential. The image is that a structure of class relations generates an array of "empty places" filled by individuals. To pursue micro-level class analysis we must both figure out how to define these empty places and what it means for an individual to be linked to those places.

Traditional understanding

Traditional Marxism developed a systematic conceptualization of class structure only at the highest levels of abstraction. The "empty places" in class relations were defined by the social property relations within specific modes of production. In capitalist societies this led to the rigorous specification of two basic class locations: *capitalists* and *workers* within capitalist relations of production. To these could be added class locations that were rooted in various kinds of precapitalist relations of production, especially the *petty bourgeoisie* within simple commodity production, and in some times and places, various class locations within feudal relations of production. In many concrete analyses loose references were also made to other class locations, especially to the new middle class of managers and professionals, but these were not given firm conceptual status.

In the traditional account, individuals were linked to these empty places through their direct relationship to the means of production: capitalists owned the means of production and employed workers; workers sold their labor power on a labor market and worked within capitalist firms; the petty bourgeoisie were direct producers using their own means of production. Every class location was therefore in one and only one class. Individuals might, of course, change their class in the course of their lives, but at any given point in time they were located within a specific class.

Initial reconstructions

The framework elaborated in this book attempts to reconstruct the traditional Marxist concept of class structure in two different ways. First, the map of empty places has been transformed through the development of the concept of *contradictory locations within class relations*. Instead of defining class locations simply at the level of abstract modes of production, I have tried to develop a more concrete, multidimensional understanding of how jobs are tied to the process of exploitation. Specifically, I have argued that, in addition to the relationship to the ownership of the means of production, the linkage of jobs to the process of exploitation is shaped by their relation to domination within production (authority) and to the control over expertise and skills. This generates the more complex map of locations we have used throughout the book. In this new conceptualization, the "middle class" is not simply a residual category of locations that do not comfortably fit the categories "capitalist" and "worker." Rather, middle-class locations in the class structure are those that are linked to the process of exploitation and domination in contradictory ways. The "empty places" in the class structure, therefore, are no longer necessarily in one and only one class.

The second way in which the traditional view of class locations has been modified is through the concept of mediated class locations. The central point of trying to assign a class location to an individual is to clarify the nature of the lived experiences and material interests the individual is likely to have. Being "in" a class location means that you do certain things and certain things happen to you (lived experience) and you face certain strategic alternatives for pursuing your material well-being (class interests). Jobs embedded within social relations of production are one of the ways individuals are linked to such interests and experiences, but not the only way. Families provide another set of social relations which tie people to the class structure. This is especially salient in families within which different members of the family hold jobs with different class characters. Individuals in such families have both direct and mediated class locations, and these two links to class relations may or not be the same. This introduces a new level of complexity into the micro-analysis of class which is especially relevant to the interaction of class and gender.

Empirical confirmations

Empirically "testing" concepts is a tricky business. Indeed, there are some traditions of social science which regard concepts as simply linguistic conventions, and thus there is no sense in which a particular conceptualization can be shown to the *wrong*; at most a given concept can be more or less *useful* than others. There is, however, an alternative view which claims that at least some concepts should be treated as attempts at specifying real mechanisms that exist in the world independent of our theories. For such "realist concepts," a definition can be incorrect in the sense that it misspecifies some crucial feature of the relevant causal properties.[6]

The concept of class being proposed in this book is meant to be a realist concept, not simply an arbitrary convention. The appropriate way of evaluating the concept, therefore, is to examine a variety of effects that the hypothesized class-defining mechanisms are supposed to generate. If a given conceptualization is correct, then these effects should follow certain expected patterns. Anomalies with respect to these expectations, of course, need not invalidate the concept, since

[6]   The general perspective offered here is that social science, Marxist and other, should be seen as containing a variety of different kinds of concepts: some are pure conventions; some are merely commonsense categories from everyday language; others are systematically worked out ideal-types; and still others are realist concepts that attempt to define the criteria for a given concept in terms of real mechanisms operating in the world. For a general discussion of realist concepts, see Wright (1985: 1–37).

failures of prediction of this sort can be due to the presence of all sorts of confounding mechanisms (including the special kind of confounding mechanism we call "measurement problems"). Nevertheless, as in more straightforward hypothesis testing, such surprises pose challenges which potentially provoke reconstructions.

In one way or another, nearly all of the results of this book bear on the problem of evaluating the adequacy of the proposed conceptualization of class structure, even though little of the research is directly geared toward "testing" this conceptualization against its rivals. Still, a few of the results have a particularly clear relation to the theoretical logic which underlies the conceptualization of class in this book.

First, in the analysis of class consciousness, the variation across class locations in individual attitudes toward class issues broadly follows the predictions derived from the three-dimensional class structure matrix. Particularly in Sweden and the United States, the extent to which individuals were likely to hold procapitalist or proworking-class attitudes varied monotonically across the three dimensions of the matrix. This does not, of course, decisively prove that this is the appropriate way of specifying the concept of class location within a Marxist framework, but it lends credibility to the approach.

The second specific way the results of this research support the proposed reconceptualization of class is more complex. In the various analyses of the permeability of class boundaries, it was demonstrated that the probabilities of permeability events (mobility, friendships, cross-class marriages) occurring between specific class locations were not simply additive effects of permeability across the three class boundaries we studied – the property boundary, the authority boundary and the skill boundary. For example, the probability of a friendship between a person in a working-class location and a capitalist location was not simply the sum of the probabilities of a friendship across the property boundary and across the authority boundary. If the effects of these three boundaries had been strictly additive, then this would have suggested that aggregating the dimensions into a "class structure" was simply a conceptual convenience. Nothing would be lost by disaggregating the class structure into these more "primitive" dimensions and treating them as separate, autonomous attributes of jobs. The consistent interactions among these dimensions in the patterns of class permeability support the claim that these three dimensions should be considered dimensions of a conceptual gestalt – "class structure" – rather than simply separate attributes of jobs.

Third, the credibility of the concept of mediated class locations is demonstrated in the analysis of the class identity of married women in two-earner households. At least in Sweden, the class identity of such women was shaped both by their own job-class and by the class of their husband. While there are complications in this analysis which we will review in the discussion of class consciousness below, these results generally support the idea that individuals' locations in a class structure should be conceptualized in terms of the multiple ways in which their lives are linked to class relations.

Surprises

Most of the empirical results in this book are consistent with the proposed reconceptualization of class structure. There are, however, two specific sets of results that are somewhat anomalous and thus raise questions about the concept of contradictory class locations. Both of these involve the relationship between the authority and skill dimensions of the class structure matrix, one in the analysis of permeability of class boundaries, the other in the investigation of class consciousness. We will discuss these results in more detail later when we examine the general results for class permeability and for class consciousness. Here I will only focus on how these results bear on the conceptualization of contradictory class locations.

First, in the analyses of permeability of class boundaries, for each of the kinds of permeability we studied the authority boundary was always much more permeable than the skill boundary (and in some analyses not significantly impermeable in absolute terms), yet within a Marxist framework, authority is more intimately linked than is skill or expertise to the fundamental class cleavage of capitalism, the capital–labor relation. This relatively high permeability of the authority boundary compared to the skill boundary is thus in tension with my reconstructed Marxist class concept in which authority constitutes a dimension of the *class* structure among employees rather than simply an aspect of "stratification" or even merely role differentiation.

Second, in Japan the extremely muted ideological differences across levels of managerial authority compared to a rather sharp ideological cleavage between experts and nonexperts at every level of the authority hierarchy also runs against the implications of the contradictory class location concept. Since the items we use as indicators of class consciousness center around capital–labor conflict, if it were the case that managerial authority defines the basis for a contradictory location linked to the capitalist class, then it is surprising that ideological differences along this dimension are so muted in a thoroughly capitalist society like Japan, and it is especially surprising that the skill cleavage is so much more striking than the authority cleavage.

Further possible reconstructions?

Both of these anomalous results may simply be the result of measurement problems. The Japanese results are obviously vulnerable to all sorts of measurement errors on the attitude questions. But measurement issues may equally undermine the permeability results. Even though we tried to restrict the permeability of the managerial boundary to events that linked proper managers (not merely supervisors) to employees outside of the authority hierarchy, in several of the analyses it was impossible to rigorously distinguish managers and supervisors. Furthermore, even the "manager" category includes people near the bottom of authority structures. The fact that throughout the book we have amalgamated managers in small businesses with managers in multinational corporations may also confound the analyses. It is one thing for the manager of a locally owned retail store or a McDonald's franchise to be good friends with workers and to have come from a working-class family, and another thing for a manager in the headquarters of IBM (let alone an executive) to have such ties. It may well be the case, therefore, that these results would be quite different if we restricted managers to people with decisive power over broad organizational resources and policymaking and distinguished large-scale capitalist production from small business.

However, if these anomalous results turn out to be robust, they may indicate that the concept of "contradictory class locations" does indeed meld a relational concept of class rooted in capitalist property relations with dimensions of gradational stratification. This is most obvious for the skill dimension, which seems to have a natural gradational logic of having more or less of something. Authority is inherently a relational property of jobs, but yet its place within class analysis might better be understood in terms of strata within classes rather than a distinctive kind of class location. This line of reasoning might suggest a fairly radical conceptual shift away from the idea of contradictory locations within class relations: authority and skill would be treated as the bases for gradational strata within the class of employees defined by capitalist relations of production. Such a class analysis could still claim to be Marxist insofar as the class concept itself remained deeply linked to the problem of exploitation and capitalist property relations, but it would no longer attempt to specify differentiated *class* locations at concrete, micro-levels of analysis among employees. If this conceptual move were embraced, then the distinctively Marxist class concept would primarily inform analyses at the more abstract levels of class analysis, whereas something much more like a gradational concept of social stratification would inform concrete levels of analysis.

I do not believe that these particular results for managers are so compelling as to call for this kind of conceptual transformation. For most of the analyses in this book, the divisions among employees which we have mapped along the authority and skill dimensions appear to have class-like effects, and the concept of contradictory locations within class relations does a good job of providing an explanatory framework for understanding the results. Taken as a whole, the results of the studies in this book affirm the fruitfulness of the concept of contradictory class locations. Thus, while the conceptual framework does not achieve the level of comprehensive coherence, either theoretically or empirically, which I had hoped for when I first began working on the problem of the middle class, the anomalies are not so pressing as to provoke a new conceptual metamorphosis.

17.2 Class structure and its variations in advanced capitalist societies

Traditional understanding

The traditional Marxist view of the variations across time and place in the class structure of capitalist societies revolves around three broad propositions:

1 *The distribution of the population into different classes within capitalism should depend largely upon the level of development of the "forces of production" (technology and technical knowledge).* This should be particularly true for the distribution of class locations within capitalist production itself. Since our sample is of countries which are all at roughly the same level of economic development, it

would be expected that their class distributions should not differ greatly.

2 *The broad tendency of change over time in class distributions within capitalist societies is toward an expansion of the working class.* There are two principal reasons for this expectation: first, the petty bourgeoisie and small employer class locations are eroded by competition from larger capitalist firms, thus expanding the proportion of the labor force employed as wage-earners; and second, rationalization and technical change within production, designed to maximize capitalist profits, tend to generate a "degradation of labor" – the reduction in the skills, autonomy and power of employees – which results in a relative expansion of proletarianized labor among wage-earners.[7]

3 *As a result of these two propositions, the expectation is that the working class should be the largest class within developed capitalist societies.* The image of developed capitalist societies as becoming largely "middle class societies" would be rejected by most Marxists, regardless of the specific ways in which they elaborate the concept of class.[8]

Confirmations

Some aspects of these traditional understandings are supported by the data in Part I of this book. In all six of the capitalist societies we examined, the working class remains the single largest location within

---

[7] Marx cited an additional tendency with advanced development of the forces of production: after capitalism has matured, the increasing capital intensity of production tends to continually displace workers, especially out of industrial production. Some of these workers become part of "the reserve army of labor" (the unemployed) and some become part of the surplus population (the marginalized underclass). This reduction in industrial working-class employment may also indirectly contribute to the expansion of "middle-class" employment opportunities, especially in the state, although Marx himself is not very clear on this. In any event, while these tendencies certainly make the picture more complex, the most common view among Marxists has been that the working class, perhaps including the reserve army of labor, expands with capitalist development for the two reasons cited above.

[8] There are theoretical currents within Marxism which present a very different picture from this standard view because of their definition of "working class." Nicos Poulantzas (1975), for example, limits the working class to productive, manual, nonsupervisory labor. The result, as I have argued (Wright, 1976: 23), is that the working class becomes less than 20% of the US labor force. Most contemporary Marxist discussions adopt a class concept which defines the working class in much less restrictive terms.

the class structure, and when nonskilled supervisors and skilled workers are combined with the working-class location, in every country we have examined the "extended working class" is a clear majority (55–60%) of the labor force, and a large majority of employees (generally around 75%). It may well be the case that in terms of the distribution of income and life-styles – the characteristic way that the "middle class" is defined in popular culture – a substantial majority of the population is middle class. But in terms of relationship to the process of production and exploitation, the majority of the labor force is either in the working class or in those contradictory class locations most closely linked to the working class. Also as expected, the variation in class distributions, at least among employees, across the six countries we examined is relatively modest: the extended working class constitutes about three-quarters of employees in all of these countries while the most privileged segment of the middle class (the extended expert-manager location) constitutes about one-ninth of employees.

Surprises

Two principal surprises stand out in the results on class structure. First, there is strong evidence that, at least in the United States, the working class is declining as a proportion of the labor force, and, what is more, this decline is occurring at an accelerating rate. While in the 1960s the decline in the relative size of the working class was entirely attributable to changes in the sectoral composition of the labor force (i.e. the sectors with the smallest proportion of workers were growing the fastest), by the 1980s the working class was declining in all major economic sectors. Experts and expert managers, on the other hand, have generally been expanding as a proportion of the labor force. Second, it also appears in the United States that the long, continuous decline of the petty bourgeoisie ended in the early 1970s and that since the middle of that decade self-employment has increased almost steadily. A similar growth in self-employment occurred in a variety of other developed capitalist countries. By the early 1990s the proportion of the labor force self-employed in the US was perhaps as much as 50% greater than twenty years earlier. In the 1980s this expansion of self-employment was occurring within most economic sectors. Furthermore, between 1980 and 1990 there was an expansion of small employers – not just the petty bourgeoisie – due to sectoral changes, indicating that the expansion of self-employment is unlikely to be simply a question of disguised forms of wage labor.

Reconstructions

These trends suggest that while the working class is hardly disappearing, there is clear evidence of an expansion of class locations which are relatively "privileged" in various ways – in terms of autonomy, authority and access to surplus, and even access to capital. The traditional Marxist thesis of deepening proletarianization within developed capitalist economies is therefore called into question.[9]

There are two strategies for rethinking the problem of the transformation of capitalist class structures in light of these results. The first response leaves the basic theory of proletarianization intact, but identifies a misspecification of the empirical context of the analysis. It is possible, for example, that these trends are artifacts of the restriction of the analysis to changes in class structures *within* specific nation-states. It has long been recognized that capitalism is a global system of production. This suggests that the proper unit of analysis for understanding the transformation of capitalist class structures should be the world, not specific firms, countries or even regions. It could be the case, for example, that the proportion of the employees of American corporations world-wide who are in the working class has increased, but that there has been a shift of employment to workers outside the borders of the US. Global capitalism could thus be characterized by increasing proletarianization even if developed capitalism is not.

The second response calls into question more basic elements of the traditional Marxist understanding. As various theorists of "post-industrial" society have argued, the dramatic new forces of production of advanced capitalist societies may have fundamentally altered the developmental tendencies of capitalist class relations. Of particular

---

[9] These observations are consistent with the claim that within the working class there has been a relative expansion of badly paid service employment and a decline of highly paid factory jobs. There may indeed be deepening proletarianization within the working class and yet declining proletarianization in the labor force as a whole. These results also do not address the problem of the expansion of the so-called "underclass" – the part of the population that is economically oppressed but marginalized from the process of capitalist exploitation. It is certainly plausible that one of the ramifications of the relative decline of the working class in the labor force is the expansion of the "relative surplus population," the part of the population that cannot find a place within capitalist class relations.

importance in this regard are the implications of information technologies for the class location of various kinds of experts and managers. One scenario is that a decreasing proportion of the population is needed for capitalist production altogether, and among those who remain employed in the capitalist economy, a much higher proportion will occupy positions of responsibility, expertise and autonomy. This implies a broad decline of the working class and purely supervisory employees, an increase of the "relative surplus population," and an expansion of experts and proper managers. Of course, this may simply be a short-lived phase, not a permanent reconfiguration of capitalist class structures. It is possible that once these new technologies have been in place for a while, a process of systematic deskilling and proletarianization might once again dominate changes in class distributions. But it may also be the case that these new forces of production stably generate a class structure different from earlier industrial technologies.

17.3 Individual lives and the class structure

Traditional understanding

Marxism has never developed a systematic theory of the way the lives of individuals intersect class structures, and thus there is not a strong set of expectations about the class patterns of intergenerational mobility, friendship formation and family composition. There is nothing in the Marxist concept of class to logically preclude the possibility of two class structures with very similar distributions of *locations* having quite different trajectories of individual lives across locations.

Nevertheless, the underlying spirit of Marxist class analysis suggests that in a stable capitalist class structure most people's lives should be fairly well contained within specific class locations. Specifically, Marxism suggests three general propositions about the permeability of class boundaries:

1 *The relative impermeability of the property boundary.* The antagonistic material interests and distinctive forms of lived experience linked to class locations should make friendships, marriages and mobility across the basic class division of capitalist societies – the division between capitalists and workers – relatively rare. Such events should certainly be less common than parallel events that spanned the authority and skill dimensions of the class structure.

In the language developed in Part II of the book, the property boundary in the class structure should be less permeable to mobility, friendships and families than either the skill or authority boundary.

2 *The authority boundary.* A weaker expectation within a Marxist class analysis is that the authority boundary should be less permeable than the skill boundary. Insofar as the class antagonisms generated by managerial authority are more closely linked to the basic class cleavage of capitalism than is skill or expertise, there should be greater barriers to intimate social interaction across the authority boundary than across the skill boundary.

3 *Variations in permeability across capitalist societies.* On the assumption that the degree of impermeability of a class boundary is based on the antagonism of material interests generated around that boundary, then the more purely capitalistic is a class structure, the less permeable its property boundary should be, both absolutely and relative to other class boundaries.

Confirmations

The core results of our investigations of the permeability of class boundaries in Part II are quite consistent with the first and third of these expectations. In particular, the property boundary is generally less permeable than either the authority or skill boundaries to intergenerational mobility, friendship formation and cross-class marriages. Also, as expected, the property boundary is generally less permeable in North America than in Scandinavia, especially for intergenerational mobility. The contrast is especially striking in the comparison of the United States and Sweden: the chances of intergenerational mobility or friendships across the property boundary are over twice as great in Sweden as in the United States. Where capitalism is the most unconstrained and thus capitalist property relations make the biggest difference in the material interests of actors, the barriers to intergenerational mobility and friendship ties across the property boundary appear to be greatest.

Surprises

Not all of the results in our analyses of class boundary permeability fit comfortably with Marxist intuitions. First, even though the property boundary is the least permeable of the three class boundaries we explored, nevertheless it can hardly be described as highly impermeable. Roughly speaking, mobility, friendships and cross-class marriages across the property boundary occur at about 25–30% of the rate that would be expected if the boundary were completely permeable. Furthermore, in the broader analysis of the petty bourgeoisie in the United States in Chapter 4, we observed that well over 50% of all workers say that they would like to be self-employed some day, and over 60% have some kind of personal connection with the petty bourgeoisie – through previous jobs, class origins, second jobs, spouses or close personal friendships. The extent to which the lives of people in capitalist societies cross the property boundary is thus greater than suggested by the traditional Marxist image of capitalist class relations.

Second, as already noted in the discussion of anomalies in the concept of contradictory class location, the authority boundary turns out to be highly permeable to all three social processes we have explored in all four countries. Recall that for the purposes of these analyses we have tried to define the permeability of the authority boundary relatively restrictively – except for the mobility analysis, it involves a connection between proper managers (not mere supervisors) and nonmanagerial employees. With that definition, for many of the results the authority boundary creates almost no barriers. Again, while Marxist theory does not contain strong predictions about how individual lives intersect authority relations within work, given the importance of domination within production to Marxist class analysis, this degree of permeability is at least in tension with certain traditional Marxist themes.

Third, cross-class families are more common in all of the countries we studied than many Marxists would have expected. In roughly a third of all dual-earner families in these countries, husbands and wives were in different class locations. This is particularly important theoretically since families are units of consumption with shared material interests. The existence of cross-class families, therefore, means that for many people their direct and mediated class locations will be different.

Reconstructions

It is an old theme in sociology, especially in the Weberian tradition, that social mobility is a stabilizing process in contemporary societies. It is generally assumed that a class structure that rigidly constrains the lives of individuals will ultimately be more fragile than one with relatively high levels of fluidity. These issues have been largely neglected within the Marxist tradition of class analysis. Much more attention has been paid to the levels of inequality across class locations and the exploitative practices thought to generate that inequality than to the way individual lives are organized within those class structures.

The patterns of class-boundary permeability which we have explored indicate that this issue needs to be taken seriously within Marxist class analysis. The results suggest that the durability of capitalism in the developed capitalist societies is probably not simply due to its capacity to generate growth and affluence for a substantial proportion of their populations, but also because of the extent to which individual lives and interactions cross the salient divisions within the class structure. This is particularly the case for the permeability of the secondary class divisions in capitalist societies – class boundaries constituted by authority and skill – but it is also true for the primary class division. Of course, none of our analyses examine the probability of life events linking the working class and large capitalists, let alone the "ruling class." Nevertheless, the personal linkages between workers and small employers are not rare events in developed capitalist societies.

This permeability of class boundaries has potentially important consequences for both the class identities and interests of actors. Insofar as identities are shaped by biographical trajectories of lived experiences, the relative frequency of cross-class experiences would be expected to dilute class identity. Even more significantly, to the extent that class boundaries are permeable to *intra*generational mobility (a problem we have not explored) and family ties, then class interests would no longer be narrowly tied to individual class locations. Class interests define the strategic alternatives individuals face in pursuing their material welfare. Those alternatives are quite different where individual families contain members in different class locations or where individuals have a reasonable expectation that their future class location might be different from their present one. Class analysis needs to incorporate these facts about the interweaving of lives and structures.

17.4 Effects of class structure: class consciousness and class formation

Traditional understanding

Forms of consciousness – at least those aspects of consciousness bound up with class – are deeply affected by the ways class structure shapes lived experiences and material interests. While political and cultural processes may affect the extent to which such consciousness develops a coherent ideological expression and becomes linked to collectively organized social forces, nevertheless, a strong and systematic association between class location and the subjectivities of actors should be generated by the class structure itself. While Marxism does not predict politically conscious, collectively organized class struggles to be a universal feature of capitalism, it does predict that at the level of individual subjectivity, there should be a systematic association between location in the class structure and forms of class consciousness.

This general Marxist perspective on class location and class consciousness suggests five broad theses about the empirical problems we have been exploring:

1 *The point of production thesis.* Within the Marxist tradition, class has its effects on people's subjectivity not mainly through the standard of living generated by class positions (the "sphere of consumption"), but by the experiences and interests generated within production itself. Therefore, in cases in which there is a disjuncture between direct class location and mediated class location, class consciousness should be more powerfully shaped by direct class.

2 *The polarization thesis.* Class structures should be ideologically polarized between workers and capitalists on aspects of consciousness concerning class interests.

3 *The multidimensional exploitation thesis.* Among employees, the extent of working-class consciousness should vary monotonically with a person's location within the two-dimensional matrix of class locations among nonproperty-owners. Even if one does not buy into all of the details of the concept of contradictory class locations, still most Marxists would predict that the more fully

proletarianized is a class location along either the skill or authority dimensions, the more likely it is that persons in that class location will have proworking-class consciousness.

4 *The macro-mediation thesis.* While class location should be systematically linked to class consciousness everywhere, the strength of this linkage at the micro-level will vary across countries depending upon the strength of working-class formations.

5 *Class formation thesis.* Within the common patterns postulated in the polarization thesis and the multidimensional exploitation thesis, the specific line of demarcation between class formations will vary cross-nationally depending upon a range of historically contingent processes, especially the political legacies of class struggles.

Confirmations

With the partial exception of some results concerning the point of production thesis (see below), the basic patterns of the relationship between class location and class consciousness in our various analyses are broadly consistent with these hypotheses. Even though we only have data on relatively small capitalist employers, in all three of the countries we studied, capitalists and workers are ideologically polarized in their attitudes toward class issues. Among employees, workers and expert managers are also polarized, with nonexpert managers and nonmanagerial experts having ideological positions somewhere between these extremes. Furthermore, as suggested by the macro-mediation thesis, the strength of the micro-level association between class location and various aspects of class consciousness does vary across countries. Specifically, this association is consistently very strong in Sweden where working-class formations are politically and ideologically strong, while the association is moderate in the United States and quite weak in Japan. Finally, as suggested by the class formation thesis, the specific ideological coalitions that are formed on the basis of these common underlying patterns are quite different in the three countries we examined. At least for Sweden and the United States, these differences can plausibly be interpreted in terms of the divergences in the two countries in the historical trajectories and institutional legacies of political class struggles.

Surprises: direct and mediated class locations

The results of the study of the effects of family class composition on class identity partially contradict the point of production thesis. For men, the thesis holds in both the United States and Sweden: class identity is much more decisively shaped by the class character of the individual's own job than by the class composition of the household within which men live. For women, in contrast, mediated class locations (i.e. their links to the class structure through their spouses' job) matter much more than they do for men. In Sweden, for wives in two-earner households, direct and mediated class locations have roughly the same impact on the probability of their having a working-class identity; in the United States, for wives in two-earner households, direct class location has almost no effect on class identity net of the effect of mediated class location. At least for the study of the class identity of married women in two-earner households, therefore, this aspect of class subjectivity is affected at least as much by mediated class locations as by their direct position within the system of production, contradicting the point of production thesis.

Surprises: class consciousness and class formation

While the patterns of class structure and consciousness we observed are broadly consistent with Theses 2–5, the extent of cross- national variation in the strength of association of class location and consciousness is greater than suggested by traditional Marxist intuitions. In particular, the Japanese case falls outside of the range of variability that would be expected within Marxist class analysis. While class location is a statistically significant predictor of class consciousness in Japan, nevertheless it accounts for a very modest amount of the variance in our attitude scales in Japan (about 5%) – about half of the variance accounted for by class in the United States and less than a third of the figure for Sweden. Even when an array of other class-related experiences and conditions are added to the equation, the explained variance in the Japanese data remains quite small compared to the other two countries.

The patterns of ideological class formation in Japan also do not conform with standard Marxist expectations. While it is the case that the basic monotonic relationship between class location and consciousness postulated in the multidimensional exploitation thesis roughly holds for Japan, the variation in consciousness along the authority dimension is highly attenuated compared to either the United States or Sweden. Divisions along the dimension of skill (especially between experts and skilled employees) clearly have much deeper effects on consciousness in Japan than divisions along the dimension of managerial authority. As already noted, given that domination (and thus managerial authority) is more closely linked to capitalist exploitation than is skill, Marxism would generally expect that proworking-class consciousness should not vary more sharply across categories of skill and expertise than across levels of managerial hierarchies. Sweden and the United States conform to this expectation; Japan does not.

Reconstructions: direct and mediated class locations

The results for Swedish and American married women in the study of class identity suggest that the relative weight of the sphere of production compared to the sphere of consumption in shaping class consciousness depends upon the nature of the class formations within which class experiences are generated and translated into subjectivity. In Sweden, as a result of the cohesiveness of the labor movement and its strength within production, "class" is formed collectively at the point of production itself. In the United States, class is highly disorganized and atomized at the point of production, and is formed as a collective category primarily within the sphere of consumption, especially in terms of standards of living and the character of residential neighborhoods. When politicians talk about a "middle-class tax cut" they mean "a middle-income tax cut." This difference between Sweden and the United States in the sites within which class is constructed, then, accounts for the difference between the two countries in the causal salience of production and consumption in the formation of class identities. The point of production thesis, therefore, is not wrong; it is simply underspecified. To the extent that class becomes collectively organized within production, class experiences and interests generated within production itself will more strongly shape class identity than will experiences and interests in the sphere of consumption; where class formations remain highly disorganized within production, the sphere of consumption will have greater weight in shaping class subjectivities.[10]

---

[10] This is not a circular argument, for the collective organization of the class within production is logically distinct from the patterns of variations across individuals in forms of identity and consciousness.

Reconstructions: class consciousness and class formation

The main results for class consciousness and class formation which are somewhat anomalous for the traditional Marxist understanding of these issues come from Japan. As in other cases, it is always possible that the surprising results for Japan are simply artifacts of measurement problems. The survey instrument used in this project was designed and tested within a broadly Western European cultural context. While there are still potential problems in the comparability of the meaning of identically worded questions between countries such as the United States and Sweden due to the differences in their political cultures, we tried to minimize such problems in the selection and wording of questions. The Japanese research team was not part of that process, and in any event it is possible that the differences in cultural meanings between Japan and the other countries might have undermined any attempt at generating genuinely comparable questions. With a more suitable survey instrument, therefore, it might turn out that Japan was not so different from the United States and Sweden after all.

On the assumption that these results do not merely reflect measurement issues, they are consistent with the conventional image of Japanese society in which significant segments of the working class have high levels of loyalty to their firms and in which the social distance between managers and workers is relatively small. In terms of the Marxist understanding of class consciousness, this suggests that the concrete organizational context of class relations may have a bigger impact on the micro-relationship between an individual's class location and class consciousness than is usually suggested within Marxist class analysis. Capitalism may be universally characterized by processes of exploitation and domination, but firms can be organized in ways which significantly mute the subjective effects of these relations. These organizational contexts may thus not merely affect the extent to which the class experiences and class interests of workers can be mobilized into collective action, but also the way these experiences and interests are transformed into identities and beliefs.

17.5 Class and other forms of oppression: class and gender

Traditional understanding

While there has always been some discussion within the Marxist tradition of the relationship between class and other forms of oppression, until recent decades this has not been given concentrated theoretical attention. Traditionally, Marxist discussions have emphasized two somewhat contradictory themes. On the one hand, there is the classical formulation by Marx that the development of capitalism will destroy all traditional, ascriptive forms of oppression which act as impediments to the expansion of the market. Racism and sexism erect barriers to the free movement of labor and thus block the functioning of fully commodified, competitive labor markets. Marx – along with many contemporary neoclassical economists – believed that the long-term tendency in capitalism is for these barriers to be destroyed.

On the other hand, many contemporary Marxists have downplayed the corrosive effects of the market on ascriptive oppressions, and instead have stressed the ways in which both racial and gender oppression are functional for reproducing capitalism, and therefore are likely to persist and perhaps even be strengthened with capitalist development.[11] A variety of possible functional effects are then posed: racism divides the working class and thus stabilizes capitalist rule; racial oppression facilitates super-exploitation of specific categories of workers; gender oppression lowers the costs of labor power by providing for unpaid labor services in the home; gender oppression underwrites a sharp split between the public and private spheres of social life, which reinforces consumerist culture and other ideological forms supportive of capitalism.

Such functionalist accounts do not necessarily imply the absence of any autonomous causal mechanisms for gender and racial oppression, and they certainly do not logically imply that the best way to combat racism and sexism is simply to struggle against class oppression. The

---

[11] The functionalist analysis of racism and sexism treat these relations, and the ideologies which sustain them, as part of the "superstructure" of capitalist society. The superstructure, following Cohen's (1978) analysis, consists of all those noneconomic phenomena which (a) have the effect of reproducing the economic base, and (b) take the form they do because they reproduce the economic base. The first of these criteria establishes a functional *description* of racism and sexism; the second establishes a functional *explanation*.

existence of specific forms of racism or sexism could be functionally explained by their beneficial effects for capitalism, yet the ultimate *destruction* of these forms of oppression could require concentrated struggle directly against them and could be achieved in spite of their functionality for capitalism.[12] Nevertheless, these kinds of arguments do imply an explanatory primacy to class and suggest that whatever autonomy racial and gender mechanisms might have is circumscribed by the functional imperatives of the class system.

More recent discussions have tended to reject such functionalist arguments and have stressed greater autonomy for nonclass forms of oppression. Nevertheless, there is still a general expectation by Marxists that class and nonclass forms of oppression will tend to reinforce each other. This generates two broad theses about the interconnection of class and other forms of oppression:

1 *Nonclass oppression translates into class oppression.* Marxists would generally expect that social groups that are significantly oppressed through nonclass mechanisms will tend to be especially exploited within class relations. This can be either because the nonclass oppression affects the access of groups to the resources which matter for class, or because of direct discriminatory mechanisms within class relations themselves. In either case, it would be predicted that nonclass oppressions will be translated into class oppressions so that women and racially oppressed groups should be overrepresented in the working class and underrepresented in the most privileged class locations.

2 *Class oppression translates into nonclass oppression.* "Oppression" is a variable, not a constant. While all capitalist societies may be exploitative, the degree of inequality generated by capitalist relations varies considerably across capitalisms. Similarly, both

---

[12] Even if one accepts a strong class-functionalist explanation of racial and gender oppression, it still would not follow that the destruction of such oppression presupposes the destruction of capitalism. Capitalism can functionally explain racism (e.g. racism occurs because it divides the working class which helps to stabilize capitalism), and still racism could in principle be eliminated within capitalism with a result that either capitalism would find a functional substitute for racism, or that capitalism would simply function less well. Unless a functional explanation also involves an argument that there are no functional alternatives and that the given functional arrangement is indispensable for the very survival of the system in question, then functional explanations do not prevent an account of autonomous gender and racial causal mechanisms.

racial and gender oppressions vary considerably. One of the factors which shape such variation in the intensity of nonclass oppression, Marxists would argue, is the power and interests of exploiting classes. Nonclass oppression will be more intense to the extent that exploiting classes, on the one hand, are able to take advantage of nonclass oppressions to further their own interests, and, on the other, are able to block popular mobilizations which might effectively challenge these forms of nonclass oppression. This does not imply that nonclass oppressions are *created* by exploiting classes, but it does imply that exploiting classes have interests in perpetuating such oppressions and have the capacity to act on those interests. A class analysis of nonclass oppression, therefore, would generally predict that, at any given level of capitalist development, *the more oppressive and exploitative are class relations within capitalism, the more oppressive these other forms of oppression will tend to be as well.*[13]

Confirmations

The results in our various explorations of class and gender distributions are broadly consistent with the expectations of the first thesis. In particular, in every country we examined, women in the labor force are universally much more proletarianized than are men. In general, roughly 50–60% of women in the labor force are in the working class, compared to only 35–45% of men. Similarly, in our analysis of gender and authority, significant gender inequality in authority was present in all of the countries we examined. This gender gap in authority was quite robust, being present for a variety of different measures of authority as well as in equations in which a wide range of individual, job and firm attributes were included as controls. Our brief exploration of race and class also indicates that blacks are significantly more proletarianized than whites, and black women – subjected to both racial and gender forms of oppression – are the most proletarianized of all race and gender categories. These results correspond to the general

---

[13] The specification "at any given level of capitalist development" captures the traditional Marxist view that capitalist development will itself generate pressures for the erosion of racial and gender oppression. The use of racial and gender oppression by ruling classes to disorganize subordinate classes and in other ways reproduce capitalism, therefore, is always constrained by the degree to which these forms of oppression have been eroded by capitalist development itself.

expectation that inequalities generated by nonclass forms of oppression will be reflected in class inequalities as well.

Surprises

Two results run counter to broad Marxist expectations about the intersection of class and gender. Most striking, perhaps, are the results for the rank ordering of countries in the gender gap in authority. The thesis that class exploitation intensifies nonclass oppressions would lead to the prediction that the Scandinavian countries should have the smallest gender gap in authority. On every measure, the United States has considerably greater class inequality than Sweden and Norway, yet the gender gap in workplace authority is much smaller in the US than in these social democratic countries. These results run directly counter to the expectation in the second thesis that gender inequalities will be greatest where class inequalities are greatest.

The results for the study of housework also run counter to Marxian expectations. While Marxist theory does not explicitly generate explanations of the *variations* in the sexual division of labor across households, nevertheless, most Marxists would expect the class composition of households to have at least some effects on the amount of housework men do, specifically, in those dual-earner households in which women were in relatively more privileged and powerful class positions than their husbands, Marxists would generally expect men to do more housework than in households in which men occupied more privileged class positions than their wives. This simply was not the case in either Sweden or the United States – husbands did little housework regardless of the class composition of the household.

Reconstructions

The results for authority and housework reinforce the standard feminist thesis that gender relations are quite autonomous from class relations. While many Marxists acknowledge this thesis, nevertheless there remains an expectation that empirically class and gender inequalities will be closely tied to each other. While the specific issues we have been exploring here are fairly limited in scope, they indicate that these two forms of oppression can vary quite independently of each other.

This does not imply that struggles for women's liberation do not confront obstacles generated by existing class relations. Demands for quality, inexpensive childcare, for example, may be constrained by the difficulty of democratic states raising taxes in the context of global capitalism; equal pay for equivalent work may be impeded by the labor market for credentialed labor, an important aspect of the skill/expert dimension of class relations; and fully degendered authority hierarchies may be undermined by the competitive pressures of corporate organizations. Nevertheless, the degree of independent variation of class and gender relations supports the general claim that the struggles over gender inequality may have more scope for success inside of capitalism than Marxists have usually been willing to acknowledge.

This book was written for two rather different audiences: non-Marxists who are skeptical about the fruitfulness of Marxism as a theoretical framework for pursuing systematic empirical research, and radicals who are skeptical about the fruitfulness of quantitative research as a strategy for pursuing class analysis.

To the first audience I wanted to show that Marxist class analysis could be carried out with the same level of empirical rigor as non-Marxist stratification research and that it could generate sociologically interesting empirical results. To accomplish this I faced three principal tasks. First, I had to clarify the core concepts of Marxist class analysis so that they could be deployed in quantitative empirical research. Second, I had to show that Marxist theory generated interesting questions which could be addressed productively using quantitative methods. And third, I had to operationalize the concepts in such a way as to generate answers to these questions. Much of this book has attempted to carry out these tasks.

To the left-wing audience my central objective was not mainly to affirm the importance of class analysis, but to show that knowledge within class analysis could be pursued using conventional quantitative research methods. Left-wing scholars, especially Marxists, are generally skeptical of quantitative analysis and have traditionally relied primarily on historical and qualitative methods in their empirical research. In part this skepticism is rooted in the substantive concerns of Marxism – social change and epochal transitions, transformative struggles, dynamic processes in the historically specific lived experiences of actors. Since these themes in the Marxist tradition are not easily amenable to precise measurement and quantitative treatment, Marxist scholars understandably have engaged primarily in qualitative research.

The traditional Marxist skepticism toward quantitative methods, however, goes beyond simply a judgment about the appropriate kinds of data needed to answer specific theoretical and empirical questions. It has also reflected a general hostility by many (although not all) Marxists to anything that smacked of "bourgeois social science." The terms of this hostility are familiar to anyone who has engaged the Marxist tradition of scholarship: Marxism, it has been claimed, is dialectical, historical, materialist, antipositivist and holist, while bourgeois social science is undialectical, ahistorical, idealist, positivist and individualist. This litany of antinomies has frequently underwritten a blanket rejection of "bourgeois" research methods on the grounds that they were irredeemably tainted with these epistemological flaws.

One of the main objectives in this book has been to counter this current within Marxist thought by demonstrating that quantitative methods could illuminate certain important problems in class analysis. This objective is part of a larger project for reconstructing Marxist thought in which the distinctiveness of Marxism is seen as lying not in its "method" or epistemology, but in the concepts it deploys, the questions it asks, and the answers it proposes. Here I have attempted to show that there are important problems of class analysis in which knowledge can usefully be generated with systematic quantitative research.

In pursuing this dual agenda of demonstrating the usefulness of class analysis to non-Marxists and the usefulness of quantitative analysis to Marxists and other radical scholars, we have examined a diverse set of substantive problems. Some of these, like the study of patterns of class formation, the transformation of the class structure, or the problem of the class location of married women in dual-earner households, are central to class analysis. Others, like the permeability of class boundaries to friendships or the relationship between class and housework, are somewhat more peripheral. For all of these topics, however, I believe that our knowledge of class analysis has been pushed forward in ways that would not have been possible without systematic quantitative investigation.

In some cases this advance in knowledge has taken the form of confirming various expectations that were grounded in less systematic observations. In other cases, the new knowledge has emerged from surprises, from unexpected results. And, out of these unexpected results, new questions and unresolved problems have been posed for future empirical research and theoretical reconstruction.

References

Abbott, Pamela and Geoff Payne (eds.). 1990a. *The Social Mobility of Women: Beyond Male Mobility Models*. London: Falmer Press.

——— 1990b. "Women's Social Mobility: The Conventional Wisdom Reconsidered." Pp. 12–24 in Geoff Payne and Pamela Abbot (eds.) *The Social Mobility of Women: Beyond Male Mobility Models*. London: Falmer Press.

Acker, J. 1973. "Women and Social Stratification: A Case of Intellectual Sexism", *American Journal of Sociology* 78, 4: 936–945.

——— 1990. "Hierarchies, Jobs, Bodies: A Theory of Gendered Organization," *Gender and Society* 4: 139–158.

Agresti, Alan. 1984. *Analysis of Ordinal Categorical Data*. New York: Wiley.

——— 1990. *Categorical Data Analysis*. New York: Wiley.

Akerloff, G. A. and J. L. Yellen (eds.). 1986. *Efficiency Wage Models of the Labor Market*. Cambridge: Cambridge University Press.

Alston, Roland. 1978. "How to Incorporate Yourself and Make it Pay," *Black Enterprise* 8, 9: 37–38, 57.

Althusser, Louis. 1971. *Lenin and Philosophy*. London: NLB.

Atwood, Margaret. 1987. *The Handmaid's Tale*. New York: Ballantine Books.

Barrett, Michele. 1980. *Women's Oppression Today*. London: Verso.

——— 1984. "Rethinking Women's Oppression: A Reply to Brenner and Ramas," *New Left Review* 146: 123–128.

Baudelot, Christian, Roger Establet and Jacques Malemort. 1974. *La Petite Bourgeoisie en France*. Paris: Maspero.

Baxter, Janeen and Emily Kane. 1994. "Dependence and Independence: The Relationship between Gender Inequality and Gender Attitudes in the United States, Canada, Australia, Norway and Sweden" (unpublished manuscript).

Beach, Charles and James McKinnon. 1978. "A Maximum Likelihood Procedure for Regression with Correlated Errors," *Econometrica* 46: 51–58.

Bechhofer, Frank and B. Elliott. 1978. "The Voice of Small Business and the Politics of Survival," *Sociological Review* 26: 57–88.

Bechhofer, Frank and B. Elliott (eds.), 1981. *The Petite Bourgoisie: Comparative Studies of the Uneasy Stratum*, London: Macmillan.

Bechhofer, Frank and B. Elliott. 1985. "The Petite Bourgeoisie in Late Capitalism," *Annual Review of Sociology* 11: 181–207.

Beck, E. M., Patrick M. Horan and Charles M. Tolbert II. 1978. "Stratification in a Dual Economy: A Sectoral Model of Earnings Determination," *American Sociological Review* 43: 704–720.

Becker, Eugene H. 1984. "Self-employed Workers: An Update to 1983," *Monthly Labor Review* 107: 7.

Becker, Gary S. 1981. *A Treatise on the Family*. Cambridge: Harvard University Press.

Bell, Daniel. 1973. *The Coming of Post-Industrial Society*. New York: Harper and Row.

Bennett, J. T. and W. P. Orzechowski. 1983. "The Voting Behavior of Bureaucrats: Some Empirical Evidence," *Public Choice* 41.

Berk, Sarah. 1979. "The Organization of the Husbands' Household Day." In K. W. Feinstein (ed.) *Working Women and Families*. Beverly Hills: Sage.
    1985. *The Gender Factory: The Apportionment of Work in American Households*. New York: Plenum Press.

Berk, Sarah and R. A. Berk. 1979. *Labor and Leisure at Home: Content and Organization of the Household Day*. Beverly Hills: Sage.

Berk, Sarah, and A. Shih. "Contribution to Household Labor: Comparing Wives' and Husbands' Reports," in S. Berk (ed.) *Women and Household Labor*. Beverly Hills: Sage.

Berger, Suzanne. 1981. "The Uses of the Traditional Sector in Italy: Why Declining Classes Survive." Pp. 71–89 in Frank Bechhofer and B. Elliott (eds.) *The Petite Bourgeoisie: Comparative Studies of the Uneasy Stratum*. London: Macmillan.

Bergman, Barbara. 1986. *The Economic Emergence of Women*. New York: Basic Books.

Bertaux, Daniel. 1977. *Destins personnels et structure de class*. Paris: Presses Universitaires de France.

Bielby, William T. and James N. Baron. 1986. "Men and Women at Work: Sex Segregation and Statistical Discrimination," *American Journal of Sociology* 91: 759–799.

Blau, Francine D. and Marianne A. Ferber. 1990. "Women's Work, Women's Lives: A Comparative Perspective," National Bureau of Economic Research, Working Chapter No. 3447. Cambridge.

Blau, Peter M. 1988. "Structures of Social Positions and Structures of Social Relations." Pp. 43–59 in J. H. Turner (ed.) *Theory Building in Sociology: Assessing Theoretical Cumulation*. Newbury Park, CA: Sage.

Blau, Peter M. and Otis Dudley Duncan. 1967. *The American Occupational Structure*. New York: Wiley.

Bluestone, Barry and Bennet Harrison. 1982. *The Deindustrialization of America*. New York: Basic Books.

Blumstein, Philip and Pepper Schwartz. 1984. *American Couples, Money, Work and Sex*. New York: Pocket Books.

Bögenhold, Dieter. 1985. *Die Selbstständigen. Zur Soziologie dezentraler Produktion*. Frankfurt/Main: Campus.

Bourdieu, Pierre. 1984. *Distinction: A Social Critique of the Judgement of Taste.* Translated by Richard Nice. London and New York: Routledge and Kegan Paul.

1985. "The Social Space and the Genesis of Groups," *Theory and Society* 14: 723–744.

1987. "What Makes a Social Class? On the Theoretical and Practical Existence of Groups," *Berkeley Journal of Sociology* 32: 1–17.

Bourdieu, Pierre and Jean-Claude Passeron. 1990. *Reproduction in Education, Society and Culture.* 2nd ed. London: Sage.

Bowles, Samuel and Herb Gintis. 1986. *Capitalism and Democracy.* New York: Basic Books.

1990. "Contested Exchange: New Microfoundations for the Political Economy of Capitalism," *Politics & Society* 18, 2: 165–222.

Bowles, Samuel, David M. Gordon and Thomas E. Weisskopf. 1990. *After the Wasteland: A Democratic Economics for the Year 2000.* New York: M. E. Sharpe.

Braverman, Harry. 1974. *Labor and Monopoly Capital: The Degradation of Work in the Twentieth Century.* New York: Monthly Review Press.

Breen, Richard. 1987. "Sources of Cross-national Variation in Mobility Regimes: English, French and Swedish Data Reanalysed," *Sociology* 21: 75–90.

Breen, Richard and Christopher Whelan. 1985. "Vertical Mobility and Class Inheritance in the British Isles," *British Journal of Sociology* 36: 175–192.

Bregger, John E. 1963. "Self-Employment in the United States, 1948–62," *Monthly Labor Review* (January): 37–43.

Brenner, Johanna. 1989. "Work Relations and the Formation of Class Consciousness," in Wright, Becker, et. al (1989), 184 190.

Brenner, Johanna and Maria Ramas. 1984. "Rethinking Women's Oppression," *New Left Review* 144: 33–71.

Brint, Steven. 1984. " 'New-Class' and Cumulative Trend Explanations of the Liberal Political Attitudes of Professionals," *American Journal of Sociology* 90, 1: 31– 71.

Brinton, Mary C. 1988. "The Social-Institutional Bases of Gender Stratification: Japan as an Illustrative Case," *American Journal of Sociology* 94, 2 (September): 300–334.

Brinton, Mary and Hang-Yue Ngo. 1991. "Occupational Sex-Segregation in Comparative Perspective," unpublished manuscript, University of Chicago.

Browning, Harley L. and Joachim Singleman. 1978. "The Transformation of the U.S. Labor Force: The interaction of Industry and Occupation," *Politics & Society* 8, 3–4: 481–509.

Brubaker, Rogers. 1985. "Rethinking Classical Theory: The Sociological Vision of Pierre Bourdieu," *Theory and Society* 14, 6 (November): 745–775.

Burawoy, Michael. 1979. *Manufacturing Consent.* Chicago: University of Chicago Press.

1985. *The Politics of Production.* London: Verso.

1990. "Marxism as Science: Historical Challenges and Theoretical Growth," *American Sociological Review* 55, 6: 775–793.

1992. *The Radiant Past*. Chicago: University of Chicago Press.

1993. *Ethnography Unbound*. Berkeley: University of California Press.

Burawoy, Michael and Erik Olin Wright. 1990. "Coercion and Consent in Contested Exchange," *Politics & Society*, June, reprinted in Wright (1994), chapter 4.

Burris, Val. 1987. "The Neo-Marxist Synthesis of Marx and Weber on Class," in N. Wiley (ed.) *The Marx–Weber Debate*. Newbury Park, CA: Sage Publications.

Burt, Ronald. 1983. *Corporate Profits and Cooptation: Network of Market Constraints and Directorate Ties in the American Eoconomy*. New York: Academic Press.

Capp, Al. 1992. *Li'L Abner*, vol. 14: 1948. Princeton, WI: Kitchen Sink Press.

Carchedi, G. 1977. *The Economic Identification of Social Classes*. London: Routledge & Kegan Paul.

Catalyst. 1990. *Women in Corporate Management: Results of a Catalyst survey*.

Census of the Population 1940. Public Use Microdata Sample [Machine-readable Datafile] / Prepared by the Bureau of the Census. Washington, DC: The Bureau [Producer and Distributor], 1983.

1950. Public Use Microdata Sample [Machine-readable Datafile] / Prepared by the Bureau of the Census. Washington, DC: The Bureau [Producer and Distributor], 1983.

Centers, Richard. 1949. *The Psychology of Social Classes*. Princeton: Princeton University Press.

Chalmers, Norma. 1989. *Industrial Relations in Japan: The Peripheral Workforce*. London and New York: Routledge.

Chant, David and Mark Western. 1991. "The Analysis of Mobility Regimes: Implementation Using SAS Procedures and An Australian Case Study," *Sociological Methods and Research* 20: 256–286.

Charles, Maria. 1992. "Cross-National Variations in Occupational Sex Segregation," *American Sociological Review* 57 (August): 483–502.

Charles, Nicola. 1990. "Women and class – a problematic relationship," *Sociological Review* 38: 43–89.

Chase, Ivan D. 1975. "A Comparison of Men's and Women's Intergenerational Mobility in the United States," *American Sociological Review* 40: 483–505.

Cohen, G. A. 1978. *Karl Marx's Theory of History: A Defense*. Princeton: Princeton University Press.

1988. *History, Labour, and Freedom*. Oxford: Oxford University Press.

Conk, Margo. 1979. *The United States Census and Labor Force Change: A History of Occupation Statistics*. Ann Arbor: UMI Research Press.

Costello, C. 1991. *We're Worth It: Women and Collective Action in the Insurance Workplace*. Champaign, IL: University of Illinois Press.

Coverman, Shelley. 1985. "Explaining Husbands' Participation in Domestic Labor," *The Sociological Quarterly* 26, 1: 81– 97.

Cowan, Ruth Schwartz. 1983. *More Work for Mothers: The Ironies of Household Technology from the Open Hearth to the Microwave*. New York: Basic Books, Inc.

Crossick, Geoffrey. 1978. *An Artisan Elite in Victorian Society. Kentish London 1840–1880*. London: Croom Helm.

Curran, James and Roger Burrows. 1986. "The Sociology of Petit Capitalism: A Trend Report," *Sociology* 20, 2: 265–279.

Currie, Elliott and Jerome H. Skolnick. 1983. *America's Problems: Social Issues and Public Policy*. 2nd ed. Glenview, IL: Scott, Foresman.

Curtis, J. 1963. "Differential Association and the Stratification of the Urban Community," *Social Forces* 42: 68–77.

Dahrendorf, Ralf. 1959. *Class and Class Conflict in Industrial Society*. London: Routledge and Kegan Paul.

Dahrendorf, Ralf, P. Fedoseyev, U. Himmelstrand, R. Richta, Y. Singh, A. Touraine, K. Tsurami. 1977. *Scientific-Technological Revolution: Social Aspects*. Beverly Hills: Sage Publications.

Dale, Angela. 1986. "Social Class and the Self-Employed," *Sociology* 20, 3: 430–434.

Daly, Patricia. 1982. "Unpaid Family Workers: Long-term Decline Continues," *Monthly Labor Review* (October): 3–5.

Delphy, Christine. 1984. *Close to Home: A Materialist Analysis of Women's Oppression*. London: Hutchinson.

Diprete, Thomas A. and T. Whitman Soule. 1988. "Gender and Promotion in Segmented Ladder Systems," *American Sociological Review* 53 (February): 26–40.

Dohse, Knuth, Ulrich Jurgens and Thomas Malsch. 1985. "From 'Fordism' to 'Toyotism'? The Social Organization of the Labor Process in the Japanese Automobile Industry," *Politics & Society* 14, 2: 115–146.

Domhoff, G. William. 1971. *The Higher Circles*. New York: Vintage Books.

Dore, Ronald. 1987. *Taking Japan Seriously: A Confucian Perspective on Leading Economic Issues*. Stanford, CA: Stanford University Press.

Duncan, G. J. and S. D. Hoffman. 1985. "A Reconsideration of the Economic Consequences of Divorce," *Demography* 22, 4: 485–497.

Duncan, Otis Dudley. 1966. "Methodological Issues in the Analysis of Social Mobility." In N. J. Smelser and S. M. Lipset (eds.) *Social Structure and Mobility in Economic Development*. Chicago: Aldine.

Dunton, Nancy and David L. Featherman. 1983. "Social Mobility Through Marriage and Through Careers: Achievement Over the Life Course." Pp. 285–320 in Janet T. Spence (ed.) *Achievement and Achievement Motives: Psychological and Sociological Approaches*. San Francisco: W. H. Freeman.

Edwards, Meredith. 1982. "Financial Arrangements Made by Husbands and Wives: Findings of a Survey," *Australian and New Zealand Journal of Sociology* 18: 320–338.

Elster, Jon. 1985. *Making Sense of Marx*. Cambridge: Cambridge University Press.

Engels, Frederick. 1968 [1884]. *The Origin of the Family, Private Property and the State*. Reprinted in *Karl Marx and Frederick Engels, Selected Works in One Volume*. London: Lawrence and Wishart. 455–593.

Erikson, Robert. 1984. "Social Class of Men, Women and Families," *Sociology* 18: 500–514.

Erikson, Robert and John H. Goldthorpe. 1985. "Are American Rates of Social Mobility Exceptionally High? New Evidence on an Old Issue," *European Sociologial Review* 1: 1–22.

1987a. "Commonality and Variation in Social Fluidity in Industrial Nations. Part I: A Model for Evaluating the 'FJH hypothesis'," *European Sociological Review* 3: 54–77.

1987b. "Commonality and Variation in Social Fluidity in Industrial Nations. Part II: The Model of Core Social Fluidity Applied," *European Sociological Review* 3: 145–166.

1993. *The Constant Flux.* Oxford: Oxford University Press.

Erikson, Robert, John H. Goldthorpe and Lucienne Portocarero. 1979. "Intergenerational Class Mobility in three Western European Societies: England, France and Sweden," *British Journal of Sociology* 30: 415–441.

1982. "Social Fluidity in Industrial Nations: England, France and Sweden," *British Journal of Sociology* 33: 1–34.

1983. "Intergenerational Class Mobility and the Convergence Thesis: England, France and Sweden," *British Journal of Sociology* 34: 303–343.

Esping-Anderson, Gosta. 1990. *The Three Worlds of Welfare Capitalism.* Princeton: Princeton University Press.

Esping-Anderson, Gosta, Roger Friedland and Erik Olin Wright. 1976. "Modes of Class Struggle and the Capitalist State," *Kapitalistate* 4.

Eurostat. 1980 and 1985. *Employment and Unemployment.* Luxemburg: Statistical Office of the OECD.

Fain, T. Scott. 1980. "Self-employed Americans: Their Number Has Increased," *Monthly Labor Review* (November): 3–8.

Farkas, George. 1976. "Education, Wage Rates and the Division of Labor between Husband and Wife," *Journal of Marriage and the Family* 38: 473–483.

Featherman, David and Robert M. Hauser. 1978. *Opportunity and Change.* New York: Academic Press.

Featherman, David L., Frank L. Jones and Robert M. Hauser. 1975. "Assumptions of Social Mobility Research in the US: The Case of Occupational Status," *Social Science Research* 4: 329–360.

Feld, Scott L. 1981. "The Focussed Organization of Social Ties," *American Journal of Sociology* 86: 1015–1035.

Fenstermaker, Deborah. 1985. "Changes in Estimation Procedure in the Current Population Survey Beginning in January 1985," *Employment and Earnings* (January).

Fierman, Jaclyn, 1990. "Why Women Still Don't Hit the Top," *Fortune* 122, 3: 40.

Folbre, Nancy. 1994. *Who Pays for the Kids? Gender and the Structures of Constraint.* New York: Routledge.

Fraad, Harriet, Stephen Resnick and Richard Wolff. 1994. *Bringing it All Back Home: Class, Gender and Power in the Modern Household.* London: Pluto Press.

Fraser, Nancy. 1993. "After the Family Wage: What Do Women Want in Social Welfare?" Unpublished manuscript. Department of Philosophy, Northwestern University.

Froebel, Folker, Jurgen Heinrichs and Otton Kreye. 1980. *The New International Division of Labor: Structural Unemployment in Industrialized Countries and Industrialization in Developing Countries.* Cambridge: Cambridge University Press.

Fuchs, Victor R. *The Service Economy.* New York: Columbia University Press, 1968.

Fujita, Wakao. 1973. "Labor Disputes," in Kazuo Okochi, Bernard Karsh and Solomon B. Levine (eds.) *Workers and Employers in Japan: The Japanese Employment Relations System.* Tokyo: Tokyo University Press.

Gaillie, Duncan. *In Search of the New Working Class.* Cambridge: Cambridge University Press, 1978.

Ganzeboom, Harry, Ruud Luijkx and Donald Treiman. 1989. "Intergenerational Class Mobility in Comparative perspective." Pp. 3–84 in *Research in Social Stratification and Mobility,* vol. VIII, edited by Arne L. Kalleberg. Greenwich: JAI Press.

Ganzeboom, Harry, Donald Treiman and Wout Ultee. 1991. "Comparative Intergenerational Stratification Research: Three Generations and Beyond," *Annual Review of Sociology* 17: 277–302.

Gardiner, Jean. 1975. "Women's Domestic Labour." *New Left Review* 89 (January–February): 47–58. Reprinted in Z. Eisenstein (ed.) *Capitalist Patriarchy and the Case for Socialist Feminism.* New York: Monthly Review Press, 1979.

Garland, Susan. 1991. "Throwing Stones at the Glass Ceiling," Business Week, August 19: 29.

Geerken, M. and W. R. Gove. 1983. *At Home and at Work: The Family' Allocation of Labor.* Beverly Hills: Sage.

Geiger, Theodor. 1932. *Die soziale Schichtung des deutschen Volkes.* Stuttgart: Enke Verlag.

Gellately, Robert. 1974. *The Politics of Economic Despair. Shopkeepers and German Politics 1890–1914.* London.

Germany, Statistisches Bundesamt. 1972. *Bevölkerung und Wirtschaft 1872–1972.* Stuttgart.

Gerth, Hans and C. W. Mills. 1958. *From Max Weber.* New York: Oxford University Press.

Giddens, Anthony. 1973. *The Class Structure of the Advanced Societies.* New York: Harper and Row.

Ginsberg, Norman. 1992. *Divisions of Welfare: A Critical Introduction to Comparative Social Policy.* London: Sage.

Glenn, Evelyn Nakano. 1992. "From Servitude to Service Work: Historical Continuities in the Racial Division of Paid Reproductive Work," *Signs* 18, 11: 1–43.

Gnanaskaran, K. S. 1966. "Interrelations between Industrial and Occupational Changes in Manpower, United States, 1950–1960." Analytical and Technical Report No. 6. Philadelphia: University of Pennsylvania Population Studies Center.

Goldberg, Gertrude Schaffner and Eleanor Kreman (eds.). 1990. *The Feminization of Poverty: Only in America?* New York: Praeger.

Goldthorpe, John. 1980. *Social Mobility and Class Structure in Modern Britain.* Oxford: Oxford University Press.

1983. "Women and Class Analysis: In Defence of the Conventional View," *Sociology* 17: 465–488.

1984. "Women and Class Analysis: A Reply to the Replies," *Sociology* 18: 491–499.

1987. *Social Mobility and Class Structure in Modern Britain.* 2nd ed. Oxford: Clarendon Press. (With Catriona Llewellyn and Clive Payne.)

Goldthorpe, John H. and Clive Payne. 1986. "On the Class Mobility of Women: Results from Different Approaches to the Analysis of Recent British Data," *Sociology* 20: 531–555.

Goodman, Leo A. 1979. "Simple Models for the Analysis of Association in Cross-Classifications Having Ordered Categories," *Journal of the American Statistical Association* 74: 537–552.

1984. *The Analysis of Cross-Classified Data Having Ordered Categories.* Cambridge, MA: Harvard University.

Gordon, Andrew. 1985. *The Evolution of Labor Relations in Japan: Heavy Industry, 1853–1955.* Cambridge, MA: Council on East Asian Studies, Harvard University.

Gordon, David M. 1994. "Bosses of Different Stripes: A Cross National Perspective on Monitoring and Supervision," *American Economic Review* 84, 2 (May).

Gorz, Andre. 1967. *Strategy for Labor.* Boston: Beacon Press.

Gouldner, Alvin. 1979. *The Future of Intellectuals and the Rise of the New Class.* New York: Seabury Press.

Gramlich, Edward M. and Daniel L. Rubinfeld. 1980. *Public Employment, Voting and Spending Tastes: Some Empiricial Evidence.* Ann Arbor, MI: Institute of Public Policy Studies, University of Michigan.

Grandjean, Burke D. 1981. "History and Career in a Bureaucratic Labor Market," *American Journal of Sociology* 86, 5: 1057–1092.

Granovetter, Mark S. 1973. "The Strength of Weak Ties," *American Journal of Sociology* 78: 1360–1380.

Grusky, D. B. and R. M. Hauser. 1984. "Comparative Social Mobility Revisited: Models of Convergence and Divergence in 16 Countries," *American Sociological Review* 49: 19–38.

Haas, Linda. 1981. "Domestic Role Sharing in Sweden," *Journal of Marriage and the Family* (November): 955–967.

Halaby, Charles. 1979. "Job Specific Sex Differences in Organizational Reward Attainment: Wage Discrimination vs. Rank Segregation," *Social Forces* 58: 108–127.

Halaby, Charles and Michael Sobel. 1979. "Mobility Effects in the Workplace," *American Journal of Sociology* 85, 2: 385–416.

Halaby, Charles and David Weakliem. 1993. "Ownership and Authority in the Earnings Function," *American Sociological Review* 58, 1 (February): 16–30.

Hartmann, Heidi. 1979a. "The Unhappy Marriage of Marxism and Feminism," *Capital & Class* 8: 1–33.

1979b. "Capitalism, Patriarchy and Job Segregation by Sex." Pp. 206–247 in Zillah Eisenstein (ed.) *Capitalist Patriarchy and the Case for Socialist Feminism*. New York: MR Press.

1981. "The Family as the Locus of Gender, Class and Political Struggle: The Example of Housework," *Signs* 3: 311–394.

1987. "Internal Labor Markets and Gender: A Case Study of Promotion." Pp. 59–92 in Clair Brown and Joseph A. Pechman (eds.) *Gender in the Workplace*. Washington DC: The Brookings Institution.

Haupt, Heinz-Gerhard. 1985. *Die Radikale Mitte. Lebensweise und Politik von Handwerkern und Kleinhändlern in Deutschland seit 1848*. Munich: DTV.

Hauser, R.M. 1981. "The Structure of Social Relationships: Cross-Classifications of Mobility, Kinship, and Friendship," *IHS Journal* 5: 1–51.

1984. "Vertical Class Mobility in Great Britain, France and Sweden," *Acta Sociologica* 27: 87–110.

Hauser, Robert M. and David B. Grusky. 1988. "Cross-national Variation in Occupational Distributions, Relative Mobility Chances, and Intergenerational Shifts in Occupational Distributions," *American Sociological Review* 53: 723–741.

Hayes, Bernadette. 1990. "Intergenerational Occupational Mobility Among Employed and Non-employed Women: The Australian Case," *Australian and New Zealand Journal of Sociology* 26: 368–388.

Heath, A. and N. Brittain. 1984. "Women's Jobs Do Make a Difference: A Reply to Goldthorpe," *Sociology* 18, 4: 475–490.

Hill, Martha. 1980. "Authority at Work: How Men and Women Differ." Pp. 107–146 in Greg J. Duncan and James Morgan, *Five Thousand American Families*, vol. 8. Ann Arbor: University of Michigan Press.

Hirschhorn, Larry. 1984. *Beyond Mechanization: Work and Technology in a Post-industrial Age*. Cambridge: MIT Press.

Hoff, Jens. 1985. "The Concept of Class and Public Employees," *Acta Sociologica* 28: 3.

Hoffman, Walther G. 1965. *Das Wachstum der deutschen Wirtschaft seit der Mitte des 19. Jahrhunderts*. Berlin: Springer Verlag.

Holland, Paul W. and Samuel Leinhardt. 1973. "The Structural Implications of Measurement Error in Sociometry," *Journal of Mathematical Sociology* 3: 85–111.

Hollingshead, August B. 1949. *Emlstown's Youth*. New York: John Wiley.

Hood, Jane C. 1983. *Becoming a Two-Job Family*. New York: Praeger.

Hout, Michael. 1983. *Mobility Tables*. Beverly Hills: Sage.

1984. "Status, Autonomy and Training in Intergenerational Mobility," *American Journal of Sociology* 89: 1379–1409.

1988. "More Universalism, Less Structural Mobility: The American Occupational Structure in the 1980s," *American Journal of Sociology* 93: 1358–1400.

1989. *Following in Father's Footsteps: Social Mobility in Ireland*. Cambridge, MA: Harvard University Press.

Hout, Michael and Robert M. Hauser. 1991. "Symmetry and Hierarchy in Social Mobility: A Methodological Analysis of the CASMIN Model of

Class Mobility." CDE Working Paper 92–5, Center for Demography and Ecology, University of Wisconsin-Madison.

Hout, Michael and John A. Jackson. 1986. "Dimensions of Occupational Mobility in the Republic of Ireland," *European Sociological Review* 2: 114–137.

Howe, Carolyn. 1987. *Class Structure and Class Formation in Advanced Capitalism: A Comparative Study of Sweden and the United States.* Ph.D. Dissertation, Department of Sociology, University of Wisconsin-Madison.

Huber, Joan and G. Spitze. 1983. *Sex Stratification: Children, Housework and Jobs.* New York: Academic Press.

Huckfeldt, R. R. 1983. "Social Contexts, Social Networks, and Urban Neighborhoods: Environmental Constraints on Friendship Choice," *American Journal of Sociology* 89: 651–669.

Huff, D. L. and L. A. Sperr. 1967. "Measures for Determining Differential Growth of Markets," *Journal of Marketing Research* 4: 391–395.

Humphries, Jane. 1977. "Class Struggle and the Persistence of the Working Class Family," *Cambridge Journal of Economics* 1, 3: pp. 241–258.

Ichiyo, Muto. 1986. "Class Struggle in Postwar Japan." In G. McCormack and Y. Sugimoto (eds.) *Democracy in Contemporary Japan.* London: M. E. Sharpe.

Institute for Labor Education and Research. 1982. *What's Wrong with the US Economy?* Boston: South End Press.

International Labor Organization.1992. *The Yearbook of Labor Statistics.* Geneva: International Labor Organization, 51st ed.

Ishida, Hiroshi, John H. Goldthorpe and Robert Erikson. 1991. "Intergenerational Class Mobility in Postwar Japan," *American Journal of Sociology* 96: 954–992.

Jackman, Mary. 1972. "The Political Orientation of the Socially Mobile in Italy: A Re-Examination," *The American Sociological Review* 37 (April): 213–222.

Jackman, Mary R. and Robert W. Jackman. 1983. *Class Awareness in the United States.* Berkeley: University of California Press.

Jackson, R. M. 1977. "Social Structure and Process in Friendship Choice." In C. S. Fischer, R. M. Jackson, C. A. Stueve, K. Gerson (eds.) *Networks and Places: Social Relations in the Urban Setting.* New York: Free Press.

Jacobs, Jerry A. 1989. *Revolving Doors. Sex Segregation and Women's Careers.* Stanford: University Press.

1992. "Women's Entry into Management. Trends in Earnings, Authority and Values Among Salaried Managers," *Administrative Science Quarterly* 37: 282–301.

Jaffee, David. 1989. "Gender Inequality in Workplace Autonomy and Authority," *Social Science Quarterly* 70, 2. (June): 375–390.

Jefferson, Thomas. 1786. [1984] *Writings.* New York: Literary Classics of the United States, Viking Press.

Jenkins, Robert M. 1988. *Procedural History of the 1940 Census of Population and Housing.* Madison: University of Wisconsin Press.

Jenson, Jane, Elizabeth Hagen and Cellaigh Reddy (eds.). 1988. *Feminization of the Labor Force: Paradoxes and Promises.* Oxford: Polity.

Jones, Frank L. and Peter Davis. 1986. *Models of Society: Class, Gender and Stratification in Australia and New Zealand.* Sydney: Croom Helm.

1988a. "Class Structuration and Patterns of Social Closure in Australia and New Zealand," *Sociology* 22: 271–291.

1988b. "Closure and Fluidity in the Class Structure," *The Australian and New Zealand Journal of Sociology* 24: 226–247.

Joppke, Christian. 1986. "The Cultural Dimensions of Class Formation and Class Struggle: on the Social Theory of Pierre Bourdieu," *Berkeley Journal of Sociology* 31: 53–78.

Kalleberg, Ahrne and Rachael Rosenfeld. 1990. "Work in the Family and in the Labor Market," *Journal of Marriage and the Family* 52 (May): 331–346.

Kamata, Satoshi. 1982. *Japan in the Passing Lane.* New York: Pantheon.

Kanter, Rosabeth Moss. 1977. *Men and Women of the Corporation.* New York: Basic Books.

Katzenstein, Mary Fainsod. 1987. "Comparing the Feminist Movements of the United States and Western Europe: An Overview." In Mary Fainsod Katzenstein and Carol McClurg Mueller (eds.) *The Women's Movements of the United States and Western Europe.* Philadelphia: Temple University Press.

Kitagawa, E. 1955. "Components of a Difference between Two Rates," *Journal of the American Statistical Association* 50: 1168–1174.

Knoke, David. 1973. "Intergenerational Mobility and the Political Party Preferences of Men," *American Journal of Sociology* 78, 6: 1448–1468.

Kohn, M. 1969. *Class and Conformity.* Holmwood: The Dorsey Press.

Kurz, Karin and Walter Muller. 1987. "Class Mobility in the Industrial World," *Annual Review of Sociology* 13: 417–442.

Laclau, Encsto and Chantal Mouffe. 1985. *Hegemony and Socialist Strategy.* London: Verso.

Ladd, Everett. Jr. 1979. "Pursuing the New Class: Social Theory and Survey Data." Pp. 101–122 in Bruce Briggs (ed.) *The New Class?* New Brunswick: Transaction Books.

Laumann, Edward O. 1966. *Prestige and Association in an Urban Community.* Indianapolis: Bobbs-Merrill Company.

1973. *Bonds of Pluralism: the Form and Substance of Urban Social Networks.* New York: John Wiley and Sons.

Lerner, Gerda. 1986. *The Creation of Patriarchy.* New York: Basic Books.

Leuilfsrud, Hakon and Alison Woodward. 1987. "Women at Class Crossroads: Repudiating Conventional Theories of Family Class," *Sociology* 21: 393–412.

Lewis, Jane. 1985. "The Debate on Sex and Class," *New Left Review* 149: 108–120.

Lincoln, Abraham. 1907 [1865]. *Life and Works of Abraham Lincoln: Centenary Edition*, Marion Mills Miller (ed.). New York: Current Literature.

Linder, Marc. 1983. "Self-Employment as a Cyclical Escape from Unemployment: A Case Study of the Construction Industry in the United States During the Postwar Period," *Research in Sociology of Work: Peripheral Workers* 2: 261–274.

Lipset, S. M. and H. Zetterberg. 1959. "Social Mobility in Industrial Societies." Pp. 11–75 in Seymour M. Lipset and Reinhardt H. Bendix (eds.) *Social Mobility in Industrial Society*. Berkeley: University of California.

Lukacs, George. 1971 [1922]. *History and Class Consciousness*. Cambridge: MIT Press.

Maddala, G. S. 1983. *Limited-dependent and Qualitative Variables in Econometrics*. New York: Cambridge University Press.

Mallet, Serge. 1963. *La nouvelle class ouvriere*. Paris: Seuil.

Manski, Charles F. 1989. "Anatomy of the Selection Problem," *The Journal of Human Resources* 24, 3 (Summer): 343–360.

Mare, Robert D. 1986. "Further Evidence on Sibship Size and Educational Stratification," *American Sociological Review* 51: 403–412.

Marsh, A., P. Heady and J. Matheson. 1981. *Labour Mobility in the Construction Industry*. London: HMSO.

Marshall, Gordon. 1983. "Some Remarks on the Study of Working Class Consciousness," *Politics & Society* 12, 3: .263–302.

Marshall, Gordon, David Rose, Howard Newby and Carolyn Vogler. 1988. *Social Class in Modern Britain*. London: Unwin Hyman.

Mayer, Nonna. 1977. "Une filière de mobilité ouvrière: l'accès à la petite entreprise artisanale et commerciale," *Revue française de sociologie* 18: 25–45.

McGuire, Gail M. and Barbara Reskin. 1993. "Authority Hierarchies at Work: The Impacts of Race and Sex," *Gender and Society* 7, 4: 487–506.

McLanahan, Sara, Annemette Sorensen and Dorothy Watson. 1986. "Sex Differences in Poverty, 1950–80," unpublished paper.

McRae, Susan. 1986. *Cross-Class Families: a Study of Wives' Occupational Superiority*. Oxford: Clarendon Press.

Meissner, M., E. W. Humphreys, S. M. Meis and W. J. Sheu. 1975. "No Exit for Wives: Sexual Division of Labor and the Accumulation of Household Demands," *Canadian Review of Sociology and Anthropology* 12: 424–439.

Milkman, Ruth. 1987. *Gender at Work*. Chicago: University of Illinois Press.

Mishel, Lawrence and David Frankel. 1991. *The State of Working America*. New York.

Moen, Phyllis. 1989. *Working Parents: Transformations in Gender Roles and Public Policies in Sweden*. Madison: University of Wisconsin Press.

Molyneux, Maxine. 1979. "Beyond the Domestic Labour Debate," *New Left Review* 116: 3–27.

Morgan, J. M., I. A. Sirageldin, and N. Baerwaldt. 1971. *Productive Americans*. Ann Arbor: Institute for Social Research, University of Michigan.

Morrison, Ann M., R. P. White, E. Van Velsor, and the Center for Creative Leadership. 1987. *Breaking the Glass Ceiling*. New York: Addison Wesley.

Morrison, Ann M. and Mary Ann Von Glinow. 1990. "Women and Minorities in Management," *American Psychologist* 45: 200–208.

Nahemow, L. and M. P. Lawton. 1975. "Similarity and Propinquity in Friendship Formation," *Journal of Personality and Social Psychology* 32: 205–213.

Nash, June. 1983. "The Impact of the Changing International Division of Labor on Different Sectors of the Labor Force." In June Nash and Patricia Fernandez-Kelly (eds.) *Women, Men and the International Division of Labor.* Albany: State University of New York Press.

Nash, June and Patricia Fernandez-Kelly (eds.) 1983. *Women, Men and the International Division of Labor.* Albany: State University of New York Press.

National Committee on Pay Equity. *Closing the Wage Gap: An International Perspective.* Washington DC: National Committee on Pay Equity.

O'Connor, James. 1973. *The Fiscal Crisis of the State.* New York: St. Martin's Press.

OECD. 1977. *The Development of Industrial Relations Systems: Some Implications of Japanese Experience.* Paris: OECD.

Offe, Claus. 1974. "Structural Problems of the Capitalist State: Class Rule and the Political System." In C. von Beyme (ed.) *German Political Studies,* vol. I. Russle Sage.

1984. *Contradictions of the Welfare State.* London: Hutchinson.

Ollman, Bertell. 1986. "How to Study Class Consciousness," chapter presented at the annual meeting of the American Sociological Association, New York, August.

Ossowski, Stanislaw. 1963. *Class Structure in the Social Consciousness.* London: Routledge & Kegan Paul.

Pahl, Jan. 1983. "The Allocation of Money and the Structure of Inequality within Marriage," *Sociological Review* 31: 313–335.

Pahl, R. E. 1984. *Divisions of Labor.* Cambridge: Cambridge University Press.

Palmer, G. and A. Miller. 1949. *Industrial and Occupational Trends in National Employment.* Industrial Research Department. Wharton School of Finance and Commerce. Philadelphia: University of Pennsylvania.

Parkin, Frank. 1974. "Strategies of Social Closure in Class Formation." In Frank Parkin (ed.) *The Social Analysis of the Class Structure.* London: Tavistock.

1979. *Marxism and Class Theory: A Bourgeois Critique.* New York: Columbia University Press.

Payne, Geoff and Pamela Abbott (eds.). 1990. *The Social Mobility of Women: Beyond Male Mobility Models.* London: Falmer Press.

Perloff, H., E. S. Dunn Jr., E. E. Lampard and R. F. Muth. 1960. *Regions, Resources and Economic Growth.* Baltimore: Johns Hopkins Press.

Philips, Joseph D. 1962. "The Self-Employed in the United States," *University of Illinois Bulletin* 59, 91: 1–100.

Pindyck, Robert S. and Daniel L. Rubinfeld. 1981. *Econometric Methods and Economic Forecasts.* New York: McGraw-Hill.

Piore, Michael and Charles Sabel. 1984. *The Second Industrial Divide.* New York: Basic Books.

Pleck, Joseph. 1985. *Working Wives/Working Husbands.* Beverly Hills: Sage.

Portocarero, Lucienne. 1983a. "Social Mobility in Industrial Nations," *Sociological Review* 31: 56–82.

1983b. "Social Fluidity in France and Sweden," *Acta Sociologica* 26: 127–139.

Poulantzas, Nicos. 1975. *Classes in Contemporary Capitalism.* London: New Left Books.

Presser, Harriet B. and Virginia S. Cain. 1983. "Shift Work Among Dual-Earner Couples with Children," *Science* 219: 876–879.

Przeworski, Adam. 1985. *Capitalism and Social Democracy*. Cambridge: Cambridge University Press.

Przeworski, Adam and John Sprague. 1985. *Paper Stones: A History of Electoral Socialism*. Chicago: University of Chicago Press.

Public Reports of the Presidents of the United States. Ronald Reagan. 1983. Book 1. Washington DC: United States Government Printing Office, 1984.

Rainey, Hal, Carol Traut and Barrie Blunt. 1986. "Reward Expectancies and Other Work-Related Attitudes in Puboic and Private Organizations: A Review and Extention," *Review of Public Personnel Administration* 8, 3: 50–72.

Ray, Robert N. 1975. "A Report on Self-employed Americans in 1973," *Monthly Labor Review* (January): 49–54.

Reich, Robert. 1991. *The Work of Nations: Preparing Ourselves for 21st Century Capitalism*. New York: Knopf.

Reinerman, Craig. 1987. *American States of Mind: Political Beliefs and Behavior Among Private and Public Workers*. New Haven: Yale University Press.

Reskin, Barbara 1984. (ed.) *Sex Segregation in the Workplace: Trends, Explanations, Remedies*. Washington DC: National Academy Press.

Reskin, Barbara. 1988. "Bringing Men Back In: Sex Differentiation and the Devaluation of Women's Work," *Gender and Society* 2, 1: 58–81.

Reskin, Barbara and Heidi Hartmann. 1986. *Women's Work, Men's Work: Sex Segregation on the Job*. Washington DC: National Academy Press.

Reskin, Barbara and Lrene Padavic. 1994. *Women and Men at Work*. Thousand Oaks, CA: Pine Forge Press.

Reskin, Barbara and Catherine Roos. 1992. "Jobs, Authority and Earnings Among Managers: The Continuing Significance of Sex," *Work and Occupations* 19, 4 (November): 342–365.

Resnick, S. and R. Wolfe. 1988. *Knowledge and Class*. Chicago: University of Chicago Press.

Richta, Radovan and a Research Team. 1968. *Civilization at the Crossroads: Social and Human Implications of the Scientific and Technological Revolution*. Czechoslovakia: International Arts and Sciences Press.

Robinson, J. P. 1977. *How Americans Used Time in 1965*. New York: Praeger.

Robinson, John, Vladimir G. Andreyenkov and Vasily D. Patrushev. 1988. *The Rhythm of Everyday Life: How Soviet and American Citizens Use Time*. Boulder: Westview Press.

Robinson, R. and J. Kelley. 1979. "Class as Conceived by Marx and Dahrendorf," *American Sociological Review* 41: 209–234.

Roemer, John. 1982. *A General Theory of Exploitation and Class*. Cambridge: Harvard University Press.

    1985. "Should Marxists be Interested in Exploitation?" *Philosophy and Public Affairs* 14: 30–65. Reprinted in John E. Roemer (ed.) *Analytical Marxism*. Cambridge: Cambridge University Press, 1986.

Rogers, Joel. 1990. "Divide and Conquer: Further Reflections on the Distinctive Character of American Labor Laws," *Wisconsin Law Review* 1, 1: 1–147.

Roos, Patricia. 1981. "Sex Stratification in the Workplace: Male–female Differences in Economic Returns to Occupation," *Social Science Research* 10: 195–224.

1985. *Gender and Work. A Comparative Analysis of Industrial Societies*. Albany: State University of New York Press.

Rosenbaum, James E. 1984. *Career Mobility in a Corporate Hierarchy*. New York: Academic Press.

Rosenfeld, Rachel A. and Anne L. Kalleberg. 1990. "A Cross-national Comparison of the Gender Gap in Income," *American Journal of Sociology* 96: 69–106.

Ruggie, M. 1984. *The State and Working Women: A Comparative Study of Britain and Sweden*. Princeton: Princeton University Press.

1988. "Gender, Work and Social Progress: Some Consequences of Interest Aggregation in Sweden." In Jane Jenson, Elizabeth Hagen and Cellaigh Reddy (eds.) *Feminization of the Labor Force: Paradoxes and Promises*. Oxford: Polity.

Ryan, William. 1981. *Equality*. New York: Pantheon.

Scandura, Terri 1. 1992. *Breaking the Glass Ceiling in the 1990s*. US Department of Labor, Women's Bureau. Washington, DC.

Secombe, Walley. 1974. "The Housewife and her Labour under Capitalism," *New Left Review* 83 (January–February): 3–24.

Seeman, Melvin. 1977. "Some Real and Imaginary Consequences of Social Mobility: A French-American Comparison," *American Journal of Sociology* 82, 4: 757–782.

Sen, Amartya. 1984. "Family and Food: Sex Bias in Poverty." In Amartya Sen, *Resources, Values and Development*. Blackwell, 1984.

Shelton, Beth and Ben Agger. 1993. "Shotgun Wedding, Unhappy Marriage, No-Fault Divorce? Rethinking the Feminism–Marxism Relationship." Pp. 25–42 in Paul England (ed.) *Theory on Gender / Feminism on Theory*. New York: Aldine de Gruyter.

Singelmann, Joachim. 1978. *From Agriculture to Services*. Beverly Hills: Sage Publications.

Sorensen, Annemette and Sara McLanahan. 1987. "Married Women's Economic Dependency, 1940–1980," *American Journal of Sociology* 93, 3: 659–687.

Sorokin, Pitirim A. 1929. *Social Mobility*. New York: Harper.

Spaeth, J. L. 1985. "Job Power and Earnings."*American Sociological Review* 50: 603–617.

Stanworth, Michelle. 1984. "Women and Class Analysis: A Reply to John Goldthorpe," *Sociology* 18: 159–170.

Steinmetz, George. 1983. *Economic Crisis and Collective Action: Working-Class Protest Against Unemployment in Paris During the 1880s*. M.S. Thesis. University of Wisconsin-Madison.

Steinmetz, George and Erik Olin Wright. 1989. "The Fall and Rise of the Petty Bourgeoisie: Changing Patterns of Self-employment in the post-War United States," *The American Journal of Sociology* 94, 5 (March) 973–1018.

Stephens, John. 1979. *The Transition From Capitalism to Socialism*. Urbana and Chicago, IL: University of Illinois.

Stier, Haya and David Grusky. 1990. "An Overlapping Persistence Model of Career Mobility," *American Sociological Review* 55: 736–756.

Stolzenberg, Ross M. and Daniel A. Relles. 1990. "Theory Testing in a World of Constrained Research Design," *Sociological Methods and Research* 18, 4 (May): 395–415.

Strasser, Susan. 1982. *Never Done: A History of American Housework*. New York: Pantheon.

Strober, Myra and Carolyn L. Arnold. 1987. "The Dynamics of Occupational Segregation among Bank Tellers." Pp. 107–148 in Clair Brown and Joseph A. Pechman (eds.) *Gender in the Workplace*. Washington DC: The Brookings Institution.

Szalai, Alexander. 1966a. "The Multi-national Comparative Time Budget Research Project: A Venture in International Research Cooperation," *The American Behavioral Scientist* 10: 1–30.

1966b. "Trends in Comparative Time Budget Research," *American Behavioral Scientist* 3: 3–8.

Szalai, Alexander, P. E. Converse, P. Feldheim, E.K. Scheuch and P. F. Stone (eds.) 1972. *The Use of Time: Daily Activities of Urban and Suburban Populations in Twelve Countries*. The Hague: Mouton.

Szelenyi, Ivan and William Martin. 1985. *New Class Theory and Beyond*. Unpublished book manuscript, Department of Sociology, University of Wisconsin, Madison.

Szymanski, Albert. 1983. *Class Structure: A Critical Perspective*. New York: Praeger.

Taylor-Gooby, Peter. 1985. "Personal Consumption and Gender," *Sociology* 19: 273–284.

Therborn, Göran. 1982. *The Power of Ideology and the Ideology of Power*. London: Verso.

Thompson, E. P. 1968. *The Making of the English Working Class*. Harmondsworth: Penguin.

Thompson, Kenneth H. 1971. "Upward Social Mobility and Political Orientation: A Re-evaluation of the Evidence," *The American Sociological Review* 36 (April): 223–235.

Touraine, Alain. 1971. *The Post Industrial Society*. New York: Random House.

Toutain, J.-C. 1963. *La population de la France de 1700 à 1959*. In *Histoire quantitative de l'économie Française*, vol. III, in *Cahiers de L'Institut de Science Économique Appliquée*. Paris: ISEA.

Treiman, Donald and Heidi Hartmann. 1981. *Women, Work and Wages*. Washington DC: National Academy Press.

Treiman, Donald and Patricia Roos. 1983. "Sex and Earnings in Industrial Society," *American Journal of Sociology* 89: 612–650.

Tsuda, Masumi. 1973. "Personnel Administration at the Industrial Plant Level." In K. Okochi, B. Karsh and S. B. Levine (eds.) *Workers and Employers in Japan: The Japanese Employment Relations System*. University of Tokyo Press.

Tyree, Andrea and Judith Treas. 1974. "The Occupational and Marital Mobility of Women," *American Sociological Review* 39: 293–302.

US Department of Commerce. 1940. *Instructions to Enumerators. Population and Agriculture. 1940.* Washington: Bureau of the Census.

Van Parijs, P. 1986. "A Revolution in Class Theory," *Politics & Society.* Reprinted in Wright et al. (1989), 213–242.

Van Regemorter, Denise. 1981. "Evolution du nombre et du revenu des commerçants et des artisans de 1953 à 1977," *Cahiers économiques de Bruxelles* 89.

Vanek, J. 1974. "Time Spent in Housework," *Scientific American* 231: 116–120.

Verbrugge, L. M. 1977. "The Structure of Adult Friendship Choices," *Social Forces* 56: 576–597.

1979. "Multiplexity in Adult Friendships," *Social Forces* 57: 1286–1309.

Vogel, Ezra F. 1979. *Japan as No. 1: Lessons for America.* Cambridge, MA: Cambridge University Press.

Volko v, Shulamit. 1978. *The Rise of Popular Antimodernism in Germany. The Urban Master Artisans, 1873–1896.* Princeton: Princeton University Press.

Walker, Kathryn. 1970. "Time Used by Husbands for Household Work," *Family Economics Review* 4: 8–11.

Walker, Kathryn, and Margaret Woods. 1976. *Time Use: A Measure of Household Production of Goods and Services.* Washington DC: American Home Economics Association.

Warren, Bill. 1978. *Imperialism: Pioneer of Capitalism.* London: New Left Books.

Watson, Dorothy. 1990. "Dimensions of Class: the Impact of Interests, Workplace Experiences and Network Ties on Class Consciousness in Four Western Democracies," Ph.D. Dissertation, University of Wisconsin-Madison.

Weiss, Linda. 1984. "The Italian State and Small Business," *Archives Européennes de Sociologie* 25: 214–241.

Westergaard, John and Henrietta Resler. 1975. *Class in a Capitalist Society: A Study of Contemporary Britain.* Harmondsworth: Penguin.

Western, Mark and Erik Olin Wright. 1994. "The Permeability of Class Boundaries to Intergenerational Mobility: A Comparative Study of the United States, Canada, Norway and Sweden," *American Sociological Review,* 59, 4: 606–629.

Wilson, Franklin D., Marta Tienda and Lawrence Wu. 1992. "Racial Equality in the Labor Market: Still an Elusive Goal?" Discussion chapter no. 968–92. University of Wisconsin-Madison: Institute for Research on Poverty.

Wilson, William Julius. 1982. *The Declining Significance of Race.* Chicago: University of Chicago Press.

1987. *The Truly Disadvantaged.* Chicago: University of Chicago Press.

Winkler, Heinrich August. 1972. *Mittelstand, Demokratie und National Sozialismus. Die Politische Entwicklung von Handwerk und Kleinhandel in der Weimarer Republik.* Cologne: Kiepenhauer & Witsch.

Wolf, Wendy C. and Neil D. Fligstein. 1979a. "Sex and Authority in the Workplace: The Causes of Sexual Inequality," *American Sociological Review* 44 (April): 235–252.

1979b. "Sexual Stratification: Differences in Power in the Work Setting," *Social Forces* 58, 1 (September): 94–107.

Wong, Raymond Sin-Kwok. 1990. "Understanding Cross-national Variation in Occupational Mobility," *American Sociological Review* 55: 560–573.

1992. "Vertical and Non-Vertical Effects in Class Mobility: Cross-National Variations," *American Sociological Review* 57: 396–410.

Wright, Erik Olin. 1976. "Class Boundaries in Advanced Capitalist Society," *New Left Review* 98 (July–August): 3–41.

1978. *Class, Crisis and the State.* London: New Left Books.

1979. *Class Structure and Income Determination.* New York: Academic Press.

1985. *Classes.* London: New Left Books.

1986. *Class Structure and Class Consciousness: Merged Multi-Nation File: United States Survey, 1980, Sweden Survey, 1980, Norway Survey, 1982, Canada Survey, 1983, Finland Survey, 1981* [Machine-Readable Data File]. Principal Investigator, Erik Olin Wright. ICPSR ed. Madison, WI: University of Wisconsin, Institute for Research on Poverty [Producer], 1986, Madison, WI: Distributor Inter-University Consortium for Political and Social Research [Distributor], 1986. Ann Arbor, MI.

1989a. "Rethinking, Once Again, The Concept of Class Structure." Pp. 269–348 in Wright, et al. (1989).

1989b. "Women in the Class Structure," *Politics and Society* 17: 35–66.

1989c. *Comparative Project on Class Structure and Class Consciousness* [MRDF]. Madison, WI: Institute for Research on Poverty [producer]. Ann Arbor, MI: Inter-University Consortium for Political and Social Research [distributor].

1989d. "The Comparative Project on Class Structure and Class Consciousness: An Overview," *Acta Sociologica* 32, 1: 3–22.

1993. "Typologioes, Scales and Class Analysis: A Comment on Halaby and Weakliem," *American Sociological Review* 58, 1 (February): 31–34.

1994. *Interrogating Inequality.* London: Verso.

Wright, Erik Olin and Bill Martin. 1987. "The Transformation of the American Class Structure, 1960–1980," *American Journal of Sociology* 93, 1 (July).

Wright, Erik Olin and Kwang-Yeong Shin. 1988. "Temporality and Class Analysis: A Comparative Analysis of Class Structure, Class Trajectory amd Class Consciousness in Sweden and the United States," *Sociological Theory* (Spring).

Wright, Erik Olin and Joachim Singelmann. 1982. "Proletarianization in the American Class Structure." In Michael Burawoy and Theda Skocpol (eds.) *Marxist Inquiries, Supplement* to the *American Journal of Sociology* 83.

Wright, Erik Olin, Carolyn Howe and Donmoon Cho. 1989. "Class Structure and Class Formation." In Melvin Kohn (ed.), *Comparative Sociology.* Beverly Hills: Sage ASA Presidental Volume.

Wright, Erik Olin, Andrew Levine and Elliott Sober. 1992. *Reconstructing Marxism: Essays on Explanation and the Theory of History.* London: Verso.

Wright, Erik Olin, Cynthia Costello, David Hachen and Joey Sprague. 1982. "The American Class Structure", *American Sociological Review* (December).

Wright, Erik Olin, Uwe Becker, Johanna Brenner, Michael Burawoy, Val Burris, Guglielmo Carchedi, Gordon Marshall, Peter Meiksins, David Rose,

Arthur Stinchcombe, Phillipe Van Parijs. 1989. *The Debate on Classes*. London: Verso.

Wuthnow, Robert and Wesley Schrum. 1983. "Knowledge Workers as a New Class," *Work and Occupations* 10, 4: 471–487.

Xie, Yue. 1992. "The Log-Multiplicative Layer Effect Model for Comparing Mobility Tables," *American Sociological Review* 57: 380–395.

Yamaguchi, Kazuo. 1987. "Models for Comparing Mobility Tables: Toward Parsimony and Substance," *American Sociological Review* 52: 482–494.

Yearbook of Labor Statistics. 1986. Japan: Policy Planning and Research Department, Minister's Secretariat, Ministry of Labor.

Zaretsky, Eli. 1976. *Capitalism, the Family and Personal Life*. New York: Harper & Row.

Index of names

Index of subjects